European Yearbook of International Economic Law

For further volumes:
http://www.springer.com/series/8165

Christoph Herrmann • Markus Krajewski •
Jörg Philipp Terhechte
Editors

European Yearbook of International Economic Law 2013

Springer

Editors
Christoph Herrmann
Chair for Constitutional and
Administrative European Law,
European and International
Economic Law
University of Passau
Passau, Germany

Markus Krajewski
Chair for Public Law and International Law
University of Erlangen-Nürnberg
Erlangen, Germany

Jörg Philipp Terhechte
Chair for Public Law,
European and International Law,
Regulatory and Competition Law
Director of the Competition & Regulation Institute
Leuphana University Lüneburg
Lüneburg, Germany

ISBN 978-3-642-44710-5 ISBN 978-3-642-33917-2 (eBook)
DOI 10.1007/978-3-642-33917-2
Springer Heidelberg New York Dordrecht London

Softcover re-print of the Hardcover 1st edition 2013

Printed on acid-free paper

Springer is part of Springer Science+Business Media (www.springer.com)

Editorial EYIEL 4 (2013)

Volume 4 (2013) of the European Yearbook of International Economic Law (EYIEL) offers a special focus on recent developments in International Competition Policy and Law.

International competition law is emerging as a distinct subfield of international economic law in recent years even though international agreements on competition cooperation date back into the 1970s. Competition law became a prominent subject of political and academic debates in the late 1990s when competition and trade were discussed as one of the Singapore subjects in the WTO. Today, international competition law is a complex multi-layered system of rules and principles encompassing not only the external application of domestic competition law and traditional bilateral cooperation agreements but also competition provision in regional trade agreements and non-binding guidelines and standards. Furthermore, the relevance of competition law for developing countries or the relationship between competition law and public services raise controversial debates.

The contributions to this volume reflect the growing diversity of the issues and elements of international competition law. The effectiveness of competition law is intrinsically linked to the institutional design of competition authorities. In his distinguished essay, *William E. Kovacic* revisits this classical theme of competition law and develops characteristics of good agency practice reflecting in particular his own experience and expertise as a former Chairman of the US Federal Trade Commission.

The next set of essays addresses the relationship between trade law and competition law. *Alden Abbott* and *Shanker Singham* argue that both fields serve similar welfare-enhancing goals despite distinct legal traditions and support their case with an analysis of anticompetitive market distortions in the WTO and the International Competition Network (ICN). The essays by *Hanspeter Tschaeni* and *Valérie Engammare* and by *Peter Hilpold* supplement the trade and competition debate by studying the role of competition law in regional trade agreements (RTAs). *Tschaeni* and *Engammare* recall the growing importance of RTAs for competition law and share insights from the negotiators perspective. *Hilpold* takes the debate one step further and asks whether RTAs can serve as a stepping stone towards a plurilateral (or even multilateral?) agreement on competition law.

For EYIEL as a European yearbook on economic law it seems fitting to include a specific perspective on European law issues. *Anestis Papadopoulos* exposes us to the external competition law and policy of the EU showing that the EU plays an important role in all areas of international competition law. Focussing on public services in transnational competition law, *Johan van de Gronden* addresses a decisively "European" subject. His question is whether the complex relationship between public services and competition law in the internal legal order of the EU is equally relevant at the international level.

It is often argued that limiting cartels and abusive behaviour by dominant players would also be beneficial for developing countries. In fact, competition law is certainly on the rise in the Global South. *Trudi Hartzenbergs* contribution on competition policy in Africa contains ample evidence of this development, but also highlights the diversity of approaches in Africa at the national and regional level. *Yane Svetiev* approaches the subject from a conceptual and policy perspective. Offering an optimistic view, he shows how competition law can indeed function as an element of the international law of development.

The last essay of the special focus on competition law places competition law in a broader theoretical and constitutional perspective. *Gralf-Peter Calliess*, *Jens Martens,* and *Moritz Renner* ask how the institutional prerequisites of the world market, in particular undistorted competition, can be reproduced. They show that to a certain extent, market-based solutions and private law regimes can contribute to this reproduction leading—at least partly—to a privatisation of the economic constitution.

Part II of EYIEL 4 (Regional Integration), as usual, is devoted to selected questions of regional economic integration development around the world, especially new aspects of the next generation of US and European Free Trade Agreements with third countries, and new developments in Southeast Asia.

Part III (International Economic Institutions) contains analytical reports on recent developments within the International Monetary Fund (IMF), the World Trade Organization (WTO), the World Intellectual Property Organization (WIPO), and the United Nations Conference on Trade and Development (UNCTAD) as Part IV (Reviews) provides for detailed information about recent publication in the field of International Economic Law. The contribution on the World Customs Organization (WCO) addresses the developments with regard to customs valuation in particular.

The editors are happy to introduce Professor *Markus Krajewski*, University of Erlangen-Nürnberg as a new editor of EYIEL. Markus is an internationally recognised expert in the field of International Economic Law and a most valuable addition to the editorial team.

We are also delighted to welcome Professor *Eleonor M. Fox*, New York University School of Law and Professor *William E. Kovacic*, George Washington University School of Law to the Advisory Board of EYIEL. Both are globally well-known experts in the field of International Economic Law, in practice as well as in scholarship.

Very sadly, one of the initial members of the Advisory Board, Prof. Dr. Horst G. Krenzler, former Director General for Trade of the Commission of the European

Union and honorary professor of the Ludwig-Maximilians-University Munich, passed away shortly before this volume went into production. He was not only an extremely supportive board member and extraordinarily competent trade lawyer, who knew trade from all perspectives (as trade negotiator, as of counsel, and as honorary professor), but also constantly strived to hand his knowledge on to others by lecturing at the university and by editing a leading commentary on European external trade law (in German). To Christoph, he was also a personal friend and honoured him greatly by making him his co-editor (and now successor) of the aforementioned commentary. We grieve for him as a trade lawyer and as a most enjoyable, kind and lovely person, and we will do our very best to honour his memory.

Finally, we are indebted to a great number of people, again primarily to our contributors. The collaboration with Springer and especially with Dr. *Brigitte Reschke* was—once more—very enjoyable, cooperative, and fruitful. We have to extend our thanks to the member of the EYIEL Advisory Board, too. Lastly, we would like to thank our research assistants at the Universities of Lüneburg and Passau (in particular to *Sören Räthling*) for their invaluable support in handling the manuscripts and proofs.

Passau/Erlangen-Nürnberg/Lüneburg
August 2012

Christoph Herrmann
Markus Krajewski
Jörg Philipp Terhechte

Contents

Part II Regional Integration

Part III International Economic Institutions

Part IV Book Reviews

Contributors

Alden Abbott is a Director of Global Patent Law and Competition Strategy for Research in Motion. He previously was a senior public servant in the US Government, having served as Deputy Director for International Affairs and Director of Policy and Coordination (Bureau of Competition), Federal Trade Commission, among other positions. Alden is an Adjunct Professor at George Mason Law School. He has published and lectured extensively on competition policy and regulation, and has advised foreign governments on competition law reform. Alden's biography appears in Who's Who in America.

Wolfgang Bergthaler is a senior counsel at the International Monetary Fund's Legal Department, where he works on legal aspects of IMF financing operations, governance and financial issues, exchange system issues, financial sector issues, corporate and household insolvency, sovereign debt issues, and judicial reform issues. Before joining the IMF in 2006, he practiced as an attorney in Vienna and Brussels. Wolfgang is a graduate of Karl-Franzens Universität Graz (Magister iuris and Doctor iuris), Georgetown University Law Center (LL.M.), and the Université III Robert Schuman, Strasbourg (Certificate Erasmus). Wolfgang is admitted to practice in the State of New York and the District of Columbia and was admitted to practice in Vienna, Austria. He lectures and publishes on issues related to international finance.

Chester Brown is Associate Professor at the Faculty of Law, University of Sydney. He is also a Barrister at 7 Selborne Chambers, Sydney, and a door tenant at Essex Court Chambers, London, and Maxwell Chambers, Singapore. He practices, teaches, and researches in the fields of public international law, international arbitration, and international investment law. He formerly served as Assistant Legal Adviser to the British Foreign and Commonwealth Office, and prior to this, he was a Senior Associate in the International Arbitration Group of Clifford Chance LLP, London. He was educated at the Universities of Melbourne, Oxford, and Cambridge.

Colin M. Brown is a lawyer in Unit F.2 (Legal Aspects of Trade Policy) of the Directorate General for Trade of the European Commission where he works on trade and energy and trade and environment issues as well as international procurement issues. He advises on bilateral trade negotiations and coordinates DG Trade's legal work on bilateral negotiations. Colin is also responsible for institutional issues, including the roll-out of the changes to EU trade policy brought about by the Lisbon Treaty. Before joining DG Trade in October 2006, he served for 6 years for the Legal Service of the European Commission. Previously, he worked on trade law issues in private practice in Brussels. Colin has been the Chair of the Legal Advisory Committee of the Energy Charter Treaty since January 2004. He is visiting lecturer in WTO law at the Université Catholique de Louvain, Belgium. He holds an LL.B. (first class Honours) from the Faculty of Law of the University of Edinburgh, Scotland (1996), a Diploma in International Relations from the Bologna Center of the School of Advanced International Studies (SAIS), John Hopkins University, Bologna, Italy (1997), and an LL.M. in European Law from the College of Europe, Bruges (1998). He is a member of the New York Bar.

Marc Bungenberg is Professor of Public Law, European Law, Public International Law, and International Economic Law at the University of Siegen, Visiting Professor at the University of Lausanne and academic advisor to the International Investment Law Centre Cologne. He studied law in Hannover and Lausanne (LL.M. 1995). Marc received his doctorate in law at the University of Hannover (1999) and his Habilitation at the Friedrich Schiller University Jena (2006). His main fields of research are European and international economic law (in particular common commercial policy of the EU, state aid law, public procurement, and international investment law).

Gralf-Peter Calliess, Ph.D. (law) University of Göttingen, Habilitation, University of Frankfurt, is a Professor of Law at the University of Bremen. He leads an interdisciplinary research project on "The Constitution of Global Commerce" at the DFG (Deutsche Forschungsgemeinschaft—German Research Foundation) Collaborative Research Centre "Transformations of the State" (http://www.sfb597.uni-bremen.de/).

Christopher Dallimore is a Senior Researcher in the Department of Customs and Excise at the University of Münster, Germany. A graduate of Cardiff University, Wales, UK, he holds a Magister Iuris from the University of Trier and Doctor Iuris from the University of Münster. He specialises in the legal implications of supply chain security measures as well as customs-related problems in European and international law. Christopher is also the Head of Studies of the Master of Customs Administration programme offered by the University of Münster and sub-editor of the World Customs Journal.

Valérie Engammare is a Legal Adviser at the International Economic Law Division of the Swiss State Secretariat for Economic Affairs. She holds a doctorate degree from the University of Zurich.

James Thuo Gathii is Wing-Tat Lee Chair in International Law and Professor of Law at Loyola University Chicago. James is a member of the Global Faculty of the Trade Policy Training Institute (TRAPCA) in Arusha, Tanzania. He is an independent expert on the Working Group on Extractive Industries, Environment and

Human Rights Violations in Africa, of the African Commission on Human and Peoples' Rights. He is a founding member of the Third World Approaches to International Law network and currently the Co-Chair of the African Interest Group of the American Society of International Law. James is a member of the International Law Association's Study Committee on the Meaning of War. James received his LL.B. from the University of Nairobi and his SJD from Harvard Law School.

Andrew Giddings is Counsel in the Legal Department of the International Monetary Fund, where he works on legal aspects of IMF financing operations, governance and financial issues, exchange system issues, sovereign debt issues, and corporate and household insolvency. Before joining the IMF in 2009, he practiced as an attorney in New York working on international financial transactions and litigation. Andrew is a graduate of Harvard Law School (J.D.), the Fletcher School of Law and Diplomacy (M.A.L.D.), Tufts University (B.A.), and the Institut d'études politiques de Paris (Undergraduate Exchange Programme Certificate). He is a member of the New York and Massachusetts bars.

Johan van de Gronden, born on 31 October 1966, studied law at Utrecht University and Free University Amsterdam. He received his Ph.D. on 30 September 1998, defending a thesis on the Implementation of European environmental law by decentralised authorities. Johan worked at the Europa Institute University Utrecht, from 2003-2007 as senior lecturer. On 1 September 2007, he was appointed as a full time professor of European law at the Radboud University Nijmegen, The Netherlands. Johan frequently lectures and gives international and national presentations on issues of EU Internal Market and competition law. He publishes extensively on subjects such as Services of General Economic Interest, Services Directive and health care & EU law (in international and national journals, volumes, and books). Since 2003, Johan is a Deputy Judge at the District Court of Rotterdam. Since 2006, he is a member of the Committee Consumer Affairs of The Social and Economic Council of the Netherlands and since 2009, he is also a member of the Committee International Affairs of this council.

Trudi Hartzenberg is the Executive Director of the Trade Law Centre (tralac). Her research interests include international trade and regional integration in Africa, competition, investment and industrial policy issues in Africa.

Peter Hilpold is a Professor for International Law, European Law, and Comparative Public Law at the University of Innsbruck. He has taught at several European Universities and is the author of more than 150 academic publications. He is member of the scientific board or permanent collaborator of several academic journals.

Rhea Tamara Hoffmann is a doctoral candidate and member in the Research Group "The Change in Transnational Labour and Economic Law" at the Cluster of Excellence "The Formation of Normative Orders" at Johann Wolfgang Goethe-University Frankfurt, Germany. Her doctoral thesis explores the implications of international investment law and arbitration from a constitutional theory perspective.

Edwini Kessie is currently on leave from the World Trade Organization (WTO) and is the Chief Trade Adviser of the Forum Island Countries and Head of the Office of the Chief Trade Adviser (OCTA). Edwini is admitted as a solicitor to the Supreme Courts of England & Wales, New South Wales, Australia, and Ghana. He is also a part-time lecturer in international trade law at the World Trade Institute in Berne, Switzerland and the University of Technology in Sydney, Australia. He has a Doctorate Degree in Law from the University of Technology, Sydney, Australia and Masters' Degrees in Law from the University of Toronto, Canada and the University of Brussels, Belgium and a Bachelor's Degree in Law from the University of Ghana.

Moritz Keller is an associate in the international arbitration group of Freshfields Bruckhaus Deringer LLP. He regularly acts as counsel for states, governmental agencies, and private parties in litigation proceedings as well as international investment and commercial arbitration proceedings under various arbitration rules such as the Arbitration Rules of the International Centre for the Settlement of Investment Disputes (ICSID) or the Arbitration Rules of the International Chamber of Commerce. Moritz has completed his legal education at the Justus-Liebig-Universität Gießen and the University of Wiconsin (Madison) Law School in the US. He has obtained a doctor of laws (Dr. iur.) in Gießen and a degree of master of laws (LLM) in Madison. Moritz regularly publishes on various issues of commercial and procedural law, including arbitration and investment law and has given lectures and seminars at various universities.

William E. Kovacic is a Professor of Global Competition Law and Policy at George Washington University, Washington D.C., where he also is the director of the Competition Law Center. Before joining the George Washington Law School in 1999, William was the George Mason University Foundation Professor at the George Mason University School of Law, Arlington, Virginia. From June 2001 to December 2004, he served as the general counsel for the US Federal Trade Commission (FTC). William was an FTC Commissioner from January 2006 to October 2011, and served as Chairman of the agency from March 2008 to March 2009. Since 1992, he has served as an adviser on antitrust and consumer protection issues to the governments of Armenia, Benin, Egypt, El Salvador, Georgia, Guyana, Indonesia, Mongolia, Morocco, Nepal, Panama, Russia, Ukraine, Vietnam, and Zimbabwe. William obtained his J.D. from Columbia University and a B.A. from Princeton University.

Andreas Krallmann is a lawyer in the Federal Ministry of Economics and Technology in Berlin. He currently works in the unit for export financing. From 2007 to 2012, he was seconded as a Legal Adviser to the WTO unit of the Permanent Mission of Germany to the Office of the United Nations and other International Organisations in Geneva, Switzerland. From 2011 to 2012, he chaired the WTO Committee on Subsidies and Countervailing Measures. Prior to his Geneva posting, Andreas worked in the European departments of the German Federal Ministry of Finance and the Federal Ministry of Economics and Technology. He reads law at the Free University Berlin and obtained an LL.M. in International Commercial Law from the University of Nottingham, England, before taking his bar exam in Berlin.

Jens Mertens, Ph.D. (law) University of Bremen, wrote his dissertation in the course of the interdisciplinary research project "The Constitution of Global Commerce" at the DFG (Deutsche Forschungsgemeinschaft—German Research Foundation) Collaborative Research Centre "Transformations of the State" (http://www.sfb597.uni-bremen.de/) and still works thereat as a research assistant.

Anestis Papadopoulos is a lawyer at KPP Law in Athens, Greece. He practises in the field of commercial law, with a focus on competition law and market regulation. He has previously worked as a legal expert of the Hellenic Competition Commission. He has also worked for the European Commission (stage at DG Competition), and the British Institute of International and Comparative Law (Fellow). He has acted as an international consultant for UNCTAD and has been for three years a teaching fellow at the Law School of Athens. He has given lectures at the London School of Economics and University College Dublin and is research affiliate at the Centre for Competition Law and Policy at the University of Oxford. Anestis holds an LL.B. from the University of Athens, an LL.M. from Manchester University and a Ph.D. from the London School of Economics.

Joost Pauwelyn is a Professor of International Law at the Graduate Institute of International and Development Studies (IHEID) in Geneva, Switzerland and Co-Director of the Institute's Centre for Trade and Economic Integration (CTEI). He is also Senior Advisor with the law firm of King & Spalding LLP. Before joining the Graduate Institute in 2007, Joost was a tenured professor at Duke Law School, USA. He also served as legal officer at the World Trade Organization from 1996 to 2002 and practiced law at a major Brussels law firm. Joost received degrees from the Universities of Namur and Leuven, Belgium as well as Oxford University and holds a doctorate from the University of Neuchâtel. He is the author of, most recently, International Trade Law (2012, 2nd ed., with A. Guzman) and Global Challenges at the Intersection of Trade, Energy, and the Environment (2010). He is General Editor of the Journal of International Dispute Settlement and was appointed on the roster of WTO panellists and as arbitrator under Free Trade Agreements.

Alexander Proelß is a Professor for International and European Law at the University of Trier and Director of the Institute of Environmental and Technology Law of that University.

Ashique Rahman is an Australian solicitor and an Associate at the law firm Volterra Fietta, London. He advises and represents States, international organisations, and private entities on a wide range of contentious and non-contentious public international law and related international dispute resolution issues. He has worked as counsel on a number of investment arbitration proceedings pursuant to the ICSID and UNCITRAL Rules. He is a graduate of the Universities of New South Wales and Sydney.

Patrick C. Reed is a member of the New York and District of Columbia Bars and a lawyer with the firm of Simons & Wiskin in New York City. His law practice concentrates on customs, international trade, and import-export regulatory law, including the World Trade Organization agreements and other international trade and investment agreements. He is an adjunct assistant professor in the Business Law Department, Baruch College, City University of New York, and a Fellow at the Weissman Center for International Business, Baruch College. He is also an adjunct professor in the Center for Global Affairs, New York University. He holds a J.D. degree from Columbia University School of Law, a master's degree and a Ph.D. in international relations from The Fletcher School of Law and Diplomacy, Tufts University, with concentrations in international law and international economic relations.

Moritz Renner, Ph.D. (law) University of Bremen, wrote his dissertation in the course of the interdisciplinary research project "The Constitution of Global Commerce" at the DFG (Deutsche Forschungsgemeinschaft—German Research Foundation) Collaborative Research Centre "Transformations of the State" (http://www.sfb597.uni-bremen.de/) and now works at Humboldt-University, Berlin.

Diana Rosert works in UNCTAD's Section on International Investment Agreements (IIA) in the Investment and Enterprise Division. She holds a Master of Arts in International Political Economy from the University of Warwick, United Kingdom. Her research interests are in international economic relations, especially international trade and investment agreements and their sustainable development impact.

Shanker Singham is a partner in the antitrust and international trade groups of Squire Sanders. He is the leader of the firm's Global Market Access/International Trade Agreements group and is a frequent author and speaker on topics related to antitrust, international antitrust, and international trade. He is the author of A General Theory of Trade and Competition; Trade Liberalization and Competitive Markets (CMP Publishing, 2007), and is Chairman of the International Roundtable on Trade and Competition Policy.

Yane Svetiev is a Research Fellow at the Law Department of the European University Institute (EUI) in Florence, as part of the project on European Regulatory Private Law. Previously he was a Max Weber Fellow at the EUI. His research focuses on EU intervention to promote competition or for regulatory purposes, the relationship between the various sectoral regimes and their interface with national private law and the national administrations of the Member States. Yane did his doctoral studies at Columbia University.

Christian J. Tams is a Professor of Law at the University of Glasgow, Scotland. Before joining the University of Glasgow in 2008, he was an assistant professor at the Walther Schücking Institute of International Law at the University of Kiel. His research in international law focuses on the law of state responsibility, dispute settlement, and investment protection, but is based on a generalist approach to the discipline. In addition to his academic work, he has advised states in proceedings before the International Court of Justice (ICJ) and the International Tribunal for the Law of the Sea (ITLOS). He is an adjunct professor at the Europa-Kolleg Hamburg, and serves on the German Court of Arbitration for Sports and the ILA Committee on the Use of Force. He is a member of the Royal Society of Edinburgh Young Academy and has held visiting positions at universities in France, China, Germany, and Lithuania. Christian studied law at the universities of Kiel, Lyon III and Cambridge (LL.M, 2000; Ph.D., 2004), and is a qualified German lawyer (admitted in 2005).

Catharine Titi is a doctoral candidate at the University of Siegen, Germany. She has studied law in Greece and France, and holds two postgraduate academic qualifications from the University of London. Catharine has previously worked in management consulting for PricewaterhouseCoopers, London. Her research interests include international economic law, public international law, and EU law.

Hanspeter Tschaeni is Head of the International Economic Law Division of the Swiss State Secretariat for Economic Affairs SECO. He holds degrees in Law (doctorate, University of Zurich) and Political Science (M.A., Temple University, USA).

Elisabeth Tuerk is an Officer in Charge of UNCTAD's Section on International Investment Agreements (IIA) in the Investment and Enterprise Division. She manages the Section's work across all three pillars of UNCTAD activities (i.e. research and analysis, capacity-building, and consensus-building). In her previous UNCTAD assignment, Elisabeth worked as an Economic Affairs Officer at UNCTAD's Division on International Trade and Commodities. Prior to joining UNCTAD, Elisabeth worked as a staff attorney for the Trade and Investment Program of the Center for International Environmental Law (CIEL, Geneva). She holds a Magistra Degree in Law and a Magistra Degree in International Management from the Karl-Franzens University, Graz, Austria as well as a Masters Degree (MILE, Masters of International Law and Economics) from the World Trade Institute (WTI) in Bern, Switzerland.

Lucrezia Tuis works as a legal officer in the Directorate General for Trade of the European Commission. She has provided legal advice on EU bilateral relations in particular the EU-Central America Association Agreement and EU-Colombia and Peru FTA, trade and development (including the drafting of the new Generalised System of Preferences (GSP) Regulation), trade and environment and trade in services issues. She was also involved in the management of WTO dispute settlement cases (e.g. DS 426 Canada–FIT Program; DS 425 China–scanners; DS 400/401 EU–seal products). She holds an LL.M in International Economic Law and Policy (IELPO) from the University of Barcelona (UB), a Master's degree in International trade economics and a Bachelor's degree in International economics both from Ca' Foscari University of Venice.

Andrea Wechsler is a Max Weber Fellow at the European University Institute, Florence, Italy, Affiliated Research Fellow at the Max Planck Institute for Intellectual Property and Competition Law, Munich, and Schöller Fellow at the Dr. Theo and Friedl Schoeller Research Center for Business and Society, Nürnberg. Her expertise is in international, European and Asian economic law and its theory, international trade, trade agreements, business transactions, international commercial arbitration and mediation, law and technology, as well as (comparative) legal method and the economic analysis of the law. Her work experience includes management consulting with McKinsey & Company, Inc., court clerking at the European Court of Justice in the Chambers of Judge Ninon Colneric, and lecturing at the Ludwig Maximilians University Munich, in the China-EU School of Law, Beijing, at the European University Institute and at James Madison University, Florence. Andrea received her education at the University of Oxford (M.A. (Oxon)), Columbia University School of Law (LL.M. (Columbia)), Ludwig Maximilians University (LL.M., Dr. iur.), Munich, and Beijing University (Chinese language diploma).

Wolfgang Weiß, born 1966, studied law and economics at the University of Bayreuth (Germany), where he also received his doctorate in law and his Habilitation. He holds a Chair in Public Law, European Law, and Public International Law at the German University of Administrative Sciences in Speyer. Furthermore, he is affiliated with Oxford Brookes University, where he was a Reader and Professor previously. His main research areas are public international law and WTO law, European constitutional and administrative Law, and German public law.

Hans-Michael Wolffgang is a Professor of International Trade and Tax Law and Head of the Department of Customs and Excise that forms part of the Institute of Tax Law at the University of Münster, Germany. He is a director of the Münster Master studies in Customs Administration, Law and Policy and has written extensively on international trade law, customs law, and export controls in Europe.

Part I
Topics

Distinguished Essay: Good Agency Practice and the Implementation of Competition Law

William E. Kovacic

Introduction

In recent decades, the community of jurisdictions with systems of competition laws has experienced a stunning enlargement. By 1990, fewer than 20 jurisdictions had established competition laws and mechanisms for their enforcement. Today, the number of systems stands at over 120.[1] By 2020, new additions will bring the number of adopters to over 130.

The dramatic international expansion of competition law, with a significant commitment of public and private resources for its implementation, begs a basic question about this remarkable global endeavour: how is it working?[2] How many of the newer systems are performing effectively? By what standards do we assess system quality in any competition policy regime? Which institutional traits or practices, of old agencies or new, tend to generate good policy outcomes?

The search for answers to these questions assumes greater importance. Within the past decade, many jurisdictions have made fundamental changes to the management, organization, and structure of their competition systems.[3] France, Spain,

I am grateful to David Hyman and Marc Winerman for many useful discussions about the subject of this essay. The views expressed here are mine alone.

[1] Kovacic, The Institutions of Antitrust Law: How Structure Shapes Substance, Michigan Law Review 110 (2012) 6, p. 1019 (1019, 1042 and fn. 82) ("Institutions of Antitrust Law").

[2] Kovacic, Hollman & Grant, How Does Your Competition Agency Measure Up?, European Competition Journal 7 (2011) 1, p. 25; Kovacic, Rating the Competition Agencies: What Constitutes Good Performance?, George Mason Law Review 16 (2009) 4, p. 903.

[3] These changes are described in Kovacic, "Institutions of Antitrust Law" (1042–43).

W.E. Kovacic (✉)
George Washington University, 2000 H Street, N.W, Washington, DC 20052, USA
e-mail: wkovacic@law.gwu.edu

C. Herrmann et al. (eds.), *European Yearbook of International Economic Law (EYIEL), Vol. 4 (2013)*, European Yearbook of International Economic Law 4,
DOI 10.1007/978-3-642-33917-2_1,

and Portugal have consolidated the antitrust enforcement competence of two agencies into a single new institution. Brazil has combined the antitrust functions of three bodies into a single agency. The Netherlands has added consumer protection and public utility oversight to the portfolio of the competition agency. The United Kingdom has proposed the formation of a new competition body to replace an existing two-agency configuration. Jurisdictions such as Australia and Mexico have amended their laws to treat certain antitrust infringements as criminal offenses. Numerous authorities, including the Competition Directorate of the European Commission and the Bundeskartellamt, have established a new office of the chief economist and engaged this unit more extensively in the development of individual cases.

These and related developments have not gone unnoticed. There are many signs that institutional considerations are beginning to receive the attention they deserve. Academic researchers have turned greater attention to crucial questions of institutional design and its influence upon competition system performance. Some recent contributions have provided detailed studies of individual jurisdictions.[4] Others have examined trends across systems.[5] The programmes of International bodies such as the International Competition Network, the Organization for Economic Cooperation and Development, and the United Nations Commission on Trade and Investment reflect expanded emphasis upon matters of policy implementation.[6]

Careful attention to the institutions of competition law could not have happened too soon. The increasing focus on institutional considerations is a welcome departure from the tendency, well-documented by political scientists, of academicians, policy makers, and practitioners to overlook the vital role of bureaucracy in determining policy outcomes.[7] The global competition policy community has

---

[4] See Crane, *The Institutional Structure of Antitrust Enforcement*, 2011 (studying the US competition policy system); Wilks, Institutional Reform and the Enforcement of Competition Policy in the UK, European Competition Journal 7 (2011) 1, p. 1 (discussing proposed reforms to structure of UK's competition system).

[5] Terhechte, *Internationales Kartell- und Fusionskontrollverfahrensrecht*, 2008, pp. 1–23; Sokol, Monopolists Without Borders: The Institutional Challenge of International Antitrust in a Global Gilded Age, Berkeley Business Law Journal 4 (2007) 1, p. 37; Fox, Antitrust and Institutions; Design and Change, Loyola University Chicago Law Review 41 (2010) 3, p. 473; Trebilcock & Iacobucci, Designing Competition Law Institutions: Values, Structure, and Mandate, Loyola University Chicago Law Journal 41 (2010) 3, p. 455.

[6] These adjustments are described in Hollman & Kovacic, The International Competition Network: Its Past, Current, and Future Role, University of Minnesota International Law Review 20 (2011) 2, p. 274.

[7] One formative treatment of this point in the political science literature is Allison, *Essence of Decision: Explaining the Cuban Missile Crisis*, 1971, p. 266: Allison explained decision-making by US and Soviet policy makers in the Cuban Missile Crisis as a function of bureaucratic customs, habits, and routines. He noted that "bureaucracy is indeed the least understood course of unhappy policy outcomes produced by the U.S. government." He concluded on pp. 267–268: "If analysts and operators are to increase their ability to achieve desired policy outcomes, we shall have to find ways of thinking harder about the problem of 'implementation,' that is, the path between the preferred solution and the actual performance of government." For another excellent diagnosis, see Wilson, *Bureaucracy: What Government Agencies Do and Why They Do It*, 2000.

suffered from a tendency to focus chiefly upon the substance of doctrine and policy and to slight the means by which policy is developed and implemented. The physics of substantive standards routinely eclipses the engineering of implementation. The physics of competition policy is unmistakably important, and no system can prosper without a foundation in sound analytical concepts. To have elegant physics without excellent engineering is a formula for policy failure. To be adapted successfully to practice, theory cannot be suspended in air. Unless grounded in the engineering of effective institutions, theory will not work in practice. The engineering of policy making involves basic questions of implementation. It is one thing to conceive a locomotive able to propel a bullet-train at hundreds of kilometers per hour. It is another to engineer the infrastructure of rails, roadbeds, bridges, and tunnels that must function effectively if the train is to realize its performance capabilities. Institutions constitute the infrastructure over which competition policy must travel. The quality of institutional arrangements determines how far, fast, and effectively a system of competition law can go.

The tendency to underinvest attention and effort to the infrastructure of competition policy is partly rooted in the incentives that confront the leadership of competition agencies and other public regulatory bodies. Incumbent political leaders in regulatory agencies have relatively few incentives to invest in the engineering of institution building and implementation, which are the agency's equivalent of durable infrastructure. Instead, the political process (with its emphasis on short-term credit claiming) and the activity-based measures of performance often used in popular commentary and scholarly writing create powerful incentives to engage in consumption and too little motivation to make capital investments that improve regulatory policy making.[8] As used here, "consumption" consists of engaging in activities that generate readily observable events for which one can claim credit. This can imbue policymaking with a highly short-term perspective. By contrast, investments in creating a strong institutional infrastructure generate returns that tend to extend mainly beyond the period of leadership of individual political appointees, of which I am one. Given the choice between consumption and investment, the interior voice that urges incumbent leaders to consume easily can drown out the voice that calls for investment. Given the mismatch between long term policy needs and the short term incentives that confront regulatory agency appointees, it is a major challenge to establish norms that press the agency to examine its institutional arrangements regularly and pursue measures to improve them.

The imperative to strengthen institutional arrangements as a way to increase competition agency effectiveness grows more intense as the complexity and pace of commerce increase. Competition agencies operate in highly dynamic environments characterized by rapid change in technology, business organization, and patterns of commerce at home and abroad. These forms of dynamism demand

[8] See Cooper & Kovacic, Behavioral Economics: Implications for Regulatory Behavior, Journal of Regulatory Economics 41 (2012) 1, p. 41.

routine upgrades and experiments in the regulatory framework. The upgrades in the regulatory policy framework must take place on a recurring basis. A central characteristic of good regulatory design and performance involving the internet is a norm that emphasizes continuous improvements, identifies relevant commercial phenomena on a regular basis, upgrades the knowledge base of the agency routinely, and always asks questions about what the appropriate institutional design should be. On the report card by which the quality of regulatory bodies is evaluated, a vital criterion is the demonstrated capacity of an agency to account for new commercial, political, and social phenomena and to adapt the agency's infrastructure to address them.

A positive modern trend among the world's competition and consumer protection authorities is a growing recognition that skill in implementation and the quality of institutional arrangements shape policy results. Instead of conferences that dwell exclusively upon the big issues of substance—what is the right standard for abuse of dominance, what does net neutrality mean, and how might its specific operational criteria be designed—there is more discussion about the proper design of regulatory frameworks and how regulatory agencies can make things work effectively in practice. There is a very healthy inclination to elevate questions about how to set priorities, how to structure operations, how to recruit and retain a capable professional staff, and how to measure effectiveness. This is producing a better balance between deliberations about questions of normative principles of policy on the one hand and matters of institutional infrastructure and management on the other.

Greater appreciation for the importance of institutional design and policy implementation may have the useful effect of spurring a redefinition of what constitutes a "good" regulatory agency. In scholarly papers and in casual conversation, students of regulation often discuss how well agencies are doing. There is no readily observable market index by which one can see how the "shares" of competition agencies are trading. What does it mean to say that a regulatory body is performing well, adequately or deficiently? A properly designed report card would reward an agency that consciously devotes effort to improving its institutional infrastructure. This requires capital investments in institutional capacity, a commitment that collides with the short-term orientation of much policymaking. An aphorism urged upon policy makers is "to pick the low hanging fruit." This summons up images of fruit gatherers roaming about the regulatory landscape with baskets in search of easily reached tree limbs. Public policy lacks a good aphorism that says it is the duty of agency leaders to plant trees. The trees of good policy can take years to grow, and the maturation process can easily outrun the tenure of the political appointee who will serve 2, 3, or 4 years. A policymaking culture that emphasizes short-term credit-claiming regards one who would plant trees as a fool. The consequence is an underinvestment in the kinds of capital improvements that improve agency performance over time.

One cannot readily design binding commands that compel leaders to make capital investments in agency capacity. A sustained commitment to institution-building arises instead from the establishment of norms (inside and outside the agency) that treat enhancements to institutional infrastructure and agency capacity as an essential duty of leadership. Such a norm presses regulators to describe in each budget cycle what steps the agency is taking today to make it a better institution 5 and 10 years into the future.

In the discussion that follows, this essay spells out approaches to creating stronger competition policy institutions. The essay builds upon three principal sources. First, it uses my earlier experiences in seeking to derive lessons from the process of competition law reform in countries undergoing the transition from central planning toward greater reliance on market systems.[9] In the course of advising various governments on the design and implementation of competition systems in the 1990s, it became apparent that donor organizations had overlooked the importance of institutional considerations in proposing specific reforms. Despite this shortcoming, a number of the newer systems proved to be a source of significant institutional innovation. The new systems started the process of building new competition policy frameworks without the path dependency and preconceptions that tend to beset older systems and limit their capacity to embrace innovations. The newer regimes asked important, basic questions about regulatory design and governance that older regimes might view as asked and answered.

The second major basis for the essay is a self-assessment exercise that the Federal Trade Commission (FTC) carried out in 2008 and published in 2009.[10] The self-study sought to assess the FTC's institutional framework in light of the exceptional institutional innovation and upheaval, noted earlier, among competition agencies. Called *The FTC at 100*, the self-study had three dimensions. The agency conducted internal assessments, held roundtables with a various observers in the United States, and had extensive public consultations abroad. The exercise benchmarked the Commission with many of its foreign counterparts.

The third perspective comes from recent experience working with individual jurisdictions on the management, organization, and strategy of competition systems. With greater frequency, agencies are seeking to improve their effectiveness by strengthening the methods by which they allocate resources, take decisions, and assess the economic outcomes of their programmes. The renewed modern attention to agency effectiveness is one of the most heartening developments in the field of competition policy.

---

[9] Kovacic, Institutional Foundations for Economic Law Reform in Transition Economies: The Case of Competition Policy and Antitrust Enforcement, Chicago-Kent Law Review 77 (2001) 1, p. 265.

[10] The Federal Trade Commission at 100: Into Our 2nd Century (Jan. 2009), available at http://www.ftc.gov/ftc/workshops/ftc100/docs/ftc100rpt.pdf. This project is summarized in Kovacic, The Digital Broadband Migration and the Federal Trade Commission: Building the Competition and Consumer Protection Agency of the Future, Journal on Telecommunications and High Technology Law 8 (2010) 1.

Characteristics of Good Agency Practice

What is a good competition agency? One valuable way to answer this question is to consider how an agency does its business. An important assumption here is that improvements in *how* an agency is organized and operates will increase the social value of *what* it does. Presented below are techniques that characterize good agency practice.

Clear Statement of Goals

One necessary foundation for effective agency performance is a clear definition of the agency's aims. Everything an agency does flows from the development of a clear statement of what the agency is about and what it means to do. It is a great challenge for leaders to state their aims clearly and to persuade the agency's staff that the stated aims are worth pursuing. The agency's administrative and professional staff have heard a sequence of political appointees offer their vision for the future. They are familiar with a wide array of slogans, clichés, and motivational techniques. The staff has heard them all. With each new group of political appointees, the staff seeks to learn the new vocabulary and re-flag existing projects to please the new regime. It is no small matter to overcome concerns that each collection of new leaders takes some comfort from knowing they will not fully internalize the effects of choices taken during their tenure. It requires considerable effort to make a credible commitment to build durable norms and to identify goals that serve the public and the institution well over time.

The formulation and statement of goals has two elements. One is internal discussion, and the other is external consultation with academics, consumers, business officials, and other public officials. The statement of goals is not a one-time endeavour. The agency's aims require reexamination and reformulation as conditions change. The clear statement and restatement of aims have a number of important advantages. The process provides valuable guidance to the agency's staff, and it helps affected firms organize their affairs to satisfy their obligations under the law. It facilities debate over what the agency ought to be trying to achieve. Further, it sets a baseline for measuring the results of the agency's activities. Maybe most important, the exercise of preparing a clear statement of aims forces the agency to define its purpose and to decide, among all of the choices available to it, what goals most warrant its attention.

Process to Set a Strategy

Good agencies have a conscious plan to set strategy. No responsibility of agency leadership is more important. A good strategy planning process does not consist simply of doing what the agency has done the year before. The tyranny of the daily routine has a powerful tendency to discourage planning and the forward-looking establishment of priorities. In the interviews for the FTC's self-study, one head of a competition agency said, "I'm so busy that I have no time to think, much less to plan." Many agencies operate with what might be called a fire department model of prioritization. The fire bell rings, the agency takes out the trucks, puts out the fire, returns to the station, and waits for the bell to ring again. In this model, nobody has time to think about fire prevention—to determine what causes fires and to figure out how best to stop them from happening in the first place.

A good process of setting strategy forces the agency to consider which outlays of resources yield the best returns. The United Kingdom's Office of Fair Trading (OFT) has one of the best management approaches for measuring proposed projects according to their likely economic effects or their contribution to the development of doctrine. The champions for each proposed initiative must answer essentially the following five questions: What are the expected gains in economic impact, doctrine, or staff experience? Who among our staff will do the project? How long will it take? What are the risks—especially, what are the costs to the agency if it fails? How will we know it is working?

Central to the OFT planning process is the definition of anticipated returns of a project and the comparison of these expected returns to the project's likely cost in staff and time. Project teams also are asked to provide practical tests by which the agency can tell whether expected gains are being realized in practice. OFT clearly communicates its planning framework to its staff and requires staff to relate proposed projects to the framework.

OFT takes individual projects and considers them as elements of an agency-wide portfolio. Individual matters are classified according to their likely risks and returns. Some matters pose relatively low risks and promise relatively small returns. Some present modest risks and offer modest returns. Others entail high risks but, if successful, are likely to generate substantial returns. By examining projects as parts of a portfolio, OFT is able to assess whether its programme is balanced in two respects. It helps the agency assess whether its commitments are well-matched to its capabilities to perform successfully, and it supplies a useful means of seeing whether the agency is taking acceptable political risks. In selecting projects, an agency can envision itself as either accumulating political capital or spending it. An agency can afford to incur deficits in political capital temporarily, but not chronically. If an agency runs deficits in political capital consistently over time, it will melt down and fail. Proposed projects must be measured by their impact upon the political capital account.

Strategic planning assumes special importance in the current context. The financial crisis has created enormous pressure to reduce public expenditures and to make wise choices among possible application of competition agency funds. For example, the FTC is responsible for enforcing approximately 55 statutes. To do this we receive an annual appropriation of roughly US$300 million, which supports the work of 1,100 employees. The imperative to select good projects increases with the possibility that federal regulators in the years ahead will do well to protect existing budgets or, perhaps, obtain small increases. There is no surplus of capacity to cope with improvident programme decisions that entail commitments that outrun our capabilities to deliver good results. Now more than ever a competition agency cannot rely on path dependence—a simply repetition of past patterns of behaviour—to decide what it will do.

From Case-Centrism to Effective Problem Solving

There is a healthy movement on the part of many competition authorities to move from a case-centric approach to policy making and resource allocation toward a philosophy that emphasize problem solving. The traditional focus of project selection has responded to the way in which many regulators bodies are evaluated. To a large degree, the popular measure of a competition agency is the number of cases it prosecutes: you are whom you sue. The commencement of a case is a readily measurable event, and cases often serve as a proxy for the more meaningful and difficult exercise of determining whether the agency's programmes are improving economic performance. In a case-centric measurement scheme, there often is extra credit for the big case that gets prominent media coverage.

There are serious problems with a norm that treats the number of prosecutorial events as the chief index of an agency's worth. The agency can become the equivalent of an airline that measures effectiveness by its number of takeoffs. At the agency's airport, an observer would see a large display board labeled "Departures." If the observer asked, "Where is the board for arrivals?," the agency would reply, "We do not track arrivals. Instead, look at our impressive number of departures." For purposes of good public policy, one needs to monitor arrivals carefully. Are projects arriving on time? Are projects taking the agency where it is supposed to be going? Did the agency set out on a case with a clear idea of where it was going—the difference between departing Washington, D.C. and saying "Fly to Los Angeles" versus saying "Fly to the West Coast."?

An indifference to how projects come to earth—smooth touchdowns, hard landings, or smash-ups?—can afflict leaders with relatively short-term appointments if the agency is graded by the number of cases it initiates. If the policymaking world and the community of academics, consumer groups, and practitioners measure the agency and its leaders by the number of cases launched, agency leaders may be induced to give them what they want. This is a terribly short-sighted structure of incentives.

There is strong evidence of an emerging, superior view among competition policy makers about how agencies should approach the application of their authority. The appropriate measure of an agency's value is how well it solves competition policy problems, not merely how many cases it prosecutes. A problem-solving orientation asks two basic questions about each problem the agency faces. The first is to ask what is the best policymaking tool or collection of tools to address the problem. The best problem-solving approach may often involve a mix of techniques. In the case of serious fraud involving electric commerce, it has become increasingly evident that effective competition policy making must draw upon a wide array of policy instruments.

The successful agency of the future will possess a broad, flexible portfolio of tools. For example, in the United States the FTC ought to be a central participant in forming policy for the internet and for a wide range of other challenging competition and consumer protection issues precisely because Congress has given the agency an unusually broad range of policy instruments. The Commission's Bureau of Economics has over 80 industrial organization economists with doctorates. Among other accomplishments, this team has done truly superior empirical research on many pressing issues of public policy, including recent path-breaking work on mortgage disclosures.[11] The Commission also has the distinctive capacity to compel firms to provide information for the preparation of studies unrelated to the prosecution of individual cases. The application of this capacity has enabled the FTC to make significant contributions to public understanding of matters such as the food advertising directed toward children[12] and the interaction between producers of branded pharmaceuticals and manufacturers of generic equivalents.[13]

A further distinctive capability of many competition agencies is the joining up of the competition and consumer protection perspectives that are inherent in a multi-purpose mandate. For a number of matters involving the operation of the internet, it can be valuable to bring both substantive disciplines to be in deciding when and how policymakers should intervene. For examine, in addressing subjects relating to privacy, the FTC's Bureau of Consumer Protection's experience in bringing cases, designing regulations, and conducting education programmes has generated useful insights about the design of privacy protections. The agency's experience as a competition policy authority makes the agency sensitive to possibilities for rivalry among firms to elicit private initiative to satisfy consumer tastes concerning privacy, and it highlights the need to ensure that privacy related rules are not set in a way that endangers practices that bring significant benefits to consumers. The mix of competition and consumer protection duties creates a healthy dynamic tension inside the agency and increases our capacity to see all major dimensions of a problem and devise appropriate solutions.

No agency can assume that it has achieved the optimal regulatory regime. Changing economic conditions and experience gathered from regulatory policy in other jurisdictions supply reasons for continuing reassessment. One question worth considering is whether the results of collective decision making by a multi-member commission are superior to those achieved from a regulatory body headed by one individual.

[11] Lacko & Pappalardo, Federal Trade Commission, Bureau of Economics, Staff Report, Improving Consumer Mortgage Disclosures: An Empirical Assessment of Current and Prototype Disclosure Forms (June 2007), available at http://www.ftc.gov/os/2007/06/p025505mortgage disclosurereport.pdf.

[12] Federal Trade Commission, Marketing Food to Children and Adolescents: A Review of Industry Expenditures, Activities, and Self-Regulation (July 2008), available at http://www.ftc.gov/os/2008/07/p064504foodmarketingreport.pdf.

[13] Federal Trade Commission, Generic Drug Entry Prior to Patent Expiration: An FTC Study (July 2002), available at http://www.ftc.gov/os/2002/07/genericdrugstudy.pdf.

Many agencies are governed by a single official or a team consisting of a chief executive and a chief operating officer. A potential benefit of having a unitary governance mechanism is an increase of accountability. The head of an institution with a unitary governance framework may be more likely to internalize the costs and benefits of decisions taken during her tenure. The unitary framework also eliminates the circumstance where one member of a governing board acts in a manner that diminishes the value of the partnership but advances the individual's interests.

Comparative experience also raises serious questions about procedural conventions governing the operation of multi-member commissions in some jurisdictions. The US Government in the Sunshine Act,[14] for example, severely limits opportunities for collective discussion and consultation that are assumed to the strengths of a decision making by a college rather than by a single executive. For a broad range of matters, the Sunshine Act forbids a quorum of commission members (for a five member body, the quorum is three) from discussing agency business without the prior issuance of a public notice that such conversations will take place and, in many instances, without making the conversation open to the public. It is difficult to imagine a measure that is better calculated to diminish agency effectiveness by forbidding spontaneous conversations among a plurality of members of the board. At the FTC, conversations about FTC cases or broader policy issues are permitted if only two commissioners participate. For instance, if a third member of the commission appears in the cafeteria and joins two colleagues who are discussing FTC business over lunch, the conversation about Commission work immediately ceases and discourse turns to topics of culture, sport, or holiday plans. Consequently, discussions about agency matters take place in bilateral conversations between commissioners, with the inevitable misinterpretation and loss of meaning that takes place as information is relayed in a chain of seriatim encounters, two-by-two, among the five. Another accepted circumvention of the Sunshine Act is to have the advisors of the commissioners meet as a group to discuss what board's collective preferences might be. Rather than encourage private face-to-face discussions among the five board members, the multi-member federal commissions rely heavily on the insane alternative of having their staffs collectively and privately perform key functions of debate and consensus-building.

When the strictures of the Sunshine Act are explained to the FTC's foreign counterparts, there is an evident disbelief that a nation nominally would choose to avail itself of the benefits from collective decision making and proceed to disable, or severely encumber, the process of collective discussion that for most tribunals is an essential means by which the benefits of governance by college are realized. A rethink of this debilitating limitation is an appropriate part of a larger assessment about how the FTC and other federal regulatory commissions might improve effectiveness. If existing limits on spontaneous private discussions involving a plurality of commission members are not relaxed, there is considerable merit to abandoning the collective governance model and replacing it with a unitary executive.

[14] 5 U.S.C. 552b (1994).

Effective System of Internal Quality Control

Modern experience has underscored the importance of strong quality control as an element of good agency practice. Agencies with competition or consumer protection responsibilities are using a variety of means to test the legal theory and factual support for proposed cases and administrative regulations. Some have designated staff to participate on "scrutiny panels" or to serve as "devil's advocates" to test the work of the case handling teams. A key focus of these measures is to avoid a tendency to underestimate the quality of conceptual arguments and facts that an opponent will raise in litigation.

Beyond attaining an accurate view of an opponent's likely litigation positions, the effort to build robust, internally driven quality control techniques is to set policy and process in the right place—to do the right things and to do things the right way. The enhancement of internal quality control mechanisms reflects an awareness that an agency will not achieve good policy results consistently if it relies principally on outsiders to come in from time to time and exhort the agency to do this, that, or the other thing. External assessments can help guide the design of an internal quality control and usefully supplement the agency's own internal measures.[15] Yet the urgency to test theories, facts, programmes, and processes must come foremost from within.

Investments in Building Knowledge

The most important input to what competition and consumer protection agencies do is knowledge. Agencies rise or fall according to how well they understand commercial developments and stay attuned to current thinking in business strategy, economics, law, and public administration. The commercial environment that the agencies oversee and the intellectual disciplines on which they rely feature high levels of dynamism and increasing complexity. A recurring criticism of public policy making that involves the internet and other dynamic commercial developments is that the knowledge base of the government agencies is the equivalent of a bicycle and the rate of change in the industry resembles a Porsche. From this perspective, the agency cyclists struggle in vain to catch up. On a good day, they feebly get their arms around developments that took place 5 years ago. Policy

[15] An excellent example of this form of external assessment is the framework that Paul Malyon and Bernard J. Phillips have developed in recent years under the auspices of a project sponsored by the Competition Committee of the Organization for Economic Cooperation and Development. Malyon and Phillips have constructed an evaluation tool that assists competition authorities to examine their management processes and, based on the results of extensive interviews with agency officials and employees and outside observers, to construct an action plan for improvements. The competition authorities of Hungary, Mexico, and Portugal have participated in this exercise.

is set based on stale knowledge, new developments rush onward, and the agency never achieves the capacity to addresses current problems effectively.

A competition policy or consumer protection agency resembles a high technology company whose well-being depends upon the quality of its research and development programmes. Imagine a conversation between the executives of a pharmaceutical company and investment analysts. Suppose the analysts ask the chief executive to describe the firm's R&D programme. What conclusions would the analysts form if the CEO said the firm has fired its scientists, shuttered its laboratories, abandoned plans to develop new drugs, and chosen to focus solely on turning out its existing products as fast as it can? That is a formula for going out of business.

To cope with change and complexity, the agency must obtain regular, substantial additions to its base of knowledge. Without routine upgrades, an agency is prone to misdiagnose problems, select harmless or perverse cures, or find itself trapped in analytical models that once represented the state of the art but have become threadbare. The successful agency of the future is one that invests heavily in building knowledge and in refreshing its intellectual capital. These investments are the public administration equivalent of research and development.[16] These outlays do not occur spontaneously or by accident. Good agency practice requires a conscious process of building R&D outlays into every budget cycle. Regulators should be pressed to explain what part of their budgets is being spent on making their agencies smarter.

R&D for competition policy and consumer protection can take several forms. One method is to convene public consultations in the form of hearings or workshops. In these proceedings, an agency asks knowledgeable outsiders to share their views about important developments in commerce and in academic disciplines central to the agency's work. These proceedings do not necessarily seek to identify definitive policy making paths. In many instances, they serve to teach the agency what it must know to apply its authority wisely.

Since the early 1990s, the FTC has made external consultations a more central element of its portfolio of activities.[17] This reflects the Commission's recognition that the only way for the agency to stay current is to use its policy instruments to improve its understanding of the commercial and intellectual environment where it operates. This highlights another respect where case-centric measures of agency effectiveness give false signals about what an agency should do. In a case-centric world, the incentive to make substantial R&D investments goes down the drain.

---

[16] During his tenure as FTC Chairman from 2001–2004, Timothy Muris underscored the need for the FTC and similar institutions to invest in "competition policy research and development" and to make these expenditures a routing element of the agency's budget process. Muris, Looking Forward: The Federal Trade Commission and the Future Development of Competition Policy, Colum. Bus. L. Rev. (2003) 2, p. 359.

[17] More Than Law Enforcement: the FTC's Many Tools—A Conversation with Muris & Pitofsky, Antitrust L.J. 72 (2005) 3, p. 773 (774–780) (discussing FTC's expanded use of public consultations).

In any period, an agency faces the question of how much to consume (i.e. bring new cases or issue new rules) and how much to invest (e.g. undertaking projects that improve the agency's base of knowledge or its administrative infrastructure and thus increase its capacity to select the optimal mix of policy measures). If it embraces case-centrism as the measure of its worth, an agency will emphasize current consumption and slight investments in capability.

Another approach to building knowledge is to engage the skills of institutions outside the agency. The FTC cannot accumulate the capability it needs with its own resources alone. One promising way for the FTC to augment its own efforts is to form partnerships with academic research centers. In 2008, the agency initiated a prototype with Northwestern University, which has a superb complex of researchers in business, economics, and law who specialize in topics closely related to the FTC's responsibilities. The FTC programme with Northwestern could become a platform that the agency can duplicate elsewhere in the United States and abroad. One can look forward to a day when the FTC has links with institutions such as the Department of Economics at the University of Toulouse, the Centre for Competition Policy at the University of East Anglia, the faculties of economics and law at Oxford University, the London School of Economics, the National University of Singapore, and any number of other leading research centers. Through partnerships with academic research centers, the FTC can learned about state of the art developments in theory and empirical research and, by reviewing current Commission initiatives, can seek to encourage researchers to study topics related to the agency's work. To this end, the FTC might make greater efforts to make agency data accessible to researchers who have an interest in doing applied work related to competition law and consumer protection. Without these kinds of collaborations, the FTC and its counterpart agencies overseas are unlikely to keep up with the demands that developments in commerce and in the intellectual framework of competition and consumer protection place upon government authorities to strengthen their pool of knowledge.

Recruiting and Retaining Human Capital

As suggested above, increased cooperation with external institutions can help the FTC expand its capabilities and improve its effectiveness. Even with these and other forms of collaboration, the public agencies can prosper only if they succeed in recruiting and retaining a high quality staff. At some point, the United States will have to confront the political and social hypocrisy by which its citizens and elected officials demand Mercedes-like performance from public institutions and insist on paying nothing more than Chevrolet prices to get it. In no area of our experience as consumers do we expect there to be no general link between the quality of what we are willing to pay and what we get. On what basis might one reasonably expect that this relationship is largely or completely irrelevant in the field of public administration?

The current recession has raised the FTC's personnel retention rates and made public service a more attractive career option for many individuals. No agency can count on national economic distress to preserve and enhance its human capital indefinitely. As economic conditions improve, the economic enticements of the private sector again will hammer at the fragile structure of civil service compensation schemes. Even amid conditions of economic crisis, there are many skills necessary to agency effectiveness that cannot be had on the cheap. For example, good information technology specialists remain in high demand. The FTC and its foreign counterparts depend ever more heavily on their communications infrastructure and electronic data sets to conduct routine operations and improve productivity. An agency can suffer grievously if it does not sustain and enhance its information technology systems. How long will a superb information technology officer remain with the Commission if the civil service salary ceiling remains at about $150,000—or perhaps $20,000 more with a Senior Executive Service bonus?

Public agencies are no different from any number of other institutions whose quality of performance is a function of their human capital. A major reason for the FTC's progression from near death in 1969[18] and from a severe legislative pummeling in the late 1970s and early 1980s[19] to a position in the front ranks of the world's public agencies is that the overall quality of its personnel improved dramatically. One major enhancement was the development of a larger number of highly skilled teams to prepare and litigate the agency's cases. Despite these improvements, the FTC and many other public agencies lack the depth of skills that private sector institutions such as law firms can assemble. The Commission resembles a sports team with an excellent first team and a substantial number of skilled players on the bench. However, the roster is thinner than one would like in several areas, and the departure of certain valued performers could cause a drop off in performance.

The FTC's position is not unique among competition and consumer protection authorities. If one makes the safe assumption that salaries for civil servants are not about to rise significantly, agencies will have to find novel ways to attract and keep the human talent they need to perform effectively. Several strategies come to mind. One way is to give agency employees a better experience by devoting extensive attention to individual professional development. Another is to cooperate more extensively with the academic community to establish internships for students, to recruit promising graduates, and to encourage faculty members to spend time in the agencies as visiting scholars. If substantial turnover is to be an inevitable, chronic condition, the agencies must build methods to retain institutional memory and other

[18] Ibid (592–602), p. 587 (592–602) (discussing critical assessments of FTC issued by Ralph Nader's consumer organization and by a blue ribbon commission of the American Bar Association).

[19] Ibid (592–602).

forms of important knowhow when people leave. Agencies can develop an electronic repository of research memoranda, checklists used to perform interviews and conduct investigations, and other practical tools that can be used by others and do not need to be reconstructed from scratch. Staff can establish and maintain data sets that track activity and permit managers and case handlers to obtain a clear, accurate profile of what the agency has done and to identify the nature and status of existing matters. Many of these endeavours require the agency to make regular capital outlays for information systems.

Constructing and Improving Networks with Other Institutions

The FTC self study underscored a point that many agencies have come to realize in the course of working in legal environments where many public agencies share responsibility for specific functions. Individual initiative will not enable competition and consumer protection agencies to carry out their mandates successfully. The performance of national competition policy and consumer protection systems will degrade over time if agencies do not improve their capacity to cooperate effectively with other institutions that have the same or similar mandates.

A number of jurisdictions are realizing that it can be a tremendous source of national economic advantage to improve the design of regulatory institutions, either by reordering the assignment of regulatory responsibility or by strengthening cooperation among existing institutions. This advantage consists of achieving the existing level of regulatory performance at a lower cost or improving regulatory results at the same cost. If the United States complacently regards the existing configuration of competition policy and consumer protection regulatory authority as immutable and fails to engage existing institutions in more substantial collaborative programmes, the nation will fall behind other jurisdictions that are experimenting actively with institutional reforms to achieve superior policy solutions.

The present configuration of competition policy authority is a striking example of the problem. In recent years, three jurisdictions—France, Portugal, and Spain—have consolidated their two national competition agencies into a single entity. Brazil has combined most functions performed by the three national bodies with competition policy authority into a single institution. These developments ought to be a stimulus for Americans to ask whether the existing distribution of policy making and prosecutorial power is sensible. What benefits does the country gain from having two federal antitrust agencies? Is it sensible for sectoral regulators at the national and state levels to conduct reviews of mergers and impose conditions that go beyond remedies attained by the federal antitrust authorities? Should state governments have competence to enforce the national competition laws and conduct proceedings parallel to those undertaken by the Department of Justice and the FTC? Is the existing form of private rights of action well conceived?

A closely related question of institutional design is the wisdom of maintaining jurisdictional boundaries that were set in the first half of the twentieth century. The FTC has advocated the abandonment of the common carrier exception to its jurisdiction to account for the transformation of the telecommunications sector in the past 30 years.[20] The Commission has developed substantial expertise in dealing with false advertising and the litigation of claims involving unfair or deceptive acts or practices. This expertise usefully could be brought to bear upon a range of matters involving telecommunications services providers, but the common carrier exception precludes this.

If the answer to all of these queries is to leave the status quo in place, then it is incumbent upon the public agencies with competition or consumer protection duties to spend more effort than they do today to achieve a greater convergence of approaches and to see how collaboration can permit them to achieve results that exceed the grasp of single agencies acting alone. One place to start is to create a domestic competition network and a domestic consumer protection network to engage the public authorities in the kind of discussions and cooperation that US agencies pursue with their foreign counterparts.[21] There is no forum where the US public institutions assemble regularly to discuss what they do and consider, as a group, how the complex framework of federal, state, and local commands might operate more effectively. At best, the US public authorities perform these network building functions in piecemeal fashion at bar association conferences and other professional gatherings. There also are bilateral discussions involving some public bodies.[22] These measures are useful, but they are not good substitutes for the establishment of a more comprehensive framework of interagency regulatory cooperation. The US competition agencies spend more time seeking to develop effective mechanisms for cooperation with foreign authorities than they devote to the integration of policymaking across federal and state agencies domestically.

Good examples of how to achieve greater levels of cooperation exist abroad. In the middle of the previous decade, the European Union (EU) created the European Competition Network (ECN) to coordinate the work of the national competition authorities of the EU member states and the European Commission's Competition Directorate (DG COMP). The ECN meets regularly to discuss matters of common

[20] See Prepared Statement of the Federal Trade Commission, Before the Subcommittee on Interstate Commerce, Trade, and Tourism, Committee on Commerce, Science and Transportation, US Senate (Apr. 8, 2008), available at http://www.ftc.gov/os/testimony/p034101reauth.pdf.

[21] See Kovacic, Toward a Domestic Competition Network, in: Epstein/Greve (eds.), *Competition Laws in Conflict: Antitrust Jurisdiction in the Global Economy*, 2004, p. 316 (describing value of establishing a domestic competition network).

[22] These initiatives facilitate discussion about current law enforcement matters and the examination of larger policy issues. Since 2006, the FTC and many of the state attorneys general have convened an annual workshop to address topics of common interest. The workshops have addressed competition and consumer protection issues in the petroleum industry, the pharmaceutical industry, and the retailing sector. This recently developed custom will continue In the autumn of 2009, when the FTC, DOJ, and the states convene a workshop on energy issues.

concern and to promote information sharing and other forms of cooperation. The network has achieved considerable success in avoiding conflicts that might have arisen from the EU's decision to devolve greater levels of responsibility to the member states as part of a modernization of the EU's competition policy framework.

As suggested above, government agencies in the United States would do well to emulate the European experience and create domestic networks for competition policy and consumer protection, respectively. A domestic competition network could begin with a memorandum of understanding adopted by the public agencies with competition policy duties, including the two federal antitrust agencies, sectoral regulators such as the Federal Communications Commission (FCC) and the antitrust units of the state attorneys general. The agreement might commit the participants to participate in regular discussions about matters such as the coordination of inquiries involving the same transaction or conduct, the development of common analytical standards, information sharing about specific cases, staff exchanges, and the identification of superior investigative techniques. Cooperation could progress toward the pursuit of joint research projects and the preparation of a common strategy to address various commercial phenomena. The network would be a platform for replicating activities that have become core elements of the ECN, such as interagency sharing of practical knowledge and sector-specific experience, the development of common training exercises, and benchmarking of procedures across agencies.

The same approach could be applied to consumer protection. Shared concurrent authority is common for a variety of consumer protection matters involving the internet and other aspects of commerce. For the internet, the consumer protection portfolio is shared by, among others, the FCC, the FTC, state attorneys general, and state consumer protection offices. Focal points for collaboration within a domestic consumer protection network would include the development of common analytical techniques, coordination of investigations, and the preparation of common research projects.

Communication with External Constituencies

Effective internal and external communications are key ingredients of good agency performance. One dimension of effective communications is to communicate the agency's aims and intentions clearly to its own staff and to external audiences. Another element is education directed to consumers and to businesses. Consumer and business education programmes can encourage precaution taking that reduces exposure to internet fraud and spurs greater reporting of episodes of apparent misconduct.

Education programmes can build upon what the FTC learns through the application of its research and data collection tools. As noted above, FTC researchers have done excellent work to examine how individuals absorb information and understand disclosures associated with various products and services. The work of the FTC's Bureau of Economics has identified a number of ways where disclosures involving mortgage transactions might be improved to enable consumers to make better choices among product alternatives. These efforts supplement the agency's litigation programme, which challenges instances of misrepresentation and related misconduct involving the sale of financial services products. The mix of initiatives—research, consumer education, and litigation—is another illustration of the application of a multidimensional problem solving approach to address problems the FTC has encountered.

Ex Post Evaluation

A necessary element of the policy life cycle is a conscious process to assess whether specific agency initiatives achieved their intended aims. There is a great temptation to treat ex post evaluation as a luxury to be dispensed with in order to handle the press of new business. It is easier to issue a press release that gives assurances about the efficacy of a chosen course of action than it is to attempt to measure actual effects. Too often public agencies behave like a hospital that performs surgeries, discharges its patient, and declines to provide post-operative monitoring. Upon discharge, the patient asks the surgeon, "When do I come back to see you?" The surgeon replies, "Never. We have a press release that says we removed every malignant cell, we leave every bit of healthy tissue in place, and you are in great shape." No responsible hospital practices medicine in that manner, and the same should go for competition or consumer protection agencies. The measurement of outcomes can be difficult, but difficulty does not excuse a failure to try.

An ex post evaluation programme ought to have three basic elements.[23] The first is to test the results of the agency's substantive initiatives—to assess the impact of cases, rules, education programmes, and advocacy. Agencies can avail themselves of a growing body of experience concerning the design of evaluation techniques. Means to this end include reviews conducted by agency insiders, consultations with outside experts, and peer review exercises performed by representatives from other competition authorities.

The second is to evaluate the agency's procedures and management methods. For example, by measuring the time required for matters to progress through the agency's investigation and decision making processes, it may be possible to identify ways to accelerate the disposition of individual matters without diminishing the quality of the agency's analysis.

The third approach is to conduct periodic reviews of the institutional framework through which the jurisdiction develops and applies competition and consumer

[23] For a more comprehensive discussion, see Kovacic, Using Ex Post Evaluations to Improve the Performance of Competition Policy Authorities, J. Corp. Law 31 (2006) 2, p. 503.

protection policy. An important element of good administrative practice is to embrace a norm that treats periodic assessment as an essential foundation for agency improvement. A culture that regards routine assessment and refinement has to be built from within and not imposed by outsiders.

One focal point for this type of assessment is the US framework for privacy. A review could consider whether the country should take the disparate elements of privacy oversight and create a uniform data protection regime. Alternatively, should the country leave existing industry specific and activity specific privacy commands in place and construct a new, overarching statute that would cover conduct not subject to existing oversight? A third possibility is to rely mainly on the application of Section 5 of the FTC Act to fill in the interstices in the system. Whatever path is taken, the process of reform should be the result of a well-considered deliberative assessment and not merely a quick response to crisis.

Conclusion: A Report Card on Good Administrative Practice

What do we mean when we speak of a competition authority as being a "good" agency? By what standards should we measure whether a competition authority is performing its responsibilities properly with respect to matters subject to its oversight?

One vital approach to measure a public regulatory authority is to assess the quality of its institutional infrastructure. Good agency performance does not take shape in a vacuum. Policy travels across an infrastructure of institutions, and the strength of the institutional framework and operational methods determines whether agencies can deliver superior policy results.

As suggested above, successful competition policy agencies are likely to feature several characteristics. Good competition agencies (1) clearly and coherently specify their goals, (2) devise and apply a conscious, thoughtful mechanism for selecting strategies to attain their aims, (3) measure themselves not by the number of cases they prosecute but by their capacity to solve problems by recourse to a broad, flexible portfolio of policy tools, (4) develop rigorous internal quality control systems, (5) invest heavily in building knowledge, increasing human capital, and enhancing the infrastructure of information systems, (6) routinely engage in ex post evaluation exercises to determine how specific initiatives turned out and to identify the need for refinements of the agency's analytical approach, statutory powers, and institutional design.

Doing these things well requires incumbent agency leadership to make capital investments whose benefits may come to pass mainly during into the tenure of future appointees. A telling sign of a good leader is the intensity of commitment to take actions today that generate positive externalities for one's successors. For an agency, the aim is to create a norm that discourages individual credit-claiming in the short term and emphasizes contributions to the long-term success of the institution.

One person whose ideas helped inform the FTC's self study is Fred Hilmer, who played a formative role in the modern development of Australia's competition and consumer protection system and now serves as the Chancellor of the University of New South Wales. Among other duties, Chancellor Hilmer teaches executive MBA classes. He tells his students that the successes their companies are experiencing today probably are rooted in long-term investments that their predecessors made 5 or 10 years ago. Hilmer advises them, upon returning to their offices, to pose the following question to themselves every day: "What have I done to make the lives of leaders who follow me better off 5 or 10 years from now?" That is good advice for public officials, as well.

Competition Policy and International Trade Distortions

Alden F. Abbott and Shanker Singham

Introduction

Competition law and international trade law ("trade law") traditionally have "sailed under different flags." Competition laws sanction business conduct that is deemed to harm the competitive process—in particular, collusive or exclusionary agreements among competitors, anticompetitive mergers, and abuses of monopoly power. Trade laws, by contrast, generally impose specific limitations (tariffs and non-tariff barriers) on business transactions that cross national boundaries. Furthermore, national trade laws, unlike competition laws, increasingly have been constrained by international agreements, and litigation generated by those laws has been reviewed by international tribunals.

However, notwithstanding their distinct legal traditions, international trade policy and competition policy, properly applied, are mutually reinforcing methods for promoting welfare. Changes to trade laws and regulations that reduce or eliminate national barriers to trade and investment (such as high tariffs, quotas, and investor nationality restrictions) promote welfare-enhancing contractual relations that expand trade and, more generally, raise aggregate welfare in the

---

The views expressed herein are solely attributable to the authors and do not necessarily represent the views of their employers. This article draws substantially on Abbott/Singham, Enhancing Welfare by Attacking Anticompetitive Market Distortions, Concurrences 8 (2011) 4. The authors benefited greatly from the comments of Randolph W. Tritell, Director, Office of International Affairs, Federal Trade Commission.

A.F. Abbott (✉)
Director for Global Patent Law and Competition Strategy, Research in Motion,
1611 Westmoreland Street, McLean, VA 22101-5166, USA
e-mail: alden.abbott@gmail.com

S. Singham
Partner, Squire Sanders, 1200 19th St., N.W., Suite 300, Washington, DC 20036, USA
e-mail: Shanker.singham@squiresanders.com

C. Herrmann et al. (eds.), *European Yearbook of International Economic Law (EYIEL), Vol. 4 (2013)*, European Yearbook of International Economic Law 4,
DOI 10.1007/978-3-642-33917-2_2,

liberalising nations.[1] The benefits of trade liberalisation are magnified by competition law rules that lower the incidence of consumer welfare-reducing restrictions on the competitive process.[2]

Multilateral welfare-enhancing initiatives characterise modern trade policy. In the post-World War II era, the General Agreement on Tariffs and Trade (GATT) negotiating framework, and its successor, the World Trade Organization (WTO), have substantially reduced tariffs and non-tariff trade barriers, promoting global trade liberalisation import competition and thus economic growth.[3] Also, regional and bilateral trade liberalisation compacts, such as the European Union (originally a "customs union" that was transformed into a vehicle for large scale European economic integration), the North American Free Trade Agreement ("NAFTA," covering the United States, Canada, and Mexico), and the US-Korea Free Trade

---

[1] The beneficial effects of trade liberalisation are summarised at OECD, Benefits of Trade Liberalisation, available at: http://www.oecd.org/about/0,3347,en_2649_36442957_1_1_1_1_1,00.html. Technical questions regarding the welfare effects of specific trade liberalisation policies (such as whether the welfare benefits due to "trade creation" associated with bilateral or regional "free trade" outweigh the welfare losses due to "trade diversion" that reduces trade with non-liberalising jurisdictions) are beyond the scope of this article. A classic work that explores trade diversion and trade creation is Viner, *The Customs Union Issue*, 1950. For a more recent review of the literature on trade creation versus trade diversion, see, e.g., Eicher/Henn/Papageorgiou, Trade Creation and Trade Diversion Revisited: Accounting for Model Uncertainty and Natural Trading Partner Effects, Journal of Applied Econometrics 27 (2010) 2, available at: http://faculty.washington.edu/te/papers/EHP.pdf.

[2] We use the term "consumer welfare" as including the sum of consumers' and producers' surplus. This is consistent with the approach recommended by the legal scholar Robert H. Bork, see Bork, *The Antitrust Paradox*, (Revised ed.) 1993, pp. 90–106 (deeming the maximisation of allocative and productive efficiency (that are associated with consumers' surplus and producers' surplus, respectively) to be the appropriate goal of US antitrust enforcement). Consumer welfare-reducing restrictions could be either private (such as, for example, "naked" price fixing, division of markets among competitors, and other anticompetitive contracts) or public (such as, for example, onerous licensing requirements, other restrictions on entry into businesses or professions, and prohibitions on truthful advertising). Public restraints tend to be the most pernicious, because the normal market forces that tend to undermine private restraints (for instance, entry by new competitors) cannot undermine such restraints, which are backed by the force of law. Only changes to the law, which will be lobbied against by the beneficiaries of the anticompetitive status quo, can undo restraints imposed by government. For an overview of the growing international consensus regarding the harmful nature of government restraints on competition, see Cooper/Kovacic, US Convergence with International Competition Norms: Antitrust Law and Public Restraints on Competition, Boston University Law Review 90 (2010) 4, p. 1555, available at: http://www.ftc.gov/speeches/kovacic/2010convergencecomment.pdf.

[3] The WTO has also established a binding trade dispute resolution framework for assessing complaints regarding the alleged illegal application of anti-dumping and countervailing standards, among other rules. This framework, albeit imperfect, has provided a means for somewhat constraining international "trade wars" and constraining the application of protectionist policies. The WTO has been characterised as a multinational structure that, by reducing the power of protectionist interest groups found in individual countries, can simultaneously promote welfare-enhancing trade and accountable government. See McGinnis/Movsesian, The World Trade Constitution, Harvard Law Review 114 (2000) 2, p. 511 (558).

Agreement (one of several such agreements entered into by the United States), have been a force for increasing welfare by extending the geographic extent and scope of trading and investment opportunities.[4]

However, as the WTO-led trade law system has expanded, it has not wisely brought national competition laws within its purview.[5] Currently, national competition laws embody a host of different assumptions about the role of economics; the proper scope and nature of competition law prohibitions, rules, and remedies; procedural issues; and the influence non-competition policy concerns should have on competition law enforcement decisions. Any effort at reaching a consensus on these questions that could inform decision-making under a WTO competition code would be doomed to failure if it related to private behaviour. There is a role for international competition law policy in an increasingly globalised economy through voluntary efforts at building understanding across jurisdictions and thereby gradually converging towards best (or "better") practices. The role of the International Competition Network (ICN) in furthering this aim is touched upon later in this article. In addition, in the area of public sector restraints on trade there may be scope for an international agreement (initially among countries whose consumer welfare enhancing policy goals are more closely aligned) as we also discuss later.

In any event, as the number of ACMDs rises, the WTO system is being forced to deal with a number of regulatory restrictions that reduce welfare by harming the competitive process and have a trade effect. Specifically, the WTO has embraced disciplines on anti-competitive private sector restraints (GATS Article IX), and specific anti-competitive restraints on a sectoral basis (Basic Telecom Agreement and Reference Paper on Competition safeguards). These initiatives extend beyond GATT 1947 provisions that are drawn from the competition lexicon. They include Article III 2 of GATT 1947, which prohibits discriminatory taxation interpreted by the cases to require "equality of competitive opportunity," and GATT Article XVII, which limits the range of activities of State-Trading Enterprises (STEs). Under Article XVII, STEs are subject to commercial considerations when operating in commercial markets and "fair and equitable" standards when buying for themselves. Both of those standards are really competition standards. Indeed, in *Canada*

[4] As explained in the references in note 1, such agreements diminish welfare, however, to the extent that they divert more trade away from the rest of the world than they create within the liberalised trade bloc.

[5] For a good description of the European Union's proposal for inclusion of competition within the WTO framework, and, the failure of this initiative in light of opposition from the United States and developing countries, see generally Papadopoulos, *The International Dimension of EU Competition Law and Policy*, 2010, pp. 211–245. As explained therein, the United States was particularly concerned about the lack of experience of many developing countries with competition law and policy, and the risk that application of the WTO dispute resolution system would risk politicising the application of competition rules (due to the second-guessing of discretionary prosecutorial decisions based on complex evidentiary evaluations). The European proposal dealt with competition laws and policies as they related to private restraints, as opposed to limiting the WTO's jurisdiction over the Anti-Competitive Market Distortions we discuss in this article, and therefore prompted many of these concerns.

Wheat Board,[6] the leading case on Article XVII, the US agreed that "commercial considerations" meant profit-maximising behaviour (in other words, any behaviour that was not profit-maximising was not "commercial").

Nevertheless, the WTO and other trade agreements simply do not reach a variety of anticompetitive welfare-reducing government measures that create de facto trade barriers by favouring domestic interests over foreign competitors. Moreover, many of these restraints are not in place to discriminate against foreign entities, but rather exist to promote certain favoured firms. We dub these restrictions "anticompetitive market distortions" or "ACMDs," in that they involve government actions that empower certain private interests to obtain or retain artificial competitive advantages over their rivals, be they foreign or domestic.

This article assesses the nature of ACMDs, and the limited efforts of government and international institutions in dealing with them. It briefly demonstrates that the WTO has not been able (and in the near term almost certainly will not be able) to cope adequately with these restraints. However, it then strikes a more hopeful note by suggesting that the multilateral International Competition Network ("ICN")—and, in particular, the ICN's Advocacy Working Group—may be a possible near term vehicle for beginning to confront (or at least beginning to highlight) the harm of ACMDs. With that in mind, this article proposed the development of a metric to estimate the net welfare costs of ACMDs. Such a metric could help strengthen the hand of the ICN—and of reform-minded public officials—in building the case for the dismantling of these restraints, or their replacement by less costly means for benefiting favoured constituencies. Eventually, "soft convergence" under the aegis of the ICN might begin to lead some jurisdictions to chip away at, if not wholly dismantle, harmful ACMDs—or at least to begin to replace ACMDs with less harmful means of benefiting favoured constituencies. The dismantling of ACMDs might also be facilitated by the negotiation of a WTO plurilateral agreement (or some other agreement among like-minded countries) to prohibit the most egregious types of ACMDs. As these reforms gradually are implemented, restrictions on welfare-enhancing international commerce will further diminish and national competition policies may be expected to be deployed more effectively in the consumer (and public) interest.

Nature of ACMDs

ACMDs have up to now largely avoided competition law sanction. For purposes of our discussion, ACMDs include: (1) governmental restraints that distort markets and lessen competition; and (2) anticompetitive private arrangements that are

[6] Report of the Appellate Body, WT/DS276/AB/R, *Canada – Measures Relating to Exports of Wheat and Treatment of Imported Grain*. This case is discussed later in this article following note 11.

backed by government actions, have substantial effects on trade outside the jurisdiction that imposes the restrictions, and are not readily susceptible to domestic competition law challenge. Among the most pernicious ACMDs are those that artificially alter the cost-base as between competing firms. Such cost changes will have large and immediate effects on market shares, and therefore on international trade flows.

With the growing internationalisation of commerce, ACMDs not only diminish domestic consumer welfare—they increasingly may have a harmful effect on foreign enterprises that seek to do business in the country imposing the restraint. The home nations of the affected foreign enterprises, moreover, may as a practical matter find it not feasible to apply their competition laws extraterritorially to curb the restraint, given issues of jurisdictional reach and comity (particularly if the restraint flies under the colors of domestic law). Because ACMDs also have not been constrained by international trade liberalisation initiatives, they pose a serious challenge to global welfare enhancement by curtailing potential trade and investment opportunities.

Inspired by our focus on harm to competition, we believe that the most fruitful method for assessing ACMDs is to assess them from the perspective of how they affect market participants. This methodology is drawn from the OECD Competition Assessment Toolkit ("Toolkit"),[7] which seeks to help "governments to eliminate barriers to competition by providing a method for identifying unnecessary restraints on market activities and developing alternative, less restrictive means that still achieve government policy objectives." The Toolkit focuses specifically on rules and regulations that (1) limit the number and range of suppliers, (2) limit the ability of suppliers to compete, (3) reduce the incentives of suppliers to compete, (4) limit the choices and information available to consumers, and (5) apply to state-owned enterprises (SOEs).

Rules That Limit the Number and Range of Suppliers

These include the grant of exclusive rights for a company to supply a service or product; license requirements; limitations on public procurement opportunities; geographic limitations on the ability of firms to supply goods or services, invest capital, or supply labour; and the bestowal of exclusive rights on government to supply a good or perform a service. Within this category, restrictions on entry are the most common source of complaints from foreign and domestic firms. Entry restrictions can take the form of direct bans or indirect restrictions, such as quality standards, certification rules, capital adequacy requirements for banks, and other administrative or bureaucratic barriers. Entry restrictions not only may confer market power and restrict output of favoured firms, they may inhibit the realisation

[7] The OECD Competition Assessment Toolkit is available at: http://www.oecd.org/document/48/0,3746,en_2649_37463_42454576_1_1_1_37463,00.html.

of economies of scale and discourage investment. State or local rules that limit entry at the sub-national level may prove particularly pernicious in this regard, and retard economic growth as they diminish consumer welfare.

Rules That Limit the Ability of Suppliers to Compete

Such rules can take the form of anything that reduced the intensity with which firms compete. For instance, regulations limiting advertising can chill interfirm competition. Some countries impose restrictions on direct to consumer advertising that limit consumer information about products and services and may lock in consumer preferences based on imperfect information. This may particularly affect new foreign market entrants that seek to build a reputation in a new market. Similarly, some regulations can raise the costs of established domestic firms with respect to new entrants from abroad, by setting particularly high product standards that are geared to goods that are produced by a favoured domestic company. Rules on content can also have the effect of limiting variety and choice, thereby damaging consumer welfare.

Rules That Reduce the Incentive of Suppliers to Compete

Some regulatory structures may lead to cartel formation or otherwise dampen or eliminate firms' incentive to compete. This may happen, for example, when a government exempts a certain group of firms (such as state-owned companies) from national competition laws, or imposes restrictions that make it highly costly for consumers to switch from one supplier to another.

Rules That Limit the Choice and Information Available to Consumers

There are many types of rules of this sort. Some of these relate to the advertising restrictions described above. Others relate to systems of self-regulation and co-regulation, where the regulatory burden falls to market participants themselves through voluntary systems of regulation.

Rules That Apply to State-Owned Enterprises

In many jurisdictions, governments provide special subsidies or legal exemptions (for example, exemptions from competition law) to state-owned enterprises. In addition, regulatory systems often are skewed to favour a particular national champion or champion technology. These distortions artificially skew competitive outcomes and may entrench or create monopoly power in the hands of the favoured enterprises. As described later in this article, the ICN has issued recommendations regarding tools that competition enforcers might use to curb competitive harm created by such rules.

In addition to these particular practices, ACMDs may take the form of tax legislation that confers benefits on preferred companies, as well as regulatory and enforcement actions—for example, environmental agency decisions, decisions by government boards regarding locations of investments or product standards, exemptions from building permits, and preferences in public procurements.

We now turn to the efforts of the trading system thus far to come to grips with these types of restraints.

The WTO and ACMDs

The WTO has only a limited ability to combat ACMDs. Most such restraints either fall outside the strictures found in the various WTO Codes and Agreements, or, even if they do not, the WTO has proven itself largely unable to tackle them or to apply the right metric to analyse them.[8] The three notable examples of efforts to reach ACMDs through WTO enforcement actions deserve brief scrutiny, for they illustrate not only the limitations inherent in the current WTO framework, but also the direction of WTO policy.

Kodak/Fuji Film

Kodak claimed that it was seriously handicapped in its efforts to enter the Japanese film market by a combination of Japanese government and private restraints that, cumulatively, blocked efficient entry into the Japanese film market by foreign firms. Kodak asserted that its market share in Japan had been kept to less than 10 % by anticompetitive actions by the Fuji Photo Film Company and counter-liberalisation measures taken by the Japanese government. In particular, the four largest wholesale distributors of photographic film products in Japan handled Fuji products exclusively.

[8] One of the authors has advocated the creation of a multilateral public sector restraints agreement, building on existing WTO jurisprudence and introducing more centrally concepts of consumer welfare enhancement into the discussions of trade restricting government measures. See Singham, *A General Theory of Trade and Competition: Trade Liberalisation and Competitive Markets*, 2007, pp. 542–546. Although the authors strongly support such an approach, political constraints may preclude its adoption (or even serious consideration) in the near future. The more modest short-term approach advocated in this article, which emphasises reliance on non-binding advocacy, is fully consistent with the more ambitious long-term goal of establishing a binding international agreement; the two approaches are complements, not substitutes.

These exclusive relationships allegedly resulted from various Japanese Government actions and regulations designed to offset the opening of Japan's film market to foreign firms and from certain allegedly anticompetitive actions by Fuji. Fuji claimed that it had not engaged in anticompetitive behaviour and asserted that Kodak actually had access to all film retailers in Japan. The fact that Fuji had exclusive ties to the major wholesalers did not keep Kodak from distributing to retailers through its own channels, according to Fuji. Fuji also emphasised that Kodak had taken similar actions in the US market to maintain its high market share there. Citing these concerns, the US Trade Representative initiated WTO dispute resolution proceedings against Japan in 1996. The WTO Appellate Body in 1998 found that the restraint in question—involving practices that included government-supported restrictions on film distribution channels—did not implicate violations of Japan's WTO trade commitments.[9]

Mexican Telecoms[10]

COFETEL, Mexico's telecommunications regulatory agency, conferred on Telmex, the dominant Mexican telecommunications company (initially state-owned and then privatised), the power to fix the rate to be paid to all foreign telecommunications carriers terminating calls in Mexico. COFETEL rules, which mandated that those companies charge no less than the Telmex fee for termination, decreed a market-sharing system in support of the high price. The United States filed a claim with the WTO, arguing that these cartel-like incumbent protection regulatory arrangements violated Mexico's WTO commitments to open up its telecommunications market. In particular, the United States included a competition law charge in its complaint that Mexico had violated its commitments under the General Agreement on Trade in Services (GATS), the GATS Telecommunications Annex, and the accompanying Reference Paper. The panel in large part ruled in favour of the United States, finding that Mexico had failed to ensure interconnection at cost-oriented rates; had failed to prevent anticompetitive practices by a major telecommunications supplier (Telmex); and had failed to ensure reasonable and non-discriminatory access to and use of telecommunications networks. Particularly noteworthy were the panel's holding that the term "anticompetitive practices" (found in section 1 of the Reference Paper) necessarily includes cartels; that the "state action" defence for anticompetitive behaviour shielded by regulation

[9] Report of the Panel, WT/DS44/R, *Japan – Measures Affecting Consumer Photographic Film and Paper*.

[10] See Report of the Panel, WT/DS204/R, *Mexico – Measures Affecting Telecommunications Services*, paras. 7.222-7.224. The discussion of the *Mexican Telecoms* matter is based on Fox/Crane, *Global Issues in Antitrust and Competition Law*, 2010, pp. 413–417, and on Dispute Settlement: Dispute DS-204, *Mexico – Measures Affecting Telecommunications Services*, available at: http://www.wto.org/english/tratop_e/dispu_e/cases_e/ds204_e.htm.

should be disfavoured in the international context (a state should not be allowed to mandate trade-harming anticompetitive behaviour to evade its international commitment to prohibit such conduct); and that the adopted anticompetitive regulations were not "appropriate" measures to promote regulatory sovereignty and to protect Mexican investment in domestic infrastructure.

In 2005, Mexico announced that it had fully complied with the panel's recommendations by promulgating new resale regulations allowing for the commercial resale of long distance and international long distance services originating in Mexico, and the United States expressed satisfaction with these changes. The procompetitive resolution of the *Mexican Telecoms* matter, however, it did not lead to a series of similar WTO cases. This is probably because of the limited coverage of the WTO's General Agreement on Trade and Services ("GATS") and the difficulty of proving the violations of the Basic Telecoms Agreement and Reference Paper. The Telmex case represented a particular trade-distortive and anticompetitive activity that could be shown to have violated very specific WTO commitments partly because of the extreme nature of the behaviour involved. Moreover, the satisfactory settlement of this matter undoubted was also strongly influenced by the fact that the United States was Mexico's major trading partner and was linked (with Canada) to Mexico through a comprehensive free trade accord, the North American Free Trade Agreement (NAFTA). Indeed, at the time the case was brought there was a lively debate about whether it should be brought as a NAFTA or a WTO case, and the WTO was chosen as a forum partly to signal a global precedent.

Canada Wheat Board[11]

WTO jurists also applied competition disciplines to a WTO provision drawn from the competition lexicon in the "Canada Wheat Board" case. The Panel and Appellate Body were asked to interpret Article XVII of GATT 1947. Article XVII, as we noted previously, provided that where an STE was buying or selling in the commercial market, it should be subject to "commercial considerations." The US asserted that "commercial considerations" meant that behaviour had to be profit-maximising, and any revenue-maximising behaviour could not be seen to be "commercial." The case concerned the role of an STE, the Canada Wheat Board (CWB) in the purchase and sale of wheat on international markets. The US challenged the CWB's practices as violating Article XVII. The US contended that Canada and the CWB must afford competing wheat sellers as well as potential wheat buyers an "adequate opportunity ... to compete for participation in [the CWB's] sales." The US argued that the CWB had to act like a commercial seller, and that it could not use its special privileges to the disadvantage of other

[11] The following discussion of this case draws upon Singham, *A General Theory of Trade and Competition: Trade Liberalisation and Competitive Markets,* 2007, pp. 203–218.

commercial actors. The US charged that because the CWB Act was a mandate to promote sales, rather than profits this necessarily led CWB to take unfair advantage of its privileges. Unfortunately, the Panel took a very simplistic view of "commercial considerations," noting that this merely required STEs not to act like "political actors." The panel rejected the US's thesis that the structure of the CWB necessarily resulted in sales inconsistent with Article XVII. It is noteworthy that the Appellate Body reviewing the case returned to the principle of non-discrimination as axiomatic in WTO cases. Proof of discriminating conduct had to come first, and then (and only then), evidence had to be adduced of conduct that did not satisfy "commercial considerations." The Appellate Body was very specific:

> We see no basis for interpreting that provision as imposing comprehension competition-law-type allegations on STEs as the United States would have us do. [Appellate Body Report 145]

Measuring the Welfare Effects of ACMDs

In order to better assess and compare individual ACMDs—and to build the case for phasing out or dismantling them—a metric might be devised to produce estimates of the welfare effects of particular restrictions. Below we briefly sketch a proposal for developing such a metric. Although any metric is bound to be imprecise in application, it should be possible to produce "rough and ready" estimates of the social costs of ACMDs through this exercise. The metric, which could be refined in light of economic learning and case studies, might help inspire a broader international dialogue on welfare-reducing government measures.

A Metric for Measuring ACMDs

The metric would estimate the impact of the ACMD on domestic markets as well as global markets, to the extent possible. The purpose of the metric would be to quantify the difference between the market equilibrium with the market distorted by the regulation, and the equilibrium where the regulatory distortion was not present.

The question is what is the best metric for measuring ACMDs? Historically, analysis of behind-the-border trade barriers or regulatory protection has focused on the impact of these barriers on trade flows. However, we suggest that this metric does not properly evaluate the true impact of ACMDs. While it clearly measures the impact of the barrier to external trade, it does not properly measure the true impact of the ACMD under scrutiny on the domestic economy in the country where the ACMD exists. A better measure of this is a welfare-based metric based on the implications of the measure for consumer welfare (as previously defined). The type of analysis would be a standard partial equilibrium analysis[12] where the ACMD itself would act as an external shock and the effect measured would be how far the external shock moves the equilibrium from a consumer welfare enhancing market equilibrium. In other words, one would ask how introduction of a particular ACMD altered cost curves and demand curves in the affected market or markets, and the net effect of such alterations on consumer welfare. The estimate would not need to be exact—it could be stated as a rough estimate, plus or minus a certain percentage (error tolerance). Such an approach could add credibility by recognising imperfections in estimation and limitations on knowledge, while at the same time highlighting the real harm to domestic interests flowing from the ACMD. More generally, by highlighting the aggregate deleterious effects of ACMDs on the domestic public at large, broad adoption of this metric might marginally weaken *ex ante* private and public incentives to adopt new ACMDs in the first place.

The ICN and ACMDs

Although *ACMDs* may not readily be reached by direct antitrust law enforcement (as yet) or formal WTO trade enforcement mechanisms, they nevertheless may be susceptible to being undermined through targeted "competition advocacy" initiatives. Such initiatives involve efforts by competition agencies to ensure that competition considerations are weighed in the formulation of laws, regulations, and public policies. Often competition advocacy may involve critiques of draft rules or laws on the grounds that the proposed formulations would block or distort consumers and thereby reduce consumer welfare.

Historically, competition advocacy has been directed at sister agencies at the national level or at subordinate levels of government. In recent years, in discussions with emerging competition regimes, major competition agencies (such as the US Federal Trade Commission, the US Department of Justice, and the European

[12] A partial equilibrium analysis "analyses the behaviour of a single market, household, or firm, taking the behaviour of all other markets and the rest of the economy as given." See Samuelson/ Nordhaus, *Economics*, (14th ed.) 1992, p. 287. We do not consider the possibility, suggested by the "theory of the second best," that the welfare harm in the market primarily affected by the ACMD would be more than offset by welfare gains elsewhere, due to the interaction among markets. Leading antitrust commentators have consistently upheld partial equilibrium approaches as key to the carrying out of competition policy, and have dismissed second best concerns, based on the real world impossibility of analysing all potential interactions among markets and on the high likelihood that market-specific partial equilibrium competition analyses "get it right." See, e.g., Bork, *The Antitrust Paradox*, (Revised ed.) 1993, pp. 113–114; Posner, *Antitrust Law*, (2nd ed.) 2001, p. 13 n. 5.

Commission's Directorate General for Competition) have promoted competition advocacy as a valuable method for consumer welfare enhancement.[13]

Consistent with this recent trend, the international "virtual network" dedicated to competition policy, the ICN, established an Advocacy Working Group ("Advocacy Group") in 2001.[14] The ICN consists of competition agencies, not national governments. This might appear at first blush to be a weakness, since its constituent members lack the ability to bind their jurisdictions internationally and some may lack substantial domestic political influence. Properly understood, however, we believe the nature of ICN membership is actually a strength, in that it may allow agencies to sign on to recommendations that do not necessarily reflect current national government policies. Over time, the agencies may be able to secure home state support for such recommendations, to the extent they become more broadly accepted and are seen as reflecting international "best practices."

The initial efforts of the Advocacy Group centred on the identification of advocacy "best practices" and the provision of information to ICN members in support of their advocacy activities. In 2008, the Advocacy Group redirected its efforts to the carrying out of case-specific "market studies," with the goal of identifying good practices for conducting studies. During 2009-2010, the Group conducted five teleseminars where ICN member agencies described their experiences in advocating competition. The teleseminars focused on building relationships between a competition authority and the private bar; government involvement in markets; the role of international organisations in advocacy; competition in the financial markets; and evaluation of particular agencies' competition advocacy programmes. The Advocacy Group promoted an advocacy best practices handbook and Competition Advocacy "Toolkit" in 2010-2011, with the aim of spreading the "culture" of advocacy studies. It also has established an ICN data bank of advocacy studies ("Market Studies Information Store"). The Advocacy

[13] For a good overview of the importance of competition advocacy as a tool to combat government-sponsored restraints on competition, see Cooper/Kovacic, US Convergence with International Competition Norms: Antitrust Law and Public Restraints on Competition, Boston University Law Review 90 (2010) 4, p. 1555, available at: http://www.ftc.gov/speeches/kovacic/2010convergencecomment.pdf.

[14] The ICN was established in 2001 as an international "virtual network" for the promotion of "soft convergence" among competition policy regimes through the exchange of information among competition agencies and expert "non-governmental advisors." The ICN states that it "provides competition authorities with a specialized yet informal venue for maintaining regular contacts and addressing practical competition concerns. This allows for a dynamic dialogue that serves to build consensus and convergence towards sound competition policy principles across the global antitrust community. The ICN is unique as it is the only international body devoted exclusively to competition law enforcement and its members represent national and multinational competition authorities. Members produce work products through their involvement in flexible project-oriented and results-based working groups. Working group members work together largely by Internet, telephone, teleseminars and webinars." See http://www.internationalcompetitionnetwork.org/about.aspx. Information on the ICN's Advocacy Working Group is available at: http://www.internationalcompetitionnetwork.org/working-groups/current/advocacy.aspx. The following main textual discussion is drawn from this web entry.

Group also liaises with the ICN's "Advocacy and Implementation Network" in order to generate advocacy recommendations for new competition regimes ("beneficiary agencies").

The Advocacy Group is ideally suited to promote the study and, hopefully, the gradual elimination of, ACMDs that harm consumer welfare. As part of a consensus-building international body, the Advocacy Group can shed a spotlight on a regime's regulatory practices that reduce consumer welfare, without the coercive aspect associated with litigation or state-to-state negotiations.[15] Interjecting the ICN into critiques of anticompetitive government practices is not without precedent—the ICN already has adopted consensus materials that can be applied to advocate against abuses of state-sponsored market power. In particular, the ICN has adopted a document drafted by the ICN's Unilateral Conduct Working Group entitled "State Created Monopolies Analysis Pursuant to Unilateral Conduct Laws—Recommended Practices" ("RP"). The RP include giving competition authorities "an effective role" for promoting competition in connection with privatisation and market liberalisation efforts. The RP also endorse bestowing on competition authorities "effective competition advocacy instruments," including providing "expert reports" and "recommendations" to government bodies responsible for liberalisation/privatisation; participation in meetings and briefings with key government officials; an ability to bring legislative and administrative actions before the courts; and publication of competition authority opinions in order to spark public debate. Aggressive ICN efforts to advance the role of domestic competition agencies in taking on international hybrid restraints would be very much in keeping with the tradition embodied in the State Created Monopolies RP.[16]

Furthermore, ICN-commissioned studies that illuminate the nature and extent of welfare losses stemming from international hybrid restraints may empower fledgling competition agencies to push for domestic reforms, by invoking the importance of being seen as following the "international consensus." Application of a well-regarded metric for measuring the effects of ACMDs, such as the one proposed above, could heighten the impact of individual studies and strengthen the hands of national competition officials—invoking the imprimatur of the ICN—in arguing for welfare-enhancing reforms.

The Advocacy Group could perhaps further advance competition advocacy efforts by publicising economic techniques that may be used to estimate the magnitude of welfare losses associated with particular restraints. Estimates derived from specific case studies that highlight the extent of foregone welfare due to lack of competition may spur efforts to "phase out" *ACMDs* in favour of less socially costly support for favoured constituencies, such as direct targeted subsidies. Eventually, well-supported empirical welfare loss estimates might build the case for

---

[15] See http://www.internationalcompetitionnetwork.org/uploads/library/doc318.pdf.

[16] Indeed, we believe that the long-term plan of the Advocacy Working Group is in harmony with our proposed reform. See http://www.internationalcompetitionnetwork.org/uploads/library/doc763.pdf.

avoiding less costly "substitute" policies altogether, and lead to the actual elimination of *ACMDs*. In particular, the Advocacy Working Group might formulate some additional general principles from such studies, which could be included in its Competition Advocacy Toolkit—and publicised by the ICN as a whole. To the extent it succeeded, such an ICN-facilitated attack on *ACMDs* might over time also strengthen the hand of competition officials in arguing for the rescission of the more egregious "state action" restraints that have been put in place specifically to shield favoured commercial actors from competitive forces.

Plurilateral Agreement Concerning ACMDs

ICN efforts to limits ACMDs through competition advocacy hopefully could eventually build support for a plurilateral agreement limiting ACMDs, perhaps under the aegis of the WTO.[17] Like-minded jurisdictions could join such an agreement on a voluntary basis as the domestic harm caused by ACMDs and the benefits to be gleaned from limiting or prohibiting them became apparent. Below we briefly sketch possible features that a plurilateral agreement might embody. This discussion is merely suggestive, meant to stimulate further thinking about possible cooperative actions to constrain ACMDs.

The plurilateral agreement could have proactive measures that discipline ACMDs, as well as defensive measures that enable members to take unilateral actions against them, where clearly warranted. These unilateral actions might be in the form of a proportionate trade retaliatory measure that an affected state could invoke upon showing that there was a market distortion that had an anticompetitive effect that led to specific welfare losses in its domestic markets, either to firms or to consumers (the size of the trade retaliation would be bounded by the magnitude of the welfare loss). Such a retaliatory mechanism would have to pass muster under the rules of the global agreement, and there would be full dispute resolution if a party violated these rules.

A key question would be whether full WTO style dispute resolution procedures should be available to ensure that signatories conformed their policies to disciplines applied to ACMDs under the agreement. While full dispute resolution (in the WTO sense, complete with trade sanctions) might not be immediately available, the dispute resolution process could include a referral back to the competition agency of the country that had failed to act against the specific ACMD. The referral might

[17] For the most part, all WTO agreements apply to all GATT members. However, when the WTO was established in 1995, four "plurilateral" agreements were made applicable only to those WTO members that had agreed to them: the Agreement on Trade in Civil Aircraft, the Agreement on Government Procurement, the International Dairy Agreement, and the International Bovine Meat Agreement (the latter two agreements were scrapped in 1997). See http://www.wto.org/english/thewto_e/whatis_e/tif_e/agrm10_e.htm. The WTO framework would allow for the creation of additional plurilateral agreements.

include a series of benchmarks that would have to be met within a time certain. Failure to comply with the benchmarks would be a violation of the agreement, and would be subject to fuller dispute resolution.

Conclusion

Interest group politics and associated rent-seeking by well-organised private actors are endemic to modern economic life, guaranteeing that *ACMDs* (not to mention many other sorts of restrictions that are directly shielded by state action immunity) will not easily be rooted out. Nevertheless, the ICN's Advocacy Working Group may provide a good vehicle to assist competition agencies worldwide in their efforts to highlight the baleful effects of such restraints. While this proposed solution is not the only pathway that must be followed, the Advocacy Working Group may provide the tools that, over time, convince state actors to phase out or eliminate particularly egregious restraints. As the benefits of curbing ACMDs become increasingly apparent, individual member states may wish to consider entering into a plurilateral agreement (perhaps under WTO auspices) by which they agree to curb these anticompetitive measures. To the extent such reforms are implemented, consumer welfare will benefit, and trade and competition policy will prove more effective in promoting a welfare-enhancing economic growth agenda that benefits all nations.

The Relationship between Trade and Competition in Free Trade Agreements: Developments since the 1990s and Challenges

Hanspeter Tschaeni and Valérie Engammare

Introduction

Since the 1990s, the number of free trade agreements (FTAs) has dramatically increased. According to the WTO, 336 regional trade agreements were in force in June 2012.[1] While these agreements 20 years ago covered primarily trade in goods-related issues, their scope and complexity have since been steadily extended. Today, they often contain "WTO plus" provisions in the field of services, intellectual property rights or government procurement and also increasingly address issues that are not covered by WTO Agreements in a comprehensive way, such as investment or competition. This can in particular be explained by the fact that once tariff barriers have been removed, domestic policies and regulations become more salient as potential obstacles to trade.[2]

In this context, many FTAs contain a chapter on competition as well as other provisions with a competition dimension. According to the WTO World Trade Report 2011, competition represents the main policy area covered by preferential trade agreements among the issues not addressed in the WTO agreements,[3] which is

The views expressed in this article are solely those of the authors and do not necessarily represent the views of the Swiss State Secretariat for Economic Affairs.

[1] Source: WTO Website. Note that this figure includes customs unions that are not considered in this article.

[2] See WTO, World Trade Report 2011: The WTO and Preferential Trade Agreements—From Coexistence to Coherence, 2011, p. 109.

[3] WTO, World Trade Report 2011: The WTO and Preferential Trade Agreements—From Coexistence to Coherence, 2011, p. 132.

H. Tschaeni • V. Engammare (✉)
State Secretariat for Economic Affairs, International Economic Law Division, Holzikofenweg 36, 3003 Berne, Switzerland
e-mail: hanspeter.tschaeni@seco.admin.ch; v.engammare@gmail.com

C. Herrmann et al. (eds.), *European Yearbook of International Economic Law (EYIEL), Vol. 4 (2013)*, European Yearbook of International Economic Law 4,
DOI 10.1007/978-3-642-33917-2_3, © Springer-Verlag Berlin Heidelberg 2013

essentially due to the wide range of provisions—both horizontal and sector-specific—found in FTAs.

In this contribution, the authors analyse from a negotiator's perspective the developments that took place over the last 20 years concerning competition and competition-related provisions in FTAs and their implications for the relationship between trade and competition. The contribution starts by outlining the context in which competition disciplines in FTAs emerged and recalls the rationales for such provisions. It then presents an overview of competition and competition-related provisions that can typically be found in FTAs, using as examples the agreements concluded by the European Union (EU), the United States (US), which are often identified as the two main "families" of FTAs as far as competition is concerned, and, as a middle way, the FTAs concluded by the members of the European Free Trade Association (EFTA).[4] Customs unions and regional trade agreements creating an internal market fall into a different category of integration and provide for another environment for competition rules. Therefore, they are not included in this analysis. Based on this overview, some of the challenges for the negotiator are addressed that arise from the inclusion of comprehensive disciplines on competition in FTAs: How to ensure compliance with the relevant provisions? How can the different rules concerning competition coexist in a single agreement? How to ensure that competition provisions of an FTA, which are sometimes very close to those of antitrust cooperation agreements, lead to effective cooperation on competition matters?

The Emergence of Competition Provisions in International Trade Agreements

Attempts to Address the Relationship between Trade and Competition in a Multilateral Setting

Trade relations have been substantially liberalised in the last 50 years. A key instrument was the GATT 1947, which managed through successive negotiation rounds to reduce the tariffs of its members to a very low level overall. With the entry into force of the WTO in 1995, the focus was extended to services, trade-related intellectual property rights and, in a plurilateral setting, government procurement. An efficient dispute settlement mechanism ensured that the respective rules could also be enforced. Liberalisation of trade relations and the establishment of harmonised rules and procedures for trade between states have thus been to a large degree a multilateral development and have, with a WTO membership of 155 as of June 2012, taken on a global dimension. The development also changed considerably the overall conditions for competition for economic operators involved in cross-border economic activities.

[4] The Member States of EFTA are Iceland, Liechtenstein, Norway, and Switzerland.

In contrast, drafting and enforcing competition rules, understood as rules addressing anti-competitive practices of private and public enterprises, have remained primarily a national prerogative. To be sure, there has been a large degree of convergence among domestic rules and developing countries benefit from experiences and often use as a model rules and institutions from nations with a longer tradition of competition. However, there does not exist a set of multilateral rules with an efficient enforcement mechanism for competition as is the case for trade in the context of the WTO.

Attempts to adopt multilateral rules on competition can be traced back to the genesis of the multilateral trade system. The basis for the GATT 1947, the Havana Charter, devoted a full chapter (Chapter V) to restrictive business practices and admonished Members to "*take appropriate measures. . .to prevent, on the part of private or public commercial enterprises, business practices affecting international trade which restrain competition, limit access to markets, or foster monopolistic control, whenever such practices have harmful effects on the expansion of production or trade. . .*"[5] The drafters also provided for compliance mechanisms by granting the International Trade Organization, which was to be created through the Charter, the right to conduct investigations and the power to request members to take remedial action, in accordance with their respective laws, if the conditions of Article 46 of the Charter were not fulfilled.[6]

The Havana Charter was not adopted and Chapter V did not find its way into the GATT 1947. However, some parts of that Agreement, as well as other WTO Agreements, address competition-related matters in relationship with, for instance, national treatment, state-trading enterprises or monopolies and exclusive business suppliers.[7] It took nearly 50 years until another attempt was made to address the relationship between trade and competition in the WTO in a comprehensive way. The WTO Ministerial Meeting in Singapore established in December 1996 a working group on the interaction between trade and competition policy. The theme was further addressed in the Work Programme of the Doha Declaration of November 2001 where Ministers recognised "*the case for a multilateral framework to enhance the contribution of competition policy to international trade and development. . .*" In spite of these ministerial declarations and the intensive discussions in the working group,[8] a consensus on the modalities to start

[5] Art. 46(1) of the Havana Charter.

[6] Art. 46(1) of the Havana Charter.

[7] See Hoekman/Mavroidis, Competition, Competition Policy and the GATT, The World Economy 17 (1994) 2, p. 121; OECD Joint Group on Trade and Competition, Competition Elements in International Trade Agreements: A Post-Uruguay Round Overview of the WTO Agreements, 1999.

[8] The working group dealt with the following issues: core principles, including transparency, non-discrimination and procedural fairness, and provisions on hardcore cartels; modalities for voluntary cooperation; and support for progressive reinforcement of competition institutions in developing countries through capacity building. Full account was to be taken of the needs of developing and least-developed country participants and appropriate flexibility provided to address them.

negotiations could not be found at the Ministerial Meeting in Cancún, Mexico, in September 2003. However, the reasons of this failure lie rather in the fear of imbalances and overload of the agenda that negotiations on competition could have generated than in opposition on substantive issues.[9] No further attempts have been undertaken in the WTO since then.

To this date, the only multilaterally agreed set of rules on competition, albeit non-binding, is the "Set of Multilaterally Agreed Equitable Principles and Rules of the Control of Restrictive Business Practices," adopted in December 1980 by the United Nations General Assembly and since implemented under the auspices of the United Nations Conference on Trade and Development (UNCTAD). Taking the form of recommendations, the Set contains principles and rules for enterprises as well as for states at national, regional, and sub-regional levels. In its preamble, the Set clearly recognises the negative consequences of restrictive business practices for international trade, in particular for trade affecting developing countries. It includes provisions on international measures and establishes an international institutional machinery, providing in particular for the possibility of holding consultations between states and establishing an Intergovernmental Group of Experts (IGE) with the task of providing a forum for discussion on any matter related to the Set. In spite of its comprehensive scope, the effects of the Set have been limited. Consultations are rarely held and the rules and principles have not been further developed since 1980. On the other hand, in line with the increased importance attributed to competition rules worldwide, the meetings of the IGE have become a useful forum for the exchange of experiences, especially among developing countries, and the efforts of the UNCTAD Secretariat in organising technical assistance and capacity building are given high marks by these countries.[10] However, the IGE's focus is clearly on competition-related issues and the relationship between competition and trade is only occasionally discussed.

International Developments concerning Cooperation on Competition Matters

Competition provisions in FTAs are not only influenced by ideas and rules that originated in the trade field. Equally important are models and instruments that had been developed by competition experts with a view to improving international cooperation between competition authorities. It became increasingly evident in the

[9] On the reasons for the failure to reach an agreement on the launching of negotiations, see Anderson/Evenett, Incorporating Competition Elements in Regional Trade Agreements: Characterization and Empirical Analysis, Working Paper, 2006, Section 2.2.3.

[10] This finding is also supported by Anderson/Evenett, Incorporating Competition Elements in Regional Trade Agreements: Characterization and Empirical Analysis, Working Paper, 2006, Section 2.2.2.

early 1990s that globalisation did not only have an impact on the interaction between trade and competition but also provided new challenges for competition authorities to enforce their respective laws in light of anti-competitive practices that increasingly took place between actors located in different jurisdictions. An international standard that is still accepted today was set in 1995 by the Recommendation of the Organisation for Economic Cooperation and Development (OECD) concerning Co-operation between Member Countries on Anticompetitive Practices Affecting International Trade. The Recommendation encourages OECD Member countries to cooperate more closely to deal effectively with anti-competitive practices by way of notification, exchange of information, coordination of action, consultation, and conciliation. The Appendix to the Recommendation entails detailed guiding principles for the implementation of these means of cooperation.

Many of the modes of cooperation provided for in the OECD Recommendation of 1995 were taken over and made operational in the context of bilateral cooperation agreements[11] between economic partners, leading to increased and improved cooperation and contacts between the competition authorities of those parties. In addition, the content of the Recommendation also served as model for the cooperation provisions in FTAs, as will be shown in the following sections. Provisions in FTAs providing for notification, coordination, positive and negative comity and exchange of information are in most cases based on this standard.

FTAs as an Instrument for Competition Rules

While the motivations for including provisions on competition in FTAs may vary from agreement to agreement, some common rationales can nonetheless be distinguished:

First, anti-competitive practices may nullify the effects achieved through trade liberalisation: Practitioners and academic literature[12] are in agreement that benefits agreed in FTAs such as elimination of tariffs, market access opportunities and entry

[11] International Competition Network (ICN), Cooperation between Competition Agencies in Cartel Investigations, Report of the Cartels Working Group to the ICN Conference, May 2006, p. 5. For examples of bilateral cooperation agreements on competition, see the EU-Japan Agreement concerning Cooperation on Anti-Competitive Activities, signed on 10 July 2003, in force since 9 August 2003; see also United States-Canada Agreement of 1995 concerning the Application of Their Competition and Deceptive Marketing Practices Laws, signed on 1 and 3 August 1995, in force since its signature.

[12] Holmes/Papadopoulos/Kayali/Sydorak, Trade and Competition in RTAs: A Missed Opportunity?, in: Brusik/Alvarez/Cernat (eds.), *Competition Provisions in Regional Trade Agreements: How to Assure Development Gains*, 2005, p. 67 (71); Anderson/Evenett, Incorporating Competition Elements in Regional Trade Agreements: Characterization and Empirical Analysis, Working Paper, 2006, Section 2.1; Desta/Barnes, Competition Law in Regional Trade Agreements: An Overview, in: Bartels/Ortino (eds.), *Regional Trade Agreements and the WTO Legal System*, 2006, p. 239 (242).

possibilities for foreign enterprises can be severely restricted or nullified through dominant positions of firms in certain markets, anti-competitive agreements between market participants and even cross-border mergers having an anti-competitive effect. This argument, focusing on the relationship between trade and competition, was also put forward in the discussions on competition disciplines in the context of the WTO.[13] This danger is even more pronounced with regard to state-owned enterprises or undertakings granted special and exclusive rights by the state. Confinement of the reach of competition rules to national territories makes it often impossible for competition authorities to track down, and proceed in a concerted manner against such activities, which provides an incentive for the conclusion of competition disciplines, inclusive cooperation mechanisms, in the context of trade agreements.

Second, deeper integration through an FTA creates a demand for cooperation on competition policy: FTAs often aim to create a true "economic partnership" between the parties, which also calls for intensified relations on competition issues between them. This objective may be brought about by certain cooperation mechanisms, for instance exchange of information between competition authorities, or via technical assistance activities. In addition, it is now widely acknowledged in the international competition community that cooperation is crucial to prevent cross-border anti-competitive practices.[14] This awareness as well as efforts to foster cooperation on competition matters also contributed to the demand for competition provisions in FTAs.

Third, there has been a general move from the multilateral to the bilateral/plurilateral agenda: Since the Doha Round negotiations of the WTO have not been concluded yet, many countries have turned their attention to bilateral or regional negotiations instead, leading to a proliferation of FTAs. This had its effect on competition-related issues as well.[15] Given that it is reasonably clear that there will be no comprehensive multilateral rules on competition in the WTO in the near future, FTAs provide the natural venue to address such issues. In doing this, FTA negotiators could draw from the attempts described above in international organisations such as the OECD, the WTO and the UNCTAD.

Recognising the growing importance of competition provisions in FTAs, several attempts have been made at classifying them according to the contents of their competition provisions. A conclusion often referred to is the one by Solano/Sennekamp,[16] who distinguished two "families" of agreements, the EC-style

---

[13] See Mitchell, Broadening the Vision of Trade Liberalisation—International Competition Law and the WTO, World Competition 24 (2001) 3, p. 343.

[14] International cooperation is thus for several years a key topic for the International Competition Network, the OECD Competition Committee and the UNCTAD IGE on Competition Law and Policy.

[15] Holmes/Papadopoulos/Kayali/Sydorak, Trade and Competition in RTAs: A Missed Opportunity?, in: Brusik/Alvarez/Cernat (eds.), *Competition Provisions in Regional Trade Agreements: How to Assure Development Gains*, 2005, p. 67 (71–72).

[16] Solano/Sennekamp, Competition Provisions in Regional Trade Agreements, OECD Trade Policy Working Paper, (2006) 31.

agreements (focusing on substantive provisions addressing anti-competitive practices) and the North American-style-agreements (focusing on cooperation). Although the study by Solano/Sennekamp has been subject to criticism,[17] and the authors themselves cautioned that the categorisation has to be seen with a certain degree of flexibility and that there is overlap in cross-regional FTAs, the distinction was later found to be still valid and the finding "robust," also when including competition-related provisions contained in other chapters of FTAs than the competition chapter.[18]

Looking at this distinction from a negotiator's point of view, its usefulness is somewhat mixed. Its most evident consequence is that, expressing the preferences of two of the largest economic powers in the world, the features of their "families" have been "exported" to partner countries with whom the EU and the United States concluded FTAs. Such partners then tend in turn to use that model in their agreements with other parties. While this may have a certain clustering effect, it obviously has its limits where parties from the two "families" negotiate an agreement with each other.[19] A further observation is that although economic powers like the EU and United States are in a better position to have their model texts prevail, the examination in this Article concludes that even they vary in their approaches and more recent agreements point in the direction of a certain convergence between the core features of the two families.[20]

Overview of Competition Provisions in the EU, US and EFTA FTAs

Classification

For the purpose of this article, we distinguish the following types of competition and competition-related provisions in FTAs[21]:

---

[17] Anderson/Evenett, Incorporating Competition Elements in Regional Trade Agreements: Characterization and Empirical Analysis, Working Paper, 2006, Section 3.1.

[18] Teh, Competition Provisions in Regional Trade Agreements, in: Estevadeordal/Suominen/Teh (eds.), *Regional Rules in the Global Trading System*, 2009, p. 418 (483); WTO, World Trade Report 2011: The WTO and Preferential Trade Agreements—From Coexistence to Coherence, 2011, p. 144.

[19] Therefore, it is no coincidence that Solano/Sennekamp also listed as agreements where there is overlap between the features of the two styles agreements such as Chile-Korea, EC-Chile, EC-Mexico, EFTA-Mexico or Korea-Singapore.

[20] See infra.

[21] For other classifications, see Solano/Sennekamp, Competition Provisions in Regional Trade Agreements, OECD Trade Policy Working Paper, (2006) 31; Holmes/Papadopoulos/Kayali/Sydorak, Trade and Competition in RTAs: A Missed Opportunity?, in: Brusik/Alvarez/Cernat (eds.), *Competition Provisions in Regional Trade Agreements: How to Assure Development Gains*, 2005, p. 67 (73–74) and Desta/Barnes, Competition Law in Regional Trade Agreements: An

The first type of rules consists in substantive provisions on competition policy. Such provisions state the parties' rights and obligations under the agreement with regard to anti-competitive practices, and provide for measures and mechanisms to address such practices. They may refer to the internal laws of the parties, provide for certain principles to be respected when enforcing such laws,[22] or set common concepts in order to achieve a certain degree of harmonisation of competition rules.[23] FTAs may also include substantive provisions on state monopolies and public enterprises, and cover various other issues such as transparency or due process in the context of competition policy and enforcement. In this category, particular attention will be paid to compliance mechanisms foreseen in the agreements to enforce competition provisions.

Formally, these rules are usually part of a horizontal chapter on competition matters. However, other chapters of an FTA, for instance those on services, intellectual property, government procurement and investment may also include provisions that refer in a more or less specific manner to competition.[24] Similarly, FTAs may contain horizontal provisions that apply in principle to all sectors covered by the FTA and may have specific implications for competition.[25] This covers for instance obligations set by the agreements with regard to non-discrimination, transparency or administrative procedures. These competition-related provisions represent the second category of provisions. As far as compliance is concerned, these rules are in principle subject to the dispute settlement procedures of the FTA.

The third type of competition provisions consists in rules on cooperation. These rules range from broad provisions to detailed rules. They may cover issues such as notification, coordination, positive and negative comity, exchange of information and consultation between the parties and/or their competition authorities. Cooperation may take place between competition authorities directly. It is important to stress the link between substantive rules and cooperation mechanisms: the latter can be a complementary—and in practice very relevant—means of enforcement for substantive rules, since the scope of jurisdiction of the competition authorities is limited to the national territory.[26]

Overview, in: Bartels/Ortino (eds.), *Regional Trade Agreements and the WTO Legal System*, 2006, p. 239 (244–245).

[22] The FTAs concluded by the United States for instance include obligations related to non-discrimination, due process and judicial review. See for instance Art. 16.1.(2) US-Chile FTA.

[23] See Desta/Barnes, Competition Law in Regional Trade Agreements: An Overview, in: Bartels/Ortino (eds.), *Regional Trade Agreements and the WTO Legal System*, 2006, p. 239 (244).

[24] Pursuing a different objective than this article, the study conducted by Teh provides a broad and comprehensive analysis of these provisions. See Teh, Competition Provisions in Regional Trade Agreements, in: Estevadeordal/Suominen/Teh (eds.), *Regional Rules in the Global Trading System*, 2009, p. 418.

[25] See Anderson/Evenett, Incorporating Competition Elements in Regional Trade Agreements: Characterization and Empirical Analysis, Working Paper, 2006, Section 3.1.

[26] See Grewlich, Globalisation and Conflict in Competition Law: Elements of Possible Solutions, World Competition 24 (2001) 3, p. 367 (382).

FTAs Concluded by the European Union

General Observations

The content of the competition rules provided for in agreements concluded by the EU depends on the type of agreement concerned. Those concluded since the mid-1990s with North African and Mediterranean countries (Euromed agreements) and Stabilisation and Association Agreements (SAA) entered into with the Southern European states—potential accession candidates—since 2004 usually contain few provisions on competition. Inversely, agreements with partners outside the Europe/Euromed zone, all in force or provisionally applied after 2000,[27] often contain detailed rules. Provisions on state aid play a prominent role in most Euromed agreements[28] and in the SAAs, relating in particular to obligations with regard to assessment and transparency of state aid.[29] This can be explained by the fact that, in EU's conception, state aid is part of competition law.

Substantive Provisions in the Competition Chapter

In the 1970s already, competition was addressed in the FTAs concluded by the European Community by setting out a list of anti-competitive practices deemed incompatible with the proper functioning of the agreement, insofar as they affect trade between the parties.[30] This approach, which creates a common standard, was maintained up to now and is present in most agreements.[31] However, a few agreements concluded with partners outside the Europe/Euromed zone refer to the competition laws of the parties.[32]

The SAAs and the Euromed agreements provide for adjustment of state monopolies with the aim of removing discriminations of a commercial character[33] and contain obligations with regard to public undertakings and undertakings to

[27] These include the agreements with South Africa (in force since 1 January 2000), Mexico (in force since 1 July 2000), Chile (in force since 1 February 2003/1 March 2005), CARIFORUM States (signed in 2008 and provisionally applied since 29 December 2008), Korea (signed in 2010 and provisionally applied since 1 July 2011).

[28] Szepesi, Comparing EU Free Trade Agreements: Competition Policy and State Aid, ECDPM inBrief 6E, 2004, p. 2.

[29] See for instance Art. 53 EU-Jordan Association Agreement.

[30] See Art. 23 EU-Switzerland FTA.

[31] See for instance Art. 35 EU-South Africa Trade, Development and Co-operation Agreement; Art. 41(1) EU-Algeria Association Agreement; Art. 11.1(3) EU-Korea FTA.

[32] Annex XV EU-Mexico Global Agreement; Art. 172(1) EU-Chile Association Agreement; Art. 11.1(1) and 11.3(2) EU-Korea FTA.

[33] See for instance Art. 39 EU-Macedonia SAA; Art. 37 EU-Tunisia Association Agreement.

which special and exclusive rights have been granted.[34] Among agreements with overseas partners, various solutions appear, but most agreements also tend to include provisions on public enterprises and designated monopolies.[35]

Compliance Mechanisms Specific to Competition

With regard to compliance mechanisms, the Euromed agreements and the SAAs provide for the possibility to take appropriate measures, after consultation in the Association Council, the monitoring body of the agreement, against practices violating the agreement.[36] The agreements concluded with partners outside the Europe/Euromed zone do not allow for such measures. For instance, the EU-Korea FTA only provides for consultations.[37]

The Euromed agreements and most of the SAAs do not exclude competition from the dispute settlement mechanisms, which are usually not very detailed and of a political nature. It is interesting to note that recent SAAs that provide for arbitration exclude competition provisions from the dispute settlement mechanism.[38] Similarly, the agreements concluded with overseas partners, which provide for detailed and arbitration-based dispute settlement procedures, usually exclude competition from such procedures.[39]

Provisions related to Competition in Other Chapters

The agreements concluded by the EU comprise relatively few references to competition in chapters other than the competition chapter, except in the more recent agreements, including those with Euromed and Southern European partners.[40]

Provisions can be found with regard to telecommunications services, and consist in provisions concerning competitive safeguards and universal services based on the WTO 1996 Reference Paper on Telecommunications Services.[41] A few

---

[34] See for instance Art. 70 EU-Macedonia SAA; Art. 55 EU-Jordan Association Agreement; Art. 38 EU-Morocco Association Agreement.

[35] Art. 179 EU-Chile Association Agreement; Art. 11.4 and 11.5 EU-Korea FTA. Inversely, the EU-Mexico Global Agreement contains no such provisions.

[36] See for instance Art. 34(5) EU-Egypt Association Agreement; Art. 73(10) EU-Montenegro SAA.

[37] Art. 11.7 EU-Korea FTA.

[38] See Art. 2 of Protocol 7 of the EU-Montenegro SAA; Art. 2 of Protocol 7 of the EU-Serbia SAA.

[39] Art. 180 EU-Chile Association Agreement; Art. 11.8 EU-Korea FTA.

[40] Art. 39(1) EU-Jordan Association Agreement; Art. 34(3) EU-Algeria Association Agreement; Protocol 4 on Land Transport and Art. 91 concerning financial services of the EU-Serbia SAA. However, competition is in this context conceived as a goal for cooperation and does not give rise to specific obligations with regard to anti-competitive practices.

[41] Art. 112 EU-Chile Association Agreement; Art. 7.30 EU-Korea FTA.

agreements also refer to competition in the section on government procurement, usually in a general manner[42] or similarly to the WTO Plurilateral Agreement on Government Procurement, for instance with respect to technical specifications.[43]

Certain agreements with partners outside the Europe/Euromed region contain provisions based on Articles XVI (2) and XVII (3) GATS, which refer to competition in connection with market access[44] and national treatment.[45] The FTAs with partners outside the Europe/Euromed zone include in their trade in goods chapters provisions based on Article III GATT regarding national treatment on internal taxation and regulation. They provide *inter alia* for non-discrimination with regard to internal laws and regulations,[46] which may also have an impact on competition laws and regulations.[47]

The FTAs with partners outside the Europe/Euromed zone also tend to include horizontal provisions that are relevant for competition. This is in particular the case for transparency issues (exchange of information, publication of laws and regulations).[48] The EU-Korea Agreement includes an entire chapter on transparency, addressing issues of publication, enquiries, due process, non-discrimination and regulatory quality.[49]

Cooperation Provisions

Euromed agreements usually only provide for an exchange of information, within the limits set by the requirements of professional and business secrecy.[50] Beyond that, they do not provide for specific cooperation and leave it to the Association Council to adopt the rules necessary for the implementation of the agreements' provisions addressing anti-competitive practices.[51] Such rules were adopted in

---

[42] Art. 139(1) EU-Chile Association Agreement; Art. 167(2) EU-CARIFORUM States Economic Partnership Agreement.

[43] Art. 173(2) EU-CARIFORUM States Economic Partnership Agreement.

[44] See for instance Art. 97 EU-Chile Association Agreement; Art. 67 EU-CARIFORUM States Economic Partnership Agreement; Art. 7.5 EU-Korea FTA.

[45] Art. 68(3) and 77(3) EU-CARIFORUM States Economic Partnership Agreement; Art. 7.6(3) EU-Korea FTA.

[46] See Art. 27 EU-CARIFORUM States Economic Partnership Agreement; Art. 2.8 EU-Korea FTA.

[47] See Mitchell, Broadening the Vision of Trade Liberalisation—International Competition Law and the WTO, World Competition 24 (2001) 3, p. 343 (360).

[48] Art. 190-192 EU-Chile Association Agreement; Art. 235 EU-CARIFORUM States Economic Partnership Agreement.

[49] Art. 12.1-12.8 EU-Korea FTA.

[50] See Art. 36(6) EU-Israel Association Agreement; Art. 53(7) EU-Jordan Association Agreement; Art. 34(6) EU-Egypt Association Agreement.

[51] See for instance Art. 36(3) EU-Tunisia Association Agreement; Art. 36(3) EU-Morocco Association Agreement.

2004 in the case of Morocco.[52] They contain detailed provisions on notifications, exchange of information, coordination of enforcement activities as well as negative and positive comity and technical cooperation. The Euromed Agreement between the EU and Algeria—which entered into force in 2005—contains similar rules.[53] SAAs for their part do not provide for cooperation on competition issues.

Cooperation plays a more important role in the agreements concluded with partners outside of Europe, with varying degrees of detail. Some agreements contain rather broadly formulated provisions, addressing in particular certain aspects of cooperation such as comity[54] or exchange of information.[55] Others contain more detailed rules on notification requirements, coordination of procedures, comity, technical cooperation and exchange of information subject to the standards of confidentiality applicable in each party.[56]

Again, the example of the EU-Korea Agreement is interesting, since a full-fledged agreement concerning cooperation on anti-competitive activities had been concluded between the parties in 2009. The competition chapter of the agreement thus merely recognises the importance of cooperation between competition authorities and refers for details to the cooperation agreement.[57] In addition, the FTA provides for consultations between the parties.[58]

FTAs Concluded by the United States

General Observations

For the United States, the North American Free Trade Agreement (NAFTA), which came into force in 1994, was the precursor of subsequent FTAs with regard to competition. However, only a few of them feature a competition chapter,[59] while most of the agreements include competition provisions in sector-specific chapters

---

[52] EU-Morocco Association Council Decision No. 1/2004 (2005/466/EC) of 19 April 2004 adopting the necessary rules for the implementation of the competition rules, OJ [2005] L 165/10.

[53] See Annex 5.

[54] Art. 38-40 EU-South Africa Trade, Development and Co-operation Agreement.

[55] Art. 128 EU-CARIFORUM States Economic Partnership Agreement.

[56] Annex XV EU-Mexico Global Agreement; Art. 172 et seq. EU-Chile Association Agreement. The EU-Mexico Agreement is more detailed than the EU-Chile Agreement and provides for instance for provisions on avoidance of conflicts and specifies what kind of information may be exchanged. See also Szepesi, Comparing EU Free Trade Agreements: Competition Policy and State Aid, ECDPM inBrief 6E, 2004, p. 6.

[57] Art. 11.6 EU-Korea FTA.

[58] Art. 11.7 EU-Korea FTA.

[59] Among the 18 US FTAs in force as of May 2012, only 6—i.e. a third—have a competition chapter: NAFTA, US-Chile FTA, US-Singapore FTA, US-Australia FTA, US-Peru FTA and US-Korea FTA.

such as government procurement or telecommunications services. The US FTAs are very homogeneous with regard to both the competition chapter and sector-specific provisions, with some specificities.

Substantive Provisions in the Competition Chapter

The FTAs concluded by the United States containing a competition chapter provide that each party shall adopt or maintain measures or competition laws to proscribe anti-competitive conduct.[60] They do not define what such conduct is, leaving this issue to the internal laws of the parties. Some agreements also indicate that the parties shall maintain an authority[61] responsible for competition matters.

Contrary to NAFTA, which does not contain such provisions, the competition chapters of US FTAs include standards that apply to enforcement, for instance the respect of the right to be heard and a possibility of judicial review of sanctions and remedies imposed in case of violations of competition laws.[62] The US-Korea FTA includes very detailed provisions concerning the procedural rights that must be respected in relation with competition law enforcement.[63]

All US FTAs with a competition chapter include provisions on designated monopolies and state enterprises. The agreements recognise the right of the parties to designate a monopoly and set an obligation to ensure that designated monopolies operate in a certain manner.[64] As far as state enterprises are concerned, US FTAs provide in particular that the parties shall ensure that such enterprises do not act in a manner inconsistent with the agreement, and accord non-discriminatory treatment in the sale of their goods and services.[65] The US-Singapore FTA imposes additional detailed and far-reaching obligations on Singapore regarding government enterprises.[66]

---

[60] See for instance Art. 1501(1) NAFTA; Art. 16.1 US-Chile FTA; Art. 16.1 US-Korea FTA.

[61] Art. 12.2 US-Singapore FTA; Art. 14.2(2) US-Australia FTA; Art. 13.2 US-Peru Trade Partnership Agreement.

[62] See for instance Art. 12.2 US-Singapore FTA; Art. 14.2(1) US-Australia FTA; Art. 14.2(3) US-Peru Trade Partnership Agreement.

[63] Art. 16.1(2)-(6) US-Korea FTA. These provisions address non-discrimination, the right to be heard, the opportunity to cross-examine witnesses, judicial review, possibility of settlements for competition authorities, and rules of procedures for administrative hearings.

[64] See for instance Art. 14.3 US-Australia FTA; Art. 13.5 US-Peru Trade Partnership Agreement; Art. 16.2 US-Korea FTA. Certain agreements provide for additional obligations, in particular in the form of notifications, when the designation of a monopoly may affect the interests of persons of another party, see Art. 1502(2) NAFTA, and Art. 16.3 US-Chile FTA.

[65] See for instance Art. 1503 NAFTA; Art. 14.4 US-Australia FTA; Art. 16.3 US-Korea FTA.

[66] Art. 12.3(2) US-Singapore FTA. See Desta/Barnes, Competition Law in Regional Trade Agreements: An Overview, in: Bartels/Ortino (eds.), *Regional Trade Agreements and the WTO Legal System*, 2006, p. 239 (257).

Except for NAFTA, the FTAs concluded by the United States having a competition chapter also include provisions on transparency with regard to competition,[67] each party committing in particular to make available to the other, upon request, public information on competition enforcement, state enterprises and monopolies and exemptions provided under the competition laws.

Compliance Mechanisms Specific to Competition

With regard to compliance, the agreements usually provide for consultations between the parties in order to foster understanding and address specific matters.[68] Certain agreements also specifically foresee consultations on the effectiveness of measures taken to proscribe anti-competitive conduct.[69] They usually provide for a partial application of the dispute settlement procedures of the agreement to competition matters.[70] In NAFTA, dispute settlement was excluded concerning the article on competition laws (adoption of measures and cooperation),[71] but possible regarding the provisions on monopolies and state enterprises. In the other agreements, dispute settlement applies in principle, but several provisions are excluded. In effect, dispute settlement procedures apply essentially to provisions on designated monopolies and state enterprises and transparency.

Provisions Related to Competition in Other Chapters

Most FTAs concluded by the United States, including those without a competition chapter, contain references to competition in the chapters on telecommunications services, intellectual property, government procurement and investment.

In the chapter on telecommunications services, most agreements, like those of the EU, provide for competitive safeguards and universal service provisions based on the WTO 1996 Reference Paper on Telecommunications Services.[72] NAFTA, which was concluded before the adoption of the WTO Reference Paper, also

---

[67] Art. 16.6 US-Chile FTA; Art. 12.5 US-Singapore FTA; Art. 14.8 US-Australia FTA; Art. 13.8 US-Peru Trade Partnership Agreement; Art. 16.5 US-Korea FTA.

[68] Art. 16.7 US-Chile FTA; Art. 16.7 US-Korea FTA; Art. 13.9 US-Peru Trade Partnership Agreement.

[69] Art. 1501(1) NAFTA; Art. 14.2(1) US-Australia FTA.

[70] See for instance Art. 16.8 US-Chile FTA; Art. 14.11 US-Australia FTA; Art. 16.8 US-Korea FTA.

[71] Art. 1501(3) NAFTA.

[72] See for instance Art. 12.4(2) and 12.8 US-Bahrain FTA; Art. 13.4(2) and 13.8 US-Dominican Republic/Central America FTA.

includes provisions aimed at preventing anti-competitive conduct in the telecommunications sector.[73]

Some of the services chapters also contain references to competition, for instance by allowing certain conditions for the supply of value-added services if they are imposed as remedies to anti-competitive practices or if their goal is to promote competition.[74] As far as investment is concerned, remedies to anti-competitive practices are also reserved in the context of disciplines concerning investment performance requirements.[75]

Most of the US FTAs also include references to competition in the chapter on government procurement, in particular with regard to technical specifications, tendering procedures, and supply of information.[76] The provisions refer to competition as an objective and are similar to those of the WTO Plurilateral Agreement on Government Procurement.

In addition, with regard to trade in goods, several agreements refer to or incorporate Article III of the GATT providing for non-discrimination with regard to internal laws and regulations.[77]

Finally, the US agreements include a chapter on transparency that applies horizontally, addressing issues of publication, supply of information, requirements that administrative proceedings have to fulfil, and review of administrative action.[78] These provisions in principle also apply to competition proceedings.

Cooperation Provisions

All US FTAs with a competition chapter contain provisions on cooperation, which are usually stated in general terms. The agreements merely provide that the parties shall cooperate, via their competition authorities, on issues of competition law enforcement, and list examples for such cooperation, such as notifications, consultations, and information exchange.[79] Working groups are sometimes created to promote cooperation.[80]

---

[73] Art. 1305 NAFTA.

[74] See Art. 12.16(1) US-Australia FTA.

[75] Art. 1106(1) NAFTA; Art. 15.8(3)(b)(ii) US-Singapore FTA; Art. 11.8(3)(b) US-Korea FTA.

[76] See for instance Art. 1007(4), 1008(2), 1013(2), 1016 and 1019(3), (5) NAFTA; Art. 15.6(6), 15.7(6), 15.8 and 15.9(2) US-Australia FTA. The US-Singapore FTA on its part incorporates provisions of the WTO Government Procurement Agreement, including Art. VII, X and XV, which refer to competition concerns (Art. 13.3(1) US-Singapore FTA).

[77] Art. 301 NAFTA; Art. 3.2(1) US-Chile FTA.

[78] See for instance Art. 1802-1805 NAFTA; Chapter 19 US-Singapore FTA; Chapter 18 US-Oman FTA.

[79] See Art. 1501(2) NAFTA; Art. 12.4 US-Singapore FTA; Art. 14.2(3) US-Australia FTA.

[80] Art. 14.2(4) US-Australia FTA; Art. 13.4 US-Peru Trade Partnership Agreement.

The FTAs with Australia and Korea also include, in general terms, cooperation on consumer protection.[81] Furthermore, the US-Australia FTA provides for cooperation on competition *policy* in order to promote policies that foster free trade, investment and competitive markets.[82]

It can also be noted that the United States have concluded bilateral cooperation agreements regarding competition with certain of their free trade partners. Such agreements exist in particular with Mexico (2000), Canada (2004) and Chile (2011).

FTAs Concluded by the EFTA Member States

General Observations

Among agreements concluded by the Member States of EFTA, one can distinguish between the FTAs concluded with countries in the Euro-Mediterranean zone in the 1990s and early 2000s, which cover essentially trade in goods and provide for provisions similar to those of the EU agreements, and later agreements with overseas partners, which tend to be more comprehensive.

Substantive Provisions in the Competition Chapter

With regard to competition, the FTAs concluded with Euromed and Southern European partners focus on the potential harm that anti-competitive practices represent for trade. The agreements list certain anti-competitive practices that are considered as incompatible with the proper functioning of the agreement in so far as they affect trade between the parties.[83] The agreements specify that these provisions also apply to the activities of public undertakings and undertakings to which the parties grant special or exclusive rights, in so far as the application of these provisions does not obstruct the performance of the tasks assigned to them.[84] Certain agreements also provide for adjustment of state monopolies with the aim of removing discriminations,[85] while later agreements refer to Article XVII GATT on state-trading enterprises.[86]

---

[81] Art. 14.6 US-Australia FTA; Art. 16.6 US-Korea FTA.

[82] Art. 14.9 US-Australia FTA.

[83] See for instance Art. 17(1) EFTA-Israel FTA; Art. 17(1) EFTA-Morocco FTA; Art. 18(1) EFTA-Albania FTA.

[84] See for instance Art. 18(2) EFTA-Jordan FTA; Art. 17(2) EFTA-Albania FTA.

[85] See Art. 10 EFTA-Morocco FTA; Art. 14 EFTA-Tunisia FTA; Art. 9 EFTA-Croatia FTA.

[86] See for instance Art. 15 EFTA-Albania FTA; Art. 16 EFTA-Serbia FTA.

The agreements concluded with overseas partners in the 2000s contain more comprehensive provisions on competition and tend to have a separate chapter on competition matters. They usually include a list of practices deemed incompatible with the agreement.[87] The FTAs with Mexico and Canada are closer to the NAFTA approach, as the parties commit to adopt or maintain measures to proscribe anti-competitive business conduct.[88] The agreements with overseas partners usually do not provide for specific provisions in the competition chapter on monopolies and state enterprises.[89]

Compliance Mechanisms Specific to Competition

As far as compliance is concerned, the agreements with Euromed and Southern European partners enable a party to take appropriate measures, after consultations in the Joint Committee, the monitoring body of the agreement, if it considers that a practice violates the competition provisions of the agreement.[90] The mechanism is similar to the one provided for in the agreements concluded by the EU with the same partners.[91] The agreements with overseas partners usually foresee consultations in the Joint Committee,[92] but do not allow a party to take appropriate measures unilaterally. The competition chapter is systematically excluded from the dispute settlement procedures provided for under the agreements.[93]

Provisions Related to Competition in Other Chapters

Other provisions related to competition can be found in agreements that cover issues such as government procurement, services and in particular telecommunications services, and intellectual property rights. Such provisions are usually contained in agreements with overseas partners that include comprehensive disciplines on services and government procurement,[94] but not in agreements

---

[87] See for instance Art. 50(1) EFTA-Singapore FTA; Art. 72(3) EFTA-Chile FTA; Art. 5.1(2) EFTA-Korea FTA.

[88] Art. 51 of the EFTA-Mexico FTA; Art. 14(1) EFTA-Canada FTA.

[89] References are only punctual, for instance, Art. 72(3) of the EFTA-Chile FTA provides that anti-competitive practices may be carried out by private and public enterprises.

[90] See for instance Art. 17(3) EFTA-Morocco FTA; Art. 17(4) EFTA-Tunisia FTA; Art. 18(4) EFTA-Albania FTA.

[91] On EU Agreements, see Solano/Sennekamp, Competition Provisions in Regional Trade Agreements, OECD Trade Policy Working Paper, (2006) 31, para. 47.

[92] See for instance Art. 75(4) EFTA-Chile FTA; Art. 5.1(6) EFTA-Korea FTA; Art. 8.4 EFTA-Colombia FTA.

[93] See for instance Art. 50(3) EFTA-Singapore FTA; Art. 78 EFTA-Chile FTA; Art. 8.6 EFTA-Colombia FTA.

[94] The agreements with Canada and SACU do not contain such provisions.

with Euromed and Southern European countries, which primarily cover trade in goods.

Concerning the services chapter, certain FTAs include provisions based on Articles VIII and IX GATS (monopolies and unfair practices),[95] either by incorporating them or containing a similar content.[96] Certain FTAs also refer to competition in the provisions on market access and national treatment.[97] In this regard, the rules are similar to Articles XVI (2) and XVII (3) GATS.

The agreements with an annex on telecommunications services include provisions inspired by the 1996 WTO Reference Paper on Telecommunications Services regarding competitive safeguard and universal services.[98]

The agreements with a chapter on government procurement contain references to competition concerns similar to those of the WTO Plurilateral Agreement on Government Procurement, in particular in relation with the provision of information,[99] as well as technical specifications and limited tendering.[100]

In their trade in goods chapters, the agreements usually refer to Article III GATT with regard to internal regulations.[101]

The agreements providing for the non-application of anti-dumping measures between the parties refer to competition rules as a means to prevent dumping.[102]

FTAs with overseas partners and recent agreements with Southern European countries also include horizontal provisions on transparency, providing in particular for the public access to laws and regulations and dealing with information requests.[103]

Cooperation Provisions

The agreements concluded with Euromed partners and Southern European countries do not include cooperation provisions, contrary to the FTAs concluded

[95] See Art. 3.11 and 3.12 EFTA-Korea FTA.

[96] Art. 4.11 and 4.12 EFTA-Korea FTA.

[97] See for instance Art. 21, 23(3), 29(4) and 31(4) EFTA-Mexico FTA with regard to services and financial services; Art. 25(2) EFTA-Chile; Art. 25(3) EFTA-Singapore; Art. 4.5(3) EFTA-Colombia FTA.

[98] See for instance Art. 5 and 7 of Annex IX EFTA-Chile FTA; Art. 5 and 7 of Annex X EFTA-Korea FTA.

[99] Art. 63(3) EFTA-Mexico FTA; Art. 59(3) and 65(3) EFTA-Chile FTA.

[100] Art. 7.8(6) and 7.10(7) EFTA-Colombia FTA. The EFTA-Mexico FTA has a special approach, Mexico committing to apply certain NAFTA rules and the EFTA States certain provisions of the Government Procurement Agreement of the WTO, see Art. 61(1) and Annex XVII EFTA-Mexico FTA.

[101] See for instance Art. 11 EFTA-Tunisia FTA; Art. 2.6 EFTA-Korea FTA; Art. 10 EFTA-Albania FTA.

[102] See Art. 16(2) EFTA-Singapore; Art. 17(2) EFTA-Albania FTA.

[103] Art. 79 EFTA-Mexico FTA; Chapter VIII EFTA-Chile FTA; Art. 10.1 EFTA-Korea FTA; Art. 5 EFTA-Albania.

with overseas partners, which often contain such provisions. These provisions vary in their degree of detail, but a tendency to include specific provisions on cooperation can be observed. The FTA with Mexico, in force since 2001, is the first agreement concluded by the EFTA States to include cooperation provisions on competition. The agreement provides for notification and positive comity.[104] Later FTAs include detailed provisions concerning cooperation, in particular notifications.[105] Other issues addressed include coordination of enforcement activities, negative and positive comity, consultations, and exchange of information.[106] The respective laws of the parties dealing with communication of information are usually reserved.[107] The agreements often provide that cooperation may be carried out by the competition authorities of the parties.[108]

Stocktaking—Developments Since the 1990s

Several conclusions can be drawn from the analysis of EU, US and EFTA FTAs in the previous sections:

The nature, content and scope of competition provisions included in the agreements appear to **depend on the type of the agreement and the partner concerned**. This is especially true for the agreements concluded by the EU and the EFTA countries. For them, a distinction has to be made between agreements with, on the one hand, Euromed and Southern European partners that do not include a comprehensive competition chapter and contain only few competition-related provisions in other chapters, and, on the other hand, overseas partners, which include more comprehensive competition provisions. By contrast, the FTAs concluded by the United States appear to be more homogeneous, although only a few of them include a competition chapter. This finding is consistent with what has been described in the literature as "hub-and-spoke" and "cross-regional" patterns.[109]

The three parties differ in the **definition**, or the absence thereof, **of anti-competitive practices** covered by the FTA. This observation is consistent with

[104] Art. 52(2)-(4) of the EFTA-Mexico FTA.

[105] Art. 73 EFTA-Chile FTA; Art. 15 EFTA-Canada FTA.

[106] Art. 73 et seq. EFTA-Chile FTA; Art. 15 EFTA-Canada FTA; Chapter 8 of the EFTA-Colombia FTA.

[107] See for instance Art. 76(2) EFTA-Chile FTA.

[108] See for instance Art. 79 EFTA-Chile FTA; Art. 15(4) EFTA-Canada FTA.

[109] Teh, Competition Provisions in Regional Trade Agreements, in: Estevadeordal/Suominen/Teh (eds.), *Regional Rules in the Global Trading System*, 2009, p. 418 (421).

the findings made in previous studies.[110] Typically, the United States do not describe anti-competitive activities in their FTAs in substantive terms and normally focus on national competition laws and their enforcement. In their enforcement practices, parties are required to respect certain general principles such as non-discrimination, due process and judicial review. It can be presumed that the reliance on national competition legislation and its enforcement is based on the understanding that this will also have a positive effect on trade relations and will benefit the economic environment in general. The EU and EFTA, on the other hand, set out minimal substantive elements of what could constitute anti-competitive practices and establish an explicit link between them and trade. In several of their agreements, such activities are declared incompatible with the agreement to the degree that they have an influence on trade relations between the parties. Some FTAs concluded by EFTA complement these substantive elements with the same requirements as the United States to proscribe such practices via the parties' national competition laws.

It is also interesting to note that the EU, the United States and the EFTA countries have chosen different ways of dealing with **compliance** in the context of competition provisions. The US agreements normally provide in general terms for consultations to foster understanding between the parties and address specific matters. The EU and EFTA FTAs as a rule contain in addition to consultations in the Joint Committees the explicit objective of facilitating or achieving thereby a solution to the problem caused by the anti-competitive practices. If no solution can be achieved, some EU and EFTA agreements give the affected party the possibility to take appropriate measures. The three parties again differ in their use of the dispute settlement mechanisms of the FTA. The agreements concluded by the United States make the respective provisions applicable for certain competition-related issues, such as the practices of monopolies and state-owned enterprises and in case of violation of transparency requirements. It can be presumed that the intention of the US approach is to apply dispute settlement provisions to practices for which the state as the contracting party can be held accountable or that it can at least influence, which is not the case for anti-competitive activities of private enterprises. The practice of the EU is mixed. In older agreements, the competition chapters are subject to the dispute settlement provisions, while in more recent agreements that provide for more detailed and arbitration-based mechanisms, such provisions are not applicable. In many of the FTAs concluded by the EFTA countries, the competition chapters are excluded from the reach of dispute settlement provisions.

The examination further reveals that **cooperation provisions increasingly gained importance**, with some recent agreements providing for rules similar to those

[110] Solano/Sennekamp, Competition Provisions in Regional Trade Agreements, OECD Trade Policy Working Paper, (2006) 31; Desta/Barnes, Competition Law in Regional Trade Agreements: An Overview, in: Bartels/Ortino (eds.), *Regional Trade Agreements and the WTO Legal System*, 2006, p. 239.

foreseen in the 1995 OECD Recommendation[111] and in antitrust agreements providing for cooperation between competition authorities. This trend is particularly strong in the agreements concluded by EFTA Members with overseas partners. It can also be observed in the provisions of the more recent Euromed agreements concluded by the EU, for instance with Algeria and Morocco. In agreements concluded by the United States, cooperation appears to be a central element, but is usually stated in general terms. It is interesting to note that the tendency to include comprehensive cooperation provisions can also be observed in FTAs concluded by other countries: Japan's FTAs for instance usually provide for comprehensive cooperation provisions such as notification, coordination of enforcement activities, exchange of information, transparency and treatment of confidential information, as well as positive and negative comity.[112]

As far as the **relationship between trade and competition** is concerned, certain agreements contain an obligation to address anti-competitive practices insofar as they may affect trade between the parties, while others include obligations that apply to competition policy in general, independently of an effect on trade. As mentioned above, in the US FTAs the link between competition and trade is usually addressed in a general manner,[113] and sometimes not at all. For instance, according to the US-Chile and US-Korea FTAs,[114] the aim of measures proscribing anti-competitive conduct is to promote economic efficiency and consumer welfare and not to preserve the benefits of trade liberalisation.[115] There appears to have been a change in policy in the United States because the link between trade and competition was present in NAFTA, where even a working group on trade and competition was established.[116] As far as the agreements by the EU and EFTA Members are concerned, the fact that cooperation provisions tend to become more important, providing for instance for cooperation between competition authorities directly, might also signal a looser link to trade.

Finally, not only competition chapters tend to become more detailed, but also **competition-related provisions in other chapters as well as horizontal provisions**. This development is especially pronounced in the case of FTAs

---

[111] See *supra*.

[112] See for instance Chapter 5 of the Implementing Agreement of the Economic Partnership Agreement between Japan and Indonesia, signed on 27 August 2007, in force since 1 July 2008; Chapter 3 of the Implementing Agreement of the Free Trade and Economic Partnership Agreement between Japan and Switzerland, signed on 19 February 2009, in force since 1 September 2009; Chapter 2 of the Implementing Agreement of the Agreement between Japan and the Republic of Peru for an Economic Partnership, signed on 31 May 2011, in force since 1 March 2012.

[113] See for instance Art. 12.1 US-Singapore FTA and Art. 14.1 US-Australia FTA.

[114] Art. 16.1 US-Chile FTA; Art. 16.1 US-Korea FTA.

[115] See also Teh, Competition Provisions in Regional Trade Agreements, in: Estevadeordal/Suominen/Teh (eds.), *Regional Rules in the Global Trading System*, 2009, p. 418 (464).

[116] Art. 1504 NAFTA. This working group no longer meets, see Jones, Competition Dimensions of NAFTA and the European Union: Semi-Common Competition Policy, Uncommon Rules, and No Common Institutions, Jean Monnet/Robert Schuman Paper Series, 6 (2006) 18, p. 8.

concluded by the United States.[117] This has to do with the coverage of the FTAs concerned, in particular with the inclusion of comprehensive provisions on services, telecommunications or government procurement. In this regard, the more recent agreements concluded by the EU, the United States and EFTA show more similarities than with regard to the content of the competition chapters. Largely, this can be explained by the fact that these provisions are similar to the corresponding WTO provisions. More detailed provisions also tend to be provided for with regard to horizontal obligations, such as transparency and procedural requirements. This development is significant in terms of compliance, since the dispute settlement procedures provided for under the FTA in principle apply to such competition-related and horizontal provisions.

By way of conclusion, it can be stated that, in spite of the different approaches in some matters, a certain **convergence** can be observed between the agreements concluded by the EU, the United States and the EFTA countries, in particular as far as FTAs with partners outside the Europe/Mediterranean region are concerned. Cooperation on competition matters over time gained importance in the EU and EFTA agreements, which indicates that the distinction between agreements addressing anti-competitive behaviour affecting trade and agreements focusing on cooperation has lost some of its relevance.[118] In addition, the EU and EFTA agreements with overseas partners do not provide for the possibility to take appropriate (unilateral) measures against anti-competitive practices, which brings them closer to US agreements. Provisions relating to antitrust matters are excluded from the dispute settlement procedures in the recent agreements concluded by all three parties. Likewise, the provisions referring to competition in specific chapters of the agreements, such as telecommunications and government procurement, are very similar in their scope and content in the different agreements. This development can, as already mentioned, to a large extent be explained by the influence of WTO disciplines.

Challenges

The inclusion of competition-related questions in a complex trade agreement such as a modern FTA, the necessity to strike a balance between requirements typical for competition and trade as well as the potential problems caused by addressing competition issues in a general chapter entirely devoted to this question and in other chapters present considerable challenges to the negotiators. They have to find efficient solutions to these and related issues since these solutions may have a strong impact on the implementation of competition and competition-related

[117] See Teh, Competition Provisions in Regional Trade Agreements, in: Estevadeordal/Suominen/Teh (eds.), *Regional Rules in the Global Trading System*, 2009, p. 418 (484).
[118] See *supra*.

provisions of FTAs. Three areas where such challenges are particularly noticeable are discussed in this section in more detail: compliance, coexistence between specific competition provisions and a competition chapter, and effective cooperation.

Compliance

One of the main reasons for including competition provisions in an FTA is to address problems caused by anti-competitive activities for the realisation of trade concessions under the agreement. In the first place, such activities are subject to scrutiny by competition authorities charged with the enforcement of national competition laws. It is recognised international standard that competition authorities should be independent from political and other influence when pursuing their tasks. This raises the question how such anti-competitive activities can be addressed in the context of the FTA without interfering with the independence of national competition authorities. A different but related issue is the degree to which the contracting party itself can be held accountable for complying with the provisions concerning competition of the agreement, be they formulated in a general competition chapter or in specific sections of the FTA.

For a negotiator for the United States, addressing these questions should be reasonably clear. US FTAs rely primarily on the respective national competition laws and their enforcement by national competition authorities. Problems or disputes arising in the implementation of competition-related provisions can be discussed between the parties and to the degree that they are caused by practices or actors over which the state has sufficient influence, they can be subject to the dispute settlement provisions of the agreement.[119] EU and EFTA negotiators face a more complicated task. EU and EFTA agreements normally contain descriptions of anti-competitive practices that are most likely to have a negative influence on trade. While there is an implicit assumption that such practices will be pursued and eliminated by the national competition authorities, the agreements also address the eventuality that this is not the case and the practices continue to affect trade between the parties. The EU and the EFTA countries thus squarely address the relations between competition and trade aspects and take into consideration that there might be limits for national competition laws to eliminate all the practices that have a negative influence on trade. In such a case, since the authorities tasked with monitoring the FTA have no authority to directly pursue the behaviour or practice at stake, they have to rely on an instrument typical of the trade field, namely appropriate measures. Although not explicitly stated, it can be presumed that such measures are similar to compensatory or rebalancing measures provided for in other parts of the FTA, such as in trade remedies and dispute settlement. Therefore, it is also consistent to require, as some

---

[119] See *supra*.

agreements do,[120] that such measures should be proportionate and least disturb the functioning of the agreement. An interesting question is whether such measures in turn could not be questioned under the terms of the dispute settlement provisions if the party against which they are directed feels that they do not fulfil these requirements or are contrary to accepted practices of customary international law. This issue is normally not addressed in FTAs.

Competition provisions in FTAs are often explicitly excluded from the dispute settlement mechanism of the agreement. To the degree that competition provisions in most cases do not contain specific requirements for the contracting parties, this is understandable. It can also be presumed that this exclusion reflects the understanding that the dispute settlement provisions of the FTA should not be used to interfere with the sole competence of the competition authorities to decide in a binding way whether a given practice is anti-competitive or not. Other possible explanations include sovereignty concerns and the fact that competition policy is a new area for certain partner countries.[121] In the context of the GATT, some authors have raised the question whether, under certain conditions, contracting parties could be held accountable for negative effects of anti-competitive practices on other parties under the terms of Article XXIII dealing with nullification or impairment.[122] Whether so-called non-violation complaints,[123] i.e. complaints against measures that are not in conflict with the provisions of an agreement but have the effect of nullifying or impairing a benefit accruing to a party directly or indirectly, could be considered in an FTA depends in the first place on whether such complaints are admitted under the terms of the dispute settlement chapter of an agreement.[124] On the other hand, it also depends on the interpretation of the term "measure." Would for instance the fact that a contracting party provided for large-scale exemptions in its competition law be sufficient to qualify as "measure" and for a case under the dispute settlement chapter of an FTA if anti-competitive practices harming trade between the parties would occur in a field exempted from the national competition law[125]? No such case has to our knowledge been addressed in the GATT or in an FTA.

[120] See Art. 17(4) in conjunction with Art. 37 EFTA-Tunisia FTA.

[121] See Teh, Competition Provisions in Regional Trade Agreements, in: Estevadeordal/Suominen/Teh (eds.), *Regional Rules in the Global Trading System*, 2009, p. 418 (482).

[122] See Hoekman/Mavroidis, Competition, Competition Policy and the GATT, The World Economy 17 (1994) 2, p. 121; Roessler, Should Principles of Competition Policy Be Incorporated into WTO Law through Non-Violations Complaints?, Journal of International Economic Law 2 (1999) 3, p. 413.

[123] See Report of the Panel, *Japan—Measures Affecting Consumer Photographic Film and Paper*, WT/DS44/R.

[124] For an example of such inclusion, see the Free Trade and Economic Partnership Agreement between Japan and Switzerland, signed on 19 February 2009, in force since 1 September 2009.

[125] On the issues raised by non-violation complaints in relationship with competition, see Hoekman/Mavroidis, Competition, Competition Policy and the GATT, The World Economy 17 (1994) 2, p. 121 (141).

Coexistence between Specific Competition Provisions and a Competition Chapter

The trend towards the inclusion of more and increasingly comprehensive competition provisions in FTAs raises the question of their relationship to one another. In the same agreement, such provisions may appear in a competition chapter while others are sector-specific. In addition, also horizontal provisions may have an impact on competition provisions.

As mentioned above, most provisions related to competition in sector-specific chapters are based on WTO rules. In the WTO, the issue of their relationship with general competition provisions does not arise, since there is no comprehensive multilateral agreement in this field. Therefore, this matter is specific to the FTAs. Where competition is merely referred to as an objective,[126] or as a means to interpret national treatment obligations,[127] the relationship is unproblematic, since the provisions in the sector-specific chapters do not have the same scope as the obligations included in the competition chapters. Similarly, if certain measures are excepted from a prohibition contained in a sector-specific chapter if they are imposed as remedies to anti-competitive practices,[128] the relationship is not problematic.

Other obligations, for instance the duty to adopt or maintain appropriate measures to prevent anti-competitive practices by major suppliers of telecommunications services,[129] give rise to questions, in particular if the competition chapter but not the sector-specific chapter is excluded from the dispute settlement procedures of the agreement. If, as an example, a party fails to adopt appropriate measures to prevent anti-competitive practices in the telecommunications sector, may the other party have recourse to dispute settlement under the agreement, or shall it first use the possibilities provided for under the competition chapter, namely consultations between competition authorities? Agreements seldom address this issue. An exception is the US-Singapore FTA, which contains a rule of conflict in the telecommunications services chapter, stating that in the event of an inconsistency between the telecommunications chapter and another chapter, the former shall prevail to the extent of the inconsistency.[130]

The relationship between competition-related provisions in the competition chapter and other chapters is also invoked if an agreement contains in its chapter on trade in services provisions based on Article IX GATS on consultations between the parties in case of business practices by service suppliers restraining

---

[126] For instance, goal to achieve "optimum effective competition," see Art. 15.7(6) US-Australia FTA.

[127] See for instance Art. 7.6(3) EU-Korea Agreement.

[128] See examples from the US FTAs cited *supra*.

[129] See for instance Art. 5 of Annex IX EFTA-Chile FTA.

[130] Art. 9.15 US-Singapore FTA.

competition.[131] Such provisions may be less detailed than the consultations provided for in the competition chapter. In principle, both sets of provisions may apply concurrently, if they do not contain conflicting requirements. However, also in this case it may occur that the provisions in the chapter on trade in services, provided they are formulated in a binding manner, are subject to dispute settlement procedures of the agreement.[132] In order to avoid difficulties in the application and interpretation of the agreement in case of coexistence of different competition provisions, some FTAs offer a solution. As an example, the EU-CARIFORUM Agreement stipulates that appropriate measures must be taken in accordance with the chapter on competition matters.[133]

The relationship between horizontal obligations such as transparency or due process and provisions included in the competition chapter appears to be more straightforward, since horizontal obligations in principle apply to all sectors and procedures covered by the agreements. A horizontal obligation to publish laws, regulations and administrative rulings of general application, for instance, would also apply to competition acts. In some agreements, the competition chapter contains more specific obligations than the horizontal provisions.[134] This is the case in the US-Korea FTA, which provides for the review *in a court* of the sanction or remedy for the violation of competition laws[135] whereas, the horizontal obligation in the transparency chapter only stipulates that the parties shall establish judicial, quasi-judicial, or administrative tribunals or procedures for the review of matters covered by the agreement.[136]

It can thus be concluded that the relationship between the provisions in a competition chapter with other provisions of the agreement addressing competition-related issues is of practical relevance for the interpretation and the implementation of the agreement. This issue is likely to intensify in the future because of the inclusion of more competition-related provisions in FTAs. Negotiators need to identify overlaps and potential conflicts and may find it useful, where appropriate, to introduce rules dealing with the relationship between the different chapters and the application and interpretation of the agreement.

[131] See for instance Art. 4.12 EFTA-Colombia FTA.

[132] As stressed by Teh, depending on the carve-out of dispute settlement procedures in the competition chapter, provisions in specific chapters may be the only competition-related provisions of a regional trade agreement that may be subject to such procedures. See Teh, Competition Provisions in Regional Trade Agreements, in: Estevadeordal/Suominen/Teh (eds.), *Regional Rules in the Global Trading System*, 2009, p. 418 (482).

[133] Art. 90, 97 and 111 EU-CARIFORUM Agreement.

[134] Teh, Competition Provisions in Regional Trade Agreements, in: Estevadeordal/Suominen/Teh (eds.), *Regional Rules in the Global Trading System*, 2009, p. 418 (465).

[135] Art. 16.1(4) US-Korea FTA.

[136] Art. 21.4(1) US-Korea FTA.

Effective Cooperation

As pointed out above, comprehensive provisions on cooperation in competition matters increasingly tend to be included in FTAs concluded by the EU and the EFTA countries, while the United States always put more emphasis on cooperation, albeit in a less detailed way.[137] In most cases, the instruments resorted to stem from the OECD Recommendation from 1995, which today still sets the international standard in this field. While being able to draw from a common basis, the negotiator is nevertheless confronted with a number of questions when deciding on how to shape the cooperation provisions:

First, what is the main purpose of cooperation? In agreements focusing on eliminating anti-competitive practices that undermine the benefits of trade liberalisation, it would seem that cooperation should primarily aim at overcoming the shortcomings caused by national competition laws in pursuing cross-border anti-competitive practices. Instruments assisting the respective authorities to cooperate with each other, such as notifying cases being of interest to the other side, exchanging information, coordinating their activities, providing for negative and positive comity, etc. are therefore to be preferred. If, on the other hand, cooperation primarily serves to improve the parties' knowledge of each other's competition regime, exchange experiences and practices or provide technical assistance or capacity building in establishing efficient competition regimes, the emphasis and the wording of the provisions will be different.

Second, who are the main actors for cooperation? In order to improve the chances of eliminating cross-border anti-competitive practices, in the first instance cooperation between the respective competition authorities should be strengthened. Since most national competition authorities are independent, there needs to be a common understanding between them and the authorities responsible for trade that the instruments referred to in the FTA will also be used by the competition authority. Therefore, in many negotiations, cooperation provisions are handled by representatives of the national competition authorities. These authorities may also be in charge of technical assistance or capacity building. It is interesting to note that many FTAs explicitly refer to competition authorities in their cooperation provisions.[138]

Third, does it always make sense to include comprehensive cooperation provisions on competition in FTAs? Entering into a preferential agreement is a sign that a substantial trade flow and economic cooperation already exists between the parties or is expected to intensify. While this speaks generally in favour of including also competition provisions in the FTA, there are also reasons for a

---

[137] See *supra*.

[138] Annex V EU-Algeria Association Agreement; Art. 16.2 US-Chile FTA; Art. 5.2(5) EFTA-Korea FTA.

differing approach vis-à-vis different categories of partner countries.[139] On the one hand, even between FTA partners are there various strengths of economic ties that may lead to different assessments of the likelihood of cross-border anti-competitive activities. On the other, parties may differ in their economic development or in the degree to which they have a well-established competition regime.[140] There may also be different legal traditions that will have an influence on the result of negotiations. For all these reasons, parties may be inclined to vary the content of the cooperation provisions in their agreements. They may also decide for a progressive approach by setting certain basic requirements that would be valid at the moment of entry into force of the agreement. More comprehensive cooperation could be agreed when either the country at stake has consolidated its competition regime or a higher degree of mutual trust has been established after some years of cooperation.[141]

Finally, are there limits to cooperation? The main obstacle for effective cooperation in fighting large international cartels or other cross-border anti-competitive practices are national confidentiality and secrecy laws. In most countries, such laws prevent the competition authorities from exchanging relevant information and documents. It is often explicitly stated in competition chapters of FTAs that no party is required to submit information or documents that would be counter to such national laws. Although an increasing number of countries have drafted laws that would allow the competition authorities, under certain conditions, to also exchange confidential information, it is in rare cases only that agreements are concluded that provide for this.

Conclusion

The examination of the agreements concluded by the EU, the United States and the EFTA countries illustrates how FTAs have over the last 20 years become an important vehicle for addressing competition matters and concluding competition rules. Although differences exist, and are likely to continue to exist, a trend towards a certain convergence can be observed that may facilitate the further conclusion of such rules in FTAs, in particular between parties from different "families." This

[139] Cernat, Eager to Ink, But Ready to Act? RTA Proliferation and International Cooperation on Competition Policy, in: Brusik/Alvarez/Cernat (eds.), *Competition Provisions in Regional Trade Agreements: How to Assure Development Gains*, 2005, p. 3 (8–9).

[140] Rosenberg/Araújo, Implementation Costs and Burden of International Competition Law and Policy Agreements, in: Brusik/Alvarez/Cernat (eds.), *Competition Provisions in Regional Trade Agreements: How to Assure Development Gains*, 2005, p. 191 (208).

[141] UNCTAD, Experiences Gained so far on International Cooperation on Competition Policy Issues and the Mechanisms Used, TD/B/COM.2/CLP/21/Rev.5, 2007, para. 28; WTO Working Group on the Interaction between Trade and Competition Policy, Modalities for Voluntary Cooperation, Background Note by the Secretariat, WT/WGTCP/W/192, 2002, para. 13.

convergence may in particular be useful in order to provide solutions to the challenges that the negotiators face when drafting competition and competition-related provisions and integrating them in the general architecture of an FTA.

The trend towards more comprehensive competition provisions in FTAs implies that competition matters in trade agreements are increasingly seen as fostering competition values and regimes *per se* in the parties as opposed to being mainly seen as offsetting the harmful effects of anti-competitive practices on trade. The growing importance of cooperation provisions makes the competition chapters of FTAs also more similar to antitrust cooperation agreements, which provide for specific mechanisms to be used by competition authorities. This influences the way trade agreements will need to be negotiated and implemented. Competition and competition-related provisions in an international trade agreement require that both competition and trade authorities work together in defining their respective roles and join efforts in both designing and implementing such provisions. Otherwise, there is a risk that competition provisions bear little relation to the reality of the competition authorities and as a result are not used by them.

The growing importance and the comprehensiveness of competition provisions in FTAs also raise the question on how they integrate in the general architecture of FTAs. For instance, such provisions do not necessarily fit in the institutional framework provided for under an FTA, as illustrated by the fact that they are usually excluded from the dispute settlement procedures. Specific mechanisms, such as consultations between competition authorities directly or more detailed cooperation provisions, possibly including the exchange of confidential information and documents, may thus in the future become increasingly relevant in order to ensure compliance with competition provisions, in particular between parties with well-established competition regimes. Anticipating these difficulties, in particular by ensuring that competition provisions are compatible with the general system of the agreement as well as with specific provisions addressing competition matters is thus likely to be a critical task for competition negotiators in the years to come.

Appendix: List of Agreements Quoted[142]

Agreements Concluded by the European Union

EU-Switzerland FTA, signed on 22.7.1972, in force since 1.1.1973
EU-Tunisia Association Agreement, signed on 17.7.1995, in force since 1.3.1998.
EU-South Africa Trade, Development and Co-operation Agreement, signed on 11.10.1999, in force since 1.1.2000
EU-Morocco Association Agreement, signed on 26.2.1996, in force since 1.3.2000

[142] According to their date of signature.

EU-Israel Association Agreement, signed on 20.11.1995, in force since 1.6.2000
EU-Mexico Global Agreement, signed on 8.12.1997, in force since 1.7.2000
EU-Jordan Association Agreement, signed on 24.11.1997, in force since 1.5.2002
EU-Chile Association Agreement, signed on 18.11.2002, in force since 1.2.2003/ 1.3.2005
EU-Macedonia SAA, signed on 9.4.2001, in force since 1.5.2004
EU-Egypt Association Agreement, signed on 25.6.2001, in force since 1.6.2004
EU-Algeria Association Agreement, signed on 22.4.2002, in force since 1.9.2005
EU-Montenegro SAA, signed on 15.10.2007, in force since 1.5.2010.
EU-CARIFORUM States Economic Partnership Agreement, signed on 15.10.2008, provisionally applied since 29.12.2008
EU-Serbia SAA, signed on 29.4.2008
EU-Korea FTA, signed on 6.10. 2010, provisionally applied since 1.7.2011

Agreements Concluded by the United States

North American Free Trade Agreement (NAFTA), signed on 17.12.1992, in force since 1.1.1994
US-Chile FTA, signed on 6.6.2003, in force since 1.1.2004
US-Singapore FTA, signed on 6.5.2003, in force since 1.1.2004
US-Australia FTA, signed on 18.5.2004, in force since 1.1.2005
US-Bahrain FTA, signed on 14.9.2004, in force since 11.1.2006
US-Dominican Republic/Central America FTA, signed on 5.8.2004, in force since 2006
US-Oman FTA, signed on 19.1.2006, in force since 1.1.2009
US-Peru Trade Partnership Agreement, signed on 12.4.2006, in force since 1.2.2009
US-Korea FTA, signed on 30.6.2007, in force since 12.3.2012

Agreements Concluded by the EFTA Members

EFTA States-Israel FTA, signed on 17.9.1992, in force since 1.7.1993
EFTA States-Morocco FTA, signed on 19.6.1997, in force since 1.12.1999
EFTA States-Mexico FTA, signed on 27.11.2000, in force since 1.7.2001
EFTA States-Croatia FTA, signed on 21.6.2001, in force since 1.1.2002
EFTA States-Jordan FTA, signed on 21.6.2001, in force since 1.9.2002
EFTA States-Singapore FTA, signed on 26.6.2002, in force since 1.1.2003
EFTA States-Chile FTA, signed on 26.6.2003, in force since 1.12.2004
EFTA States-Tunisia FTA, signed on 17.12.2004, in force since 1.6.2006
EFTA States-Republic of Korea FTA, signed on 15.12.2005, in force since 1.9.2006

EFTA States-Egypt FTA, signed on 27.1.2007, in force since 1.8.2007
EFTA States-Canada FTA, signed on 26.1.2008, in force since 1.7.2009
EFTA States-Colombia FTA, signed on 25.11.2008, in force since 1.7.2011
EFTA Sates-Serbia FTA, signed on 17.12.2009, in force since 1.10.2010
EFTA States-Albania FTA, signed on 17.12.2009, in force since 1.11.2010

Regulating International Competition Issues by Regional Trade Agreements: A Stepping Stone Towards a Plurilateral Trade Agreement?

Peter Hilpold

Introduction

There is widespread consensus that international rules for the regulation of the (anti-)competitive behaviour of private economic actors are sorely needed.[1] In fact, the competition issue is not a merely internal question, specific to each individual jurisdiction. The globalisation of the international economy has gone hand in hand with the creation of international competition problems. Nonetheless, on the broader multilateral level it is hard to find a consensus for such provisions. At the same time, this gap is filled, at least in part, by provisions inserted in bilateral agreements as well as in Regional Trade Agreements (RTAs). This development raises a series of questions that need to be addressed. First, we have to ask what International Competition Law actually means and what these rules are supposed to achieve. WTO law does not totally ignore the competition agenda but several factors worked against having this subject integrated in a consistent and coordinated manner in the broader WTO framework. At a next step, it appears worth to examine to what extent competition provisions in bilateral agreements and in RTAs may constitute a substitute for the lack of an international framework agreement in this area. As it is known, the process of regionalisation has both been qualified

This contribution builds on an earlier article entitled "International Competition Law and Regional Trade Agreements," published in Manchester Journal of International Economic Law 2 (2005) 3, p. 82.

[1] See for example, Heinemann, Le nécessité d´un droit mondial de la concurrence, Revue Internationale de Droit Économique 18 (2004) 3, p. 293.

P. Hilpold (✉)
Universität Innsbruck, Innrain 52, A-6020 Innsbruck, Österreich
e-mail: Peter.Hilpold@uibk.ac.at

C. Herrmann et al. (eds.), *European Yearbook of International Economic Law (EYIEL), Vol. 4 (2013)*, European Yearbook of International Economic Law 4,
DOI 10.1007/978-3-642-33917-2_4,

a "building block" and a "stumbling block"[2] on the way towards a further strengthening of the multilateral order.[3] We have to ask, what would be the appropriate qualification with regard to the provisions on competition.

It is interesting to note that states that have opposed the insertion of competition provisions in WTO law appear not to have had any problem in agreeing to such rules on a regional level. The special mechanisms shall be explored that were conducive to such a development. Proceeding on in the analysis, we have to note that there is not one single approach to regulate competition on the regional level. There are rather different philosophies in this field. In a comparative analysis, these various approaches shall be juxtaposed. Finally, an outlook shall be tried as to possible future developments in this field. It appears tempting to ask whether the increasing efforts to regulate the competition issue bilaterally and regionally constitute a stepping stone towards the creation of a true international competition law or whether this might be considered a "second-best"-policy[4] that makes a multilateral framework superfluous.

Why Do We Need International Competition Rules?

As liberalisation of international trade within the GATT/WTO order has torn down state created barriers to trade on a wide scale private anticompetitive measures, taking first of all the form of cartels and the abuse of dominant positions have not only become more visible but also more pernicious.[5] In fact, such measures not only make some markets impenetrable replacing governmental protectionism by private barriers but they may empower some businesses in such a way as to allow them to disrupt competitive structures in other countries. Both the internal as the external effects of anticompetitive behaviour threaten international trade.

Nonetheless, as it has been said, while the competition problem has become international, the competition laws remained national,[6] thereby creating a "regulatory disjunction."[7]

---

[2] See Sutherland et al., The Future of the WTO, 2004, p. 22, para. 83, available at: http://www.wto.org/english/thewto_e/10anniv_e/future_wto_e.pdf.

[3] The proliferation of RTAs is a matter of fact. As of 31 July 2010, 474 RTAs have been notified to GATT/WTO and 283 of those are effectively in force. See WTO, Regional Trade Agreements, at: http://www.wto.org/english/tratop_e/region_e/region_e.htm.

[4] With regard to the theory of the "second-best," see Lipsey/Kelvin Lancaster, The General Theory of Second Best, in: The Review of Economic Studies 24(1) (1956-1957), p. 11.

[5] See also Ostry, *The Post-Cold War Trading System: Who's on First*, 1997; Bila/Olarreaga, Regionalism, Competition Policy and Abuse of Dominant Position, Journal of World Trade 32 (1998) 3, p. 153. On present developments in international competition law, see also Terhechte (ed.), *Internationales Kartell- und Fusionskontrollverfahrensrecht*, 2008.

[6] See Taylor, *International Competition Law – A New Dimension for the WTO*, 2006, p. 1.

[7] See Taylor, *International Competition Law – A New Dimension for the WTO*, 2006, p. 1.

For various reasons national competition law cannot make up for the lack of an effective international regulation of competition. First, many legal orders still do not regulate competition in detail. Second, it will be shown that international aspects cannot be tackled in all details on a unilateral way. Third, governments are usually interested to regulate anticompetitive behaviour that affects the domestic markets while they might be less interested to counter anticompetitive activities of domestic enterprises that damages only foreign markets.

As the international dimension of anticompetitive behaviour and, even more so, the perception of this dimension, is, to a large extent, only a consequence of trade liberalisation, it is understandable that attempts to regulate this area stood for a long time in the shadow of traditional trade negotiations. Further, there is a second reason why International Competition Law (ICL) was a late-comer on the scene of international trade negotiations. These negotiations followed a clear path according to which measures with the least impact on national sovereignty were tackled first while more sensitive issues, in particular those associated with internal regulations, were postponed for later negotiating agendas.

According to this ranking, it was clear that competition issues that are usually strictly interwoven with national regulations should be among the last issues governments were willing to set on the agenda for multilateral negotiations. As all countries have chosen individual approaches to the competition issue from an international perspective the overall picture was a very incoherent one. With regard to the international repercussions of these various approaches, if a government had chosen not to regulate anticompetitive behaviour or if it strictly avoided any extraterritorial effect of its own competition law no conflict with other jurisdictions, so it was thought, could arise. However, as anticompetitive behaviour is, as shown, also an international phenomenon, in both cases an important aspect of this phenomenon remained unregulated. Some jurisdictions, especially the US American and the Canadian one, had taken up this challenge and had tried to regulate this issue comprehensively, i.e. both under its national and its international aspects, thereby, however, provoking immediate conflicts with other jurisdictions. On a whole, over the time it had become ever more clear that by acting unilaterally governments were caught between a rock and a hard place, damned as they were either to leave an important regulatory problem unsolved or to enter squarely into potential jurisdictional conflicts. The only solution to this problem could be to look for some sort of an international approach. To this avail a large array of possible techniques were at disposal, everyone with its own advantages and drawbacks so that again no universal common ground could be found on this issue.

First Attempts to Find Multilateral (Universal) Solutions

As it is known, the need for a multilateral regulation of this area was sensed rather early in time. A very bold attempt in this regard was made in the immediate aftermath of World War II during the Havanna Conference when it was planned to create an International Trade Organization (ITO). In this context, considerable energy was spent to draft rules on "restrictive business practices" as the need was perceived to tackle the issue of trade barriers comprehensively.

The respective subject was regulated in Chapter V of the Havanna Charter. The Charter took a broad approach:

> Each Member shall take appropriate measures and shall co-operate with the Organization to prevent, on the part of private or public commercial enterprises, business practices affecting international trade which restrain competition, limit access to markets, or foster monopolistic control, whenever such practices have harmful effects on the expansion of production or trade and interfere with the achievement of any of the other objectives act forth in Article 1.

The range of cases indicated as specifications of restrictive business practices was equally held broad. Art. 46 para. 2 of the Charter mentions, i.a. fixing prices, terms or conditions, excluding enterprises from, or allocating or dividing, any territorial market or field or business activity, discriminating against particular enterprises, limiting production or fixing production quotas, extending the use of rights under patents, trade marks or copyrights granted by any member to matters that, according to its laws and regulations, are not within the scope of such grants.

Finally, the ITO could declare, by a majority of two-thirds of the Members present and voting, further similar practices as restrictive business practices.[8] Therefore, the ITO had enormous potential to become active in the field of competition law. However, this enormous purview of the competition law provisions was in the final end more of a drawback than an advantage, especially in view of the fact that basic notions about international competition law were still unclear.

As it is known, the ITO never entered into force. Many reasons were given for this failure, among which the fact that this whole framework was ahead of its time as well as the suspicion that the relevant rules would unduly impinge on national sovereignty rank high. Both arguments find a good basis in the rules on restrictive business practices, as, on the one hand, little practical experience was given with such provisions and, on the other, the large powers for intervention awarded to an international organisation in competition issue[9] was unprecedented and could explain very well the fears by many governments as to their sovereign powers.

In 1948, only part IV of the Havanna Charter containing mainly provisions on trade liberalisation was enacted but the need for a broader framework remained nonetheless a pressing issue. Also, attention for competition issues remained high,

---

[8] Art. 46(2) (g) of the Charter.

[9] According to Art. 48 of the Charter the ITO, subsequent to complaints by Members, was endowed with an investigative power in competition issues. The whole competence had evolutive characteristics as it was planned, i.a., to undertake further studies on restrictive business practices (see Art. 49 of the Charter). Members were under an obligation to ensure, within their jurisdiction, that enterprises would not engage in restrictive business practices as listed in Art. 46(2) and (3) of the Charter and to assist the Obligation in preventing these practices (Art. 50 of the Charter).

at least in the first years. However, in 1960, a Group of Experts appointed by the GATT in 1958 concluded that:

> the complexities of the subject and the impossibility of obtaining accurate and complete information on private commercial activities in international trade [make it] impracticable to set up any procedures for investigating or passing judgment on individual cases within the framework of GATT.[10]

This statement did not find unanimous approval in political practice and literature but nonetheless it introduced a long hiatus where competition was an absolute non-starter in international trade negotiations. It was studiously avoided to tackle this issue. On the positive side of this situation stood the fact that negotiating resources, which by their nature are always scarce, could be concentrated on some core topics. Furthermore, this halt on negotiations in the field of competition meant that time was bought for further studies in this area. Thereby a better understanding of the main questions to be tackled should be achieved. However, on the other side stood the fact that several states took recourse to unilateral measures in order to come to terms with competition problems arising from the universal sphere.

Possible Ways to Tackle the International Competition Issue

As has been shown, the attempt to devise a full-blown multilateral regulation on international competition, undertaken at the outset of the creation of modern International Economic Law, was doomed to fail, primarily because there was much uncertainty both about the nature of international competition itself as on the appropriate instruments to tackle the ensuing challenges in an appropriate way. Furthermore, as will be evidenced in the following, the United States had found their own, unilateral, approach to deal with this subject. As the US in the immediate after-war time had the decisive say on the further development of international economic regulations this fact exercised enormous influence on all the ensuing attempts to deal with international competition law.

Usually, two diametrically opposed approaches are distinguished when ways are looked for to address problems of international competition policy: the unilateral and the internationalist one.

The Unilateral Approach

According to the unilateral approach, competition issues are mainly a question of national law and the national legislation is the appropriate place to deal with this subject even with regard to its international perspectives. The possibility both of

[10] See GATT Basic Instruments and Selected Documents, 9 S, p. 172.

lacunae and of jurisdictional conflicts is not denied but these negative aspects are considered to be the smaller price to be paid for a situation where some compromise is unavoidable.

Up to a certain extent, the unilateral approach is aware of the international background against which all unilateral acts take place. In fact, usually conflicts will be avoided as far as possible when international measures are implemented. This attitude takes the name of (negative) comity.[11] On the basis of this position states try to avoid conflicts with other states when exercising their sovereign powers. Therefore, the existence of an international order is not denied and neither are the obligations resulting from an international legal system where its constitutive subjects pay each other consideration and respect.

The decisive question is rather how far this respect will reach or, to put it otherwise, when will the subjective interests of the state trump the reasons of comity?

We see that there is a smooth transition from the unilateral to the internationalist approach.

The unilateral approach can best be exemplified by the attitude taken by the US, both when acting from a position of strength and willing to impose its position on the international plane as in those cases when it tried to pay respect to other states´ interests in this field.[12]

The case usually reported as standing at the outset of the Supreme Court´s ruling on its jurisdiction in international competition cases, *American Banana Co v. United Fruit Co.* of 1909,[13] seems to devise a very restrictive position bearing out clear jurisdictional restraint. The Sherman Act, the US antitrust law, should apply only on conduct taken place on US territory (and not in Panama and Costa Rica as was here the case). Therefore, according to this position, US antitrust law should apply strictly according to the territoriality principle. Anticompetitive behaviour relating to the US territory only with regard to its effect should therefore not fall into the jurisdiction of US courts.

A radical reversal of this jurisprudence took place after the 2nd World War in *United States v. Aluminium Co. of America*[14] (Alcoa). In this case the Supreme

---

[11] See extensively in this regard Papadopoulos, *The International Dimension of EU Competition Law and Policy*, 2010, p. 66. With regard to the concept of "comity" see also Paul, Comity in International Law, Harvard International Law Journal 32 (1991) 1, pp. 1–7 and Kämmerer, Comity, Max Planck Encyclopedia of Public International Law (online edition) 2006; for a critical analysis as to the actual relevance of the comity principle see Terhechte, WTO und Wettbewerb, in: Hilf/Oeter (eds.), *WTO-Recht*, 2010, p. 643 (652).

[12] For these cases see Guzman, International competition law, in: Guzman/Sykes (eds.), *Research Handbook in International Economic Law*, 2007, p. 418; Matsushita, Trade and Competition Policy, in:Bethlehem et al. (eds.), *The Oxford Handbook of International Trade Law*, 2009, p. 646 and Papadopoulos, *The International Dimension of EU Competition Law and Policy*, 2010, p. 67 et seq.

[13] 213 US 347 (1909).

[14] 148 F.2d 416 (2d Cir. 1945).

Court adopted the effects theory: Conduct that has consequences within the borders of another state can be judged by the courts of that state.[15]

The same position was confirmed and further strengthened in various judgments, even though, in *Timberlane Lumber Co.,*[16] the court, inspired by the comity position, reminded that it was in the interest of the US to consider other states´ interests. In *Hartford Fire Insurance Co v. California*[17] of 1993 the Supreme Court tried to mediate between comity and the effects theory. Only in cases of "true conflicts" between US law and foreign law comity should apply and prevail.[18] There is also a problem of unequal treatment of firm. In fact, already in 1982 legislation was passed according to which the application of US antitrust laws on conduct of US enterprises should be widely limited while the Sherman Act should continue to apply to foreign enterprises.[19]

On a whole it can be seen that US Antitrust law displays considerable extraterritorial effects and that comity considerations for a long time have been taken into regard only to a very limited extent. This attitude is closely associated with the position of strength of the USA on the international plane. However, this strength is not limitless and therefore, lately, the US is trying to harness the extent of its antitrust jurisdiction by the conclusion of agreements containing provisions on competition. In the end, the fight against anticompetitive measures shall thereby be made more effective and less disruptive in the international relations.

The European Union, on the other hand, had tried for a much longer time to give comity aspects greater consideration. This position changed when it first applied, in the Wood Pulp case,[20] EC competition law to conduct of foreign enterprises abroad. In the GE/*Honeywell* case[21] the EC prohibited an acquisition between US firms

[15] See the statement by Judge Learned Hand according to whom it "[is] settled law [...] that any state may impose liabilities, even upon persons not within its allegiance, for conduct outside its borders that has consequences within its borders which the state reprehends," *United States vs. Aluminium Co. of Am.*, 148 F.2d 416, 443 (2d Cir. 1945).

[16] *Timberlane Lumber Co. vs. Bank of America Nat´l Trust & Sav. Ass´n*, 549 F. 2d 597 (9th Cir. 1976).

[17] 509 US 764 (1993).

[18] See also Guzman, International competition law, in: Guzman/Sykes (eds.), *Research Handbook in International Economic Law*, 2007, p. 421.

[19] See Matsushita, Trade and Competition Policy, in: Bethlehem et al. (eds.), *The Oxford Handbook of International Trade Law*, 2009, p. 650 et seq., referring to the Foreign Trade Antitrust Improvements Act of 1982, 96 Stat. 1233 of 8 October 1982, 15 USC 6 (a). According to this Act, only foreign conduct that has a "direct, substantial, and reasonably foreseeable effect" on US trade could be challenged. The overall assessment of this Act has been negative. See i.a. Springman, Fix Prices Globally, Get Sued Locally? US Jurisdiction over International Cartels, University of Chicago Law Review 72 (2005) 1, p. 265 (271 et seq.).

[20] ECJ, Joined Cases C-89/85, 104/85, 114/85, 16/85, 117/85 and 125-129/85, *Ahlstrom and others vs. EC Commission*, ECR [1988] 5193.

[21] Commission Decision 2004/134/EC of 3 July 2001, OJ [2004] L 48/01.

because it created a dominant position while the US authorities had cleared before this act. A conflict between the US and the EC competition authorities ensued.[22]

In the meantime, some emerging countries are beginning to apply their competition policy in an extraterritorial way.[23]

The Internationalist or Globalist Approach

According to the internationalist or globalist approach, national competition law, with both its active and reactive instruments, is not sufficiently equipped to deal with the international dimension of competition. This approach is not a closed or monolithic one. It can rather be further differentiated according to the stringency of the instruments adopted and according to the reach of the respective competition policy.

The most far-reaching internationalist approach would consist in the adoption of a plurilateral agreement both with procedural and substantive provisions on competition to be inserted in the WTO framework. Many arguments would militate for such an approach. In fact, there can be no doubt that an effective competition policy is co-conducive to the achievement of the goals pursued by the traditional WTO rules. On the other hand, it is also known that the respective attempt to create such a framework have failed at an early stage of the Doha Round, even though the Doha agenda recognised "the case for a multilateral framework to enhance the contribution of competition policy to international trade and development." Even before the effective launching of the Doha Round, a WTO Working Group on the Interaction between Trade and Competition Policy was established as part of the so-called "Singapore issues" where, soon after the success of Marrakesh, much hope was set for a continuous strengthening of the international trade order (December 1996).[24] Although this Working Group managed to provide important insights in the interaction of trade and competition law, its work was finally abandoned because no consensus was given on the sensibility of such a far-reaching approach. As will be seen in the following, the main reason for the failure of this attempt can be found in the fact that different stages of development imply different needs in the area of competition policy. This implies that binding agreements with both procedural and substantive provisions on competition law will be attainable, first, between countries of a similar development stage and with a comparable economic structure. This does not exclude the feasibility of such agreements between

[22] See Matsushita, Trade and Competition Policy, in: Bethlehem et al. (eds.), *The Oxford Handbook of International Trade Law*, 2009, Trade and Competition Policy, note 13, p. 653, with further details.

[23] See Papadopoulos, *The International Dimension of EU Competition Law and Policy*, 2010, p. 70, referring to the respective practice of South Korea.

[24] See Hilpold, Die Fortentwicklung der WTO-Ordnung, Recht der Internationalen Wirtschaft 44 (1998) 2, p. 90 (93 et seq.).

industrialised and developing countries and in fact a considerable number of such agreements have been concluded. Nonetheless, in these agreements the rules on competition usually make part of a greater whole. While the interest for such rules may be differently strong, the overall framework allows compensating those parties that would prefer to do without them. It is obvious that it is easier to achieve such a compensation within a smaller group of countries than on the multilateral level.

An important obstacle for the inclusion of provisions on competition law was further the question how to define the extent of this subject. Thus, there was considerable uncertainty about the relationship between competition law and anti-dumping measures. For some, these instruments should be combined at least provisionally in order to buy time for a systematic substitution of anti-dumping measures by provisions on competition law.[25] There can be no doubt that anti-dumping measures have often been abused for protectionist purposes.[26] However, others stressed the utility of anti-dumping law even in an international economic order based on free trade and independently from competition law in a narrower sense.[27]

And finally, for developing countries there was an information problem, a cost problem and a problem of economic sovereignty with such a plurilateral agreement. With next to no experience in this field and lacking further the institutional requisites for effectively implementing the required measures they feared the legal and economic consequences that would ensue from dispute settlement proceedings in case of shortcomings in this area.[28] As to the aspect of economic sovereignty, several developing countries feared they could lose their ability to conduct an autonomous industrial policy (including the de facto possibility to discriminate in favour of national industries).[29]

To fill the gap resulting from the demise of the respective endeavours within the WTO "soft" forms of multilateral cooperation for the creation of an international competition policy have come to life. In this context, the International Competition

---

[25] See, i.a., Hoekman/Mavroidis, Dumping, Antidumping and Antitrust, in: Journal of World Trade 30 (1996) 1, p. 27.

[26] See Hilpold, Die Ergebnisse der Uruguay-Runde—eine Bestandsaufnahme, Zeitschrift für vergleichende Rechtswissenschaft (1994) 4, p. 419 (452 et seq.). As it has been seen, while antitrust policy is designed to protect *competition*, anti-dumping policy protects *competitors*. See Bhattacharjea, The Case for a Multilateral Agreement on Competition Policy: A Developing Country Perspective, Journal of International Economic Law 9 (2006) 2, p. 293 (300).

[27] See, i.a., Stewart, Why Antidumping Laws Need Not be Cloned After Competition Law Nor Replaced by Such Laws, paper presented at the conference "Antidumping and Competition Policy: Complements or Substitutes?," Center for Applied Studies in International Negotiations, Geneva, 11–12 July 1996, cited according to Hoekman, Competition Policy and Preferential Trade Agreements, 2002, p. 2, mentioning several further arguments why the inclusion of competition law in the multilateral trade system has been opposed in literature.

[28] See Bhattacharjea, The Case for a Multilateral Agreement on Competition Policy: A Developing Country Perspective, in: Journal of International Economic Law 9 (2006) 2, note 27, p. 297.

[29] See Bhattacharjea, The Case for a Multilateral Agreement on Competition Policy: A Developing Country Perspective, in: Journal of International Economic Law 9 (2006) 2, p. 297.

Network (ICN) has to be mentioned. This is an informal cooperation network between national and multinational competition authorities that also includes academics, practitioners, representatives from business, consumer groups, and the legal and economic professions. In the meantime, it encompasses over 100 competition agencies that try to promote "more efficient and effective antitrust enforcement worldwide to the benefit of consumers and business."[30] While the emphasis of this network is on enforcement, there can be no doubt that it may pave the way for some sort of "soft harmonisation" of national competition legislations, even beyond the national orders directly involved.

On a whole, it can be said that the particular appeal of this network lies in its extension, its flexible working methods and its problem orientation. The lesser degree of bindingness in comparison to traditional multilateral agreements may constitute, at first sight, a drawback but, on the other hand, the working method of this network fits well to the main characteristics of the norm creation process in international law, based as it is on discussion and persuasion.[31]

Nonetheless, soft forms of cooperation like that in the ICN, attractive as they may seem, cannot replace more stringent agreements, be they of a smaller or of a more extensive geographic reach, be they only procedural in nature or comprehensive of substantive provisions.

For a long time it has been tried to overcome the deficits resulting from the lack of a true international framework on competition law by bilateral cooperation agreements, regarding information sharing, notifications requirements, the introduction of choice of law rules as well as substantive cooperation.[32] While the so-called "first generation agreements" consisted mainly in soft law instruments designed to ensure effective (negative) comity, the second generation of these agreements provided for more substantive measures, in particular for enforcement measures, and setting precise obligations to investigate alleged anticompetitive practices at the other party´s request (positive comity).

An important basis for favouring this sort of cooperation was laid by an OECD recommendation of 1967.[33]

It is interesting to note that agreements of this kind were first and foremost concluded by those countries that had the most developed antitrust law and that had displayed the most extensive preparedness to apply these laws in an extraterritorial way, the US and Canada. Over the years, a whole network of such agreements was woven around these countries. The EC, for a long time, remained more prudent in this regard, first of all because it tried to avoid any sort of conflict in competition

[30] See ICN Factsheet and Key Messages, April 2009, http://www.internationalcompetitionnetwork.org/uploads/library/doc608.pdf.

[31] See in this context, in particular, the so-called "New Haven Approach" by McDougal/Lasswell.

[32] See for more details on these agreements Guzman, International competition law, in: Guzman/Sykes (eds.), *Research Handbook in International Economic Law*, 2007, and Papadopoulos, *The International Dimension of EU Competition Law and Policy*, 2010, pp. 52 et seq.

[33] See OECD, Recommendation on Cooperation between Member Countries on Restrictive Business Practices Affecting International Trade, 1967.

matters with other jurisdictions and afterwards because high hopes were set in the creation of a plurilateral framework on competition within the WTO system. As these hopes were disappointed, the EU had to partially reorient itself. Nonetheless, it already concluded in 1991 an agreement on bilateral cooperation with the US that was extended to an enforcement agreement (positive comity) in 1998.

Of a wholly different nature are those agreements that establish a separate trade regime where competition provisions constitute a natural and essential element. These agreements may be bilateral or regional (RTAs). An important characteristic of these agreements lies in the fact that they deal with competition issues as part of an attempt to liberalise trade—in the respective area—on a broader scale.

International Competition Provisions as Part of Special Trade Regimes

While attempts to establish a fully-fledged international competition law regime have not been successful, at least in so far as a binding plurilateral agreement with substantive provisions and provisions on dispute settlement was aspired at, a process has taken place over the last decades, widely unnoticed by the community of competition law experts, on the basis of which provisions on competition law were inserted in Regional Trade Agreeements (RTA).[34] As it is known, in this context the term "regional" should not be understood according to its traditional meaning. Here, it means nothing else than the opposite of "multilateral." Therefore, RTAs are exceptions to the Most-Favoured-Nation-Principle according to Art. I GATT, an exception especially provided for in Art. XXIV GATT and this provision does not set any requirement as to the geographic closeness of the cooperation partners.

As it is known, Art. XXIV does neither tell anything about competition rules in RTAs but the doctrine has developed a so-called "stage approach" according to which the following five stages of economic integration can be distinguished:[35] Free trade area (members retain national tariffs); Customs Union (a common external tariff is introduced); Common market (barriers to free factor movement are abolished); Economic union (national economic policies are harmonised to some extent) and Total economic integration (the integration zone resembles an autonomous state as economic policies are unified and supranational institutions are created to supervise their implementation).

[34] On the following see in more detail Hilpold, *Die EU im GATT/WTO-System*, 2009, pp. 19 et seq., and Hilpold, International Competition Law and Regional Trade Agreements, Manchester Journal of International Economic Law 2 (2005) 3.

[35] See L. Hog Ta, Will Asean Economic Integration progress beyond a Free Trade Area?, International and Comparative Law Quarterly 53 (2004) 4, p. 935 (942-943), referring to Balassa 1961.

This stages approach implies that a natural development takes place according to which integration in RTAs become ever deeper. At the last stage, rules on competition are an important, perhaps even necessary element of an RTA. It is probably no coincidence that the most successful integration zones so far, the European Union and NAFTA, have both devoted much importance to rules on competition. As for the European Union, competition policy is at present one of the most efficient policies of this entity.

In the last years several studies have been published that gave a decisive contribution to shed light on this issue and to furnish, first of all, empirical information about this subject. In this context, two studies have primarily to be mentioned: the UNCTAD study on "Competition Provisions in Regional Trade Agreements: How to Assure Development Gains" of 2005[36] (UNCTAD study) and the OECD study on "Competition Provisions in Regional Trade Agreements" of 2006.[37] Three years later a further study appeared that is to be seen as a specification in respect to the former two.[38] In fact, it extended the purview of the inquiry, examining the effect of provisions that did not formally relate to competition in the traditional sense but had repercussions on competition policy in a practical sense. In the following, some of the most salient results of these studies shall be summarised and briefly commented:

- The insertion of competition rules in RTAs is part of a broader attempt to foster trade liberalisation. Therefore, *competition* policy has a complementary role with respect to trade liberalisation. If an RTA adopts rules on competition law, the relevant provisions have, first of all, an instrumental function with regard to the primary intent to promote trade liberalisation. "Trade is the overriding principle."[39] The respective agreements themselves leave no doubt as to this "hierarchy of goals and values."[40]

[36] Brusick/Alvarez/L. Cernat (eds.), Competition Provisions in Regional Trade Agreements: How to Assure Development Gains, UNCTAD Study, 2005.

[37] Solano/Sennekamp, Competition Provisions in Regional Trade Agreements, OECD Study, COM/DAF/TD (2005) 3/FINAL, March 2006.

[38] See Teh, Competition provisions in regional trade agreements, in: Estevadeordal et al. (eds.), *Regional Rules in the Global Trading System*, 2009, p. 418.

[39] So explicitly Solano/Sennekamp, Competition Provisions in Regional Trade Agreements, OECD Study, COM/DAF/TD (2005) 3/FINAL, March 2006, para. 12.

[40] See, for example, the relevant provision in agreements where the EC is a party:

> The following [anti-competitive practices] are incompatible with the proper functioning of the Agreement, in so far as they may affect trade between the parties.

The NAFTA agreement contains a similarly worded provision:

> [...] adopt or maintain measures to proscribe anticompetitive business conduct and take appropriate action with respect thereto, recognizing that such measures will enhance the fulfillment of the objective of this Agreement.

Both provisions are cited according to Solano/Sennekamp, Competition Provisions in Regional Trade Agreements, OECD Study, COM/DAF/TD (2005) 3/FINAL, March 2006.

- Deeper forms of integration are not only likely to contain competition provisions but these provisions are also usually more sophisticated than those in RTAs with a lesser depth of integration.
- There is a great variety in the nature of the competition rules in the various agreements. Nonetheless, by and large, two "families" can be distinguished in the important category of North-South RTAs. RTAs of this kind concluded by Canada and the US emphasise cooperation of competition authorities, thereby extending main elements of the North American antitrust philosophy to their cooperation partners. As a consequence they oppose supranational supervisions, dispute settlement and adjudication. In the same vein, the EU also "exports" main characteristics of its competition policy to its cooperation partners in the South. Consequently, these RTAs contain substantive provisions on competition law, they are designed to engender a harmonisation process and they favour even the creation of supra-national agencies to supervise competition law on the blueprint of the EU Commission.[41] At the same time it has to be remarked that these families are "flexible" categories.[42] On a whole, it is interesting to see that both the US and Canada on the one hand and the EU on the other managed to implant their visions on competition policy on a world-wide scale. The EU philosophy on competition law seems to exercise a particular attraction. In fact, several South-South agreements are now adopting the EU perspective, probably because this approach is seen as a recipe for successful "deep" integration.[43]

  In the European area, the competition provisions in RTAs resemble the more the EU competition rules the closer the RTA as a whole is to EU law. As a consequence, RTAs conceived as a form of "accession association" are regularly endowed with very detailed and "strong" rules on competition. This comes not really as a surprise as the main goal of these agreements is the preparation of full membership that implies the adoption of penetrating rules on competition law.[44]
- Not all sectors of the economy are equally affected by the attempts to introduce competition policies. Like in the case of trade rules, agriculture also constitutes an area of competition policy, a special case that is generally not easily accessible for international regulations.
- In addition to competition rules in the proper sense, sectoral provisions (for example in the field of telecommunications and financial services, government procurement, and intellectual property) and so-called horizontal competition principles (non-discrimination, transparency, and procedural fairness) have to

[41] See Brusick/Alvarez/Cernat (eds.), Competition Provisions in Regional Trade Agreements: How to Assure Development Gains, UNCTAD Study, 2005, p. x.

[42] See Solano/Sennekamp, Competition Provisions in Regional Trade Agreements, OECD Study, COM/DAF/TD (2005) 3/FINAL, March 2006, para. 44.

[43] This is in particular true for MERCOSUR. See, for example, Bischoff-Everding, *Wettbewerbsrecht im MERCOSUR*, 2003.

[44] This aspect is closely dealt with in Papadopoulos, *The International Dimension of EU Competition Law and Policy*, 2010, note 12, pp. 93 et seq.

be considered if a more complete picture is seeked.[45] Of course, further complexity is added to the study. This broader perspective can change somewhat the overall assessment even though no or few provisions on competition law in the traditional understanding (such as those examined in the UNCTAD and in the OECD study) are present.[46] And even if competition law provisions in a narrower sense are excluded from dispute settlement,[47] competition rules in a broader sense can again be subject to such scrutiny.[48]

– There can be no doubt that competition issues assume a particular connotation with developing countries. This particular situation where they find themselves was a main reason why many of them opposed the creation of a plurilateral regime that would tackle the competition issue mainly from the perspective of the industrialised countries. On the other hand, the lack of competition in these economies can be a remarkable hindrance to development. Furthermore, developing countries are much exposed to pressures by international cartels.[49] For this reason—and because the introduction of provisions on competition is often part of a greater package deal characterised by the do ut des-principle—developing countries have agreed to provisions on competition in this context. However, to these rules, the special and differential treatment principle applies. This principle finds expression in the flexibility of commitments, provisions on technical assistance and capacity building as well as in the granting of transition periods.[50]

Conclusion

RTAs are a phenomenon that is here to stay. An ever-growing part of international trade takes place within such areas. They fulfil an important role both as a surrogate for further liberalisation steps on the multilateral level and as a stimulus to proceed

---

[45] This is the approach chosen by Teh, Competition provisions in regional trade agreements, in: Estevadeordal et al. (eds.), *Regional Rules in the Global Trading System*, 2009, note 39, p. 489.

[46] Teh, Competition provisions in regional trade agreements, in: Estevadeordal et al. (eds.), *Regional Rules in the Global Trading System*, 2009, note 39, p. 489.

[47] This is the case in about one third of RTAs examined by Teh, Competition provisions in regional trade agreements, in: Estevadeordal et al. (eds.), *Regional Rules in the Global Trading System*, 2009, note 39, p. 489, in particular around the US-hub.

[48] Teh, Competition provisions in regional trade agreements, in: Estevadeordal et al. (eds.), *Regional Rules in the Global Trading System*, 2009, note 39, p. 489.

[49] Brusick/Alvarez/Cernat (eds.), Competition Provisions in Regional Trade Agreements: How to Assure Development Gains, UNCTAD Study, 2005, p. xi.

[50] Solano/Sennekamp, Competition Provisions in Regional Trade Agreements, OECD Study, COM/DAF/TD (2005) 3/FINAL, March 2006, note 38, para. 10, lit. h). For a rather critical assessment of these achievements see Evenett, What Can We Really Learn From the Competition Provisions of Regional Trade Agreements, 2005, available at: http://www.evenett.com/research/chapters/RevisedEvenettUNCTADRTAvolume.pdf.

globally on the liberalisation path.[51] As integration becomes ever deeper within these zones, the inclusion of rules on competition policy becomes a natural consequence. As of yet it is not clear whether these regional regimes may equally assume the characteristics of a role model for a multilateral regulation of competition as it is the case for the general trade regime. As it is known, the different visions on how to craft multilateral trade rules are a permanent bone of contention between North and South in the relevant negotiation fora. It seems that in the field of competition law the respective divide is even greater. It has been argued that in multilateral negotiations on competition rules developing countries might have a greater levy to obtain rules that are of a more immediate concern to them.[52]

Further, beyond an agreement on a closer core meaning, there is no real consensus on how to define competition law or, respectively, on what anticompetitive measures really are. For this reason, some RTAs make only a general reference to anti-competitive measures while others content themselves with giving some examples.[53] Of course, in these cases, considerable uncertainties remain but the more homogenous perspective on the regional level (in respect to the multilateral one) should permit to overcome the impasse.

Therefore, the strong criticism levied against the UNCTAD and the OECD studies is only partly justified. While the extension of the perspective may have been useful for gaining a better insight in this difficult subject the main contribution by this new approach has to be seen in the following: It bears further evidence to the fact that the concept of competition is not yet consensually defined in all its ramifications.[54]

If it is difficult to find a consensus on the meaning of competition law on the regional level this must the more so be the case on the multilateral level and this explains to a considerable extent why it has not been possible up to this day to devise such an agreement. In this sense, the experiences made at the regional level

[51] See Hilpold, Regional Integration According to Article XXIV GATT—Between Law and Politics, Max Planck Yearbook of United Nations Law 7 (2003), p. 1, and Hilpold, *Die EU im GATT/WTO-System*, 2009.

[52] In particular, developing countries would be more interested in regulating the abuse of dominant positions and in countering the deleterious trans-border effects of cartels. See Evenett, What Can We Really Learn From the Competition Provisions of Regional Trade Agreements, 2005, note 51, p. 16, available at: http://www.evenett.com/research/chapters/RevisedEvenettUNCTADRTAvolume.pdf.

[53] See Solano/Sennekamp, Competition Provisions in Regional Trade Agreements, OECD Study, COM/DAF/TD (2005) 3/FINAL, March 2006, note 38, para. 18.

[54] By the way, if we adopt such a broad concept of competition law then the WTO is already active in this field. In fact, provisions on competition can be found in several parts of WTO law, such as Art. III (4) GATT, Art. VIII (2) GATS, Art. 40 TRIPS, Art. 8 TRIMS, Art. 3 Anti-Dumping Agreement, Art. 8.1 TBT Agreement and Art. 11.1(a) and Art. 11.3 Safeguards Agreement. See Matsushita, Trade and Competition Policy, in: Bethlehem et al. (eds.), *The Oxford Handbook of International Trade Law*, 2009, note 13, pp. 648 et seq. For a detailed analysis of WTO provisions relating to competition law see Terhechte, WTO und Wettbewerb, in: Hilf/Oeter (eds.), *WTO-Recht*, 2010, pp. 643 (653 et seq.).

bode ill for any aspiration to find such a consensus in the near future. In sum, we can say that the regional level offers a most valuable field for an in-depth inquiry into the intricacies of international competition law. The—often neglected—results in this area, as incomplete as they may be, deserve much greater attention if further attempts to conceive a plurilateral agreement on international competition rules are made. The particularities of the various RTAs stand against any attempt to transfer these provisions lock, stock, and barrel to the multilateral level.[55] On the regional level, it is far easier to overcome diversities in competition policy cultures than on the multilateral level. Consequently, the enforcement of substantive rules is easier to achieve regionally. Therefore, with regard to the multilateral level, it is more realistic to assume that a strengthening of substantive cooperation and enforcement of competition rules could take place in an evolutionary process starting from the existing loose forms of international cooperation in competition matters. The inclusion of rules on competition law in RTAs might therefore be seen as a provisional second best solution. On the longer run it might offer important insights for a multilateral solution based on true consensus, it might engender a learning process and finally a de-facto harmonisation of central elements of national competition policy so that a multilateral framework can bridge the remaining gaps.

[55] In a comprehensive study by Evenett, Levenstein, and Suslov it has been very well explained that for the time being the diversities in national competition policies effectively bar the conclusion of a broader multilateral framework agreement in this field. There is the danger that an agreement that is not really universal and comprehensive (and we have yet to find out what this really means) would immediately open new spaces for circumvention and the creation of new safe havens. See Evenett/Levenstein/Suslow, International Cartel Enforcement: Lessons from the 1990s, World Bank Policy Research Working Paper No. 2680, 2001.

External Competition Law of the EU

Anestis Papadopoulos

Setting the Context

Competition law is a legal tool whose origins go back to the fifteenth century, and even earlier, with the aim of regulating practices that have an anticompetitive effect on the markets. While competition law has been a prominent feature of economic policies in the US for more than a 100 years and the EU for more than 60 years, in the last three decades the number of the countries that have adopted competition law has been significantly increased. In this regard, competition law and policy is gradually becoming a legal tool used not only by industrialised countries but also by developing, and least developed countries.

Several factors have led to this increase of countries that adopted competition law recently, including the dominance of liberal national political frameworks and subsequent development of market oriented economies, coupled with the collapse of the Soviet Union; the expansion of the EU and subsequent obligation of the new Member States to have and apply EU compatible competition law and policy; the support by a number of International Institutions, such as the IMF, UNCTAD, the World Bank and the OECD of the adoption of competition rules by countries members to those institutions. Today, more than 110 countries have adopted competition law, and of these countries, 80 have adopted such law within the last 30 years.[1]

While in most of the industrialised countries it is accepted that provisions on cartels, abuse of dominance, and some sort of merger control should be the basis of competition law, it is also a fact that in most of the countries that have recently

---

This paper is based on my book entitled "*The international dimension of EU competition law and policy,*" 2010.

[1] See Papadopoulos, *The international dimension of EU competition law and policy*, 2010, pp. 15–17.

A. Papadopoulos (✉)
Partner, KPP Law, Athens
e-mail: a.papadopoulos@kpplaw.eu

C. Herrmann et al. (eds.), *European Yearbook of International Economic Law (EYIEL), Vol. 4 (2013)*, European Yearbook of International Economic Law 4,
DOI 10.1007/978-3-642-33917-2_5,

adopted competition legislation, courts have not had the time to examine many competition cases, relevant academia has not had the time to discuss and develop competition related principles, and competition authorities have not had much time to review many competition cases and apply competition policy widely.

In this context, it is also widely acknowledged, that the understanding about the broader scope of competition law in different countries and the evaluation of particular practices varies. Four main factors that lead to such a varied application of competition law, which in turn become the subject matter of discourse at the international level may be distinguished: the importance of economics in the application of competition law, and the fact that a number of sometimes divergent economic theories have been used in the context of the assessment of a business practice and subsequent application of the competition-related rules; the fact that certain sectors of national economies are regulated by sectoral regulation and not competition, and such sectors and regulations vary from country to country; the relationship between competition law and policy and other national policies that sometimes may have a scope divergent to that of competition law and policy; and the social structure and traditions of particular national societies that have an effect on the way that competition law is applied in these countries.[2]

Competition Law Goes International

In parallel, in the last decades, economic globalisation[3] that refers to improvements in technology and communications,[4] liberalisation of international trade through the provisions of the GATT and more recently the WTO, which to a great extent has opened up national boarders to multinational firms, and the subsequent increase of economic flows through the operation of those firms, have led to the "internationalisation" of several fields of economic activity, and the subsequent need of regulation of such activities at the international level.[5]

---

[2] See Papadopoulos, *The international dimension of EU competition law and policy*, 2010, pp. 18–35.

[3] Economists would probably prefer the term "international economic integration," referring to the integration of markets due to the increase of international economic activity. These are probably over-simplified definitions, in view of the debate regarding the meaning, or even the existence of globalisation. See Held, Golblatt, McGrew, and Perraton, *Global Transformations: Politics, Economics and Culture*, 1999, pp. 2–10, where the authors provide a number of alternative definitions on globalisation.

[4] Rodrik, How Far will International Economic Integration Go?, The Journal of Economic Perspectives, 14 (1999) 1, p. 177; Archibugi, and Pietrobelli, The Globalisation of Technology and its Implications for Developing Countries. Windows of Opportunity or Further Burdens?, Technological Forecasting and Social Change 70 (2002) 9, p 861 (864), where the authors identify three main categories of (economic) globalisation: the international exploitation of nationally produced technology, the global generation of innovation, and global technological cooperations.

[5] The list of such fields, includes, (not exclusively) intellectual property, corporate governance, money laundering, telecommunications, energy, environmental, transport, tax, and banking regulations that may also deal with business practices.

Being a basic tool of regulation of the markets, competition law and policy has been considered one of the domestic policies that should be included in the list of topics for negotiation at the international level,[6] since it is suggested that ineffective domestic competition policies could be a substantial obstacle in the process of trade liberalisation.[7]

Two sets of competition related practices have been considered as having such a negative effect on trade liberalisation: practices conducted by private firms that may have an international effect, and hybrid public-private practices that may have the same effect. As to the former, it has been suggested, that the most directly linked to international trade are anticompetitive practices that have an exclusionary effect, thus hindering the entrance and expansion of foreign firms in the markets where the anticompetitive practices take place.[8] These practices may include cartels, abuse of dominance and vertical agreements that may have a foreclosure effect. On the procedural side, differences in the procedures provided by national competition laws for the review of mergers, has been also considered as creating problems to firms that have to notify the merger to multiple authorities.

As to the latter (public-private practices), there are also competition-related governmental practices that may also have an influence on the operation of international trade. These may include industrial policy considerations, which may imply the lack of law, exemptions, and exclusions from the application of competition rules or lack of enforcement or strategic enforcement of law, with the aim of strengthening particular firms, and creating national champions that would be able to become protagonists at the international level.[9]

Layers of Internationalisation of Competition Law

The appearance of the above practices that have an effect on multiple states, has generated the need for international arrangements to address these practices, or at least to provide for some sort of coordination on the way that states apply the rules that regulate such practices. As noted above, the way that competition law is applied by the various nations that have such a law in place varies, and this may lead to conflicts, in cases where more than one jurisdictions review the same practice.

With the aim of securing the uniform application of competition law at the international level, attempts for a multilateral agreement on competition first

[6] Howse, From Politics to Technocracy-and Back Again: The Fate of the Multilateral Trading Regime, American Journal of International Law, 96 (2002) 1, p. 94 (96).

[7] OECD, Trade and Competition Policies- Options for a Greater Coherence, 2001.

[8] Marsden, *A Competition Policy for the WTO*, 2003, Chapter 3, and especially pp. 91–108.

[9] See International Competition Policy Advisory Committee (2000), ICPAC Final Report to the Attorney General and the Assistant Attorney General for Antitrust, (hereinafter ICPAC report) http://www.usdoj.gov/atr/icpac/finalreport.htm, at pp. 202–215.

appeared almost a century ago, without success to date.[10] That being said, in the absence of multilateral agreement to regulate anticompetitive practices that have an international effect, a number of alternative options have been pursued by the states that have faced similar issues, and these options put in context the different layers of the internationalisation of competition law.

The formation of international norms is dominated by the concept of state sovereignty, which is the basis of international political order.[11] This model stems from the presumption that "*the coherence of society has to be provided through the unitary power of the state. Since the split of multitudes of individuals and the disorder of society cannot create collective reason, it is the homogeneity and unity 'of the state' and its sovereign power, which forges and represents the quasi-transcendental destiny of society.*"[12]

From an international law perspective, it follows that sovereign states have sole responsibility for regulating any matter that occurs within their territory,[13] and that they are therefore the primary subjects of international law.[14] Based on these two assumptions, when problems that affect multiple countries emerge, two possible options may provide with solutions to the resolution of conflicts.

The first is based on the principle that sovereign states have the power to regulate all matters that arise within their territory, and leads to unilateral solutions, which in the field of competition law and policy take the form of extraterritorial application of national competition laws. The second assumption, i.e. that sovereign states are the primary subjects of international law, is the basis for the conclusion of international agreements with which contracting states agree on particular competition law related commitments.[15] Thus, in the field of international competition law, on the one end of the spectrum there is extraterritorial application of competition law and on the other end, there is the possibility of adopting a binding multilateral agreement to regulate competition practices with an effect on multiple states.

---

[10] See Papadopoulos, *The international dimension of EU competition law and policy*, 2010, chapter 6.

[11] Burley, Law Among Liberal States: Liberal Internationalism and the Act of State Doctrine, Columbia Law Review 92 (1992) 8, p. 1907 (1923–1926); See also Dabbah, *The Internationalisation of Antitrust policy* , 2003, at pp. 141–142.

[12] Preub, Political Order and Democracy: Carl Schmitt and his Influence, in: Ch. Mouffe, (ed.), *The Challenge of Carl Schmitt,* 1999, p. 167. Cited by Jayasuriya, Globalization, Sovereignty, and the Rule of Law: From Political to Economic Constitutionalism?, Constellations 8 (2001) 4, p. 442 (445).

[13] Philpott, Sovereignty: An Introduction and Brief History, Journal of International Affairs 48 (1995) 2, p. 353 (356–357).

[14] Shaw, *International Law*, 2004, 5th edition, pp. 175–223.

[15] Further, in this context, international agreements have been considered equivalent of a contract. Guzman, The Design of International Agreements, European Journal of International Law 16 (2005) 4, p. 579 (585).

In between these opposites, there are a number of variations. For instance, Terhechte, in discussing the process of the evolution of international competition law with a focus on the enforcement of the law, identifies the two main pillars of the internationalisation of the relevant rules, i.e. improved *cooperation* between the authorities and courts and gradual *convergence* of the relevant rules of the states.[16] The author further identifies a number of relevant sub-categories of these pillars.

In addition, international agreements that are devoted to competition law or include competition provisions in the broader framework of issues they address may be categorised based on various factors. The number of participating countries is a relevant factor, and therefore there are bilateral, plurilateral[17] and multilateral agreements. The extent to which such agreements have been concluded between neighbouring countries or not may also lead to the characterisation of an agreement as regional or transnational. From a different perspective, the extent to which the agreements are devoted to enforcement cooperation on competition law matters, or they include competition law in a broader trade framework is another factor; thus, there are enforcement cooperation agreements and free trade agreements that include competition provisions. Whether the agreements oblige the signing parties to apply the agreed clauses (hard law) or whether the parties just express an intention to cooperate (soft law) is also a factor to be taken into account in the context of classifying agreements.

Furthermore, in parallel with the conclusion of agreements on competition and the subsequent development of norms, it has been identified in the relevant literature, that such development has been characterised by the emergence and impact of transnational networks of competition officials and experts, which have resulted in the diffusion of competition law and have contributed to the development of common understandings among officials and experts as to the notion of competition law and its optimum application.[18]

The External Competition Law of the EU: A Definition

The EU itself has been a protagonist in the development of international competition norms and more generally in the internationalisation of competition rules. This position is firstly based on the fact that the EU is considered an international organisation where the participating states retain to a certain extent their

[16] Terhechte, International Competition Enforcement Law Between Cooperation and Convergence—Mapping a New Field for Global Administrative Law, The University of Oxford Centre for Competition Law and Policy, Working Paper CCLP(L) 26 (2009), p. 7.

[17] Referring to agreements concluded by more than three states.

[18] See Maher, Competition Law in the International Domain: Networks as a New Form of Governance, 29 (2002) 1, Journal of Law and Society, p. 111; see Maher and Papadopoulos, Competition Agency Networks Around the World, in Ezrachi (ed): *International Research Handbook on Competition Law*, 2013.

sovereignty.[19] To this end and based on detailed substantive rules and effective enforcement of the rules by the European Commission and the regional courts, competition law in the EU has been developed in a transnational rather in a national context, and this is itself a strong indication of the international perspective of EU competition law.[20] The commitment of the EU in the development of international competition rules has been also evident in the context of the unsuccessful attempts of the administration of the Union for the adoption of competition law in the WTO framework.[21] In parallel, the EU has also been active in the conclusion of bilateral enforcement cooperation agreements on competition and bilateral trade agreements that include competition law provisions.

Against this background, the external competition law of the EU, which is the central theme of the paper, may be defined as the law that the Union has developed in relation to anticompetitive practices and mergers that have an effect in the territories of the EU and one or more other states. In other words, is the law that, when applied, has a potential effect on the territories of states, and/or on subjects—residents of, or registered at countries outside the EU. In this regard, external competition law of the EU is automatically linked to the system of international law, i.e. law that regulates the relations between and among nations and states.

In an attempt to identify the various sources of international competition law that form the external competition law of the EU, and on the basis of the above analysis there are two alternatives: extraterritorial application of competition law, that, as will be showed below, is a feature of the EU competition regime, and international agreements that include competition provisions or are devoted to competition. The EU has concluded two types of such agreements, i.e. bilateral trade agreements that include competition provisions, and enforcement cooperation agreements. The next sections of the paper discuss the way that extraterritoriality and the various international agreements formulate the external competition law of the EU.

Extraterritoriality

In the absence of a multilateral agreement on competition, and in view of the fact that most of the international (bilateral and regional) agreements that have been concluded to date are in the form of soft law the application of competition rules on

[19] On the relation between EU law and international law and the various perspectives from which this relation has been discussed in the relevant literature, see Ziegler, International Law and EU Law: Between Asymetric Constitutionalisation and Frangmentation, in Orakhelashvili (Ed) *Research Handbook on the Theory and History of International Law*, 2011, p. 268.

[20] See Papadopoulos, *The international dimension of EU competition law and policy*, 2010, chapter 5, where it is suggested that the EU in general and its competition regime in more particular has had an influence in the development of other similar regional settings.

[21] See Papadopoulos, *The international dimension of EU competition law and policy*, 2010, chapter 6.

an extraterritorial manner, has been a practice-principle with an important impact in the field of international law. As with most features of national competition regimes, extraterritorial application of competition law was initially a feature of the US competition law, which has been subsequently followed by a number of countries.[22] In particular, in the US the courts have consistently applied US antitrust rules in an extraterritorial manner in the last 65 years,[23] on the basis of the "effects doctrine" that was introduced in the 1945 *Alcoa* case,[24] and according to which, the US courts have the competence to apply US competition rules to conduct that has taken place wholly or partly in a foreign state, and as far as such conduct intends to affect the United States and has in fact such an effect. The Ninth Circuit mitigated the effects test in 1976 in the *Timberlane* decision,[25] by taking into account a consideration of comity for foreign defendants creating thus a rule-of-reason comity analysis. Comity is a principle first developed in continental Europe in the seventeenth century and while there is no universal consensus on the notion of comity, it is widely accepted that comity is a principle applied solely through courtesy of the state that implement its laws and according to which extraterritorial determinations are often grounded in considerations of politeness or respect to the respective laws of the states that may be affected by the extraterritorial application of competition rules.[26]

The rule of reason comity analysis was codified in the Foreign Trade Antitrust Improvements Act of 1982 (FTAIA),[27] which provides that the challenged conduct must have a "direct, substantial and reasonable foreseeable effect" on US commerce or on the trade of a US citizen/company engaged in export commerce. That said the impact of the FTAIA as a statute, has not been significant.[28] As opposed to the trend towards growth of significance of the principle of comity in the assessment of jurisdiction on cases with an effect on multiple markets, in the 1993 *Hartford* decision[29] the Supreme Court held that practically comity would be applied only in exceptional cases where there would be "true conflict" in the

---

[22] See IBA (2006) Report of the Task Force on Extraterritorial Jurisdiction, p. 50 and p. 70, where it is noted that competition laws have been applied in an extraterritorial manner by Argentina, Austria, Belgium, Brazil, Canada, China, Czech Republic, Denmark, Finland, France, Germany, Italy, Japan, Norway, Portugal, Russia, South Africa, South Korea, Spain, Switzerland and the UK.

[23] See generally Barnet, Conflicts of Jurisdiction and International Comity in Extraterritorial Antitrust, Emory International Law Review 18 (2004), p. 555.

[24] United States Court of Appeals for the 2nd Circuit, *United States v. Aluminum Co. of America,* 148 F.2d 416 (2ed Cir. 1945).

[25] United States Court of Appeals for the 9nd Circuit, *Timberlane Lumber Co. v Bank of America,* 549 F.2d 597 (9th Cir. 1976).

[26] See Papadopoulos, *The international dimension of EU competition law and policy*, 2010, pp. 64–67.

[27] 15 U.S.C s 6a (1994).

[28] Springman, Fix Prices Globally, Get Sued Locally? US Jurisdiction Over International Cartels, University of Chicago Law Review 72 (2005), p. 265 (271–273).

[29] United States Supreme Court, *Hartford Fire Ins. Co. v. California*, 509 U.S.764 (1993).

assessment of jurisdiction. This position was later confirmed by the Supreme Court in the *Nippon Paper* case, where it held that comity is "more an aspiration" than an established rule, confirming in the process that the growth of comity in competition matters was stunted by *Hartford Fire*.[30]

More recently though, in the *Empagran* decision,[31] the Supreme Court, further developed the principle of extraterritoriality, by taking the position that foreign purchasers of vitamins based outside the US did not have the right to bring a claim for treble damages in a US court for conduct that had taken place solely outside the US market, even where it was part of a wider cartel that did affect US market. On remand from the Supreme Court,[32] the Court of Appeals took the position that, in order to obtain relief, plaintiffs have to show that there is a "direct casual relationship" or put differently a "proximate causation" between the effect that the anticompetitive practices have in the US market and the injuries they have suffered[33] While the *Empagran* case showed that there may be a tendency to mitigate the extent and impact of extraterritoriality in the US, it may also be suggested that such mitigation may not be overstated in view of the fact that extraterritorial application of competition rules by the US courts, remains the norm, something that is supported by the fact that the US has been very active in recent years in seeking extradition of foreign nationals who are involved in cartels.[34]

Similarly, the application of the effects doctrine, leading to extraterritorial application of competition rules has been actively pursued by the European Commission in the last two decades in a number of cases, with the EU courts nonetheless, being more hesitant in applying the doctrine.[35] It is noted that the territorial limits of application of competition law in the EU is provided directly by the founding Treaty, and all its amended versions, which clearly state that the competition related articles are applied in relation to anticompetitive conduct, as far as such conduct "may affect trade between Member States."

---

[30] *United States of America v. Nippon Paper Industries Co. LTD, et al.*, p. 9, 109 F.3 d (1st Cir. 1997).

[31] United States Court of Appeals for the District of Columbia Circuit, *Hoffman La Roche vs. Empagran*, SA 124 2359 (2004). See Reinker, Case Comment: Roche vs. Empagran, Harvard Journal of Law and Public Policy 28 (2004) 1, p. 297.

[32] See Opinion of the Court of Appeals, *Empagran S.A. v. Hoffman La Roche LTD., et al.*, No 01-7115c (2005).

[33] See Opinion of the Court of Appeals, *Empagran S.A. v. Hoffman La Roche LTD., et al.*, No 01-7115c (2005).

[34] As Watson–Doig notes, in the period between 2000 and 2005, of the 80 individuals serving jail sentences in the US for cartel activity, 18 were foreign nationals. See Watson-Doig, Crime and Competition, Competition Law Insight of 10.4.2007 (2007), p. 8 (9). See also the discussion on the *Ian Norris case*, section 3.4.2.

[35] See Sato, Extraterritorial Application of EU Competition Law—Is it Possible for Japanese Companies to Steer Clear of EU Competition Law?, Journal of Political Science and Sociology (2009) 11, p. 23 (pp. 30 et seq.).

The notion of the effect on trade between Member States as a prerequisite for enforcement of competition rules (anticompetitive agreements and abuse of dominance), has been an issue widely discussed in relation to practices conducted by firms registered in the EU.[36] In relation to practices with an effect on multiple (EU and non EU) markets and jurisdiction, the seminal, to date, decision is *Wood Pulp*,[37] where the Commission found that 36 out of 42 suppliers of wood pulp were violating European competition law (what is now Art 101(1) TFEU). Forty out of these 42 undertakings were not resident within the European Union. On appeal, the Court of Justice ruled that an agreement concluded by undertakings that are not within the borders of the European Union would be an infringement of European competition law, as far as the agreement is "implemented" within the EU.[38] In taking this decision, the Court of Justice refrained from relying on the effects doctrine as opposed to the position of the Commission, which was in favour of the effects doctrine, and this position was supported by Advocate General Darmon who opined on the Case.[39] Thus, the extent to which EU competition law has embraced the effects doctrine is still not clear, or at least not the same as the US, and at least as far as the European Court is concerned.[40]

In mergers, nevertheless, the situation is clearer. In particular, in *Gencor*,[41] Commission took the decision to block a merger that was cleared by the South African competition authorities, despite the fact that both the companies involved in the merger were registered in South Africa, but fell within the EU turnover thresholds that determine jurisdiction.[42] Judging on the case the Court of First Instance (CFI) declared that "the application of the [Merger] Regulation is justified under public international law when it is foreseeable that a proposed concentration will have an immediate and substantial effect in the Community."[43] This position

[36] The Commission has also published guidelines in relation to the assessment of the effect. See EU Commission, Guidelines on the effect of trade concept contained in Articles 81 and 82 of the treaty (2004/C 101/07), OJ C 101/81.

[37] ECJ, Joined Cases C-89, 104, 114, 116, 117 and 125-129/85, *Ahlstrom and Others v. E.C. Commission (Re Wood Pulp Cartel),* [1988] E.C.R. 5193.

[38] ECJ, Joined Cases C-89, 104, 114, 116, 117 and 125-129/85, *Ahlstrom and Others v. E.C. Commission (Re Wood Pulp Cartel),* [1988] E.C.R. 5193, para. 16: the decision reads: "[A]n infringement of Article 85 ... [is] made up of two elements, the formation of the agreement, decision or concerted practice, and the implementation thereof."

[39] See ECJ, Opinion of Advocate-General Darmon of 25 May 1988 in joined cases 89, 104, 114, 116, 117 and 125-129/85 [1988] E.C.R. 5214, para.57. See Geradin, Reysen and Henry, Extraterritoriality, Comity and Cooperation in EC Competition Law (2008), p. 6. Available at SSRN: http://ssrn.com/abstract=1175003.

[40] Banks, The Development of the Concept of Extraterritoriality under European Merger Law and its Effectiveness under the Merger Regulation following the Boeing/Mc Donnell Douglas Decision 1997, European Competition Law Review 19 (1998) 5, p. 306 (308).

[41] CFI, Case T-102/96, *Gencor Ltd v Commission*, [1999] ECR II-0753.

[42] CFI, Case T-102/96, *Gencor Ltd v Commission*, [1999] ECR II-0753, paras. 78–88.

[43] CFI, Case T-102/96, *Gencor Ltd v Commission*, [1999] ECR II-0753, para. 90.

was welcomed by senior officials of the EU Commission, which as noted above had been in favour of the application of the effects doctrine in relevant cases.[44]

This brief presentation of the development of extraterritoriality just highlights the fact that given the absence of binding international norms to be applied in the field of competition law, the EU institutions, and mainly the Commission, have been eager in expanding the scope of extraterritorial application of the Union's competition law. In this regard, and while from an international law perspective this trend may not be welcomed in view of the fact that international problems require international solutions, it may not be doubted, that extraterritorial application of competition rules is an important feature of the EU's external competition law.

That being said, it should not be underestimated either what has been mentioned above, that the EU as a polity has been a protagonist in the attempts for the development of international competition law. In relation to the more specified theme of the paper, i.e. the external competition law of the EU, two types of agreements that have been concluded between the EU and third countries, i.e. bilateral enforcement cooperation agreements on competition and bilateral trade agreements that include competition provisions, have had an effect on the development of the external competition law of the European Union, and these two groups of agreements are further discussed in the paper.

Bilateral Trade Agreements of the EU

Bilateral trade agreements have been in recent years the most important tool in the development of the EU's external policy. The first group of relevant agreements and basis for the development of the network of such agreements by the EU has been the so-called Europe Agreements, which were the agreements signed in the 1990s between the EU and the countries that pursued accession in the Union.[45] These agreements covered all fields of the *acquis communautaire*, which is the legal framework that regulates the relations of its Member States and were based on a set of accession criteria adopted in 1993, and further detailed in 1995 with the

[44] Former Commissioner Monti stated that "I am confident, however, that this uncertainty is now behind us: the European Court of First Instance . . . clearly states that the Community's exercise of jurisdiction over a merger taking place wholly outside of the Community is compatible with the principles of public international law, where the merger produces direct substantial and foreseeable effects within the EU." Monti, Cooperation Between Competition Authorities: A Vision for the Future," speech delivered at the Japan Foundation Conference, Washington, DC, 23. June 2000, speech/00/234, available at: http://europa.eu/rapid/pressReleasesAction.do?reference=SPEECH/00/234&f.

[45] Such agreements were signed with countries that eventually entered the EU in 2004 and 2007, and in particular with: Bulgaria, Czech Republic, Cyprus, Estonia, Hungary, Latvia, Lithuania, Malta, Poland, Romania, Slovakia, and Slovenia.

issuance of a White Paper by the Commission.[46] In order to enter the EU, these countries had to fulfil all the criteria set by the EU and this process of adoption of the *acquis* by these countries was very closely scrutinised by the EU Commission.[47] As the Commission notes, "*membership will only happen when the necessary requirements are met,*"[48] a statement that shows that the room for negotiation of the relevant requirements is minimum. This policy of the EU has been criticised by various commentators who stated that the EU was not eager to cooperate in this process and was only interested in imposing its rules to countries that pursued accession.[49] That said one should not ignore that the willingness of the EU's partners to accept the prerequisites of the EU was based in the context of their political and economic decision to join the regional bloc, which would in turn improve and strengthen those states' economies.

In the field of competition law in particular, the supervision of the adoption and implementation of EU compatible competition rules was carried out primarily by DG Competition in cooperation with DG Enlargement, which is the Directorate of the Commission in charge of the enlargement process.

Europe Agreements eventually led to the accession of 12 signing countries in the EU, ten of them in 2004 and another two, Romania and Bulgaria in 2007. Today, Croatia is an acceding county and the date of its entrance into the EU is set for 2013, while another five countries have the status of candidate countries, namely, FYROM, Iceland, Montenegro, Serbia, and Turkey. In addition, three countries, Albania, Bosnia and Herzegovina, and Kosovo have the status of potential candidate countries. The relationship between the EU and these countries is also based on relevant bilateral trade agreements, which in the context of the broader themes they cover, also include competition law.

Furthermore, and apart from the category of bilateral FTAs that includes the agreements with acceding, candidate and potential candidate countries, another two

---

[46] White Paper EC Commission Preparation of the Associated Countries of Central and Eastern Europe for Integration into the Internal Market of the Union, (1995) COM (95) 163 final.

[47] See Devuyst, Kankanen, Lindberg, Orssich, and Roebling, EU enlargement and competition policy: where are we now?, Competition Policy Newsletter (2002) 1, p. 3; Geradin (ed) *Modernization and Enlargement: Two Major Challenges for EC Competition Law*, 2004, in particular chapters 13 to 17; Holscher and Stephan, Competition Policy in Central Eastern Europe in the Light of EU Accession, Journal of Common Market Studies 42 (2004) 2, p. 321; Sceres, Multi-Jurisdictional Competition Law Enforcement: The Interface Between European Competition Law and the Competition Laws of the New Member States, European Competition Journal 3 (2007) 2, p. 465.

[48] See the website of the Commission at http://ec.europa.eu/enlargement/the-polic7y/index_en.htm.

[49] In particular, it has been argued that in the context of their accession, candidate countries had to "swallow all 80,000 pages of European laws and adapt their own legislation to accommodate them," and this whole process has been closely reviewed by EU officials. Leonard, *Why Europe Will Run the 21st Century?*, 2005, p. 45. On the way that the EU monitors the adoption and implementation of the Acquis, see the EC Commission website at http://ec.europa.eu/enlargement/enlargement_process/accession_process/how_does_a_country_join_the_eu/negotiations_croatia_turkey/index_en.htm#acquis.

categories of EU bilateral FTAs may be distinguished; agreements with countries included in the ENP and agreements with other—selected trading partners.

More specifically, as to the former, following the accession of ten Member States in 2004, the EU launched the so-called European Neighbourhood Policy with the aim at establishing closer cooperation with the Union's neighbouring countries and from a broader perspective strengthening the prosperity, stability and security in the neighbourhood.[50] A network of bilateral partnership or association agreements has been concluded by the EU in order to put in context its relations with two sub-groups of countries that are included in ENP: Southern Mediterranean countries, with which the EU has signed the so-called Euro-Mediterranean agreements,[51] and East European and Central Asian Countries,[52] with which the EU has concluded partnership and cooperation agreements. Finally, as to the latter, the EU has entered into bilateral FTAs with a number of non neighbouring trade partners, such as Chile, Mexico, South Africa, and Korea.[53]

Competition Law in Trade Agreements

While bilateral trade agreements of the EU include provisions relating to commercial, political and cultural issues, the common denominator and starting point for further cooperation are rules relating to trade liberalisation. The reduction of tariffs and the gradual creation of a free trade area is the goal of most of these agreements.[54] In this context, the role of competition law is to reduce as much as possible anticompetitive practices conducted by private firms that may have an effect on (the liberalised) trade between the contracting parties and therefore competition is a tool for achievement of market integration. To this end, the role of competition law in bilateral FTAs is similar to the role of competition law within the EU.

Having managed to successfully develop a system of competition law internally, the EU, as mentioned above, has imposed the same model to countries that have

[50] ENP was first outlined in a 2003 Commission Communication. Commission (EC), Wider Europe— Neighbourhood: A New Framework for Relations with our Eastern and Southern Neighbours, COM (2003) 104 final, which was followed by a more detailed Communication in 2004: Commission EC, Communication from the Commission, European Neighbourhood Policy; Strategy, COM (2004) 373 final.

[51] Such agreements have been signed with Algeria, Egypt, Israel, Jordan, Lebanon, Morocco, the Palestinian Authority, and Tunisia.

[52] Armenia, Azerbaijan, Georgia, Kazakhstan, Kyrgyzstan, Moldova, Russia, Ukrain and Uzbekistan.

[53] See http://ec.europa.eu/enterprise/policies/international/facilitating-trade/free-trade/index_en.htm. The EU is also in the process of negotiating agreements with India, Malaysia, Singapore, and a more comprehensive agreement with Canada.

[54] In particular, this goal is explicitly expressed in agreements with candidate and accession countries, in the Euro-Med agreements, and in the agreements signed with Chile, South Africa, and Mexico.

pursued accession to the Union. In the same context, in relation to ENP, where the relation between the EU and the neighbour countries is not as tight as it is with candidate and acceding countries, the EU has expressed the opinion that in the context of the proposed regulatory and legislative approximation, "*Convergence towards comparable approaches and definitions, legislative approximation on anti-trust as well as State aid regulations, will eventually be needed for partners to advance towards convergence with the Internal Market.*"[55] In relation to non-neighbouring trade partners, once more, competition is used to complement the aim of achieving a free trade area that is the goal of the contracting parties.

Type of Provisions Included in the Agreements

It may be observed that, depending on the particular category of the agreements (i.e. agreements with candidate countries, agreements with countries included in the ENP, which may be further distinguished between the agreements with Mediterranean countries and agreements with Eastern European and Central Asian countries, and finally agreements with other trading partners), the wording of the competition-related provisions is very similar, or even identical, and this may be attributed to the fact that by using same provisions as a standard starting point of negotiations, it is faster to conclude such negotiations.

Furthermore, the various bilateral agreements of the EU include substantive competition provisions (i.e. provisions that regulate anticompetitive practices) and in this context, the EU agreements may be differentiated by agreements where either the US or Canada is a signing party, which do not contain substantive competition law provisions, but provisions dedicated to cooperation and coordination of enforcement activities.[56] While this distinction may not be absolute, as certain bilateral FTAs signed by the EU include particular provisions on cooperation,[57] and in practise these agreements are the basis for further cooperation between the signing parties, the distinction is still useful as it highlights the fact that the main feature of the policy of the EU in this field is to export its competition model to other countries.

In more particular, all the agreements with candidate countries include provisions declaring void anticompetitive agreements and abuse of dominance, by using wording identical to that of articles 101 and 102 TFEU. Similar provisions

[55] Commission EC, Communication from the Commission, European Neighbourhood Policy; Strategy, COM (2004) 373 final, p. 16.

[56] OECD Joint Group on Trade and Competition, Competition Provisions in Regional Trade Agreements, OECD Trade Policy Working Paper COM/DAF/TD(2005)3/FINAL (2006) 31. Available at: http://search.oecd.org/officialdocuments/displaydocumentpdf/?doclanguage=en&cote=com/daf/td(2005)3/final.

[57] See in detail Papadopoulos, *The international dimension of EU competition law and policy*, 2010, pp. 127–138.

are included in the agreements with the Mediterranean countries. The difference is that while candidate countries are under the obligation to harmonise their legislation to that of the EU (with a view to entering the EU), in the case of the Mediterranean countries, some of the agreements provide that the aim of cooperation is to assist the Euro-Mediterranean countries to approximate their legislation to that of the EU, while in the agreements concluded with three of these countries,[58] the wording is slightly different, as it is provided that the parties agree to make best efforts to approximate their laws in order to facilitate the application of the agreement. Finally in relation to the Eastern European and Central Asian countries, the parties recognise that an important condition for strengthening the economic links between the EU and the co-signing party is the approximation of the co-signing party's existing and future legislation to that of the Community; and the agreements include competition in the extensive list of the relevant fields that have to be approximated countries, without reference to particular substantive provisions.[59]

Similarly, in relation to state aids, the agreements with candidate countries include provisions on state aids, similar or even identical to those of the TFEU. In the context of accession, the adoption and application of the state aid rules is scrutinised by the Commission, and this is ensured in practice with the creation of inventories of state aid where the candidate and acceding countries notify any aid granted in their territory.[60] State aid provisions are also included in most of the agreements with the Mediterranean countries,[61] nevertheless none of these countries has adopted state aid rules to date.[62] As opposed to these agreements, the agreements with former Soviet Union States do not include such provisions.

Furthermore, the agreements with candidate and Mediterranean countries and the agreements with Moldova, Russia and Ukraine, also include provisions on state monopolies of a commercial character and public undertakings, according to which the parties undertake a commitment to progressively adjust any state monopolies of a commercial character, so as to ensure that, by the end of the fifth year following the entry into force of the respective agreements, no discrimination regarding the conditions under which goods are procured and marketed exists between nationals of the Member States and of the candidate country. These agreements also include provisions on public undertakings and undertakings granted exclusive rights. As in the case with the provisions on state aids nevertheless, and given the fact that the implementation of the agreements are closely scrutinised by the EU only in

---

[58] Egypt, Israel and Jordan.

[59] See in detail, Papadopoulos, *The international dimension of EU competition law and policy*, 2010, pp. 105–115.

[60] This has been in practice a demanding task. See Papadopoulos, *The international dimension of EU competition law and policy*, 2010, p. 120.

[61] With the exemptions of Algeria and Lebanon.

[62] See Papadopoulos, *The international dimension of EU competition law and policy*, 2010, p. 123.

relation to candidate countries, these provisions gradually have a practical effect only in relation to candidate countries and not to the other EU's signing partners.[63]

The Impact of Bilateral FTAs as External Competition Law of the EU

As mentioned above, and briefly analysed in this section, the EU has used bilateral FTAs as a tool for the exportation of its competition model. In this context, and from a conceptual and strategic point of view, these agreements are an important feature of the external competition law of the EU, as they contribute to the building up of a legal environment in the co-signing countries that is similar to that of the EU.

Nevertheless, the extent to which it has achieved this goal and the extent to which these agreements have been implemented in practice vary. In particular, the closer the political and economic relations of the co-signing party with the EU, the more rigorous the implementation of the agreement. For example, the competition provisions found in the agreements with candidate countries have been most rigorously applied in the context of those countries' aim to access the EU.[64] At the opposite side of the spectrum and concerning the provisions included in the agreements with former Soviet Union states, the competition provisions are looser and include only general statements from the parties that they will have competition rules in place.

Enforcement Cooperation Agreements

One of the instruments that puts into context the external competition law of the EU, are bilateral enforcement cooperation agreements. These agreements have followed the relevant Recommendation of the OECD on enforcement cooperation on competition, which was first adopted in 1967 and most recently amended in 1995.[65] The Recommendation, based on the principle of comity, provides with a number of practices that may increase the level of cooperation and the impact of such cooperation between competition authorities on cases of mutual interest. Such practices include notification of cases, coordination of parallel investigations on the same case, exchange of information and positive comity, i.e. a mechanism according to which, the competition authority of a member country may request

[63] See Papadopoulos, *The international dimension of EU competition law and policy*, 2010, pp. 122–126.

[64] Glenn, From Nation-States to Member States: Accession Negotiations as an Instrument of Europeanization, Comparative European Politics 2 (2004) 1, p. 3.

[65] OECD, Recommendation of the Council, 27 and 28 July 1995, C(95)130 final.

the competition authorities of another member country to take action if the member considers that one or more undertakings situated in that country are or have been engaged in anticompetitive practices that are substantially and adversely affecting the member country's interests.[66]

Based on the Recommendation and following the emergence of conflicts that arose in the context of the application of US antitrust rules on an extraterritorial manner, the US entered into such agreements in the 1970s and early 1980s with Germany and Australia. The US has been the country most eager to enter such agreements, the underlying arguments for such a policy being that these agreements have been considered as an alternative to the negotiations for a multilateral agreement on competition, during which the US has been consistently sceptical. In addition, it has been further suggested that bilateral agreements increase national power in the sense that it is easier for strong industrialised states to handle their relationship with other states on a bilateral, rather on a multilateral level, an argument also relevant to the bilateral FTAs discussed in the previous section of the paper.[67]

It has been also observed that the EU, at least until recently, has not been as active as the US in the adoption of bilateral enforcement cooperation agreements, and the main reasons leading to this position is that the EU throughout the 1990s and until the collapse of the WTO talks on competition focused on the WTO and considered enforcement cooperation agreements as of secondary importance.[68] Furthermore, in view the voluntary nature of the agreements, the Commission considered for some time and until recently, such agreements of limited value, since cooperation could be carried out anyway, irrespective of the existence of such agreements.[69]

That being said, the EU Commission has been involved in some of the most important relevant enforcement cooperation agreements with important players in the international field. The first and most influential to date, has been the agreement with the US of 1991, which eventually entered into force in 1995,[70] and has been supplemented by the agreement of the same parties on positive comity of 1998. The EU Commission has signed relevant agreements with Canada and Japan, in 1999 and 2003 respectively. In more recent years, and following the collapse of the WTO talks, it seems that the Commission has shifted its interest to the building up of its

[66] OECD, Recommendation of the Council, 27 and 28 July 1995, C(95)130 final, Art I.A and I.B.

[67] See Papadopoulos, *The international dimension of EU competition law and policy*, 2010, pp. 58–62.

[68] See Papadopoulos, *The international dimension of EU competition law and policy*, 2010, chapter 6.

[69] This position has been expressed by Stephen Ryan, of the European Commission at a CEPR meeting in Paris, December 2005.

[70] Due to an action brought by France that questioned the competence of the Commission to sign such an agreement on behalf of the EU. The agreement was later approved by the European Council and in this way, the conflict was resolved. See Riley, The Jellyfish Nailed? The Announcement of the EC/US Competition Co-operation Agreement, European Competition Law Review 16 (1995) 3, p. 185.

bilateral competition enforcement relations with major countries, and in this regard the EU has signed an enforcement cooperation agreement with the Republic of Korea, while on a more informal level, the DG for Competition has signed memoranda of understanding with the relevant competition enforcers of Brazil in 2009 and the Federal Antimonopoly Service of Russia in 2010.[71] Furthermore, in 2003 the EU and China agreed to start a "Competition Policy Dialogue," which is an initiative built upon conferences workshops on competition related issues where officials from the two parties participate.[72]

Bilateral enforcement cooperation agreements and MOUs signed by the EU largely follow the OECD model, and include provisions on notification of cases, cooperation and consultations on cases that are reviewed by the Authorities of both parties to the agreement, exchange of information between the competition authorities, meetings between competition officials, as well as negative and positive comity. The MOUs with Brazil and Russia, also include provisions for technical assistance and exchange of officials of the Authorities.

While the cooperation between the EU and the US, on the basis of the relevant agreements, and with very few exemptions,[73] has been considered as effective and thus successful,[74] it has been also noted above, that the extent to which such agreements have an actual effect on the relations between the signing states, is a matter mostly decided upon the actual willingness of the parties to cooperate. This assumption is based on the fact that these agreements are considered soft law instruments, as they all include the so called "confidentiality clause" on the basis of which the parties may refuse disclosure of any information if the law of the party that possesses the information prohibits it or if this would be incompatible with the possessing party's important interests. In case such restrictions apply, the Competition Authorities may exchange the relevant information, only if there is a "waiver"

[71] See the website of the EU Commission at http://ec.europa.eu/competition/international/bilateral/index.html.

[72] See Wu, EU-China Competition Dialogue: A New Step in the Internationalisation of EU Competition Law?, European Law Journal 18 (2012) 3, p. 461 (466–467).

[73] The prominent examples here are the conflicts that arose in two merger cases in the 1990s and early 2000s, and the one between Boeing and McDonnell Douglas in 1996 and the other between GE and Honeywell in 2001, where the EU and US Authorities reached diverse outcomes. See Boeder and Dorman, The Boeing/Mc Donnell Douglas Merger: The Economics, Antitrust Law and Politics of the Aerospace Industry, Antitrust Bulletin XLV (2000) 1, p. 119; Patterson and Shapiro, Trans-Atlantic Divergence in GE/Honeywell Causes and Lessons, Antitrust Magazine (2001), p. 18. A similar conflict, not of the same scale nevertheless arose in relation to the recent Microsoft case, where the EU Commission imposed a very big fine to Microsoft for abuse of dominance, a decision that has been upheld by the Court (CFI, Case T-201/04, *Microsoft v. Commission*, [2007] ECR II-03601) and despite the fact that the company had reached a settlement on the same case with the US Authorities, more than two years before the issuance of the EU Commission's decision.

[74] See Blauberger, The Governance of Overlaping Jurisdictions: How International Cooperation Enhances the Autonomy of Competition Authorities, TransState Working Papers (2009) 102, at p. 8.

of confidentiality from the party—company involved in the practice under review by the Authorities.[75]

This inability to exchange confidential information, along with the inability of such agreements to resolve conflicts in cases where important interests of both parties are at stake, have led a number of commentators and officials to question the usefulness of these soft law agreements in the field of international competition. In this regard, countries such as the US, Canada and Australia have moved forward by signing agreements that allow for the exchange of confidential information (the so called "second generation of agreements"), and have also used Mutual Legal Assistance Treaties (MLATS) and extradition treaties, to cooperate in cases relating to practices that constitute violations of criminal law.

The EU has not managed to date to conclude second generation agreements, due to the certain limitations provided by Regulation 1/2003,[76] and in this regard, the question that emerges is whether enforcement cooperation agreements have in practice any effect in the development of the external competition law of the EU. From a broader perspective, the question that arises in more general is whether soft law may have an effect in the development of international competition law.

This distinction of soft law and hard law and their effect at the international legal and political arena, has been a topic widely debated in the relevant literature, especially in the last few years.[77] Hard law refers to legally binding obligations that are precise (or can be made precise through adjudication or the issuance of detailed regulations) and that delegate authority for interpreting and implementing the law. Each of these features of law (obligations, precision and delegation) may be present in varying degrees along a continuum, and each can vary independently of the others.[78] At the other end of the spectrum, soft law is used in cases where legal arrangements are weakened along one or more of the dimensions of hard law, i.e. obligations, precision, and delegation. To this end, it has been suggested that

---

[75] See Papadopoulos, *The international dimension of EU competition law and policy*, 2010, pp. 78–81.

[76] According to Article 12(3) of Regulation 1/2003 any exchange of information between the Commission and the Member States cannot be used by the receiving authority to impose custodial sanctions. Thus, Member States that have penalised cartels (such as the United Kingdom) may not use information received by the Commission or other Member States in order to impose custodial sanctions. In this regard, if the Commission entered into a second generation agreement that allowed for exchange of confidential information with the United States, where cartels are considered a criminal offence, it would in practice discriminate against certain other Member States that could only use such relevant information to a limited extent. See Papadopoulos, *The international dimension of EU competition law and policy*, 2010, p 84.

[77] See Schaffer and Polla, Hard vs Soft Law: Alternatives, Complements and Antagonists in International Governance, Minessota Law Review 94 (2009) 3, p. 706.

[78] Abbott, Keohane, Moravcsik, Slaughter and Snidal, The Concept of Legalisation, International Organisation, 54 (2000) 3, p. 401.

soft law stands between hard law and purely political arrangements,[79] and includes both legal provisions, which is a feature of hard law, which provisions nonetheless are not binding in practice, which is a feature of purely political arrangements.

While from a purely legal perspective hard law would be preferable as it would put into very specific context the relations between the contracting parties, the use of soft law seems unavoidable since it may overcome deadlocks in the relations of states that result from economic or political differences among them, when efforts to overcome such deadlocks through the use of hard law have been unsuccessful.[80] It has also been documented, that soft law is used where there are differences in the economic structures and economic interests of different states,[81] and competition law is a field where one may observe variations in the application of competition rules by different states. As mentioned earlier in the paper such variations in the application of national competition rules are regular, due mainly to the different political aims of the states that apply national competition rules and differences in the economic approach they follow in the context of application of the rules coupled with the fact that competition law has been adopted by states that are at different levels of development. In this regard, cooperation based on soft law instruments is more flexible than traditional international agreements with binding provisions, and to this end, such first generation of enforcement cooperation agreements have been used by various states and the EU.

Furthermore, a significant facet of such soft law agreements, is that the mechanisms for cooperation, meetings, consultation and exchange of information, create channels for diffusion of information about technical aspects of competition law. Such diffusion creates in turn common understandings among competition officials that cooperate in the context of the respective agreements, as to the proper application of competition law provisions.[82] In this context, Parisi notes that the cooperation of EU and US competition officials and the work of the US –EU

---

[79] Abbott, Keohane, Moravcsik, Slaughter and Snidal, The Concept of Legalisation, International Organisation, 54 (2000) 3, p. 401 (421–422). For a critique on this analysis, see Finnemore and S. J, Alternatives to "Legalization": Risher Views of Law and Politics, International Organization 55 (2001) 1, p. 743, where the authors hold that the distinction made by Abbott and Snidal has certain limitations, as it does not take into account other important ingredients of law, such as the features and effects of legitimacy, including the need for a certain link between law and underlying social practice.

[80] Reismann, A Hard look at Soft Law: Panel Report, American Society of International Law, 82 (1991), p. 371 (427).

[81] Reismann, A Hard look at Soft Law: Panel Report, American Society of International Law, 82 (1991), p. 371 (375).

[82] From an international relations theory perspective, the outcome of such cooperation and development of common understandings, is the creation of transgovernmental networks. See Raustiala, The Architecture of International Cooperation: Transgovernmental Networks and the Future of International Law, Virginia Journal of International Law 43 (2002) 1, p. 51, where the author notes that power still plays a role in the relations between cooperating states and officials, nonetheless, such power is defined as "power to attract, which is different from traditional hard power, defined as the power to coerce."

working group on mergers, set up in 1999 led to such development of common understandings in the field of merger review, which in turn led to convergence in the application of the relevant rules in the EU and the US.[83]

In a broader context, Wu argues, that the competition political dialogue between the EU and China, has had as an effect that China adopted competition rules that are close to the EU model of competition.[84] To this end, when such a common understanding has been achieved, it could be argued that cooperation through soft law instruments may lead to stronger forms of cooperation. In relation to the core theme of the paper, i.e. the external competition law of the EU, it may be argued that bilateral enforcement cooperation agreements, even in the form of soft law, contribute to the development of the EU's external competition law, in two ways: inbound, in the sense that on the basis of the cooperation with other states the EU may change its rules so as to become compatible with those of the state with which the EU cooperate,[85] and outbound, in the sense that through cooperation the EU may persuade other states to adopt rules similar to those of the EU.[86]

Conclusion: Evaluation of EU's External Competition Law

This paper has attempted to observe the development of the external competition law of the EU. The first section of the paper has provided with an introduction to the concept of competition law and the position that the way that competition law is being applied in various states varies due to a number of reasons linked to the particular legal, cultural, political, and economic environment of the states that apply these rules. On the other hand, the emergence of economic globalisation and subsequent practices that have an effect on multiple states, has generated the need for international norms to regulate those practices.

In a world where international relations to a great extent are based on the concept of sovereignty of nation states, there are two alternative ways to address practices that have an effect on multiple markets; the one is extraterritorial application of

---

[83] See Parisi, Cooperation Among Competition Authorities in Merger Regulation, Cornell International Law Journal 43 (2010) 1, p. 55 (63–66), where the author nevertheless also notes that the convergence achieved is not absolute, and gives as an example the fact that the Merger Regulation of the EU provides that in the context of review of mergers a number of factors have to be taken into account, including the "economic and financial power of the merging parties," a factor not taken into account by the US Authorities.

[84] See Wu, EU-China Competition Dialogue: A New Step in the Internationalisation of EU Competition Law?, European Law Journal 18 (2012) 3, p. 461.

[85] A notable example here is the development of EU merger rules, as noted in Parisi, Cooperation Among Competition Authorities in Merger Regulation, Cornell International Law Journal 43 (2010) 1, p. 55.

[86] This argument may be also linked to the work carried out in the context of international initiatives such as the ICN.

national competition laws, and the other is the adoption and application of agreements that are devoted to or include competition provisions. These two alternatives formulate the development of the external competition law of the EU, which is itself an international organisation that has applied competition law on a transnational rather on a national level.

Section 2 has discussed the development of extraterritoriality as a principle of EU competition rules and made reference to three main points: That the concept of extraterritoriality first appeared and developed in the US; that the EU Commission has for decades been trying to apply the effects doctrine and that the regional Courts have been to date more hesitant to apply the doctrine, something though that has changed in the case of mergers with the *Gencor* decision; and that irrespective from the particular principle to be applied, extraterritoriality is a standard feature of EU competition law. When important interests are at stake, recent history has showed that the EU (especially the Commission) has been eager to apply EU rules in an extraterritorial manner.

This statement nevertheless should not lead to the conclusion that in the field of international competition law extraterritoriality is the main feature of EU competition law. Instead, as mentioned above, the EU is itself a plurilateral—regional agreement that has developed competition rules, it has been active at all levels of development of international competition norms, and this has been very obvious in the context of the unsuccessful multilateral negotiations on competition at the WTO. This paper has discussed two types of such agreements; bilateral trade agreements signed by the EU with third countries and include competition provisions, and bilateral enforcement competition agreements.

As to the former, it has been noted that such agreements have been the main tool with which the EU has put the enlargement project into context, and/or has pursued strengthening and improvement of its relations with neighbouring countries, and selected trade partners. In this regard, relevant agreements have been signed with acceding and candidate countries, with countries included in the ENP and with selected trade partners. In parallel, these agreements have been the main tools for the development of the EU's external competition law. In particular, competition law has been included in these agreements with the aim of addressing practices conducted by private firms that may put at risk the trade liberalisation process that is the central aim of the agreements. The main point made in the paper, is that depending on the particular category of the agreements and in more particular, the closer the political and economic relations of the co-signing party with the EU, the more rigorous the implementation of the agreement. It has been noted for instance that the agreements with acceding and candidate countries have been rigorously applied in view of those countries' willingness to enter the EU, and their commitment to adopt and apply the full range of the EU regulations, competition law included. On the other hand, the agreements with neighbouring countries, and in particular those with former Soviet Union states are looser in terms of obligations and to a certain extent on precision of the provisions.

Finally the paper presented the bilateral enforcement cooperation agreements and arrangements adopted and developed by the EU. It has been noted in this context, that until recently, these type of agreements have not been the main preference of the EU administration, and that was partly due to the fact that the EU administration was focused on the negotiations at the multilateral level (at least until the collapse of the WTO talks on competition) and partly because the EU bureaucracy was of the opinion that the usefulness of such soft law—non binding agreements is limited, on the basis of the argument that in case the relations with another national competition authority is close, there is no need to have non binding agreements in place in order to cooperate.

That said, it has also been pointed out that the EU has signed the most important and tested agreement of this kind with the US in 1991 (and 1998), has been involved in such agreements with its most important partners (Canada and Japan), and more recently with Brazil and Russia, and has also tried to formalise its relations on competition law with China. To this end, and despite the fact that the EU has not managed to conclude the so-called second generation enforcement cooperation agreements that would allow for exchange of confidential information without the need of a consent by the involved companies, the paper takes the view that these soft law agreements have still had an effect on the development of the external competition law of the EU, as they formalise, even in a non binding way, the EU's cooperation with important trade partners, and on the other hand the network created by such agreements and the formalisation of cooperation, form a basis for diffusion of ideas, norms, and principles of the EU's competition norms to the co-signing parties.

This network has been expanded in recent years with the creation and work of the ICN and the work carried out under the auspices of the OECD and UNCTAD (the latter mostly in relation to developing countries), which have played an important role on the development of common understandings in the field of competition law. As in the case of the WTO talks on competition, the EU has been actively participated in all these initiatives. While this work is very important in delineating the policy of the EU at the international level, it has not been further discussed in this paper, which has focused on agreements signed by the EU.

From a broader perspective, and even though the discussion carried out here has been limited to the concept of extraterritoriality and bilateral agreements concluded by the EU, without detailed reference to the developments at the plurilateral and multilateral levels, this discussion just emphasises what is widely accepted in the field of international competition law, that the EU has been one of the most active players in both the strengthening of cooperation and development of competition norms in the international arena. From a different perspective, in the absence of a binding multilateral competition agreement, both these processes are dynamic ones, and as the analysis of the paper indicates, so is the external competition law of the EU.

Transnational Competition Law and Public Services

Johan van de Gronden

Introduction

International trade agreements aim at opening up national markets and remove obstacles to free trade. The majority of the trade agreements impose obligations upon states to remove these obstacles. However, over the years treaties tend to govern competition law as well.[1] As a result, these treaties also require that companies refrain from anti-competitive practices. In fact, such agreements are capable of completing the process of trade liberalisation, as the competiveness of international markets is not only dependent on the removal of obstacles coming from state laws but also on the absence of anti-competitive practices of companies. However, at the same time, the fear exits that progressive trade liberalisation could put under pressure the provision of essential services every citizen should have access to. In various systems of national law States have developed special concepts in order to reconcile the need to open-up markets with the right of every citizen to have access to particular essential services or goods (such as the supply of water, the provision of particular health care services[2] etc.). Due to the globalisation process (big enterprises are engaged in trans boundary business activities) and trade agreements concluded by States or International Organisations such as the EU it goes without saying that these concepts developed at national level fall short in addressing the tensions between trade liberalisation and the access to essential services.

[1] See the Treaties discussed in section "Regional Trade Agreements and Public Services" of this article.

[2] Cf. Hervey, If Only It Were So Simple: Public Health Servies and EU Law, in: Cremona (ed.), *Market Integration and Public Services in the European Union*, 2011, pp. 209–214.

J. van de Gronden (✉)
Faculty of Law, Radboud University Nijmegen, P.O. Box 9049 6500 KK Nijmegen, The Netherlands
e-mail: j.vandegronden@jur.ru.nl

C. Herrmann et al. (eds.), *European Yearbook of International Economic Law (EYIEL), Vol. 4 (2013)*, European Yearbook of International Economic Law 4,
DOI 10.1007/978-3-642-33917-2_6, © Springer-Verlag Berlin Heidelberg 2013

The aim of this contribution is to examine whether in international economic law a concept that is capable of addressing these tensions is emerging. In this regard, it should be noted that an important terminological matter is how to describe the services (and, in fact, also the goods) that play such an important role in the society of many states that they entail issues of collective concern. It is clear from the outset that the terms used to indicate these services differ from jurisdiction to jurisdiction. Nevertheless, it is also obvious that these services and goods are subject to all kinds of measures in order to realise objectives of public interests. In other words, these services and goods have a public dimension. Therefore, I will refer to these services and goods as "public services," which is a term that is widely used in legal doctrine.[3] Furthermore, it should be pointed out that in essence the term public services does not only encompass particular essential services but also concerns goods that citizens should have access to, such as the supply of water. However, as the majority of the access issues concern services and the supply of essential goods has undeniably a "service dimension," the term used in this article is "public *services*."

Another important terminological matter is what the term "competition law" constitutes. On first sight, this area of law suggests to encompass every rule that is capable of stimulating the competition process. However, it should be borne in mind that both measures taken by States (such as abolishing burdensome authorisation schemes) and commercial practices of companies (such as setting up a new business in order to compete with other firms already operating on a given market) could give a boost to this process. It is of great importance to draw a sharp line between rules that oblige States to remove obstacles to trade and rules that prohibit companies from engaging in anti-competitive behaviour. As the first category is directed at States and the second one deals with companies, these two sets of rules are subject to different principles. Furthermore, it should be noted that it is common ground that the term "competition law" refers to rules directed at companies,[4] i.e. entities engaged in some kind of commercial or economic activities. Therefore, this contribution will (mainly) confine itself to the competition rules directed at companies/firms/undertakings. After all, at the heart of this study is the provision of public services, which implies the presence of companies on the market, willing and able to supply these services (and goods). Moreover,

---

[3] See e.g. Cremona, Introduction, in: Cremona (ed.), *Market Integration and Public Services in the European Union*, 2011, pp. 1–10; Nistor, *Public Services and the European Union. Healthcare, Health Insurance and Education Services*, 2011, pp. 2 et seq.; Krajewski, Protecting a Shared Value of the Union in a Globalized World: Services of General Economic Interest and External Trade, in: van de Gronden (ed.), *EU and WTO Law on Services. Limits to the Realisation of General Interest Policies within the Services Markets?*, 2009, p. 188; Adlung, Public Services and the GATS, Journal of International Economic Law 2006, p. 455; Krajewski/Neergaard/van de Gronden, Introduction, in: Krajewski/Neergaard/van de Gronden (eds.), *The Changing Legal Framework for Services of General Interest for Europe. Between Competition and Solidarity*, 2009, p. 1.

[4] Art. 101 and 102 TFEU, for example, are directed at "undertakings."

it should be pointed out that public services issues do usually not raise in merger control cases. Therefore, the analysis carried out below will not include the rules on concentration. However, as various enterprises are financed by States in order to supply particular public services, State aid issues will be touched upon.

In sum, the central question is whether a concept of public services is emerging in transnational competition law. In order to solve this question, I will start with discussing a body of supranational law that has a comprehensive set of competition rules and a specific model for public services: EU competition law. The EU, which is currently based on the Treaty establishing the EU (hereafter: TEU) and the Treaty on the functioning of the EU (hereafter: TFEU),[5] has a longstanding tradition of using competition rules for the purpose of trade liberalisation, or in EU terminology, for the purpose of market integration (of their Member States). In addition, it should be noted that the EU is one of the most important trading blocks in the world and, therefore, models developed in EU law are of great interest for understanding issues of international competition law. However, the cradle of competition law is the US (where the term anti-trust law is preferred over competition law) and, therefore, this contribution will also explore how US anti-trust law deals with public services. After that, attention will be paid to the overarching agreement for international trade: the WTO. Admittedly, the WTO contains rules directed at States, rather than obligations imposed on companies.[6] Though, in delineating its scope WTO law makes use of a concept that is (partly) based on the notion of competition between companies.[7] Accordingly, it is of great importance to include this overall legal framework for international trade in the analysis. In what follows, various regional trade agreements, including agreements concluded by the EU with other countries, will be examined. At the end the findings will be brought together and some conclusions will be drawn.

The EU Rules on Competition and Public Services

The Treaty on the Functioning of the European Union (hereafter: TFEU) lays down the competition rules in Articles 101 up and to 109.[8] In the EU, the European Commission is the competition authority, which has the task to implement and enforce these Treaty provisions, in close cooperation with the national competition authorities of the Member States. It would be beyond the scope of this article to discuss all aspects of European competition law, as the EU experience with this area

[5] Before the Treaty of Lisbon, OJ [2007] C 306/1, entered into force, the EU was based on the Treaty on the European Union (EU) and the Treaty establishing the European Community (EC).

[6] On the question whether a competition law system should be introduced in the WTO framework, see Taylor, *International Competition Law. A New Dimension for the WTO?*, 2006, pp. 147 et seq.

[7] On the role of the notion of competition in WTO law, see pp. 126 et seq.

[8] Before the entering into force of the Treaty of Lisbon, Art. 81-89 EC contained these rules.

of law has resulted into a huge body of case law, decisional practices and legislation. Therefore, this section will focus on the issues, which are of particular interest for public services. It must be noted that even a discussion limited to these aspects forces one to make a selection of subjects to be covered and to be left out.

Overview of the EU Competition Rules

Article 101 (1) TFEU contains a ban on agreements between undertakings, concerted practices between undertakings and decisions of associations of undertakings that have the object or effect to restrict competition, in so far as the trade between the EU Member States is influenced. Article 101 (3) TFEU exempts these agreements, concerted practices and decisions of undertakings, if (1) they contribute to the improvement of production, distribution and innovation, (2) consumers get a fair share of this improvement, (3) they are indispensable and (4) competition is not totally eliminated. It is controversial to what extent this exemption, which is drafted to justify practices based on objectives of an economic nature, is capable of providing a safe harbour for contracts pursuing public interests.[9] As a result, it is difficult to base a public service policy on a broad reading of this provision.

Nevertheless, it should be noted that in Wouters[10] and Meca-Medina,[11] the CJEU has held that particular agreements on professional ethics[12] respectively on anti-doping rules in sports were permitted, as long as these agreements pursue legitimate objectives and do not go beyond what is necessary. It is striking that in these judgments the CJEU did not base its conclusion on Article 101 (3) TFEU but on the finding that competition within the meaning of Article 101 (1) TFEU was not restricted. However, to date, it is not clear whether the approach developed in Wouters and Meca-Medina could also be applied to other issues than those that were at stake in these two cases.

In EU competition law various block exemptions, which exempt specific categories of agreements from the cartel prohibition of Article 101 (1) TFEU, are in place. However, none of them apply to public services.

Article 102 TFEU prohibits undertakings from abusing their dominant position, in so far as intra-Union trade is affected. While as a rule Article 101 (1) TFEU only covers multilateral behaviour, Article 102 TFEU targets both unilateral (single dominance) and multilateral conduct (collective dominance). In contrast with Article 101 TFEU, "dominance-specific" exceptions are absent in EU competition law.

---

[9] On this matter, see Townley, *Article 81 EC and Public Policy*, 2009, pp. 141 et seq. See also the Commission Guidelines on the application of Article 81(3) [now Article 101(3)] of the Treaty, OJ [2004] C 101/97, para. 42.

[10] ECJ, Case C-309/99, *Wouters*, ECR [2002] I-1577.

[11] ECJ, Case C-519/04P, *Meca-Medina*, ECR [2006] I-6991.

[12] The *Wouters* case concerned professional ethics of practicing lawyers.

Of special interest for public services is Article 106 TFEU. Pursuant to the first section of this Article, Member States are not allowed to take measures with regard to public undertakings and undertakings having exclusive and special rights contrary to the competitions rules or other provisions laid down in the Treaty. It is apparent from the case law that most of the cases arising under Article 106 (1) concern Member State measures that facilitated abusive behaviour.[13] Even more important for the public services than the first section of Article 106, is the second limb of this provision. Pursuant to Article 106 (2) TFEU particular restrictive practices are permitted, if they are necessary for the provision of "Services of General Economic Interest." The Section "Public Services: The Emerging Role of Services of General Economic Interest" will discuss this concept in more detail.

Article 107 (1) TFEU provides that it is not permitted for Member States to grant state aid to undertakings, if this causes distortions of competition on the European Internal Market and influences the trade between the Member States. In various cases, the Court of Justice of the EU (hereafter: CJEU) was called upon to solve problems resulting from the application of this Treaty provision to measures taken by the Member States in order to finance the provision of public services. The approach adopted by the CJEU with regard to these problems will be discussed below. In this respect it should be noted that the Commission has the authority to clear national state aid measures that satisfy the conditions of the various exceptions laid down in sections 2 and 3 of Article 107 TFEU. It is settled case law that it is not allowed to effectuate national state aid measures that are not notified to the Commission for approval or are not cleared yet.[14] If this so-called standstill provision is not observed by the Member States, both the Commission and domestic courts have the power to order the recovery of this illegal state aid.[15]

Establishing the Scope of EU Competition Law: The Concept of Undertaking

The rules laid down in Articles 101, 102, 106 and 107 come only into play, if undertakings are involved in a particular case. Over the years, the CJEU has developed a huge body of case law on how to interpret the concept of undertaking. For public services, this concept is of great importance, as particular "entities" providing these services may be immune from EU competition law, as they do not satisfy the conditions for undertaking developed in the CJEU's case law.

---

[13] See e.g. Jones/Sufrin, *EU Competition Law. Text, Cases and Materials*, 2011, pp. 577–599.

[14] See e.g. ECJ, Case C-39/94, *La Poste*, ECR [1996] I-3547. This rule is derived from Art. 108(3) TFEU.

[15] See previous note. See also Council Regulation (EC) No. 659/1999 of 22 March 1999, OJ 1999 L 83/1, Art. 14.

It is settled case law that every entity engaged in an economic activity is an undertaking for the purposes of EU competition law.[16] An economic activity is defined as the offering of goods or services on the market.[17]

In applying this definition to public services the CJEU has developed two lines in its case law. If the provision of a particular service comes down to the exercise of State prerogatives (the performance of tasks that are typical for the public domain), the activity concerned is not of an economic nature and, as a result, EU competition law does not apply according to the first line of the CJEU's case law.[18] For example, in Eurocontrol[19] the CJEU held that air traffic control was not covered by the Treaty provisions on competition. Strikingly, this means that competition law applies if the given good or service potentially can be supplied on the market, as it may be assumed that State prerogatives only concern tasks that cannot be performed in a market-based environment.[20]

The second line of the case law on the concept of undertaking is concerned with the principle of solidarity[21] and is only relevant for national social security schemes. If the management of such a scheme is predominately based on solidarity and the bodies administering this scheme are subject to substantial State control,[22] the CJEU will find that these bodies are not engaged in economic activities.[23] In case of a mix of solidarity and competition or in absence of substantial State control, the bodies managing social security schemes are undertakings within the meaning of EU competition law and, as a consequence, they must observe the competition rules of the Treaty.[24]

[16] The leading judgment for this definition is ECJ, Case C-41/90, *Höfner*, ECR [1991] I-1979.

[17] See e.g. ECJ, Case 118/85, *Commission vs. Italy*, ECR [1987] 2599.

[18] See ECJ, Case C-343/95, *Diego Calì*, ECR [1997] I-1547.

[19] ECJ, Case C-364/92, *Eurocontrol*, ECR [1994] I-43

[20] See van de Gronden, Purchasing care: economic activity or service of general (economic) interest?, European Competition Law Review 25 (2004) 2, p. 84 (85).

[21] Cf. Schweitzer, Services of General Economic Interest: European Law's Impact o the Role of Markets and of Member States, in: Cremona (ed.), *Market Integration and Public Services in the European Union*, 2011, p. 22.

[22] See e.g. ECJ Case C-437/09, *AG2R Prévoyance vs. Beaudout Père et Fils SARL*, 3 March 2011 n.y.r.; ECJ Case C-350/07, *Kattner Stahlbau GmbH vs. Maschinenbau- und Metall-Berufsgenossenschaft*, ECR [2009] I-1513; ECJ, Joined Cases C-264/01, C-306/01, C-354/01 and C-355/01, *AOK Bundesverband, et al. vs. Ichthyol-Gesellschaft Cordes, Hermani & Co., et al.*, ECR [2004] I-2493, and ECJ, Joined Cases C-159/91 and C-160/91, *Christian Poucet vs. Assurances Générales de France and Caisse Mutuelle Régionale du Languedoc-Roussillon*, ECR [1993] I-637.

[23] See van de Gronden/Sauter, Taking the temperature: EU competition law and healthcare, Legal Issues of Economic Integration 38 (2011) 3, p. 213 (218–223).

[24] See, for example, ECJ, Case C-67/96, *Albany International BV vs. Stichting Bedrijfspensioenfonds Textielindustrie*, ECR [1999] I-5751, ECJ, Joined Cases C-115/97, C-116/97 and C-117/97, *Brentjens' Handelsonderneming BV vs. Stichting Bedrijfspensioenfonds voor de Handel in Bouwmaterialen*, ECR [1999] I-6025; ECJ, Case C-219/97, *Maatschappij Drijvende Bokken BV vs. Stichting Pensioenfonds voor de Vervoer- en Havenbedrijven*, ECR [1999] I-6121, and ECJ, Case C-244/94, *Fédération Française des Sociétés d'Assurance, et al. vs. Ministère de l'Agriculture et de la Pêche (FFSA)*, ECR [1995] I-4015.

So, organisations providing public services escape from EU competition law, if these organisations exercise State prerogatives or manage a social security scheme predominantly based on solidarity and subject to substantial State control. As the CJEU has decided that the nature of purchase activities are depended on the subsequent use of the goods or services bought,[25] such organisations are also not caught by EU competition law, if they purchase goods and services.

Nonetheless, it should be noted that a great deal of public service providers do fall within the scope of EU competition law either for the reason that the provision of their services is not typical for the public domain or for the reason that their social security scheme is not entirely based on the principle of solidarity. Apart from social security schemes, EU competition law seems to adhere to the view that as soon as a service or good can be provided through the market, the Treaty provisions on competition are applicable.

Public Services: The Emerging Role of Services of General (Economic) Interest

The finding that EU competition law applies to many public services does not mean that no due consideration is paid to the special characteristics of these services. Article 106 (2) TFEU provides that restrictive measure could be justified in the light of the concept of Services of General Economic Interest (hereafter: SGEI). It is clear that in EU competition law, the term "public services" is not used; rather, the key term Services of General Economic Interest is preferred.

Both Member States infringing Article 106 (1) TFEU and companies violating Article 101 or 102 TFEU are entitled to invoke Article 106 (2) TFEU. It is apparent from the settled case law of the CJEU that two conditions must be met: (1) the company concerned must be entrusted with a SGEI mission and (2) the restriction of competition should not go beyond what is necessary.[26] It should be noted the exception of Article 106 (2) could be invoked by both undertakings with exclusive and special rights and by undertakings without any of such rights. What only matters, is whether the enterprise concerned is entrusted with a the operation of SGEI.

The entrustment of the special task could be derived from decisions taken by public bodies and (general obligations laid down in) legislation.[27] The necessity test is not interpreted in a strict way, as this test is met as soon as the undertaking entrusted with a special task can only provide the services concerned under economically acceptable circumstances by restricting competition.[28]

---

[25] ECJ, Case C-205/03 P, *Federación Española de Empresas de Tecnología Sanitaria (FENIN) vs. Commission*, ECR [2006] I-6295.

[26] See e.g. ECJ, Case C-475/99, *Ambulanz Glöckner*, ECR [2002] I-8089.

[27] See, for example, ECJ Case C-437/09, *AG2R Prévoyance vs. Beaudout Père et Fils SARL*, 3 March 2011 n.y.r.

[28] This test was carried out for the first time in the landmark decision ECJ, Case C-320/90, *Corbeau*, ECR [1993] I-2533.

In legal doctrine it is argued that the approach of economically acceptable circumstances comes down to a flexible and Member State friendly test.[29] In balancing the merits of competition and the need to provide essential services the CJEU is prepared to tip the balance in favour of the Services of General Economic in a relatively great amount of cases. The EU approach to public services/Services of General Economic Interest is based on the autonomy of Member States to ensure the continuous and stand-by provision of these services. Also worth mentioning is that the test of economically acceptable circumstances is especially suited for tackling problems of cherry picking: one of the main problems regarding SGEI is that commercially oriented enterprises will deploy themselves to the most profitable activities, leaving the other activities to undertaking entrusted with the task to guarantee access for all to a particular essential service. It goes without saying that such practices would prevent this undertaking from performing its task under economically acceptable circumstances. In other words, market failures may give raise to take action and to invoke Article 106 (2) TFEU.[30]

Member States can solve these market failures by granting exclusive or special rights to the undertakings with a SGEI mission. However, another way of address this problem is to grant state aid to these undertakings.

Here, the Treaty provisions on state aid come in. In the landmark decision of Altmark[31] the CJEU has acknowledged that financing particular services plays a significant role in the SGEI policies of the Member States. Therefore, it decided that such aid given in order to compensate the costs of the provision of these services does not constitute a violation if the following conditions are fulfilled: (1) the undertaking concerned is charged with the execution of a SGEI mission, (2) the parameters of the amount of the compensation are established in an objective and transparent way (3) the compensation does not go beyond what is necessary, and (4) the amount of the compensation is determined on the basis of the expenses of a well-run undertaking (if the contract to perform the task concerned has not been subject to a public procurement procedure). In this regard it should be noted that in Altmark, the CJEU did no use the term SGEI, rather it referred to Public Service Obligations (hereafter: PSO). However, it is apparent from the BUPA case[32] that SGEI and PSO are identical concepts. Although the Altmark judgment was an important development, a lot of questions remained unsolved. Therefore, the Commission has adopted several measures in order to clarify how the Treaty

---

[29] See Buendia Sierra, *Exclusive Rights and State Monopolies cf. also EC Law. Article 86 (Former Article 90) of the EC Treaty*, 1999, pp. 319, 320; cf. also Schweitzer, Services of General Economic Interest: European Law's Impact on the Role of Markets and of Member States, in: Cremona (ed.), *Market Integration and Public Services in the European Union*, 2011, pp. 38–41.

[30] See Van de Gronden, The Internal Market, the State and Private Initiative. A Legal Assessment of National Mixed Public-private Arrangements in the Light of European Law, Legal Issues of Economic Integration 33 (2006) 2, p. 105 (135–136), and Sauter, Services of General Economic Interest and Universal Service in EU law, European Law Review 33 (2008) 2, p. 167 (179–180).

[31] ECJ, Case C-280/00, *Altmark*, ECR [2003] I-7747.

[32] See ECJ, Case T-289/03, *British United Provident Association*, ECR [2008] II-81, paras. 161–162.

provisions on State aid should be applied to PSO and SGEI. In December 2011 these measures are updated, as the Commission then issued the Decision on the application of Article 106 (2) of the Treaty to State aid granted in form of public service compensation granted to certain undertakings entrusted with the operation of services of general economic interest,[33] the Communication on the application of the European Union State aid rules to compensation granted for the provision of services of general economic interest[34] and the Communication on the European Union framework for State aid in the form of public service compensation.[35] In this regard also Directive 2006/111 on the transparency of financial relations between Member States and public undertakings.[36a]

The Altmark judgment and the post Altmark developments demonstrate that the importance of SGEI has grown over the years. Therefore, it is no surprise that the Commission has published several official (soft law) documents on these services.[36] The position of SGEI is further reinforced by the Treaty of Lisbon. This treaty has added Article 14 to the TFEU. According to this provision the EU and the Member States are under the obligation to ensure that SGEI fulfill their mission. Article 14 TFEU even assigns the competence to adopt regulations on SGEI to the European legislature. Furthermore, it should be pointed out that according to Article 6 of the Treaty establishing the European Union the Charter of Fundamental Rights of the European Union[37] has the same legal status as the Treaties. This is of great importance for SGEI, as Article 36 of this Charter provides that the EU recognises and respect access to Services of General Interest as provided for in national laws and practices, in accordance with EU law, in order to promote the social and territorial cohesion of the Union. The Charter does not only assign a constitutional dimension to SGEI, but it also refers to a broader concept, i.e. Services of General Interest (SGI). From Protocol 26[38] (annexed to the Treaty of Lisbon), it could be derived that SGI are an overarching concept: it encompasses both economic SGI (which are, of course, SGEI) and non-economic SGI.[39] It is not a great surprise that

---

[33] Commission Decision 2012/21/EU of 20 December 2011, OJ [2012] L 7/3.

[34] OJ [2012] C 8/4.

[35] OJ [2012] C 8/15.

[36a] OJ [2006] L 318/17.

[36] See e.g. the Commission Communication, A Quality Framework for Services of General Interest in Europe, COM(2011) 900 final, 20 December 2011. On these Commission documents, see Neergaard, The Commission's Soft Law in the Area of Services of General Economic Interest, in: Szyszczak/Davies/Andenaes/Bekkedal (eds.), *Developments in Services of General Interest*, 2011, pp. 37 et seq.

[37] OJ [2010] C 83/389.

[38] Protocol on Services of General Interest to be annexed to the Treaty on the European Union, to the Treaty on the Functioning of the European Union and, where applicable, to the Treaty establishing the European Atomic Energy Community, OJ [2007] C 306/148.

[39] On the various concept related to SGEI, see e.g. Neergaard, Services of General Interest: the Nature of the Beast, in: Krajewski/Neergaard/Van de Gronden (eds.), *The Changing Legal Framework for Services of General Interest for Europe. Between Competition and Solidarity*, 2009, pp. 19 et seq.

Protocol 26 acknowledges that it is for the EU Member States to regulate non-economic SGI. Interestingly, after having stressed the Member States' competences in providing SGEI, it lays down requirements that SGEI should comply with. These requirements are related to issues of high quality, safety and affordability, equal treatment, and the promotion of universal access and of user rights. In other words, by adopting Protocol 26 the Treaty framers have started to develop EU principles for SGEI.

The Role of the State and Public Services: The Useful Effect Doctrine

The State could endorse arrangements made by undertakings providing public services. However, these State measures should be compatible with the special rules for State and competition developed in the CJEU's case law. It is settled case law that it is not permitted for Member States to deprive the useful effect of the competition rules laid down in the Treaty. As this rule is rooted in the obligation to respect the effectiveness of EU competition law, it is known as the useful effect doctrine.[40] On the basis of Article 4 (3) TEU, which contains the principle of Union Loyalty, and Article 101 TFEU, the CJEU has held that the Member States are prohibited from requiring or encouraging the adoption of restrictive agreements, decisions or concerted practices or from reinforcing their effects.[41] Furthermore, Member States are not allowed to delegate their powers to intervene on the market to private economic operators.[42] It is apparent from cases such as Arduino[43] and Cipolla[44] that national measures that involve undertakings in the decision process but leave the final responsibility to decide on what intervention should be made to the State, do not constitute a violation of the useful effect doctrine. It is very important, in other words, that the final responsibility to take the necessary decisions remains in the hands of the State. Therefore, in its case law the CJEU assigns great significance to the institutional structure: in case of preventive State supervision, the CJEU is likely to find no infringement of EU competition law, whereas the risk of such an infringement is substantial, if State supervision is limited to ex-post actions.[45]

[40] See e.g. Vedder, *Competition Law and Environmental Protection in Europe: Towards Sustainability?*, 2003, pp. 5, 237–246.

[41] See e.g. ECJ, Case 267/86, *Pascal Van Eycke vs. ASPA*, ECR [1988] 4769.

[42] ECJ, Case 267/86, *Pascal Van Eycke vs. ASPA*, ECR [1988] 4769.

[43] ECJ, Case C-35/99, *Criminal proceedings against Manuele Arduino*, ECR [2002] I-1529.

[44] ECJ, Case C-202/04, *Federico Cipolla against Rosaria Portolese and Stefano Macrino and Claudia Capoparte against Roberto Meloni*, ECR [2006] I-11421.

[45] See Verschuur, *Overheidsmaatregelen en het toezicht van nationale mededingingsautoriteiten. De consequenties van het arrest CIF voor nationale mededingingsautoriteiten en overheden*, 2010, pp. 106–114.

In sum, public bodies cannot simply declare generally binding, for example, price fixing agreements, as this would lead to a violation of the useful effect doctrine. The European Commission could decide to take action against such practices. It should even be noted that in the landmark decision of CIF,[46] the CJEU has held that this doctrine should not only be applied by domestic courts, but also by national competition authorities. As a result, national measures reinforcing, for example, the effects of price fixing agreements may prompt actions from the part of a national competition authority.

An important issue is to what extent undertakings obliged by a national measure to conclude a cartel could be liable for violation of competition law. In Ladbroke[47] the CJEU has decided that undertakings only escape liability, if they had no freedom to engage in competitive behaviour; if some kind of margin of freedom was left, however, they are supposed to have infringed competition law. Accordingly, undertakings providing public services are not liable under EU competition law, if they were forced to be engaged in anti-competitive practices and had no discretion whatsoever to prevent these practices.[48]

US Anti-trust Rules and Public Services

Although the rules on competition laid down in US statutes are not part of trade agreements, it is of utmost importance to analyse them. As already stated, the US is the cradle of competition law. Therefore, it may be assumed that virtually all competition law systems are rooted in these rules somehow. A proper understanding of the dynamics of international competition law, including issues related to public services, requires an analysis of US anti-trust law.

Below a general and brief overview of the main rules will be given. Subsequently, attention will be paid to the US anti-trust Immunity for State Action. It should be noted that, unlike EU competition law, US anti-trust law does not contain any public service-specific exemptions. However, in US anti-trust law several exceptions of general nature are available.[49] For the purpose of the issue of public services the State Action Doctrine is relevant. This doctrine, which was recognised by the Supreme Court in Parker v. Brown[50] for the first time, entails that the US anti-trust laws do not apply, if a State of the US takes a measures leading to

---

[46] ECJ, Case C-198/01, *Consorzio Industrie Fiammiferi (CIF) vs. Autorità Garante della Concorrenza e del Mercato*, ECR [2003] I-8055.

[47] ECJ, Joined Cases C-359/95 P and C-379/95 P, *Commission and France vs. Ladbroke Racing Ltd.*, ECR [1997] I-6265. See also GC, Case T-387/94, *Asia Motor France and others vs. Commission*, ECR [1996] II-961.

[48] See Elhauge/Geradin, *Global Competition Law and Economics*, 2011, p. 67.

[49] See e.g. Elhauge/Geradin, *Global Competition Law and Economics*, 2011, pp. 38–47.

[50] *Parker vs. Brown*, 317 U.S. 341, 63 S.Ct. 307 (1943).

displacing competition by creating a particular regulatory regime.[51] As such state measures could concern public services, the State Action Doctrine will be discussed below.

Overview of US Antitrust Law

Above, it was outlined that undertakings are the addressees of EU competition law and that the CJEU has developed a functional approach to the concept of undertaking; according to this definition, the nature of the activities concerned could lead to the application of the competition rules to particular State bodies. Such an approach is absent in US anti-trust law. US government agencies enjoy sovereign immunity from anti-trust liability (irrespective of the nature of the activities they carry out), unless there is a statutory waiver.[52] Furthermore, it is dependent on the State Action Doctrine to what extent public bodies of the States of the US are caught by anti-trust law (which doctrine will be discussed below). It is clear that in US law private firms are the addressees of the anti-trust rules. Accordingly, many State bodies providing public services are immune from these rules for the sole reason that they are part of the federal government or of a State of the US.

First Section of the Sherman Act

In so far as public services are provided by private operators, US anti-trust law should be observed. The most important piece of legislation of this area of law is the Sherman Act. The First section of the Sherman Act reads as follows:

> Every contract, combination in the form of trust or otherwise, or conspiracy, in restraint of trade or commerce among the several States, or with foreign nations, is declared to be illegal. Every person who shall make any contract or engage in any combination or conspiracy hereby declared to be illegal shall be deemed guilty of a felony, and, on conviction thereof, shall be punished by fine not exceeding $10,000,000 if a corporation, or, if any other person, $350,000, or by imprisonment not exceeding three years, or by both said punishments, in the discretion of the court.

It is beyond the scope of this article to discuss every aspect of this provision. Nevertheless, it is clear that in essence the first section of the Sherman Act comes down to a ban on cartels, although this section cannot be interpreted in exactly the

[51] See Hovenkamp, *Antitrust*, (4th ed.) 2005, p. 332.

[52] Elhauge/Geradin, *Global Competition Law and Economics*, 2011, p. 40. They point out that even if a general waiver is in place, "persons" are not deemed eligible to be defendants under anti-trust law, unless the agency statute provides otherwise.

same way as Article 101 TFEU.[53] An important difference with the EU-style ban on cartels is that in US anti-trust law a sharp difference must be made between the per se rule and the Rule of Reason. A few practices are considered to cause so much harm to the competition process (such as price cartels) that they will be condemned by the US courts without any deep investigation into the effects of these practices.[54] It is common ground in US anti-trust law that most restraints must be analysed under the Rule of Reason: after the market has been defined the pro and anti competitive effects must be assessed.[55] If the pro competitive effects outweigh the restrictive effects, the practice under review is legal. In contrast, if more restrictive effects are found, section 1 of the Sherman act is violated. In this regard, it should be borne in mind that the Rule of Reason of US anti-trust law differs considerably from the Rule of Reason approach developed in EU free movement law. Whereas US antitrust law is concerned with efficiencies and pursues economic objectives and consumer welfare, EU free movement law aims at striking a good balance between market integration (an economic value) and general interest issues (non-economic values).[56]

As a result, it is difficult to accommodate considerations merely based on the general interest in the application of section 1 of the Sherman Act. Consequently, if contracts or other practices concern public services and also contain competition constraints, it must be examined whether they lead to economic efficiencies.[57] If not, these practices will be condemned.

In this regard attention should be paid to the way US anti-trust laws are enforced in health care. There is a longstanding tradition of applying these rules to all kinds of practices carried out in the health care industry and, therefore, this tradition is a nice case in point when it comes to public services and US anti-trust law. After all, in many countries, a considerable amount of services that are supplied in the health care industry is regarded to be of a public nature.

The competent US antitrust authorities have codified their decisional practice in the State of Health Care Antitrust Enforcement Policy.[58] Section B of these

---

[53] For example, under current US anti-trust law, predatory pricing (too low prices) is condemned under both section 1 of the Sherman Act and section 2 of the Sherman act (which deals with matters of market power). See Sullivan/Hovenkamp/Shelanski, *Antitrust Law, Policy and Procedure: Cases, Materials, Problems*, (6th ed.) 2009, pp. 669–670. However, in EU competition law, predatory pricing is only assessed under Art. 102 TFEU. AKZO, which is the leading case in this respect, is solely based on Art. 102 TFEU. See ECJ, Case C-62/86, *AKZO Chemie BV vs. Commission*, ECR [1991] I-3359. Cf. also Jones/Sufrin, *EU Competition Law. Text, Cases and Materials*, (4th ed.) 2011, pp. 395–399.

[54] See Hovenkamp, *Antitrust*, (4th ed.) 2005, p. 116.

[55] Hovenkamp, Antitrust, (4th ed.) 2005, p. 116.

[56] See Van de Gronden, The Treaty provisions on Competition and Health Care, in: van de Gronden/Szyszczak/Neergaard/Krajewski, *Health Care and EU Law*, 2011, p. 277.

[57] See Elhauge/Geradin, *Global Competition Law and Economics*, 2011, pp. 180–208.

[58] See the State of Health Care Antitrust Enforcement Policy, issued by the U.S. Department of Justice and the Federal Trade Commission, August 1996, available at: http://www.ftc.gov/bc/healthcare/industryguide/policy/hlth3s.pdf.

guidelines outlines how arrangements made by physicians will be assessed. It is stressed, for example, that joint ventures set up by physicians, where the participants share substantial risks, should be reviewed under the anti-trust laws if (some degree of) market power is involved.[59] The key question is whether the joint venture at issue is not anti-competitive on balance. The following quote taken from the State of Health Care Antitrust Enforcement Policy explains in clear wording what approach the US authorities have adopted with regard to their assessment of the practices in the health care industry[60]:

> The Agencies emphasize that it is not their intent to treat such networks either more strictly or more leniently than joint ventures in other industries, or to favour any particular pro-competitive organization or structure of health care delivery over other forms that consumers may desire. Rather, their goal is to ensure a competitive marketplace in which consumers will have the benefit of high quality, cost-effective health care and a wide range of choices, including new provider-controlled networks that expand consumer choice and increase competition.

It is clear that what counts the most are the economic benefits resulting from the arrangements made. It could be argued that restrictive contracts and other practices concerning public services may be justifiable under section 1 of the Sherman Act. However, the justification of these practices must be based (mainly) on economic benefits. A trade-off between public interest goals that are not rooted in economic benefits and anticompetitive effects does not seem possible.

The Second Section of the Sherman Act

Like EU competition law, US anti-trust law addresses issues of market power. In this respect section 2 of the Sherman Act is of great importance

The text of this section is as follows:

> Every person who shall monopolize, or attempt to monopolize, or combine or conspire with any other person or persons, to monopolize any part of the trade or commerce among the several States, or with foreign nations, shall be deemed guilty of a felony, and, on conviction thereof, shall be punished by fine not exceeding $10,000,000 if a corporation, or, if any other person, $350,000, or by imprisonment not exceeding three years, or by both said punishments, in the discretion of the court.

Although section 2 deals with firms having market power, it is drafted differently from Article 102 TFEU. Whereas the point of departure for the EU provision on market power is the concept of dominance, the equivalent US rule is based on "monopolization" and the "attempt to monopolize." As US anti-trust law stands now, a two-prong test must be carried out: (1) a firm must have a large amount of market power and (2) it must have engaged in particular monopolistic or

[59] See the State of Health Care Antitrust Enforcement Policy, p. 70.

[60] See State of Health Care Antitrust Enforcement Policy, p. 71.

anticompetitive acts.[61] In order to measure the market power of a particular form, in the US the competent authorities usually define the relevant market.[62] Most US courts are reluctant in finding monopolisation in cases, where the relevant market shares are not in excess of 70%.[63] However, the prohibition on the attempt to monopolise may kick in at lower market shares.[64]

All kinds of conducts could be found illegal under section 2 of the Sherman Act, such as predatory pricing and tying. As in section 1 of the Sherman Act, in monopolisation cases the rule of reason plays a major role. The pro-competitive (and efficient) effects must be distinguished from anti-competitive/exclusionary effects (which are inefficient).[65] Consequently, it may be assumed that anti-competitive conduct related to public services will be allowed, only in so far as it contributes to efficiency improvements.

The Antitrust Immunity for "State Action"

As already mentioned, for the purpose of public services the State Action Doctrine is of great importance. The provision of public services could be framed in such a way by a State of the US that based on this doctrine the restrictive practices caused by the operators are immune from the US antitrust rules. For instance, in the past several States of the US have enacted laws authorising physicians to engage in collective bargaining with health insurers.[66] Another example is the issuing by a municipality of exclusive franchise contracts with waste companies, cable television companies or taxicab companies.[67] Under normal circumstances, collective bargaining by physicians is likely to give raise to antitrust liability. In contrast, in case of legal protection by a State of the US the question arises whether the professionals are shielded from anti-trust claims.

To start with, it should be noted that in essence the State Action Doctrine is a principle of federalism: it is about resolving tensions arising from US federal laws

[61] See e.g. Sullivan/Hovenkamp/Shelanski, *Antitrust Law, Policy and Procedure: Cases, Materials, Problems*, (6th ed.) 2009, p. 591.

[62] See e.g. Sullivan/Hovenkamp/Shelanski, *Antitrust Law, Policy and Procedure: Cases, Materials, Problems*, (6th ed.) 2009, p. 592.

[63] See Hovenkamp, *Antitrust*, (4th ed.) 2005, p. 137.

[64] See the report of the US Department of Justice (Antitrust Division), Competition and Monopoly: Single-Firm Conduct Under Section 2 of the Sherman Act, 2008, p. 7, available at: http://www.justice.gov/atr/public/reports/236681.pdf.

[65] See Hovenkamp, *Antitrust*, (4th ed.) 2005, p. 138. Cf. also *Standard Oil Co. of N.J. vs. U.S.*, 221 U.S. 1, 31 S.Ct. 502 (1911).

[66] Blair/Coffin, Physician Collective Bargaining: State Legislation and the State Action Doctrine, Cardozo Law Review 26 (2004–2005), p. 1732.

[67] Areeda/Hovenkamp, *Antitrust Law, An Analysis of Antitrust Principles and Their Application, Volume IA*, (3rd ed.) 2006, p. 43.

on anti-trust and State business regulation.[68] Consequently, its aim is to delineate the competences at federal and state level. Although the State Action Doctrine is relevant for public services, its rationale is to settle disputes resulting from conflicting competences.

As was pointed out above, the starting point of the State Action Doctrine was the Parker v. Brown case. Originally, the State Action Doctrine applied only to conduct mandated by the State.[69] However, in the Midcal case,[70] the US Supreme Court has refined the approach developed in Parker v. Brown by formulating a two-prong test: (1) the restraint under review must be a practice that is clearly articulated and affirmatively expressed as State policy and (2) the policy concerned must be actively supervised by the state itself.[71] The first condition comes down to the requirement that a State has authorised the activity in double sense, i.e. that the state permits the activity and intends to displace the federal anti-trust scrutiny.[72] The anti-competitive effect of the State regulation concerned must be foreseeable[73] and this regulation must be read to embody the view that it is in the public interest to displace market forces.[74] The second condition requires that the private conduct concerned must be adequately supervised by a State organ having the power of both disapproving and evaluating/regulating the conduct concerned.[75] Rubber stamping the private parties' decisions by a State organ is not enough for the State Action doctrine to be applicable.[76] It should be prevented that private parties act in their own interest and not in public interest of the State; to put it differently, State policies should not be captured by the industry being regulated.[77] To illustrate

[68] Inman/Rubinfeld, Making Sense of the Antitrust State-Action Doctrine: Balancing Political Participation and Economic Efficiency in Regulatory Federalism, Texas Law Review 75 (1996–1997) 6, p. 1205.

[69] See Hovenkamp, *Antitrust*, (4th ed.) 2005, p. 332.

[70] *California Retail Liquor Dealers Ass'n vs. Midcal Aluminum Co.*, 445 U.S. 97, 100 S.Ct. 937 (1980).

[71] Hovenkamp, *Antitrust*, (4th ed.) 2005, p. 333.

[72] See Areeda/Hovenkamp, *Antitrust Law, An Analysis of Antitrust Principles and Their Application, Volume IA*, (3rd ed.) 2006, p. 73.

[73] On the Foreseeability Standard, see Trujillo, State Action Antitrust Exemption Collides With Deregulation: Rehabilitating the Foreseeability Doctrine, Fordham Journal of Corporate & Financial Law 11 (2005–2006) 2, p. 349 (367–372).

[74] See Semeraro, Demystifying Antitrust State Action Doctrine, Harvard Journal of Law and Public Policy 24 (2000) 1, p. 203 (211–212).

[75] See Areeda/Hovenkamp, *Antitrust Law, An Analysis of Antitrust Principles and Their Application, Volume IA*, (3rd ed.) 2006, p. 73.

[76] See Areeda/Hovenkamp, *Antitrust Law, An Analysis of Antitrust Principles and Their Application, Volume IA*, (3rd ed.) 2006, p. 65, and Shenefield, The Parker v. Brown State Action Doctrine and the New Federalism of Antitrust, Antitrust Law Journal 51 (1982), p. 344.

[77] Inman/Rubinfeld, Making Sense of the Antitrust State-Action Doctrine: Balancing Political Participation and Economic Efficiency in Regulatory Federalism, Texas Law Review 75 (1996–1997) 6, p. 1262. Cf. also *Federal Trade Commission vs. Ticor Title Ins. Co.*, 504 U.S. 621 (1992).

this finding, attention has to be paid to the above-mentioned example of the laws enacted by several States in order to authorise collective bargaining by physicians. These laws are only compatible with US antitrust law, if the supervision carried out by the competent authorities is adequate.[78]

To my mind, the institutional framework is of great importance for successfully invoking the State Action Doctrine. What matters the most, is not the objective pursued by a particular State measure but its institutional framework.[79] The underlying principle is the protection of State legislative sovereignty in a federal system.[80] Nevertheless, there is a "substantive dimension" to the second prong of the State Action test: the question of the degree of State involvement must be resolved by the US courts by taking into account the nature of the policy concerned and by examining the appreciation of a particular State that the public interest is furthered by the anti-competitive restraints concerned.[81]

Another important question is whether municipalities could invoke the State Action Doctrine. The point is that under the US constitution individual States are sovereigns and, therefore, not liable under the anti-trust laws. This is not true for municipalities and their actions may, as a result, give raise to anti-trust liability.[82] However, municipalities can derive immunity from the authority of an individual State. If a US State authorises a municipality to regulate a particular market, the State Action Doctrine applies (provided that the condition of active supervision is also met).[83]

The State Action Doctrine is hard to interpret and to apply,[84] and it is beyond the scope of the present article to provide a comprehensive discussion of every aspect of this doctrine. However, it is clear that this doctrine is not predominately driven by considerations of public interest, but by the aim to safeguard State powers against federal laws. The organisation and delivery of public services, such as sewage disposal or the supply of medical services, could benefit from the exemption developed in Parker v. Brown and Midcal. Nonetheless, the main argument for

[78] See Blair/Coffin, Physician Collective Bargaining: State Legislation and the State Action Doctrine, Cardozo Law Review 26 (2004–2005), p. 1732 (1747–1749).

[79] Cf . Stine/Gorman, Putting the Lid on State-Sanctioned Cartels: Why the State Action Doctrine in its Current Form Should Become a Remnant of the Past, University of Miami Law Review 66 (2011) 1, pp. 128–131.

[80] Inman/Rubinfeld, Making Sense of the Antitrust State-Action Doctrine: Balancing Political Participation and Economic Efficiency in Regulatory Federalism, Texas Law Review 75 (1996–1997) 6, p. 1252.

[81] See Semeraro, Demystifying Antitrust State Action Doctrine, Harvard Journal of Law and Public Policy 24 (2000) 1, p. 203 (212).

[82] See *Lafayette vs. Louisiana Power & Light Co.*, 435 U.S. 389, 98 S. Ct. 1123 (1978).

[83] See e.g. Hovenkamp, *Antitrust*, (4th ed.) 2005, p. 335–337, and Inman/Rubinfeld, Making Sense of the Antitrust State-Action Doctrine: Balancing Political Participation and Economic Efficiency in Regulatory Federalism, Texas Law Review 75 (1996–1997) 6, p. 1259.

[84] See Areeda/Hovenkamp, *Antitrust Law, An Analysis of Antitrust Principles and Their Application, Volume IA*, (3rd ed.) 2006, pp. 71 et seq.

invoking the State Action Doctrine for public services does not lie in the need to provide these services in the general interest; rather it is the institutional design of the applicable legal framework that could make the provision and delivery of the public services immune from US antitrust law. This approach largely differs from the stance to public services taken in EU competition law, as the application of Article 106 (2) TFEU requires scrutiny of the necessity of the restrictions of competition in order to ensure that Services of General Economic Interest are provided. Nevertheless, also resemblances between the US and EU approach should be identified. As is the case with the US State Action Doctrine, the EU Useful Effect Doctrine is not violated, if the institutional structure of the State measures under review allow for sufficient State supervision.[85]

WTO Law and Public Services: Services Supplied in the Exercise of Governmental Authority

The WTO does not lay down any provisions on competition, in the sense of rules directed at companies that prohibit them from being engaged in anticompetitive behaviour.[86] However, the General Agreement on Trade in Services (GATS) does contain an Article that is closely related to the issue of public services and refers indirectly to competition matters. Article I:3 (b) GATS states that the Agreement does not apply to "services supplied in the exercise of governmental authority." Pursuant to Article I:3 (c) GATS a service supplied in the exercise of governmental authority constitutes any service that is supplied neither on a commercial basis, nor in competition with one or more service providers. To my mind, it is clear that these two articles of the GATS are of great relevance for public services, as many of these services are provided in a non-commercial or non-competitive environment. Furthermore, the notion of competition plays an important role, and therefore the concept of service supplied in the exercise of governmental authority within the meaning of the GATS should be analysed in this contribution.

The Definition of Services Supplied in the Exercise of Governmental Authority

Article I:3 (b) and Article I:3 (c) GATS determine the applicability of the GATS rules. In other words, a service that satisfies the conditions of Article I:3 (c) GATS is not covered by the provisions contained in the GATS.

[85] See the section on the Useful Effect Doctrine in EU competition law.

[86] Furthermore, it should be pointed out, as Taylor noted, that international trade and competition rules considerably overlap, as they both aim at increasing efficiency and global welfare. See Taylor, *International Competition law. A new Dimension for the WTO?*, 2006, pp. 167–184.

The key question is what is meant by the words "commercial basis or in competition." So far, no WTO dispute settlement case law is available on the definition of these words. In legal doctrine, it is argued that the words "commercial basis" point to services provided by companies in order to seek profit.[87] Krajweski[88] points out that the word commercial should be interpreted in the light of the definition of the concept of "commercial presence" used in Article XXVIII (d) GATS. This Article defines "commercial presence" as "any type of business or professional establishment." As businesses are usually prepared to pursue activities if they are profitable, it may be assumed that the aim to make a profit is key to the words "commercial basis." Therefore, these services provided by profit-seeking companies do fall within the ambit of the GATS. If a WTO member allows profit-seeking entities to be engaged in the organisation and delivery of particular public services, the conclusion should be that these services are governed by the GATS. Only in so far as these services are supplied by providers that are not for profit, the GATS may not apply.

However, it is apparent from Article I:3 (c) GATS that services that are applied in competition do also not escape from the GATS. It is not clear from the drafting of Article I:3 (c) GATS, which degree of competition is required. Does potential competition, that is, the possiblity that the provision of a particular service can be made subject to market forces/competition, suffice? Or does the GATS require some form of actual competition (on a given market where several providers supply comparable services, or in the terminology of the WTO, the like-products)? Adlung[89] and VanDuzer[90] argue that Article I:3 (c) GATS could be based on a "one-way" conception of competition: does the supplier concerned strive for customers? If not, the service at hand is not supplied in competition, irrespective of the fact whether other operators providing "the like-services" on the market seek to poach customers. This finding is derived from the Panel report in "Mexico-Measures Affecting Telecommunications Services," where competition is described as "rivalry in the market, striving for custom between those who have the same commodities to dispose."[91] In this view actual competition is required,

---

[87] See Krajewski, Protecting a Shared Value of the Union in a Globalized World: Services of General Economic Interest and External Trade, in: van de Gronden (ed.), *EU and WTO law on Services. Limits to the Realisation of General Interest Policies within the Services Markets?*, 2009, p. 200.

[88] See Krajewski, Protecting a Shared Value of the Union in a Globalized World: Services of General Economic Interest and External Trade, in: van de Gronden (ed.), *EU and WTO law on Services. Limits to the Realisation of General Interest Policies within the Services Markets?*, 2009, p. 199 and 200.

[89] Adlung, Public Services and the GATS, Journal of International Economic Law 9 (2006) 2, p. 465.

[90] See VanDuzer, Health, Education and Social Services in Canada: The Impact of the GATS, in: Curtis/Ciuriak (eds.), *Trade Policy Research 2004*, 2004, p. 396.

[91] See Report of the Panel, *Mexico – Measures Affecting Telecommunications Services (Mexico-Telmex)*, WT/DS204/R, para. 7.230. The definition is taken from the Oxford English Dictionary.

and even a particular mode of actual competition, that is, rivalry coming from the supplier that provide the services under review. This means that a particular university that does not seek to poach students does not supply services in competition, even not if other educational institutions providing the "like-services" on the same market do attempt to attract students from other providers.

It is not clear whether this approach to the definition of "competition" will be adhered to in future decisions of the WTO dispute settlement body and the WTO Appellate Body. Another possible approach to the word "competition" of Article I:3 (c) GATS is that as soon as a certain degree of elasticity of substitution exists between two or more services, these services are supplied in competition.[92] As a result, the services provided by, for example, a waste removal company that does not seek to poach customers are, nevertheless, supplied in competition, if according to the relevant laws of a particular WTO member other companies are also allowed to operate on the market.

A question that remains to be answered is whether all possibilities of substitution should be considered. For instance, does substitution that could take place between private and public schools, or even substitution of the services offered by universities in different countries suffice for assuming that the WTO rules apply? Given the difficulties surrounding the definition of the concept of service, it should be awaited whether the WTO dispute settlement bodies would be prepared to give this far-reaching interpretation to the term "competition."

Evaluation

Although many issues need still to be settled yet, it is apparent from the analysis above that the approach developed at WTO level is based on a "black and white" view. As soon as a particular service has a market dimension, the provisions of the GATS apply. As a result, only public services that are (sufficiently) sheltered from market forces escape the applicability of this Treaty. However, in this regard, it should be noted that it eventually depends on the commitments made by a WTO member to what extent the organisation and delivery of public services covered by the GATS are affected by the disciplines/prohibitions laid down in this Agreement. Nevertheless, some important conclusions can be drawn with regard to the WTO approach to public services. In this approach, a sharp distinction must be made between public services that are subject to market forces and public services, which are not subject to these services. The first category should be made subject to the GATS provisions, which are apparently regarded as the rules for the market.

[92] See Krajewski, Protecting a Shared Value of the Union in a Globalized World: Services of General Economic Interest and External Trade, in: Van de Gronden (ed.), *EU and WTO law on Services. Limits to the Realisation of General Interest Policies within the Services Markets?*, 2009, p. 201. He argues that such an elasticity should be determined on a case-by-case basis.

However, the last category remains unregulated by the GATS. Furthermore, in WTO law the distinction between the two categories of public services is based on a substantive criterion. Only public services with a commercial or competitive nature are caught by the GATS. Therefore, the level of State supervision over the provision of public services does not provide an argument for the interpretation of the term "services supplied in the exercise of governmental authority." This is remarkable, as the words "governmental authority" suggests on first sight that some kind of State control seems to be of interest. However, a WTO member is able to influence the applicability of the GATS rules on public services, not by introducing substantial State control but by not allowing any elements of profitability or competition in the organisation of the delivery of public services.

Services that are considered to be of public interest by a particular WTO member, but are provided on a commercial basis or in competition do fall within the scope of the GATS. As a result, the WTO member concerned must observe the GATS disciplines (obligations contained in the GATS, such as the provisions on market access[93]). Nevertheless, in this regard it should be noted that apart from the provision on Most Favoured Nation,[94] which applies to all services, the GATS disciplines only apply in so far as a particular WTO member has made particular services subject to these disciplines. Specific commitments should be inscribed in the schedule of the country concerned. Consequently, it is in the hands of the WTO members to which extent the GATS trade rules have an impact on public services that have a commercial or competitive nature. This is also true for Article VIII GATS, which contains a discipline for monopolies and exclusive service suppliers. WTO members may be tempted to make limited commitments in order to ensure that public facilities, such as universities and hospitals, are not inscribed in the schedule of their country.[95] For, example it is apparent form the WTO Services Database Output[96] that the EU has made limitations on the Market Access discipline for "higher educational services" and for "public utilities that are subject to public services and to exclusive rights granted to private operators."[97] This bits and pieces approach makes clear that at WTO level no coherent approach to "public services of an economic nature" has

[93] See Art. XVI GATS.

[94] See Art. II GATS.

[95] See Adlung, Public Services and the GATS, Journal of International Economic Law 9 (2006) 2, p. 468.

[96] This database is available at: http://tsdb.wto.org/default.aspx.

[97] Strikingly, this limitation refers only to exclusive rights and to special rights. As already was pointed out in the section on the EU rules on competition and public services, the TFEU contains not only provisions for firms with exclusive rights but also for firms with special rights. This raises the question whether the limitations are not applicable special rights. If this is true, certain special rights in the EU might be found incompatible with the GATS, irrespective of whether the special rights concerned are justifiable under Art. 106(2) TFEU.

been developed. All in all, in legal doctrine it is argued that the efficiency of the existing disciplines is limited due to their conditional character.[98]

Regional Trade Agreements and Public Services

In the WTO treaties, competition provisions are absent. However, increasingly such provisions are included in Regional Trade Agreements (hereafter: RTAs). Consequently, it is necessary to examine to which extent these RTAs take into account the role of public services in competition law. Below various representative Regional Trade Agreements will be explored. As the EU has made a big effort in incorporating competition rules in the RTAs it has concluded, these trade agreements will be discussed in a separate section.

The Role of Public Services in the Competition Rules Contained in Various Regional Trade Agreements

At the heart of this section are RTAs, the EU is no party to. As it would be beyond the scope of this contribution to discuss all agreements, a selection is made. Four RTAs will be analysed: one from Africa, two from North and South America and one from Asia.

Of particular interest is the West African Economic and Monetary Union (hereafter: WAEMU), as this RTA has introduced a comprehensive set of competition rules that is also applied in practice.[99] The "Traite de l'Union Economic et Monetaire Ouest Africaine" (Treaty establishing the Economic and Monetary Union of West-Africa, hereafter TUEMOA) contains three provisions on competition. Article 88 prohibits the conclusion of anti-competitive agreements, abusive behaviour of dominant firms and public state aid that restricts competition. So, in comparison with the EU rules on competition the TUEMOA lays down the basic competition provisions in one Article. In this regard, it should be noted that the TUEMOA establishes a special body vested with the task to monitor the compliance with the obligations laid down in this Treaty. An important part of this task is concerned with the enforcement of the competition rules. Article 26 TUEMOA refers to this body as the Commission.

Of further importance is Article 89 TUEMOA, which gives the Council of Ministers the power to adopt laws on competition. Several regulations and

---

[98] See e.g. Poretti, *The Regulation of Subsidies within the General Agreement on Trade in Services of the WTO. Problems and Prospects*, 2009, p. 175.

[99] See Papadopoulos, *The International Dimension of EU Competition Law and Policy*, 2010, p. 184.

directives dealing with competition law issues are based on this provision. Regulation 02/2002[100] is very interesting, since it contains specific provisions about public services and competition. Article 6.1 of this regulation stipulates that it is not permitted for the States that are member of the WAEMU to take measures with regard to public enterprises or firms having exclusive or special rights that run contrary with the TUEMOA provisions on competition (laid down in Article 89 of this Treaty). More in general, Article 6.1 of Regulation 02/2002 obliges the WAEMU States to refrain from every measure incompatible with the rules contained in this regulation. It is clear from the outset that Article 6.1 is modelled after EU competition law. The section of Article 6.1 governing public enterprises and firms having exclusive and special rights is similar to Article 106 (1) TFEU (discussed above). The limb of Article 6.1 imposing the general duty upon WAEMU States to respect the proper functioning of the competition rules has great resemblance with the useful effect doctrine (developed in the case law of the CJEU on the basis of the principle of Union loyalty and discussed above). It is not a surprise that the TUEMOA has derived its approach to public services from the EU experience, as the European Treaties constitute the general model for the WAEMA.[101] As was already stated above, a significant provision of European competition law is Article 106 (2) TFEU, which sets out to what extent the competition rules apply to public services (that are of an economic nature). A similar provision is laid down in Article 6.2 of Regulation 02/2002 of the WAEMA. This provision starts with acknowledging that the enterprises entrusted with the operation of a mission to provide Services of General Economic Interest (hereafter: SGEI) are governed by the competition rules. So, like in EU law, public services are referred to as SGEI in WAEMA law. Nevertheless, enterprises with a SGEI mission could claim that compliance with these rules would obstruct the performance of the special task assigned to them. If this claim is correct, they are allowed to restrict competition, in so far as this is necessary with a view to their special task. In this respect, a very important difference with the EU approach should be noted. The enterprise or the WAEMA State involved should apply for prior authorisation from the WAEMA Commission. Consequently, under the WAEMA competition rules the exemption for SGEI has no direct effect; rather it is in the hands of a supranational body to what extent national measures taken with regard to a specific SGEI mission escape from the competition rules. Another striking difference is that Article 6.2 of Regulation 02/2002 explicitly provides that SGEI missions are capable of justifying violations of Article 88 sub a (cartel prohibition) and sub b (the ban on the abuse of a dominant position) TUEMOA. However, no reference is made to Article 88 sub c of this Treaty, which deals with

---

[100] Règlement 02/2002/CM/UEMOA relatif aux pratiques anticoncurrentielles à l'intérieur de l'UEMOA, available at: http://www.uemoa.int/Pages/Actes/NewPages/reglement_2_2002_CM_UEMOA.aspx.

[101] See Papadopoulos, *The International Dimension of EU Competition Law and Policy*, 2010, p. 290.

state aid. Therefore, a strict reading of Article 6.2 of Regulation 02/2002 would lead to the conclusion that aid given in order to finance the provision of SGEI cannot benefit from the exception laid down in this provision. Such a finding could cause problems, as the EU experience that has resulted in cases such as Altmark has shown. The application of the state aid rules to public service should be moderated in order to prevent that the proper functioning of these services are put under pressure. So, it cannot be excluded that in the future the WAEMA institutions will have to develop an approach that is capable of coping with the problems caused by the need to finance particular public services. In this regard, it should be noted that the WAEMA Council did pay attention to financial issues related to public undertakings. It has adopted Directive 01/2002,[102] which has imposed on the WAEMA States the obligation to make their financial relations with public undertakings transparent. As a result, the WAEMA Council has introduced obligations similar to those introduced by the EU in its Transparency Directive (see above).

CARICOM

An important RTA from the region of North and South America is the Treaty establishing the Caribbean Community including the CARICOM Single Market and Economy (hereafter: the CARICOM Treaty).[103] This Treaty has introduced a comprehensive institutional framework for the implementation of the competition rules. Articles 171-176 establish the Competition Commission, which has the authority to take action upon infringement of the competition rules. Furthermore, judicial protection against these actions is in the hands of the Court of Justice, which is the judicial body of the CARICOM Treaty. As for the substantive competition rules, Article 177 of the CARICOM Treaty is of significance. The first section of this Article, under a, provides that agreements between enterprises, decisions by associations of associations of enterprises and concerted practices by enterprises that have the effect or object to restrict competition within the (Caribbean) community are prohibited. Article 177 (1) sub b of this Treaty condemns abuse of a dominant position. Article 179 and further set out which practices qualify as abusive practices, whereas Article 178 defines the term dominant position. Strikingly, Article 177 (1) sub c adds a third prohibition to the (classical) "two prong list" of the cartel prohibition and the ban on the abuse of a dominant position. This "third" provision forbids any other like conduct by enterprises whose object or effect is to frustrate the benefits expected from the CARICOM common market.

[102] Directive 01/2002 relative à la transparence des relations financières d'une part entre lest états membres et les entreprises publiques, et d' autre part entre les Etats membres et les organisations internationale sou étrangères, available at http://www.uemoa.int/Pages/ACTES/Conseildes-Ministres.aspx.

[103] This treaty is available at: http://www.caricom.org/jsp/community/revised_treaty-text.pdf.

In comparison with the EU and US antitrust law systems, the CARICOM competition rules contain an extra tool for tackling restrictive practices.

Furthermore, it should be noted that Article 177 (4) CARICOM Treaty provides that restrictive practices caught by the first section of Article 177 are exempted, if they contribute to the improvement of the production of goods and services or to the promotion of technical or economic progress. On top of that, these practices should allow consumers a fair share of the benefits concerned, should be indispensible and must not eliminate competition in respect of the market for the goods or services at issue. This exemption has great resemblance with the EU exemption contained in Article 101 (3) TFEU. However, an important difference is that in EU competition law, the exemption only applies to practices caught by the cartel prohibition, whereas in CARICOM law every conduct can be justified irrespective of whether it is condemned by the cartel prohibition or by any other provision of competition law.

The overall structure of the CARICOM competition rules is similar to EU competition law,[104] but there are differences with regard to some important details. A striking derogation from the EU system is related to public services. Provisions on Services of General Economic Interest are absent in the CARICOM Treaty. Then again, Article 183 seems to contain a mechanism that may be capable of addressing issues related to public services. The first section of this provision gives the Council for Trade and Economic Development (COTED) the authority to suspend or exclude the application of the Treaty provisions on competition for specific sectors. What is more important, the second section of this Article explicitly states that the COTED is competent to exclude or to suspend the application of the competition rules to any sector or any enterprise in the public interest. It may be assumed that companies providing public services or sectors, where such services play an important role, could benefit from these exemptions.[105] In this regard, it is important to note that pursuant to Article 31 of the CARICOM Treaty it is permitted for the Member States to restrict the freedom of establishment in the public interest by having in place a monopoly. Consequently, the creation of monopolies in order to guarantee the provision of public services is not necessarily incompatible with CARICOM law.[106] This does not call into question that discrimination resulting

[104] Papadopoulos, *The International Dimension of EU Competition Law and Policy*, p. 182.

[105] However, it should be noted that a UNCTAD report issued in 2005 noted that it was not clear whether COTED has exercised this power to exempt agriculture, a sector that is of great interest for CARICOM states, from the competition rules. See the UNCTAD Report, Competition Provisions in Regional Trade Agreements: How to Assure Development Gains, 2005, p. 456.

[106] Beckfor, The Appropriate Design and Enforcement of Competition Law and Policy in Countries at Different Stages of Market Development, paper submitted at the second Regional Seminar UNCTAD/SELA on Trade and Competiveness, p. 16. This paper is available at: http://www.jftc.com/Libraries/Speeches_and_Presentations/The_Appropriate_Design_and_Enforcement_of_Competition_Law_and_Policy_in_Countries_at_Different_Stages_of_Market_Development_The_case_of_CARICOM_-_Dr_Delroy_Beckford.sflb.ashx.

from these monopolies is prohibited. Furthermore, the monopoly rights ought not to be exercised in violation of the competition rules.[107] What this exactly means, is not clear. More in particular, the CARICOM treaty does not explain the relationship between the competition rules and the public monopolies. In sum, monopoly rights may be created by the Member States, but to what extent the enterprises vested with these rights are subject to competition law remains unclear. Of further importance, is Article 94 of the CARICOM Treaty, which provides that Member States must ensure "...the elimination in the practices of public undertakings...", in so far as these practices lead to trade distortions, trade discrimination or competition restrictions. In other words, the way public services are provided could also lead to problems, if no monopolies are present. Strikingly, no further clarification on what is meant by trade distortions, trade discrimination or competition restrictions in this respect is given. Thus, to what extent competition and trade may be restricted in order to ensure access for all to a particular public service is not clear. As a result, the application of the CARICOM competition rules to public services is in a state of limbo. Nonetheless, it is apparent from the foregoing that the system introduced by these rules is based on the presumption that competition could apply to public services.

NAFTA

The North American Free Trade Agreement[108] (hereafter: NAFTA) contains a modest set of competition rules. This finding does not come as a surprise, because the NAFTA members do not aim to transfer their trading block into an advanced form of integration.[109] However, it is salient that most of the NAFTA competition provisions deal with a subject matter, which is of great importance for public services, i.e. Monopolies and State Enterprises. The chapter of the NAFTA governing competition policy (chapter 15) starts with imposing the general obligation on its Member States to have in place a system of competition law and to co-operate with the other Member States in enforcement matters.[110] In other words, the Treaty itself does not contain any substantive rules on cartels or dominance; rather it takes the national systems of the Members as point of departure for these rules.

Then, the duties with regard to monopolies and State enterprises are set out in great detail. Article 1502 NAFTA provides that its Members are entitled to create monopolies. It is apparent from Article 1505 that a monopoly is an entity (including a consortium or government agency) that is designated as the sole provider or purchaser of a good or service. The same provision clarifies that the grant of an IP right cannot lead to the creation of a monopoly within the meaning of NAFTA law.

[107] See Art. 31(2) sub a CARICOM Treaty.

[108] This treaty is available at: http://www.nafta-sec-alena.org/en/view.aspx?x=343.

[109] See Nsour, *Rethinking the World Trade Order. Towards a Better Legal Understanding of the Role of Regionalism in the Multilateral Trade Regime*, 2010, p. 200.

[110] See Art. 1501 NAFTA.

Article 1502 does not only acknowledge the right of Member States to maintain or establish a monopoly, but it also introduces monopoly-specific competition rules. A Member State introducing a monopoly must, "...wherever possible...", make a prior notification of this to the other NAFTA members. Furthermore, a privately owned monopoly should be designated in such a way that (1) its practices are consistent with the other obligations resulting from the NAFTA, (2) it acts solely in accordance with commercial considerations, (3) it provides non-discriminatory treatment to investors coming from other NAFTA Members and (4) it does not use its monopoly position in order to engage in anti-competitive practices in a non-monopolised market adversely affecting investments of enterprises of another NAFTA party. These four monopoly-specific rules do not apply to procurement by governmental agencies of goods and services, as long as these purchase activities serve governmental purposes. Conversely, if the aim of these agencies lies in commercial resale or in the production of goods and services for commercial sale, the exemption does not apply and the purchase activities concerned are caught by the four monopoly-specific rules. There is a clear resemblance with the EU FENIN judgment of the CJEU discussed above. In this judgment, it was held that the nature of purchase activities was determined by the subsequent use of the products or services concerned. If these goods and services are applied for non-economic purposes, such as the exercise of state prerogatives, EU competition law does not apply; if their subsequent use is of an economic nature, the EU competition rules must be observed. Under the NAFTA system a similar approach to purchase activities is present, as these activities only escape from the competition rules in so far as they concern goods and services that public bodies use for governmental purposes (and not for commercial purposes). Consequently, also in NAFTA law the subsequent use of the products or services purchased is decisive.

Article 1503 NAFTA acknowledges that Member States have the right to maintain or establish a state enterprise. In other words, public services provided by such enterprises are, in principle, compatible with NAFTA law. Nonetheless, it should be noted that it is not permitted for State enterprises to adopt measures inconsistent with the NAFTA provisions on investments and financial services. Furthermore, State enterprises must accord non-discriminatory treatment in the sale of its goods or services to investments made by companies of other NAFTA members.

The NAFTA provides for a dispute settlement procedure, but, unfortunately, Article 1501 (3) NAFTA excludes the competition rules from this mechanism. Where the EU experience has resulted into an enormous body of case law and decisional practice, no classical competition law cases are handled on the NAFTA level. However, the exclusion of Article 1501 (3) NAFTA does not apply to the provisions on Monopolies and State enterprises. Therefore, the International Centre for Settlement of Investment Disputes handled a case[111] resulting from a complaint

[111] See NAFTA/UNCITRAL/ICSID, *United States Parcel Service of America, Inc vs. Government of Canada*, 2007. This case is available at: http://www.state.gov/s/l/c3749.htm.

against the Canadian government, which was alleged to allow Canada Post to restrict competition by using privileges from its letter mail monopoly for the benefit of its express delivery services. It was claimed that these practices would lead to reduction of the costs of Canada Post in providing its non-monopoly courier and parcel services. However, the dispute settlement body found that the subsidisation of particular services was justified for reasons of culture policy.[112]

ASEAN-Australia-New Zealand Agreement

Unlike important other RTAs, to date no competition rules are adopted in the framework of the Association of Southeast Asian Nations (hereafter: ASEAN). However, this does not mean that the ASEAN members do not recognise the importance of competition law for international trade. In the Agreement Establishing the ASEAN-Australia-New Zealand Free Trade Area (hereafter: AANZ) some attention to the role of competition is paid in order to improve the trade between the ASEAN countries, Australia and New Zealand. Chapter 14 of this agreement sets out the general competition rules. These rules come down to promoting cooperation between the Member States in competition law matters and to further exploring the principles of competition law. Consequently, compared to many other trade blocks, the competition rules are drafted in a modest way in the AANZ. This finding is further supported by Article 4 of chapter 14 of AANZ, which provides that the Consultation and Dispute Settlement procedure, laid down in chapter 17, does not apply to competition law matters.

Interestingly, provisions dealing with, inter alia, public services are laid down in AANZ as well, but in other chapters than the one on competition. Chapter 11 lays down provisions on investment. It could be argued that Article 1 (2) sub c excludes public services from the scope of these provisions, because it says that services supplied in the exercise of governmental authority are not caught by the AANZ investment rules. Such activities are defined as any services, which are supplied neither on a commercial basis nor in competition with one or more service suppliers. It is clear from the outset that this definition is taken from the GATS. In sum, public services that are not provided in a competitive or commercial environment benefit from this exemption.

Also Chapter 8 AANZ, which contains the rules for the trade in services, is concerned with public services. Like Chapter 11, it creates a safe harbour for services supplied in the exercise of governmental authority.[113] Article 2 sub q defines these services likewise as Chapter 11 did, by referring to the GATS definition (which assigns great value to the absence of competition or commerciality). Furthermore, a carve-out for specific public services is laid down in Article 1

[112] See Nsour, *Rethinking the World Trade Order. Towards a Better Legal Understanding of the Role of Regionalism in the Multilateral Trade Regime*, 2010, p. 151.

[113] See Art. 1(4) sub d of chapter 8.

(4) sub d. According to this provision particular measures affecting traffic rights are also excluded from the Treaty provisions on the trade in services.

To conclude an exemption for public services based on the GATS model is found in the Annex on financial services. However, this exemption is formulated in positive wording (in contrast with the GATS definition, which takes the services supplied in the exercise of governmental authority as starting point): Article 1 (3) of this Annex states that the rules on financial services are applicable to financial services, with regard to which the AANZ members have allowed that they are provided in competition with a public entity or financial service suppliers. Two aspects are worth noting. In the first place, only competition is regarded as a decisive argument for finding a particular set of trade rules to be applicable. Reference to commerciality is absent. In the second place, the involvement of a public entity, which is defined as any entity that is part of the government, does not automatically mean that the rules of financial services do not apply. If competition is allowed, the public entities do not benefit from the exemption of Article 1 (3) of the Annex.

The Role of Public Services in the Competition Rules Contained in Various Free Trade Agreements Between the EU and Its Trading Partners

Increasingly, the EU concludes trade agreements that include competition rules with other countries. These agreements can take the shape of a bilateral agreement (an agreement between the EU and one particular country) or of a plurilateral agreement (an agreement between the EU and a group of countries). It would go beyond the scope of this article to discuss all these agreements. Therefore, in order to give a representative overview, a few trade agreements concluded with neighbouring countries and a few treaties concluded with countries from other parts of the world will be analysed.[114] The analysis below will not include agreements with candidate countries, as the aim of these agreements is to guide the countries concerned through the process of accession to the EU, which implies that in essence the competition rules contained in such agreements are derived from the TFEU. As a result, the analysis of these rules would be of limited value.

EU Trade Agreement with Algeria

The Euro-Mediterranean Agreement establishing an Association between the European Community and its Member States, of the one part, and the People's Democratic

[114] Cf. Papadopoulos, *The International Dimension of EU Competition Law and Policy*, 2010, p. 97.

Republic of Algeria, of the other part[115] (hereafter: Euro-Mediterranean Agreement with Algeria) aims at promoting the political dialogue and the trade between the parties to this agreement. Competition rules are an important part of the policy of the parties to remove obstacles to trade. Article 41 (1) sub a Euro-Mediterranean Agreement with Algeria prohibits all agreements between undertakings, decisions by associations of undertakings and concerted practices between undertakings that have as the object or effect the restriction of competition. Article 41 (1) sub b Euro-Mediterranean Agreement with Algeria prohibits undertakings to abuse their dominant position. It is clear from the outset that these provisions are taken from the TFEU. Furthermore, the Agreement introduces an institutional framework for the implementation of the rules, such as mechanisms for cooperation.

Article 42 obliges the parties to progressively adjust any State monopolies in order to ensure that discrimination in the marketing of goods is abolished. The Association Council (which is composed of the representatives of the EU and the government of Algeria) must be informed about the measures taken in this respect. This provision is of interest for public services, as the supply of essential goods (such as water) can be guaranteed through a State monopoly. Of even more importance is Article 43 of the Euro-Mediterranean Agreement with Algeria, which provides that the Association Council must ensure that no measures are taken with regard to public enterprises and enterprises having exclusive or special rights, in so far as these measures disturb the trade between the EU and Algeria in a manner that runs counter to the interests of the parties to the agreement. In rather complicated wordings, which are clearly modelled after Article 106 (1) TFEU, the Euro-Mediterranean Agreement with Algeria bans particular restrictive measures that are in place in order to govern the provision of public services by certain companies. However, in line with its EU model (Article 106 (2) TFEU), Article 43 Euro-Mediterranean Agreement with Algeria moves on by providing that that this Article should not obstruct the performance in law or in fact of the particular tasks assigned to the enterprises concerned. Article 43 incorporates the approach of Services of General Economic Interest in the EU-Algeria trade rules without using the term Services of General Economic Interest.

EU Trade Agreement with Egypt

An agreement that is similar to the one concluded with Algeria is the Euro-Mediterranean Agreement establishing an Association between the European Community and its Member States, of the one part, and the Arab Democratic Republic of Egypt, of the other part[116] (hereafter: Euro-Mediterranean Agreement with Egypt). Article 34 of this treaty also prohibits cartels and abusive practices of dominant undertakings, in the same wording as the Algeria Agreement does, and as a result,

[115] OJ 2005 L265/1.

[116] OJ [2004] L 345/39.

as the TFEU does. On top of that, public aid is also banned in this provision. Furthermore, Article 36 Euro-Mediterranean Agreement with Egypt stipulates that the Association Council (composed of representatives of the EU and the government of Egypt) must ensure that with regard to public undertakings and undertakings having exclusive and special rights no measures are taken that could affect trade and are not in the interest of the parties. However, this Article should not obstruct the special tasks assigned to these undertakings. This provision highly mirrors Article 43 Euro-Mediterranean Agreement with Algeria. It must be noted that both agreements with Algeria and Egypt link the application of the exemption of the special tasks only to the public undertakings and the undertakings having exclusive and special rights. This means that the "special task derogation" can solely be invoked by these undertakings. This is not consistent with the way Article 106 (2) TFEU is applied in EU competition law. As already lined out above, the exception of Services of General Interest can be relied upon by every undertaking entrusted with a SGEI mission, irrespective of whether such an undertaking is vested with exclusive or special rights (or is owned by the State).

EU Trade Agreement with Chile

As already noted, the EU has also concluded agreements with states in parts of the world further away than the neighbouring countries. Of special interest is the Agreement establishing an association between the European Community and its Member States, of the one part, and the Republic of Chile, of the other part[117] (hereafter: the EU Chile Association Agreement). This agreement obliges the competition authorities of the EU and Chile to co-operate in enforcing the competition rules. The model introduced is that the competition law system of both parties should be applied and, as a result, no substantive competition provisions on cartels and dominant position are laid down in the EU Chile Agreement. Strikingly, the Agreement does lay down substantive rules dealing with issues that are of great relevance for public services. Article 179 (1) of the Agreement provides that, in principle, it is permitted for parties to designate or to maintain public or private monopolies. However, the second section of this Article contains a provision that highly mirrors the provisions on special undertakings of the agreements that EU has concluded with Algeria and Egypt. Measures taken with regard to public undertakings or undertakings having special and exclusive rights are not allowed, if these measures distort trade in goods or services between the parties. Furthermore, these undertakings should be subject to the competition rules, in so far as the application of these rules does not lead to the obstruction of the performance of the special task assigned to these undertakings. Consequently, also the EU Chile Association Agreement acknowledges the special role of (what is called in EU

[117] OJ [2002] L 352/3.

law) Services of General Economic Interest. The position of these services is reinforced by Article 115 of this agreement. Pursuant to this provision, each party has the right to define the kind of universal service obligations it wishes to maintain in Telecommunication law. It may be assumed that this provision allows parties to guarantee access to essential telecommunication services for all, which comes down to ensuring that particular Services of General Economic Interest are provided in the Telecommunication sector. Furthermore, Article 115 of the EU Chile Agreement sets out that the national rules governing these obligations should be transparent, objective and non-discriminatory. On top of that, they must be neutral with respect to competition and be no more burdensome than necessary.

It is remarkable, that the EU Chile Association Agreement, which does not come up with its own rules for cartels and dominance, pays so much attention to public services. However, no precedents on the application of Article 179 are available, as Article 180 of the EU Chile Association Agreement stipulates that the dispute settlement rules of this agreement does not apply to matters of competition law.

EU Trade Agreement with the CARIFORUM States

An important agreement concluded by the EU with another group of countries is, of course, the European Economic Area.[118] However, as the EEA agreement largely overlaps with the TFEU, when it comes to economic matters such as the internal market and competition, the added value of an analysis of this agreement would be limited. Therefore, the agreement the EU has concluded with the CARIFORUM states will be analysed instead. The EU has concluded with these States the Economic Partnership Agreement between the CARIFORUM states,[119] of the one part, and the European Community and its Member States, of the other part[120] (hereafter: the CARIFORUM treaty). This treaty contains a comprehensive set of competition rules, dealing with both substantive issues and matters of cooperation. Article 126 of the CARIFORUM treaty prohibits the conclusion of cartels by undertakings and the abuse of dominance by one or more undertakings, in wordings that are clearly taken from Articles 101 and 102 TFEU. Interestingly, a provision on public enterprises and enterprises with exclusive and special rights is laid down in the CARIFORUM treaty. The first part of Article 129 of this Treaty is clearly

[118] This Agreements is available at: http://www.efta.int/~/media/Documents/legal-texts/eea/the-eea-agreement/Main%20Text%20of%20the%20Agreement/EEAagreement.pdf.

[119] The following states belong to this category: Antigua and Barbuda, Barbados, Belize, the Commonwealth of Dominica, the Dominican Republic, Grenada, the Co-operative Republic of Guyana, the Republic of Haiti, Jamaica, Saint Christopher and Nevis, Saint Lucia, Saint Vincent and the Grenadines, the Republic of Surinam and the Republic of Trinidad and Tobago.

[120] OJ [2008] L 289/I/3.

modelled after Article 179 of the EU Chile Treaty. Section 1 acknowledges that the parties are allowed to have public and private monopolies in place. Section 2 bans national measures taken with regard to public undertakings and undertakings having special and exclusive rights, in so far as these measures distort trade in goods and services between the parties to an extent contrary to the interest of these parties. Furthermore, such companies must be subject to competition law, provided that the application of this area of law does not lead to the obstruction of the particular task assigned to them. It is clear that the concept of Services of General Economic Interest plays an important role in the CARIFORUM treaty. Although this term is not explicitly used, the last sentence of Article 129 section 2 is clearly modelled after the concept of Article 106 (2) TFEU. The role of these services is further reinforced in other Articles of the CARIFORUM treaty. Article 100 of this treaty acknowledges that it is permitted for the parties to have universal service obligations in place in Telecommunication law.[121] According to Article 94 section 1 sub f a universal service is constituted by a set of services of specified quality that must be made available to all users on the territory of a CARIFORUM state or a EU Member State at affordable prices. Since access for all at affordable prices is emphasised in this definition, it is clear that Article 94 refers to a service, which would qualify as a Service of General Economic Interest in EU law.

The second part of Article 129 of the CARIFORUM treaty contains some interesting provisions. The third section thereof stipulates that public enterprises in a CARIFORUM state do not fall within the scope of the Treaty provisions on competition, if they are governed by specific sectoral rules of regulatory frameworks. It should be noted that it is apparent from the wording of this provision that this exemption does not apply to the public enterprises of the EU. Section 4 requires that no discrimination resulting from State monopolies of a commercial nature or character should exist 5 years after the entering into force of the CARIFORUM treaty. In this regard, it should be noted that the agreement applies provisionally as from 29 December 2008.[122]

Some Observations on the Implementation

Unfortunately, to date the implementation of the competition rules laid down in the trade agreements concluded by the EU with neighbouring countries in the Mediter-

[121] Art. 91 of the CARIFORUM Treaty.

[122] See the announcement made at: http://www.crnm.org/index.php?option=com_content&view=article&id=276&Itemid=76.

ranean region is very limited: only a few measures are taken by the Association Councils established by these trade agreements.[123] This finding does not come as a surprise, as, for example, a report from 2007 on Algeria shows that the competition law framework of this country should be further improved and upgraded.[124] Moreover, in the EU Chile Agreement the section on competition law is excluded from the dispute settlement mechanism. This means that unlike the similar provisions laid down in the EU model, no precedents on public services (Services of General Economic Interest) are available, when it comes to the trade agreements the EU has concluded.

Then again, it is save to conclude that the EU has exported its model to public services to the trade agreements concluded with its partners. In EU law, it is common ground to treat these matters as competition law issues. As a result, the partners of the EU are now forced to reconsider their stance to public services at the background of the EU experience with these services and to examine whether their measures regarding these services are anti-competitive.[125]

Conclusions

In many States a considerable amount of public services are provided through monopoly and similar rights.[126] In trade agreements, these rights meet with a hostile approach as they are regarded as obstacles to free trade. In other words, national measures taken to organise and deliver public services are deemed to give raise to trade problems. This does not mean that all monopoly and similar rights are condemned, but the members to many trade agreements must examine with great care whether these rights cause unjustified distortions of competition or trade.

Strikingly, whereas in many national jurisdictions it is acknowledged that public services play a key role on the market, trade agreements tend to treat the organisation and delivery of these services as a problem that must be resolved. How do the trade agreements address this problem? Or to put it differently, which model for public services is developed in international competition law?

---

[123] See Geradin/Petit, Competition Policy in the Southern Mediterranean Countries, Review of Network Economics 3 (2004) 1, p. 78.

[124] See European Neighbourhood and Partnership Instrument—Algeria. Strategy Paper 2007–2013 & National Indicative Programme 2007–2010, p. 36, available at: http://ec.europa.eu/world/enp/pdf/country/enpi_csp_nip_algeria_en.pdf.

[125] See Papadopoulos, *The International Dimension of EU Competition Law and Policy*, 2010, p. 115.

[126] Art. 106(1) TFEU, for example, forbids Member States to take measures with regard to companies having a special position on the market contrary to the competition rules. A similar provision is found in many trade agreements the EU is a party to. Also, in other trade blocks such as those of the WAEMU countries or the parties to the NAFTA, monopolies and similar rights are placed under critical scrutiny.

It is apparent from the analysis carried out in the previous sections that two categories of solutions are created in international economic law. The first category is based on a black and white approach and the second one is based on a "balancing act."

The "Black and White Solution" for Public Services

In the first category of solutions, it is examined whether a particular service falls within the ambit of the competition (and trade) rules. If not, the States remain free to regulate them. In contrast, if competition law applies, public services are treated in the same way as other services, which entails that the providers of these services must fully observe the duty not to conclude cartels or to make misuse of their market power.

In establishing the applicability of the competition (and trade) rules, a test that takes the organisation of the delivery of public services as point of departure is developed. In some systems, this test is predominately based on formal criteria. The institutional design of the public services organisation plays a key role in these systems. If the State bears the final responsibility with regard to particular important decisions, the public services are immune from competition law. This test is mostly deployed in US anti-trust law and in the EU rules on the useful effect doctrine. An important point in case is State supervision and, more in particular, ex ante supervisory mechanisms, as the absence of these mechanisms is a significant argument for not excluding the public services from the scope of competition law.

In other systems, the test focuses on how much room for competition or commercial activity is allowed for in national law. In these systems, the test is not based on formal considerations, rather it resolves around substantive benchmarks. In essence, it should be examined whether the State has introduced genuine elements of competition as to justify the application of the rules of the "market game," i.e. the provisions on competition (and trade). In WTO law (GATS), in RTAs that took their definition of services supplied in the exercise of governmental authority from WTO law and in the EU cases dealing with social security schemes and the concept of undertaking, the test of the organisation of the delivery of public services is deployed in this way. In these systems, the applicability of the norms are depending on whether the public services concerned are supplied in competition or in a commercial environment.

Although the details of the "Black and White" approach may differ from system to system (as to whether formal or substantive considerations are decisive), such systems do have one important feature in common. Eventually, all "Black and White systems" draw on the will of the legislature of the State concerned, for the key question is whether this legislature has introduced a public services organisation that justifies the application of the competition (and trade) rules. The issue concerned can be approached from either a formal or a substantive angle, but this does not call into question that the legislature of a State can model the measures regarding public services in such a way that these are immune from competition law. Therefore, to a certain extent, it is in the hands of the national legislature whether the competition (and trade) rules should be observed in matters concerning public services.

The "Balancing Solution" for Public Services

The second category of solutions is mainly created in EU competition law. As outlined at the beginning of this chapter, the interpretation given to the concept of undertaking, which is defined as every entity engaged in an economic activity, is decisive for the applicability of the competition rules contained in Articles 101 and 102 TFEU. Apart from the management of social security schemes, only the exercise of State prerogatives (powers that are typical for the pubic domain) escapes from competition law. This approach comes down to applying the competition rules to all services and goods that can be supplied through the market. The benchmark is not whether the national legislature of a State has introduced a model eligible for competition; rather, the main question is whether from an abstract point of view it is possible to make the provision of particular public services subject to market forces, irrespective of whether such a role for the market is envisaged by the State concerned. Consequently, in EU competition law—except in cases concerning social security schemes—the mere observation that public services can be offered on the market place will suffice for finding that the providers of these services are undertakings. When it comes to the applicability of Articles 101 and 102 TFEU, in general the will of the national legislature is not of great importance in EU competition law, since this legislature cannot prevent these Treaty provision from being applicable to public services (with the exception of social security services). EU competition law is capable of covering more public services than US anti-trust law. Furthermore, it is consistent with this finding to point out that the same might be true for trade agreements that have derived their competition law model from the EU experience. Then again, it should be recalled that these agreements are hardly applied in practice, which considerably moderates the high expectations of the role that the international competition rules could play in the States concerned.

A very important difference with the "Black and White systems" is that the TFEU lays down a public services-specific exception. As was pointed out at the beginning of this chapter, Article 106 (2) TFEU provides that restrictive measures and practices are permitted, if this is necessary with a view to the provision of Services of General Economic Interest (SGEI). As already noted, the TFEU prefers the term SGEI over public services. In any event, in Article 106 (2) TFEU cases the role of the national legislature is of importance, as this legislature should ensure that particular enterprises are entrusted with a SGEI mission. Furthermore, Article 106 (2) TFEU only applies, in so far as SGEI operators can only perform the task entrusted to them under economically acceptable circumstances by restricting competition. As was already explained above, the test of the economically acceptable circumstances is developed in order to address the market failure of cherry picking. It is even apparent from the Altmark developments that SGEI are suitable to justify state aid measures taken in order to finance services that the market fails to deliver (adequately).[127] Furthermore, it should be pointed out that in many trade agreements provisions are laid down modelled after Article 106 (2) TFEU. A salient difference is that most of these provisions do not speak of "Services of General Economic Interest"; rather they refer to special tasks. In fact, the term "task" reflect better the core elements of the "Article 106 (2) TFEU concept" than the word "service," as also the supply of goods could satisfy general interest needs.

Which lesson could be learned from the EU experience (that is also exported to other treaties)? Only a limited number of public services escape from competition law, namely those that cannot be offered on the market place. The broad scope of the competition rules is moderated by a public service-specific exception. Therefore, States are forced to balance the benefits resulting from competition and free trade with the need to ensure access to public services for all. The test of economically acceptable circumstances shows that market failure is a good justification for tipping the balance in favour of public services. Furthermore, as the market failures concerned relate to the need to ensure access for all to particular essential services, it should be noted that solidarity also plays a key role in this respect.[128] Therefore, if the "balancing solution" for public service is adopted, the national legislature should not be concerned with trying to carve out public services from the scope of competition law, but with addressing market failures that could put the provision of these services under pressure. In so far as market failures are absent, competition should not be restricted.

Final Observations

In international competition law two approaches to public services are developed, in this contribution labelled as the "White and Black solution" and the "Balancing solution." Although significant differences exist between both solutions, it is clear that a considerable number of public services are brought within the scope of competition law, in order to remove obstacles to free trade. However, an important problem should be pointed to: apart from the EU and US anti-trust rules, the international competition rules laid down in trade agreements are (hardly) enforced.[129] It implies that this problem justifies the conclusion that international

[127] In EU state aid law, the term Public Service Obligations is used, next to the concept of SGEI.

[128] See Krajewski, Conclusion, in: Krajewski/Neergaard/van de Gronden (eds.), *The Changing Legal Framework for Services of General Interest for Europe. Between Competition and Solidarity*, 2009, pp. 504–505.

[129] See in this respect the UNCTAD Report, Competition Provisions in Regional Trade Agreements: How to Assure Development Gains, 2005, p. 31 and Nsour, *Rethinking the World Trade Order. Towards a Better Legal Understanding of the Role of Regionalism in the Multilateral Trade Regime*, 2010, p. 153.

competition law cannot yet, deliver in trade matters, what it promises. Therefore, the question is whether the States party to trade agreements have the courage to improve the effectiveness of the competition rules they have agreed upon. It can certainly not be ruled out that the fear exists that better enforcement of the competition rules could have adverse effects on the access for all to particular public services. This problem could be resolved by combing the "White and Black solution" with the "Balancing solution": as long as a particular essential service should be shielded from market forces in the view of a State, its national legislature could make the provision of the service concerned subject to intense regulation. This regulation can be lifted, if the public service industry concerned is ready for competition. It is important to note that it is not necessary to expose this industry to unbridled competition, as long as a public service-specific exception suitable for addressing various kinds of market failures is in place. To conclude, introducing smart competition law systems is a significant challenge the international community faces nowadays, as competiveness contributes to economic growth and prosperity.

Competition Policy in Africa

Trudi Hartzenberg

Introduction

During the past two decades, many African countries have adopted competition policy as an important instrument of economic and, more specifically, market governance. The proliferation of competition policy regimes in Africa has taken place during a phase of broad-based economic liberalisation, including trade liberalisation, and domestic economic reforms such as privatisation. In some cases, these reforms were part of structural adjustment programmes, were supported by the International Monetary Fund and the World Bank, and in other cases the economic adjustment programmes were homegrown. The World Trade Organisation (WTO) was established in 1995 after the conclusion of the Uruguay Round of Multilateral trade negotiations. The first WTO Ministerial Conference, held in Singapore in 1996, brought new generation trade issues, including competition policy, on to the multilateral trade agenda. However, at the 2003 Cancun Ministerial Conference, competition was dropped from the Doha Development Agenda, following debates among developing countries about the benefits of a competition regime. Despite the fact that competition no longer features on the multilateral trade agenda, many regional trade agreements include provisions on competition. In many cases, the provisions cover cooperation in competition enforcement. Perhaps the most important experience to date has been in the context of the negotiations with the European Union to conclude Economic Partnership Agreements. Many countries have still to conclude these negotiations; the provisions being discussed focus specifically on cooperation in enforcement. However, in Africa, there are several regional integration arrangements that provide for a regional competition law and the establishment of a regional competition authority.

T. Hartzenberg (✉)
Executive Director, Trade Law Centre (tralac), PO Box 224, Stellenbosch 7600, South Africa
e-mail: trudi@tralac.org

C. Herrmann et al. (eds.), *European Yearbook of International Economic Law (EYIEL), Vol. 4 (2013)*, European Yearbook of International Economic Law 4,
DOI 10.1007/978-3-642-33917-2_7,

This paper starts with a brief review of the important fault lines of competition governance development in Africa. It traces some of the competition policy developments at national level, highlighting experiences of select countries. From a national focus, the paper then moves to consider competition developments at regional level, specifically within Africa's regional economic communities. Finally conclusions regarding the implementation experience in African countries reflect on the requirements for effective implementation, as well as, the development of a competition culture in African economies, are presented with an update on the establishment of the African Competition Forum.

National Competition Policy Development in Africa

Since the early 1990s, many African governments have been actively developing competition policy and law and establishing competition authorities for enforcement. Various approaches to competition governance have been adopted; some have established independent competition authorities, while others have authorities that are housed within a government ministry, where decisions are subject to ministerial approval. A number of African countries including Mauritius, Kenya, South Africa, The Gambia, Tanzania and Zambia have amended their competition legislation or adopted entirely new legislation. Some of these competition regimes have set important benchmarks for effective enforcement of competition policy in developing countries.

Substantive provisions in the competition law in Africa cover a broad range of issues including restrictive practices, abuse of a dominant position, and merger review provisions, in many countries requiring pre-merger notification. While in most cases the central focus is the promotion of competition to enhance economic efficiency, there is also increasingly focus on public interest and broader economic development objectives, with explicit inclusion of consumer welfare provisions. It is also common to have extensive jurisdictional coverage; all economic activity within the country, bar some exceptions, is usually covered by the competition law. In some cases, competition law provides for extra-territorial jurisdiction, covering all economic activity in the country or having an effect in the country. This is of course important with respect to growing cross-border economic activity as Africa's regional integration initiatives make progress and the global integration of Africa's economies.

The inclusion of public interest objectives in competition law makes sense for African countries, since their markets are likely to be small and market processes weakly developed. In many African countries, economic governance institutions such as property rights (including intellectual property rights) protection are also in their infancy, and many countries are still negotiating privatisation programmes. The private sector, especially the small business sector, often lacks the capacity or information to respond effectively to both competitive and anti-competitive challenges. Explicit incorporation of public interest objectives can give expression to the market development and broader development imperatives for these countries.[1] However, there are challenges when it comes to enforcement of public interest provisions. In many jurisdictions, the development of a jurisprudence will amplify and clarify the scope of such provisions. This takes time to develop.

Many African markets are characterised by very specific size and ownership configurations. Small businesses in African countries tend to be, predominantly, indigenously owned, while larger businesses are often foreign owned. It is important, in this context, to note the important linkages between competition and investment issues, in particular foreign direct investment. New market entrants, through, for example, greenfield investment or merger and acquisition activity, in addition to changing the market structure, can have an important impact on the nature and intensity of competition in a market. Therefore, the growing interest in Africa as an investment destination increases the importance of competition policy, and specifically increases the importance of merger review for African countries.

For effective enforcement, it is not only the capacity of the competition authority that matters. The development of a competition culture among business, consumers and civil society organisations, as well as knowledge of the nature of anti-competitive practices and their pernicious effect both for business and consumers is also important, so that these practices may be brought to the attention of the competition authority. Some competition authorities have included advocacy and the development of a competition culture in their capacity programmes. A good example, referred to later in the paper, is Zambia.

Annexes 1–5[2] of this paper provide an overview of the current status of national competition law and policy, and competition authorities in African countries. Annex 1 provides a review of competition policy in southern Africa. This sub-region has been particularly active in competition policy development in recent years. South Africa and Zambia provide very interesting case studies of competition policy in this region. In both cases, there has been strong focus on developing the credibility of the competition authority, as well as building a competition culture.

Annex 2 provides a summary of competition regimes in East Africa. In this region, there are countries that have long experience of competition governance, such as Kenya and Tanzania, while others are still in the early phase of developing competition policy and establishing competition authorities. Rwanda, for example, is currently engaged in a programme to establish a competition authority. Following the development of a competition policy and law, government officials in the Ministry of Trade and Industry have been appointed to focus on competition matters and to begin a programme of capacity building. The assistance of other

[1] It is important to keep in mind that there may be other policies that may impact more directly on some of the public interest issues included in competition policy. The risk of policy-overload, especially if policy is effectively enforced, needs to be considered carefully. Policy complementarities and coherence are important principles to consider.

[2] These annexes provide a summary of competition law and policy in Africa; the delineation into sub-regions is done for convenience, rather than following the regional economic groupings since there is significant membership overlap amongst these.

authorities, such as the South African Competition Commission has been sought. Such initiatives are important to build institutional capacity and bode well for cooperation in enforcement in Africa.

Annex 3 provides an update on competition policy developments in Central Africa. Although much progress has been made in the development of law and policy, none of the countries in this region has functioning competition authorities yet. Cameroon and the Democratic Republic of the Congo are expected to have functioning authorities in the near future.

Annex 4 shows that in West Africa, there is much activity in the competition policy field. Some countries, including Benin, are in the early stages of developing a policy and law, while others, such as Burkina Faso, have had a law and functioning competition authority for some years. In some cases, it is evident that the development of a policy and law may not be expeditiously followed by the establishment of a competition authority. This observation, which is also true of other African subregions, raises important questions about the capacity requirements for effective competition law enforcement. The United Nations Conference on Trade and Development (UNCTAD) has played an important role assisting African countries to develop competition policy and law. This has to be further supported by the development of both technical expertise and institutional capacity development to manage the enforcement of competition law. Such capacity development can take considerable time.

Annex 5 presents the status of competition policy in North Africa. There is also considerable diversity among these countries as regards the status of competition governance. In some countries, such as Egypt, there is considerable experience over a number of years, while in others, such as Libya and Mauritania development is still in the early stages, with no competition authorities established yet.

From this summary overview of competition policy in Africa, it is possible to conclude that there has been an increased focus on competition policy during the past two decades; however, much remains to be done to provide for effective competition enforcement. Effective enforcement requires technical capacity, financial resources and an independent authority to review and adjudicate competition matters. Access to information is essential; this is a major challenge in many African countries. Market and company information may not be systematically collected and readily available to the competition authority. In cases where foreign companies are involved there may also be challenges associated with access to information. Cooperation with other competition authorities may also assist with capacity constraints in the conduct of investigations. Enforcement also requires expertise in the legal and economics professions. South Africa's experience has shown that the adoption of a robust competition regime has led to the development of expertise in the legal profession, with most law firms now having competition law expertise, and competition economics has become an important focus of postgraduate economics programmes at many universities.

The three country case studies presented below provide an indication of the nature of competition governance in Africa and the experience of competition enforcement.

Zambia's Competition Policy

In 1991, Zambia's new government adopted a strategy for liberalisation and privatisation of the economy; the development of a national competition law and policy took place during this era of policy revamp. The specific aim was to ensure a level playing field in the economic sector in order to avoid market distortions, which could lead to stagnation of the economy or diminished growth over time.[3] As the Government no longer had control over the production, distribution, or pricing of goods and services, the potential benefits of a more market-oriented economy would only be realised if anti-competitive practices could be prevented. In addition, as the private sector became the driver of economic growth, consumer protection from businesses and manufacturers that engaged in unfair trading practices became important.[4] The Competition and Fair Trading Act (CFTA), No. 18 of 1994,[5] was passed and entered into force in February 1995, establishing a regulatory and institutional framework for competition and consumer welfare in the country. This legislation aimed to ensure that there was fair competition amongst economic actors and that the fruits of liberalisation did not only accrue to firms but were passed on to consumers.[6] The CFTA called for the establishment of the Zambia Competition Commission (ZCC), operational since March 1997, as an autonomous body responsible for the enforcement of the Act. The objectives of the CFTA, as stated in the Preamble, were:

- To encourage competition in the economy by prohibiting anti-competitive trade practices;
- To regulate monopolies and concentrations of economic power;
- To protect consumer welfare;
- To strengthen the efficiency of production and distribution of goods and services;
- To secure the best possible conditions for the freedom of trade;
- To expand the base of entrepreneurship; and
- To provide for matters connected with or incidental to the foregoing.[7]

The experience of ZCC provides an important example for what can be achieved, even in least developed countries, as regards competition governance.

---

[3] Competition and Consumer Protection Commission (CCPC), 'Our background', 2012, available at: http://www.ccpc.org.zm/index.php?option=com_content&view=article&id=90&Itemid=96.

[4] Republic of Zambia Ministry of Commerce, Trade and Industry, Draft Competition and Consumer Protection Policy, 2009, available at: http://www.ccpc.org.zm/index.php?option=com_docman&task=doc_download&gid=20&Itemid=51.

[5] Competition and Fair Trading Act, Chapter 417 of the Laws of Zambia of 1994.

[6] Republic of Zambia Ministry of Commerce, Trade and Industry, Draft Competition and Consumer Protection Policy, 2009, available at: http://www.ccpc.org.zm/index.php?option=com_docman&task=doc_download&gid=20&Itemid=51.

[7] Preamble of the Competition and Fair Trading Act.

To support strict enforcement of competition law, ZCC was careful to build its credibility. In addition ZCC, with the assistance of, for example, UNCTAD and the International Competition Network (ICN), prioritised building capacity of the competition authority. Partnerships with competition authorities in both developed and developing countries, including the Australian and South African competition authorities, saw ZCC officers develop technical capacity for investigating complaints and doing merger impact assessments. ZCC also engaged in ongoing activities to build a competition culture; broadcasts in national print media and television were used not only to communicate ZCC's decisions but also to engage with chambers of business, consumer organisations and academic institutions thus broadening the scope and impact of competition law enforcement in Zambia.

However, by 2009, the Zambian Government recognised that the existing legal framework was inadequate to deal with some of the challenges faced by businesses and consumers and that consumer welfare provisions could be enhanced.[8] As a result, a Competition and Consumer Protection Policy was drafted in November 2009 to promote the development of competitive and fair markets that would lead to industrial and economic growth and development as well as protection of businesses and consumers.[9] The Policy recognises transparency, accountability and due process, as well as non-discrimination (national treatment) and engagement with market participants (promoting research and development, and education and information), as guiding principles in policy enforcement, in line with international best practices.[10] Following approval of the Policy, the Competition and Consumer Protection Act, No. 24 of 2010, was passed and entered into force in October 2010, repealing and replacing the Competition and Fair Trading Act. Although the new law is intended to continue the policies reflected in the earlier statute, it is a more comprehensive law that deals more comprehensively with both competition and consumer protection issues.[11] The new Act applies to the Zambian economy in general, including all economic activity within or having an effect within Zambia, except where otherwise indicated.[12]

Amongst the objectives of the new legislation, as stated in the Preamble to the Act, is to safeguard and promote competition in Zambia. To achieve this objective,

---

[8] Republic of Zambia Ministry of Commerce, Trade and Industry, Draft Competition and Consumer Protection Policy, 2009, available at: http://www.ccpc.org.zm/index.php?option=com_docman&task=doc_download&gid=20&Itemid=51.

[9] Republic of Zambia Ministry of Commerce, Trade and Industry, Draft Competition and Consumer Protection Policy, 2009, available at: http://www.ccpc.org.zm/index.php?option=com_docman&task=doc_download&gid=20&Itemid=51.

[10] International Chamber of Commerce (ICC) Commission on Competition, Recommended framework for international best practices in competition law enforcement proceedings, Paris: ICC, Document No. 225/666, 2010, available at: http://www.iccwbo.org/uploadedFiles/ICC/policy/competition/pages/ICC%20International%20Due%20process%2008%2003%2010%20FINAL.pdf.

[11] Competition and Consumer Protection Commission (CCPC), 2012, available at: http://www.ccpc.org.zm/index.php?option=com_content&view=article&id=90&Itemid=96.

[12] § 3(1) Competition and Consumer Protection Act.

Part III of the Act prohibits restrictive business and anti-competitive trade practices, defined as any agreement, decision or concerted practice that has as its object or effect the prevention, restriction or distortion of competition to an appreciable extent in the local market.[13] Certain horizontal and vertical agreements between enterprises are prohibited, although exemptions are allowed if the agreement is likely to, among other things, maintain or promote exports from Zambia; promote or maintain efficient production, distribution or provision of goods and services; promote the competitiveness of micro and small enterprises; or obtain a public benefit that is likely to outweigh the lessening of competition that would result from the agreement.[14] A corporate leniency programme is also provided to assist specifically with the prosecution of cartels. This programme is not yet developed.

Abuse of a dominant position of market power, which can take the form of charging an unfair price, an excessive price or a price below marginal or variable cost; limiting or restricting production, market access, investment or technological development in a manner that affects competition; applying dissimilar conditions to equivalent transactions; and charging an excessive price to the detriment of consumers, is also prohibited.[15] The Competition Commission is empowered in Part V to initiate market inquiries when there are reasonable grounds to suspect that a restriction or distortion of competition is occurring within a particular sector or type of agreement.[16]

The control of mergers is contained in Part IV of the Act. A merger is said to occur when an enterprise acquires or establishes control over the whole or part of the business of another enterprise, or when two or more enterprises mutually agree to arrange common ownership or control over the whole or part of their respective businesses.[17] The Act gives the Commission power to review proposed mergers and acquisitions when the agreement meets the prescribed threshold for authorisation,[18] or when there are reasonable grounds to believe that an agreement that falls below the prescribed threshold would create a dominant position; substantially lessen or prevent competition; result in competition or public interest concerns that need to be taken into account; or when the merger is to be concluded outside of Zambia but having consequences inside Zambia that require further consideration.[19] In either case, upon receipt of the proposed merger notification, the Act directs the Commission to carry out a market assessment to determine the likely effects of the proposed merger in the relevant market, on trade and the economy in general,[20] as well as a

[13] § 8 Competition and Consumer Protection Act.

[14] § 19(2) Competition and Consumer Protection Act.

[15] § 16 Competition and Consumer Protection Act.

[16] § 38 Competition and Consumer Protection Act.

[17] § 24(1) Competition and Consumer Protection Act.

[18] As stipulated in the Competition and Consumer Protection (General) Regulations, 2011, contained in Statutory Instrument No. 97 of 2011 dated 19 August 2011.

[19] § 27(1) Competition and Consumer Protection Act.

[20] § 29 Competition and Consumer Protection Act.

competition assessment to determine whether the merger is likely to prevent or substantially lessen competition in a market in Zambia.[21] The Commission may also take into account any factor that bears upon the public interest in the proposed merger when making its consideration to assess the extent to which a proposed merger is likely to result in a benefit to the public.[22] At the end of its review, the Commission may approve the merger, approve the merger with conditions, or reject it in its entirety.

In addition to promoting competition, the new Act aims to protect consumers against unfair trade practices,[23] recognising consumer protection as the ultimate goal of competition regulation in the country.[24] Unfair trading practices are prohibited under Part VII of the Act, defined as any practices that mislead consumers, compromise the standard of honesty and good faith that an enterprise can reasonably be expected to meet, or place pressure on consumers by use of harassment or coercion.[25] In addition, the Act prohibits false or misleading representations by a person or enterprise with respect to any material fact about a product or service or the conditions attached to the purchase of the product or service; the display by shop owners of any signs or notices that purport to disclaim any liability or deny any right that a consumer has under the Act or any other written law; the supply of defective, unsuitable, or substandard goods or services; and the supply of goods that do not conform to the mandatory safety standard for that class of goods.[26] Other consumer protection provisions contained in Part VII relate to product labelling, price display, unfair contract terms and consumer complaints.

The new Act provides for the institutional architecture to implement and enforce the competition regulations in Zambia. The continued functioning of the Zambia Competition Commission, re-named the Competition and Consumer Protection Commission (CCPC)[27] is provided for. The functions of the Commission, contained in Part II of the Act, include the review of the operation of markets in Zambia and the conditions of competition in those markets; review the trading practices pursued by enterprises doing business in Zambia; investigate and assess restrictive agreements, abuse of dominant positions, and mergers; and investigate

[21] § 30 Competition and Consumer Protection Act.

[22] § 31 Competition and Consumer Protection Act.

[23] Preamble of the Competition and Consumer Protection Act.

[24] Lingela, Balancing competition and the public interest, 2012, available at: http://www.ccpc.org.zm/index.php?option=com_content&view=article&id=117:balancing-competition-a-the-public-interest&catid=47:articles&Itemid=128.

[25] §§ 45-46 Competition and Consumer Protection Act.

[26] §§ 47-49, 52 Competition and Consumer Protection Act.

[27] Preamble of the Competition and Consumer Protection Act.

unfair trading practices and unfair contract terms and impose such sanctions as may be necessary.[28] Provisions relating to investigations and determinations by the Commission are contained in Part VIII of the Act. Among the Commission's most important missions is that of advocacy. The Act charges the Commission to undertake and publish general studies on the effectiveness of competition; to act as a primary advocate for competition and effective consumer protection; to advise Government on laws affecting competition and consumer protection; and to inform the public on competition and consumer protection issues. The advocacy mandate is important as it provides a check on overly restrictive governmental regulations that may otherwise hinder the competitive process, among other things.[29] However, the Commission is aware that there is still a lot of work to be done in the years to come in order to raise awareness on competition and consumer protection issues in the country.[30] Furthermore, given the Commission's broad mandate and budgeted staff of only 26, may be too small to allow for the focus on, and to develop expertise in all markets. The perceived lack of independence of the institution has also been criticised. For the Commission to have a proper role in promoting competition in Zambia, more resources and long-term assistance would therefore be needed, as well as greater independence in its functioning.[31]

Also established under the Act is the Competition and Consumer Protection Tribunal, allowing parties aggrieved by a Commission decision to appeal adverse determinations within 30 days.[32] The provision for a Tribunal marks a milestone in Zambia's efforts to ensure that appeal cases are dealt with expeditiously.[33] According to the provisions contained in Part XI of the Act, the Tribunal will constitute a part-time panel with members appointed by the Minister of Commerce. It will also have its own investigatory powers and may compel testimony and documents as appropriate. From the Tribunal, parties may further appeal adverse decisions to the High Court.[34] Efforts to establish the Tribunal are currently underway, although as of February 2012 it was not yet operational.

---

[28] § 5 Competition and Consumer Protection Act.

[29] United States Agency for International Development (USAID) and Agribusiness Commercial Legal and Institutional Reform (AgCLIR), Legal and Institutional Reform in Zambia's Agricultural Sector, 2011, available at: http://www.fintrac.com/cpanelx_pu/EAT/15_33_7791_Zambia%20AgCLIR.pdf.

[30] Competition and Consumer Protection Commission (CCPC), 'Welcome to CCPC', 2012 available at: http://www.ccpc.org.zm.

[31] United States Agency for International Development and Agribusiness Commercial Legal and Institutional Reform, Legal and Institutional Reform in Zambia's Agricultural Sector, 2011, available at: http://www.fintrac.com/cpanelx_pu/EAT/15_33_7791_Zambia%20AgCLIR.pdf.

[32] § 60 Competition and Consumer Protection Act.

[33] Competition and Consumer Protection Commission (CCPC), 'Our background', 2012, available at: http://www.ccpc.org.zm/index.php?option=com_content&view=article&id=90&Itemid=96.

[34] United States Agency for International Development and Agribusiness Commercial Legal and Institutional Reform, Legal and Institutional Reform in Zambia's Agricultural Sector, 2011, available at: http://www.fintrac.com/cpanelx_pu/EAT/15_33_7791_Zambia%20AgCLIR.pdf.

Egypt's Competition Policy

In 1991, Egypt embarked on a comprehensive Economic Reform and Structural Adjustment Programme (ERSAP), in collaboration with the World Bank and the International Monetary Fund, with the aim of transforming the economy into a market-based economy and eradicating the major imbalances the economy faced in the 1970s and 1980s.[35] In particular, the Government aimed to reduce the size of the public sector and expand the role of the private sector. Privatisation and other free market policies followed, although for many years Egypt was unable to achieve a free, competitive and stable business environment as the regulatory reforms concerning competition law and policy remained absent.[36] Although Egypt's competition law was first drafted in 1995, numerous revisions and modifications were made over the next 10 years before the law was finally passed by Parliament in February 2005.[37] The Law on the Protection of Competition and the Prohibition of Monopolistic Practices, No. 3 of 2005, entered into force on 16 May 2005. The title of this Law indicates Government's desire to couple the protection of competition with the struggle against monopoly, while at the same time omitting any provisions related to consumer protection in the belief that separate laws for competition and consumer protection would be the best course of action.[38] The Law provided for the establishment of the Egyptian Competition Authority (ECA) that would be responsible for monitoring the market and enforcing the provisions of the Law, launched in 2006. Following adoption of the Law, a set of Executive Regulations was issued in August 2005.[39] The Law and Executive Regulations have since been amended, in

[35] Abdel Latif/Ghoneim, Competition, Competition Policy and Economic Efficiency in the MENA Region: The Case of Egypt, International Development Research Centre, 2005, available at: http://idl-bnc.idrc.ca/dspace/bitstream/10625/26939/1/124654.pdf.

[36] Ghoneim, Egypt, in: Mehta (ed.), *Competition Regimes in the World – A Civil Society Report*, 2006, available at: http://competitionregimes.com/pdf/book/africa/42-egypt.pdf.

[37] Rasromani, "Regulating a free market: Competition Authority formation underway," Daily News Egypt, 8 February 2006, available at: http://www.dailystaregypt.com/article.aspx?ArticleID=590.

[38] Abdel Latif/Ghoneim, Competition, Competition Policy and Economic Efficiency in the MENA Region: The Case of Egypt, International Development Research Centre, 2005, available at: http://idl-bnc.idrc.ca/dspace/bitstream/10625/26939/1/124654.pdf. The Consumer Protection Law, No. 67 of 2006, entered into force in May 2006. It is accompanied by a set of Executive Regulations. The law created the Consumer Protection Agency (CPA) as the supervisory authority in charge of enforcing the law.

[39] Prime Ministerial Decree No. 1316 of 2005 issuing the Executive Regulations of Protection of Competition and Prohibition of Monopolistic Practices Law No. 3 of 2005.

2008 and 2010 respectively.[40] In late 2011, further amendments to the Law were proposed, which have been approved by Cabinet.[41]

The objective of Egypt's competition legislation is to ensure that all economic activities are undertaken in a manner that does not prevent, restrict or harm competition.[42] This objective emphasises the right for all persons transacting in the market (including natural and legal persons, economic entities, unions, financial associations and groupings, and groups of persons regardless of their means of incorporation[43]) to undertake economic activity provided it does not negatively affect competition or diminish economic freedom.[44] Public utilities controlled by the State are not subject to the Law unless the utility is privately owned and operated.[45] The Law is applicable to all economic activities related to both goods and services, and is extended to include practices, contracts or agreements committed abroad that negatively impact on competition in Egypt.[46] The relevant market to which the Law applies is defined in terms of two elements, namely the relevant products and the geographical area, which are described in the Executive Regulations.[47]

Egypt's competition law is very specific about the considered violations[48] that could have a negative impact on economic activity. In the first instance, Article 6 of the Law contains a list of prohibited practices and agreements between competing persons (horizontal agreements). These include raising, decreasing or stabilising the sale or purchase prices of products; dividing product markets on the basis of geographical area, distribution centres, types of customers, goods, market shares

---

[40] Law No. 190 of 2008 Amending Certain Provisions of the Law on Protection of Competition and Prohibition of Monopolistic Practices promulgated by Law No. 3 of 2005; Law No. 193 of 2008 adding a new article numbered (26) to the Law on Protection of Competition and Prohibition of Monopolistic Practices promulgated by Law No. 3 of 2005; Prime Ministerial Decree No. 2957 of 2010 to Amend Some Provisions of the Executive Regulations of Protection of Competition and Prohibition of Monopolistic Practices Law No. 3 of 2005.

[41] Egypt State Information Service (SIS), "Egypt's cabinet approved amendments of anti-monopoly law," 27 September 2011, available at: http://www.sis.gov.eg/en/Story.aspx?sid=58147.

[42] § 1 Protection of Competition and the Prohibition of Monopolistic Practices Law; § 2 Executive Regulations.

[43] § 2(a) Protection of Competition and the Prohibition of Monopolistic Practices Law.

[44] Abdel Latif/Ghoneim, Competition, Competition Policy and Economic Efficiency in the MENA Region: The Case of Egypt, International Development Research Centre, 2005, available at: http://idl-bnc.idrc.ca/dspace/bitstream/10625/26939/1/124654.pdf.

[45] Trade-Related Assistance Centre (TRAC), Competition Policy and Law in Egypt: Report on the Seminar, 2006, available at: http://www.amcham-egypt.org/Trac/reports/Competition_Law_Dec_2006.pdf.

[46] § 5 Protection of Competition and the Prohibition of Monopolistic Practices Law; § 3 Executive Regulations.

[47] § 6 Executive Regulations.

[48] Trade-Related Assistance Centre, Competition Policy and Law in Egypt: Report on the Seminar, 2006, available at: http://www.amcham-egypt.org/Trac/reports/Competition_Law_Dec_2006.pdf.

or seasons or periods of time; coordination with regards to proceeding or refraining from participating in tenders, auctions, bids and other calls for procurement; and restraints on the manufacturing, production, distribution or marketing of goods or services. The Law adopted a per se rule in addressing horizontal agreements where the agreement in itself is considered a violation and not the result of such agreement.[49]

Restrictive business practices between a person and his/her clients or suppliers (vertical agreements) are prohibited under Article 7. Whether or not an agreement or contract is likely to restrict competition is determined by the Competition Authority on a case by case basis in light of the evaluation of various criteria, including the effect it would have on the freedom of competition in the market; the existence of benefits to be accrued to consumers; considerations of preserving the quality of the product or its reputation; and the extent of compliance of the conditions of the arrangement with established commercial customs in the economic activity under examination.[50]

Egypt's competition law also prohibits abuse of a dominant position in a market, as provided for in Article 8. A firm is said to occupy a dominant position in the market when the firm owns more than 25% of the market share; the firm has the power to manipulate the prices and the volume of supply of the product within its relevant market; and the firm's competitors lack the ability or fail to curb these manipulative practices.[51] Practices constituting abuse of a dominant position include, among other things, acts that would lead to the non-manufacturing, non-producing or non-distributing of a product for a certain period of time; discriminating between sellers or buyers, who have similar commercial standings, with regards to sale or purchase prices or in the conditions of the contract; refusing to produce or provide a product that is circumstantially scarce when its production or provision is economically possible; limiting the distribution of a specific product on the basis of geographic areas, distribution centres, clients, seasons or periods of time within vertical agreements; selling products below their marginal cost or average variable cost; and obliging a supplier not to deal with a competitor. The conditions and procedures for implementing the provisions of Article 8 are contained in the Executive Regulations.[52] It is noteworthy that the size of the firm does not in itself represent a violation. The Law is concerned only with the *abuse* of dominant position by persons who practice their economic activity in the market that may lead to harming their clients, suppliers or competitors.[53]

[49] Egyptian Competition Authority (ECA), Annual Report 2006–2007, 2008, available at: http://www.eca.org.eg/ECA/upload/Publication/Attachment_A/15/annual%20report%20english.pdf.

[50] § 12 Executive Regulations.

[51] § 4 Protection of Competition and the Prohibition of Monopolistic Practices Law; § 7 Executive Regulations.

[52] § 13 Executive Regulations.

[53] Egyptian Competition Authority, Frequently Asked Questions, 2012, available at: http://www.eca.org.eg/ECA/StaticContent/View.aspx?ID=14.

The Law does not cover merger control, as is the case in many other African countries and also internationally.[54] However, amendments to the Law in 2008 included the provision that economic entities with an annual turnover that exceeds one hundred million Egyptian pounds are required to notify the Competition Authority upon their acquisition of assets, proprietary rights or shares; establishment of unions; mergers or amalgamations; or establishment of joint management of two or more enterprises, according to the rules and procedures set forth in the Executive Regulations.[55] This notification is to be submitted to the Authority within 30 days from the date of concluding the procedures of a merger or an acquisition.[56]

Exemptions to the provisions of Articles 6, 7, and 8 are contained in the Law. Private firms managing a public utility are eligible for a 2-year exemption period upon submission of a proposal requesting such an exemption to the Competition Authority. Exemptions may be granted when this would be in the public interest or when the benefits to consumers of the agreements, contracts or works of the company exceed the effects it has on restricting the freedom of competition.[57] In addition, the Law does not apply to any agreements concluded by the Government for the purpose of applying sale prices of one or more essential basic products as determined by a decree of the Cabinet of Ministers.[58] However, Egypt's competition law does not include a *de minimis* provision, which would mean that certain agreements are too small to do any real harm to competition and would therefore be exempted from the Law.[59]

The Egyptian Competition Authority (ECA), established under Article 11 of the Law, acts as a regulatory body in safeguarding a competitive environment and prohibiting monopolistic practices in the country.[60] Activities of the ECA include, among other things, receiving appeals for inquiry, inspection and investigation of violating agreements and practices; implementing appropriate fair actions in relation to anti-competitive agreements and practices based on the evidence obtained; coordinating with similar authorities in other countries on matters of common

---

[54] Trade-Related Assistance Centre, Competition Policy and Law in Egypt: Report on the Seminar, 2006, available at: http://www.amcham-egypt.org/Trac/reports/Competition_Law_Dec_2006.pdf.

[55] § 19 Protection of Competition and the Prohibition of Monopolistic Practices Law; §§ 44-45 Executive Regulations.

[56] Egyptian Competition Authority, Frequently Asked Questions, 2012, available at: http://www.eca.org.eg/ECA/StaticContent/View.aspx?ID=14.

[57] § 9 Protection of Competition and the Prohibition of Monopolistic Practices Law; § 15 Executive Regulations.

[58] § 10 Protection of Competition and the Prohibition of Monopolistic Practices Law; §§ 18-20 Executive Regulations.

[59] Abdel Latif/Ghoneim, Competition, Competition Policy and Economic Efficiency in the MENA Region: The Case of Egypt, International Development Research Centre, 2005, available at: http://idl-bnc.idrc.ca/dspace/bitstream/10625/26939/1/124654.pdf.

[60] Trade-Related Assistance Centre, Competition Policy and Law in Egypt: Report on the Seminar, 2006, available at: http://www.amcham-egypt.org/Trac/reports/Competition_Law_Dec_2006.pdf.

interest; and policy advocacy and public awareness.[61] Although the ECA was originally affiliated with the Prime Minister's office, the Authority is a fully independent body with powers separate from those of the Minister of Trade and Industry.[62] The Authority is managed by a Board of Directors that includes a Chairperson, a Counsellor from the State Council, representatives from the relevant ministries, specialists and experts, and members from various federations and unions.[63] The autonomy of the Authority derives from its decision-making process of the ECA Board, whose resolutions are passed by a majority vote from its 15 members.[64] The transparency of the ECA's operations is embodied in a regular publication covering the decisions and recommendations taken by the Authority, the procedures and measures it adopts, and related matters, as well as an annual report on the activities of the Authority and its future agenda.[65]

The procedures of inquiry, inspection and collection of information regarding potential anti-competitive agreements and practices or other breaches of the provisions of Articles 6, 7, and 8 of the Law are carried out in accordance with the provisions in the Executive Regulations.[66] Any person may notify the Authority of any violation of the provisions of the Law of which they are aware.[67] Upon establishing a breach of any of the Law's provisions, the ECA is required to order the violator to readjust his position and to redress the violation forthwith or within a period of time specified by the Board.[68] However, provision is made for the Board to allow violators to rectify their position before taking legal action against them.[69] The great advantage of this provision is that it promotes fuller cooperation between market players and the ECA.[70] The Executive Director of the ECA is required to notify the concerned person or persons of the decision taken by the Board regarding the complaint.[71]

The ECA is responsible for implementing penalties with respect to any violations of the Law. Sanctions in the Egyptian law are confined to fines: any entity found guilty of violating the provisions is punished by a fine of not less than one hundred thousand Egyptian pounds and not more than three hundred million

---

[61] § 11 Protection of Competition and the Prohibition of Monopolistic Practices Law.

[62] Authorised through Decree No. 571/2006 to exercise the Prime Minister's powers stipulated under the Law.

[63] § 12 Protection of Competition and the Prohibition of Monopolistic Practices Law.

[64] Trade-Related Assistance Centre, Competition Policy and Law in Egypt: Report on the Seminar, 2006, available at: http://www.amcham-egypt.org/Trac/reports/Competition_Law_Dec_2006.pdf.

[65] Trade-Related Assistance Centre, Competition Policy and Law in Egypt: Report on the Seminar, 2006, available at: http://www.amcham-egypt.org/Trac/reports/Competition_Law_Dec_2006.pdf.

[66] §§ 35-43 Executive Regulations.

[67] § 19 Protection of Competition and the Prohibition of Monopolistic Practices Law. The procedures for initiating such complaints are contained in §§ 31-32 Executive Regulations.

[68] § 20 Protection of Competition and the Prohibition of Monopolistic Practices Law.

[69] § 20 Protection of Competition and the Prohibition of Monopolistic Practices Law.

[70] Trade-Related Assistance Centre, Competition Policy and Law in Egypt: Report on the Seminar, 2006, available at: http://www.amcham-egypt.org/Trac/reports/Competition_Law_Dec_2006.pdf.

[71] § 43 Executive Regulations.

pounds.[72] Criminal lawsuits are not initiated in relation to acts violating the provisions of the Law unless a request by the Minister is presented.[73]

South Africa's Competition Policy

South Africa's first democratic elections were held in 1994, after which the new government embarked on a comprehensive policy review exercise. This economic policy review process included South Africa's competition law and policy. Competition law and policy had been adopted under the Apartheid regime; however, several shortcomings of the 1979 Maintenance and Promotion of Competition Act were noted; there were no provisions related to vertical or conglomerate configurations or ownership concentration. There were also no pre-merger notification requirements in the law and no explicit prohibitions. The final yardstick for competition decisions was the "public interest" that was not defined in the Act. The *ad hoc* and inconsistent decisions of the then Competition Board were thus not unexpected. The Competition Board was not independent; it could only make recommendations to the Minister of Trade and Industry. A regulation issued by the Minister of Trade and Industry in 1984 declared some practices *per se* unlawful. These included resale price maintenance, horizontal collusion on price, terms or market share and bid rigging. Despite this regulation, there were no prosecutions. It was clear to the new government that the 1979 Act did not provide for a robust competition regime.

Effective implementation of a strong competition policy was viewed as an important tool to regulate private enterprise, given that the African National Congress's policy of nationalisation had been abandoned by 1994. Specific goals of competition policy included the dilution of the concentration of economic power because this was detrimental to balanced economic development and the promotion of greater private sector efficiency.

Following a comprehensive policy process, which included debates within the National Economic Development and Labour Council (Nedlac), a new competition law, the Competition Act, no. 89 of 1998 was promulgated and became effective in September 1999.

The Competition Act provides for a robust institutional architecture for competition enforcement. Three agencies are provided for, to enforce and implement competition regulations. The Competition Commission, the Competition Tribunal, and the Competition Appeal Court have exclusive jurisdiction over competition matters.

The Competition Commission is the investigatory agency. It is an autonomous statutory body that monitors competition and market transparency by investigating

[72] § 22 Protection of Competition and the Prohibition of Monopolistic Practices Law.

[73] § 21 Protection of Competition and the Prohibition of Monopolistic Practices Law.

anti-competitive conduct.[74] It is empowered to investigate, control, and evaluate restrictive practices, abuse of dominant position, as well as mergers and acquisitions.[75] The Commission is independent from the Department of Trade and Industry and its decisions may be appealed to the Competition Tribunal and the Competition Appeal Court. This is very different from the situation of the previous Competition Board. The Competition Board, which existed until 1999, functioning under the Maintenance and Promotion of Competition Act of 1979, was basically an administrative body, within the Department of Trade and Industry.[76] The 1979 Act granted the Board extensive scope to investigate both mergers and restrictive practices.[77] However, with effective decision-making resting with the Minister, it was to be expected that political dictates would lead to challenges to credibility and consistency.

The Competition Tribunal is the adjudicatory body or court of first instance, adjudicating matters referred to it by the Commission or by a complainant who, under Section 51(3) and (4) of the Competition Act, can refer matters directly to the Tribunal, subject to the Tribunal's rules of procedure, after a decision of non-referral has been made by the Commission.[78] In brief, the key functions of the Tribunal are to grant exemptions, authorise or prohibit large mergers[79] and adjudicate prohibited practices and mergers under Chapters 2 and 3 of the Act respectively.[80] The Tribunal also acts as an appeal body for decisions of the Commission and may grant orders for costs on matters presented to it by the Commission.[81]

The Competition Appeal Court (CAC) may consider any appeal or review of a decision of the Tribunal. It may confirm, amend or set aside any decision or order and give any judgment or make any order that the circumstances require.

The Competition Act incorporates features that reflect South Africa's unique development challenges. In certain cases, it permits and requires consideration of public interest issues such as empowerment, employment, and impact on small and

---

[74] See Competition Act of the Republic of South Africa, 1998, Chapter 4.

[75] Competition Commission, Functions, available at: http://www.compcom.co.za/aboutus/aboutus_competition_commission_function.asp?level=3&child=2&desc=9.

[76] Republic of South Africa, Maintenance and Promotion of Competition Act 96 of 1979, available at: http://www.compcom.co.za/thelaw/thelaw_act_maintenance.asp?level=1&child=3.

[77] Republic of South Africa, Maintenance and Promotion of Competition Act 96 of 1979, available at: http://www.compcom.co.za/thelaw/thelaw_act_maintenance.asp?level=1&child=3.

[78] See Republic of South Africa Competition Tribunal, Case 72/CR/Dec03, *Nationwide Poles and Sasol (Oil) Pty Ltd*, 2005, available at: http://www.saflii.org/za/cases/ZACT/2005/17.pdf (describing a case of alleged price discrimination referred by a complainant to the Tribunal after a non-referral decision by the Commission.); see also Republic of South Africa Competition Appeal Court, Case 49/CAC/Apr05, *Sasol Oil (Pty) Ltd vs. Nationwide Poles CC*, 2005, available at: http://www.saflii.org/za/cases/ZACAC/2005/5.pdf (overturning the Competition Tribunal).

[79] The Commission has first-instance jurisdiction over smaller mergers. See Competition Act of the Republic of South Africa, 1998, Chapter 4, Sec. 21.

[80] Competition Act of the Republic of South Africa, 1998, Chapter 2 (Prohibited Practices), Chapter 3 (Merger Control).

[81] Competition Act of the Republic of South Africa, 1998, Chapter 4 (Part B).

medium enterprises. Although equity considerations are explicitly incorporated into South Africa's competition law, political channels as a means of appealing these issues, are not permitted. There is also no ministerial power to override the decisions of the competition agencies, as there had been previously. The competition institutions are independent.

The overall purpose of the Competition Act is to promote and maintain competition, in order

(a) to promote the efficiency, adaptability and development of the economy;
(b) to provide consumers with competitive prices and product choices;
(c) to promote employment and advance the social and economic welfare of South Africans;
(d) to expand opportunities for South African participation in world markets and recognise the role of foreign competition in the Republic;
(e) to ensure that small and medium-sized enterprises have an equitable opportunity to participate in the economy; and
(f) to promote a greater spread of ownership, in particular to increase the ownership stakes of historically disadvantaged persons.

Government of South Africa: Competition Act, No 89 of 1998

Development concerns also featured strongly in the debates on the role of competition policy in addressing both structural features of the economy, as well as corporate behaviour, especially of the large conglomerates.[82] The challenges of addressing poverty and unemployment were as much a part of the policy discussion as was the promotion of competition and economic efficiency.[83]

The Competition Act covers "all economic activity within, or having an effect within, the Republic," thus providing for extraterritorial jurisdictional coverage. The nature and scope of the extra-territorial reach was tested in a case involving the export of soda ash from the United States to Botswana.[84] Both Botswana and South Africa are members of the Southern African Customs Union (SACU) and implement a common external tariff.[85] Hence, imports into Botswana, for example, can be expected to have an effect within South Africa. It was argued in this case that the

---

[82] Lewis, The Objectives of Competition Law and Policy and the Optimal Design of a Competition Agency, presented at the OECD Global Forum on Competition, 10–11 February 2003, p. 4.

[83] Lewis, The Objectives of Competition Law and Policy and the Optimal Design of a Competition Agency, presented at the OECD Global Forum on Competition, 10–11 February 2003, p. 4.

[84] Republic of South Africa Competition Tribunal, Cases 49/CR/Apr00 and 87/CR/Sep00, *Competition Commission and Botswana Ash (Pty) Ltd*, 2001, available at: http://www.saflii.org/za/cases/ZACT/2001/46.pdf (ruling on the effect of an American export cartel of soda ash to Botswana).

[85] For more detail on the Southern African Customs Union, see the 2002 Customs Union Agreement, available at: http//www.tralac.org/scripts/content.php?id=3031.

exports of soda ash from the United States into Botswana were actually destined for the South African market.

In addition to the coverage of restrictive practices and abuse of a dominant position, South Africa's competition law makes provision for pre-merger notification and assessment of the impact of merger transactions. A merger (or acquisition) takes place when one or more firms directly or indirectly acquire or establish, directly or indirectly, control over the whole or part of the business or the whole firm. A merger may occur through the purchase or lease of assets, joint ventures and/or the amalgamation of the businesses. Pre-merger notification is required for intermediate and large mergers (thresholds for these categories are determined periodically). Included in the scope of the merger-notification provisions is foreign direct investment (FDI).

In light of the surge in FDI through mergers and acquisitions in recent years, the impact of cross-border mergers and acquisitions (M&As)—as opposed to green-field FDI—on host economies has raised some concern. In some cases, M&As can be used to deliberately reduce or eliminate competition altogether. The impact on domestic competition is arguably the most common concern regarding cross-border M&As. The sheer size of some of the multinational firms involved, and their large share of global markets, raises fears about growing international oligopolies and market power.[86] Many of these concerns were recently highlighted in the landmark merger between US-based Walmart and South Africa's Massmart. It is clear that effective competition policy is vital to the management of FDI, through M&As in particular as well as more generally.[87] In addition, this merger highlights the importance of international trade obligations, a clear case of managing a very tricky policy interface, in the context of specific domestic development imperatives. The implications of both international agreements and domestic policy and laws for policy space, and policy coherence are important lessons from this transaction. South Africa had extensively liberalised the distribution services sector in the context of the General Agreement on Trade in Services in the WTO; this meant that the competition commission and the competition tribunal could not impose strict conditions on the merging parties related to product sourcing for example. Concerns had been raised in the merger hearings regarding the impact of the global sourcing strategy that Walmart uses, which could result in more imports and hence adversely affect domestic producers. The conditional approval of the merger by the Competition Tribunal was appealed by three government ministers and a trade union. The Competition Appeal Court delivered its judgment on 9 March 2012,[88] upholding the approval of the merger, with any conditions pertaining to domestic sourcing of products.

---

[86] UNCTAD, 2000, op. cit.

[87] UNCTAD, 2000, op. cit.

[88] The decision of the Competition Appeal Court is available on the Competition Tribunal website at: http://www.comptrib.co.za.

A strategic decision was made in the early phase of the new competition regime to focus very strongly on merger review. This decision was deemed important to the development of expertise within the competition authority as well as to building the credibility of the authority and its institutions. Despite the fact that not many mergers were prohibited, it is arguable that the aim of building competence and the reputation of the authority was achieved. Recently, there has been a definite focus on restrictive practices, specifically cartel activities. This has been supplemented by the Corporate Leniency Programme,[89] in terms of which a cartel member may be granted lenience, subject to certain conditions, if it provides information on cartel activities to the competition authority. The concerted effort to eradicate restrictive practices and specifically cartel activities has met with some considerable success; resulting in serious fines for firms in a range of sectors including bread and telecommunications.

Regional Competition Regimes in Africa

Regional integration features in the development strategies of most African countries. This makes sense given the small markets, small economies and the specific geo-political configuration of African countries. The African continent is home to the largest number of least developed countries of all continents, and many are land-locked. Therefore, it can be argued that regional integration offers an opportunity to enhance market size and to address some of the competitiveness constraints that African countries face. The enthusiastic embrace of regional integration finds expression in membership of some times more than one regional economic community (REC). Most of the regional economic communities start with a commitment to establish a free trade area characterised by intra-regional trade liberalisation, they then aim to become a customs union with a common external tariff and a single customs territory. Many RECs aim to further integrate to become a common market, then to establish a monetary union and eventually a political union.

These integration ambitions are also enshrined at the continental level by the African Union (AU), to establish an African Economic Community (AEC). Eight RECs have been recognised by the AU to serve as building blocks to achieve the AEC.[90] These are the Southern African Development Community (SADC), the

[89] Details of the corporate leniency programme and application forms for the programme are available on the Competition Commission website at: http://www.compcom.co.za/corporate-leniency-policy.

[90] The RECs that have been identified as building blocks by the African Union for the AEC are the Southern African Development Community (SADC), the East Africa Community (EAC), the Common Market for East and Southern Africa (COMESA), the Economic Community of West African States (ECOWAS), the Intergovernmental Authority on Development (IGAD), the Economic Community of Central African States (ECCAS), the Community of Sahel-Saharan States (CEN-SAD) and Arab Maghreb Union (AMU).

East Africa Community (EAC), the Common Market for East and Southern Africa (COMESA), the Economic Community of West African States (ECOWAS), the Intergovernmental Authority on Development (IGAD), the Economic Community of Central African States (ECCAS), the Community of Sahel-Saharan States (CEN-SAD), and Arab Maghreb Union (AMU). In addition to these RECs there are also a number of others; the Southern African Customs Union (SACU) the Mano River Union (MRU), the Indian Ocean Commission (IOC), the West African Economic and Monetary Union (UEMOA) and the Central African Monetary and Economic Community (CEMAC).

Annex 6 of this paper provides a summary of the status of competition law and policy in the RECs. The current situation ranges widely; in some RECs there are provisions for cooperation[91] among Member States on competition law matters, while others have advanced to the establishment of a regional competition authority.

Cooperation provisions feature in the SACU[92] Agreement. SACU is the oldest functioning customs union in the world; it was established in 1910. South Africa is by far the largest and most-developed of the Member States with a diversified industrial base. The SACU Agreement of 2002 provides in Article 40 Part 8 that all Member States should have a competition policy and that they should cooperate in the enforcement of competition law and regulations. The modalities of cooperation are not specified. Currently South Africa, Namibia, Swaziland and Botswana have a competition policy, law and a competition authority. Only Lesotho has not yet drafted a law or established a competition authority. Article 41 of the SACU Agreement requires that policies and instruments to address unfair trade practices between Member States be developed. SACU has enlisted the assistance of UNCTAD to draft two annexes to the 2002 Customs Union Agreement to address unfair trade practices and to delineate mechanisms for cooperation among Member States on competition law and policy. This process is still underway.[93]

The Member States of SADC[94] signed a Declaration on Regional Cooperation in Competition and Consumer Policies in 2008. However, this has not been implemented. SADC launched a free trade area in August 2008. Implementation should have been complete by the beginning of 2012. However, several Member States have applied for derogations from their agreed tariff phase downs, and Mozambique had negotiated an extended time frame for implementation to 2015. SADC had aimed to be a customs union by 2010, but failed to meet this deadline. At this stage, the focus is very much on the full implementation of the free trade area.

---

[91] Competition matters are covered differently in the RECS; for example, this may be found in the Treaty or Agreement or in a Protocol on Trade or a separate legal instrument.

[92] South Africa, Botswana, Lesotho, Namibia and Swaziland are members of SACU.

[93] Information on the development of the Annexes is available on the SACU Secretariat's website at: http://www.sacu.int/policy.php?id=409.

[94] Angola, Botswana, Democratic Republic of the Congo, Lesotho, Namibia, Swaziland, Zambia, Zimbabwe, Tanzania, Malawi, Seychelles, Mauritius, and Mozambique are members of SADC. Madagascar is the fifteenth member, but currently suspended.

The Heads of State and Government of ECOWAS[95] adopted a Regional Competition Policy Framework (RCPF) in 2008, along with two Supplementary Acts (Supplementary Act No. A/SA.1/06/08 of 19 December 2008 and Supplementary Act No. A/SA.2/06/08 of 19 December 2008). The RCPF seeks to clarify the basic elements of a competition policy within the context of regional integration. The Supplementary Acts provide for the adoption of the Community Competition Rules and the modalities of their application within ECOWAS, and the establishment, functions and operation of the Regional Competition Authority (RCA). Both Supplementary Acts are annexed to the ECOWAS Treaty. The coverage of these instruments is broad, including:

- Agreements and concerted practices restraining trade
- Abuse of dominant position
- Mergers and acquisitions
- State aid
- Public enterprises
- Compensation for victims of anti-competitive practices
- Authorisations and exemptions

Although the groundwork for a regional competition policy has been laid, the ECOWAS Competition Policy has yet to be implemented. Steps to facilitate the full implementation of the RCPF are currently underway as the RCA is being established.

The most advanced REC on regional competition matters is COMESA.[96] The regional competition law (COMESA Competition Regulations 2004), was drafted in accordance with the provisions of Article 55 of the COMESA Treaty, which prohibits any practice that violates the objective of trade liberalisation, including any "agreement between undertakings or concerted practice which has as its objective or effect the prevention, restriction of distortion of competition within the Common Market."[97]

The COMESA Competition Regulations articulate the objectives of the regional competition law to address cross-border competition concerns, with the purpose "to promote and encourage competition by preventing restrictive business practices and other restrictions that deter the efficient operation of markets, thereby

[95] The Member States of ECOWAS are Benin, Burkina Faso, Cape Verde, Sierra Leone, Cameroon, Côte d'Ivoire, The Gambia, Ghana, Guinea, Guinea Bissau, Liberia, Mali, Niger, Nigeria, Senegal and Togo.

[96] Burundi, Comoros, the Democratic Republic of Congo, Djibouti, Eritrea, Ethiopia, Kenya, Libya, Madagascar, Mauritius, Rwanda, Seychelles, Sudan, Swaziland, Uganda, Zambia, Zimbabwe, the Republics of the Egypt and Malawi are members of COMESA.

[97] The COMESA Treaty is available on the COMESA website at: http://about.comesa.int/index.php?option=com_content&view=article&id=77&Itemid=116.

enhancing the welfare of the consumers in the Common Market."[98] A range of restrictive business practices are prohibited. These include:

- Price fixing agreements
- Collusive tendering and bid-rigging
- Market or customer allocation agreements
- Quota allocation of sales and production
- Concerted refusal to supply goods to services to a potential purchaser
- Collective denial of access to an arrangement or association that is crucial to competition.

Abuse of a dominant position is also prohibited, if it restricts or is likely to restrict entry into a market; prevents or deters any undertaking or is likely to deter any undertaking from engaging in competition in a market, directly or indirectly imposes unfair purchase or selling prices or other restrictive business practices; engages in any business activity that results in the exploitation of its customers or suppliers, to frustrate the benefits expected from the establishment of the Common Market. Merger control provisions aim to prohibit those mergers or acquisitions that are likely to substantially prevent or lessen competition in the Common Market.

The scope of application (Article 3 of the Regulations) provides that all activity within or having an effect within the Common Market shall be covered. This broad reach of the Regulations provides a regulatory framework to address competition matters within the Common Market, but also to deal with global mergers and international cartels. The COMESA Competition Commission[99] was launched in December 2008 and is due to begin operations early in 2012.

Promoting Cooperation for Better Competition Enforcement: Concluding Remarks

Competition policy in African countries varies considerably; ranging from countries that provide examples of best practice not only for developing countries, but also globally. However, there remains much to be done to ensure that competition governance permeates the African continent. Both global economic developments and Africa's own regional integration provide motivation for the

[98] The COMESA Competition Regulations are available at: http://www.tralac.org/wp-content/blogs.dir/12/files/2011/uploads/COMESACompetitionRegulations.pdf.

[99] The COMESA Competition Commission's website is http://www.comesacompetition.org. This portal provides information on the scope of regional competition matters as well as guides for business and consumers on accessing competition law in COMESA.

development of competition policy Africa. The particular structure of many of Africa's markets and economies; small markets, small economies, as well as the asymmetric size distribution of firms in many markets underscores the importance of effective competition governance. In the final analysis, the negative impact of restrictive practices on market outcomes and the development compromise that this entails, provides very strong motivation for competition policy to enhance market outcomes.

While to some extent there is evidence that competition law and policy development has advanced significantly in the past two decades, effective enforcement remains a challenge in many African countries. Effective enforcement of competition law and policy is dependent on many factors. An independent authority, unshackled by political interference, is important to safeguard the "rule of law" for market governance. Expertise within the competition authority is of course imperative; both legal and economic expertise is essential for competent investigations and assessments of the competition matter at hand, whether it be a merger review case or a restrictive practices case. As noted earlier, the development of a competition culture is an important component of effective enforcement. Appreciation of the benefits of competition and the pernicious effects of restrictive practices by a broad range of stakeholders will assist the competition authority by identifying competition matters. Cooperation among competition authorities can also assist in effective enforcement, through for example, the sharing of information. There is much to be gained through capacity building programmes by experienced African competition authorities for newly established authorities. This is already happening; the South African Competition Commission regularly hosts experts from other authorities. Practical experience on investigations and assessments are an important means of building capacity and developing good practice for effective enforcement.

An important development for building competence and strengthening enforcement, and developing a competition culture in Africa is the establishment of the African Competition Forum. Although this is not the first attempt at regional cooperation,[100] the establishment of this forum dedicated to discussing competition issues pertaining specifically to Africa is an important development.[101] The notion

[100] The South African competition authorities were instrumental in the establishment of the Southern and Eastern African Competition Forum (SEACF), involving Kenya, Malawi, Mauritius, Mozambique, Seychelles, Swaziland, Tanzania, Zambia, Zimbabwe and the Secretariats of SADC and COMESA. The objective of a SEACF in the SADC region is to create a coherent group of countries in the region to assist countries in the development of competition policies and establishment of competition agencies.

[101] CUTS Centre for Competition, Investment & Economic Regulation (CUTS CCIER), Broad-based support key to competition enforcement in Africa, ReguLetter 12 (2011) 1, p. 1, available online at: http://www.cuts-ccier.org/pdf/reguletter1-11.pdf.

of an African Competition Forum (ACF)[102] was first proposed by the UK's Department for International Development (DFID) in its 2009 White Paper[103] with the aim being to assist African countries to "identify and address obstacles to fair competition."[104] An Africa Stakeholder Workshop (ASW) was subsequently held in Nairobi, Kenya on 11–12 March 2010 to discuss the establishment of such a Forum. The ASW, organised by the DFID in collaboration with Kenya's Monopolies and Prices Commission (MPC), was attended by 34 officials from African competition authorities, regional and international organisations, consumer groups, and academia.[105] The establishment of an ACF was unanimously endorsed, and it was agreed that the Forum would be a primarily "virtual" organisation.[106] An Interim Steering Committee was set up with the task of drafting the organisation and governance structure, funding, and membership of the ACF; preparing a draft business and strategic plan to direct the ACF in the short-term (the first 3 to 5 years); and identifying and proposing projects and activities to be undertaken by the Forum.[107] Recognising the wide disparities that exist in the economic and social development of countries in Africa that would need to be taken into account in the

[102] The concept of a competition "Forum," as opposed to a "programme," brings with it the idea of something more visible, permanent, and dynamic, and perhaps a requirement for formal membership and related terms of reference. Such a forum would bring together various experiences, achievements, challenges, and competencies, and could provide a useful platform for the sharing of ideas and knowledge; refocusing the direction of a vision, mission, or strategic direction of participating members; as well as allowing for common research into competition law and policy reform issues. See Kaira, The possibility of establishing an Africa Competition Forum, Presentation prepared for the Workshop on Competition Law and Policy in African Small States, 26–27 July 2010.

[103] Department for International Development (DFID), Eliminating world poverty: Building our common future, White Paper Presented to Parliament by the Secretary of State for International Development, 2009.

[104] Department for International Development (DFID), Eliminating world poverty: Building our common future, White Paper Presented to Parliament by the Secretary of State for International Development, 2009, p. 34.

[105] Kaira, The possibility of establishing an Africa Competition Forum, Presentation prepared for the Workshop on Competition Law and Policy in African Small States, 26–27 July 2010; Small States Network for Economic Development (SSNED) and Namibian Competition Commission (NCC), Final Report. Prepared for the Workshop on Competition Law and Policy in African Small States: Small-Size Constraints, Institution Design and Regional Cooperation, 26–27 July 2010, Project ref: WK NMB 01, available at: http://www.ssned.org/file.aspx?f=539.

[106] Kaira, The possibility of establishing an Africa Competition Forum, Presentation prepared for the Workshop on Competition Law and Policy in African Small States, 26–27 July 2010; Small States Network for Economic Development (SSNED) and Namibian Competition Commission (NCC), Final Report. Prepared for the Workshop on Competition Law and Policy in African Small States: Small-Size Constraints, Institution Design and Regional Cooperation, 26–27 July 2010, Project ref: WK NMB 01, available at: http://www.ssned.org/file.aspx?f=539.

[107] Kaira, The possibility of establishing an Africa Competition Forum, Presentation prepared for the Workshop on Competition Law and Policy in African Small States, 26–27 July 2010.

design and activities of the ACF,[108] a first activity undertaken by the Committee was a needs assessment of the various African countries to establish the competition needs on the ground. Findings from this exercise[109] were shared at the first Conference of the ACF in early March 2011 in Nairobi, co-hosted by the MPC and the International Development Research Centre (IDRC) with support from the DFID. The ACF was officially launched at this conference on 3 March 2011.[110] The second meeting of the ACF was held during the 11th Organisation for Economic Cooperation and Development (OECD) Global Forum on Competition on 16–17 February 2012 in Paris, France.[111]

The ACF is envisaged to be "African driven" and to propagate members' specific concerns[112] by building capacity in competition agencies in the region while promoting awareness and appreciation of competition principles amongst government and other stakeholders in order to support the creation of strong competition regimes in Africa.[113] The ACF will facilitate the exchange of information, dissemination of knowledge and experience, building of staff and institutional capacity through provision of technical assistance, and undertaking of various studies and related programmes to promote the development and strengthening of competitive markets.[114] Specifically, the ACF aims to create awareness and build support for competition policy both within and outside of government (competition advocacy); strengthen implementation of competition policies by providing advice and building capacity; and encourage regional integration. In terms of the latter, the ACF seeks to facilitate cooperation and collaboration amongst various regional

---

[108] Kaira, The possibility of establishing an Africa Competition Forum, Presentation prepared for the Workshop on Competition Law and Policy in African Small States, 26–27 July 2010.

[109] The needs assessment report indicated that assistance required by African agencies would include strategic planning and management, practical aspects of competition law enforcement such as investigative and litigation skills and techniques, foundational training on the basics of competition law and economics, technical assistance in drafting competition policy, laws and regulations and in designing agency procedures, guidelines, and operational manuals, and advocacy and engagement with other stakeholders. It is cited in CUTS Centre for Competition, Investment & Economic Regulation, Broad-based support key to competition enforcement in Africa, ReguLetter 12 (2011) 1, p. 1, available online at: http://www.cuts-ccier.org/pdf/reguletter1-11.pdf.

[110] Competition Commission of South Africa, African Competition Forum launched in Nairobi, Press release of 8 March 2011, available at: http://www.compcom.co.za/assets/Uploads/AttachedFiles/MyDocuments/ACF-Launch-Conference-press-release-final.pdf.

[111] Remarks by Angel Gurría, OECD Secretary-General, at the opening of the eleventh meeting of the OECD Global Forum on Competition, Paris, 16–17 February 2012, available at: http://www.oecd.org/document/61/0,3746,en_21571361_44315115_49692733_1_1_1_1,00.html.

[112] Kaira, The possibility of establishing an Africa Competition Forum, Presentation prepared for the Workshop on Competition Law and Policy in African Small States, 26–27 July 2010.

[113] Competition Commission of South Africa, African Competition Forum launched in Nairobi, Press release of 8 March 2011, available at: http://www.compcom.co.za/assets/Uploads/AttachedFiles/MyDocuments/ACF-Launch-Conference-press-release-final.pdf.

[114] Kaira, The possibility of establishing an Africa Competition Forum, Presentation prepared for the Workshop on Competition Law and Policy in African Small States, 26–27 July 2010.

organisations as well as enhance participation of member countries in international forums "to represent and put forward 'African' points of view."[115] To distinguish the ACF from other such Forums, priority would be given to addressing issues impacting on poverty and economic development in African countries rather than focusing on competition law and policy per se, thereby giving due recognition to other national socio-economic priorities facing governments.[116] In light of the above, the flagship objective of the ACF can be summarised as follows:

> [To] promote the adoption of competition principles in the implementation of national and regional economic policies of African countries, in order to alleviate poverty and enhance inclusive economic growth, development and consumer welfare by fostering competition in markets, and thereby increasing investment, productivity, innovation and entrepreneurship.[117]

The establishment of the ACF marks a milestone in competition management in Africa by providing a platform for mobilising and harnessing experiences and ideas in competition regulation, which is necessary for improving the organisation of competition policy and law in the continent and thereby deepen the gains to be made from local, regional, and international liberalised markets and reduce poverty.[118] As the ACF rolls out its activities, it becomes critical, however, to identify which programmes and initiatives would really be of benefit to African countries and their consumers.[119] Strong leadership and continued funding will be needed in order for the initiative to be a success.[120]

---

[115] Kaira, The possibility of establishing an Africa Competition Forum, Presentation prepared for the Workshop on Competition Law and Policy in African Small States, 26–27 July 2010.

[116] Kaira, The possibility of establishing an Africa Competition Forum, Presentation prepared for the Workshop on Competition Law and Policy in African Small States, 26–27 July 2010.

[117] Competition Commission of South Africa, African Competition Forum launched in Nairobi, Press release of 8 March 2011, available at: http://www.compcom.co.za/assets/Uploads/AttachedFiles/MyDocuments/ACF-Launch-Conference-press-release-final.pdf. p. 1.

[118] Competition Commission of South Africa, African Competition Forum launched in Nairobi, Press release of 8 March 2011, available at: http://www.compcom.co.za/assets/Uploads/AttachedFiles/MyDocuments/ACF-Launch-Conference-press-release-final.pdf. p. 1, as stated by Uhuru Kenyatta, Kenyan Deputy Prime Minister and Minister of Finance.

[119] CUTS Centre for Competition, Investment & Economic Regulation, Broad-based support key to competition enforcement in Africa, ReguLetter 12 (2011) 1, p. 1, available online at: http://www.cuts-ccier.org/pdf/reguletter1-11.pdf.

[120] Bakhoum, A dual language in modern competition law? Efficiency approach versus development approach and implications for developing countries, World Competition 34 (2011) 3, p. 495.

Annex 1. Competition Laws in Southern Africa

	Overview	Competition legislation	Issues covered	Competition authorities
SOUTHERN AFRICA				
Angola	In the early stages of adopting a competition law. A Competition Bill was drafted in 2004.			
Botswana	A National Competition Policy was prepared by the Ministry of Trade and Industry in July 2005 as a stepping stone towards the formulation of a competition law for the country. Although the Competition Act was passed by Parliament in December 2009, establishing the Commission and the Competition Authority, some 2 years passed until October 2011, before regulations were passed in terms of the Act.	Competition Act, No. 17 of 2009	– Competition Authority and Commission – Control of restrictive agreements and dominant position – Investigation of horizontal and vertical agreements – Determination of cases, penalties and remedies – Market inquiries – Merger control – Appeals	Botswana Competition Authority, launched January 2012
Comoros	There is currently no competition law in place. However, the Commercial Code of 1984 states that "trade is carried on the principle of free competition."			
Lesotho	There is currently no competition law or authority. However, with the help of UNCTAD, a draft Competition Bill was presented to stakeholders and Government in 2009. Consultations are ongoing.			

(continued)

Annex 1. (continued)

	Overview	Competition legislation	Issues covered	Competition authorities
SOUTHERN AFRICA				
Madagascar	A regulatory framework for competition was adopted in 2005 with the promulgation of the Law on Competition and the Malagasy Commission in October 2005. Madagascar is in the process of establishing a Competition Council.	Law No. 2005-020 on Competition	– Fair competition – Obligation of transparency – Anti-competitive practices – Institutional framework – Competition offences	
Malawi	Government adopted a Competition Policy in September 1997, following which the Competition and Fair Trading Act was passed and entered into force in 2000. The Malawi Competition and Fair Trade Commission, entrusted with the responsibility to implement the national competition law, has been operational since 2005, but administration is still weak.	Competition Policy for Malawi, 1997 Competition and Fair Trading Act, No. 43 of 1998	– Competition and Fair Trade Commission – Anti-competitive trade practices, including merger control	Competition and Fair Trade Commission, established in 2005
Mauritius	Competition law was introduced with the promulgation of the Competition Act of 2007 on 24 October 2008 (Parts I and II). The Act established the legal framework for the control of restrictive business practices. The Competition Commission established by the Act became operational in 2009.	Competition Act, No. 25 of 2007	– Competition Commission – Restrictive business practices – Investigations – Penalties and remedies – Appeals	Competition Commission of Mauritius, established in 2009 Website: http://www.gov.mu/portal/sites/ccm/index.htm

Mozambique	Government approved a national Competition Policy in July 2007, although the regulatory framework is still in discussion and development.	Competition Policy, published in BR no. 45, 12 November 2007, 1st grade, 3rd Supplement		
Namibia	Regulation of competition issues was introduced in 2003 through the Competition Act. The Act resembles in many aspects the South African Competition Law enacted in 1998, as the inspiration flowed from models and patterns of the latter. The Namibian Competition Commission was formally launched on 9 December 2009, and is the principal organ promoting competition in the market.	Competition Act, No. 2 of 2003	– Namibian Competition Commission – Restrictive business practices – Mergers – Offences and penalties	Namibian Competition Commission, launched in 2009 Website: http://www.mti.gov.na/ncc.htm
Seychelles	Competition laws were enacted in late 2009. The Fair Competition Act was enacted in November 2009 and came into operation on 5 April 2010. The Fair Trading Commission Act of 2009 was also enacted to create the Fair Trading Commission, which is vested with investigative and other enforcement powers as well as an educational and advisory role in relation to fair competition laws and practices.	Fair Competition Act, No. 18 of 2009 Fair Trading Commission Act, No. 17 of 2009	– Fair Trading Commission – Restrictive business practices – Investigation by and hearing before Commission – Assessment of restrictive business practice – Determination of cases by Commission, penalties and remedies – Appeals	Seychelles Fair Trading Commission, established in 2009 Website: http://www.ftc.sc/
South Africa	A well-developed and regulated competition regime based on best international practice is in place. Following the advent of democracy, the Competition Act was passed in 1998 and entered into force on 1 September 1999. The Act made	Competition Act, No. 89 of 1998 Competition Amendment Act, No. 1 of 2009	– Prohibited practices – Merger control – Competition Commission, Tribunal and Court – Investigation and adjudication procedures	Competition Commission of South Africa, launched in 1998 Website: http://www.compcom.co.za Competition Tribunal of South Africa, launched in 1998

(continued)

Annex 1. (continued)

	Overview	Competition legislation	Issues covered	Competition authorities
SOUTHERN AFRICA				
	provisions for the establishment of three enforcement agencies: the Competition Commission, the Competition Tribunal, and the Competition Appeal Court. The Competition Amendment Act was signed in August 2009.		– Enforcement – Offences	Website: http://www.comptrib.co.za/
Swaziland	An incipient structure for competition policy was contained the Fair Trading Act of 2001. Later, a dedicated competition law was passed by Government in 2007, through which the Swaziland Competition Commission was established.	Fair Trading Act, 2001 The Competition Act, No. 8 of 2007	– Competition Commission – Anti-competitive trade practices	Swaziland Competition Commission, established in 2007 Website: http://www.compco.co.sz/
Zambia	Competition legislation was introduced in 1994 with the Competition and Fair Trading Act. The Zambia Competition Commission (ZCC) was established in 1997. In 2010, the Competition and Consumer Protection Act was signed into law, thereby repealing the Act of 1994 and re-naming the ZCC the Competition and Consumer Protection Commission.	Competition and Consumer Protection Act, No. 24 of 2010	– Restrictive business and anti-competitive trade practices – Mergers – Market inquiries – Sector regulated activities – Consumer protection – Investigations and decisions by the Commission – Competition and Consumer Protection Commission and Tribunal	Competition and Consumer Protection Commission (formerly Zambia Competition Commission), established in 1997 Website: http://www.ccpc.org.zm/

Zimbabwe	A competition policy and law was formally adopted in 1996 with the enactment of the Competition Act [Chapter 14:28]. However, the Act only came into operation in 1998, the same year that the Competition Agency was established to implement it. In 2001, the Act was amended, and the Industry and Trade Competition Commission and Tariff Commission were merged to form the Competition and Tariff Commission.	Competition Act, No. 7 of 1996, as amended by the Competition Amendment Act, No. 29 of 2001	– Competition and Tariff Commission – Investigation and prevention of restrictive practices, mergers and monopoly situations – Investigation of tariff charges and related unfair trade practices – Authorisation of restrictive practices, mergers and other conduct – Appeals	Competition and Tariff Commission, launched in 2002

Annex 2. Competition Regimes in East Africa

EAST AFRICA				
Burundi	A Bill on a Legal Regime on Competition was passed in 2010. The application of the Competition Law is subject to the establishment of a Competition Commission; this is not yet in place. At this stage, there are no competition regulations.	Law No. 1/06 of 25 March 2010, regarding the Legal Regime on Competition	– Unfair competition – Anti-competitive practices – Regulation of prices and invoices – Commercial information – Hindrances to free competition – Repressive procedure of infringements	
Comoros	There is no competition law in place. However, the Commercial Code of 1984 states that "trade is carried on the principle of free competition."			
Djibouti	Government plans to draft a law on competition, but at present the relevant national technical competence is lacking. The Commercial Chamber of the Court of First Instance rules on competition disputes on a case-by-case basis.			
Eritrea	There is currently no competition law/policy enforced.			
Ethiopia	Government pledged its commitment to enforce free market economic policy with the passing of the Trade Practices Proclamation in	Trade Practice and Consumer Protection Proclamation, No. 685 of 2010	– Anti-competitive trade practices, including regulation of mergers and unfair competition – Protection of consumers	Trade Practice and Consumers Protection Authority, forthcoming

	2003. This was later repealed when the Trade Practice and Consumer Protection Proclamation was passed in 2010 in an effort to increase the effectiveness of the regulating authority and overall consumer protection. The Government is currently in the process of establishing a new body, the Trade Practice and Consumers Protection Authority (TPCPA).		– Trade Practice and Consumers Protection Authority – Instituting of actions and conducting investigations	
Kenya	Competition law is enshrined in the Competition Act of 2009 that came into force in July 2011. The Act replaced the Restrictive Trade Practices, Monopolies and Price Control Act of 1989. The Act has expanded the scope of enforcement in Kenya through adoption of international best practices.	Competition Act, 2009, CAP. 504	– Establishment of the Powers and functions of the Competition Authority – Restrictive trade practices – Mergers – Control of unwarranted concentration of economic power – Consumer welfare – Establishment and Powers of the Competition Tribunal	Competition Authority of Kenya, established in 2011 Website: http://www.cak.go.ke/
Rwanda	First steps towards specific legislation governing competition were made in December 2008 when a Competition and Consumer Protection Policy was drafted. This was later published in final version in September 2010. The Competition and Consumer Protection Bill was passed by Government in November 2011.	Competition and Consumer Protection Bill, 2009	– Anti-competitive practices – Mergers – Consumer protection – Criminal provisions	

(continued)

Annex 2. (continued)

EAST AFRICA				
	The legislation, among other things, prescribes punitive measures for any company that violates consumers' rights or abuses competition principles.			
Somalia	Although no competition laws are in place, there have been recent calls for sub-national reforms to improve competition and safeguard against anti-competitive practices. Progress in this regard has yet to be made.			
Sudan	Efforts have been made in recent years to adopt competition laws as part of several economic and structural reforms. A competition law is in place, and competition regulations were drafted in 2010. No competition authority has been established. Note: Since the referendum in 2011,	The Competition (Organisation) and Monopoly (Prevention) Law, 2008	– Restrictive practices – Merger control	
Tanzania	Competition policy was introduced in 1994 with the adoption of the Fair Trade Practices Act. This was repealed by the Fair Competition Act of 2003, which entered into force on 12 May 2004. The 2003 Act has strengthened competition	Fair Competition Act, No. 8 of 2003	– Restrictive trade practices – Misleading and deceptive conduct – Unfair business practices – Unconscionable conduct – Implied conditions in consumer contracts – Offences, penalties and remedies	Fair Competition Commission, launched in 2004 Website: http://www.competition.or.tz/ Fair Competition Tribunal, operational since 2005

	law in Tanzania, in particular by establishing the Fair Competition Commission and the Fair Competition Tribunal.		– Fair Competition Commission – Fair Competition Tribunal – National Consumer Advocacy Council	Website: http://www.fct.or.tz/
Uganda	Although there is no competition law at present, Government drafted a Competition Bill in 2004. The Bill calls for the establishment of a Competition Commission for Uganda. The Draft bill was tabled to Parliament and returned with a request to draft a policy to accompany the law. Uganda is now developing a National Competition and Consumer Protection policy. The policy will bridge the gap between competition and consumer protection.	Draft Competition Bill, 2004	– Competition Commission of Uganda – Offences and penalties – Prohibition of anti-competitive agreements – Prohibition against abuse of dominant position – Regulation of combinations, including mergers and acquisitions – Competition advocacy	

Annex 3. Competition Regimes in Central Africa

CENTRAL AFRICA				
Cameroon	Competition legislation was introduced in 1998. The Competition Law calls for the establishment of a National Competition Commission to ensure the enforcement of competition policy in the country.	Act on Competition, Law No. 98/013 of 14 July 1998	– Anti-competitive agreements – Abuse of a business or group of dominant firms on the market – Mergers and acquisitions – The National Commission of Competition – Offences and penalties	National Competition Commission, forthcoming
Central African Republic	In the absence of a comprehensive competition policy, the current regulatory framework for competition dates from 1992. This Law covers free pricing and its limits; some anti-competitive practices; the rules governing commercial transactions (with a view to protecting consumers); and the suppression of economic fraud. In 2006, this framework was supplemented, in particular by strengthening the definition of anti-competitive practices and the penalties for the offences covered by the law.	Act No. 92.002 of 26 May 1992, bearing on Price Liberalisation and Competition Regulation Decree No 06.229, laying down rules for implementing certain provisions of Law No. 92.002 of May 26, 1992	– Price freedom – Anti-competitive practices – Transparency and restrictive practices – Repression of fraud – Organisation of supervision – Penalties – Offences and sanctions	
Chad	At present, there are no national regulations on competition. A draft law on competition was drawn up by the Ministry of Commerce, Industry			

	and Handicrafts in 2002 to fill this legislative gap but has still to be adopted. A Directorate for Competition and Price Control has been established within the Ministry to assist in the management of competition.			
Democratic Republic of Congo	There is no formal law on competition, although efforts to regulate it have been made since 1950. A Competition Commission was established in theory in 1987, although it is not yet operational.	Legislative Ordinance No. 41-63 of 24 February 1950, on the Suppression of Unfair Competition Departmental Order No. DENI/CAB/06/013/87 of 26 May 1987, on the Establishment and Operation of the Competition Commission		Competition Commission, to begin operations
Congo	No comprehensive competition policy exists, although some aspects are covered by the current regulatory framework that dates from 1994. This law covers pricing regimes for products, goods and services; market transparency; anti-competitive practices (although these provisions have not yet been implemented); trading standards; stockholding; and the investigation and repression of fraud. Consumer protection is also one of the objectives of the law.	Act No. 6-94 of 1 June 1994, regulating Prices, Trading Standards, Finding and Fraud	– Price regulations – Advertising prices and market transparency – Anti-competitive practices – Commercial standards and possession of stocks – Investigation and repression of fraud and other offences – Sanctions and penalties	
Equatorial Guinea	A competition law is currently being developed although nothing is yet in place.			

(continued)

Annex 3. (continued)

CENTRAL AFRICA			
Gabon	The competition regime was established in 1998 and has not changed since then. The law prohibits anti-competitive practices such as unlawful understandings or abuse of a dominant market position, and certain trade practices, including dumping. However, the planned Competition Commission has not yet been set up, and the regulatory framework is therefore not in effect.	Law No. 14/98 of 23 July 1998, fixing the Regime of Competition in Gabon	– Freedom of prices and exchanges – Anti-competitive practices – Transparency and commercial transactions – Regulation and economic concentration – Repression of obstacles to the freedom of competition

Annex 4. Competition Regimes in West Africa

WEST AFRICA				
Benin	A Draft law on competition is presently being finalised that will cover anti-competitive practices and consumer protection and provide for the creation of a national Competition Council. The Draft competition law was considered by the Commission of Legislation and Consolidation at its meeting in July 2011 before being submitted to the Supreme Court for comment.			
Burkina Faso	The regulatory framework for competition policy has not changed since 2001. This legislation aims to ensure fair and healthy competition in the market, ensure consumer protection, and consolidate the common market UEMOA. The National Commission on Competition and Consumption (CNCC) was established in 1984 and became operational on 1 August 1998.	Act No. 033-2001/ANamending the LawNo. 15/84/ADP of May 5, 1994, on the Organisation of Competition in Burkina Faso	– Price freedom and rules in Competition Law – National Commission of Competition and Consumption – Agreements and abuses of dominance – Market transparency practices restrictive of competition – Illegal competition practices, including procedures and penalties	National Commission of Competition and Consumption (*Commission nationale de la concurrence et de la consummation*), operational since 1998

(continued)

Annex 4. (continued)

WEST AFRICA				
Cape Verde	Competition has been regulated since 2003. A Competition Advisory Council, an independent quasi-judicial government entity, has been created although is not yet operational. The Council's primary function would be to adjudicate unfair trade claims, but it would also propose draft legislation to Government. Decisions of the Council would be appealed to the courts.	Decree-Law No. 53/2003 of 24 November 2003, on Competition	– Competition rules, including prohibited practices – Enforcement of competition, including the Competition Council – Process, including procedures related to prohibited practices and mergers – Offences and penalties	Competition Advisory Council, forthcoming
Côte d'Ivoire	The Competition Act was passed in 1991 and amended in 1997. Two bodies are responsible for implementing competition policy: the Competition Commission, operational since January 1994; and the Department of Competition created by decree of the Council of Ministers.	Act No. 97-10 of 6 January 1997, amending Act No. 91-999 of 27 December 1991, on Competition	– Price freedom and trade – Competition Commission – Anti-competitive and restrictive business practices – Information on price and conditions of sale – Concentration and mergers – Common provisions	The Competition Commission, operational since 1994
Gambia	Consultations on a proposed competition law were launched in 2001, although the Competition Act was only	Competition Act, No. 4 of 2007	– The Competition Commission – Restrictive business practices	Gambia Competition Commission, established in 2008 Website: http://www.gcc.gm/

	passed in October 2007. The overall objective of the Act is to foster a viable competition culture that favours investment, fair trade, growth, and poverty reduction.		– Investigation by or on behalf of the Commission – Penalties and remedies – Appeals	
Ghana	In September 2000, a Competition Bill was presented to Parliament although this is yet to be enacted into law. The Bill sought, among others things, to establish a Commission that would ensure fair competition in trade practices, as well as a Trade Practices Court. Government has embarked on the process of developing a new Competition Bill. To deal with unfair business practices in particular, an Act was passed in 2000.	Competition and Fair Trade Practices Bill, 2000 Protection against Unfair Competition Act, No. 589 of 2000	– Regulation of restrictive trade practices – Mergers and acquisitions – Unfair trade practices – Competition Commission and Trade Practices Court – Consumer protection	Ghana Competition Commission, forthcoming
Guinea	The regulatory framework for competition and pricing was developed in 1994. In September 2004, a Standing Consultative Committee on Competition and Prices (CCPCP) was established, although this is barely operational. The National Competition and Prices	Law No. L/94/40/CTRN of 28 December 1994, and Decree No. D/94/119/PRG/SGG		Standing Consultative Committee on Competition and Prices, established in 2004

(continued)

Annex 4. (continued)

WEST AFRICA				
	Observatory (ONCP), within the National Trade and Competition Directorate, oversees the application of free competition and related legal texts.			
Guinea-Bissau	There is currently no competition law in place although steps have been taken towards the drafting of relevant laws and policies with the help of UNCTAD.			
Liberia	There is currently no competition law.			
Mali	The competition regime was established through a Government Ordinance in 1992, which entered into force in 1998. The National Competition Council (CNC) was established in 1999 in order to develop and enforce regulations related to trade and competition, among other things. The CNC also gives its opinion on matters related to price controls and business concentration. The Ordinance was replaced in 2007.	Ordinance No. 07-025/P-RM DU of July 18, 2007, on the Organisation of Competition	– Unfair competition – Information and consumer protection – Community anti-competitive practices – National Competition Council	National Competition Council (*Conseil National de la Concurrence*), established in 1999

Niger	No dedicated domestic regime dealing with anti-competitive practices exists. However, a basic text on competition and prices was passed in 1992 that aims to protect consumers and ensure fair competition between traders, manufacturers and service providers. A Bill on Freedom of Pricing, Competition and Consumer Protection has been proposed.	Ordinance No. 92-025 of 7 July 1992		
Nigeria	The Federal Government is yet to adopt a competition law for the country. Several efforts have been made since 2002 to adopt legislation, although such attempts have never been successful. Some of the efforts are indicated to the right.	Federal Competition Bill, 2002 Competition (Antitrust) Bill, 2007 Nigerian Trade and Competition Commission Bill, 2008 Federal Competition and Consumer Protection Bill, 2009		
Sao Tome & Principe	A draft Competition Bill is being prepared in order to introduce competition law into the country.			
Senegal	The regulatory framework for competition and price control was most recently revised in 1994. The Law on Prices, Competition and Economic Litigation brought about price liberalisation and market	Law No. 94-63 of 22 August 1994, on Prices, Competition and Economic Disputes, and various Decrees of application	– Competition Commission – Anti-competitive practices – Price regulations – Offences and seizures – Powers and duties of officers	National Competition Commission, established in 1994

(continued)

Annex 4. (continued)

WEST AFRICA	
	forces. The Law established the National Competition Commission to regulate market practices. The Ministry of Commerce shares jurisdiction for enforcing competition law. However, at present, the competition law has not been effectively enforced.
Sierra Leone	No domestic legislation on competition currently exists, although the Ministry of Trade and Industry has undertaken to develop a Competition Policy and Law that will promote competition in the market by ensuring a level playing field for all actors, limiting anti-competitive behaviour, promoting the efficient use of resources, and encouraging innovation, in turn improving quality of products and consumer welfare.

Togo	The regulatory framework for competition policy was amended in 1999 when a law was passed on the Freedom of Prices and Applicable Rules of Competition. The law covers some aspects of competition and provides for free pricing, as well as consumer protection.	Law No. 99-012 of 28 December 1999, and Decrees No. 2001-207/PR and No. 2001-208/PR of 16 December 2001	– Freedom of prices – Information on prices and conditions of sale – National Commission for Competition and Consumer Protection – Agreements and abuse of dominance – Market transparency and restrictive competition practices – Illicit competition practices and penalties

Annex 5. Competition Regimes in North Africa

NORTH AFRICA				
Algeria	Regulations on competition were first introduced in 1989, and were later repealed by an Ordinance in 1995. The Ordinance set out regulations and mechanisms for competition as an economic policy instrument. It also established a competition authority responsible for enforcing compliance with competition regulations and market transparency. A new Ordinance was added to the legislation on competition and came into force in July 2003.	Ordinance No. 03-03 of July 19, 2003, on Competition Law No. 10-05 of August 15, 2010, amending and supplementing Ordinance No. 03-03 of July 19, 2003	– Price freedom – Restrictive competition practices – Economic concentrations – The Competition Council – Sanctions – Appeals	Competition Council, established in 2003 but currently inactive
Egypt	In February 2005, the People's Assembly adopted Egypt's first comprehensive Competition Law that concerns the protection of competition and the prohibition of monopolistic practices. The Law provided for the establishment of a Competition Agency, which would have the right to receive and investigate complaints, initiate its own investigations, and take decisions and necessary steps to stop anti-competitive practices. Following adoption of the law, a set of Executive Regulations was issued. The Competition Law was amended in June 2008, following which the Executive Regulations were	Law No. 3 of 2005,on the Protection of Competition and the Prohibition of Monopolistic Practices, as amended by Laws No. 190 and 193 of 2008 Decree No. 1316 of 2005, issuing the Executive Regulations of Protection of Competition and Prohibition of Monopolistic Practices Law No. 3 of 2005, as amended by Decree No. 2957 of 2010	– Agreements and contracts – Anti-competitive and restrictive business practices, including abuse of dominant position – The Authority for the Protection of Competition and the Prohibition of Monopolistic Practices – Filing complaints and the procedures of inquiry, inspection, collection of information and receiving notifications	Egyptian Competition Authority, operational since 2006 Website: http://www.eca.org.eg/ECA/default.aspx

	amended in November 2010. In late 2011, the Cabinet approved further amendments to the Competition Law.		– Penalties and sanctions – Exemptions	
Libya	Steps have been taken to introduce a national Competition Law and establish a Competition Authority, but do not exist yet.			
Mauritania	Regulation on free prices and competition dates back to 1991, although this law was replaced in 2000 by a Code of Commerce that contains a number of rules relating to these matters. The Code prohibits anti-competitive practices and sanctions are in place. However, there is no vision or plan defining a clear approach to scoping competition policy. By-laws have to be developed for the implementation of the Code's principles. In the absence of a strong, independent Competition Agency, the enforcement of the competition law and policy advocacy actions are limited.	Law No. 2000-05 on The Code of Commerce, Book V: Award of Freedom and Competition	– Freedom of pricing – Transparency and open market operations – Anti-competitive practices	
Morocco	Competition policy and price controls have been governed by law since 2001. The Law defines the rules for protection of competition to boost economic efficiency and improve the welfare of consumers. It also aims to ensure transparency and fairness in trade relations. A Competition Council was established, initially with a purely advisory role. However, with the new constitution, the Council has been raised to the rank of an independent	Law No. 06-99 on Free Pricing and Competition (promulgated by Dahir No. **1-00-225** of 5 June 2000), implemented by Decree No. 2-00-854 of 17 September 2001	– Freedom awards – Anti-competitive practices – Operations of economic concentration – The Competition Council – Restrictive competition practices – Investigations and sanctions	National Competition Council, operational since 2008 Website: http://conseil-concurrence.ma/

(continued)

Annex 5. (continued)

NORTH AFRICA				
	constitutional authority with extended prerogatives. A Draft Bill of amendment has been submitted to Government to recognise this new situation.			
Tunisia	After its enactment in 1991, the national law on competition has been amended several times, most recently in 2005. The Competition Law lays down the rules of transparency and smooth operation of the market, and prohibits any behaviour that distorts competition. The Law also provides for the supervision of mergers. The Competition Council was established in 1995, replacing the Competition Board.	Law No. 91-64 of July 29, 1991, on Competition and Prices As amended and completed by Law No. 93-83 of 1993, Law No. 95-42 of 1995, Law No. 99-41 of 1999, Law No. 2003-74 of 2003, Law No. 2005-60 of 2005, and Decree No. 1215 of 1995	– Freedom of pricing – Competition and anti-competitive practices – The Competition Commission – Transparency of prices and restrictive practices – Special provisions for property products and services not subject to the regime of freedom of prices – Offences and sanctions – Procedures and transaction tracking	Competition Council (*Conseil de la Concurrence*), established in 1995

Annex 6. Status of Competition Legislation in Regional Economic Communities in Africa

	Overview	Competition legislation	Issues covered	Competition authorities
Southern African Development Community (SADC)	The SADC Declaration on Regional Cooperation in Competition and Consumer Policies was adopted by Trade Ministers in 2008 and subsequently signed by SADC Heads of State and Government in 2009. The Declaration was based on Article 25 of the SADC Protocol on Trade, which calls for Member States to *implement measures within the Community that prohibit unfair business practices and promote competition*. The Declaration provides for a cooperation framework in the application of member States' respective national competition laws. It is the instrument currently in place to facilitate the investigation and elimination of anti-competitive practices that have cross-border effects.	SADC Declaration on Regional Cooperation in Competition Law and Consumer Policies, 2009	– Effective cooperation on competition and consumer protection laws – The Competition and Consumer Policy and Law Committee – Functions of the Secretariat	
Southern African Customs Union (SACU)	In 2004, an UNCTAD document was prepared entitled "The Southern African Custom Union Regional Cooperation Framework on Competition Policy and Unfair Trade Practices." The report provides an analysis of the legal provisions in the			

(continued)

Annex 6. (continued)

	Overview	Competition legislation	Issues covered	Competition authorities
	2002 SACU Agreement relating to regional cooperation on competition policy (Article 40) and anti-competitive and unfair trade practices (Article 41). The SACU Treaty does not, however, provide for a common and binding SACU Competition Law. Nevertheless, draft annexes to the 2002 SACU Agreement on Unfair Trade Practices and Cooperating Mechanisms on Competition Policy, Competition Law and Regulations are currently being finalised.			
East African Community (EAC)	The East African Competition Policy was adopted by the Council of Ministers in 2004. Subsequently, the East African Legislative Assembly adopted the EAC Competition Act in 2006. The Act seeks to promote and protect fair competition in the Community through, among other things, prohibiting anti-competitive practices; enhancing consumer welfare; guaranteeing equal opportunities and a level playing field for all market participants in the Community; and establishing the East African Community Competition Authority. The Act is applicable to all economic activities and sectors having cross	The East African Community Competition Act, 2006 The East African Community Competition Regulations, 2010	– Restraints by enterprises – Abuse of market dominance – Mergers and acquisitions – Partner State subsidies – Public procurement – Enforcement procedure – Consumer welfare – EAC Competition Authority	EAC Competition Authority, forthcoming

	border effect. Competition regulations for the Community were adopted in 2009.			
Common Market for Eastern and Southern Africa (COMESA)	COMESA adopted a regional competition policy in the form of the COMESA Competition Regulations in 2004. The purpose of the Regulations is to promote and encourage competition by preventing restrictive business practices and other restrictions that deter the efficient operation of markets, and to protect consumers against offensive conduct by market actors. The Regulations apply to all economic activity within the COMESA region, whether the activities are conducted by private companies or public enterprises. Due to the absence of the institutional framework necessary for their enforcement, however, the Regulations have not yet been implemented. It was expected that the COMESA Competition Commission, responsible for the enforcement of the Regulations, would commence its official operations in early 2012.	COMESA Competition Regulations, 2004	– Institutional arrangements – Anti-competitive business practices and conduct – Mergers and acquisitions – Consumer protection – Investigations and enforcement	COMESA Competition Commission, launched in 2009 Website: http://www.comesacompetition.org/
SADC-EAC-COMESA Tripartite FTA	Member States of SADC, EAC and COMESA agreed in October 2008 to negotiate a Tripartite Free Trade Area (FTA). A Draft Agreement and Annexes were published in 2009 and subsequently revised in 2010. Annex 7 concerns Competition Policy and	Draft Annex on Competition Policy and Consumer Protection, under Article 23(3) of the Draft Agreement Establishing	– Prohibition of anti-competitive business behaviour – Determination and abuse of a dominant position – Prohibited practices	

(continued)

Annex 6. (continued)

	Overview	Competition legislation	Issues covered	Competition authorities
	Consumer Protection within the Tripartite FTA. The Annex states that Members from the respective economic blocs shall *work together in tackling anti-competitive practices, regulating mergers and acquisitions, and protecting consumers from unfair trade practices*. The DRAFT Agreement calls for the establishment of a Competition Policy and Consumer Protection Forum which would serve as a platform for sharing information, experience and expertise, as well for undertaking peer review and monitoring the implementation of competition policy and consumer protection laws across the region.	the COMESA, EAC And SADC Tripartite Free Trade Area, 2010	– Mergers and acquisitions – Consumer protection – Sanctions – Cooperation and exchange of information – Tripartite Competition Policy and Consumer Protection Forum – Cooperation between national and regional authorities for competition	
Central African Economic and Monetary Union (CEMAC)	Regional legislation on anti-competitive practices has been in place since 1999 and subsequently amended in 2005. The Regulation prohibits any practices that result in a barrier to free competition in the region, and provides for the control of such practices. The Regulation also calls for the establishment of a Regional Competition Council responsible for the application of the Regulation and competition investigations, among	Regulation of Anti-Competitive Business Practices, Regulation No. 1/99/UEAC-CM-639 of 25 June 1999, as amended by Regulation No. 12/05-UEAC-639 U-CM-SE of 25 June 2005 Regulation of State Practices Affecting Trade between Member	– Anti-competitive practices, including mergers and abuse of dominant positions – Control of anti-competitive practices, including the establishment of a Regional Competition Council – Penalties – Sanctions	Regional Council of Competition

	other things. In February 2010, following a request from the Council of Ministers in 2008, a revision to the Regulation was proposed in the form of a set of Rules for the Protection of Competition.	States, Regulation No. 4/99-UEAC-CM-639 of 18 August 1999		
Economic Community of West African States (ECOWAS)	A Regional Competition Policy Framework (RCPF) and two Supplementary Acts were adopted by the ECOWAS Heads of State and Government in 2008. The RCPF sought to clarify the basic elements of a competition policy within the context of regional integration. The Supplementary Acts provided for the adoption of the Community Competition Rules and the modalities of their application within ECOWAS, and the establishment, functions and operation of the Regional Competition Authority (RCA). Both Supplementary Acts were annexed to the ECOWAS Treaty. Although the groundwork for a regional competition policy has been laid, the ECOWAS Competition Policy has yet to be implemented. Steps to facilitate the full implementation of the RCPF are currently underway as the RCA is being established.	ECOWAS Regional Competition Policy Framework, 2008 Supplementary Act No. A/SA.1/06/08 of 19 December 2008 Supplementary Act No. A/SA.2/06/08 of 19 December 2008	– Agreements and concerted practices restraining trade – Abuse of dominant position – Mergers and acquisitions – State aid – Public enterprises – Compensation for victims of anti-competitive practices – Authorisations and exemptions – Competition Authority – Sanctions or measures against anti-competitive practices	Regional Competition Authority, forthcoming

(continued)

Annex 6. (continued)

	Overview	Competition legislation	Issues covered	Competition authorities
West African Economic and Monetary Union (WAEMU) ***(Union Économique et Monétaire Ouest-Africaine, UEMOA)***	The WAEMU Treaty of 1994 contained various provisions related to the establishment of common rules on competition applicable within the Community. However, specific legislation on competition, in the form of three Regulations and two Directives of the WAEMU Council of Ministers, was only introduced in 2002. The legislation aims to deal with anti-competitive practices; curb restrictions and the abuse of a dominant position; regulate state aid; ensure transparency in financial relations; and promote cooperation between the WAEMU Competition Commission and the national competition agencies of the Member States. The regulations came into effect on 1 January 2003 while the Directives entered into force on 1 July 2002.	Regulations No. 02/2002/CM/WAEMU, 03/2002/CM/WAEMU, and 04/2002/CM/WAEMU of 23 May 2002 Directives No. 01/2002/CM/WAEMU and 02/2002/CM/WAEMU of 23 May 2002	– Anti-competitive agreements – Abuses of dominant position – State aid – Anti-competitive practices attributable to Member States – Exemptions – Public interventions (practices emanating from States) – Inquiries and audits – Penalties	Advisory Committee on Competition, established in 2002 WAEMU Competition Commission, forthcoming

Privatizing the Economic Constitution: Can the World Market Reproduce its own Institutional Prerequisites?

Gralf-Peter Calliess, Jens Mertens, and Moritz Renner

"Commerce ... can seldom flourish long in any state ..., in which the faith of contracts is not supported by law ..."
Adam Smith[1]
"The inability of societies to develop effective, low-cost enforcement of contracts is the most important source of both historical stagnation and contemporary underdevelopment ..."
Douglass C. North[2]

Introduction

Markets are a result of social organization rather than a natural phenomenon. Commerce, defined as the marketing of goods and services, is dependent on a complex set of institutions among which commercial and competition law figure quite prominently. Commercial law, understood as a set of efficacious institutions for the enforcement of contracts, enables and facilitates at-arm's-length market

This article is based on the authors' joint research conducted within the framework of the Collaborative Research Center 597 "Transformations of the State" in Bremen, http://www.staat.uni-bremen.de/?SPRACHE=en. It especially builds on work published in the following articles: Calliess/Mertens, Transnational Corporations, Global Competition Policy, and the Shortcomings of Private International Law, Indiana Journal of Global Legal Studies 18 (2011) 2, p. 843; Calliess/Renner, The Public and the Private Dimensions of Transnational Commercial Law, German Law Journal 10 (2009) 10, p. 1341; Renner, Towards a Hierarchy of Norms in Transnational Law?, Journal of International Arbitration 26 (2009) 4, p. 533.

[1] Smith, *An Inquiry into the Nature and Causes of the Wealth of Nations*, 1778, Book II pp. 539–540.

[2] North, *Institutions, Institutional Change and Economic Performance*, 1990, p. 54.

G.-P. Calliess • J. Mertens • M. Renner (✉)
Fachbereich Rechtswissenschaft, Universität Bremen, Universitätsallee GW1, 28353 Bremen, Germany
e-mail: calliess@uni-bremen.de; jens.mertens@gmx.de; moritz.renner@uni-bremen.de

C. Herrmann et al. (eds.), *European Yearbook of International Economic Law (EYIEL), Vol. 4 (2013)*, European Yearbook of International Economic Law 4,
DOI 10.1007/978-3-642-33917-2_8, © Springer-Verlag Berlin Heidelberg 2013

exchange. Competition law, consisting of a ban on cartels, a prohibition of the abuse of dominant positions, and merger control, regulates freedom of contract in order to protect it from self-abolition. Taken together, commercial and competition law make up the core pillar of what was called the 'economic constitution' of market economies by German ordo-liberalism.[3] Historically, the evolution of the economic constitution was tied to the nation state, and in case of the European internal market to the EU supranational legal system as backed by the Member States. After globalization, which entity provides the economic constitution of the world market? The WTO might be a candidate, but for now does not qualify as a provider of commercial and competition law. In the absence of a world state as a regulator, can the world market produce its own economic constitution by means of private ordering?

Indeed, many scholars claim that the global economy has generated private legal regimes for the enforcement of contracts, e.g. the New Law Merchant as a transnational commercial law.[4] Moreover, Gunther Teubner suggests that such private regimes are subject to auto-constitutional processes that enable them to reflect public policy considerations.[5] In the context of the economic constitution, this would imply that private actors on 'the law market'[6] do not only provide efficacious contract enforcement institutions, but also that they are able to prevent contracting parties from distorting competition through cartel agreements, for example. So are 'merchants of law' also acting as 'moral entrepreneurs'[7] when it comes to competition policy as a public good?

In this article, we intend to analyze in some detail the potential anti-competitive effects of a privatization of commercial law and we discuss to what extent the self-constitutionalization of private regimes may be understood as a privatization of competition law. In a first step, we will argue that the institutional organization of

---

[3] Böhm, *Wettbewerb und Monopolkampf. Eine Untersuchung zur Frage des wirtschaftlichen Kampfrechts und zur Frage der rechtlichen Struktur der geltenden Wirtschaftsordnung*, 1933; Behrens, *Weltwirtschaftsverfassung, Jahrbuch für Neue Politische Ökonomie Band 19*, 2000, p. 5.

[4] Teubner, 'Global Bukowina': Legal Pluralism in the World Society, in: Teubner (ed.), *Global Law without a State*, 1997, p. 3; Berger, *The creeping codification of the lex mercatoria*, 1999; Stone Sweet, The New Lex Mercatoria and Transnational Governance, Journal of European Public Policy 13 (2006) 5, p. 627; Calliess, Transnational Civil Regimes: Economic Globalisation and the Evolution of Commercial Law, in: Gessner (ed.), *Contractual Certainty in International Trade – Empirical Studies and Theoretical Debates on Institutional Support for Global Economic Exchanges*, 2009, p. 215; Calliess et al., Transformations of Commercial Law: New Forms of Legal Certainty for Globalized Exchange Processes?, in: Hurrelmann et al. (eds.), *Transforming the Golden Age Nation State*, 2007, p. 83.

[5] Teubner, Global Private Regimes: Neo-spontaneous Law and Dual Constitution of Autonomous Sectors in World Society, in: Teubner/Ladeur (eds.), *Globalization and Public Governance*, 2004, p. 71; Teubner, *Constitutional Fragments. Societal Constitutionalism and Globalization*, 2012.

[6] O'Hara/Ribstein, *The law market*, 2009.

[7] Dezalay/Garth, Merchants of Law as Moral Entrepreneurs: Constructing International Justice from the Competition for Transnational Business Disputes, Law & Society Review 29 (1995) 1, p. 27.

cross-border commerce differs in fundamental ways from what we know from domestic markets due to the lower level of legal certainty created by the state legal system. Secondly, we will illustrate how international traders adapt to these differences by employing private governance mechanisms such as vertical integration (uniform governance) or international commercial arbitration (trilateral governance) in order to support their trade. Thirdly, we will assess the potential effects of this privatization of commercial law on competition policy, namely the potential abuse of market-dominating positions resulting from a rise in the level of vertical integration on the world market as well as the potential of contracting around the ban on cartels by choosing arbitration rather than litigation as a means of commercial dispute resolution.

Quality of Commercial Law as Crucial Factor for the Institutional Organization of Commerce

Institutions are the foundation of economic exchange. Prominently defined by Douglass C. North as "the rules of the game in a society or, more formally, [...] the humanly devised constraints that shape human interaction,"[8] institutions allow economic actors to predict the behaviour of potential trade partners, turning uncertainty into calculable risk and thus allowing transactions to take place. However, what kind of institutions a society will develop is largely dependent on external factors. In the following sections we will show that due to the deficiencies of private law on the international level, the 'society of traders' engaged in cross-border commerce has developed institutions different from those employed in domestic trade, calling for differentiated considerations as far as competition in international market structures is concerned.

Deficient Contract-Enforcement and Protection of Property Rights in International Trade

Transactions are always threatened by uncertainty, resulting from the opportunistic behaviour of human beings. Only if payment and delivery happen simultaneously, no further institutional embedding of a transaction seems necessary. However, in a modern society based on the division of labour and credit, it is inevitable that goods and services are exchanged across large distances and time spans. With no direct

[8] North, *Institutions, Institutional Change and Economic Performance*, 1990, p. 3. For more specific information on the role of institutions in cross-border trade cf. Dietz, *Institutionen und Globalisierung – Eine empirische Untersuchung am Beispiel grenzüberschreitender Softwareentwicklungsverträge*, 2010.

means of control left, any party making an advance delivery or payment risks losing its transaction input, since for the other party it is the economically most reasonable behaviour to refrain from making delivery or payment and thus to double profits. Because of this risk, no party will move in advance. Consequently, the transaction will not take place at all.

In order to overcome this so-called 'prisoner's dilemma', a party that moves in advance must be able to expect with sufficient certainty that its counterpart will fulfil its contractual obligations. Within the modern nation state, this protection is granted by a judicial system that creates legal certainty with regard to the enforcement of contracts. Acting "in the shadow of law,"[9] traders have a strong incentive to fulfil their contractual obligations since the costs of losing a lawsuit exceed the gain from cheating.[10] The enforcement of contracts and the protection of property rights—in short commercial law—thus form part of the economic constitution allowing economic exchange between anonymous parties. Commercial law, therefore, is a prerequisite for the emergence of competitive market structures.

However, in the absence of a 'world state', there is no supranational world private law regime that would generate a similar level of contractual certainty for cross-border trade. The judicial settling of conflicts concerning cross-border transactions, therefore, poses always three questions: (1) Which nation's courts are responsible for resolving the conflict? (2) Which national contract law are these courts supposed to apply in resolving the conflict? (3) Is a judgment from one nation state recognized and enforced in another nation state?[11]

In theory, these issues are addressed by private international law (PIL). However, contrary to the wording, PIL does not represent international uniform law. Instead, each state's legal system has its own conflict of laws provisions. Although the idea of a global private law based on contracts under international law emerged already at the end of the nineteenth century,[12] more than a century of work in different international organizations, such as the Hague Conference on Private International Law (since 1893), the International Institute for the Unification of Private Law (UNIDROIT, since 1926) and the United Nations Commission on International Trade Law (UNCITRAL, since 1966), have only produced piecemeal results, like the UN Convention on the International Sale of Goods (CISG) of 1980.[13] Hence, the transacting parties are confronted with a plethora of different conflict of laws rules and substantive norms. They cannot rely on enforcement by state courts, as there is still no global agreement on the recognition and enforcement

[9] Cf. Dixit, *Lawlessness and Economics: Alternative Modes of Governance*, 2004, p. 10.

[10] For an in-depth analysis of the function of a state-organized private law system cf. Mertens, *Privatrechtsschutz und vertikale Integration im internationalen Handel*, 2011, pp. 31 et seq.

[11] Calliess, The Making of Transnational Contract Law, Indiana Journal of Global Legal Studies 14 (2007) 2, p. 469 (473) with further references.

[12] Zitelmann, Die Möglichkeit eines Weltrechts, Allgemeine österreichische Gerichts-Zeitung 39 (1888), p. 193.

[13] For the CISG see Ferrari, *Quo Vadis CISG? Celebrating the 25th Anniversary of the United Nations Convention on Contracts for the International Sale of Goods*, 2005.

of judgments.[14] Instead, domestic courts control autonomously whether a foreign judgment is in conformity with public policy. At least in Europe, these issues have partly been mitigated due to intensive integration efforts.[15] However, on the global scale, the problems remain largely unresolved.

In sum, the economic constitution for the world market lacks a functioning commercial law component. The resulting 'constitutional uncertainty'[16] on the international level causes additional transaction costs that often make the unassisted market unavailable as a form of organizing cross-border transactions.[17]

Private Ordering as the Institutional Basis of Cross-Border Trade

As a reaction, traders engaged in cross-border commerce have developed a variety of private governance mechanisms as functional equivalents to a state-organized private law system. It is not a question *whether* trade works without the protection of a state-organized private law system; it is only a question of *how* and *how well* it works. Not only in the modern age but also throughout history, traders have managed to protect transactions in a way sufficient to allow economic exchange. There are a great number of studies on the ancient *Lex Mercatoria* or medieval Law Merchant supporting this fact.[18] More recently, research covered a variety of

---

[14] For The Hague Convention on Jurisdiction and Foreign Judgments in Civil and Commercial Matters of 2005, which has still not taken effect, cf. Baumgartner, *The Proposed Hague Convention on Jurisdiction and Foreign Judgments: Trans-Atlantic Lawmaking for Transnational Litigation*, 2003.

[15] Especially through the Council Regulation (EC) No. 44/2001 of 22 December 2000 (Brussels I—Regulation), OJ [2001] L 12/1, the Convention of 16 September 1988 on jurisdiction and the enforcement of judgments in civil and commercial matters (Lugano Convention), the Regulation (EC) No. 805/2004 of the European Parliament and of the Council of 21 April 2004, OJ [2004] L 143/15, the Rome Convention on the law applicable to contractual obligations, adopted on 19 June 1980, the Regulation (EC) No. 593/2008 of the European Parliament and of the Council of 17 June 2008, OJ [2008] L 177/6, and the Council Regulation (EC) No. 1206/2001 of 28 May 2001, OJ [2001] L 174/1.

[16] Schmidt-Trenz/Schmidtchen, Private International Trade in the Shadow of the Territoriality of Law: Why does It Work?, Southern Economic Journal 58 (1991) 2, p. 329 (331).

[17] In this vein already Schmidtchen/Schmidt-Trenz, *Private Law, The World Production Possibility Frontier and the Need for an International "Private Law Community": German Theory of Order and Constitutional Economics at Work*, 1989, p. 34: '[...] trades between 'faceless buyers and sellers' [...] hardly work in international trade. They require a developed legal system and protective safeguard that we encounter only in an ideal domestic economy.'; Cf. also Rühl, Effizienzprobleme bei grenzüberschreitenden Rechtsstreitigkeiten, German Working Papers in Law and Economics (2006) 17, p. 6: 'Constitutional uncertainty caused by the plurality of law can prevent rationally acting parties from concluding cross-border transactions and, hence, lead to the failure of these transactions; whereas national transactions would not fail.'.

[18] Among the most popular are: Greif, Reputation and Coalitions in Medieval Trade: Evidence on the Maghribi Traders, The Journal of Economic History 49 (1989) 4, p. 857; Greif, The Organization of Long-Distance Trade: Reputation and Coalitions in the Geniza Documents and Genoa During the Eleventh and Twelfth Centuries, The Journal of Economic History 51 (1991) 2, p. 459; Greif, The fundamental problem of exchange: A research agenda in Historical Institutional

private governance mechanisms employed in modern cross-border trade. Relational contracts, trade intermediaries and trade clubs, letters of credit, arbitration tribunals and unilateral control through firm structures are just a selection of popular instruments.[19]

Recent empirical data confirms that in international trade, the case-load of commercial courts is by far lower than in domestic trade.[20] As a general rule, it can be said that in international trade the relative weight of public governance mechanisms decreases while the importance of private governance mechanisms increases when compared to domestic trade.

Global Economic Constitution Outside the "Shadow of Law": Can Private Ordering Support Global Competitive Market Structures?

So how does this shift towards private governance affect the economic constitution of global markets? In the following sections, we will discuss two concerns that put into question whether private ordering is able to reproduce the elements of the economic constitution necessary for competitive market structures on the global

Analysis, European Review of Economic History 4 (2000) 3, p. 251; Greif, *Institutions and the path to modern economy: Lessons from medieval trade*, 2006; North, Institutions, transaction costs, and the rise of merchant empires, in: Tracy (ed.), *The Political Economy of Merchant Empires*, 1991, pp. 22–40; Milgrom et al., The Role of Institutions in the Revival of Trade: The Law Merchant, Private Judges, and the Champagne Fairs, Economics and Politics 2 (1990) 1, p. 1; Clay, Trade Without Law: Private-Order Institutions in Mexican California, Journal of Law, Economics & Organization 13 (1997) 1, p. 202.

[19] See Calliess et al., Transformations of Commercial Law: New Forms of Legal Certainty for Globalized Exchange Processes?, in: Hurrelmann et al. (eds.), *Transforming the Golden Age Nation State*, 2007, pp. 83–108; Dietz/Nieswandt, The Emergence of Transnational Cooperation in the Software Industry, in: Gessner (ed.), *Contractual Certainty in International Trade – Empirical Studies and Theoretical Debates on Institutional Support for Global Economic Exchanges*, 2009, pp. 87–106; Dietz, *Institutionen und Globalisierung – Eine empirische Untersuchung am Beispiel grenzüberschreitender Softwareentwicklungsverträge*, 2010, pp. 65 et seq.; Sosa, Cross-Border Dispute Resolution from the Perspective of Mid-sized Law Firms—The Example of International Commercial Arbitration, in: Gessner (ed.), *Contractual Certainty in International Trade – Empirical Studies and Theoretical Debates on Institutional Support for Global Economic Exchanges*, 2009, pp. 107–156; Konradi, The Role of Lex Mercatoria in Supporting Globalised Transactions: An Empirical Insight into the Governance Structure of the Timber Industry, in: Gessner (ed.), *Contractual Certainty in International Trade – Empirical Studies and Theoretical Debates on Institutional Support for Global Economic Exchanges*, 2009, pp. 49–86.

[20] Hoffmann, Schiedsgerichte als Gewinner der Globalisierung?—Eine empirische Analyse zur Bedeutung staatlicher und privater Gerichtsbarkeit für den internationalen Handel, Zeitschrift für Schiedsverfahren 8 (2010) 2, p. 96 (100); Hoffmann/Maurer, Entstaatlichung der Justiz—Empirische Belege zum Bedeutungsverlust staatlicher Gerichte für internationale Wirtschaftsstreitigkeiten, Zeitschrift für Rechtssoziologie 31 (2010) 2, p. 279.

level. Firstly, the deficiencies of state-organized commercial law influence market structures, namely causing an elevated extent of vertical integration and thus reinforcing the danger of abuse of dominant positions. Secondly, private governance mechanisms are prone to neglect matters of public interest in favour of private interests. Specifically, we will ponder the question whether by choosing arbitration instead of litigation international traders are able to contract around the ban on cartels.

Vertical Integration: An Inevitable Consequence of Private Ordering

Vertical integration is the competition law issue that is most closely related to the choice of governance mechanisms. As we will show, any sort of private ordering necessarily implies vertical integration. In order to explain this relationship, we will use the theoretical model of transaction costs economics (TCE).[21]

Private Ordering, Vertical Integration, and the Assumption of Efficient Market Structures: Why Common Theory Fails on Global Markets

Based on the 'make-or-buy' decision, TCE analyzes the costs that arise when goods or services are transferred from one economic unit to another. 'Make-or-buy' characterizes the extreme points of a continuum of governance mechanisms that can be used to organize a transaction. On the one hand, an economic actor can 'make' a good or service itself, i.e. completely integrate the production and/or distribution process into its own firm structure. On the other hand, it can 'buy' the good or service externally from a third party on the market. What distinguishes 'market' from 'firm' is the way control is exerted. In a firm, no external actors are involved. Instead, there are only internal transactions between different sub-units of the same firm or corporate group, governed by means of hierarchy, i.e. a command-and-control structure based on property rights. On the market, in contrast, there is no such control over the counterparty of a transaction because both parties are completely independent from each other, i.e. 'at arm's length'-trade.

However, actors are not bound to the extremes of market or firm. They may also combine elements of both, forming 'hybrid' governance mechanisms. Graphically, the spectrum of possible modes of governance for transactions can be depicted as a straight line from market to firm with an infinite number of combinations of both

[21] For more details on the model cf. Williamson, Transaction-cost economics: The Governance of Contractual Relations, Journal of Law and Economics 22 (1979) 2, p. 233, and Williamson, Transaction Cost Economics, in: Ménard/Shirley (eds.), *Handbook of New Institutional Economics*, 2005, pp. 41–65.

mechanisms in between. Any form of private ordering means departing from market governance and moving towards the firm. Consequently, it also means employing elements of the way a firm exerts control over transactions. Thus, hybrid governance mechanisms always include elements of dependency and subordination as weaker forms of the hierarchy and orders employed in the firm.

In principle, there are three options to stabilize transactions this way.[22] First, actors can create dependency by enlarging the number of actors involved in a transaction, so a party defecting from its contractual obligations will face sanctions by third parties, e.g. a loss in reputation. Second, actors can bundle multiple transaction issues, so the counterpart will be bound to its obligations in order to gain the profit from all transactions. Third, business relations can be stretched over time, creating long-term dependencies between the actors. Moreover, these instruments can be combined in order to maximize effects. No matter if relational contracts, trade clubs, or reputation networks are analyzed: all of these mechanisms are based on the said instruments creating a certain level of dependency and/or subordination as elements of vertical integration.

Influenced by the ideas of the so-called Chicago School,[23] modern competition policy employs TCE's 'make-or-buy'-model to support its assessment that vertical integration is per se beneficial.[24] Depending on the factors specificity, uncertainty, and frequency, it is argued that for each transaction a certain governance mechanism in between market and firm is most suitable, i.e. offers the best compromise between the benefits and disadvantages of either extreme. Markets on the one hand offer low costs of organization and ideal incentives for the actors involved, but on the other hand allow no control over the counterpart's behaviour. The firm, in contrast, offers a maximum of control but suffers from high bureaucratic costs and low incentives. It is concluded that any governance mechanism chosen to organize a certain transaction must be the most efficient instrument, for if the compromise between market and firm elements was not ideal, it would eventually be crowded out by the force of competition. As a macroeconomic consequence, it is argued that due to the pressure of competition the benefits gained from this efficient choice of governance mechanisms will eventually be passed on to the consumer.

However, this reasoning is conclusive only under circumstances found within modern nation states. The 'make-or-buy'-model takes for granted an institutional framework that grants free choice between the market and the firm. However, this is the case only if there is a system of private law that reliably protects property rights

---

[22] This categorization goes back to the model of Yarbrough/Yarbrough, The Contractual Role of Boundaries: Law and Economics Meets International Organization, European Journal of International Relations 9 (2003) 4, p. 543 (551).

[23] For the main ideas of this school cf. Bork, *The Antitrust Paradox: A Policy at War with Itself*, 1978; Posner, The Chicago School of Antitrust Analysis, University of Pennsylvania Law Review 127 (1979) 4, p. 925.

[24] As one example out of many, this becomes obvious in the Commission Regulation (EC) No. 2790/1999 of 22 December 1999, OJ [1999] L 336/21, especially in recital 6.

and enforces contracts. As on the free market actors are not able to exert any influence on the counterpart's behaviour, market governance is dependent on an external governance mechanism safeguarding transactions. Such external protection is guaranteed by the private law systems that developed nation states provide for domestic trade, but—as shown above—not for cross-border trade.[25] Outside the 'shadow of law', actors in cross-border trade are forced to revert to private governance-mechanisms and thus use means of vertical integration. Consequently, the level of vertical integration in cross-border transactions will be higher than in domestic trade, given that all other factors—i.e. the frequency, uncertainty and specificity of transactions—remain unchanged.

What implications does this have on the assessment of vertical integration? Looking at single transactions it is true that vertical integration is indeed efficient. In fact, in situations where there is no system of private law enabling market transactions, private ordering and thus vertical integration is the only way to organize economic exchange. However, this does not support the conclusion that vertical integration is beneficial in general. Instead, from a macro-economical point of view, the elevated level of vertical integration on global markets is quite alarming. Due to the euphoria about the efficiency advantages of vertical integration, its costs and incentive disadvantages vis-à-vis markets are neglected. Control is costly. Hybrid governance mechanisms such as letters of credit or arbitration entail significant additional transaction costs. Trade clubs and trade intermediaries take commissions. Even to the extent that international trade is safeguarded by a transaction-specific mélange of public and private governance mechanisms,[26] already in the negotiation phase significant transaction costs arise through the involvement of international law firms. Moreover, vertical integration abolishes market incentives and causes friction within the organizational apparatus ('X-Inefficiency').

Due to these disadvantages, O. E. Williamson—one of the leading TCE scholars—called the firm-internal conduct of transactions the organizational form of last resort. He gives clear guidance: "try markets, try hybrids, and have recourse to the firm only when all else fails."[27] Vertical integration is economically beneficial only if the specificity, uncertainty and frequency of transactions justify the high level of time and effort used. Otherwise market governance is the more attractive organizational form, as it allows a leaner internal administration and offers optimal incentive structures through competition.

Not only in theory, but also in economic practice it can be observed that economic actors recognize and utilize the advantages of a low level of vertical

[25] In this vein also Dixit, *Lawlessness and Economics: Alternative Modes of Governance*, 2004, p. 3: 'Thus conventional economic theory does not underestimate the importance of law; rather, the problem is that it takes the existence of a well-functioning institution of state law for granted.'

[26] See Calliess et al., Transformations of Commercial Law: New Forms of Legal Certainty for Globalized Exchange Processes?, in: Hurrelmann et al. (eds.), *Transforming the Golden Age Nation State*, 2007, pp. 83–108.

[27] Williamson, The Economics of Governance, American Economic Review 95 (2005) 2, p. 1 (12).

integration if circumstances allow them to do so. In order to save administrative costs and to gain flexibility, corporations tend to decouple activities outside of their core competencies from the hierarchy of the firm and to transfer them to other companies by virtue of outsourcing and off-shoring. However, economic studies demonstrate that corporations tend to outsource only into those countries where legal institutions provide for an efficacious enforcement of contracts.[28]

To sum up, vertical integration does enable global economic exchange—but only at high costs. Via the final price for any good or service provided across borders, the consumer pays the profit margin of providers of private governance mechanisms. Against this background, vertical integration is not per se beneficial, but may have been chosen as an inferior type of governance mechanism only because market governance was unavailable due to the deficits of the international private law system. The tailor-made governance solutions of transnational commerce lack the economies of scale that a state-organized private law regime offers as safeguarding mechanism for the multitude of relatively unspecific transactions.[29] Thus, for the sake of a conclusive assessment of vertical integration, it is not enough to lean back and be comfortable with the lax treatment in competition law.

No Comprehensive Remedy for Vertically Concentrated Market Structures to be Expected

A solution to this problem seems hard to reach in practice, though. Adopting stricter competition rules vis-à-vis vertical integration would be counterproductive: due to the deficits of private law on the international level private ordering, and thus vertical integration, is the only mechanism enabling cross-border trade. Theoretically, only improvements of international commercial law as part of a world economic constitution—i.e. the protection of property rights and the enforcement of contracts across national borders as those parts of the economic constitution necessary for the emergence of market economies—would tackle the root of the problem.[30] However, so far all the dreams of a world private law have been disappointed, though—provided the political will—at least partial

[28] Grossman/Helpman, Outsourcing in a Global Economy, Review of Economic Studies 72 (2005) 1, p. 135; Nunn, Relationship-Specificity, Incomplete Contracts, and the Pattern of Trade, The Quarterly Journal of Economics 122 (2007) 2, p. 569.

[29] Dietz, *Institutionen und Globalisierung – Eine empirische Untersuchung am Beispiel grenzüberschreitender Softwareentwicklungsverträge*, 2010, Chapter 2, point 4.2.

[30] Cf. Behrens, *Weltwirtschaftsverfassung, Jahrbuch für neue politische Ökonomie Band 19*, 2000, p. 5; For background information on the model of an economic constitution cf. Kerber/Vanberg, Constitutional Aspects of Party Autonomy and Its Limits—The Perspective of Constitutional Economics, in: Grundmann et al. (eds.), *Party Autonomy and the Role of Information in the Internal Market*, 2001, pp. 49–79; Behrens, Die Bedeutung des Kollisionsrechts für die "Globalisierung" der Wirtschaft, in: Basedow et al. (eds.), *Aufbruch nach Europa: 75 Jahre Max-Planck-Institut für Privatrecht*, 2001, pp. 381–398 (384 et seq.).

improvements would be possible.[31] Success stories like the European Union show that unifying legal systems across national borders can work in practice. However, on the global level, no similar development is in sight. Against the background of diverse national interests and judicial conflicts, at least in the closer future no comprehensive approach has any realistic chance to succeed.

International Arbitration: An Instrument Able to Support Competitive Structures on the World Market?

Even if national systems of private law cannot sufficiently protect international transactions, does not international commercial arbitration offer a viable solution to conduct trade between anonymous parties across borders and thus allow cross-border market governance?

Arbitration as an Instrument Partially Enabling Cross-Border Market Trade

Frequently relied on in international trade, arbitration indeed serves the same function as state-based court systems as far as facilitating trade is concerned. Contractually equipped with jurisdictional powers for a specific transaction, arbitral tribunals serve as independent third parties resolving the prisoner's dilemma between anonymous actors. Most importantly, the enforcement of the tribunals' decisions does not necessarily have to rely on dependency and subordination, as is usually inherent to private ordering. Instead, decisions are enforceable via the nation states' private law systems: Having ratified the so called 1958 New York Convention, most countries enforce decisions of arbitral tribunals via the apparatus of their private law systems with only very limited options of *de novo* review of the decision.

However, it must be kept in mind that due to several shortcomings arbitration does not offer the same universal kind of protection as guaranteed by state-based private law systems; whereas the latter are accessible for any sort of claims, international arbitration favours economically powerful players and high-value transactions.[32] This mainly results from the relatively high costs of arbitration

[31] A plethora of suggestions for improving the state protection of private law can be found in Calliess/Hoffmann, Effektive Justizdienstleistungen für den globalen Handel, Zeitschrift für Rechtspolitik 42 (2009) 1, p. 1.

[32] For an extensive analysis of the role of international arbitration for small and medium-sized enterprises cf. Parise-Kuhnle, Transaktionssicherheit im Außenhandel durch prozessualen Rechtsschutz – eine Untersuchung aus der Perspektive kleiner und mittelständischer Unternehmen, CRC 597 „Transformations of the State“ Working Paper Series, forthcoming.

procedures.[33] Paying extremely high fees for arbitrators and councils alike—mostly lawyers from international law firms with hourly wages well beyond 350 €—is reasonable only, if justified by the sum at stake. Empirical research shows that a small claim procedure in front of state courts costs only a fraction of what the same procedure in arbitration.[34] While access to justice in front of public courts is granted by constitutional law, e.g. Article 6 ECHR, and backed by legal aid for destitute parties, arbitral tribunals will deny opening procedures if a party is not able to make an advance payment for the expected costs.

Further, two additional structural deficits of arbitration limit its institutional reach. First, arbitral tribunals often do not publish their awards. Thus, arbitration does not allow for the production of legal certainty for third parties that is a by-product of judicial precedent. Second, arbitral wards are final and binding, i.e. there are no stages of appeal involved where decisions are reviewed in substance for their overall consistency and coherency. This lack of control makes arbitration prone to biased and unpredictable decisions, calling into question the fairness of the proceedings. Without any objective control according to common legal standards, arbitrators might be tempted to render the decision most favourable to economically powerful parties because as repeat players they will most probably be able to channel future arbitration business to them. For experienced lawyers it is easy to justify any outcome of the proceedings in a way that is not contestable by the very limited means of control of national courts over arbitral awards. Since it takes a violation of domestic public policy in order to successfully contest an arbitral award in front of a state court, such proceedings are rarely successful. Whereas economically powerful players have the capacity to cope with the resulting unpredictability, the risks might be too high for small and medium-sized enterprises facing bankruptcy in case of unfavourable awards.[35]

To sum up, arbitration is neither accessible to the broad public, nor does it grant a level of justice comparable to a state-organized system of private law. Nevertheless, arbitration supported by public enforcement via the 1958 New York Convention is able to lay the foundation for at arm's length market transactions at least for economically powerful, repeat players. In this limited respect, international arbitration does indeed enable market transactions between independent and anonymous trade partners on the global level.

---

[33] For the cost structure of arbitration cf. Schütze, *Schiedsgericht und Schiedsverfahren*, 2007, p. 12; Henn, *Schiedsverfahrensrecht – Handbuch für die Praxis*, 2000, pp. 194 et seq.; Hoffmann, *Nationale Ziviljustiz und internationaler Handelsverkehr – ein Vorschlag zur Einrichtung von Kammern für internationale Handelssachen*, 2010, pp. 52 et seq.

[34] Lachmann, *Handbuch für die Schiedsgerichtspraxis*, 2008, marginal numbers 4682 et seq.

[35] For further details on the relation between the economic power of the parties and their access to arbitration cf. Knapp, Taking Contracts Private: The Quiet Revolution in Contract Law, Fordham Law Review 71 (2002–2003) 3, p. 761 (781); Budnitz, The High Cost of Mandatory Consumer Arbitration, Law and Contemporary Problems 67 (2004) 1–2, p. 133 (161); Drahozal, Arbitration Costs and Contingent Fee Contracts, SSRN Working Paper, 2005.

Private vs. Public Interest: Is Arbitration Able and Willing to Protect the Antitrust Law?

If arbitration enables cross-border trade between anonymous parties and thus allows for competitive international market structures, then why should it raise any issues as far as competition law is concerned? In order to answer this question one needs to look at the different interests involved in the governance of transactions.

Primarily, private governance mechanisms serve the interests of the transacting parties. They are functional equivalents to state-organized private law systems as far as the trade-facilitative function is concerned. Arbitrators, for instance, offer services as professional trade facilitators: they are engaged and paid for by the transacting parties and render their award in order to enforce contractual obligations. In other words, they are primarily bound to the *private* interests of the transacting parties as their customers.

However, the protection of competition is a goal of *public* interest. Competition law forms part of regulatory law limiting individual freedom in order to achieve better economic results for the public. Thus, at least from an ex-ante point of view it usually runs counter to the interests of private parties involved in a certain transaction. As public institutions, state courts have to consider both the facilitative and the regulatory aspects of private law. While enforcing commercial contracts and protecting property rights, at the same time they have to exercise public control functions by limiting the private autonomy of commercial actors with regard to public interests and public good.

However, it is highly doubtful whether and to what extent arbitral tribunals as private institutions have the obligation, capacity, and willingness to take into account matters of public policy. As in principle international arbitral tribunals are not bound to apply specific national regulatory rules, it comes natural to assume that interests of the public are neglected in favour of the private interests of the transaction parties. Already the German *Reichsgericht* noted that "only an unconditional submission under a specific lawmaking authority [...] guarantees that the contractual relationship will be regulated, if necessary, against the selfish will of the economically stronger partner or of both partners, with regard to those public policy concerns that are based on general principles of law."[36]

However, some proponents of the New Law Merchant do not agree with these concerns. They argue that transnational commercial law not only encompasses substantive legal norms in the interest of the contracting parties, but also creates its very own transnational public policy norms. Specifically, Gunther Teubner has proposed the idea that private governance regimes are bound to 'auto-constitutionalize', i.e. to develop a body of higher-ranking norms functionally equivalent to

[36] Reichsgericht, IV 272/35, Juristische Wochenschrift 1936, p. 2058 (2059) (our translation).

national constitutional law.[37] Therefore, the argument goes on, the transnationalization of law is not per se problematic: Law beyond the state is not necessarily inferior to state-made law when it comes to accommodating public policy concerns. From this perspective, transnational law may even be depicted as being able to overcome the public/private distinction as such, by way of establishing more inclusive processes of regulation that involve both state and non-state, civil society actors.[38]

A thorough analysis of international arbitral awards reveals that neither the fears nor the hopes voiced with regard to public policy in international arbitration are entirely justified. This follows from the precarious status of the arbitration regime itself. While international arbitration enjoys a high degree of autonomy from domestic legal systems, at the same time it is not wholly independent from the state. Arbitral tribunals do not form part of any domestic jurisdiction but are still heavily influenced by and dependent on domestic procedural law and state courts. This tension goes back to the hybrid character of international arbitration,[39] combining privately organized tribunals and proceedings with public means of enforcement, as reflected by the 1958 New York Convention. According to this almost universally ratified convention, on the one hand, the autonomy of the private character of the proceedings is respected as all State Parties to the Convention must enforce awards rendered by international arbitral tribunals on their territory without *de novo* review as to their substance.[40] On the other hand, a certain protection of public interests is granted as in a strictly limited number of situations recognition and enforcement may be refused, especially if such enforcement were contrary to the public policy of the country where enforcement is sought.[41] For the same reason, an arbitral award may be set aside by domestic courts under Art. 34 para. 2(b)(ii) of the UNCITRAL Model Law on International Commercial Arbitration (UNCITRAL Model Law) where the procedural law concerning arbitration is based in most states. Thus, the New York Convention defines both the independence and the limits of international arbitration vis-à-vis domestic regulation. While based on the will of the parties and the discretion of the arbitrators the tribunal is free to apply the law deemed appropriate to satisfy the private interests of the conflict parties, a certain protection of public interest is granted by the necessity to render a valid and enforceable award.

---

[37] Teubner, Global Private Regimes: Neo-spontaneous Law and Dual Constitution of Autonomous Sectors in World Society, in: Teubner/Ladeur (eds.), *Globalization and Public Governance*, 2004, p. 71; Fischer-Lescano/Teubner, Regime-Collisions: The Vain Search for Legal Unity in the Fragmentation of Global Law, Michigan Journal of International Law 25 (2004) 4, p. 999.

[38] See Teubner, Contracting Worlds: The Many Autonomies of Private Law, Social and Legal Studies 9 (2000) 3, p. 399.

[39] See generally Schlosser, *Das Recht der internationalen privaten Schiedsgerichtsbarkeit*, 1989.

[40] New York Convention on the Recognition and Enforcement of Foreign Arbitral Awards, 10 June 1958, 330 U.N.T.S. 38, Art. III.

[41] New York Convention on the Recognition and Enforcement of Foreign Arbitral Awards, 10 June 1958, 330 U.N.T.S. 38, Art. V para. 2 (b).

Also, the arbitration rules of the International Chamber of Commerce (ICC) in Paris, the leading provider of international commercial arbitration services worldwide, reflect this tension. According to Art. 17 para. 1 of the ICC Arbitration Rules, "[t]he parties shall be free to agree upon the rules of law to be applied by the Arbitral Tribunal to the merits of the dispute. In the absence of any such agreement, the Arbitral Tribunal shall apply the rules of law which it determines to be appropriate." Article 35 of the Rules, in contrast, provides that "[i]n all matters not expressly provided for in these Rules, the Court and the Arbitral Tribunal shall . . . make every effort to make sure that the Award is enforceable at law." In addition, Art. 6 of the Internal Rules of the ICC Court of Arbitration provides that all ICC arbitral awards are scrutinized by the ICC's central administrative body with regard to requirements of the "law of the place of arbitration."

The tension between autonomy and public oversight in arbitration is reflected on the level of the applicable substantive law, specifically with regard to the application of mandatory rules of law. In domestic legal systems, mandatory rules of law are norms that cannot be derogated from by agreement of the parties—and thus limit party autonomy. This limitation is based on the assumption that certain 'fundamental' norms must not be left at the parties' disposal. It is well established that state courts, when they enforce commercial contracts and protect property rights, at the same time exercise public control functions with regard to (1) public interests or public good such as a workable competition or a stable currency, (2) the effects of contracts on third parties, e.g. on creditors outside the contractual relationship, and (3) the protection of weaker parties within the contract itself, such as the protection of consumers or employees against the unilateral exercise of private autonomy by economically dominant actors.

Even in cross-border disputes, domestic courts apply certain mandatory norms, regardless of the law otherwise applicable, as 'overriding mandatory provisions' (e.g. Art. 9 Rome I Regulation) or with reference to the 'public policy of the forum' (e.g. Art. 21 Rome I Regulation). The doctrinal reconstruction of such mandatory norms in conflict-of-laws rules widely differs among jurisdictions and relies on very diverse doctrinal concepts.[42] Usually, the reach of 'overriding' mandatory provisions, i.e. those mandatory provisions that are applicable to cross-border disputes, is considered as more limited than that of 'ordinary' mandatory, i.e. purely domestic norms: Only those mandatory norms that protect 'essential regulatory interests' of the state concerned are applied to cross-border situations.[43] Furthermore, there is disagreement as to the question whether domestic courts should only apply the overriding mandatory provisions of the forum state or also those of third

[42] For the status of mandatory rules in conflict of laws see especially Guedj, The Theory of the Lois de Police, A Functional Trend in Continental Private International Law—A Comparative Analysis with Modern American Theories, American Journal of Comparative Law 39 (1991) 4, p. 661, as well as Hartley, Mandatory Rules in International Contracts: The Common Law Approach, Recueil des Cours 266 (1997) p. 337.

[43] Renner, in: Calliess (ed.), *The Rome Regulations. Commentary on the European Rules of the Conflict of Laws*, Art. 9 paras. 13–20.

states. Nonetheless, the concept of internationally mandatory norms protecting public policy is entrenched in every domestic system of conflict of laws.

Things become more complicated when it comes to arbitration, though. As arbitral tribunals in international cases do not serve as guardians of any national public policy, they are in principle not obliged to apply the mandatory rules of any country's jurisdiction. Instead, as recognized in the 1958 New York Convention, arbitration is based on contractual choice-of-law and choice-of-forum clauses. Consequently, the parties of a contract are free to choose the procedural and substantive rules applicable to any potentially arising conflict and thus to 'opt out of regulation'.[44]

Classical conflict-of-laws methods for dealing with this problem have proven rather unsatisfactory in arbitration as they are deeply rooted in national preconceptions of public policy and the fact that domestic courts are bound by a specific national constitutional order. International arbitral tribunals, in turn, do not have ties to any specific legal system. Though physically seated within a national jurisdiction, it is assumed by most scholars and practitioners that arbitral tribunals do not have a forum state. Instead, international arbitral tribunals operate delocalized and disconnected from domestic laws and policies. This results in the paradoxical situation that for an arbitrator, "there is no foreign law"[45] while at the same time, "every law is foreign law."[46]

Difficulties in the Emergence of Transnational Competition Law

Consequently, there is no clear-cut solution as to the application of mandatory law in international arbitration. Still, it is commonly accepted that also in arbitration, matters of public policy have to be recognized and protected at least to a certain degree. However, the question is which rules have to be applied in order to grant that protection.

For international arbitrators confronted with this question, there is not much legal guidance. The necessity to render an enforceable award forces the arbitrator to take into account the mandatory law of nation states potentially involved in the enforcement of the award, at least as far as breaches of those rules also lead to a violation of national public policy. However, the problem is that usually it is not possible to predict in which country an award is going to be enforced. Acknowledging this difficulty, there have been attempts to develop a system of

[44] O'Hara, Opting Out of Regulation: A Public Choice Analysis of Contractual Choice of Law, Vanderbilt Law Review 53 (2000) 5, p. 1551.

[45] Derains, Public Policy and the Law Applicable to the Dispute in International Arbitration, in: Sanders (ed.), *Comparative Arbitration Practice and Public Policy in Arbitration*, 1987, p. 227 (232).

[46] Voser, Mandatory Rules of Law as a Limitation on the Law Applicable in International Commercial Arbitration, American Review of International Arbitration 7 (1996) 3/4, p. 319 (330).

'transnational public policy' based on the ground-breaking work of Pierre Lalive[47] in order to carve out a concept of mandatory norms irrespective of the particularities of national law. However, apart from undisputed core elements like the recognition of the *jus cogens* of international law, anti-corruption rules, the principles of universal justice, and a minimum standard of human rights, there is no common understanding of which norms form part of transnational or truly international public policy. In absence of a 'world-constitution' the status of normative hierarchies in transnational law remains largely unresolved.

Notwithstanding these difficulties, some very important domestic courts have expressed high expectations as far as specifically the application of competition law by arbitral tribunals is concerned. In its famous Mitsubishi decision[48] in 1985 the US Supreme Court held that a contractual dispute between a Puerto Rican and a Japanese party was arbitrable although the contract potentially violated the US Sherman Act and thus American public policy in antitrust law. The Supreme Court argued that an arbitration procedure would not violate public policy since the Japanese arbitral tribunal would apply the Sherman Act just the same as an American court would do. Complementary to the Supreme Court's decision, the ECJ ruled in the Eco Swiss case[49] that all courts in EU Member States are obliged to annul arbitral awards that are contrary to Art. 81 EC Treaty (now Art. 101 Treaty on the Functioning of the European Union; TFEU). The reasoning was twofold: the ECJ argued that on the one hand antitrust law formed an integral part of European public policy, allowing annulment according to Art. 34 para. 2(b)(ii) UNCITRAL Model Law, and on the other hand a disregard of antitrust law justified refusing the recognition and/or enforcement of arbitral awards under Art. V para. 2(b) of the New York Convention.

The message to arbitral tribunals involved in both decisions is rather clear: domestic courts consider competition law to form an integral part of public policy that has to be respected by international arbitration, and any disregard thereof will result in annulment of the award and refusal of its recognition and enforcement. However, even if an arbitrator willing to render an enforceable award knows only *that* he has to take into account competition law, the courts' decisions do not give him any further guidance as to *how* he has to apply competition law, namely which rules he has to apply according to what rules of conflict.

---

[47] See Lalive, Ordre public transnational (ou réellement international) et arbitrage internationale, Revue de l'arbitrage (1986) 4, p. 327. English language version published as Lalive, Transnational (or Truly International) Public Policy in International Arbitration, in: Sanders (ed.), *Comparative Arbitration Practice and Public Policy in Arbitration, ICCA Congress Series No. 3*, 1987, pp. 257–318 (286). Similarly, the recommendations of the International Law Association Committee on International Commercial Arbitration, Report on Public Policy as a Bar to Enforcement of International Arbitral Awards, 2002, Recommendation 2(b) rely on "the existence or otherwise of a consensus within the international community as regards the principle under consideration."

[48] See US Supreme Court, 473 U.S. 614, *Mitsubishi Motors vs. Soler Chrysler-Plymouth*.

[49] See ECJ, C-126/97, *Eco Swiss China Time Ltd vs. Benetton International NV*, [1999] ECR I, 3055.

Against the background of this conflict, it must be asked how international arbitral tribunals cope with the application of competition law in practice. In order to clarify this matter, we have conducted an empirical case-by-case analysis of international arbitral awards.[50] This analysis reveals that despite all doctrinal difficulties arbitral tribunals are willing and able to apply competition law, specifically the ban on cartels as codified in Art. 101 TFEU. In the last 15 years there have been numerous cases decided by arbitral tribunals instituted by the Court of Arbitration of the International Chamber of Commerce (ICC) dealing with matters of competition law.[51] The analysis of those cases shows that arbitral tribunals do apply competition law provisions in principle. The dilemma of which rules to apply is solved in a rather pragmatic manner. Without resorting to any common methodology, arbitrators employ rules from different normative levels in order to justify the application of competition law.

However, this inconsistency of methodology and the lack of judicial review by an appellate body sometimes lead to troubling inconsistencies of arbitral case-law. This can be exemplified by two contradictory decisions in rather similar cases: whereas one tribunal held that, following the Mitsubishi case and the general consideration that arbitrators "should always be concerned about the efficacy of their awards," Art. 101 TFEU had to be applied to a contract even though the parties had chosen New York State law as applicable law,[52] another tribunal flatly ruled that antitrust disputes were not arbitrable under New York State law—and therefore left antitrust law unapplied.[53]

However, most awards that are concerned with antitrust norms simply take their applicability for granted if those rules form part of the law applicable to the contract as a whole.[54] If, for example, the parties have agreed on Belgian law as applicable to their contract, arbitrators would not engage in any further methodological reasoning but simply apply European antitrust law as part of the mandatory law common to all EU Member States. Consequently, as this focus on the chosen law regime invites parties to escape from strict regulation by choosing the most lenient law, arbitral tribunals incidentally use more sophisticated conflict-of-law

---

[50] This analysis was performed by Moritz Renner in preparation of his doctoral thesis. The full results of the study are published in Renner, *Zwingendes transnationales Recht – Zur Struktur der Wirtschaftsverfassung jenseits des Staates*, 2011, pp. 92 et seq.

[51] See, e.g., ICC Cases No. 6503, (1990), 122 J. DROIT INT'L (CLUNET) 1022-1031 (1995); 7146 (1992), Y.B. COM. ARB. XXVI 119-129 (2001); 7181 (1992), Y.B. COM. ARB. XXI 99-112 (1996); 7539 (1995), J. DROIT INT'L (CLUNET) 1030-1037 (1996); 7893 (1994), Y.B. COM. ARB. XXVII 139-152 (2002); 8423 (1994), J. DROIT INT'L (CLUNET) 1079-1082 (2002); 8626 (1996), J. DROIT INT'L (CLUNET) 1073-1079 (1999); 10988 (2003), J. DROIT INT'L (CLUNET) 1408-1417 (2006).

[52] See ICC Case No. 8626 (1996), J. DROIT INT'L (CLUNET) 1073-1079 (1999).

[53] See ICC Case No. 7893 (1994), Y.B. COM. ARB. XXVII 139-152 (2002).

[54] See ICC Cases No. 7146 (1992), Y.B. COM. ARB. XXVI 119-129 (2001); 7181 (1992), Y.B. COM. ARB. XXI 99-112 (1996); 7539 (1995), J. DROIT INT'L (CLUNET) 1030-1037 (1996); 8423 (1994), J. DROIT INT'L (CLUNET) 1079-1082 (2002); 10988 (2003), J. DROIT INT'L (CLUNET) 1408-1417 (2006).

arguments in order to justify an application of European antitrust law even if the parties have chosen the law of a third state. However, while in such cases domestic courts would rely on the so called 'loi de police' or the 'governmental interest analysis' method, arbitral tribunals prefer the 'law as a fact'-doctrine,[55] which allows them to take into account merely the factual effects of mandatory norms beyond the chosen law without, however, granting them force of law. For example, an arbitral tribunal might refer to *force majeure* provisions under the chosen law in order to rule that a contract infringing European anti-trust law is unenforceable.

Problems intensify in those arbitration proceedings that allow the decision of conflict by *amiable composition*, i.e. not according to specific rules of law but according to general considerations of equity and the customs of international trade. As by choosing this type of proceedings the parties have expressed the clear will to exempt their contractual relation from the rule of law altogether, arbitral tribunals might argue that consequently the contractual relation should not be subject to any national regulatory law, neither. In the line of this argument, the only regulatory limit to the parties' autonomy is transnational public policy as part of the *lex mercatoria*. In this vein, an arbitral tribunal sitting in Switzerland ruled that European antitrust law did not form part of transnational public policy.[56] Considering the divergent approaches to antitrust law in different jurisdictions, this reasoning is convincing. How to design competition law is a highly disputable political question traditionally decided within the democratic decision-making processes of the constitutional nation-states. For this reason it is to be doubted that beyond hard-core cases of anti-competitive behaviour there will ever be universal rules giving guidance to arbitrators in the transnational context.[57]

Conclusion

To answer the leading question of this article: The world market can reproduce its own prerequisites—but to a limited extent only.

First, it cannot be denied that private ordering is able to substitute for state-organized commercial law. However, on the one hand, the tailor-made governance mechanism employed in cross-border trade lack the economies of scale that a state-organized private law regime offers as safeguarding mechanism for the multitude of relatively unspecific market transactions. On the other hand, as private ordering

[55] See Ehrenzweig, Local and Moral Data in the Conflict of Laws, Buffalo Law Review 16 (1966), p. 55; Kay, Conflict of Laws: Foreign Law as Datum, California Law Review 53 (1965) 1, p. 47.

[56] See ICC Case No. 6503 (1990), J. DROIT INT'L (CLUNET) 1022-1031 (1995).

[57] Cf. Kahn, Les principes généraux du droit devant les arbitres du commerce international, Journal du droit international 116 (1989), p. 305 (317); Idot, Les conflits de lois en droit de la concurrence, Journal du droit international 122 (1995) 2, p. 321 (328 et seq.); for perspectives cf. Basedow, *Weltkartellrecht: Ausgangslage und Ziele, Methoden und Grenzen der internationalen Vereinheitlichung des Rechts der Wettbewerbsbeschränkungen*, 1998, pp. 94 et seq.

builds on dependency and command-and-control structures and thus necessarily implies vertical integration, international market structures suffer from a higher level of economic concentration and are more prone to the abuse of dominant market positions. Consequently, private ordering as opposed to state-organized commercial law allows cross-border trade at high costs and little market incentives only.

Second, as far as the competition law component of the world economic constitution is concerned, the example of international arbitration shows that private governance mechanisms are able to reproduce constitutional elements to a certain extent, but are still far from a comprehensive solution. As shown above, the application of competition law by arbitral tribunals suffers from several inconsistencies. Also, the development of a comprehensive 'transnational competition law' seems unlikely due to the different national approaches to antitrust regulation. However, this should not block the view from the positive results of our analysis of ICC awards. Even if the tribunals' reasoning may be inconsistent or sometimes not convincing: at least ICC tribunals—in the vast majority of cases—are able and willing to apply competition law as soon as they decide according to rules of law. It has become clear that arbitration cannot be regarded as a governance mechanism generally allowing parties to 'opt out of regulation'. Already at the current point of time, parties agreeing on an arbitration clause have to expect that a tribunal resolving any potential conflict in the contractual relation will consider the protection of competition as a goal of public interest, even if this runs counter to the ex-ante private interests of the parties. Partly this is a result of the fact that from an ex-post perspective, i.e. after a conflict has arisen, one party often has an interest in voiding the contract and, therefore, refers to the ban on cartels as an issue of public policy.

Within the European Union, the application of competition law is guaranteed by the jurisdiction of the ECJ. Since according to the decision in the Eco Swiss case awards contrary to EU competition law will be annulled by any public court in the Member States of the EU, any arbitral tribunal sensitive to the criteria laid down in Art. 35 of the ICC rules will apply competition law. Since it is one of the main goals of arbitration to render enforceable awards useful to the parties, any award potentially enforceable within the EU will consider competition law. As a large part of world trade is at least indirectly connected to the EU and thus might involve the enforcement of an award in Europe, the ECJ's legislation has great impact. If other economically powerful jurisdictions were to implement similar rules, the universal application of competition law by arbitral tribunals could be put on a more stable foundation.

Also, changes to the procedural rules of international arbitration itself could further enhance the uniform application of competition law. In the long run, it seems inevitable to push for a more thorough publication of awards in order to both allow a broader discussion of arbitral awards and enable arbitral tribunals to carve out more consistent decision-making criteria on a case-by-case basis.

The upshot for the development of a more efficient and fair world economic constitution is that public players will have to actively support the world market in reproducing its institutional prerequisites. While private ordering is able to allow a respectable level of cross-border commerce and enforce antitrust law to a certain extent, both the commercial law and the competition law element of the current world economic constitution remain under-developed in contrast to its domestic role models. In the long run, only further cooperation of national private law systems across borders will help lowering the level of vertical integration in international trade and thus allow fair market structures. Also, as far as the application of antitrust rules by arbitral tribunals is concerned, nation states will have to keep up the pressure on international arbitration organizations to apply and enforce competition law.

Competition Law and Development Policy: Subordination, Self-Sufficiency or Integration?

Yane Svetiev

Introduction

International competition lawyers often refer (with some pride) to the exponential growth of the number of jurisdictions in the world that have adopted antitrust enforcement regimes since the early 1990s. Namely, over 100 national jurisdictions now have some competition law mechanism and in addition, quite a few regional integration regimes contain competition provisions.[1] Since industrialised countries have been covered by the more established and long-standing antitrust regimes in the US and the EU, much of that growth is due to the adoption of competition laws by transition and developing economies. Some of those jurisdictions have adopted or strengthened their competition enforcement regimes of their own initiative.[2] However, frequently such a regime is implemented at the instigation or

The author acknowledges the support of the ERC Project on European Regulatory Private Law hosted at the EUI. The argument presented in this paper has benefited from discussions in research meetings with other members of the project team.

[1] Fox, In search of a Competition Law Fit for Developing Countries, NYU Law and Economics Research Paper Series, Working Paper 11-04, 2011, p. 7, available at: http://papers.ssrn.com/sol3/papers.cfm?abstract_id=1761619.

[2] The former socialist nations of Eastern Europe, for example, established competition enforcement regimes as part of their efforts at transition to a market economy.

Y. Svetiev (✉)
Research Fellow, Law Department, European University Institute, Via delle Fontanelle 10, I-50014 San Domenico, Italy
e-mail: Yane.Svetiev@eui.eu

C. Herrmann et al. (eds.), *European Yearbook of International Economic Law (EYIEL), Vol. 4 (2013)*, European Yearbook of International Economic Law 4,
DOI 10.1007/978-3-642-33917-2_9,

encouragement of international donors and development bodies, such as the World Bank, the IMF,[3] as well as the EU.[4]

While, as a result, many nations have now adopted such laws, little is known about the effects or outcomes of this trend in the developing world.[5] On the question of effectiveness, interest often tends to focus on the question of whether laws are implemented, whether there exist enforcement institutions, whether those institutions are active or whether they are regarded as successful by their peers in other countries. Yet having a highly active competition authority, which commences many investigations, even completes many of them, and collects high levels of fines is only one set of indicators of success of a nascent competition regime. The more fundamental question relates to the ultimate outcomes of this proliferation of competition laws in the developing world and the relationship to the overall objectives of public policy. Is this merely another market-opening mechanism against poorer nations that serves the trading interests of industrialised nations and their multinational companies? Alternatively, given the overriding importance of developmental objectives in these nations, does competition law contribute towards, or at least not detract from the achievement of developmental goals, such as the promotion of sustainable growth, the reduction of poverty and malnourishment, and the overall increase in human development? Moreover, are any beneficial effects worth the cost of having a domestic competition regime, or are there other less burdensome and more cost effective ways to achieve similar outcomes?

In this contribution, I explore the relationship between competition law enforcement and development policy to argue, perhaps somewhat provocatively, that these two cannot and should not be viewed as separate self-contained regimes. A number of recent developments both in advanced and other jurisdictions point towards this conclusion. In particular, I will argue that the distinctions between competition goals and developmental goals are being eroded as the conception of competition law, even in advanced jurisdictions, moves away from that of a legal instrument that protects a particular market structure or that supports an unqualified vision of business autonomy, prioritising atomistic decision-making and market transactions. Instead, competition law may increasingly be viewed as a tool for resolving the

[3] In an interview an Egyptian Competition Authority official explained that the IMF had pressed for the adoption of a competition law, but that Egypt could delay its adoption since it "wasn't one of the [top] priorities [for the IMF]," Interview with Egyptian Competition Authority official, 2 June 2009.

[4] Fingleton/Fox/Neven/Seabright, *Competition Policy and the Transformation of Central Europe*, 1996, pp. 174–176.

[5] It has been argued that the effects of antitrust enforcement in the developed world are also not well understood. For two divergent conclusions on this issue, see Crandall/Winston, Does Antitrust Policy Improve Consumer Welfare? Assessing the Evidence, Journal of Economic Perspectives 17 (2003) 4, p. 3 (23-24), and Baker, The Case for Antitrust Enforcement, Journal of Economic Perspectives 17 (2003) 4, p. 27 (42).

problems of industrial organisation more generally.[6] Moreover, the problems that competition law seeks to address cannot be described along a single dimension, such as the size (or "bigness") of firms, the opportunistic hold-up in relationships with specific investments, or even price fixing and collusion. Experience, evidence and theory have taught us that there may be good and bad reasons for, and outcomes from, both large firms and inter-firm collaboration.

The view presented in this contribution offers both an optimistic view about competition law as the "law of development" and reasons for caution. To the extent that there is no distinction between competition goals and developmental goals, the trend towards the adoption of competition laws in the developing world is a salutary one. Competition law may be calibrated to the development needs of specific jurisdictions and does not need to take a back seat in the period of pursuit of development in order to gain greater prominence in a "post-development" stage. The point of caution relates precisely to this calibration. A richer conception of the goals of competition law implies a more varied panoply of tools through which to pursue them. In particular, when developing nations adopt a competition law they tend to import the existing templates or categories contained in the laws and administrative regimes of the advanced jurisdictions—anticompetitive agreements, some form of abuse of dominance and a merger control regime. However, the meaning and significance of these categories has not been fixed and stable over time even in the mature regimes—certain aspects of anticompetitive conduct have been emphasised more at different times and in different industrial and production settings. Therefore, the importation of such categories may not be a good guide to the kinds of problems new adopters are likely to face and which of those are likely to be particularly salient to their own context and to the achievement of developmental objectives. Moreover, this kind of import may lead to early encrustations of analytical and decision-making routines for nascent antitrust authorities that may not be particularly useful, but that nonetheless become difficult to dislodge over time. In the absence of local tradition and accumulated knowledge and in an effort to mimic their colleagues from other jurisdictions, officials of newer authorities may establish a routinised approach to analysing problems and deciding cases or they may establish enforcement priorities that do not reflect the local development context. The challenge for those who promote competition enforcement in the developing world is to identify the salience of local competition problems and their relationship to developmental objectives, rather than to either speculate about competition law objectives at high levels of generality[7] or to be wedded to established antitrust categories as currently understood.

---

[6] Svetiev, Antitrust Governance: The New Wave of Antitrust, Loyola University of Chicago Law Journal 38 (2007) 3, p. 593 (634).

[7] ICN Unilateral Conduct Working Group, Report on the Objectives of Unilateral Conduct Laws, Assessment of Dominance/Substantial Market Power, and State-created Monopolies, 2007, http://www.internationalcompetitionnetwork.org/uploads/library/doc353.pdf.

Competition Law in Developing Nations: The Importance of Dynamics

Competition law as we know it today is the product of western industrialised nations. Mature antitrust jurisdictions, namely the US and the EU, have also been the principal proselytizers for the adoption of antitrust by other nations. In post-war period, US efforts to extend the reach of antitrust laws are well documented. The US advocated the adoption of antitrust laws, particularly among its European trading partners. For instance, the US was largely responsible for the implementation of a competition law in post-war West Germany and Japan, as well as the entrenchment of the competition provisions of the Treaty of Rome. US advocacy was consistent with the then regnant view of antitrust as a tool for maintaining a decentralised economy, which was also democracy-enforcing because of the link between the accumulation of economic and political power. Thus, the US imposition of antitrust laws on countries such as Germany or Japan, where pre-war totalitarian regimes had flourished, was not accidental.[8]

Apart from advocating or imposing the adoption of antitrust laws, the US also enforced its own antitrust laws extraterritorially, based on the effects doctrine, enforcement that once again, principally affected its key trading partners in Europe. Such extraterritorial extension of American values, through decisions of US litigants and courts, was resisted by the European nations. Their resistance was based, in part, on the interference of this type of enforcement with domestic policy-making with what we might call development objectives. In particular, arrangements among economic operators (including often competitors) may seem anticompetitive through the eyes of US courts and yet can be carefully calibrated arrangements among various social groups, often sponsored or supported by state policy, which seek to promote a balance of policy goals, including product quality and innovation, consumer protection, workable competition, as well as stability in production and employment.[9]

While it was the US that was to a considerable extent responsible for the inclusion of the antitrust provisions at the establishment of the European Community, the EU is regarded today as the other principal competition regime in the world. More recently, the EU has been the jurisdiction at the forefront of efforts both to induce other nations to adopt domestic or regional competition laws and to create an international competition instrument. The EU has been particularly successful in such efforts for a number of reasons. First, the processes of association and enlargement of the EU have brought a number of jurisdictions directly under the purview of the EU competition regime. Secondly, rather than relying merely on

[8] Herrigel, *Industrial Constructions: The Sources of German Industrial Power*, 1996, pp. 139–140; Gerber, *Law and Competition in Twentieth Century Europe: Protecting Prometheus*, 1998, pp. 147–148.

[9] Whitman, Consumerism versus Producerism: A Study in Comparative Law, Yale Law Journal 117 (2007) 3, p. 340.

extraterritorial enforcement, the EU has used its trading and economic relationships with other nations, as well as technical and other assistance, to induce them to adopt domestic laws or to subject them to some supranational obligations.

Despite these successes in bilateral settings, the EU failed in its efforts to include a competition instrument in the WTO agenda, as part of the package of the so-called Singapore issues. The US had never been particularly enthusiastic about being subjected to international antitrust rules more restrictive than its own, but it was developing nations that most strongly resisted the introduction of antitrust obligations in the WTO regime.[10] Developing nations were concerned about the extent to which a relatively unfamiliar set of antitrust obligations would be used as a tool for asymmetric market access for industrialised nation products, while at the same time impeding their autonomy to implement policies pursuing developmental goals. An additional concern related to the balance of enforcement priorities of their domestic institutions if they become subject to an international antitrust instrument. To avoid the breaching of international obligations domestic authorities might have to prioritise conduct of interest to foreign economic operators, while at the same time not having the resources or capacity to impose obligations and remedies on conduct of multinationals that significantly impacts domestic firms and consumers. This only heightened the suspicion that antitrust could be used as another tool for the asymmetric opening of markets placing developing nations at a disadvantage.

The academic debate stirred by the trends towards the adoption of competition law and its internationalisation focused on the issue of whether developing nations needed a competition law at all and, if so, what kind. In an oft-cited contribution, Laffont expressed scepticism about such a need based on the view that "it is not always the case that competition should be encouraged in [developing] countries" given the structure of their economies.[11] Furthermore, implementing a competition enforcement regime is both complex and costly, particularly in light of institutional and administrative weaknesses faced by those nations.[12] While in some cases competition enforcement might bring some benefits to developing nations, much of the benefits of competitive pressure could also be delivered through strictly enforced disciplines of international trade liberalisation.[13] If the trading regime can guarantee access of imports to domestic markets, this can have the effect of disentrenching incumbent market power and disciplining domestic players.

---

[10] McMahon, Developing countries and international competition law and policy, in: Faundez/Tan (eds.), *International Economic Law, Globalization and Developing Countries*, 2010, p. 252.

[11] Laffont, Competition, Information, and Development, in: Pleskovic/Stiglitz (eds.), *Annual World Bank Conference on Development Economics*, 1998, p. 237.

[12] Gerardin, Competition Law and Regional Economic Integration: An Analysis of the Southern Mediterranean Countries, World Bank Working Paper No. 35, 2004, pp. 24–26.

[13] Gerardin, Competition Law and Regional Economic Integration: An Analysis of the Southern Mediterranean Countries, World Bank Working Paper No. 35, 2004, p. 24.

Even at the conceptual level, the prescription that trade liberalisation is a sufficient substitute for competition enforcement faces two immediate shortcomings. The first is the fact that free trade does not in any way ensure competitive markets in non-tradeables, which may represent quite a significant share of the economy. The second is the fact that trade rules only impose obligations upon states and therefore can be circumvented by private arrangements seeking to block market access to foreign competitors, thus undoing the effects of trade liberalisation.[14]

Another set of arguments advanced more fundamental objections to the push for competition enforcement and an international competition instrument. For instance, in a number of contributions, Singh sought to justify the developing nations' opposition to the EU proposal for a uniform competition instrument under the WTO umbrella, arguing that this was an ill-conceived idea that would disserve the interests of developing nations. Singh argued that any "one-size-fits all" instrument would not adequately deal with the heterogeneous circumstances and development needs of such nations.[15] Specifically, he argued that an emphasis on competition enforcement in developing nations may be premature and may in fact inhibit their capacity to pursue development objectives. Instead, he suggested that East Asian late industrialising economies, such as Japan and South Korea, offered a more appropriate template for the sequencing of different policy tools for nations facing development challenges.[16]

According to Singh, these economies did not emphasise competition enforcement in the stages of early industrialisation, during which time development goals prevailed over competition goals. This also meant that industrial policy in these nations "dominated competition policy during their developmental phases i.e. if there was a conflict between the two, industrial policy prevailed."[17] According to this view, while competition policy has static goals, such as reducing prices for

[14] In fact, there is also evidence that the disciplining effect of domestic competitors is much more potent than that of imports. See Evenett, What is the relationship between competition law and policy and economic development, in: Brooks/Evenett (eds.), *Competition Policy and Development in Asia*, 2005, p. 1 (20).

[15] Singh, Competition and Competition Policy in Emerging Markets: International and Developmental Dimensions, Research papers for the Intergovernmental Group of Twenty-Four on International Monetary Affairs, No. 18, 2002, pp. 16, 19, available at: http://www.unctad.org/en/docs/gdsmdpbg2418_en.pdf.

[16] Singh, Competition and Competition Policy in Emerging Markets: International and Developmental Dimensions, Research papers for the Intergovernmental Group of Twenty-Four on International Monetary Affairs, No. 18, 2002, p. 18; Singh, Multilateral Competition Policy and Economic Development—A Developing Country Perspective on the European Community Proposals, Paper presented at the Fifth session of the Intergovernmental Group of Experts on Competition Law and Policy at Geneva, 2003, pp. 13–14, available at: http://www.networkideas.org/feathm/aug2003/MCP.pdf.

[17] Singh, Multilateral Competition Policy and Economic Development—A Developing Country Perspective on the European Community Proposals, Paper presented at the Fifth session of the Intergovernmental Group of Experts on Competition Law and Policy at Geneva, 2003, p. 16.

consumers, industry policy has dynamic goals, such as increasing investment, which requires stable profits.[18] On Singh's retelling of the relevant history, the state in these economies restricted imports and foreign investment, providing a captive market for domestic firms, which together with lax competition enforcement guaranteed high profits that could be used to "undertake high rates of investment, to improve the quality of their products, and ... to capture markets abroad."[19] It is only when development goals are achieved, with sufficient levels of industrial output and income per capita, that the state can begin to emphasise competition goals to ensure domestic competitive markets as a discipline on the now-established market players. However, in general, given the importance of dynamic (over static) efficiency for developing countries, coherence between policies will "involve competition policy being subordinated to the industrial policy during the course of economic development."[20] In other words, competition law is not the law that leads to development, but instead premature enforcement of competition law may impede the achievement of developmental objectives.

Such a view of a trade-off between competition and development goals, finds some support in the competition law doctrines of advanced antitrust regimes as well. In the US for instance, the intensity of antitrust enforcement has varied to take account of changing economic circumstances.[21] However, even in times when the purpose of antitrust was viewed as broader and more open-ended, both judges[22] and commentators[23] stated, sometimes in quite emphatic terms, that in deciding antitrust cases the focus must remain on the goal of promoting competition and that courts cannot forsake the goal of competition for other policy goals. The implication of this position appears to be that other goals are to be pursued by targeted interventions. The narrowing of the goals of antitrust policy, inspired by the so-called Chicago revolution, to harm to consumer welfare through an increase in short run prices has only further exacerbated (at least conceptually) the compartmentalisation of competition policy in the US to static efficiency goals.

---

[18] Singh, Multilateral Competition Policy and Economic Development—A Developing Country Perspective on the European Community Proposals, Paper presented at the Fifth session of the Intergovernmental Group of Experts on Competition Law and Policy at Geneva, 2003, p.15.

[19] Singh, Multilateral Competition Policy and Economic Development—A Developing Country Perspective on the European Community Proposals, Paper presented at the Fifth session of the Intergovernmental Group of Experts on Competition Law and Policy at Geneva, 2003, p. 20.

[20] Singh, Multilateral Competition Policy and Economic Development—A Developing Country Perspective on the European Community Proposals, Paper presented at the Fifth session of the Intergovernmental Group of Experts on Competition Law and Policy at Geneva, 2003, pp. 24–25.

[21] Crane, Technocracy and Antitrust, Texas Law Review 86 (2008) 6, p. 1159 (1175–1176).

[22] US Supreme Court, *National Society of Professional Engineers vs. United States*, 435 US 679 (1978), at p. 695 ("Even assuming occasional exceptions to the presumed consequences of competition, the statutory policy precludes inquiry into the question whether competition is good or bad.").

[23] Areeda, Antitrust Law as Industrial Policy: Should Judges and Juries Make It?, in: Jorde/Teece (eds.), *Antitrust, Innovation and Competitiveness*, 1992, p. 29 (32).

Similarly, in the EU the Treaty of Rome entrenched the competition provisions as foundational principles from the very beginning of the Community. However, at the same time, the Treaty provided an apparent outlet route in what is now Art. 101(3) TFEU, a provision that allows some anticompetitive arrangements to be exempted from the operation of the Art. 101(1) prohibition, if the undertakings involved could establish that the agreement or practice in question "contributes to improving the production or distribution of goods or to promoting technical or economic progress." In the original implementation Regulation 17/62, the Commission (in the exercise of its administrative role) had the monopoly of granting such exemptions. Thus, while in the EU regime the trading off of goals was integrated into the competition decision-making, this methodology does reinforce the view that the pursuit of public policy goals relating to economic progress and development may justify the suppression of competition goals.

Much ink has been spilled on the question of the appropriate goals of competition policy and the range of views of different schools of antitrust thought to this issue. In some formulations, antitrust policy should be enforced without reference to outcomes. This approach emphasises the autonomy of economic actors to make individual business decisions, absent agreements with or coercion from other traders or powerful firms. Favouring such a decentralised or atomistic economic landscape might be a value in itself, *pace* economic outcomes, and might also be beneficial to democracy if we believe that decentralised (as opposed to concentrated) economic power is incapable of dominating or completely capturing political processes. However, there are also clear potential benefits to cooperation and integration in modern economic life, particularly once we move beyond craft production destined for local buyers towards more complex industrial products that may have to be marketed to more distant markets. Autonomous decision-making by atomistic agents may be one value a community cares for (and this may not even be universally true across different communities), but there are many others, including not just lower prices, but also new and improved products, reduced poverty and malnourishment, sustainable exploitation of the local environment, improved access to water or public transport and so on.

A recognition that, in implementing competition law, various goals may need to be pursued simultaneously has at least three implications. First, it amplifies the problem caused by the absence of absolute markers that signal the need for competition intervention, such as firm size, market share, market structure or even types of conduct. Secondly, it makes decision-making multi-dimensional and therefore more complex. Finally, because of the first two, it puts an even greater strain on the institutions for implementation of law policy and this is precisely the area where developing economies often suffer from considerable weaknesses.

It is worth noting at this point that these problems are not limited to developing nations and have increasingly taken centre-stage in advanced competition regimes such as the US and the EU. In the US, the historical and ideological background to the antitrust laws, as well as their undifferentiated application through the generalist courts has made antitrust doctrine receptive to attempts to narrow the focus of interventions by essentially providing a safe harbour for conduct that is unlikely to produce an increase in consumer prices. While EU competition law has been more open to a heterodox interpretation of its purposes, in the inception the Treaty competition provisions were used quite instrumentally and quite narrowly to break down private barriers to the creation of the internal market. In other words, for a long time EU policy prioritised one particular type of competition namely cross-border competition that would challenge national systems of production and distribution.

However, more recently, both of these mature regimes have had to deal with cases that challenge narrow conceptions of competition enforcement.[24] The antitrust scrutiny of Microsoft's practices in the operating system and adjacent products, which had its iterations both in the US and the EU, placed enforcers and courts face-to-face with the production ecology of the new economy, characterised by on-going innovation, collaboration and information flows across firm boundaries. In particular, these cases brought to the fore the fact that the main forms of competition in these settings are dynamic, based not on price, but on the ability to deliver new and improved products to market. Moreover, rapidly changing technology strains the static tools of antitrust economics, by making product boundaries unstable and the sources of competitive threat matters of judgment rather than inference from current data.[25]

The focus on innovation in such cases has had a number of implications for the implementation of competition law even in mature regimes. First, it puts in sharp relief the fact that even an efficiency based competition policy need not solely focus on static allocative efficiency, but also on dynamic efficiency, particularly given that dynamic change over time makes a far more important contribution to economic growth and performance. Secondly, it suggests caution about short term prices as the sole criterion for competition intervention partly because competition can take place along many different dimensions,[26] not only price. Moreover, certain aspects of products and services may take consumers (and other players in the regulation game, such as administrators or legislators) a longer time to learn about

---

[24] Svetiev, Antitrust Governance: The New Wave of Antitrust, Loyola University of Chicago Law Journal 38 (2007) 3, p. 593.

[25] Coyle, Discussion on "Competition Economics and Antitrust in Europe," Economic Policy 21 (2006) 48, p. 786.

[26] Wright, Antitrust, Multidimensional Competition, and Innovation: Do We Have an Antitrust-Relevant Theory of Competition Now?, in: Manne/Wright (eds.), *Competition Policy and Patent Law under Uncertainty: Regulating Innovation*, 2011, p. 228.

or appreciate as a relevant dimension.[27] Finally, such cases make it necessary to confront the non-linear (or networked) inter-firm relationships in the context of complex products and applications, where there are intermingled both competitive and collaborative aspects and where innovation, production and distribution proceed continuously and simultaneously, rather than in stages.[28]

To be able to respond to antitrust problems in a dynamic environment, the advanced regimes have also had to search for ways to relax the constraints of the standard implementation tools for competition law. The remedies implemented in both the US and the EU to deal with the Microsoft litigation put into place mechanisms through which to re-establish cooperation and ensure inter-operability in the markets under scrutiny and to remove bottlenecks to innovation. The difficulties of organising production based on collaboration between independent units are staple fare in the industrial organisation literature.[29] Arguably, these interventions and remedies were not based either on an absolute distrust of business size or market concentration, nor on an absolute faith in business autonomy, but instead were attempts at solving concrete problems that arose in a particular production ecology. As such, antitrust or competition policy may be regarded as a more generic tool to resolve problems in industrial organisation to advance the public interest.[30] It follows that in such settings the once (at least conceptually) firm line between competition policy and innovation policy tends to become blurred.

This brief detour into some recent examples of competition enforcement in advanced jurisdictions also sheds some light on the issue of the sequencing of policy implementation in developing nations. In particular, to achieve

---

[27] One example of this is the issue of consumer privacy in conduct and transactions over the Internet. Before there was widespread awareness of this issue among consumers, in analysing the proposed merger between Google, Inc. and DoubleClick, Inc. on antitrust principles, the FTC recognised that the "acquisition raised concerns about consumer privacy in the online advertising marketplace that were not unique to the proposed merger." Rather than prohibiting the merger on this basis, the FTC subsequently developed and released a "set of behavioural marketing principles that could be used by businesses" to protect online privacy. See Federal Trade Commission, *The FTC in 2008: A Force for Consumers and Competition*, 2008, p. 4. Note that recently, consumer privacy issues on the Internet have taken on a far greater significance as an aspect of competition. The change in Google's privacy policy at the beginning of 2012 triggered a vocal debate with one of its rivals Microsoft, about which company offered more robust privacy protection on the Internet, triggering a response from Google in which it compared the privacy policies of the principal Internet platforms. See "Microsoft slams Google user data policy in new ads," Sydney Morning Herald, 1 February 2012, available at: http://news.smh.com.au/breaking-news-technology/microsoft-slams-google-user-data-policy-in-new-ads-20120202-1qu3b.html (reporting on Microsoft's "Putting People First" advertising campaign).

[28] Jorde/Teece, Innovation, Cooperation, and Antitrust, in: Jorde/Teece (eds.), *Antitrust, Innovation and Competitiveness*, 1992, p. 47 (49); Mathews, *Strategizing, Disequilibrium and Profit*, 2006, p. 21.

[29] Alchian/Demsetz, Production, Information Costs, and Economic Organization, American Economic Review 62 (1972) 5, p. 777.

[30] Svetiev, Antitrust Governance: The New Wave of Antitrust, Loyola University of Chicago Law Journal 38 (2007) 3, p. 593 (620, 634).

developmental objectives, do developing nations need to subsume the enforcement of competition laws to the implementation of industry policy? If it is true that the line between competition and industrial policy is being blurred by the focus on innovation and dynamic effects in competition enforcement in advanced regimes, it may be that developing nations need not be subject to this sequencing choice either. Unless of course we can argue that developing nations' circumstances are different justifying a different policy prescription. In the next section, I argue that this is not the case by relying on both some contemporary arguments and a reference to the historical "templates" discussed by Singh.

Competition Law and Developmental Objectives

Apart from the controversies presented thus far, a number of arguments have been advanced in the literature about the ways in which competition law enforcement can assist developing nations in the attainment of their developmental objectives. Brusick and Evenett, for example, have pointed to the fact that abuses of dominance are frequently alleged in developing nations against firms that provide key infrastructure, such as energy, telecommunications, banking and transport, whether state-owned or private. To the extent that such conduct leads to higher prices and lower quality, this "negatively affect[s] the efficiency of exporters and producers downstream and hence act[s] as a break to development."[31] Along a different dimension, McMahon highlights evidence that developing nations are disproportionately affected by international cartels, which raise price of staple commodities and can affect developmental goals both by hurting consumers directly and by raising costs of local producers and exporters.[32] Finally, competition law can also be a tool with which to prise open local distribution channels, where they are foreclosed by powerful economic and political interests.[33]

Note that none of the above cases need involve a conflict or a trade-off between the competition goals (even if limited to static efficiency goals) and the goals of development. Therefore, they are not inconsistent with Singh's suggestion of subordinating competition policy to industry policy where a conflict arises. If there exists a competition law and an enforcement authority, the authority should proceed against such cases (assuming it has the possibility of implementing an effective remedy, which is a different issue altogether), since competition enforcement works synergistically with and supports industry policy.

---

[31] Brusick/Evenett, Should Developing Countries Worry About Abuse of Dominant Power?, Wisconsin Law Review, (2008) 2, p. 269 (280).

[32] McMahon, Developing countries and international competition law and policy, in: Faundez/Tan (eds.), *International Economic Law, Globalization and Developing Countries*, 2010, p. 252.

[33] Fox, Economic Development, Poverty and Antitrust: The Other Path, Southwestern Journal of Law and Trade in the Americas 13 (2007), p. 211 (213).

But what about those cases where there is an apparent trade-off? In cases where in the sector that is supposed to provide the elevator for living standards through industrialisation and exports, does the achievement of such a result require protecting the prices and profits of local firms? It is precisely in those cases that Singh would suggest subordinating competition policy to industry policy. This is because the basis of the developmental strategy in the East Asian nations, according to Singh, was the use of domestic consumers as a captive market while firms in the industrialising sector build up scale, experience and knowledge to be able to capture and expand into exporting markets.

From the very outset, using such a policy prescription in many developing nations is faced with the problem that domestic markets may well be too small, both in absolute terms, but also specifically for the potential export, for this industrialisation strategy to work. If one thinks of recent developers based on high technology products for example, such as Ireland or Israel, the information technology sector was from the very outset targeted to exports and the domestic market would have been relatively insufficient to be a springboard for growth. As such, allowing harm to domestic consumers through lax competition enforcement may well not translate into the achievement of development goals down the track.

Even more fundamentally, shielding the industrialising sector from imports was another key part of the successful strategies in the East Asian template as presented by Singh. Indeed, if the key is to protect prices and profits of domestic firms, there seems to be no point in lax competition enforcement domestically, if the industrialising or development sector is subject to competition from imports. However, in a world where successive rounds of trade liberalisation have taken place over the last couple of decades and there are legal restrictions on raising protectionist barriers, it may not be feasible to implement an industrial policy that hinges critically on shielding domestic firms from imports for a period during which they can build-up competitive strength and perhaps recoup some of the outlays involved in the investments in industrial equipment.

Many in the development advocacy community have, consistently with Singh's arguments, raised their voices against the rash extension of competition policy to developing nations.[34] However, there have also been prominent voices supporting the view that credible implementation of competition and consumer protection laws in developing nations can make a meaningful and positive contribution to the achievement of development goals.

For instance, the Consumer Unity and Trust Society (CUTS) has a specific mission of extending competition and consumer protection laws and ensuring that they are effectively implemented in developing nations. CUTS is a non-governmental organisation, which seeks to advance development goals through the promotion of vibrant competition enforcement in developing nations.

---

[34] Yu, Development Challenges of Competition Policy in the Economic Partnership Agreements, 2007, available at: http://www.acp-eu-trade.org/library/files/Yu_EN_190607_South-Centre_Developmet-challenges-of-Competition-policy-in-the-EPAs.pdf.

Among its missions with respect to competition and consumer protection, CUTS includes the following: "[p]romoting fair markets to enhance consumer welfare" and "enabl[ing] people, in particular women, to achieve their right to basic needs and sustainable development through a strong consumer movement."[35] As part of pursuing those missions, since 2003 CUTS has founded a Centre for Competition, Investment & Economic Regulation,[36] which has initiated projects examining competition enforcement in a number of different sectors (healthcare, pharmaceuticals, sectoral regulation) and in different regions of the developing world (India, Africa, etc.).[37] As one CUTS official explained in an interview, the activities of CUTS are based on the premise that "healthy competition" can lead to "not only lower prices, better quality, better availability, but very importantly ... good governance."[38]

The approach followed by CUTS is to build bottom up support for competition policy enforcement, and this approach is animated by two related rationales. First, if a broader set of stakeholders, including movements promoting development goals and government authorities in general, perceive the benefits of competitive markets, it will also be easier for competition authorities to do their work. Secondly, in recognition that policy implementation and effectiveness is often the weak point in the developing world, CUTS aims to "build up that kind of awareness and that kind of a movement, which continues to pressurize the authorities ... to draft a law, adopt a law, including [to] go ahead implementing it." In other words, the aim is to contribute towards the creation of a "watch-dog" to ensure "that the law functions."[39] Thus, as opposed to the conditionality approach often followed by developing nations' foreign partners (including industrialised nations and donor organisations), organisations such as CUTS work to domesticate the competition enforcement regime, a key step for moving from the law on the books to law in action, as it builds internal support and monitoring for the implementation of competition policies.

This approach goes against the view that competition policy enforcement comes later in the sequence to industrialisation policies promoting developmental goals. On that issue, the CUTS official specifically noted that even assuming this story of shielding domestic firms from competition (domestic or foreign) as a form of industry policy presents an accurate depiction of the industrialisation process in Japan and South Korea, the problem is that "those times have gone" in light of the on-going trade liberalisation that has taken place already and the commitments that have been taken on within the WTO. From the development perspective, even if competition is not the sole force that promotes developmental goals, the CUTS collocutor suggested that there might well be lower awareness of the benefits from

---

[35] http://cuts-international.org/Capability-December2009.pdf.

[36] http://www.cuts-ccier.org/index.htm.

[37] http://www.cuts-ccier.org/Competition_Policy_and_Law.htm.

[38] Interview with Official of the Consumer Unity and Trust Society, 3 June 2009.

[39] Interview with Official of the Consumer Unity and Trust Society, 3 June 2009.

competition in many developing nations. This is because economic and personal or family affairs can often be related and deeply entwined[40] or to use the words of Rodrik, because economic life often proceeds as part and parcel of "traditional entanglements."[41]

Development Theory and Policy

Arguably, the challenge for development policy has always been to overcome different bottlenecks, whether industrial organisation, governance or social, to economic growth and progress, while simultaneously defining an appropriate role, if any, for the state in that process.[42] In other words, it is about fashioning a mix of mechanisms for the improved transformation of inputs to outputs and the appropriate distribution of the latter in order to contribute towards an alleviation of poverty and an increase in various aspects of human development.

Traditionally, theorising about development was based on the view that developing nations were stuck in a low-growth equilibrium and debates focused on what kinds of policies a government could implement to escape that equilibrium.[43] These debates had a largely macroeconomic focus. Thus, one view was that governments should promote balanced growth by way of "a coordinated, broadly based investment program" in various sectors of the economy (or in Krugman's words the "Big Push").[44] The alternative view was that governments should focus on unbalanced growth, by promoting investment in a single sector that then sets off a further chain of upstream and downstream investments. In other words, government policy should promote investment in "a few key sectors with strong linkages, then moving on to other sectors" to correct the resulting imbalances.[45]

As Rodrik has recounted, after a period of dormancy development theory subsequently turned neoclassical with an emphasis on microeconomic factors, and specifically relative prices as signals for economic activity that would produce economic development. This shift was both the result of the perceived lack of success of prior policies, changing intellectual fads, but it was also based on

---

[40] Interview with Official of the Consumer Unity and Trust Society, 3 June 2009.

[41] Rodrik, Institutions for High-Quality Growth: What They Are and How to Acquire Them, Studies in Comparative International Development 35 (2000) 3, p. 3 (8).

[42] Krugman, The Fall and Rise of Development Economics, in: Rodwin/Schön (eds.), *Rethinking the Development Experience: Essays Provoked by the Work of Albert Hirschman*, 1994, p. 39, available at: http://web.mit.edu/krugman/www/dishpan.html.

[43] Sabel, Learning by Monitoring: The Institutions of Economic Development, in: Smelser/Swedberg (eds.), *The Handbook of Economic Sociology*, 1994, p. 137.

[44] Krugman, The Fall and Rise of Development Economics, in: Rodwin/Schön (eds.), *Rethinking the Development Experience: Essays Provoked by the Work of Albert Hirschman*, 1994, p. 39.

[45] Krugman, The Fall and Rise of Development Economics, in: Rodwin/Schön (eds.), *Rethinking the Development Experience: Essays Provoked by the Work of Albert Hirschman*, 1994, p. 39.

evidence that even in developing nations "investment decisions, agricultural production, exports [were] quite sensitive to price incentives."[46] In other words, during the 1980s, development policy also turns neo-liberal, with a focus on price reform through liberalisation and privatisation programmes as a way of improving the micro signals to which economic actors must respond. Yet, according to Rodrik, in a number of different settings this turn towards a focus on liberalisation of price signals also had either unsatisfactory or disastrous consequences. In turn, such experiences "served to reveal the institutional underpinnings of market economies" and therefore "put institutions squarely on the agenda of reformers."[47] This, of course, includes the enforcement of competition law, given the recognised failures associated with private monopoly, although it also included other kinds of sectoral regulation, supervision of financial and credit markets, as well as a broader focus on good governance by, for instance, limiting the opportunities for rent-seeking and corruption. Given the conditionality mindset of international development advisors and donors, these various regimes are often seen as self-contained boxes of regulation[48] that have to be "ticked" (i.e. put in place) by developing nations. In other words, they are part of a set of pre-conditions that, when put in place, may unleash the development potential of poor countries.

Rodrik argues that production in poor countries is sensitive to price incentives, but only "as long as these are perceived to have some predictability."[49] We can think of the various regulatory regimes discussed above as mechanisms to ensure that price signals are not distorted and are more predictable; opportunities to respond to such signals by altering production decisions will not be foreclosed or expropriated by monopolists or monopsonists, or politically well-connected economic actors and so on.

However, just as unleashing price signals is not a panacea, nor is ticking the boxes for enacted regulatory regimes. The first reason is obvious: formally adopting a regulatory regime and appointing a regulator does not guarantee that the regulator will function effectively in implementing regulation or that the regime will not be captured in some way by those whom it is meant to constrain. The second reason is less obvious: even an effective regulatory regime only removes a set of forces that might distort price signals or make them unstable. There are myriad reasons why prices may shift—a shift in preferences or technology or the emergence of an alternative source of supply. For local actors to make investments that favour

[46] Rodrik, Institutions for High-Quality Growth: What They Are and How to Acquire Them, Studies in Comparative International Development 35 (2000) 3, p. 3 (4).

[47] Rodrik, Institutions for High-Quality Growth: What They Are and How to Acquire Them, Studies in Comparative International Development 35 (2000) 3, p. 3 (4).

[48] On the idea of self-sufficient regulatory regimes, see Micklitz, The Visible Hand of European Regulatory Private Law, Yearbook of European Law 28(2009), p. 3 (55–58), also Micklitz/ Patterson, From the Nation State to the Market: The Evolution of EU Private Law, unpublished manuscript, 2012.

[49] Rodrik, Institutions for High-Quality Growth: What They Are and How to Acquire Them, Studies in Comparative International Development 35 (2000) 3, p. 3 (4).

growth, they need reliable and robust information on the basis of which to make decisions about where best to direct those investments and then how to continue to make those products that are valued in markets.[50]

In offering a way forward, we might seek to synthesise the various perspectives on the elaboration of development and competition policy. One is the notion that development is favoured by a coordinated "push" in investment[51] based on the apparent common ground that "firms pursuing growth strategies together . . . were more likely to succeed than firms in isolation."[52] According to Krugman, coordinated investment would be more likely to produce economies of scale and other externalities that would push the industry "over the threshold of profitability."[53] Along similar lines, Singh emphasises the "coordination of investment activities" and argues that this was the "essential role of government" in the East Asian developers "during their developmental phase."[54]

However, as Sabel points out, apart from any coordination function there is also the task of acquiring and supplying the relevant information to those firms on what to produce and how.

On Singh's view about the proper sequencing of competition law enforcement in the developing nation, the state plays the coordination function of stimulating investments by sheltering the firms in the industrialising sector from competition allowing cartelisation and protecting their profits.[55] This, in turn, helps them to become internationally competitive exporters down the track. However, this beneficial outcome would only result if the local firms take advantage of this sheltering in order to learn to produce that which world markets demand and to deliver such products at adequate quality and price levels. Alternatively, firms may take advantage of sheltering policies to protect their profits, while the expected export performance never materialises, which may be a much more familiar story. If improved export performance does not materialise, this could be because the domestic firms failed to learn to produce well that for which there was market demand. However, they could also argue that market circumstances have changed, and that the policy of sheltering needs to continue to allow the firms to adjust to new circumstances and so on.

[50] Sabel, Learning by Monitoring: The Institutions of Economic Development, in: Smelser/ Swedberg (eds.), *The Handbook of Economic Sociology*, 1994, p. 137.

[51] Krugman, The Fall and Rise of Development Economics, in: Rodwin/Schön (eds.), *Rethinking the Development Experience: Essays Provoked by the Work of Albert Hirschman*, 1994, p. 39.

[52] Sabel, Learning by Monitoring: The Institutions of Economic Development, in: Smelser/ Swedberg (eds.), *The Handbook of Economic Sociology*, 1994, p. 137 (140).

[53] Krugman, The Fall and Rise of Development Economics, in: Rodwin/Schön (eds.), *Rethinking the Development Experience: Essays Provoked by the Work of Albert Hirschman*, 1994, p. 39.

[54] Singh, Multilateral Competition Policy and Economic Development—A Developing Country Perspective on the European Community Proposals, Paper presented at the Fifth session of the Intergovernmental Group of Experts on Competition Law and Policy at Geneva, 2003, p. 16.

[55] Singh, Multilateral Competition Policy and Economic Development—A Developing Country Perspective on the European Community Proposals, Paper presented at the Fifth session of the Intergovernmental Group of Experts on Competition Law and Policy at Geneva, 2003, p. 16.

Therefore, to understand whether a policy of sheltering is working to achieve goals of industrialisation or development and whether it needs to be continued or adjusted in some way, the government itself needs tools with which to evaluate those claims. In the absence of such tools, a policy of sheltering firms from competition and protecting their profitability can continue, imposing costs on local consumers and on the government budget without necessarily achieving improved export performance.

This brings us back to the issue of who supplies the information to the exporting sector as to which goods and how to produce them. One view might be that it is the state that must do this as part of the coordination function and this seems to be at least an unstated assumption of those who offer the export-led route to development of countries such as Japan or the East Asian tigers as a model for other developing nations to follow. However, as Sabel points out, such a view of the role of the state suggests at least three limitations in using this template for development. First, there is no reason in principle to believe that the state or the bureaucracy would have better access to such information as compared to firms.[56] Secondly, even if the Japanese or the South Korean bureaucracy did for some reason have better access to such information, this may not be the case for many of the nations currently still stuck at low levels of economic growth and development and at the same time facing serious governance and institutional limitations. Finally, even if this type of sheltering is appropriate, the state must also decide for how long to continue such a policy and when to end it, either if it is not bearing fruit or if it is no longer needed (particularly if it is also imposing costs on domestic consumers). Firms that benefit from the policy, after all, can seek to strategically supply information in an effort to continue the rents they receive from this policy, irrespective of whether they need it or whether they are indeed improving their productive and export performance.

Role of Associations, Strategic Contests, Stimulating Rivalry

It follows then that the state in the developmental context faces serious obstacles to acting as the key actor that steers the growth of export industries. It seems that the state has to stimulate the private sector to generate relevant knowledge that will enable private sector firms to produce goods that are valued and competitive in world markets and to ensure that such knowledge is also available to the administration so that it can evaluate the performance of the policy. Note that to achieve both of those purposes, it would seem preferable to foster a diversity of sources of

---

[56] Sabel points to evidence to suggest that even in Japan the state did not (ex ante) have privileged access to prescient information that would allow it to play the principal or dominant steering role in the process of industrialisation and development and that the strategies initially sponsored by state institutions were not necessarily the ones that bore fruit in Japan's path to industrialisation, see Sabel, Learning by Monitoring: The Institutions of Economic Development, in: Smelser/ Swedberg (eds.), *The Handbook of Economic Sociology*, 1994, p. 137 (150).

such information or knowledge. If all firms were pursuing precisely the same strategy, the consequences of error would be disastrous. Moreover, it is much easier for the state to be captured by a unanimous view.

Authors have pointed in particular to the importance of associations of firms in the process of implementing export-led development policies in countries such as Japan, South Korea, and Taiwan. Thus, in discussing the coordination role of the state, Sabel emphasises not so much the protection of domestic firm profits, but the learning aspect and the diffusion of learning via sectoral associations of firms. Specifically, he notes that state bureaucracies would cede regulatory authority or grant various forms of aid or subsidies only where members of firm associations could demonstrate technical expertise, knowledge of market prospects, as well as the capacity to generate knowledge about continuous and robust improvement in practices.[57] This is neither a mere cartelisation policy to protect the profits of local firms, nor a typical national champions policy, where only one or a small number of firms are selected as the subjects of the state's support. Instead, a key function of such sectoral associations is precisely to disseminate knowledge in order to improve the performance of all members, including those that might lag behind best practices.[58] Importantly, knowledge generated in this way is also available to the bureaucracy as one way of ensuring that such associations do not subvert the public interest to that of the members.

This view of the coordinating role of the state, not as a mere protector of profits, but as the facilitator of dynamic learning and the dissemination of best practices suggests that competition policy is not subordinated to, but integrated with developmental policy. Moreover, such a view of the relationship between competition law and development policy takes on an even greater significance in the current, even more globalised and disintegrated production context. As the interviewed CUTS official emphasised, nations must adjust developmental policies to the contemporary realities in trade and production.[59] Increasing trade liberalisation puts a constraint on purely protectionist policies. Even more fundamentally, trade

---

[57] Singh also highlights the importance of maintaining strategic oligopolistic rivalry in the Japanese context, together with "investment races" and "contest based competition," see Singh, Multilateral Competition Policy and Economic Development—A Developing Country Perspective on the European Community Proposals, Paper presented at the Fifth session of the Intergovernmental Group of Experts on Competition Law and Policy at Geneva, 2003, pp. 20–21, though one should be careful not to jump to the conclusion that even a very "competent" state would be capable of divining an optimal market structure for achieving developmental objectives.

[58] Sabel, Learning by Monitoring: The Institutions of Economic Development, in: Smelser/ Swedberg (eds.), *The Handbook of Economic Sociology*, 1994, p. 137 (151–152).

[59] A point also conceded by Singh, Multilateral Competition Policy and Economic Development—A Developing Country Perspective on the European Community Proposals, Paper presented at the Fifth session of the Intergovernmental Group of Experts on Competition Law and Policy at Geneva, 2003, pp. 23–24, who notes that "the focus of MITI's work, its relationship with the competition agency and its instruments for persuading firms and industries to accept its proposals, have all changed with times and with the liberalisation, globalisation and other developments in the world economy."

liberalisation has led to the fragmentation of production processes, resulting in the emergence of global value chains or production networks.[60] For firms wishing to participate in those production networks, it is not necessarily scale that provides a key advantage, but flexibility and the ability to adapt to circumstances that can change quickly, which in turn requires an ability to learn quickly and to change course in response if needed. Firms from small developing nations with small markets may not be able to rely on cartelisation of domestic markets and then wait to build up performance before seeking to access the international market; and they may not need to. Instead, such firms can seek to plug into global production chains directly even at a relatively small scale. Yet, it would still be the case that accessing foreign opportunities could be done easier in concert with other firms, given the logic of externalities in production, and multiple opportunities for learning and sources of error-correction. No doubt, inter-firm coordination or information-sharing may also be sources for antitrust concern and such concerns could be legitimate. Competition policy need not be dormant; instead, a dynamically minded competition policy would seek to understand whether learning and improved capacities to produce and participate into global production networks result from such practices or not.

In a study of developing strategies for late-developing nations, such as Ireland, Israel and Taiwan through their exploitation of opportunities in the IT industries, Breznitz points out that precisely the fragmentation in production globally provides "multiple entry points and ways to succeed" even within a single industry. Moreover, given rapid rates of technological change, an export-led development strategy could not rely on the state picking a sector and patiently waiting for selected firms to invest in order to achieve economies of scale and to efficiently supply an established and well-developed market by catching up to current technology.[61] In the IT industry, "the industry itself becomes the creation and rapid application of new technologies."[62]

In such a setting, the role and mode of state intervention to achieve developmental goals will need to adjust as well. Specifically, from the perspective of the role of competition policy vis-à-vis developmental goals, Breznitz suggests that the role of the state is to "motivate private companies to make long-term commitments to operate in rapid innovation-based industries."[63] However, implementing such a policy requires recognition that innovation is an "inherently collective endeavour," that is both "iterative and cooperative in nature." In other words, there is a need to coordinate activities across firm boundaries, and to motivate and facilitate learning

[60] Breznitz, *Innovation and the State: Political Choice and Strategies for Growth in Israel, Taiwan and Ireland*, 2007, pp. 11–12.

[61] Breznitz, *Innovation and the State: Political Choice and Strategies for Growth in Israel, Taiwan and Ireland*, 2007, pp. 14–15.

[62] Breznitz, *Innovation and the State: Political Choice and Strategies for Growth in Israel, Taiwan and Ireland*, 2007, p. 15.

[63] Breznitz, *Innovation and the State: Political Choice and Strategies for Growth in Israel, Taiwan and Ireland*, 2007, p. 29.

(including joint learning) by such private firms. Again, the developmental state here faces a dilemma in that policies aimed at coordinating and motivating innovation and learning can also result in rent-seeking, capture, foreclosure, together with stagnancy and domestic consumer harm with little or no improved export performance. The role of the developmental bureaucracy then is more challenging, since just like industry players, it must be capable of implementing and revising policies in the face of on-going change.[64] If industry players cooperate and use state incentives in a way that improves their capability to innovate robustly and deliver products to market, they are advancing the goals of both development policy (economic growth and human development) and competition policy (in the form of dynamic efficiency). If on the other hand local firms simply lobby for state protection or subsidies and, under the pretext of cooperation, seek to foreclose entry and simply exploit domestic consumers, neither development nor competition goals are being achieved.

One challenge, particularly for states with weak governance structures, is how to best create the state institutions for such dynamically minded intervention. In the contexts he studies, Breznitz describes this as a process of industry-state co-evolution, whereby the (developmental) bureaucracy ends up "less Weberian": more fragmented, less isolated and closer to industry.[65] This observation squarely poses a set of questions about the creation of sectoral (or vertical) regimes with narrowly defined objectives as opposed to regimes with horizontal objectives that cut across sectors, such as developmental or competition bureaucracies. Dividing up oversight responsibilities does multiply sources of knowledge for the state, while perhaps making capture more difficult. At the same time, having a number of different self-sufficient sectoral regimes or even regimes that cut across sectors, but with narrowly defined (intermediate) charges and little opportunity for exchange, can also mean that they end up impeding each other in the achievement of the ultimate objectives of development.

Formulating the argument in this way raises questions about the kind of advice provided by international donors and advisers about the creation of mechanisms for state intervention in developing nations. While that specific issue is beyond the scope of the paper, the argument as presented does suggest that effective regulatory mechanisms do not precede and "unleash," but go hand in hand with improved economic performance for the development sector. Moreover, it lends support to the argument that harmonisation of international antitrust norms based on a thin consensus principle, such as a suspicion of any horizontal coordination, could unwittingly foreclose mechanisms for building up the competitiveness of local firms and their capacity to plug into global production networks.

---

[64] Breznitz, *Innovation and the State: Political Choice and Strategies for Growth in Israel, Taiwan and Ireland*, 2007, p. 29.

[65] Breznitz, *Innovation and the State: Political Choice and Strategies for Growth in Israel, Taiwan and Ireland*, 2007, p. 32.

Competition Law and the Fundamentals of Human Development

The discussion so far has followed the traditional debate on the interaction between development policy and competition law, namely focusing on the goal of development by stimulating the emergence of an industrial sector vis-à-vis traditional and subsistence activities in developing nations. To close the circle, in this section we focus on the recent interest in the use of competition policy for the advancement of more immediate human development objectives. One prominent example of such application of competition law was the case by the South African Competition Commission against pharmaceutical companies for their marketing practices for HIV medicines, based on theories such as excessive pricing or the denial of an essential facility.[66] This is an instance where rather than focusing on economic objectives, such as consumer welfare, or employment or innovation, competition policy can be used to more directly influence living conditions in the developing world by improving health standards and life expectancy.[67]

Such a precedent has inspired thinking about the use of competition law in similar settings to improve access to basic necessities in developing nations. Specifically, in a briefing note the UN Special Rapporteur on the Right to Food has posed the question whether competition law should be used to address concentration and abuse of power problems in food supply chains as a way of promoting access to food and the fulfilment of the right to food in the developing world.[68] Many farmers from the developing world supply primary agricultural commodities within global food supply chains, of the kind described in the previous section. As de Schutter notes, while both farmers and final consumers of primary agricultural commodities are numerous and dispersed, the participants in the middle steps of the supply chain (commodity buyers, food processors and retailers) tend to be considerably more concentrated. Such concentration gives these intermediate buyers the capacity to depress the prices of primary agricultural products, thereby lowering the incomes of farm producers in the developing world.[69] Similarly,

---

[66] Monti, Unilateral Conduct: The Search for Global Standards, in: Ezrachi (ed.), *International Research Handbook on Competition Law*, 2012.

[67] Note that in another concrete example of the integration of policy objectives, more recently a similar result with respect to a cancer drug was obtained in India through the patenting regime and the grant of a compulsory license under the Indian Patents Act. Compulsory License Application No. 1/2011 (Controller of Patents Mumbai), *Natco Pharma Limited vs. Bayer Corporation*, available at: http://www.ipindia.nic.in/ipoNew/compulsory_License_12032012.pdf.

[68] De Schutter, Addressing Concentration in Food Supply Chains: The Role of Competition Law in Tackling the Abuse of Buyer Power, Briefing Note No. 3, 2010.

[69] This problem is not limited to the developing world. Ganesh points out that similar issues have been investigated both in the UK and in the US. See Ganesh, Right to Food and Buyer Power, German Law Journal 11 (2010) 11, p. 1190, available at: http://www.germanlawjournal.com/pdfs/Vol11-No11/PDF_Vol_11_No_11_1190-1244_Articles_Ganesh.pdf. More recently the issue has received prominence in Australia, see Battersby, "Dob in your supermarket, ACCC tells suppliers," Sydney Morning Herald, 21 February 2012, available at: http://www.smh.com.au/business/dob-in-your-supermarket-accc-tells-suppliers-20120221-1tkaw.html.

buyers (such as retailers) can seek to pass on costs of compliance with (often private) standards on hygiene or food safety. The combined effect of these reductions in the effective income for developing nation farmers is for them "to be kicked off" global supply chains, which in turn increases rural poverty and reduces access to food even for agricultural producers.[70]

The use of competition law to address this problem termed "buyer power," according to de Schutter,[71] faces the limitation that modern competition regimes focus on the welfare of final consumers as an important, even a key variable in determining the existence of an antitrust violation. While practices by intermediary buyers directed at farmers may reduce the income of producers in the developing world, if this conduct leads to lower prices of products on supermarket shelves, it may well enhance the welfare of final consumers, thus pitting the interests of rich nation consumers against poor nation farm producers. Both de Schutter and Ganesh[72] offer a number of suggestions as to how competition decision-makers and other bodies may seek to navigate that conflict, but for the purposes of the present discussion, there are three key points worth noting in understanding the role that competition law could play in this aspect of economic development.

One suggestion in their analysis of food supply chain practices is that the high concentration of the intermediary stages in the chain allows cartelisation by the buyers, namely joint concerted action to depress the prices received by developing nation farmers. However, such conduct would likely be caught under the antitrust laws of most mature regimes that typically prohibit any form of concerted action by competitors purely for the purpose of jointly fixing prices between competitors. Admittedly, if such a case was brought in the courts of an industrialised nation, where only final consumers are located, there may be an attempt to raise a jurisdictional issue based on the question of where the harmful effects of the conduct were suffered.

However, the second and more significant problem is that given the high degrees of concentration among intermediate agricultural buyers, as well as the weak market and bargaining power of the sellers (who tend to be small and dispersed farmers in the developing world), there would be no need for joint action or coordination for the buyers to depress prices. Instead, buyers can achieve the same outcome through unilateral action, which would not necessarily be caught by the competition laws of the developed regimes even if pursued by all buyers. A case based on a theory of abuse of dominance might face the obstacle of an absence of (final) consumer harm. More importantly, however, for competition law to intervene in this contracting matter between a buyer and seller, would essentially amount to a form of price regulation, if the mere aim were to maintain the income of

---

[70] De Schutter, Addressing Concentration in Food Supply Chains: The Role of Competition Law in Tackling the Abuse of Buyer Power, Briefing Note No. 3, 2010, p. 2.

[71] De Schutter, Addressing Concentration in Food Supply Chains: The Role of Competition Law in Tackling the Abuse of Buyer Power, Briefing Note No. 3, 2010, p. 3.

[72] Ganesh, Right to Food and Buyer Power, German Law Journal 11 (2010) 11, p. 1190.

the farmer (as a way of indirectly protecting her right to food). Such price regulation is problematic where the price has to be fixed by a government decision-maker in the context of a zero-sum conflict between the buyer and the farmer, since a higher price unequivocally hurts the buyer and helps the farmer. From the domestic perspective of developing nations, such protection of farm incomes attracts lobbying efforts and other forms of rent-seeking behaviour. From the global perspective, in the absence of some coordination across jurisdictions, the buyer can always threaten to go elsewhere in the face of such an effort at price control.

Yet, as de Schutter and Ganesh[73] recognise, there is a dynamic element to the buyer–supplier relationship even in the context of a traditional primary sector, such as farming or agriculture. For example, de Schutter points out that depressed incomes for developing nation farmers affect their ability to make investments for the future "and climb up the value chain."[74] Moreover, intermediate buyers who wish to place agricultural products for sale on western markets must comply with increasingly more strict requirements relating to "hygiene, food safety and traceability," both of a public and private nature. Given requirements for traceability, such safety standards are impossible to satisfy without the cooperation of the farmer who produces the primary product. Therefore, the buyer must work together with the farmer/supplier to ensure that they too have the knowledge, capacity and the means to satisfy such regulatory requirements, absent which the buyer may be unable to resell those products on western markets or be potentially subject to crippling liability. Viewed in this way, we can see some similarity between the farming context and the firms in an industrialising sector that might require some policy support while and so long as they learn how to make that which is demanded on world markets. In other words, competition authorities may structure this discussion not purely through the prism of price regulation or income protection, but in a way that stimulates dynamic learning that can advance both the right to food of local producers (thereby furthering human development goals) and the ability of buyers to resell products on world markets. While this might necessitate cooperation among local farmers, it can also contribute towards the maintenance of a disaggregated local economy, to the extent that it makes it unnecessary for foreign buyers to integrate downstream into larger agricultural holdings. If local farmers can ensure compliance with regulatory standards, continuing to buy from such decentralised farmers offers buyers greater flexibility in responding to demand shifts compared to owning the farming facilities themselves.[75]

Presented in this way, in this example also it is not entirely clear where development or innovation policy ends and where competition law begins. Perhaps

[73] Ganesh, Right to Food and Buyer Power, German Law Journal 11 (2010) 11, p. 1190 (1196).

[74] De Schutter, Addressing Concentration in Food Supply Chains: The Role of Competition Law in Tackling the Abuse of Buyer Power, Briefing Note No. 3, 2010, p. 1.

[75] Cf. Ganesh, Right to Food and Buyer Power, German Law Journal 11 (2010) 11, p. 1190 (1196), noting that costs of compliance with such standards led to the exclusion of small farmers in Kenya and a tendency towards larger farms owned by exporters.

precisely for that reason, we might be wary about policy implementation or law enforcement efforts that are centered on traditional narrow mandate bureaucracies and private law courts. Instead, as in the cases presented by Breznitz, some type of "co-evolution" between the industry and the state is required. From the industry side, such institutional forms can involve consortia where buyers help sub-contractors to develop capacities for resolving production problems.[76] From the state side, we can recall Breznitz's call for the state as a "flexible facilitating agent" and in that context a bureaucracy that is more fluid and flexible and closer to industry.[77] Part of that flexibility might involve a bias against regulatory regimes that are too specialised and focused on intermediate goals such as competition or decentralisation or price controls, without regard to how production relationships contribute towards the ultimate policy objective of improving the lot of the local population, alleviating poverty and hunger and increasing various aspects of human development.

In fashioning a development policy in the farming sector, an innovation policy logic would suggest stimulating some form of cooperation among local actors both to build capacity and to alleviate uncertainty associated with investments, but also stimulating problem-solving collaboration between local actors[78] and their foreign buyers so that they can meet the benchmarks of world markets. At the same time, a competition policy logic would urge caution about the potential effects of cooperative arrangements among local actors on both local new entrants and local consumers. Moreover, a competition policy logic might also urge caution about excessive dependence on a single product or crop, or excessive dependence on a single (or a very limited number of) foreign buyer(s).[79] A social policy or human rights logic would be attentive to the income levels received by local producers both as a source of sustenance and as a source of investments in maintaining or elevating their ability to produce the kinds of goods demanded in international production networks. It may well be both difficult and inadvisable to pursue these objectives in isolation or independently from each other.

This view echoes John Ruggie's call for a more integrated framework to the pursuit of human development objectives as opposed to a "narrow approach to

[76] Whitford/Zeitlin, Governing Decentralized Production: Institutions, Public Policy, and the Prospects for Inter-Firm Collaboration in the US, Industry & Innovation 11 (2004) 1/2, p. 11.

[77] Breznitz, *Innovation and the State: Political Choice and Strategies for Growth in Israel, Taiwan and Ireland*, 2007, p. 29, 32. Such a view of bureaucracy obviously presents a serious challenge to traditional public law visions of rigid procedures and formal hierarchies as the form of control of administrative action. However, this simply presents a challenge to be overcome to the extent that we are not forced to choose between the bureaucracy's efficacy and its accountability.

[78] It would be difficult for a single farmer to guarantee the safety of agricultural commodities from pests or diseases without the cooperation of neighbouring farmers.

[79] Sabel points to evidence that Japanese subcontractors typically sought to avoid being dependent on a single buyer, by spreading their activities across different industries and groups, while at the same time avoiding dependence on a single bank as a source of credit. Sabel, Learning by Monitoring: The Institutions of Economic Development, in: Smelser/Swedberg (eds.), *The Handbook of Economic Sociology*, 1994, p. 137 (146).

managing the business and human rights agenda,"[80] whereby regulatory efforts are confined within separate "conceptual and (typically weak) institutional box(es)"[81] each pursuing a narrow mandate or logic of its own. The co-evolving state and private sector institutions, on this view, must face policy trade-offs—as best as they can—as these trade-offs are presented, rather than leaving outcomes to fall out as imperceptible adjustments over the longer term to interventions guided by the logic of different regulatory or sectoral regimes.

Institutions, Categories and Routines

One implication of this contribution is the argument that the relationship between development and competition policy cannot be adequately captured either by idea of subordination (of the latter to the earlier) nor by compartmentalisation of narrow mandate regimes. Instead, I have argued that development policy cannot and should not be designed in isolation from competition law considerations and vice-versa. Competition law seeks to influence the modalities of production and distribution of goods and services in the economy, with the aim of both increasing the size of the pie (over time) and influencing how the pie is ultimately shared. The modes of production in the economy also influence developmental goals, such as industrialisation, the ability to take part in world production networks and the take home rewards for producers. Competition policy aimed at atomised production relationships can undermine such goals. At the same time, development policy that aims to promote cooperation and shield firm investments from some uncertainty can be captured by concentrated local economic and political interests, this again at the expense of developmental goals. While we might agree with Singh that competition policy must take into account dynamic effects, this does not mean that competition policy plays second fiddle in the developmental stage.

Based on the foregoing, it is encouraging that developing nations in the past few decades, either of their own accord or instigated by international donors or partners, have been adopting competition regimes and building implementation capacity in this field. It is also encouraging that a number of different international fora have provided focused settings for discussion of competition policy problems, including not only the initiatives within the OECD and UNCTAD, but also more recently the ICN, as a dedicated competition forum ("all antitrust, all of the time" as explained

[80] Ruggie, Protect, Respect and Remedy: a Framework for Business and Human Rights, Report of the Special Representative of the Secretary-General on the issue of human rights and transnational corporations and other business enterprises, A/HRC/8/5, 2008, p. 8, available at: http://www.reports-and-materials.org/Ruggie-report-7-Apr-2008.pdf.

[81] On this point, see also Ganesh, Right to Food and Buyer Power, German Law Journal 11 (2010) 11, p. 1190 (1227–1228).

by one of its promotors).[82] Importantly, apart from discussions about common problems, implementation strategies and enforcement cooperation, these fora also have a specific focus on the building up of regulatory capacities of decision-makers within emerging and developing economies.

However, despite this increased attention to competition law issues within a variety of settings, there is an emergent consensus that these international fora do not provide a sufficiently focused exploration of the relationship between developmental goals and competition problems or competition law implementation. In noting the paucity of specific initiatives within the ICN to address development related competition issues, Monti observes that in the realm of rules on unilateral conduct (or abuse of dominance) "the sole [ICN] effort devoted specifically to the needs of developing and transition economies is a document on recommended practices on state-created monopolies" with relatively unhelpful exhortations.[83] Elsewhere, I have argued that discussions at the annual ICN conferences are not always focused on topics that are of relevance to a broad range of member authorities from developing nations, nor are they conducted in a way that gives voice to the specific problems and experiences of such authorities.[84] With respect to UNCTAD, Monti observes that the norms elaborated within that much older competition forum, beginning with the 'Set of Multilaterally Agreed Equitable Principles and Rules for the Control of Restrictive Business Practices' from 1980 and up to the Model Law released in 2003 and revised in 2010, do not appear to have evolved much in that period. Moreover, these normative documents contain few, if any, accommodations or specific modifications tailored to the development context.[85] While it may be that the UNCTAD competition conference does a better job at giving voice to developing nation problems and experiences,[86] a relatively recent report by the UNCTAD Secretariat on abuse of dominance contains a limited number of concrete "examples of competition enforcement contributing to development."[87]

[82] James, Reconciling Divergent Enforcement Policies: Where Do We Go From Here?, in: Hawk (ed.), *International Antitrust Law & Policy 2001 Fordham Corporate Law Institute*, 2002, p. 1 (5).

[83] Monti, Unilateral Conduct: The Search for Global Standards, in: Ezrachi (ed.), *International Research Handbook on Competition Law*, 2012.

[84] Svetiev, The Limits of Informal International Law: Enforcement, Norm-generation and Learning in the ICN, in: Pauwelyn/Wessel/Wouters (eds.), *Informal International Lawmaking*, 2012, p. 271 (290).

[85] Monti, Unilateral Conduct: The Search for Global Standards, in: Ezrachi (ed.), *International Research Handbook on Competition Law*, 2012.

[86] In an interview with an official of the Consumer Unity and Trust Society, an NGO that has been operating to promote competition and consumer protection regulation in the developing world, he observed that UNCTAD has a "developing country focus." Rather than their output, the official emphasised that the UNCTAD annual conference on competition is "smaller" than the ICN meeting and "dominated by developing country authorities," which meant that "the exchange of experiences and thoughts are much better." Interview with an official of the Consumer Unity and Trust Society, 3 June 2009.

[87] UNCTAD, Abuse of Dominance, TD/B/COM.2/CLP/66, 2008, p. 12.

These limitations reflect a wider problem with international antitrust cooperation instruments, namely the tendency for guidance to new jurisdictions (whether through model rules of fora such as the ICN, UNCTAD or the OECD or through projects sponsored by donors and partners such as the World Bank or the EU) to be organised around existing antitrust categories that have emerged in different circumstances in mature regimes (i.e. the US and EU). Moreover, such guidance, being focused narrowly on competition aspects, may not address some of the issues raised in this paper. This in turn can lead officials from developing nations to view their world through those categories, influencing in turn how they normatively perceive their local experiences and examples. To take one example, Brusick and Evenett argue that most of the advice from industrialised-country experts to "nascent" competition authorities in the developing world is to give preference to actions against cartels (or horizontal restraints among competitors) and competition advocacy.[88] Hearing it repeated over-and-over again that cartels are the bane of antitrust, how does a competition official fine-tune his competition advocacy message relating to development or exporting clusters of firms of the kind mentioned earlier in this article?

There is another way in which such category based guidance from industrialised country experts can limit the ability of competition decision-makers to learn to respond to their local development context and goals, namely by encrusting decision-making procedures and establishing analytical routines. From the domain of decision-making procedures, one example is the tendency to view competition enforcement as the establishment of violations and liability that is to be decided by a court or a similar adjudicative tribunal.[89] Similarly, expert guidance may lead to the establishment of certain analytical routines within nascent antitrust authorities, such as market definition, the use of the SSNIP test and so on, without any discussion or appreciation of how, if at all, these relate to the development context and objectives.[90] Such tendencies might both rigidify and isolate the antitrust regime, impair communication across different areas of state intervention and, as a result, constrain precisely the type of flexible state-industry co-evolution that may be necessary to respond to development objectives and contexts.

[88] Brusick/Evenett, Should Developing Countries Worry About Abuse of Dominant Power?, Wisconsin Law Review (2008) 2, p. 269 (271).

[89] Svetiev, Antitrust Governance: The New Wave of Antitrust, Loyola University of Chicago Law Journal 38 (2007) 3, p. 593 (597–599). In the context of the discussion of this paper, particularly notable is the apparently emerging consensus to assign cartel offenses criminal liability.

[90] Tools of static analysis provide a framework for the step-wise breaking down of an antitrust problem and an apparently systematic method of analysing it, but as Coyle has observed they are not particularly useful or relevant in settings where unpredictable dynamics are important, see Coyle, Discussion on "Competition Economics and Antitrust in Europe," Economic Policy 21 (2006) 48, p. 786.

Concluding Remarks

Development theory in its inception tended to offer quite broad prescriptions about policy—starting from the belief in macroeconomic demand management policies (and their analogues in the development context) to the belief that unleashing price signals is a panacea for achieving economic and human development. The failures of such broad-brush prescriptions, together with evidence that successful developers did not fit neatly into existing categories has brought closer attention to both the "institutional underpinnings" of market economies and to the role that the state could play in facilitating private economic action. Regulatory regimes such as competition law or financial regulation are now firmly on the agenda of international development donors and, as a result, also on the books in many developing nations. Yet, particularly given the conditionality mindset of donors, these regulatory regimes tend to be viewed as boxes to be ticked in return for continued support. As a result, they are often implemented independently from each other, as self-sufficient regimes with narrow mandates and specialised bureaucracies, and without consideration of what role they can play in the fashioning and implementation of development policy. In such a setting, it may well be legitimate to ask whether a developing nation should prioritise developmental policies over the enforcement of competition law during the developmental stage if there is a conflict between those two regimes in a particular case.

By pointing to the growing recognition of the need to take account of dynamic effects in competition law and by seeking to identify the common ground in the various interpretations of the successes of the late developers in East Asia, this contribution has argued that the boundary between development policy and competition law is quite porous. If firms in a development sector need to coordinate their decision-making, the decision-maker needs to understand why such a need arises. An exporting cartel is not likely to be a successful strategy given that producers in developing nations tend to be price-takers in world markets. A cartel aimed at domestic consumers purely to protect profits and prices of domestic firms would ordinarily be treated with some scepticism, or at the very least, the policy-maker might seek to understand if other alternatives are available to deliver dynamic benefits over time. The need for learning spillovers across firm boundaries might be treated as a legitimate objective, but even here the policy-maker would need to learn herself in order to understand whether firms are indeed improving their capacity to participate in world markets, or whether the coordination is, or becomes, a guise for collusive conduct. The challenge then for nascent authorities, donors, advisers and international antitrust fora is not simply to build isolated competition enforcement systems based on familiar categories, but to contribute to the process of industry co-evolution with all aspects of state intervention, allowing competition (and other) considerations to be appropriately integrated into policies aiming to facilitate economic development.

Part II
Regional Integration

The European Union and Regional Trade Agreements

Lucrezia Tuis and Colin M. Brown

Introduction

This contribution provides an overview of recent activities in the European Union (EU) as regards Free Trade Agreements (FTAs) analysing the most salient activities of the EU in this domain over the last year.[1]

In general terms, it can be noted that the EU remains particularly active in the negotiation of FTAs. This has continued to intensify. While the stagnation of the Doha Development Round negotiations has led to a lower level of activity in the World Trade Organisation negotiations, the EU's FTA agenda remains dynamic. The highlights of the period surveyed include the process of signature and conclusion of the EU-Central America Association Agreement and of the EU-Columbia/Peru Trade Agreement and the conclusion of negotiations on the EU-Ukraine Association Agreement.

The views reflected in this contribution are personal and should not necessarily be attributed to the European Commission.

[1] This contribution focuses on developments between May 2011 and May 2012.

L. Tuis (✉) • C.M. Brown
Directorate General for Trade, European Commission, Rue de la Loi, 200 1049, Bruxelles, Belgium
e-mail: lucrezia.tuis@ec.europa.eu; Colin.brown@ec.europa.eu

C. Herrmann et al. (eds.), *European Yearbook of International Economic Law (EYIEL), Vol. 4 (2013)*, European Yearbook of International Economic Law 4,
DOI 10.1007/978-3-642-33917-2_10,

Developments in Particular Negotiations

EU-Central America Association Agreement

The Association Agreement between the EU and Central America[2] is the first EU "region-to-region" agreement after the Economic Partnership Agreement (EPA) negotiated with Cariforum. However, in terms of regional integration it goes beyond this EPA. In fact, the Agreement represents not only an ambitious Agreement between two regions but also an important step towards regional economic integration within Central America and consequently also towards the overall political integration process.[3]

The negotiations started in San Jose, Costa Rica, in October 2007 and were concluded in May 2010, in Madrid. After the legal revision, the Agreement was finally initialled on 22 March 2011.

The Agreement contains three pillars—Political dialogue, Cooperation and Trade.

The main objective of the Political dialogue part is to develop a privileged political partnership between the two regions based on common values and principles, as well as the reinforcement of the collaboration in areas of EU interest such as human rights, conflict prevention and good governance, regional integration, poverty reduction, the fight against inequality and sustainable development. It should be highlighted that the Agreement contains a human rights clause that constitutes one of its essential elements[4] the violation of which would enable one of the Parties to take unilateral action, including the immediate and unilateral suspension of the Agreement.[5]

[2] The full text of the Agreement is available at: http://trade.ec.europa.eu/doclib/press/index.cfm?id=689.

[3] SICA, Sistema de la Integración Centroamericana (Central American Integration System), is the economic, cultural and political organisation of Central American countries. Apart from the six Central American countries that are parties to the Agreement, Belize is also a Member.

[4] Art. 1(1): "Respect for democratic principles and fundamental human rights, as laid down in the Universal Declaration of Human Rights, and for the rule of law, underpins the internal and international policies of both Parties and constitutes an essential element of this Agreement".

[5] Art. 355: "[. . .] If a Party considers that another Party has failed to fulfil an obligation under this Agreement, it may have recourse to appropriate measures. Before doing so, except in cases of special urgency, it shall submit to the Association Council within thirty days all relevant information required for a thorough examination of the situation with a view to seeking a solution acceptable to the Parties. In selecting which measures to adopt, priority shall be given to those that are least disruptive to the implementation of this Agreement. Such measures shall be notified immediately to the Association Committee and shall be the subject of consultations in the Committee if a Party so requests. The Parties agree that the term "cases of special urgency" in paragraph 2 of this Article means a case of material breach of the Agreement by one of the Parties. The Parties further agree that the term "appropriate measures" referred to in paragraph 2 of this Article means measures taken in accordance with international law. It is understood that suspension would be a measure of last resort. A material breach of the Agreement consists in:

The second pillar of the Agreement concerns cooperation that should result in concrete actions in aspects of mutual interest, including economic development, social cohesion, natural resources, culture, justice and sciences.

As for the Trade Part, this reflects the standard structure of recent EU FTAs covering trade in goods and services, non-tariff barriers, intellectual property, dispute settlement, mediation, competition and sustainable development, among others. Therefore, it builds upon the WTO commitments that the European Union and the countries of the region owe to each other.

Finally, the Agreement establishes an institutional framework for its implementation including both an Association Council as well as an Association Committee supported by a set of Sub-Committees to allow for work and consultations on the various areas covered in the Trade Part of the Agreement as well as in the Cooperation Part.

The Agreement will be concluded by the European Union and its Member States as it covers areas that fall under the Member States shared competence (e.g. culture, by virtue of the Protocol on Cultural Cooperation attached to the Agreement). Therefore, in order for the Agreement to enter into force in the EU it needs to be ratified by the European Parliament and by the Parliaments of the Member States. However, as proposed by the Commission on 25 October 2011,[6] it is foreseen that the Trade Part will be provisionally applied pending the entry into force of the Agreement. It should be noted that, as was the case for the FTA with Korea, although according to Article 218 TFEU the consent by the European Parliament is not required for the Council decision on signature and provisional application but only for the Council decision on conclusion of the Agreement, the trade part will be provisionally applied only once the European Parliament has given such consent.

In parallel, the Commission has proposed a Safeguard Regulation[7] setting out the procedures in the EU for applying the bilateral safeguard provisions of the Agreement, notably the procedures for opening an investigation and for applying a safeguard measure once the conditions are met, as specified in the relevant Title of the Agreement (Arts. 104-116). This regulation is very similar to the one already adopted for the implementation of the EU-Korea FTA. The Regulation is expected to be adopted by the Council and the Parliament before the trade part of the Agreement is provisionally applied.

(a) repudiation of the Agreement not sanctioned by general rules of international law; (b) violation of the essential elements of the Agreement."

[6] COM(2011) 678 final, 25 October 2011.

[7] COM(2011) 599 final, 3 October 2011.

EU-Colombia and Peru Trade Agreement

In January 2009, negotiations were launched for a Trade Agreement between the EU and Colombia, Ecuador and Peru. In July 2009, Ecuador suspended its participation in the talks. Nine rounds of negotiations took place between January 2009 and March 2010, when negotiations on the Agreement were successfully concluded. This is a so-called Multi-Party Agreement that was then initialled on 13 April 2011.[8] In terms of content, apart from the differences due to the nature of the two Agreements (one is a Free Trade Agreement while the other is an Association Agreement) it is very similar to the EU Agreement with Central America. Of relevance are in particular the inclusion in Art. 1 of a Human Rights Clause (identical to the one included in the Association Agreement with Central America) and the commitments by the Parties to effectively implement core labour standards as contained in the ILO fundamental conventions (Art. 269) and eight key international environmental conventions (Art. 270).[9]

A Protocol on Cultural Cooperation was negotiated with Colombia and Peru but it is not part of the Agreement. It will be concluded separately.

The Commission, taking the view that all the areas covered by the Agreement fall within the Union's exclusive competence, proposed the Agreement to be signed and concluded as an EU-only Agreement.[10] However, the Commission's proposal was rejected on this point unanimously by the Member States of the European Union who claimed that certain provisions of the Agreement, e.g. with regard to transport matters, would fall instead under Member States shared competence and did not agree that the Union should exercise it. Consequently, the Commission proposal was amended in order to reflect the mixed nature of the Agreement as viewed by the Council. This meant that the provisional application of the agreement had to be provided for. While the decision on provisional application has not been formally adopted at the time of writing, it appears likely that provisional application will cover all, or virtually all trade matters covered by the Agreement.

---

[8] The full text of the Agreement is available at: http://trade.ec.europa.eu/doclib/press/index.cfm?id=691.

[9] The Montreal Protocol on Substances that Deplete the Ozone Layer, adopted in 1987; The Basel Convention on the Control of Transboundary Movements of Hazardous Wastes and their Disposal, adopted in 1989; The Stockholm Convention on Persistent Organic Pollutants, adopted in 2001; The Convention on International Trade in Endangered Species in Wild Fauna and Flora adopted in 1973; The Convention on Biological Diversity (CBD) and The Cartagena Protocol on Biosafety to the CBD adopted in 2000; The Kyoto Protocol to the United Nations Framework Convention on Climate Change adopted in 1997; The Rotterdam Convention on the Prior Informed Consent Procedure for Certain Hazardous Chemicals and Pesticides in International Trade, adopted in 1998. Similar provisions regarding the compliance with multilateral labour and environmental standards and agreements are included also in the Association Agreement with Central America (Art. 286 and 287).

[10] COM(2011) 570 final, 22 September 2011.

As in the case of Central America, the Commission presented to the Council on 3 October 2011 a proposal for a Safeguard Regulation[11] that mirrors the one proposed for the Association Agreement.

It is not excluded that Ecuador will participate in the Agreement in the near future.

Canada

Negotiations on the Comprehensive Economic and Trade Agreement (CETA) with Canada continued during the period under examination without yet being concluded. This agreement is likely to be one of the first agreements including provisions on investment protection.

India

Negotiations between the EU and India have been underway since June 2007. This agreement may also include provisions on investment protection. At the time of writing, the agreement was still under negotiation.

ASEAN

The EU has started negotiations with Singapore and Malaysia, in March and October 2010 respectively. The negotiations with Singapore are closest to conclusion, there being a high chance that these are completed in 2012. It is possible that the agreement with Singapore will include provisions on investment protection.

Ukraine

The EU has been negotiating an extensive Association Agreement with Ukraine since February 2008. The Association Agreement has a deep and comprehensive free trade agreement (DCFTA) embedded in it. The DCFTA is historic in that it goes far beyond the standard FTAs negotiated by the European Union in recent years by creating a mechanism for the approximation of Ukrainian legislation to EU internal market legislation on a wide range of issues. In so doing, it brings Ukraine

[11] COM(2011) 600 final, 3 October 2011.

closer to adopting EU internal market legislation than any other non-candidate country with the exception of the European Economic Area (EEA) countries and Switzerland.

A number of key questions arise that needed to be resolved in this context. One is how to ensure monitoring of Ukrainian implementation of the internal market rules. Within the EU, this is a role that is given to the European Commission which can use a number of instruments for ensuring the correct implementation of EU internal market legislation (such as, for example, the possibility of initiating infringement proceedings).

Another key issue is how to ensure that the interpretation of those internal market rules is consistent in the EU and in Ukraine. It can be questioned whether the standard WTO based dispute settlement system is well designed for issues of the interpretation of EU law. This raises similar questions to those that were examined in Opinion 1/91 of the Court of Justice of the European Union on the EEA court.[12] These issues are addressed in the agreement.

The agreement also includes a free trade agreement compatible with Article XXIV GATT and provides for the liberalisation of services consistent with Article V GATS. It contains a WTO inspired WTO dispute settlement system, comparable to those that the EU has included in other recent EU FTAs. One innovation, which is included, is the introduction of an expedited dispute settlement mechanism for energy disputes, in a reflection of the importance of trade in energy between the two parties.

Negotiations on the DFCTA were completed in October 2011 and on the Association Agreement as a whole in December 2011. At the time of writing, the agreement was subject to legal revision. The initialled text is likely to be released to the public after the completion of the legal revision.

It is possible that the agreement be presented to the Council of the European Union and the European Parliament for signature and conclusion towards the end of 2012. That will depend on an assessment of the relations between the European Union and Ukraine at the time.

DCFTAs with Georgia and Moldova

Georgia and Moldova, due in particular to their geographical proximity to the EU after the most recent enlargements of the European Union, have become of increasing strategic importance both politically and economically. The decision to launch negotiations for a Deep and Comprehensive (DC) FTA with Georgia and Moldova respectively was endorsed by the Council's Trade Policy Committee in December 2011 and followed a period of social, political and economic reforms carried out by these countries, notably in key trade and investment-related regulatory areas. The first rounds of negotiations took place at the end of March 2012. The DCFTAs would be

[12] ECJ, Opinion 1/91, [1991] ECR I-6079.

included in the Association Agreements the EU has been negotiating with Georgia and Moldova since 2010 in the framework of the Eastern Partnership. In terms of scope, the Agreements are expected to mirror mostly the DCFTA with Ukraine.

African, Caribbean, and Pacific (ACP) Countries

The EU has been actively engaged in negotiations with the ACP group of countries over an extended period of time. The EU had historically granted a unilateral preference to these countries based on a WTO waiver from Article I GATT. The waiver expired at the end of 2007.

The unilateral preferences are to be replaced by FTAs taking the form of so-called Economic Partnership Agreements (EPAs). These agreements combine an FTA with a framework for technical assistance.

A number of such agreements are being provisionally applied. These are the Cariforum EPA (Antigua and Barbuda, The Bahamas, Barbados, Belize, Dominica, Grenada, Guyana, Haiti, Jamaica, Saint Lucia, Saint Vincent and the Grenadines, Saint Kitts and Nevis, Surinam, Trinidad and Tobago and the Dominican Republic), and the Pacific EPA (with Papua New Guinea). There is also such an agreement with the countries of Eastern and Southern Africa (Mauritius, Seychelles, Zimbabwe and Madagascar, Zambia and Comoros). This agreement has been signed by Mauritius, Seychelles, Zimbabwe and Madagascar and initialled by Zambia and Comoros. It has been provisionally applied from May 2012.

Of the other agreements, the EPA with the Southern Africa Development Corporation (SADC) countries has been signed by Botswana, Lesotho, Swaziland and Mozambique but not by Namibia, which is also a member of the SADC grouping. The EPA with the Eastern African Community (Kenya, Uganda, Tanzania, Rwanda, and Burundi) has been initialled, but not signed. In the Central African region, there is an interim agreement with Cameroon that was signed in January 2009. In West Africa, interim EPAs were negotiated with Ivory Coast and Ghana. Ivory Coast has signed but Ghana has only initialled.

All countries that have at least initialled such an agreement benefit from the EPA Market Access Regulation (Council Regulation 1528/2007) which provides duty and quota free access to the EU market and serves as a transitional mechanism as these countries move from initialling to signature to full ratification of the agreement. However, benefitting from the EPA Market Access Regulation is conditional upon the agreements not just being initialled but being provisionally applied and then entering into force (see Article 2(3) of Regulation 1528/2007).

On 30 September 2011, the Commission adopted a proposal to remove all of those ACP countries that had not moved towards provisional application and entry into force from the benefits of Regulation 1528/2007[13] as of 1 January 2014 (the

[13] COM(2011) 598 final, 30 September 2011.

projected date of entry into force of the EU's new Generalised System of Preferences regime). The explanatory memorandum to the proposal states:

> Therefore, these countries no longer meet the conditions of the Market Access Regulation for advance provisional application of trade preferences which were extended to them as of 1 January 2008 in anticipation of the steps towards ratification of an EPA. According to the criteria set out in Article 2(3) of Council Regulation (EC) No 1528/2007 of 20 December 2007, trade preferences granted to these countries should no longer be maintained. The attached proposal is intended to amend the list of countries that benefit from the preferences (Annex I of Council Regulation (EC) No 1528/2007) by removing those which have still not taken the necessary steps towards ratification of an EPA. The Commission will continue to work with a view to ensuring that these countries become a contracting party to an EPA, and will use to the full the recent momentum of different negotiations to create a sustainable long term trade regime with these partners in keeping with the EPA negotiating directives and the priorities set out in the Cotonou Agreement.

The countries concerned are Botswana, Burundi, Cameroon, Comoros, Côte d'Ivoire, Fiji, Ghana, Haiti, Kenya, Lesotho, Mozambique, Namibia, Rwanda, Swaziland, Tanzania, Uganda, Zambia, and Zimbabwe (although Zimbabwe has since then taken the necessary steps). These countries will then be subject to the Generalised System of Preferences and may benefit from duty free access if they are least developed countries. This proposal is under examination at the time of writing by the European Parliament and the Council.

Conclusions

This brief overview has shown that the EU's trade policy has kept a key focus on the negotiation and conclusion of FTAs. The period surveyed has demonstrated this, with the signature of the agreements with Peru/Columbia and with Central America and the completion of negotiations with Ukraine. With the ongoing difficulties with the Doha Development Agenda negotiations, this is perhaps unsurprising. However, it is submitted that this fits rather in a pattern of increased FTA activity that has been apparent in the last 5 years than as a response to developments in the Doha negotiations. The Korea FTA has been the key major step on this route. The next few years seem likely to bring even more FTA activities.

US International Trade Agreements in the Western Hemisphere: Legal Developments in 2011

Patrick C. Reed

Introduction

To examine recent developments in international economic law and regional integration in North America, this chapter focuses on US international trade agreements in the western hemisphere during 2011. The year was significant for resolving unfinished business left over too long from previous years.

After a 4-year delay, the United States approved preferential Trade Promotion Agreements with Colombia and Panama that had been pending since 2007. Approval of these two agreements completes the current efforts of the United States to establish institutions for economic integration within the western hemisphere. The United States now is a party to six preferential trade agreements among twelve countries in a region consisting of most of North and Central America, one Caribbean country, and three countries on the Pacific coast of South America. However, the six agreements do not create a fully coherent system of economic integration within the region. Instead, they remain separate agreements in a hub-and-spoke pattern with the United States at the hub.

In addition, in 2011, the United States and Mexico entered into an agreement that settles their long dispute over cross-border trucking services under the North American Free Trade Agreement (NAFTA), which had been festering since 1995. The settlement represents a power-oriented outcome involving a partial renegotiation of NAFTA that ratifies US noncompliance with the original NAFTA provisions during a 3-year transition period.

The author wishes to express his appreciation to Claire R. Kelly and Lene Skou for their comments on a draft of this chapter.

P.C. Reed (✉)
Business Law Department, Baruch College, City University of New York, Room 9-220, 1 Bernard Baruch Way, New York, NY 10010, USA
e-mail: patrick.reed@baruch.cuny.edu

C. Herrmann et al. (eds.), *European Yearbook of International Economic Law (EYIEL), Vol. 4 (2013)*, European Yearbook of International Economic Law 4,
DOI 10.1007/978-3-642-33917-2_11,

Other developments in international economic law in 2011 in the North American region included new decisions in investment disputes under investor-state arbitrations. Investor-state arbitration continues to be used infrequently in the region. Three cases were decided in 2011, all in favour of the host state.

This chapter is divided into three parts: the US-Colombia and US-Panama Trade Promotion Agreements; the US-Mexico trucking dispute; and the recent investment dispute arbitrations.

US-Colombia and US-Panama Trade Promotion Agreements

Overview of the Agreements

The United States approved two trade agreements in 2011 that establish bilateral free trade areas with two countries in the western hemisphere: the US-Colombia Trade Promotion Agreement (the "US-Colombia TPA")[1] and the US-Panama Trade Promotion Agreement (the "US-Panama TPA").[2] The US-Colombia and US-Panama TPAs were completed in 2007, and Colombia and Panama had approved the respective agreements the same year. After a 4-year delay, the United States approved the agreements in October 2011.[3] The agreements are expected to enter into force in 2012.

The US-Colombia and US-Panama TPAs belong to the generation of eleven preferential trade agreements the United States entered into with sixteen countries between 2003 and 2007.[4] The US delay in approving these two agreements reflects

---

[1] United States–Colombia Trade Promotion Agreement, signed November 22, 2006 (modified in part in 2007; approved by Colombia in 2007 and by the United States in 2011; not yet entered into force as of March 1, 2012).

[2] United States–Panama Trade Promotion Agreement, signed June 28, 2007 (approved by Panama in 2007 and the United States in 2011; not yet entered into force as of March 1, 2012).

[3] United States–Colombia Trade Promotion Agreement Implementation Act, Pub. L. No. 112-42, 125 Stat. 462 et seq. (October 21, 2011); United States-Panama Trade Promotion Agreement Implementation Act, Pub. L. No. 112-43, 125 Stat. 497 et seq. (October 21, 2011). See also H.R. Rep. No. 112-237, 112th Cong., 1st Sess. 2 (2011) (House report on US-Colombia TPA); H.R. Rep. No. 112-238, 112th Cong., 1st Sess. (2011) (House Report on US-Panama TPA); H.R. Doc. 112-59, 112th Cong., 1st Sess. (2011) (proposed legislation and supporting documents for the US-Panama TPA, including the text of the agreement). The statutes and other documents are available on the US Government Printing Office website, http://www.fdsys.gov. However, H.R. Doc. 112-58 (2011), which should contain the legislation and supporting documents for the US-Colombia TPA, is not available on the website as of March 1, 2012.

[4] These agreements are the United States-Central America-Dominican Republic Free Trade Agreement (CAFTA-DR) with Costa Rica, El Salvador, Guatemala, Honduras, Nicaragua, and the Dominican Republic, plus bilateral agreements with Australia, Bahrain, Chile, Colombia, Morocco, Oman, Panama, Peru, Singapore, and South Korea. Before 2003, the preferential trade agreements of the United States were NAFTA with Canada and Mexico and bilateral agreements with Israel and Jordan.

a series of political obstacles in the United States. In the presidential election year of 2008, the Democrat-controlled US Congress was unwilling to approve agreements that the Bush administration had negotiated. When the Obama Administration came into office, it required Colombia and Panama to reform their labour laws and improve labour enforcement.[5] The Obama Administration also required Panama to enter into a Tax Information Exchange Agreement with the United States allowing the United States to obtain more information needed for US taxation of Panamanian businesses and financial accounts.[6] Then, for several months in 2011, an impasse arose between the Obama Administration and the Republican-controlled House of Representatives over renewal of funding for trade adjustment assistance, the US programme that helps workers displaced by import competition.

A principal goal of the United States in the US-Colombia and US-Panama TPAs is to replace unilateral US trade preferences with bilateral arrangements that would increase US market access to the two countries—something the US House of Representatives characterized as "transition[ing] the ... trading relationship[s] from one-way preferences to full partnership and reciprocal commitments ...."[7] The vast majority of imports from Colombia and Panama into the United States were already duty-free before the agreements.[8] Both countries were beneficiaries under the Generalized System of Preferences, Colombia was a beneficiary under the US unilateral preferential programme for Andean countries, and Panama was a beneficiary under the US unilateral preference programme for Caribbean Basin countries. In contrast, before the agreements, nearly all of Colombia's tariff lines and some 70% of Panama's tariff lines were dutiable for US goods.

When the agreements are implemented, immediately more than 75% of Colombia's and Panama's tariff lines for industrial and textile goods, 77% of Colombia's tariff lines for agricultural goods, and 68% of Panama's tariff lines for agricultural goods will become duty-free for US products. All of Panama's duties and most of Colombia's duties on US goods will be phased out over 5-year or 10-year periods, while some of Colombia's tariff-rate quotas will be phased out

[5] See US Trade Representative, 2012 Trade Policy Agenda, March 2012, p. 134.

[6] US Trade Representative, 2012 Trade Policy Agenda, March 2012, p. 134; see also United States–Panama Agreement on Tax Cooperation and Exchange of Tax Information, signed November 30, 2010, available on the US Treasury Department website, http://www.treasury.gov.

[7] See H.R. Rep. No. 112-237, 112th Cong., 1st Sess. 2 (2011) ("The [US-Colombia] Agreement would transition the US-Colombia trading relationship from one-way preferences to full partnership and reciprocal commitments, helping US exporters gain greater market access to the Colombian market [...]"); H.R. Rep. No. 112-238, 112th Cong., 1st Sess. 2 (2011) (same statement about the United States–Panama TPA).

[8] See US Int'l Trade Comm'n, US-Colombia Trade Promotion Agreement: Potential Economy-Wide and Selected Sectoral Effects, USITC Pub. 3896, 2006; US Int'l Trade Comm'n, US-Panama Trade Promotion Agreement: Potential Economy-Wide and Selected Sectoral Effects, USITC Pub. 3948, 2007. The US International Trade Commission is an independent investigative agency in the US government whose responsibilities include assessing the economic effects of new trade agreements. The reports are available on the International Trade Commission website, http://www.usitc.gov.

over 19 years. The US tariff lines for Colombian and Panamanian goods that are not already duty-free will be phased out over 15 years for Colombia and over 10 years for Panama.

Although the economies of Colombia and Panama are quite small compared to that of the United States, the US government forecasts that the agreements are likely to increase US exports because of increased market access in the two countries.[9] Before the agreements, Colombia was the 31st largest US import supplier and Panama was the 102nd largest, with each country representing less than 0.1% of the total value of US imports.[10] Colombia ranked as the 28th largest market for US exports, accounting for less than 1.0% of US exports, while Panama was the 45th largest, representing less than 0.5% of total US exports. Nevertheless, Colombia is the third largest market for US exports in Latin America, after Mexico and Brazil. The US government estimates that US exports to Colombia would increase by approximately 13%, or approximately $1 billion USD, and US imports from Colombia would increase by approximately 5% when the agreement is fully implemented. For Panama, it was not econometrically possible to estimate how the agreement would affect US trade in the aggregate, but the government forecasts that exports of several product categories will increase and that the agreement may have a small positive effect on the US economy.

As legal documents, the US-Colombia and US-Panama TPAs are similar in structure to each other and to other recent US preferential trade agreements.[11] In each agreement, the chapters on trade in goods include national treatment and most-favoured-nation treatment obligations, rules of origin and origin procedures, procedures for customs administration and trade facilitation, and commitments on sanitary and phytosanitary measures, technical barriers to trade, and trade remedies.[12] Under each agreement's rules of origin, if goods do not wholly originate in the territory of one of the parties, non-originating materials must be processed so as to achieve specified changes in tariff classification, plus meeting requirements for regional value content for some goods.[13] Under trade remedies, each agreement establishes a transitional safeguards procedure[14] and allows each party (as a practical matter, the United States) to apply its existing antidumping and

[9] See US Int'l Trade Comm'n, US-Colombia Trade Promotion Agreement: Potential Economy-Wide and Selected Sectoral Effects, USITC Pub. 3896, 2006; US Int'l Trade Comm'n, US-Panama Trade Promotion Agreement: Potential Economy-Wide and Selected Sectoral Effects, USITC Pub. 3948, 2007.

[10] See US Int'l Trade Comm'n, US-Colombia Trade Promotion Agreement: Potential Economy-Wide and Selected Sectoral Effects, USITC Pub. 3896, 2006; US Int'l Trade Comm'n, US-Panama Trade Promotion Agreement: Potential Economy-Wide and Selected Sectoral Effects, USITC Pub. 3948, 2007.

[11] Cf. US-Colombia TPA and US-Panama TPA with, e.g., CAFTA-DR.

[12] Chapters 2-8 of the US-Colombia TPA; Chapters 3-8 of the US-Panama TPA.

[13] Art. 4.1 and Annex 4.1 of the US-Colombia TPA; Art. 4.1 and Annex 4.1 of the US-Panama TPA.

[14] Art. 8.1-8.7 of the US-Colombia TPA; Art. 8.1-8.7 of the US-Panama TPA.

countervailing duty laws.[15] The parts of the agreements on trade in services include general commitments on cross-border trade in services, plus individual chapters on financial services, telecommunications, and electronic commerce.[16] The agreements contain chapters on government procurement, investment, and intellectual property.[17] The agreements also have separate chapters on labour, the environment, government transparency, administration of the agreement and trade-capacity building, and state-to-state dispute resolution.[18] Curiously, the US-Colombia TPA includes a chapter on competition policy,[19] but the US-Panama TPA does not.

Labour Provisions

A noteworthy change from earlier US trade agreements in the US-Colombia and US-Panama TPAs is found in the provisions governing labour standards. The US position on this issue changed in May 2007 as a result of a political agreement between the Bush Administration and congressional Democrats, who had taken control of Congress after the November 2006 elections. In previous US preferential agreements such as the 2005 Free Trade Agreement among the United States, Central America, and the Dominican Republic ("CAFTA-DR"), each party made the commitment that it "shall *strive to ensure* that its laws provide for labour standards consistent with the internationally recognized labour rights set forth [in the agreement] and shall *strive to improve* those standards in that light."[20] In the US-Colombia and US-Panama TPAs, the soft law wording of "strive to ensure" and "strive to improve" has been changed into hard law. The agreements provide that "[e]ach Party *shall adopt and maintain* in its statutes and regulations, and practices thereunder, the ... rights [set forth in the agreement]".[21] The applicable labour rights in the two agreements are "(a) freedom of association; (b) the effective recognition of the right to collective bargaining; (c) the elimination of all forms of compulsory or forced labour; (d) the effective abolition of child labour and, for purposes of this Agreement, a prohibition on the worst forms of child labour; and (e) the elimination of discrimination in respect of employment and occupation."[22]

---

[15] Art. 8.8 of the US-Colombia TPA; Art. 8.8 of the US-Panama TPA.

[16] Chapters 11, 12, 14-15 of the US-Colombia TPA; Chapters 11-14 of the US-Panama TPA.

[17] Chapters 9, 10 and 16 of the US-Colombia TPA; Chapters 9, 10 and 15 of the US-Panama TPA. The United States and Panama had a pre-existing bilateral investment treaty that was signed on October 27, 1982. This treaty will remain in effect, except that its dispute settlement procedures will be suspended in favour of those of the TPA, subject to certain exceptions during a transition period. See Art. 1-3 of the US-Panama TPA.

[18] Chapters 17, 18, 19, 20-21 of the US-Colombia TPA; Chapters 16-20 of the US-Panama TPA.

[19] Chapter 13 of the US-Colombia TPA.

[20] Art. 16.1(2) CAFTA-DR.

[21] Art. 17.2(1) of the US-Colombia TPA ; Art. 16.2(1) of the US-Panama TPA.

[22] Art. 17.2(1) of the US-Colombia TPA; Art. 16.2(1) of the US-Panama TPA. In contrast, CAFTA-DR omitted the elimination of employment discrimination, but included instead

The US-Colombia and US-Panama TPAs also modify the remedy provision if a party is found in violation of its labour obligations. Under CAFTA-DR, if a dispute settlement panel determines that a party has violated its obligations on labour standards, the prescribed remedy is a monetary assessment in an amount determined by the dispute settlement panel that "shall be paid into a fund established . . . for appropriate labor . . . initiatives, including efforts to improve or enhance labor . . . law enforcement, in the territory of the Party complained against, consistent with its law."[23] If the party fails to pay the monetary assessment, the complaining party may take steps to collect the assessment, including suspending tariff concessions as necessary to collect the assessment.[24] In contrast, the US-Colombia and US-Panama TPAs do not include a separate article providing for the monetary assessment in labour disputes. Instead, the remedy in such cases is folded into the general remedy for non-implementation. However, this remedy allows a party found in violation an option of paying a monetary assessment instead of being subject to the suspension of concessions.[25] The agreements also provide that the parties may decide to have the monetary assessment "paid into a fund . . . for appropriate initiatives to facilitate trade between the Parties, including . . . by assisting a Party in carrying out its obligations under this Agreement."[26] Therefore, as a practical matter, it appears that labour rights violations might still be remedied by a monetary assessment to be used to improve enforcement capacity.

US Trade Agreements in the Western Hemisphere in Context

When these two agreements enter into force, the United States will have six preferential trade agreements in the western hemisphere: NAFTA, CAFTA-DR, and bilateral agreements with Chile, Peru, Colombia, and Panama. The "region" in question consists of twelve countries including the United States covering most of North and Central America (except Belize), the Dominican Republic in the Caribbean, plus three Pacific-coast countries in South America. While this group of states extends beyond North America, one should note that the Office of the US Trade Representative treats the western hemisphere or the Americas as a single region.[27]

Nevertheless, when this region with its set of six agreements is viewed as a whole, the agreements still exhibit the commonly expressed criticisms of

"acceptable conditions of work with respect to minimum wages, hours of work, and occupational safety and health." See also Art. 16.8 CAFTA-DR.

[23] Art. 20.17(4) CAFTA-DR. The monetary assessment remedy applies *mutatis mutandis* to environmental standards.

[24] Art. 20.17(5) CAFTA-DR.

[25] Art. 21.16(6) of the US-Colombia TPA; Art. 20.15(6) of the US-Panama TPA.

[26] Art. 21.16(7) of the US-Colombia TPA; Art. 20.15(7) of the US-Panama TPA.

[27] See, e.g., US Trade Representative, 2012 Trade Policy Agenda, March 2012, pp. 133–137 (discussing bilateral and regional initiatives in "the Americas").

preferential trade agreements.[28] These are a failure to create a fully coherent system of economic integration among the member states, a failure to serve as building blocks toward multilateral trade liberalization or a larger geographical area of regional economic integration, and a failure to curb the negotiating leverage of the strongest member.

The first criticism, failure to create a fully coherent system of economic integration among the member states, is what Bhagwati has labeled the "spaghetti bowl" problem.[29] The six agreements remain separate, uncoordinated agreements in a hub-and-spoke pattern with the United States, lacking a mechanism for the agreements to mesh with each other. In particular, each agreement's rules of origin limit preferential treatment to goods originating in the parties to each separate agreement, thereby limiting the ability of businesses to establish multi-country supply chains. For example, finished goods produced in one country (say, Panama) from materials produced in a neighboring country with a US trade agreement (Mexico, any non-US CAFTA-DR member, Colombia, Peru, or Chile) would not qualify for duty-free treatment unless the processing in Panama transforms the materials into goods originating in Panama under the rules of origin in the US-Panama TPA.[30] (In contrast, CAFTA-DR allows multi-country supply chains among its parties because the geographic definition of "originating goods" covers the entire CAFTA-DR area.[31])

The second criticism is that preferential trade agreements rarely seem to be building blocks toward a multilateral trading system or even a larger geographic area of regional economic integration.[32] With negotiations toward the Free Trade Agreement of the Americas (FTAA) having been abandoned, the United States no longer has an on-going initiative to create a larger area of economic integration in the western hemisphere, leaving only an incomplete web of bilateral or few-party preferential trade agreements.[33]

[28] Bhagwati, *Termites in the Trading System: How Preferential Trade Agreements Undermine Free Trade*, 2008, pp. 61–88.

[29] Bhagwati, *Termites in the Trading System: How Preferential Trade Agreements Undermine Free Trade*, 2008, pp. 61–71.

[30] See Art. 4.1 of the US-Panama TPA (defining "originating goods" as goods "produced entirely in the territory of *one or both* of the Parties" or else requiring that "each of the non-originating materials used in the production of the good undergoes an applicable change in tariff classification, or [...] otherwise satisfies any applicable regional value content or other requirements [...]") (italics added).

[31] See Art. 4.1 CAFTA-DR (defining "originating goods" as goods "produced entirely in the territory of *one or more* of the Parties" (italics added)).

[32] Bhagwati, *Termites in the Trading System: How Preferential Trade Agreements Undermine Free Trade*, 2008, pp. 81–88.

[33] US Trade Representative, 2012 Trade Policy Agenda, March 2012, pp. 133–137 (discussing the continued operation of the four earlier trade agreements, approval of the US-Colombia and US-Panama TPAs, and "bilateral meetings" with non-FTA trading partners in the Americas, but no plans for new preferential trade agreements in the region).

Instead, the United States has shifted its priorities in trade negotiations to the Asia-Pacific area with the pending talks toward the Trans-Pacific Partnership ("TPP"). The Obama Administration describes TPP as "a bold initiative ... [to] advanc[e] the United States' multifaceted trade and investment interests in the dynamic Asia-Pacific region"[34] through a "comprehensive, next-generation agreement that will ... serve as a model for future free trade agreements."[35] One of the ideas in the TPP is "the long term objective of expanding the group to additional countries across the Asia-Pacific region."[36]

At this stage, then, the United States sees the TPP and not any of the existing trade agreements in the western hemisphere as the building block for a regional trade agreement covering a larger geographical area. Two parties to US agreements in the western hemisphere, Chile and Peru, are participating in the TPP negotiations.[37] Canada and Mexico have "expressed interest"[38] but have not yet joined the negotiations. If the six existing US trade agreements in the western hemisphere are to be melded into a comprehensive system of regional integration, apparently the task will involve bringing more western hemisphere countries into the TPP. The resulting "region" will not be limited to the western hemisphere, but will cover the Pacific rim. Indeed, all the parties to the US trade agreements in the western hemisphere are on the Pacific except the Dominican Republic.

The third criticism of preferential trade agreements is that they give powerful states with large markets like the United States negotiating leverage to extract concessions out of weak states with small markets.[39] Of course, this feature may be seen as an advantage of preferential agreements from the perspective of the large power. The US-Colombia and US-Panama TPAs include many features that reflect US negotiating leverage: the basic goal of replacing unilateral preferences with an agreement giving the United States enhanced market access, the US insistence on labour and tax reforms before approving the agreements, the US ability to continue to impose antidumping and countervailing duties, the stronger protection of intellectual property rights, and the chapters on labour standards and environmental protection.

---

[34] US Trade Representative, 2012 Trade Policy Agenda, March 2012, p. 4.

[35] US Trade Representative, 2012 Trade Policy Agenda, March 2012 p. 147.

[36] US Trade Representative, 2012 Trade Policy Agenda, March 2012, p. 148.

[37] Currently, the TPP negotiating parties are Australia, Brunei, Chile, Malaysia, New Zealand, Singapore, Peru, the United States, and Vietnam. See US Trade Representative, 2012 Trade Policy Agenda, March 2012, p. 147.

[38] US Trade Representative, 2012 Trade Policy Agenda, March 2012, p. 147.

[39] Bhagwati, *Termites in the Trading System: How Preferential Trade Agreements Undermine Free Trade*, 2008, pp. 71–81.

The US-Mexico Cross-Border Trucking Dispute

During 2011, the United States and Mexico reached a settlement of their long dispute over cross-border trucking services under NAFTA.[40] The trucking dispute is an example of what Robert Hudec in 1980 called "wrong cases"[41]—trade disputes that an international dispute settlement mechanism does not handle well. One type of "wrong case" is a "politically irreversible" violation: "Given political realities in most ... countries, even the most respected [trade] rules will sometimes be overcome by an industry with particularly strong influence or some peculiar economic situation."[42] Another type of "wrong case" occurs where "governments had come to regard the legal criteria in question as unrealistic, politically impossible, and, in some cases, wrong as a matter of policy."[43]

The trucking dispute showed attributes of both types of "wrong cases." It certainly featured a politically strong labour union, the International Brotherhood of Teamsters, the union representing employees of many US trucking companies. The Teamsters opposed allowing Mexican trucks to operate in the United States.[44] In addition, there was a perception among many in the United States that the NAFTA rules as negotiated did not adequately balance the goal of trade liberalization with the goal of highway safety. When the United States was supposed to open its border to Mexican trucks in 1995, "thirty-two broad-based collations, including religious, labour, and environmental groups, sent a joint letter to President Clinton

[40] Two valuable sources of information about this dispute are the 2001 NAFTA Panel Report on the dispute and the US Transportation Department's July 2011 Federal Register notice explaining the US pilot programme for allowing Mexican trucks to operate in the United States. See NAFTA, Final Report of the Panel, USA-MEX-98-2008-01, *Cross-Border Trucking Services (Mexico vs. United States)*; Pilot Program on the North American Free Trade Agreement (NAFTA) Long-Haul Trucking Provisions, 76 Fed. Reg. 40420 et seq. (Dep't of Transportation, July 8, 2011).

[41] Hudec, GATT Dispute Settlement After the Tokyo Round: Some Unfinished Business, Cornell International Law Journal 13 (1980) 2, p. 145 (159) (adopting the term "wrong cases" in discussing dispute resolution under the GATT). See also Lowenfeld, *International Economic Law*, (2nd ed.) 2008, p. 927 (observing that "the interrelation of law and politics" is found throughout international economic law and that "international economic law [...] is a process").

[42] Hudec, GATT Dispute Settlement After the Tokyo Round: Some Unfinished Business, Cornell International Law Journal 13 (1980) 2, p. 145 (159).

[43] Hudec, GATT Dispute Settlement After the Tokyo Round: Some Unfinished Business, Cornell International Law Journal 13 (1980) 2, p. 145 (160).

[44] See, e.g., Hoffa, "Keep Mexican Trucks Out", USA Today, April 1, 2009, p. 10A (James P. Hoffa, the president of the Teamsters Union, writes: "The Teamsters Union is strongly against opening the Mexican border to unsafe trucks. [...] But it's nonsense to claim that the US is being protectionist."). When the Transportation Department announced its proposed pilot programme to implement the settlement of the trucking dispute, receives comments in opposition from not only the Teamsters Union but also more than 1,000 individual union members. Pilot Program on the North American Free Trade Agreement (NAFTA) Long-Haul Trucking Provisions, 76 Fed. Reg. 40420 et seq. (Dep't of Transportation, July 8, 2011).

urging him to delay implementation of NAFTA's obligations . . . ."[45] Furthermore, Congress complicated settlement of the dispute by enacting new statutory requirements as part of Transportation Department appropriations bills. The use of appropriations bills meant that, even if a president opposed Congress's action, as a practical matter he could not veto the bill without canceling the annual funding for the Transportation Department. Ultimately, as discussed below, the settlement of the dispute essentially required renegotiating NAFTA to ratify the US position in part, by establishing a 3-year transition period to evaluate the safety compliance of Mexican trucking companies. At the same time, for NAFTA's state-to-state dispute settlement procedure, the trucking dispute has fulfilled the ominous concern about "wrong cases" that "non-compliance would become conspicuous failures for the [international institution], diminishing both its own prestige and that of its rules."[46]

The US-Mexico trucking dispute traces its origin to the early 1980s, when the United States began deregulating its trucking industry.[47] Before deregulation, the United States essentially gave national treatment to foreign trucking companies, but tight regulation of the industry meant that very few new entrants were allowed. Deregulation made it easier for Mexican and Canadian trucking companies to obtain approval to operate in the United States. In 1982, the United States imposed a moratorium on approving Mexican trucking companies for operations in the United States, because Mexico did not allow reciprocal access for US trucking companies to operate in Mexico. The moratorium was intended to encourage Mexico to ease its restrictions affecting US firms, and the US president could lift it if Mexico began to provide reciprocal access. A similar moratorium on Canada was lifted immediately in 1982 because Canada already allowed reciprocal access for US trucking operators.

The moratorium for Mexican trucks remained in place when NAFTA came into force on January 1, 1994.[48] In the US schedule of market access commitments for trade in services under NAFTA, the United States agreed to allow Mexican trucking operators to obtain operating authority to provide cross-border trucking services to or from border states (California, Arizona, New Mexico, and Texas) on December 18, 1995, or 3 years after NAFTA was signed.[49] The United States agreed further

[45] NAFTA, Final Report of the Panel, USA-MEX-98-2008-01, *Cross-Border Trucking Services (Mexico vs. United States)*, para. 80.

[46] Hudec, GATT Dispute Settlement After the Tokyo Round: Some Unfinished Business, Cornell International Law Journal 13 (1980) 2, p. 145 (159).

[47] This paragraph is based on the factual background set out in the 2001 Panel Report on the dispute. See NAFTA, Final Report of the Panel, USA-MEX-98-2008-01, *Cross-Border Trucking Services (Mexico vs. United States)*, paras. 35 et seq.

[48] NAFTA, Annex I—Reservations for Existing Measures and Liberalization Measures, Chapters Eleven, Twelve and Fourteen, I-U-18 to I-U-19.

[49] NAFTA, Annex I—Reservations for Existing Measures and Liberalization Measures, I-U-20.

that Mexican truckers could obtain authority to operate cross-border trucking services to all US states on January 1, 2000.[50]

The United States initially tried to meet the NAFTA deadline for cross-border operations in border states, but changed its position at the last moment. On December 18, 1995, instead of announcing the implementation of NAFTA, the US Transportation Secretary announced that "final disposition of pending applications [from Mexican trucking firms] will be held until consultations between the United States and Mexico to further improve their motor carrier safety and security regimes have been completed."[51] Therefore, as a practical matter, "the United States essentially continued the moratorium on Mexican trucks that had been in place prior to December 18, 1995."[52]

The United States sought to justify its actions because of alleged lack of safety in Mexican trucks.[53] The US General Accounting Office[54] issued a report that found "significant differences between United States and Mexican safety regulations" and indicated that a large percentage of Mexican trucks operating in border zones under a limited exception to the moratorium "failed to meet US truck safety standards."[55] In addition, a number of civil society groups in the United States—the "thirty-two broad-based coalitions, including religious, labour and environmental groups"[56] mentioned earlier, notably including the Teamsters Union—urged the government to delay implementing the NAFTA obligations.

By 1998, with the moratorium still in place, Mexico initiated a state-to-state dispute resolution proceeding against the United States under NAFTA Chapter 20. The US defense of the moratorium rested mainly on the proposition that the national treatment and most-favoured-nation treatment obligations in NAFTA were limited to service providers of another party who were "in like circumstances" to its own service providers (under national treatment) or to service providers of another country (under most-favoured-nation treatment). According to the United

[50] NAFTA, Annex I—Reservations for Existing Measures and Liberalization Measures, I-U-20 (6 years after NAFTA entered into force). In addition, since the moratorium operated as a restriction on Mexican investment in the United States, the United States made the commitment to allow Mexicans to establish enterprises in the United States to provide trucking services for the international transportation of cargo between points in the United States as of December 18, 1995.

[51] NAFTA, Final Report of the Panel, USA-MEX-98-2008-01, *Cross-Border Trucking Services (Mexico vs. United States)*, para. 82 (paraphrasing statement of Transportation Secretary).

[52] NAFTA, Final Report of the Panel, USA-MEX-98-2008-01, *Cross-Border Trucking Services (Mexico vs. United States)*, para. 77.

[53] NAFTA, Final Report of the Panel, USA-MEX-98-2008-01, *Cross-Border Trucking Services (Mexico vs. United States)*, para. 78.

[54] The General Accounting Office, which is now named the Government Accountability Office, is an independent agency under the US Congress that investigates how the federal government spends taxpayer dollars. See GAO website, http://www.gao.gov.

[55] NAFTA, Final Report of the Panel, USA-MEX-98-2008-01, *Cross-Border Trucking Services (Mexico vs. United States)*, para. 79.

[56] NAFTA, Final Report of the Panel, USA-MEX-98-2008-01, *Cross-Border Trucking Services (Mexico vs. United States)*, para. 80.

States, Mexican trucking operators were not "in like circumstances" to US or Canadian trucking companies because "Mexico's truck transportation regulatory system does not maintain the same rigorous standards as the systems in the United States and Canada, and . . . therefore the 'in like circumstances' language . . . means that 'service providers [in Mexico] may be treated differently in order to address a legitimate regulatory objective.'"[57]

In a decision issued in February 2001, the five-member Panel unanimously rejected the US argument and ruled that the United States had violated its NAFTA obligations. The Panel emphasized that the United States was "deny[ing] access to all Mexican trucking firms on a blanket basis, regardless of the individual qualifications of particular members of the Mexican industry, unless and until Mexico's own domestic regulatory system meets US approval."[58] In contrast, the United States reviewed applications from US and Canadian trucking firms on an individual basis. The Panel ruled that "[t]he treatment of . . . US trucking service providers by US regulatory authorities is the basis of comparison with the treatment . . . of Mexican trucking service providers . . . in determining whether the United States is providing national treatment."[59] Further, "differential treatment should be no greater than necessary for legitimate regulatory purposes such as safety, and . . . such different treatment [must] be equivalent to the treatment accorded to domestic service providers."[60] In contrast, "[i]f . . . the regulatory systems in two NAFTA countries must be substantially identical before national treatment is granted, relatively few service industry providers could ultimately qualify."[61] Accordingly, the Panel held that the United States was violating the national treatment obligation in NAFTA article 1202[62] and, for essentially the same reasons, the most-favoured-nation treatment obligation in NAFTA article 1203,[63] as well as the parallel obligations for investments under NAFTA articles 1102 and 1103.[64]

---

[57] NAFTA, Final Report of the Panel, USA-MEX-98-2008-01, *Cross-Border Trucking Services (Mexico vs. United States)*, para. 242 (quoting the US Written Submission).

[58] NAFTA, Final Report of the Panel, USA-MEX-98-2008-01, *Cross-Border Trucking Services (Mexico vs. United States)*, para. 247.

[59] NAFTA, Final Report of the Panel, USA-MEX-98-2008-01, *Cross-Border Trucking Services (Mexico vs. United States)*, para. 253.

[60] NAFTA, Final Report of the Panel, USA-MEX-98-2008-01, *Cross-Border Trucking Services (Mexico vs. United States)*, para. 258.

[61] NAFTA, Final Report of the Panel, USA-MEX-98-2008-01, *Cross-Border Trucking Services (Mexico vs. United States)*, para. 259.

[62] NAFTA, Final Report of the Panel, USA-MEX-98-2008-01, *Cross-Border Trucking Services (Mexico vs. United States)*, paras. 259 and 272.

[63] NAFTA, Final Report of the Panel, USA-MEX-98-2008-01, *Cross-Border Trucking Services (Mexico vs. United States)*, paras. 276 and 272.

[64] The panel also rejected the US argument that the moratorium could be justified under the general exception in NAFTA Art. 2101 for "measures necessary to secure compliance with laws or regulations [. . .] relating to health and safety and consumer protection." NAFTA, Final Report of the Panel, USA-MEX-98-2008-01, *Cross-Border Trucking Services (Mexico vs. United States)*,

Having found the United States in violation, the Panel "recommend[ed] that the United States take appropriate steps to bring its practices with respect to cross-border trucking services and investment into compliance with its obligations under the applicable provisions of NAFTA."[65] In doing so, the Panel explained that the United States was not obligated to approve any or all specific applications from Mexican trucking companies and could certainly ensure compliance with its trucking safety regulations, but that the blanket moratorium was not consistent with NAFTA obligations.

NAFTA provides that "[o]n receipt of the final report of a panel, the Parties shall agree on the resolution of the dispute, which normally shall conform to the determinations and recommendations of the panel ..."[66] Where the report finds that a party has violated NAFTA obligations, the complaining party has the power to impose retaliatory trade sanctions if the parties have not "reached agreement ... on a mutually satisfactory resolution ... within 30 days of receiving the final report."[67] The authorized trade sanctions are that the "complaining Party may suspend the application to the Party complained against of benefits of equivalent effect until such time as they have reached agreement on a resolution of the dispute."[68]

Mexico had initiated the proceeding in response to the US failure to meet the December 1995 deadline for allowing Mexican trucking operations in border states. While the case was pending, the January 2000 NAFTA deadline for opening the entire US market had passed without being implemented. After the Panel decision, President Bush announced that the United States and Mexico would open negotiations about implementing the Panel's recommendation and beginning a process for opening the US border to Mexican trucking companies.[69] However, near the end of 2001, the US Congress enacted legislation that set preconditions and safety requirements that needed to be met before the Transportation Department could review or process Mexican applications.[70] In late 2002, after the

para. 242. Relying on GATT jurisprudence interpreting the term "necessary to secure compliance," the panel ruled that the United States "did not [...] make a sufficient effort to find a less trade-restrictive measure than the moratorium to address its safety concerns." NAFTA, Final Report of the Panel, USA-MEX-98-2008-01, *Cross-Border Trucking Services (Mexico vs. United States)*, para. 266.

[65] NAFTA, Final Report of the Panel, USA-MEX-98-2008-01, *Cross-Border Trucking Services (Mexico vs. United States)*, para. 299.

[66] NAFTA, Art. 2018(a).

[67] NAFTA, Art. 2019(a).

[68] NAFTA, Art. 2019(a).

[69] See Pilot Program on the North American Free Trade Agreement (NAFTA) Long-Haul Trucking Provisions, 76 Fed. Reg. 40420, 40422 (Dep't of Transportation, July 8, 2011) (discussing background of the 2011 settlement).

[70] Pilot Program on the North American Free Trade Agreement (NAFTA) Long-Haul Trucking Provisions, 76 Fed. Reg. 40421 and 40422 (Dep't of Transportation, July 8, 2011) (discussing section 350 of the 2002 Transportation Department Appropriations Act, Pub. L. No. 107-87, 115 Stat. 833, 864 (December 18, 2001)). The preconditions in the legislation included a pre-authorization safety audit of the applicant company, a safety inspection of each vehicle at the border, and a requirement that the driver have a valid Mexican commercial driver's license.

Transportation Department completed the part of the statutory requirements mandating an internal review of its enforcement capacity, President Bush relaxed the moratorium in part, but only for limited operations in border states.

There followed several years with no new developments. Then, in early 2007, the US and Mexican Transportation Secretaries announced a demonstration project to allow further opening of the border to Mexican trucks.[71] Almost immediately, the US Congress, which had come under Democratic control after the fall 2006 elections, enacted new legislation containing additional requirements for approval of Mexican applications. The legislation required establishment of a so-called pilot programme, which is a test supervised by the Transportation Department and lasting up to 3 years that is intended to compile information for evaluating whether the safety goals of the applicable regulations will be met. After meeting the requirements for the pilot programme, the Transportation Department initiated a 1-year demonstration project in September 2007 and extended it into a 3-year project in 2008.

In March 2009, following the election of President Obama and continued Democratic control of Congress, Congress enacted legislation urged by the Teamsters Union that directed the Transportation Department to stop the demonstration project and stop processing applications of Mexican companies to participate in the project.[72] Until then, Mexico had been exercising forbearance and refraining from imposing retaliatory trade sanctions against the United States, although it could have done so in 2001. After the March 2009 US legislation, Mexico imposed trade sanctions in the form of special import duties that affected approximately 90 US export commodities at an estimated cost of $2.4 billion each year.[73]

After Mexico's retaliation, the US administration began discussions with members of Congress and affected US constituencies, as well as Mexican officials, to develop ideas for settling the dispute.[74] In April 2010, the United States and Mexico formed a working group to consider the next steps toward opening the US border to Mexican trucks. In January 2011, the Transportation Department released a concept document for a pilot programme for cross-border Mexican trucking. This concept document became the starting point for renewed negotiations between the

[71] Pilot Program on the North American Free Trade Agreement (NAFTA) Long-Haul Trucking Provisions, 76 Fed. Reg. 40422-40423 (Dep't of Transportation, July 8, 2011).

[72] Pilot Program on the North American Free Trade Agreement (NAFTA) Long-Haul Trucking Provisions, 76 Fed. Reg. 40423 (Dep't of Transportation, July 8, 2011). See also "Bad Example: Mexico's Justified Retaliation Against US Trucking Protectionism", Washington Post, March 23, 2009, p. A14 (editorial asserting that "the Democratic Congress's recent approval of a law, signed by Mr. Obama, [. . .] killed any chance that long-haul freight trucks from Mexico could operate in the United States, as had been promised under the North American Free Trade Agreement.").

[73] See Pilot Program on the North American Free Trade Agreement (NAFTA) Long-Haul Trucking Provisions, 76 Fed. Reg. 40420, 40423 (Dep't of Transportation, July 8, 2011).

[74] Pilot Program on the North American Free Trade Agreement (NAFTA) Long-Haul Trucking Provisions, 76 Fed. Reg. 40420, 40423 (Dep't of Transportation, July 8, 2011).

United States and Mexico. These negotiations came to fruition in time for President Calderón's state visit to the United States in March 2011. During the joint presidential press conference, President Obama announced that "after nearly 20 years, we ... finally found a clear path to resolving the trucking dispute between our two countries."[75]

Shortly after the presidential press conference, the Transportation Department published a notice that it proposed to establish the statutorily required pilot programme to compile data "to test and demonstrate the ability of Mexican motor carriers to operate safely in the United States."[76] The Transportation Department officially established the pilot programme on July 6, 2011, after receiving and evaluating extensive public comments on the proposal.[77] On the same day, the two countries formalized their settlement of the dispute by signing a Memorandum of Understanding.[78]

The Memorandum of Understanding establishes a transition period lasting not more than 3 years, known as the initial phase, which corresponds to the length of the internal US pilot programme. During the initial phase, Mexican trucking companies may apply for and receive 18-month provisional authority to perform cross-border trucking services in the United States.[79] Mexican trucks entering the United States must meet US safety standards, including carrying electronic on-board recorders to track compliance with US requirements for hours of operations.[80] Drivers of Mexican trucks must undergo a review process, including drug testing analyzed in a US laboratory as well as reading assessment to assure that they can understand US traffic signs.[81] After operating for 18 months under provisional authority, Mexican trucking companies that receive a satisfactory safety rating in a compliance review and

[75] The President's News Conference with President Felipe de Jesús Calderón Hinojosa of Mexico, 2011 Daily Comp. Pres. Doc. No. 00141 (March 3, 2011).

[76] Pilot Program on NAFTA Long-Haul Trucking Provisions, 76 Fed. Reg. 20807 (Dep't of Transportation, April 13, 2011) (notice of proposed programme and request for public comments).

[77] Pilot Program on the North American Free Trade Agreement (NAFTA) Long-Haul Trucking Provisions, 76 Fed. Reg. 40420 et seq. (Dep't of Transportation, July 8, 2011).

[78] US-Mexico Memorandum of Understanding on International Freight Cross-Border Trucking Services (July 6, 2011).

[79] US-Mexico Memorandum of Understanding on International Freight Cross-Border Trucking Services (July 6, 2011), Art. III. Before applying for the provisional authority, the trucking company must undergo a pre-authorization safety audit. US-Mexico Memorandum of Understanding on International Freight Cross-Border Trucking Services (July 6, 2011), Art. I.

[80] US Transportation Dep't Press Release, Secretary Ray LaHood's Remarks on Signing of US-Mexico Cross Border Trucking Agreement (July 6, 2011); US-Mexico Memorandum of Understanding on International Freight Cross-Border Trucking Services, Annex, § 1(2)(b) (July 6, 2011).

[81] US Transportation Dep't Press Release, Secretary Ray LaHood's Remarks on Signing of US-Mexico Cross Border Trucking Agreement (July 6, 2011); US-Mexico Memorandum of Understanding on International Freight Cross-Border Trucking Services, Annex, §§ 1(2)(b) and (d) (July 6, 2011).

continue to satisfy applicable Transportation Department regulations are to be granted permanent operating authority.[82]

In addition to the requirements applicable to Mexican trucking companies in the United States, the agreement establishes analogous provisional authority procedures for US trucking companies to operate in Mexico.[83]

The initial phase will end when the Transportation Department completes its pilot programme and notifies Congress that "the provisions of US law pertaining to the initial phase, including those regarding compliance with the statistical data collection and analysis of the initial phase, have been met."[84] At that time, "the Parties shall grant motor carriers of the other Party full access to provide international freight cross-border trucking services, subject to applicable domestic laws and regulations."[85]

As part of the July 2011 settlement, Mexico agreed immediately to suspend 50% of its retaliatory import duties on US products and to remove the remaining 50% when the first Mexican trucking company receives authorization to being transporting goods.[86] The remaining duties were removed later in 2011.[87]

The trucking dispute is a fascinating case study for international economic law of a settlement of a "wrong case." Although the July 2011 agreement apparently settles the dispute, it does not represent full US compliance with NAFTA's original provisions on cross-border trucking services. The 3-year transition period, including the pilot programme and the granting of only provisional authority, means that Mexican trucking companies do not yet receive national treatment or most-favoured-nation treatment. Nor did the United States implement the recommendations of the 2001 Panel report. Instead, the settlement represents a partial renegotiation of NAFTA to satisfy the safety concerns of the United States, the stronger party in a power-oriented outcome.[88] Assuming that Transportation Department finds in its 3-year pilot programme that Mexican trucking companies do meet US safety standards, only then will the United States fully implement its NAFTA obligations.

Mexico's NAFTA-authorized trade sanctions against the United States appear to have helped move the trucking dispute toward settlement by prompting adversely

[82] US-Mexico Memorandum of Understanding on International Freight Cross-Border Trucking Services, Annex, § 3(2) (July 6, 2011).

[83] US-Mexico Memorandum of Understanding on International Freight Cross-Border Trucking Services, Annex, §§ 2 and 4 (July 6, 2011).

[84] US-Mexico Memorandum of Understanding on International Freight Cross-Border Trucking Services, Art. 6.

[85] US-Mexico Memorandum of Understanding on International Freight Cross-Border Trucking Services, Art. 6.

[86] US Transportation Dep't Press Release, Secretary Ray LaHood's Remarks on Signing of US-Mexico Cross Border Trucking Agreement (July 6, 2011).

[87] US Trade Representative, 2012 Trade Policy Agenda, March 2012, p. 135.

[88] See Jackson, The Crumbling Institutions of the Liberal Trade System, Journal of World Trade Law 12 (1978) 2, p. 93 (98–101) (originating the term "power-oriented" dispute resolution).

affected US constituencies to urge the US government to resolve the matter.[89] In that respect, the state-to-state dispute resolution process under NAFTA Chapter 20, including sanctions, appears to have contributed to a positive solution of the dispute. Nevertheless, from another perspective, the state-to-state dispute resolution procedure may have been a victim of the trucking dispute. The 2001 panel report in the dispute was the last time the NAFTA state-to-state procedure has been used.[90] Since 2001, Canada and Mexico have instead brought a number of complaints against the United States under the WTO dispute settlement process.[91] The disuse of the NAFTA procedure undoubtedly reflects the observation expressed above that non-compliance can turn into conspicuous and damaging failures for an international institution. Perhaps a failure of this kind was to be expected in NAFTA, which no one thought would establish institutions that would severely constrain the strongest member. However, Professor Hudec also wrote in his 1980 article that "one or two disastrous failures under an obsolete provision could actually help the legal system if such failures stimulated renegotiation of the rule."[92] As the United States seeks to negotiate a better system of regional integration under the Trans-Pacific Partnership, it will be instructive to observe whether the negotiators do a better job of balancing trade liberalization with other important policy goals such as public safety,[93] as well as whether they establish a more effective system of state-to-state dispute resolution.

Investment Disputes

All the US trade agreements in the western hemisphere include investment chapters that establish investor-state arbitration to resolve investment disputes, and there are a number of bilateral investment treaties (BITs) with investor-state arbitration

[89] E.g., "No clear-cut road map on Mexican truck issue", Houston Chronicle, March 17, 2010, Business Section, p. 1 (reporting that "Business groups such as the US Chamber of Commerce have stepped up lobbying to end a standoff they say has cost American companies an estimated $2.6 billion in lost exports."); "Bad Example: Mexico's Justified Retaliation Against US Trucking Protectionism", Washington Post, March 23, 2009, p. A14 (editorial urging "a settlement of this entirely avoidable dispute, which harms both the US image in Latin America and American consumers, farmers and workers [...]").

[90] See the NAFTA Secretariat Website http://www.nafta-sec-alena.org.

[91] To cite just one example, Canada and Mexico are complainants against the United States in parallel WTO cases heard by a single panel concerning certain US country-of-origin labeling requirements, Reports of the Panel, WT/DS384/R and WT/DS386/R, *United States—Certain Country of Origin Labeling (COOL) Requirements*.

[92] Hudec, GATT Dispute Settlement After the Tokyo Round: Some Unfinished Business, Cornell International Law Journal 13 (1980) 2, p. 145 (167).

[93] See US Trade Representative, 2012 Trade Policy Agenda, March 2012, p. 4 (asserting that "Participants in the TPP negotiations are [...] addressing 21st-century trade issues, including [...] cross-cutting issues like increasing regulatory coherence [...]").

processes between states in North and Central America. During 2011, final awards were issued in three investor-state arbitrations in the region.[94] All three decisions were in favour of the host state. In this commentator's opinion, the cases were strange. They struck the commentator as misconceived or seriously mishandled on the part of the claimants. In one arbitration, the claimants tried unsuccessfully to use investor-state arbitration as the vehicle for bringing what was essentially a claim for violation of indigenous peoples' rights. Three of the four claimants had their cases dismissed for lack of jurisdiction because they did not own investments in the host country. The remaining claimant lost on the merits because NAFTA does not incorporate any legal obligation of a host country to assist businesses owned by members of an indigenous people. In a second arbitration, the case was dismissed for lack of jurisdiction because the claimant committed the tactical blunder of failing to discontinue pending litigation in the host-state court. In a third arbitration, the claim was dismissed for lack of jurisdiction because the claimant could not produce credible evidence showing that he actually owned the investment at the time the contested government measure was adopted.

The three decisions in 2001 reflect that investor-state arbitration is used infrequently under the trade agreements and BITs in North and Central America.[95] By this commentator's count, arbitral tribunals have issued final awards in thirteen investment disputes in the region during the 5 years from 2007 through 2011.[96]

---

[94] In addition to the three decisions in 2011 reviewed here, a final award was issued in late 2010 under the US-Panama Bilateral Investment Treaty in ICSID, ARB/06/19, *Nations Energy Inc. y Panamá*, Laudo (award in Spanish). In that case, the tribunal decided by a 2-1 majority that a decision by Panama's Revenue Department denying an investment tax credit for a proposed transaction and an amendment of Panama's tax law reducing the amount of the tax credit did not constitute an indirect expropriation or a denial of fair and equitable treatment. Because the award is written in Spanish, it was not practicable for this commentator to analyze the decision in detail.

[95] See Reed, International Economic Law in North America: Recent Developments in Dispute Resolution Under Regional Economic Arrangements, in: Herrmann/Terhechte (eds.), *European Yearbook of International Economic Law 2012*, 2012, pp. 457 et seq. (457) (reaching the same conclusion for the period 2008 to 2010).

[96] NAFTA/ICSID, *United Parcel Service of America vs. Canada*, Award on the Merits, available at: http://italaw.com/cases/documents/1143; NAFTA/ICSID, ARB(AF)/05/1, *Bayview Irrigation District vs. Mexico*, Award; NAFTA/ICSID, ARB(AF)/04/05, *Archer Daniels Midland Co. vs. Mexico*, Award (same dispute as *Cargill* and *Corn Products*); NAFTA, *Canadian Cattlemen for Fair Trade vs. United States*, Award on Jurisdiction, available at: http://italaw.com/cases/documents/192; NAFTA/ICSID, ARB(AF)/04/01, *Corn Products International, Inc. vs. Mexico, Decision on Responsibility* (same dispute as *Archer Daniels Midland* and *Cargill*); ICSID, ARB/05/14, *RSM Production Corp. vs. Grenada* (same dispute as *Grynberg*); NAFTA, *Glamis Gold Ltd. vs. United States*, Award, available at: http://italaw.com/documents/Glamis_Award.pdf; NAFTA/ICSID, ARB(AF)/05/2, *Cargill, Inc. vs. Mexico* (same dispute as *Archer Daniels Midland* and *Corn Products*); NAFTA, *Merrill & Ring Forestry LP vs. Canada*, Award, available at: http://italaw.com/documents/MerrillAward.pdf; ICSID, ARB(AF)/07/3, *Anderson vs. Costa Rica*; NAFTA, *Chemtura Corp. vs. Canada*, Award, available at: http://old.italaw.com/documents/ChemturaAward_000.pdf; ICSID, ARB/06/19, *Nations Energy Inc. y Panamá, Laudo*; ICSID, ARB/10/6, *Grynberg vs. Grenada* (same dispute as *RSM*); NAFTA, *Grand River Enterprises Six*

The host state was found liable in only one dispute, although it led to three separate awards, one for each of three claimants.[97] In five disputes, the claim was dismissed for lack of jurisdiction, as were the claims of three of the four claimants in a sixth dispute.[98] The small number of total disputes, the small percentage finding host-state liability, and the large percentage dismissed for lack of jurisdiction create the impression of a mismatch between existing problems and available solutions, at least in North and Central America. The available solutions are the codified international rules for protection of investments and an international institution in the form of the investor-state arbitration process. However, few cases are commenced, and nearly all are meritless, at least in North and Central America. This suggests either that government measures rarely cause grievances for international businesses or, more likely, that the existing grievances are not within the purview of the available international rules and institutions protecting investments.

The three cases from 2011 are reviewed below.

Grand River Enterprises

Grand River Enterprises Six Nations vs. United States[99] arose from cigarette regulatory laws enacted in a number of US states to implement a 1998 settlement agreement in litigation between the states and major US cigarette manufacturers over the health risks of smoking. As part of the settlement, the states enacted legislation to regulate small cigarette manufacturers that did not participate in the settlement, thereby limiting their abilities to increase their market shares at the expense of participating manufacturers. By approximately 2003, many states became concerned that the regulatory measures for nonparticipating manufacturers were not working as well as had been desired. Therefore, 38 states enacted legislation in 2003 and 2004 that amended the regulatory measures for nonparticipating manufacturers to make them stricter and more onerous. (In view of the outcome of the arbitration, the details of the complex regulatory regime need not be explained here.)

The claimants in the investor-state arbitration were Grand River, a Canadian corporation engaged in manufacturing and distributing cigarettes, and three individual claimants. The individual claimants were all Canadian-born Native

Nations, Ltd vs. United States, Award, available at http://italaw.com/sites/default/files/case-documents/ita0384.pdf; CAFTA/ICSID, ARB/09/17, *Commerce Group Corp. vs. El Salvador*, Award; NAFTA, PCA No. 55798, *Gallo vs. Canada*, Award.

[97] *Archer Daniels Midland*, *Cargill*, and *Corn Products*, contesting discriminatory Mexican taxes on soft drinks sweetened with corn syrup.

[98] *Bayview*, *Canadian Cattlemen*, *Anderson*, *Grand River* (3 of 4 claimants), *Commerce Group*, and *Gallo*.

[99] NAFTA, *Grand River Enterprises Six Nations*, Ltd. vs. United States, Award, available at: http://italaw.com/sites/default/files/case-documents/ita0384.pdf.

Americans or members of First Nations in Canadian terminology. Two lived in Canada and were controlling shareholders of Grand River. The third lived on tribal lands in New York State and owned Native Wholesale Supply ("Native Wholesale"), a US company that bought cigarettes from Grand River and distributed them in the United States.

Grand River and the individuals initiated arbitration against the United States alleging that the state regulatory legislation violated the investor protection provisions in NAFTA chapter 11. In a preliminary ruling 2006, the tribunal had ruled that claims against the original regulatory regime as enacted in 1998 were untimely under the NAFTA 3-year limitations period, thereby limiting the claim to the amendments enacted in 2003 and 2004.

In the final award, the tribunal dismissed the claims of Grand River and the two individuals living in Canada (the "Canadian-based claimants") for lack of jurisdiction, finding that they did not own any "investment" in the United States. Since Grand River's major asset was its cigarette manufacturing plant in Canada, plainly it did not qualify as an investment in the United States.[100] The claimants' main argument was that the three Canadian-based claimants and the US resident together owned an "enterprise" that consisted in their cooperative efforts to sell Grand River's cigarettes in the United States, but existed in an undocumented matter customary among indigenous peoples. The tribunal denied this theory, ruling that an "enterprise" under NAFTA requires "some form of business association with its own juridical personality constituted or organized under applicable law, rather than mere mutually beneficial business, contractual, or culturally-rooted relations."[101] In their Reply Memorial, the claimants added the theory that the "applicable law" governing their business association was Seneca tribal law, but the tribunal ruled that they failed "to show that the culturally-based or other business understandings that the Claimants describe are sufficient under Seneca law and thereby under NAFTA."[102] The tribunal also considered whether the Canadian-based claimants satisfied any of the other forms of "investment" set out in NAFTA, but held that they did not.[103]

[100] NAFTA, *Grand River Enterprises Six Nations, Ltd. vs. United States*, Award, paras. 85–89, available at: http://italaw.com/sites/default/files/case-documents/ita0384.pdf.

[101] NAFTA, *Grand River Enterprises Six Nations, Ltd. vs. United States*, Award, para. 92, available at: http://italaw.com/sites/default/files/case-documents/ita0384.pdf.

[102] NAFTA, *Grand River Enterprises Six Nations, Ltd. vs. United States*, Award, para. 103, available at: http://italaw.com/sites/default/files/case-documents/ita0384.pdf.

[103] NAFTA, *Grand River Enterprises Six Nations, Ltd. vs. United States*, Award, paras. 107–120, available at: http://italaw.com/sites/default/files/case-documents/ita0384.pdf. For example, although Grand River had lent money to Native Wholesale to finance its inventory, the loan did not qualify as an "investment" because it did not meet the NAFTA requirement that a loan to an enterprise is only an "investment" if the borrower is an affiliate of the lender. NAFTA, *Grand River Enterprises Six Nations, Ltd. vs. United States*, paras. 107–110, available at: http://italaw.com/sites/default/files/case-documents/ita0384.pdf.

The remaining claimant, the Canadian-born individual who owned Native Wholesale, definitely qualified as an "investor" under NAFTA. He asserted that the state regulatory legislation violated NAFTA by violating his legitimate expectations, expropriating a substantial part of his business, violating the national treatment and most-favoured-nation treatment obligations, and denying him fair and equitable treatment. The tribunal ruled against him on all points.

With respect to the investor's legitimate expectations, the tribunal ruled that although US laws protect the rights of Native Americans to engage in international trade and domestic business, there is no legitimate expectation to be free of state regulatory legislation on cigarettes, an area long subject to extensive state regulation.[104]

The claimant's expropriation claim was that the state legislation "resulted in the expropriation of a substantial portion of the value of his investment."[105] The tribunal, citing a number of other investment decisions, ruled that "expropriation involves the deprivation or impairment of all, or substantially all, of an investor's interests."[106] However, in the case before the tribunal, the investor's claim "involves the alleged expropriation of only part of a growing and seemingly profitable ongoing business over which he retains ownership and control."[107] Ruling that an act of expropriation cannot involve only part of an investment, the tribunal denied the expropriation claim.[108]

The claimant's remaining arguments were built on the theory that the state regulatory legislation failed in any way to help a business owned by a Native American, a member of a disadvantaged minority group, to compete with businesses not owned by members of a disadvantaged minority. In his specific arguments under NAFTA, the claimant asserted that the state regulatory legislation violated the national treatment and most-favoured-nation treatment obligations under NAFTA by discriminating against indigenous peoples. Illegal discrimination, the claimant urged, includes treating members of a disadvantaged group in the same manner as persons who are not disadvantaged: "[the claimant] should not have been subject to the disputed measures applicable to other similarly situated investors . . ., because of his situation as a First Nations trader."[109] The tribunal held that this

---

[104] NAFTA, *Grand River Enterprises Six Nations, Ltd. vs. United States*, Award, paras. 128–145, available at: http://italaw.com/sites/default/files/case-documents/ita0384.pdf.

[105] NAFTA, *Grand River Enterprises Six Nations, Ltd. vs. United States*, Award, para. 146, available at: http://italaw.com/sites/default/files/case-documents/ita0384.pdf.

[106] NAFTA, *Grand River Enterprises Six Nations, Ltd. vs. United States*, Award, para. 147, available at: http://italaw.com/sites/default/files/case-documents/ita0384.pdf.

[107] NAFTA, *Grand River Enterprises Six Nations, Ltd. vs. United States*, Award, para. 152, available at: http://italaw.com/sites/default/files/case-documents/ita0384.pdf.

[108] NAFTA, *Grand River Enterprises Six Nations, Ltd. vs. United States*, Award, para. 155, available at: http://italaw.com/sites/default/files/case-documents/ita0384.pdf.

[109] NAFTA, *Grand River Enterprises Six Nations, Ltd. vs. United States*, Award, para. 169 (stating the tribunal's understanding of the claim), available at: http://italaw.com/sites/default/files/case-documents/ita0384.pdf.

argument was not cognizable under the national treatment and most-favoured-nation treatment obligations. Instead, it ruled that the two obligations are limited to prohibiting discrimination in the form of treating a foreign investor less favourably than similarly situated US investors or other similarly situated foreign investors, neither of which occurred in this case.[110]

In his final argument, the claimant pointed to an ample body of treaty and customary international law for the protection of indigenous peoples, including at least an obligation to consult with indigenous peoples in matters affecting them. He urged that these norms are incorporated into the customary international law standard of "fair and equitable treatment" under NAFTA. The tribunal disagreed. It ruled that fair and equitable treatment does not include "the more specialized prohibitions and requirements involving indigenous peoples invoked here"[111] and "does not incorporate other legal protections that may be provided investors ... under other sources of law."[112]

Commerce Group

In *Commerce Group Corp. vs. El Salvador*,[113] a US company and its Salvadoran subsidiary (collectively "Commerce Group") were engaged in mining precious metals and related activities regulated by exploration licenses and environmental permits granted by the government of El Salvador. In 2006, the government revoked the environmental permits and did not renew the exploration licenses.

Later the same year, Commerce Group filed and began to prosecute a case in El Salvador's Court of Administrative Litigation challenging the government action and seeking reinstatement of the environmental permits. By mid-2009, the case was still pending and the parties were awaiting a decision. Then, in July 2009, Commerce Group filed a notice of arbitration against El Salvador under of the US-Central American Free Trade Agreement (CAFTA), alleging that revocation of the environmental permits violated provisions of the investment chapter. In April 2010, before the arbitral tribunal had been constituted, the Salvadoran court issued its decision where it denied Commerce Group's claim.

Under CAFTA, claimants are required to submit a "written waiver ... of any right to initiate or continue before any administrative tribunal or court under the law

---

[110] NAFTA, *Grand River Enterprises Six Nations, Ltd. vs. United States*, Award, para. 171, available at: http://italaw.com/sites/default/files/case-documents/ita0384.pdf.

[111] NAFTA, *Grand River Enterprises Six Nations, Ltd. vs. United States*, Award, para. 209, available at: http://italaw.com/sites/default/files/case-documents/ita0384.pdf.

[112] NAFTA, *Grand River Enterprises Six Nations, Ltd. vs. United States*, Award, para. 219, available at: http://italaw.com/sites/default/files/case-documents/ita0384.pdf.

[113] ICSID (CAFTA), ARB/09/17, *Commerce Group Corp. vs. El Salvador*, Award.

of any Party ... any proceeding with respect to any measure alleged to constitute a breach [of CAFTA]."[114] In an attempt to comply with this requirement, Commerce Group filed a document with the arbitral tribunal stating that "the claimants hereby waive their rights to initiate or continue any domestic proceeding with respect to any measure alleged to constitute a breach for purposes of the present Notice of Arbitration."[115]

The tribunal ruled that the mere filing of waiver was insufficient and that Commerce Group also needed to discontinue the proceedings pending before the Salvadoran court. It explained that "a waiver must be more than just words; it must accomplish the intended effect" and therefore "must comply with both a formal and a material element."[116] The tribunal rejected Commerce Group's argument that it complied with the material element of waiver because the Salvadoran case had ended in April 2010, before the tribunal had been constituted or any proceedings had been conducted. Instead, the tribunal held that the operative date for waiving and discontinuing proceedings in national courts was the date of filing the notice of arbitration, July 2009.[117] Finally, the tribunal ruled that compliance with the waiver requirement was a jurisdictional prerequisite to an investor-state arbitration, since "a waiver is required as a condition to Respondent's consent to CAFTA."[118] Therefore, the tribunal held that it "does not have jurisdiction over the Parties' CAFTA dispute."[119]

Gallo

In *Gallo vs. Canada*,[120] a Canadian corporation had been intending to use an abandoned mine it owned in Ontario as a waste disposal site, but in 2004 the Ontario legislature passed a statute prohibiting the disposal of waste in the mine. A US citizen named Gallo who was the sole shareholder of the Canadian corporation initiated an investor-state arbitration against Canada under NAFTA Chapter 11, claiming that the Ontario statute was tantamount to expropriation.

Canada asserted the surprising defense that there was no reliable, contemporaneous evidence proving that Gallo was the shareholder of the Canadian corporation in 2004 when Ontario enacted the legislation.[121] However, Canada refrained from alleging that Gallo may have acted fraudulently. When the tribunal reviewed the

[114] CAFTA, Art. 10.18.

[115] ICSID (CAFTA), ARB/09/17, *Commerce Group Corp. vs. El Salvador*, Award, para. 16 (quoting claimants' waiver).

[116] ICSID (CAFTA), ARB/09/17, *Commerce Group Corp. vs. El Salvador*, Award, para. 80.

[117] ICSID (CAFTA), ARB/09/17, *Commerce Group Corp. vs. El Salvador*, Award, paras. 97–100.

[118] ICSID (CAFTA), ARB/09/17, *Commerce Group Corp. vs. El Salvador*, Award, para. 115.

[119] ICSID (CAFTA), ARB/09/17, *Commerce Group Corp. vs. El Salvador*, Award, para. 115.

[120] NAFTA, PCA No. 55798, *Gallo vs. Canada*, Award.

[121] NAFTA, PCA No. 55798, *Gallo vs. Canada*, Award, para. 122.

record, it became "evident to the Tribunal that the acquisition, financing and management of the [mine] was not structured or documented in a way one would expect experienced business people to act when making a significant M&A (merger & acquisition) transaction."[122] Although Gallo purportedly invested Canadian $3 million in the corporation, the "factual record [was] full of unusual circumstances and mistakes,"[123] including the absence of any document in the company's records bearing Gallo's signature and dated before the Ontario legislation.

According to the corporate Shareholders' Register, Gallo became sole shareholder of the corporation in September 2002.[124] However, the corporate secretary, who was legally responsible for keeping the corporate records, and his personal assistant, who actually filled in the Shareholders' Registry, "both deposed under oath that the transfer of the share to Mr. Gallo did not happen on the date stated in the Registry, but at a later date."[125] Neither deponent could remember precisely when the share transfer was actually registered in the corporate records. Furthermore, the claimant "has not been able to produce one single shred of documentary evidence, confirming the date when [he] acquired ownership: no agreement, no contract, no confirmation slip, no instruction letter, no memorandum, no invoice, no email, no file note, no tax declaration, no submission to any authority – absolutely nothing."[126] There were also no contemporaneous shareholder resolutions Gallo signed and no contemporaneous tax filings required under US law.

For all these reasons, the tribunal held that Gallo had not proved when he acquired ownership and control of the Canadian corporation, and therefore it was impossible to ascertain whether he did so before or after the Ontario legislation was enacted.[127] Turning to the applicable law, the tribunal ruled that "for Chapter 11 of the NAFTA to apply to a measure relating to an investment, that investment must be owned or controlled by a investor of another party, and ownership or control must exist at the time the measure which allegedly violates the Treaty is adopted or maintained."[128] Therefore, "since the Tribunal has already found that the Claimant has failed to marshal the evidence to prove such ownership and control at the relevant time, the necessary consequence is that his claim must fail for lack of jurisdiction *ratione temporis*."[129]

[122] NAFTA, PCA No. 55798, *Gallo vs. Canada*, Award, para. 281.

[123] NAFTA, PCA No. 55798, *Gallo vs. Canada*, Award, para. 281.

[124] NAFTA, PCA No. 55798, *Gallo vs. Canada*, Award, para. 286.

[125] NAFTA, PCA No. 55798, *Gallo vs. Canada*, Award, para. 287.

[126] NAFTA, PCA No. 55798, *Gallo vs. Canada*, Award, para. 289.

[127] NAFTA, PCA No. 55798, *Gallo vs. Canada*, Award, para. 290.

[128] NAFTA, PCA No. 55798, *Gallo vs. Canada*, Award, para. 325.

[129] NAFTA, PCA No. 55798, *Gallo vs. Canada*, Award, para. 326.

Conclusion

The developments reviewed in this chapter reflect limits, if not limitations, of international economic law in regional economic integration in North America. The existing set of six US trade agreements in the western hemisphere liberalize trade and investment in the region, but do not create a coherent system of regional economic integration, do not provide building blocks toward such a system, and largely embody US negotiating leverage against weak trading partners (other than Canada). In the "wrong case" of the US-Mexico trucking dispute under NAFTA, state-to-state dispute resolution resulted in a power-oriented partial renegotiation of the original treaty obligations that accommodated US goals, while the formal state-to-state adjudicatory process has never been used again. The ostensibly robust but rarely successful investor-state arbitration process for investment disputes seems to suggest that unlawful host-state treatment of foreign investments is not really a serious problem in North and Central America, or at least that investors' grievances do not match the particular legal rights protected at the international level.

The Status of African Regional Trade Agreements

James T. Gathii

Introduction

This chapter comprehensively introduces all eight African Regional Trade Agreements, (RTA), that are slated to eventually combine to form the African Economic Community.[1] For each RTA, the chapter begins with an overview that includes its founding date, purposes and members as well as the sequence contemplated to be followed in the integration plan. Each of these integration schemes, free market, customs market, common market, monetary union and where there is planned political union is examined in turn. For each RTA, a section evaluating progress made in the integration agenda concludes the discussion. This chapter is therefore about the state of play in African RTAs about which there is often little written about.

Ultimately, this chapter shows that African countries have not been in short supply of detailed integration plans and schemes as well as particularly well thought out policy statements as well as the periodic statements of their highest policy making organs declaring the leadership's commitment to attaining the goals set out in integration treaties and associated documents. The fact that many of the plans discussed in this chapter have not come to fruition ought not to be a reason to dismiss what may be regarded merely as paper commitments. African RTAs must be understood in their own context rather than through the prism that the treaties underlying have necessarily lost any legal efficacy since they are observed more in breach. Yet there are challenges including multiple RTAs and memberships that compound the challenges of African trade.

[1] It is important to note that while there are numerous RTAs in the continent, only eight are recognised by the African Union for the purposes of forming the African Economic Community.

J.T. Gathii (✉)
Loyola University Chicago School of Law, 25 East Pearson Street, Chicago, IL 60661, USA
e-mail: jgathii@luc.edu

C. Herrmann et al. (eds.), *European Yearbook of International Economic Law (EYIEL), Vol. 4 (2013)*, European Yearbook of International Economic Law 4,
DOI 10.1007/978-3-642-33917-2_12,

As I have argued elsewhere, African RTAs have some defining characteristics.[2] These include as a central commitment, flexibility. Flexibility here refers to a number of features that are built into African RTAs much the same way non-discrimination principles are built into trade agreements in other parts of the world. For African RTAs non-discriminatory trade is one of a variety of features, and often non-discriminatory trade takes second place to flexibility. Flexibility elements of African RTAs include variable geometry, the principle of asymmetry, as well as compensation mechanisms. Variable geometry refers to rules allowing African RTA partners the flexibility to decide whether to make timetabled commitments in their RTA and decide the pace at which they will implement the agreements. This flexibility allows African RTA partners who want to move at a faster pace not to be held back by those unwilling to make commitments. The principle of asymmetry allows African RTA partner states to assume different levels of obligations. For example within a particular RTA, well off countries may commit to fully liberalise while not requiring the well off countries to give compensating concessions on an MFN basis. Finally, compensation mechanisms compensate the least well off countries for making liberalisation commitments.

This paper will discuss each of the eight RTAs recognised by the African Union as building blocks towards the African Economic Community. It begins with ECOWAS.

Economic Community of West African States

The Economic Community of West African States (ECOWAS) was founded in 1975 when the treaty, also known as the Treaty of Lagos, was signed.[3] ECOWAS currently consists of fifteen West African states: Benin, Burkina Faso, Cape Verde, Côte d'Ivoire, Gambia, Ghana, Guinea, Guinea-Bissau, Liberia, Mali, Niger, Nigeria, Senegal, Sierra Leone, and Togo. The objectives of ECOWAS are to "promote cooperation and integration leading to the establishment of an economic union in West Africa in order to raise the living standards of its peoples, and to maintain and enhance economic stability, foster relations among Member States and contribute to the progress and development of the African Continent."[4] ECOWAS is one of the eight regional pillars of the African Economic Community. Along with COMESA, SADC, ECCAS, and IGAD, ECOWAS signed the Protocol on Relations between the African Economic Community and the Regional Economic Communities in February of 1998.

The ultimate goal of ECOWAS is to establish an economic and monetary union to stimulate economic growth and development in the region. The ECOWAS

---

[2] Gathii, *African Regional Trade Agreements as Legal Regimes*, 2011.

[3] African Union, Profile: Economic Community of West African States, p. 2, available at: http://www.africa-union.org/root/au/recs/ECOWASProfile.pdf.

[4] Art. 3(1) of the Treaty Establishing the Economic Community of West African States, available at: http://www.worldtradelaw.net/fta/agreements/ecowasfta.pdf.

Treaty aims to achieve the goal of economic integration through the harmonisation and coordination of national policies and the promotion of integration programmes. A common market is to be established along with an economic union. A revised treaty, signed in July 1993, was designed to accelerate the process of economic integration and to increase political cooperation.[5]

Since ECOWAS' Bank for Investment and Development's (EBID) inception in 2004, the bank has loaned in excess of $702.45 million dollars in aid to Member States.[6] By 2013, the bank hopes to have funded roughly $1.5 billion dollars to fund projects.[7] The bank will continue to spend more than half of its resources on funding private sector projects that will further the goals of the community as well as 40 % of its anticipated resources on improving intra-regional trade, while the remainder of its funding will be spent on sponsoring special projects such as a regional airline, a telecommunications fund, and investment in biofuels and renewable energy.[8]

ECOWAS Member States have been negotiating Economic Partnership Agreements (EPA) with the European Union (EU). With respect to trade, ECOWAS and the EU have emphasised the "importance of regional economic integration in fighting poverty, furthering sustainable development and longer-term conflict prevention."[9] In mid-July 2009, the EU was pushing for 80 % liberalisation of the ECOWAS market for its goods, while ECOWAS leaders were pushing for 60 % liberalisation.[10]

The ECOWAS Treaty calls for the progressive establishment of a customs union during a period of 10 years beginning on 1 January 1990. Within the customs union, customs duties and other similar charges on the importation of goods originating within the region will be reduced until eliminated.[11] Article 36(4) of the ECOWAS Treaty sets forth that the Authority, (the Heads of States of ECOWAS members), may decide, at any time, that any import duties should be reduced more rapidly or eliminated earlier than laid out in any previous instrument or decision on the

[5] African Union, Profile: Economic Community of West African States, p. 2, available at: http://www.africa-union.org/root/au/recs/ECOWASProfile.pdf.

[6] African Union, Profile: Economic Community of West African States, p. 5, available at: http://www.africa-union.org/root/au/recs/ECOWASProfile.pdf.

[7] African Union, Profile: Economic Community of West African States, p. 5, available at: http://www.africa-union.org/root/au/recs/ECOWASProfile.pdf.

[8] African Union, Profile: Economic Community of West African States, p. 10, available at: http://www.africa-union.org/root/au/recs/ECOWASProfile.pdf.

[9] Seventh EU-ECOWAS Ministerial Troika Meeting, 18 May 2005, available at: http://www.europa-eu-un.org/articles/en/article_4706_en.htm.

[10] Kokutse, Trade: ECOWAS Delay on EPA Allows Ghana to Rethink, Global Issues, 29 June 2009, available at: http://www.globalissues.org/news/2009/06/29/1970.

[11] Art. 35(1), 36(1) ECOWAS Treaty, "Member States shall reduce and ultimately eliminate customs duties and any other charges with equivalent effect [...] imposed on or in connection with the importation of goods which are eligible for Community tariff treatment."

recommendation of the Council.[12] In addition, the ECOWAS Treaty requires that, "quota, quantitative or like restrictions or prohibitions and administrative obstacles to trade among the Member States shall also be removed."[13]

In order to implement this duty reduction scheme, the ECOWAS Member States have released several decisions regarding the time frames when duties should be reduced with regard to various goods under a trade liberalisation scheme.[14] For example, the Authority of the Heads of State and Government released a decision regarding the time frame and manner when duties should be reduced for industrial products originating from Member States. The decision breaks the Member States into three groups of countries with different time requirements for the reduction of duties on priority and non-priority industrial goods.[15]

A "common external tariff in respect of all goods imported into the Member States from third countries shall be established and maintained."[16] The common external tariff will be gradually established in accordance with a schedule that is to be recommended by the Trade, Customs, Taxation, Statistics, Money, and Payments Commission. Fiscal charges in excess of those charges applied to domestic goods shall not be applied directly or indirectly by Member States to imported goods from any Member State. No such charges shall be imposed for the effective protection of domestic goods.[17] Article 40(3) of the ECOWAS treaty further provides that Member States must progressively eliminate all revenue duties that are designed to protect domestic goods by the end of the period for the application of the trade liberalisation scheme.

If a Member State has an existing contract that makes it unable to comply with the provisions of Article 40 of the ECOWAS treaty, that Member State must notify the Council and not renew or extend the contract when it expires.

The ECOWAS Trade Liberalisation Scheme (TLS) aims to establish an economic and monetary union in West Africa. The ECOWAS TLS for Industrial Products originating from Member States classifies the Member States into three groups for its implementation. Group 1 consists of Cape Verde, Guinea Bissau, Gambia, Burkina Faso, Mali, and Niger. These are the weakest economies in the region. Group 2 consists of Benin, Guinea, Liberia, Sierra Leone, and Togo. Group 3 consists of Cote d'Ivorie, Ghana, Nigeria, and Senegal. These are the strongest economies in the region. The poorer economies in ECOWAS get more time to

---

[12] Art. 36(4) ECOWAS Treaty, "However, the Council shall [. . .] examine whether such reductions or eliminations shall apply to some or all goods and in respect of some or all the Member States" not later than one year before the reductions or eliminations come into effect. Once this is done, the Council must report the result for the decision of the Authority.

[13] Art. 35 ECOWAS Treaty.

[14] Documentation on the ECOWAS trade liberalisation scheme is unavailable through the internet with the exception of a scheme for the liberalisation of industrial materials.

[15] The document describing priority and non-priority industrial goods, Decision C/DEC.3/5/8, is not available online.

[16] Art. 35(2) ECOWAS Treaty.

[17] Art. 40(1) ECOWAS Treaty.

liberalise and they are required to liberalise at much lower rates. This is referred to as variable geometry.

The Community decided that priority industrial products were industrial products originating from Member States, they had to be manufactured by industries established in the sub-region, and they had to be priority products belonging to the industrial sectors approved by the Council of Ministers. "These included food, agrochemicals, telecommunication, wood, steel, and pharmaceutical industries." The implementation of the ECOWAS TLS for Industrial Products was hindered by difficulties in fulfilling the rules of origin, the minimum national participation in the equity capital or production enterprises, and the structure of the TLS involving the categorisation of industrial products as priority and non-priority goods. Part of the reason for its lack of success was Members' dependence on trade taxes for government revenue. Members were thus reluctant to implement any scheme that would threaten their interests. The ECOWAS fund, designed to compensate members for any reduction in revenue from the TLS, was not successful because of a lack of regular contributions by members and the little authority of the Secretariat to sanction those who did not contribute. Additionally there was concern over who would reap the benefits from adopting the scheme. The concern was that foreign firms with production bases located in some of the countries, specifically Cote-d'Ivoire and Senegal, would benefit more than would the ECOWAS members. This led to stringent rules of origin being adopted that only 17 manufacturing firms fulfilled. The 1983 TLS for Industrial Products was thus amended in 1992 for simplification to speed up effective implementation.

The ultimate goal of ECOWAS is to establish an economic and monetary union. Article 54(1) of the ECOWAS treaty provides that the status of an economic union shall be achieved within a maximum period of 15 years after the implementation of the regional trade liberalisation scheme. This trade liberalisation scheme was adopted by the Authority on 1983 and launched on 1 January 1990.

Article 55 of the ECOWAS treaty sets forth the goals for the completion of the economic and monetary union. The economic and monetary union is to be established within 5 years following the creation of a customs union. This is to be accomplished through the "adoption of a common policy in all fields of socioeconomic activity;" the "total elimination of all obstacles to the free movement of people, goods, capital and services and the right of entry, residence and establishment;" and the "harmonisation of monetary, financial and fiscal policies, the setting up of West African monetary union, the establishment of a single regional Central Bank and the creation of a single West African currency."[18] The Authority may decide, on the recommendation of the Council, at any time, "that any stage of the integration process should be implemented more rapidly than otherwise provided for" in the ECOWAS Treaty.[19]

[18] Art. 55(1) ECOWAS Treaty. Free movement of community citizens has been fully achieved and member states now have a common ECOWAS international passport.

[19] Art. 55(2) ECOWAS Treaty.

Under Article 51 of the ECOWAS treaty some of the steps that Member States have agreed to undertake are to harmonise their economic policies, facilitate intraregional transactions, promote a greater role for commercial banks, and establish a community central bank and a common currency.[20] In order to ensure that these goals are achieved, the ECOWAS treaty provides for the establishment of institutions that will aid in the creation of a monetary union. First, the treaty provides for a Committee of West African Central Banks to be composed of the governors of the central banks of Member nations and its main focus will be to make recommendations to the community with respect to the operation of a payment clearing system and other monetary issues.[21] In addition to the Central Banks Committee, the ECOWAS treaty provides for the creation of a Capital Issues Committee to aid in ensuring the unimpeded flow of capital throughout the community as well as to aid Member States in establishing and regulating national as well as regional stock exchanges.[22]

Regional integration has not been at the center of the national development agenda and "the potential of regionalism has not been properly explored and utilized."[23] Although West Africa was declared a free trade area in 2000, ECOWAS member countries have failed to remove tariff and non-tariff barriers to intra-regional trade.[24] One of the problems facing ECOWAS is that most of the countries are classified as least-developed by the UN. ECOWAS "accounts for 35 % of the African LDC's—making West Africa the foremost LDC region in Africa and, indeed the world as a whole."[25] Additionally, the West African region covered by ECOWAS has one of the highest amounts of poverty in the world that has led to dependence on foreign aid and loans, as well as national debt. Many countries have reduced the amount of their debt, but indebtedness remains a substantial burden for most countries. Because of these burdens, eradicating poverty and peace and security in the region have been the major focuses of the national development agenda, taking attention away from regional integration. In addition to poverty, regional challenges to integration include human insecurity, a high cost of doing business in the region giving other countries a comparative advantage, an over-dependence on commodity exports, vulnerable population groups, inadequate physical infrastructures, population growth related challenges and inadequate provision of social services including utilities such as water and waste management.

There have been recent socio-economic and political reforms in the member countries, along with structural and procedural transformations of key ECOWAS institutions. These reforms and transformations are positive developments and "hold considerable promise for enhanced regional economic development,

[20] Art. 51(1) ECOWAS Treaty.

[21] Art. 52 ECOWAS Treaty.

[22] Art. 52 ECOWAS Treaty.

[23] ECOWAS Vision 2020 Document.

[24] ECOWAS Vision 2020 Document, p. 2.

[25] ECOWAS Vision 2020 Document, p. 3.

particularly concerning efficiency, transparency and effectiveness in the administration of the Community's affairs."[26] However, these challenges pose substantial obstacles to the achievement of long-term development. One of the institutional changes has been the transformation of the Secretariat into the ECOWAS Commission. This transformation will, ideally, help to speed up the process of integration. Before the transformation, the obligations of the Member States were contained mostly in Protocols and Conventions, which are subject to prolonged Parliamentary ratification processes. This delayed their entry into force and thus slowed the integration process. Under this new legal regime, the adoption of Protocols and Conventions will be de-emphasised in an attempt to make the integration process less reliant on domestic ratification processes. It is not certain that such a shift will mean that ECOWAS members will take their responsibilities any more seriously.

The elimination of tariffs on approved industrial products was to be accompanied by the full elimination of non-tariff barriers and other administrative obstacles to trade. However, through certain norms and requirements the setting-up of administrative barriers to the entry of approved industrial products within the region seems to persist in practice. There also seems to be a lack of clear national guidelines in some ECOWAS countries regarding the implementation of the trade liberalisation scheme by the customs administrations. This constitutes an obstacle to intra-regional trade. ECOWAS achieved the status of a free trade area and has targeted to launch the ECOWAS customs union by 2009. The launch of the customs union was originally to be in 2008. As of June 2012, the customs union had not been launched.

Within ECOWAS, there is a bloc of eight countries belonging to the West African Economic and Monetary Union, (UEMOA). UEMOA was formed in 1994 by Benin, Burkina Faso, Cote d'Ivoire, Mali, Niger, Senegal, Togo, and Guinea Bissau. UEMOA has a common currency, the CFA franc, and "enjoys undeniable political recognition from Member States and notable support from Nigeria, which has made considerable effort in the resolution of many regional conflicts."[27]

Apart for UEMOA, there is the West African Monetary Zone (WAMZ), which is a group of five ECOWAS Member countries, that plan to introduce a common currency amongst its members. The WAMZ members are Gambia, Ghana, Guinea, Nigeria, Liberia and Sierra Leone. The member countries agreed to reform their economies to meet specific convergence targets prior to the introduction of the common currency, the Eco. The Eco is planned to circulate simultaneously with the CFA franc in an effort to eventually create a single monetary zone for the entire Community. The Eco was initially expected to be launched by December of 2009

[26] ECOWAS Vision 2020 Document, p. 8.

[27] African Union, Status of Integration in Africa, p. 14, para. 24, available at: http://www.africa-union.org/root/ua/conferences/2009/mai/ea/07-08mai/status%20of%20integration%20in%20africa%2027-04-09.pdf.

but as a result of the global economic downturn, the December 2009 deadline to introduce the Eco was pushed back to 2020.[28]

Due to the slow progress in implementing the fast-track approach to realising the ECOWAS common currency, the ECOWAS Authority, at its Summit in June of 2007, "mandated the ECOWAS Commission to collaborate with other regional institutions to review the current strategy with a view to recommending a single and accelerated approach to achieving the regional common currency."[29] The ECOWAS Convergence Council established an Inter-Institutional Working Group in 2008 to develop a term of reference for a revised strategy to achieve the single currency initiative. A new strategy for achieving the regional common currency was expected to have been adopted sometime after March of 2009. By April 2012, ECOWAS had not launched a common currency.

Intergovernmental Authority on Development

The Intergovernmental Authority on Development (IGAD) was created in 1996 to supersede the Intergovernmental Authority on Drought and Development (IGADD) that had been in existence since 1986. The membership of IGAD consists of Djibouti, Ethiopia, Kenya, Somalia, Eritrea, Sudan, and Uganda.

The objectives of the IGAD treaty include the harmonisation of trade policies, the promotion of free movement of goods, services and people, and the creation of an enabling environment for foreign, cross-border and domestic trade and investment.[30]

In 2003, a revised IGAD Strategy was adopted that focused on the promotion of "regional cooperation in order to achieve sustainable development, peace and security in the Region."[31] The strategic objectives emanate from the three priority areas of food security and environmental protection, peace and stability in the region, and the promotion of regional economic integration and cooperation in the region.

Two of the most important characteristics of the IGAD Strategy are flexibility and dynamism. The IGAD Strategy's flexibility allows it to "accommodate the changing interests and development needs of the Member States and its

[28] Jaidev, Governors Gloomy on Outlook for Pan-African Currency, Risk.net, 7 July 2010, available at: http://www.risk.net/risk-magazine/news/1721130/governors-gloomy-outlook-pan-african-currency.

[29] African Union, Status of Integration in Africa, p. 17, para. 39, available at: http://www.africa-union.org/root/ua/conferences/2009/mai/ea/07-08mai/status%20of%20integration%20in%20africa%2027-04-09.pdf.

[30] Art. 7 of the Agreement Establishing the Inter-Governmental Authority on Development (IGAD), available at: http://www.igad.int/etc./agreement_establishing_igad.pdf.

[31] See the IGAD Strategy, § 2.3, p. 5, available at: http://igad.int/index.php?option=com_content&view=article&id=93&Itemid=153&limitstart=2.

beneficiaries" and its dynamism allows it to "respond proactively and to address new emerging issues that may occur."[32] IGAD's work is mostly carried out in a process approach that involves intensive background studies followed by workshops and meetings in order to come up with common regional positions on the issues.[33]

The IGAD trade programme under the Economic Cooperation Sector focuses on the harmonisation of trade practices and policies of the Member States and the elimination of tariff and non-tariff barriers to trade. The long term goal of IGAD is to create an economic and customs union. This is to be accomplished in stages where IGAD will focus on changing and harmonising the policies, procedures and standards necessary to encourage increased trade among Member States in two areas—grain and livestock.[34] These two agricultural products are the most critical in terms of moving towards the achievement of food security in the region. For this purpose, efforts during the first years of the IGAD strategy will be focused on the development of mutually accepted policies and procedures to facilitate a substantial increase in trade in the two critical agricultural areas. Such policies and procedures will include "quality standards, phyto-sanitary standards, customs procedures and paperwork to ensure timely transactions and movement of commodities."[35]

IGAD's trade and infrastructure development programmes are closely interlinked. Policy harmonisation between the two areas is projected to promote trade development between Member States. The plan is that such intra-trade development will lead to the increased transportation of goods and services that requires an adequate infrastructure system. Thus, "the development of infrastructure and the removal of physical and non-physical barriers to interstate transport and communications are essential to regional cooperation and integration."[36]

The IGAD region has one of largest concentrations of livestock in the world, although this has not translated into any meaningful prosperity for IGAD Member States as individuals or as a collective body. The IGAD Livestock Policy Initiative examines the spread of disease among livestock, the inability of IGAD to influence international sanitary standards for livestock, and the inability of IGAD to form a single cohesive policy with regard to exporting livestock as the major reasons for the community's failures.

[32] IGAD Strategy, § 2.10, p. 9, available at: http://igad.int/index.php?option=com_content&view=article&id=93&Itemid=153&limitstart=2.

[33] IGAD Strategy, § 2.6, p. 7, available at: http://igad.int/index.php?option=com_content&view=article&id=93&Itemid=153&limitstart=2.

[34] IGAD Strategy, § 4.1.3.(a), p. 16, available at: http://igad.int/index.php?option=com_content&view=article&id=93&Itemid=153&limitstart=2.

[35] IGAD Strategy, § 4.1.3.(a), p. 17, available at: http://igad.int/index.php?option=com_content&view=article&id=93&Itemid=153&limitstart=2.

[36] IGAD Strategy, § 4.1.3.(b), p. 17, available at: http://igad.int/index.php?option=com_content&view=article&id=93&Itemid=153&limitstart=2.

When dealing with animal health in the IGAD region, the organisation that sets standards for animal health is the World Organization for Animal Health (OIE).[37] The OIE lists as its three main objectives: to promote and coordinate international disease research when appropriate, promote awareness to governments about the spread of epizootic diseases and methods of preventing them, and to provide a means of helping governments enforce sanitary standards for animals.[38]

The mandate of the Codex Alimentarious Commission is to "protect consumers against food borne diseases and encouraging international trade in safe food through the harmonization of food standards."[39] Since the inception of Codex almost 40 years ago, the commission has created general standards as well as over 300 product specific guidelines for food and safety standards.[40]

The export of livestock is influenced by a variety of sources including OIE, Codex, and sometimes even more stringent standards being set by some developed countries and manufacturers.[41] The result of the myriad of regulations on IGAD Member States is that they are struggling to implement these standards in part because they have little capacity. As a result, the trading interests of IGAD Member States are adversely affected. By contrast, Botswana, which has managed to keep its livestock disease free, has been able to keep its market share of beef exports to the European Union.

In addition to the inability of IGAD Member States to influence standards, the Livestock Report takes note of another crucial factor it has deemed relevant to profitability, the inability of IGAD to form a cohesive policy with regards to the export of livestock. IGAD Member States face challenges in implementing a region wide policy on livestock partly because of:

> Uncertainties signifying a weak and inefficient judiciary, disregard for the law in day to day decision making, lack of effective coordination among different levels of government in the enforcement of laws, absence of established communication channels between livestock business operators and government institutions and an overall lack of capacity to use law as an instrument in implementing policy decisions.[42]

The Livestock Report concludes by underscoring the problems that the "human, financial and technical constraints" faced by IGAD members in trying to adhere to international sanitary standards for livestock are too large to be faced by a single IGAD member alone.[43] For example, currently the EU has a host of benefits and privileges for developing countries where access is granted to their markets, of which IGAD is included.[44] The challenge here is that while the EU can treat nations

[37] IGAD Livestock Policy Initiative, p. 28.

[38] IGAD Livestock Policy Initiative, p. 29.

[39] IGAD Livestock Policy Initiative, p. 37.

[40] IGAD Livestock Policy Initiative, p. 38.

[41] IGAD Livestock Policy Initiative, p. 48.

[42] IGAD Livestock Policy Initiative, p. 78.

[43] IGAD Livestock Policy Initiative, p. 92.

[44] IGAD Livestock Policy Initiative, p. 92.

favourably with respect to market access, it has high food safety standards to admit food from developing countries. The EU offers access to its developing nations, but that access is often limited by stringent sanitary and phytosanitary that prevent even legitimate exports from regions like IGAD.

At the 12th Ordinary Summit of the Heads of State and Government in 2008, the Secretariat was directed to undertake an inventory of what had been achieved so far in the way of integration and cooperation. The Secretariat was also directed to "make recommendations on the way forward as well as develop and implement regional integration programmes" designed to make IGAD relevant as a building block of the African Union.[45] A Minimum Integration Plan has been submitted to the senior officials of the Member States and the final study was to be submitted by mid-March of 2009. Approval of the roadmap to integration will set a timeframe for the establishment of the IGAD Free Trade Area.

The 3rd Ministerial Troika Meeting between IGAD and the EU was held in Brussels on 31 March 2009. There, the parties noted that IGAD was in a stage of reform and revitalisation, "focusing its activities on priority areas of regional cooperation and strengthening the effectiveness of the IGAD Secretariat and Member States' commitments."[46] The EU stated its readiness to support these efforts at revitalisation and welcomed the Minimum Integration Plan as a means to deepen regional integration and cooperation.[47]

Common Market for Eastern and Southern Africa

The Common Market for Eastern and Southern Africa (COMESA) was formed in December of 1994. It replaced the former Preferential Trade Area (PTA) that had been in existence since 1981 with the objective of ultimately creating a larger market for greater social and economic cooperation between members and eventually resulting in a common market.[48] Its current members are Burundi, Comoros, the Democratic Republic of the Congo, Djibouti, Egypt, Eritrea, Ethiopia, Kenya,

[45] Communique of the 12th Ordinary Summit of the Heads of State and Government of IGAD, available at: http://www.igad.int/index.php?option=com_content&view=article&id=107:communique-of-the-12th-summit-of-heads-of-state-and-government-of-igad-&catid=47:communique&Itemid=149.

[46] Communique: IGAD—EU Ministerial Troika Meeting, available at: http://www.igad.int/index.php?option=com_content&view=article&id=141:communique-igad-eu-ministerial-troika-meeting&catid=47:communique&Itemid=149.

[47] Communique: IGAD—EU Ministerial Troika Meeting, available at: http://www.igad.int/index.php?option=com_content&view=article&id=141:communique-igad-eu-ministerial-troika-meeting&catid=47:communique&Itemid=149.

[48] COMESA, History of COMESA, available at: http://about.comesa.int/index.php?option=com_content&view=article&id=95&Itemid=117.

Libya, Madagascar, Malawi, Mauritius, Rwanda, Seycelles, Sudan, Swaziland, Uganda, Zambia, and Zimbabwe.

The central objective of COMESA is to form "a large economic and trading unit that is capable of overcoming some of the barriers that are faced by individual states."[49] Eventually COMESA aims to achieve a "fully integrated, competitive regional economic community."[50] The strategy chosen to attain full integration is trade development through the removal of trade and investment barriers. For the achievement of its goals, a three-stage path has been laid out. The first stage to be completed is the establishment of a Free Trade Area (FTA) where all tariffs on trade in goods between COMESA members will be eliminated.[51] Additionally in the first stage non-tariff barriers to trade between COMESA members will be eliminated.[52] The second stage is the formation of a customs union with a common external tariff, which would first allow Member States to become competitive regionally "through the process of restructuring, mergers, acquisition and privatization"[53] and eventually become internationally competitive through the application of a common tariff on imports from non-COMESA nations. The third and final step would be the formation of a monetary union[54] with a "common currency issued by a common central bank by 2025."[55]

The COMESA treaty proposes the formation of a customs union within 10 years from the effective date of the treaty.[56] Article 47 provides "the Member States agree to the gradual establishment of a common external tariff in respect of all goods imported into the Member States from third countries within a period of ten years from the entry into force of this Treaty and in accordance with a schedule to be adopted by the Council."[57] By December of 2004, according to the provisions of the treaty, a customs union with a common external tariff is supposed to have been established. The establishment of a common external tariff was intended to make Member States regionally competitive "through the process of restructuring,

[49] COMESA, Overview of COMESA, available at: http://about.comesa.int/index.php?option=com_content&view=article&id=75:overview-of-comesa-&catid=42:general&Itemid=106.

[50] COMESA, COMESA Strategy, available at: http://about.comesa.int/index.php?option=com_content&view=article&id=78:comesa-strategy-&catid=42:general&Itemid=118.

[51] Art. 45 of the Treaty Establishing the Common Market for Eastern and Southern Africa, available at: http://www.comesa.int/attachments/article/28/COMESA_Treaty.pdf.

[52] Art. 49(1) COMESA Treaty.

[53] COMESA, COMESA Strategy, available at: http://about.comesa.int/index.php?option=com_content&view=article&id=78:comesa-strategy-&catid=42:general&Itemid=118.

[54] Art. 4(4)(a) COMESA Treaty.

[55] COMESA, COMESA Strategy, available at: http://about.comesa.int/index.php?option=com_content&view=article&id=78:comesa-strategy-&catid=42:general&Itemid=118.

[56] Art. 45 COMESA Treaty.

[57] Art. 47 COMESA Treaty.

mergers, acquisitions and privatization"[58] with the ultimate goal of becoming internationally competitive.

At the 11th Meeting of the COMESA Council of Ministers, held in Cairo in May of 2001, a roadmap was created for the establishment of a customs union by December of 2004.[59] The four main objectives that the Council of Ministers set out were the creation of a common external tariff, increasing intra-COMESA trade, the further simplification of customs procedures and the finalisation of structures to implement the common external tariff as well as the customs union itself.[60] However, the customs union was not officially launched until 8 June 2009. The first of several steps taken towards the creation of the customs union was the formation of a common external tariff as authorised by Article 47 of the COMESA treaty.[61] A four band common external tariff was established at the 12th Summit of the COMESA Heads of State and Government held in Nairobi in May 2007. The four band tariff structure imposes a 10 % tariff on intermediate products, a 25 % tariff on finished goods and a 0 % tariff on capital goods and raw materials imported from non-COMESA nations.[62]

The ultimate goal of COMESA is to form a monetary union with a single currency. The short term goal leading to the achievement of this long term goal is to establish monetary stability within the region with an efficient exchange and payments system. An efficient system of exchange and payments is aimed at facilitating economic integration efforts and the attainment of sustainable economic development.[63] In 1992, the Authority of Heads of State and Government approved a programme towards the establishment of a monetary union by 2025.[64] The programme consisted of four stages. The first stage was to take place from 1992 to 1996. This stage involved the consolidation of existing instruments of cooperation in monetary and financial matters and the implementation of policy measures geared towards achieving macroeconomic convergence. As to this stage, the COMESA treaty provides that Member States were supposed to "undertake to co-ordinate their macro-economic policies and economic reform programmes with a view to promoting the economic and social balance of the Common Market and to develop a framework for macro-economic planning and programming."[65] The second stage was to take place from 1997 to 2000 and was to introduce some

[58] COMESA, COMESA Strategy, available at: http://about.comesa.int/index.php?option=com_content&view=article&id=78:comesa-strategy-&catid=42:general&Itemid=118.

[59] Final Communiqué of the Thirteenth Summit of the COMESA Authority of Heads of State and Government, 8 June 2009, p. 6.

[60] Eleventh Meeting of the COMESA Council of Ministers, 20–21 May 2001, Art. 68.

[61] Art. 47 COMESA Treaty.

[62] Communiqué of the Twelfth Summit of the COMESA Heads of State and Government, 22–23 May 2007, p. 7.

[63] Art. 72 COMESA Treaty.

[64] COMESA, COMESA Strategy, available at: http://about.comesa.int/index.php?option=com_content&view=article&id=78:comesa-strategy-&catid=42:general&Itemid=118.

[65] Art. 79 COMESA Treaty.

degree of currency convertibility and informal exchange rate union. The COMESA treaty provides that Member States shall "undertake to establish…currency convertibility which shall make their currencies convertible into one another."[66] Towards this end, all restrictions on current transactions shall be abolished by the Member States. Additionally, the treaty provides that the Member States shall "undertake to establish…an Exchange Rate Union" and "agree to the immutable fixing of the exchange rates of their currencies within a band to be prescribed by the Council."[67] The third stage is to take place from 2000 to 2024. In this stage, a formal exchange rate union is to be created and economic policies are to be coordinated by a common monetary institution. After the first three stages are completed, the fourth and final stage is the creation of a full Monetary Union with a single common currency. This is to be achieved by the year 2025 and is the ultimate goal of COMESA.

The COMESA rules of origin serve to protect the interests of COMESA Member States by ensuring that the common market tariff treatment implemented by the free trade area, which imposes no tariff on goods traded between COMESA Member States, is applied solely to those Member States[68] and that all foreign importers are subject to the common external tariff that was adopted as a part of the customs union. Article 48 of the COMESA treaty provides that goods qualify as eligible for common market tariff treatment if they are deemed to have originated in a COMESA Member State.[69] In order to help determine which goods qualify as originating in a COMESA Member State, the Rules of Origin Protocol sets forth a five part test, requiring that goods meet at least one of the enumerated criteria in order to obtain status as originating from a Member State.

The first of the criteria in determining if a good qualifies for common market tariff is to determine if the goods have been wholly produced in a Member State.[70] Rule 3 of the Rules of Origin Protocol provides a list of goods that are to be considered as produced in a Member State. Examples of these include vegetable products harvested within the borders of a Member State, products obtained from the sea, rivers and lakes of Member States, and livestock born or raised within Member States.[71] The next criteria states that goods that are produced in Member States should not have the cost, insurance and freight value of foreign materials exceed 60 % of the total cost of materials used in the production of the good.[72]

---

[66] Art. 77 COMESA Treaty.

[67] Art. 78 COMESA Treaty.

[68] Procedures Manual on the Implementation of the Protocol on the Rules of Origin for Products to be traded between the Member States of the Common Market for Eastern and Southern Africa, September 2002, Chapter 1.1, available at: http://www.mcci.org/Photos/comesarulesoforiginmanual.pdf.

[69] Art. 48(1) COMESA Treaty.

[70] Rule 2(1)(a) of the COMESA Rules of Origin Protocol, available at: http://www.iadb.org/int/intradebid/DocsPdf/Acuerdos/COMESA%20Protocol%20on%20theRules%20o%20fOrigin.pdf.

[71] Rule 3 COMESA Rules of Origin Protocol.

[72] Rule 2(1)(b)(i) COMESA Rules of Origin Protocol.

Alternatively, a good produced in a Member State may obtain common market tariff treatment if it obtains at least 35 % value added to the ex-factory cost of the goods,[73] or if non-originating goods are used in the production of a good in a Member State they may obtain common market tariff treatment if they have changed so substantially that they can no longer be classified under the same tariff heading as the original product.[74] Lastly, goods produced in Member States that have been designated to be "goods of particular importance to the economic development of Member States"[75] must contain a minimum value added of at least 25 %, in spite of Rule 2(1)(b)(ii).

COMESA sets forth specific areas for cooperation between Member States in order to further the goals of the common market. The areas of cooperation put forth in the COMESA treaty include the fields of trade liberalisation, industry, energy, transport, finance, agriculture, economic development and social development.[76] COMESA recognises that in order to have long term economic growth and prosperity in these fields, it must focus heavily on the areas of science and technology, infrastructure development, and investment development.[77]

The focus of the investment development initiative will be to enhance productivity as well as the quality of goods coming from COMESA Member States.[78] Investment development is planned to be focused in the areas of "industry, agriculture, livestock, fisheries, and irrigation"[79] as well as service-based sectors. The strategy envisaged for these sectors is to identify investment opportunities, promote higher productivity through training and collaboration, fostering a favourable investment environment, the implementation of market development programmes and the formation of programmes to mainstream gender.[80] For example, at the 12th Summit of the COMESA Heads of State and Government in 2007, the Agreement for the COMESA Common Investment Area (CCIA) was adopted.[81] The CCIA will serve as a tool where foreign and domestic investment will be promoted by guaranteeing investment against nationalisation and expropriation, offering arbitration mechanisms for resolving disputes, improving the transparency of investment

[73] Rule 2(1)(b)(ii) COMESA Rules of Origin Protocol. Ex-factory costs refers to "the value of total inputs required to produce a given product.", Rule 1 COMESA Rules of Origin Protocol.

[74] Rule 2(1)(b)(iii) COMESA Rules of Origin Protocol.

[75] Rule 2(1)(c) COMESA Rules of Origin Protocol.

[76] Art. 4 COMESA Treaty.

[77] COMESA, COMESA Strategy, available at: http://about.comesa.int/index.php?option=com_content&view=article&id=78:comesa-strategy-&catid=42:general&Itemid=118.

[78] COMESA, COMESA Strategy, available at: http://about.comesa.int/index.php?option=com_content&view=article&id=78:comesa-strategy-&catid=42:general&Itemid=118.

[79] COMESA, COMESA Strategy, available at: http://about.comesa.int/index.php?option=com_content&view=article&id=78:comesa-strategy-&catid=42:general&Itemid=118.

[80] COMESA, COMESA Strategy, available at: http://about.comesa.int/index.php?option=com_content&view=article&id=78:comesa-strategy-&catid=42:general&Itemid=118.

[81] Communiqué of the Twelfth Summit of the COMESA Heads of State and Government, 22–23 May 2007, p. 11.

rules and regulations of Member States as well as allowing for national treatment to be granted to investors by 2010, which will allow foreign investors to enjoy the same treatment as domestic investors.[82]

In order for COMESA to achieve its goals of having free movement of goods, people and services, there must be a strong infrastructure to support those goals. The current transportation and communication sectors of Member States, in COMESA and other RTAs, are not strong enough to support the organisation's goal of having a fully integrated economic zone.[83] The infrastructure development initiative will focus its efforts on facilitating transit programmes, identifying investments in the transport, communication and energy sectors as well as instituting reform in the areas of transport, telecom, postal, environmental and energy sectors.[84] For example, in order to ensure the more efficient movement of people and goods and to maximise the use of existing infrastructure, some of the measures COMESA has implemented are the harmonisation of road traffic charges and axle load limits, the creation of a COMESA carrier license and transit plates, the implementation of new transit declaration documents and more advanced cargo information systems.[85] In addition to the maximisation of current infrastructure assets such as roadways and air space, COMESA has embarked on a mission to invest in the improvement of other infrastructure assets such as energy. An example of this is the creation of initiatives such as the Eastern Africa Power Pool (EAPP) whose mission is to stabilise growth and development in the region by decreasing the cost of energy production while simultaneously increasing energy output for the region.[86]

Lastly, COMESA strives to increase cooperation and productivity in the areas of science and technology. In the past, the areas of science and technology have been neglected because investment in the research and development of new technologies has been so small among COMESA Member States.[87] UNESCO has noted that nations in Sub-Saharan Africa over the past 30 years have invested an average of only 0.3 % of their gross national product as compared with 2.2 % investment made by developed countries over that same time.[88] COMESA is striving to increase

[82] COMESA, Investment Promotion and Private Sector Development, available at: http://programmes.comesa.int/index.php?option=com_content&view=article&id=111&Itemid=149.

[83] COMESA, COMESA Strategy, available at: http://about.comesa.int/index.php?option=com_content&view=article&id=78:comesa-strategy-&catid=42:general&Itemid=118.

[84] COMESA, COMESA Strategy, available at: http://about.comesa.int/index.php?option=com_content&view=article&id=78:comesa-strategy-&catid=42:general&Itemid=118.

[85] COMESA, COMESA Strategy, available at: http://about.comesa.int/index.php?option=com_content&view=article&id=78:comesa-strategy-&catid=42:general&Itemid=118.

[86] COMESA, Infrastructure, available at: http://programmes.comesa.int/index.php?option=com_content&view=article&id=133&Itemid=201.

[87] COMESA, COMESA Strategy, available at: http://about.comesa.int/index.php?option=com_content&view=article&id=78:comesa-strategy-&catid=42:general&Itemid=118.

[88] COMESA, COMESA Strategy, available at: http://about.comesa.int/index.php?option=com_content&view=article&id=78:comesa-strategy-&catid=42:general&Itemid=118.

investment in science and technology through policy initiatives in order for the technology that is developed to serve as an engine of growth and change for the Member nations.[89] For example, the Electronic Transaction Act of 2000 was enacted with the objectives of creating a legal infrastructure for implementing secure electronic transactions, increasing the electronic filing of documents, encouraging the use of electronic signatures for online forms as well as to foster confidence in the use of electronic transactions.[90] COMESA hopes that initiatives like the Electronic Transaction Act will foster confidence, as well as investment, from the private and the public sector in research and development of technologies to be used in furthering the integration of the COMESA marketplace.[91]

COMESA Member States began tariff reduction in 1984 and were expected to have eliminated all tariffs by 2000, the anticipated date for the launching of the COMESA free trade area. Eleven COMESA Member States committed themselves to reducing tariffs regarding intra-regional trade to zero by 31 October 2000 at the COMESA Policy Organs meetings of May of 2000. These eleven Members were Djibouti, Eritrea, Egypt, Kenya, Madagascar, Malawi, Mauritius, Sudan, Uganda, Zambia and Zimbabwe.

The COMESA Free Trade Area was launched on 31 October 2000 when nine Member States eliminated tariffs on COMESA-originating products according to the schedule adopted at the 1992 Summit. The initial nine Members were Djibouti, Egypt, Kenya, Madagascar, Malawi, Mauritius, Sudan, Zambia and Zimbabwe. Burundi and Rwanda joined the free trade area on 1 January 2004, and Comoros and Libya joined in 2006. Two of the remaining 6 countries to join the free trade area, Uganda and Eritrea, have reduced tariffs by 80 %.[92] Ethiopia has reduced its tariffs by 10 %.[93] Namibia and Swaziland were granted special exemptions from the provisions of the COMESA treaty due to their membership in other regional economic communities. At the 11th Summit of the COMESA Heads of State and Government in 2006, Swaziland's derogation from reciprocating tariff preferences until the end of 2008 in order to enable her to complete consultations with her SACU partners. This was done to allow Swaziland to join the COMESA Free Trade Area.[94] The Member States that have joined the COMESA free trade area "have removed all barriers to intra-regional trade, granted trade preferences to COMESA

---

[89] COMESA, COMESA Strategy, available at: http://about.comesa.int/index.php?option=com_content&view=article&id=78:comesa-strategy-&catid=42:general&Itemid=118.

[90] Art. 3 of the Electronic Transactions Act of 2000, 1 August 2001, available at: http://programmes.comesa.int/attachments/128_Electronic%20Transaction%20Act.pdf.

[91] COMESA, COMESA Strategy, available at: http://about.comesa.int/index.php?option=com_content&view=article&id=78:comesa-strategy-&catid=42:general&Itemid=118.

[92] Non-Tariff Barriers Monitoring Mechanism, Regional Trade Facilitation Programme, available at: http://ntb.africonnect.com/.

[93] International Trade Agreements Leaflet No. 10, p. 2, available at: http://www.zra.org.zm/publications/TradeAgreement.pdf.

[94] Final Communiqué of the Eleventh Summit of the COMESA Heads of State and Government, 1 December 2006, p. 4.

members that are not yet part of FTA, and retain tariffs on imports from outside COMESA."[95] Disagreement over the Common External Tariff has contributed to the remaining COMESA members' reluctance to join the free trade area as well as to the delay in launching the COMESA Customs Union by the long past target date of 2004.[96]

The Report and Decisions of the 10th Meeting of the COMESA Council of Ministers on the 7 and 8 December 2000 published the following table:

FTA countries	Non-FTA countries			
No duties or charges of equivalent effect from 10/31/2000	Country	Rate of reduction	Country	Rate of tariff reduction
Djibouti	Burundi	60 %	Angola	Nil
Egypt	Comoros	80 %	Ethiopia	Nil
Kenya	Congo D.R.	70 %		
Madagascar	Eritrea	80 %	Namibia	Under derogation
Malawi	Rwanda	60 %	Swaziland	
Mauritius	Uganda	80 %		To Join FTA on 1/6/2001
Sudan			Seychelles	
Zambia				
Zimbabwe				

This table shows the rate of reduction of tariffs and customs duties in countries that were not participating in the free trade area at the time of the meeting. Further discussion led to the decision that trade between two non-free trade area Member States would be on a reciprocal basis at the lower customs reduction rate between the two of them. For example, if Burundi were to trade with Comoros, the tariff rate would be at a 60 % reduction. Additionally, trade with a non-free trade area Member State that has not reduced tariffs will be at full import duty rates, such as those applicable with third countries. Additionally it was decided that all Member States shall become members of the free trade area by Oct. 31, 2001. Those that have not joined by that date will trade with the free trade area Member States at full national Most Favoured Nation rates.

After the successful elimination of tariffs on originating goods, the focus turns to the elimination of restrictions and non-tariff barriers to trade. Non-tariff barriers restrict intra-regional trade and impair the ability of members to optimise on gains from preferences granted by regional trading agreements. They are seen by

[95] High Commission of India, Brief on COMESA, August 2010, available at: http://meaindia.nic.in/foreignrelation/23fr01.pdf.

[96] High Commission of India, Brief on COMESA, August 2010, available at: http://meaindia.nic.in/foreignrelation/23fr01.pdf.

COMESA as a major challenge to the realisation of the region's growth[97] and are an important step in the direction of launching the COMESA Customs Union. Potential sources of non-tariff barriers include customs clearance procedures, import regulations, sanitary and phytosanitary measures, non-tariff charges, technical regulations and transit fees. The breakdown of such barriers in COMESA is as follows: 44 % are customs clearance procedures, 8 % are import regulations, 16 % are excise duties, 12 % are sanitary and phytosanitary measures, 12 % are administrative obstacles, and 8 % are technical barriers to trade.[98] Some progress has been made in the elimination of non-tariff barriers, such as import licensing requirements, foreign exchange restrictions, the removal of import and export quotas, the easing of customs formalities, and improved functioning of border posts.[99] However, a number of non-tariff barriers continue to impede the flow of trade between COMESA Member States.

In 2001, COMESA adopted a roadmap for the elimination of non-tariff barriers, but following a period of inactivity it was decided in May of 2006 to put in place a permanent mechanism for the resolution of disputes arising from non-tariff barriers. It was also decided that advance notification of non-tariff barriers should be made by Member States and that a regional policy should be developed and all Member States should adhere to the common standards.[100] The Non-Tariff Barrier Monitoring and Reporting System also covers SADC and EAC. The implementation of the strategy regarding non-tariff barriers was designed not to be detrimental to legitimate demands for better protection of health, safety and the environment, and should not put national market regulatory regimes in jeopardy.[101] However, the application of the monitoring and elimination instrument has been constrained by a "lack of consensus over national trade laws, regulations, practices and procedures that are to be categorized as NTBs."[102]

In an effort to eliminate non-tariff barriers to trade and facilitate intra-regional, cross-border trade, COMESA has finalised the implementation of its Simplified Trade Regime.[103] The programme came into effect on 31 May 2010 and functions to reduce the cost and time of clearing goods at borders by using simplified trade

---

97 See Non-Tariff Barriers Monitoring Mechanism, Regional Trade Facilitation Programme, available at: http://ntb.africonnect.com/.

98 See Osoro, An Overview of the Elimination of Non-Tariff Barriers, available at: http://www.mcci.org/photos/ntbs.ppt.

99 High Commission of India, Brief on COMESA, August 2010, available at: http://meaindia.nic.in/foreignrelation/23fr01.pdf.

100 See Non-Tariff Barriers Monitoring Mechanism, Regional Trade Facilitation Programme, available at: http://ntb.africonnect.com/.

101 Imani Development, Inventory of Regional Non-Tariff Barriers: Synthesis Report, July 2007, p. 11, available at: http://www.tradebarriers.org/octo_upload/attachments/download/4ccff6b5-438c-45cb-b672-3a88c0a80305/ntb_synthesis_2007_final.pdf.

102 Id.

103 COMESA Finalises New Trade Regime, Trade Law Centre for Southern Africa, 29 July 2010, available at: http://www.tralac.org/2010/07/29/comesa-finalises-new-trade-regime/.

instruments. The simplified instruments include the COMESA Simplified Certificate of Origin, the COMESA Simplified Customs Document and the list of products that qualify under the programme. The value threshold for eligible goods is pegged at $500 US dollars, meaning any trade carrying goods on the eligible list that are valued at $500 or less, and which also has the COMESA Simplified Certificate of Origin, qualifies automatically for duty- and quota-free entry.[104] Goods must still have the requisite permits in compliance with the regular food safety, plant and animal health regulations.[105] The list of eligible products include tea and coffee; maize, wheat and sorghum; cotton; sisal; fish and fish products; raw milk; livestock and livestock products; fruits; nuts; oils; seeds; poultry and poultry products; vegetables; root crops; and sugar cane.[106]

COMESA has achieved the status of a free trade area and had plans to launch the COMESA customs union by 2009. The COMESA customs union was initially to be launched in 2004 but was delayed until 2008 and then again until 2009. A common external tariff was to be adopted in 2004 in accordance with the terms of Article 47 of the COMESA treaty. By 2005, the COMESA Member States had negotiated a provisional common external tariff where capital goods would be assessed at 0 %, raw materials at 5 %, intermediate goods at 15 %, and finished goods at 30 %.[107] The COMESA customs union was officially launched on 8 June 2009 at the 13th Summit of the COMESA Heads of State and Government held in Victoria Falls, Zimbabwe. The common external tariff that was officially adopted is structured as follows: raw materials, 0 %; capital goods, 0 %; intermediate goods, 10 %; and finished goods, 25 %.[108] The common external tariff will be reviewed periodically, taking into account the specific situations of Member States, in order to provide for flexibility in the customs union and to provide for evaluation and adjustment if necessary.[109] The formation of a customs union is a process, beginning with short term measures that include adopting and implementing the COMESA Tariff Nomenclature and matching national tariff structures with the COMESA common

[104] COMESA Finalises New Trade Regime, Trade Law Centre for Southern Africa, 29 July 2010, available at: http://www.tralac.org/2010/07/29/comesa-finalises-new-trade-regime/.

[105] COMESA Finalises New Trade Regime, Trade Law Centre for Southern Africa, 29 July 2010, available at: http://www.tralac.org/2010/07/29/comesa-finalises-new-trade-regime/.

[106] COMESA Finalises New Trade Regime, Trade Law Centre for Southern Africa, 29 July 2010, available at: http://www.tralac.org/2010/07/29/comesa-finalises-new-trade-regime/.

[107] Abdoulahi, Progress Report on Regional Integration Efforts in Africa towards the Promotion of Intra-African Trade, December 2005, p. 8, available at: http://repository.uneca.org/bitstream/handle/10855/12617/bib.%2053729_I.pdf?sequence=1.

[108] Official Gazette of the Common Market for Eastern and Southern Africa, Vol. 15, No. 1, 9 June 2009, Part III, Art. 7, available at: http://www.comesa.int/attachments/article/26/2009%20Gazette%20Vol.%2015%20No1.pdf.

[109] COMESA, COMESA Customs Union, available at: http://programmes.comesa.int.

external tariff in order to produce tariff alignment schedules.[110] Long term measures in the process of establishing a customs union include ensuring that all Member States adopt and implement the common external tariff, fully implementing the COMESA Regional Trade Policy, and minimising or eliminating sensitive products from the COMESA Tariff Nomenclature and the common external tariff.[111]

At the 27th meeting of the COMESA Council of Ministers held in December of 2009, the Council approved a formula to be used by Member States to adjust their national tariffs to the COMESA common external tariff. Where alignment of the national and COMESA tariffs requires a reduction in the national tariff, the national tariff should be reduced by 25 % in the first year, 25 % in the second year, and 50 % in the third year.[112] Where alignment requires an increase in the national tariff, it should be increased by 50 % in the first year, 25 % in the second year, and 25 % in the third year.[113] COMESA Secretary General Sindiso Ngwenya announced recently that the group may fail to reach the goal of achieving a duty-free trade area by 2012 because some countries have delayed in submitting their tariff alignments proposals.[114] The reluctance of some of the Member States may be due to the perceived loss of sovereignty over setting and administering the country's tariff structure. In order to complete the requisite steps in the 3-year transitional period set at the launch of the customs union, a comprehensive timetable and programme must be established so that outstanding issues and concerns are resolved and the progress made towards implementing the customs union road map can be monitored and evaluated.[115]

Steps have been taken by COMESA towards enhancing cooperation in areas other than trade. For example, COMESA Member States were recently encouraged to implement the Comprehensive Africa Agriculture Development programme (CAADP), an AU/NEPAD initiative designed to address food security and agricultural production issues.[116] The programme's objective is to develop the agriculture

---

[110] COMESA, The COMESA Customs Union: Status on Sensitive Products and Implementation of the Transition Period, p. 5, available at: http://programmes.comesa.int.

[111] COMESA, The COMESA Customs Union: Status on Sensitive Products and Implementation of the Transition Period, p. 5, available at: http://programmes.comesa.int.

[112] COMESA, The COMESA Customs Union: Status on Sensitive Products and Implementation of the Transition Period, p. 8, available at: http://programmes.comesa.int.

[113] COMESA, The COMESA Customs Union: Status on Sensitive Products and Implementation of the Transition Period, p. 5, available at: http://programmes.comesa.int.

[114] COMESA May Miss Deadline for Duty-Free Trade, Trade Law Centre for Southern Africa, 24 June 2010, available at: http://www.tralac.org/2010/06/24/comesa-may-miss-deadline-for-duty-free-trade/.

[115] COMESA May Miss Deadline for Duty-Free Trade, Trade Law Centre for Southern Africa, 24 June 2010, available at: http://www.tralac.org/2010/06/24/comesa-may-miss-deadline-for-duty-free-trade/.

[116] Masinga, COMESA Members to Implement Agriculture Policies, Trade Law Centre for Southern Africa, 21 July 2010, available at: http://www.tralac.org/2010/07/21/comesa-members-to-implement-agriculture-policies/.

sector in order to achieve regional food security, sustainable agricultural growth, sector competitiveness, and ultimately to reduce poverty levels in the region. At the COMESA Third Joint Meeting of Ministers of Agriculture, Environment and Natural Resources, Member States were urged to implement policies that prevent additional environmental degradation and ecosystems losses in order to ensure long-term growth and development.[117] Additionally, the United States Agency for International Development (USAID)/East Africa recently made a contribution to provide capacity building and technical assistance to the East African Power Pool (EAPP), a specialised COMESA institution whose objective is to improve access to affordable, clean energy through regional electricity trade exchange.[118] The Eastern Africa regional electricity market will be developed further by the Powering Progress project, which will assist the EAPP to promote reliability, to address shortages, to lower access costs, and to expand regional power capacity within the region.[119] High energy costs have been a longstanding impediment to the area's competitiveness and poverty-reducing economic growth, and the programme is expected to increase regional electricity trade exchanges that will reduce power shortages in the region. The programme will also encourage the harmonisation of regional policies and regulations for enhanced cross-border trade, address specific policy and regulatory barriers to increase investment by the private sector in electricity, and improve the performance of EAPP Member utilities.[120]

A Memorandum of Understanding has been signed between COMESA, EAC, IGAD and the Indian Ocean Commission (IOC) under which these organisations have agreed to adopt and implement the COMESA trade liberalisation and facilitation programme. Additionally, COMESA and SADC have formed a Joint Task Force to harmonise their economic integration programmes. This partnership was joined by the EAC and the first Tripartite Summit was held in Kampala, Uganda in 2008. It is important to the progress of these three organisations that the Summit decisions regarding the harmonisation of projects and programmes be implemented. It is expected that COMESA, SADC and EAC will work towards the formation of a unified free trade area and ultimately the convergence of the COMESA customs union encompassing all 26 countries. However the Tripartite free trade area has ambitious goals, for example to promote customs cooperation and trade facilitation, to combat unfair trade practices and import surges, to simplify trade structures among its large membership and to try to relax restrictions

[117] Masinga, COMESA Members to Implement Agriculture Policies, Trade Law Centre for Southern Africa, 21 July 2010, available at: http://www.tralac.org/2010/07/21/comesa-members-to-implement-agriculture-policies/.

[118] Muwanga, COMESA to Address Power Shortage, Trade Law Centre for Southern Africa, 22 July 2010, available at: http://www.tralac.org/2010/07/22/comesa-to-address-power-shortage/.

[119] Muwanga, COMESA to Address Power Shortage, Trade Law Centre for Southern Africa, 22 July 2010, available at: http://www.tralac.org/2010/07/22/comesa-to-address-power-shortage/.

[120] Muwanga, COMESA to Address Power Shortage, Trade Law Centre for Southern Africa, 22 July 2010, available at: http://www.tralac.org/2010/07/22/comesa-to-address-power-shortage/.

on the movement of business people.[121] The wide range of ambitious goals, potential conflicts over controversial issues such as rules of origin and the movement of people and capital flows, overlapping membership and existing arrangements such as EPAs with the EU have hindered any progress towards forming the tripartite free trade area.[122] In order to make sure that the smaller African countries are not negatively affected by such an arrangement, the concentration should be on encouraging diversification away from primary commodities and towards industrialisation, value-added manufacturing and sectoral industrial policy rather than focusing majorly on the reduction of tariffs.[123] One suggestion is that because the economic inequalities within the region require some kind of protection for certain industries, the free trade agreement should provide for some leeway for sensitive products in its tariff reduction schedule and also possibly a compensation mechanism to reimburse smaller countries that do not reap the benefits of the agreement.[124]

East African Community

The Treaty establishing the East African Community (EAC) was signed on November 30, 1999 and entered into force 7 July 2000. Its original members were Kenya, Uganda, and Tanzania. Burundi and Rwanda became members of the EAC in 2007. The goal of the EAC is to "widen and deepen economic, political, social and cultural integration in order to improve the quality of life of the people of East Africa through increased competitiveness, value added production, trade and investment."[125] The EAC treaty aims to establish an export-oriented economy that will enable the "free movement of goods, persons, labour, services, capital [and] information technology," as an important objective.[126] Through a series of transitional stages consisting of the establishment of a Customs Union, a Common Market, and a Monetary Union, the Treaty Establishing the EAC ultimately is aimed towards the establishment of a Political Federation.

The Treaty Establishing the EAC calls for the establishment of a Customs Union, the details of such establishment to be contained in a Protocol,[127] within

[121] African Free Trade, Trade Law Centre for Southern Africa, 5 July 2010, available at: http://www.tralac.org/2010/07/05/african-free-trade/.

[122] African Free Trade, Trade Law Centre for Southern Africa, 5 July 2010, available at: http://www.tralac.org/2010/07/05/african-free-trade/.

[123] African Free Trade, Trade Law Centre for Southern Africa, 5 July 2010, available at: http://www.tralac.org/2010/07/05/african-free-trade/.

[124] African Free Trade, Trade Law Centre for Southern Africa, 5 July 2010, available at: http://www.tralac.org/2010/07/05/african-free-trade/.

[125] See the EAC Development Strategy 2006–2010, Executive Summary, p. 7, available at: http://www.eac.int/home.html.

[126] Art. 7(c) of the Treaty Establishing the East African Community, available at: http://www.eac.int/.

[127] Art. 75(1) EAC Treaty.

4 years from the effective date of the treaty.[128] The Protocol for the Establishment of the East African Customs Union was signed on 2 March 2004 after several delays and entered into force on 1 January 2005. The Protocol sets out the requirements for the formation of the East African Community Customs Union within 5 years after the entry into force of the Protocol.[129] The objectives of the Customs Union are to "further liberalise intra-regional trade in goods on the basis of mutually beneficial trade arrangements among the Partner States; promote efficiency in production within the Community; enhance domestic, cross border and foreign investment in the Community; and promote economic development and diversification in industrialisation in the Community."[130] The Customs Union shall be established progressively over this 5 year transitional period in order to fulfill these objectives.

The Protocol provides a number of requirements to achieve the goals of trade liberalisation and the establishment of a customs union. First, Partner States must eliminate all internal tariffs and similar charges on trade among the Partner States upon the entry into force of the Protocol.[131] Tariff rates can be eliminated more quickly than set out in the Protocol if so decided by the Council. Second, to make the transition to a customs union easier, the Protocol sets out specific requirements for internal tariffs and categorisation of goods going into and out of the Partner States. For example, Article 11(2) provides that goods to and from Uganda and Tanzania are duty free and goods from Uganda and Tanzania into Kenya are duty free.

The categorisation of goods and varied tariff reduction schedules recognises the principles of variable geometry and asymmetry. The principle of asymmetry is defined by the EAC Treaty as a "principle which addresses variances for the implementation of measures in an economic integration process."[132] It allows EAC Member States to address possible negative effects that the implementation of customs union policies might have on Member States through the application of variable geometry. The EAC Treaty defines variable geometry as a principle that allows Members States to co-operate in the greater goals of the community while retaining the flexibility to work towards those goals at speeds that differ from other members.[133]

The establishment of a harmonised external tariff, or a common external tariff, in trade between Partner States and third countries is essential to the formation of a customs union. Within a customs union, Partner States must act as a single trading bloc and customs territory. The Protocol establishes a three band common external tariff. There is a minimum rate of 0 %, a middle rate of 10 % and a maximum rate of

[128] Art. 75(7) EAC Treaty.

[129] Art. 11(1) of the Protocol on the Establishment of the East African Customs Union, available at: http://customs.eac.int/.

[130] Art. 3 EAC Customs Union Protocol.

[131] Art. 10(1) EAC Customs Union Protocol.

[132] Art. 1 EAC Treaty.

[133] Art. 1 EAC Treaty.

25 % in respect of all products imported into the region.[134] After 5 years, the maximum rate of the common external tariff will be reviewed by the Partner States, and the Council can review the structure of the common external tariff and approve measures to remedy any adverse effects experienced by any of the Partner States as a result of the implementation of this Article. In exceptional circumstances, the Council may approve measures designed to safeguard Community interests.[135]

Further, Article 13 of the Protocol requires Partner States to immediately remove any non-tariff barriers to the importation of goods originating in other Partner States and to thereafter not impose any new barriers. This provision is directly mirrored by Article 75(5) of the EAC Treaty. The elimination of non-tariff barriers, as well as customs duties and tariffs, is essential to the attainment of the goal of a single market and investment area because such barriers to trade can hinder trade between the Partner States.

In order to address and efficiently manage trade and customs related matters, the East African Community Customs Management Act was assented to on 31 December 2004 and took effect on 1 January 2005. The East African Community Customs Management Act created the Directorate of Customs[136] whose duty is to coordinate and monitor the administration of the common external tariff; the enforcement of the customs laws; trade facilitation as provided for in the Protocol; the administration of the Rules of Origin; the compilation and dissemination of trade statistics; the application of information technology in customs administration; the training in customs-related matters; the quality control in customs operations and the customs negotiations.[137] In addition to creating the Directorate of Customs, the Customs Management Act also detailed standards and procedures for the implementation of trade and duties in areas such as the import, export and warehousing of goods; the departure of and clearing of vessels and aircraft; duties; inward and outward processing; and penalties for violating customs laws such as forfeitures and seizures of property.

The EAC Customs Management Act enumerates a number of goods it considers either prohibited for importation or restricted for import.[138] For example, soaps containing mercury, hazardous waste, pornographic materials, narcotics, and used car and light truck tires are all prohibited from being imported.[139] Additionally, precious metals and stones, ivory, specific types of firearms and ammunition, and historical artifacts are considered restricted imports.[140] The EAC Customs

[134] Art. 12(1) EAC Customs Union Protocol.

[135] Art. 12(2),(3) EAC Customs Union Protocol.

[136] Art. 3 of the East African Community Customs Management Act of 2004, available at: http://www.usig.org/countryinfo/laws/Uganda/East%20African%20Community%20customs%20Management%20Act%202004.pdf.

[137] Art. 4 EAC Customs Management Act.

[138] Art. 18 EAC Customs Management Act.

[139] Second Schedule, Part A of the EAC Customs Management Act.

[140] Second Schedule, Part B of the EAC Customs Management Act.

Management Act also enumerates several goods to be either prohibited or restricted for export.[141] The Act provides that prohibited goods for export are all "goods the exportation of which is prohibited under this Act or by any written law for the time being in force in the Partner States."[142] The Customs Management Act also provides a more specific list of goods that are considered restricted for export. For example, waste and scrap ferrous cast iron; timber from wood grown in partner states; fresh unprocessed fish; and wood charcoal are all goods that are restricted for export.[143] Additionally, warehoused goods, goods under duty drawback and transshipped goods are prohibited from being exported unless they are on vessels with registers greater than 250 tons.[144] In addition to providing items that may or may not be exported or imported from Member States, the Act provides procedures for unloading imports from various vessels, such as airplanes,[145] overland routes[146] and goods in transit.[147]

In addition to regulating the types of goods that may cross borders within the community, the Customs Management Act also enumerates guidelines for the administration of duties on those goods. The act specifies the duty rate for certain types of goods as well as what goods will be exempt from certain duties. For example, the Customs Management Act provides that goods "originating from member states will be accorded community tariff treatment in accordance with the rules of the protocol."[148] However, the Act also provides for exceptions to tariff duties such as the exception of goods that have entered into a Member State from another Member State from duty liability if the goods are to be exported out of that Member State.[149]

In computing the duty to be paid on goods, the Customs Management Act provides different standards for a variety of goods. For example, the duty to be paid on goods for home consumption will be the rate that is in force at the time the goods enter the country.[150] However, if the goods are imported overland, the duty rate will be that of when the duty is actually paid.[151] Further, when goods are liable to an import duty that is ad volarem, or taxed according to value, the import duty will be paid according to the fourth schedule of the Customs Management Act.[152]

---

[141] Art. 70 EAC Customs Management Act.

[142] Third Schedule, Part A of the EAC Customs Management Act.

[143] Third Schedule, Part B(1) of the EAC Customs Management Act.

[144] Third Schedule, Part B(2) of the EAC Customs Management Act.

[145] Art. 73-82 EAC Customs Management Act.

[146] Art. 83-84 EAC Customs Management Act.

[147] Art. 85-87 EAC Customs Management Act.

[148] Art. 111(1) EAC Customs Management Act.

[149] Art. 115 EAC Customs Management Act.

[150] Art. 120 EAC Customs Management Act.

[151] EAC Customs Management Act.

[152] Art. 122(1) EAC Customs Management Act.

Additionally, if there is an export duty to be paid, the rate of duty that that will be paid is the current rate at the time the goods are to be exported.[153]

Until the EAC agreed upon its own rules of origin, its Member States applied the COMESA rules of origin in their intra-community trade relations. The EAC envisaged anti-dumping, compensatory measures and safeguards to cover material damage to the industry and economy of the importing country.[154] Before the full implementation of a compensation mechanism, EAC members were allowed to invoke loss of revenue and to either wholly or partially restore the tariff and non-tariff measures that were in force before the trade liberalisation programme.[155] Article 14 of the EAC Customs Union Protocol states that the EAC Customs Union shall have rules of origin for the purpose of determining whether goods originate in Member States in order for those goods to be able to receive community tariff treatment from other Member States.[156] A good that receives community tariff treatment is a good that will be able to avail itself to the more favourable tariff rates presently available to EAC members as opposed to paying the common external tariff rate. The Rules of Origin specify criteria that will allow origin to be conferred on a good. The first criterion will allow a good to have origin conferred upon it if the good is wholly produced in a Member State.[157] Examples of products that the Rules of Origin would consider as being wholly produced in a Member State include vegetable products harvested within a Member State, products obtained from bodies of water or vessels within a state and livestock that were born and raised within a member state.[158] The second criterion will confer origin if goods have been wholly or partially produced by goods that do not originate in a Member State are transformed such that their C.I.F. (cost, insurance and freight) value does not exceed 60 % of the total cost of the materials used in production, the value added from production is at least 35 % of the ex-factory cost as detailed in the First Schedule to the Rules of Origin[159] and the goods have changed in character such that they are no longer able to be classified under the tariff heading where they were originally imported,[160] origin will be conferred.

I will now turn to another African RTA, the Arab Maghreb Union.

[153] Art. 120(2) EAC Customs Management Act.

[154] Abdoulahi, Progress Report on Regional Integration Efforts in Africa towards the Promotion of Intra-African Trade, 2005, p. 12.

[155] Abdoulahi, Progress Report on Regional Integration Efforts in Africa towards the Promotion of Intra-African Trade, 2005, p. 9.

[156] Art. 14(1) EAC Customs Union Protocol.

[157] Rule 4(1)(a) of the EAC Customs Union (Rules of Origin) Rules, available at: http://www.eac.int/customs/index.php?option=com_docman&task=doc_download&gid=2&Itemid=.

[158] Rule 5(1) of the EAC Customs Union Rules.

[159] First Schedule of the EAC Customs Union Rules.

[160] Art. 4(1)(b) of the EAC Customs Union Rules.

Arab Maghreb Union

The Arab Maghreb Union Treaty was signed on 17 February 1989 at Marrakesh, Morocco by the five Maghrebi countries—Algeria, Libya, Mauritania, Morocco, and Tunisia—its current members.[161]

The objectives and aims of the AMU, as identified in the Treaty establishing the AMU, include reinforcing the fraternal links binding together the Member States and their peoples; realising progress and prosperity for the Member States and defending their rights; contributing to the preservation of peace based on justice and equality; the pursuit of a common policy in different domains; and working towards the progressive realisation of the free movement of persons, services, goods and capital.[162] The main objectives of AMU are to strengthen all forms of ties among its Member States in order to maintain regional stability and enhance policy coordination and to gradually introduce the free movement and circulation of goods, services and factors of production. AMU's economic goals include realising the industrial, agricultural, commercial and social development of its Member States through the commitment of the necessary means to achieve this end, particularly by launching joint projects and expanding global and sectoral, economic cooperation programmes.[163]

At the third meeting of the Council of Heads of State in Libya in March of 1991, guidelines were adopted for a strategy of joint Maghreb development specifying four stages of economic integration—a free trade area was to be formed by the end of 1992, a customs union by the end of 1995, a common market by the end of 2000, and a monetary union at some point in time thereafter.[164] No clear and detailed strategy has been developed for the fulfillment of these economic goals, although technical discussions between officials of the Member States have clarified the most important economic goals.

However, despite these plans and guidelines, little progress has been made to meet these deadlines. Political instability caused a cessation in AMU's activities in 1995, disrupting the decision-making process of the organisation and preventing the countries from forming mutually beneficial economic arrangements. A lack of adequate infrastructure facilities for intra-market access, a lack of marketing institutions and incentive systems among the countries, high production costs preventing the Maghreb countries from producing internationally competitive products, and the undiversified character of the countries' productive activities

[161] Arab Maghreb Union, History, available at: http://www.maghrebarabe.org/en/uma.cfm; see also Department of International Relations and Cooperation of the Republic of South Africa, Arab Maghreb Union, available at: http://www.dfa.gov.za/foreign/Multilateral/africa/amu.htm.

[162] Art. 2 of the Treaty Establishing the Arab Maghreb Union, available at: http://www.wipo.int/wipolex/en/regeco_treaties/text.jsp?doc_id=150805&file_id=201320. A translated version is available at: http://wits.worldbank.org/GPTAD/PDF/archive/MAGHREB.pdf.

[163] Art. 3 AMU Treaty.

[164] Finaish/Bell, The Arab Maghreb Union, IMF Working Paper No. 94/55, p. 7.

have all resulted in little intra-regional trade and a stagnation in the regional integration process. However, the Member States have accrued some benefits from the creation of the AMU and subsequent negotiations, such as increased dialogue between the countries and strengthened ties among them. Despite the lack of progress, the regular meetings of the political heads of state have reinforced the Members' resolve to address their economic problems together using an integrated strategy.[165]

The highest institutional organ of the AMU is the Presidential Council, which is comprised of the Heads of State of all the Member States.[166] Only the Presidential Council has the power to make decisions, which must be made unanimously.[167] The presidency of the council rotates between the five members with each country's Head of State holding the position for a period of 1 year.[168] The Presidential Council meets regularly twice a year or extraordinarily if the circumstances so dictate.[169] A Council of Foreign Affairs Ministers also meets regularly to prepare the sessions of the Presidential Council and to examine the questions or proposals submitted to it by the Follow-Up Committee and the Specialized Ministerial Committees.[170] The Follow-Up Committee is comprised of representatives from each Member State who are in charge of the Union's affairs or follows the implementation of Presidential Council resolutions, and which submits the results of its work to the Council of Foreign Affairs Ministers.[171] A Consultative Council, which is comprised of thirty representatives from each Member State, delivers opinions on draft decisions submitted to it by the Presidential Council and makes recommendations on reinforcing the AMU's action and realising its objectives.[172] The AMU Treaty calls for a Permanent Secretariat General to be defined and a Secretary General designated by the Presidential Council.[173] Several specialised committees have been formed including committees on the interior, human resources, infrastructure, economy and finances, and food security.[174]

The AMU Treaty also establishes a Judicial Authority comprised of two judges from each Member State, for 6-year terms, to "rule on disputes related to the interpretation and application of the Treaty and agreements concluded within the framework of the Union, submitted to it by the Presidential Council or one of

[165] Finaish/Bell, The Arab Maghreb Union, IMF Working Paper No. 94/55, p. 10.

[166] Art. 4 AMU Treaty.

[167] Art. 6 AMU Treaty.

[168] Art. 4 AMU Treaty.

[169] Art. 5 AMU Treaty.

[170] Art. 7 AMU Treaty.

[171] Art. 8 AMU Treaty.

[172] Art. 12 AMU Treaty.

[173] Art. 11 AMU Treaty.

[174] Art. 10 AMU Treaty provides for the creation of Specialized Ministerial Committees set up by the Presidential Council which shall define its attributions.

the States parties to the dispute."[175] The judgments of the Judicial Authority are enforceable and final.[176] The Judicial Authority may also deliver advisory opinions submitted to it by the Presidential Council.[177]

During the 1990's, around 25 multilateral agreements have been signed by the five countries that cover a range of subjects such as taxation, customs and central banking but only five agreements have been ratified by all five Member States.[178] One of the five multilateral treaties that has been signed by all five Members is an agreement on trade and tariffs covering all industrial products.[179] This agreement is aimed at establishing free trade among the Members through the elimination of tariffs as well as the elimination of non-tariff barriers.[180] Various projects have been accomplished and initial steps towards a common market have been taken, such as a freer flow of goods and persons among the Member countries.[181] Visas are no longer required for member nationals to travel, and there are plans for a common identity card.[182] Resolutions on the integration of transportation have been reached and infrastructural improvements are underway on a railway connecting Tunis, Tunisia and Marrakech, Morocco and a pipeline to transport gas to Europe from Algeria through Morocco.[183]

Little has been done to implement the agreements or the objectives of the Treaty, and despite the creation of many working groups and the initiation of several projects, little tangible progress has been made towards economic integration. Political rivalry has consistently been an issue for cooperation in the region, particularly with respect to the Western Sahara conflict between Morocco and Algeria, the AMU's largest members. Other political issues that divided North African countries include the then international sanctions imposed against Libya and Libya's dissatisfaction with the other members for their lack of support in opposing the sanctions, civil war in Algeria, and border disputes that have

---

[175] Art. 13 AMU Treaty.

[176] Art. 13 AMU Treaty.

[177] Art. 13 AMU Treaty.

[178] See the entry on the Arab Maghreb Union, Encyclopedia of Business, available at: http://www.referenceforbusiness.com/encyclopedia/A-Ar/Arab-Maghreb-Union.html.

[179] Finaish/Bell, The Arab Maghreb Union, IMF Working Paper No. 94/55, p. 8. The other four are agreements with respect to trade in agricultural products, investment guarantees, avoidance of double taxation, and phyto-sanitary standards.

[180] Finaish/Bell, The Arab Maghreb Union, IMF Working Paper No. 94/55, p. 8; see also the Communication from the Arab Maghreb Union, Request for Observer Status, GATT Document L/7548, 2 November 1994, p. 3, available at: http://www.wto.org/gatt_docs/English/SULPDF/91820125.pdf.

[181] Martinez, Algeria, the Arab Maghreb Union and Regional Integration, EuroMeSCo Paper 59, 2006, p. 6, available at: http://www.euromesco.net/images/59_eng.pdf.

[182] See the entry on the Arab Maghreb Union, Encyclopedia of Business.

[183] See the entry on the Arab Maghreb Union, Encyclopedia of Business.

interrupted or stalled the free movement of goods and persons within the region.[184] As a result of these and other political disputes, the Heads of State met only six times before Morocco called for a suspension of the Union's activities in 1995.[185] Furthermore, an increase in terrorist activity has led the AMU Member countries to focus attention on anti-terrorism efforts, putting economic and financial reform on the back burner.[186]

The lack of progress can also be attributed to economic obstacles. Intra-regional trade has stagnated at around 3 %, a weak trade rate as compared to the EU's 60 %, 22 % for ASEAN and almost 20 % for the Mercosur countries.[187] AMU's weak intra-regional trade rate can be attributed to the numerous non-tariff and regulatory trade barriers as well as the lack of complementary economic structures between the countries.[188] Morocco and Tunisia, the AMU countries at the most advanced stage of economic development, have relatively open economies and diversified exports while the economies of Libya and Algeria are more centrally-controlled, with exports heavily concentrated in energy products.[189] Furthermore, the EU is the primary importer of products produced in the Maghreb countries and the AMU countries are heavily dependent upon European imports, resulting in less efficient AMU producers because of the proximity, diverse production structures and size of the European markets.[190] This reliance on European and other foreign suppliers is in part because of the strict border restrictions on the flow of people and goods that result in reduced commerce and less inter-regional economic activity.[191]

It has been suggested that bilateral agreements between Maghreb and European countries have the potential to create economic growth.[192] Tunisia has signed several bilateral treaties with other Maghreb and with European countries in recent

[184] Mortimer, The Arab Maghreb Union: Myth and Reality, in: Zoubir (ed.), *North Africa in Transition: State, Society, and Economic Transformation in the 1990s*, 1999; see also the entry on the Arab Maghreb Union, Encyclopedia of Business.

[185] Mortimer, The Arab Maghreb Union: Myth and Reality, in: Zoubir (ed.), *North Africa in Transition: State*, Society, and Economic Transformation in the 1990s, 1999.

[186] Hufbauer/Brunel, *Maghreb Regional and Global Integration: A Dream to be Fulfilled*, 2008, p. 10.

[187] Martinez, Algeria, the Arab Maghreb Union and Regional Integration, EuroMeSCo Paper 59, 2006, p. 6.

[188] Martinez, Algeria, the Arab Maghreb Union and Regional Integration, EuroMeSCo Paper 59, 2006, p. 6.

[189] Finaish/Bell, The Arab Maghreb Union, IMF Working Paper No. 94/55, p. 15.

[190] Finaish/Bell, The Arab Maghreb Union, IMF Working Paper No. 94/55, p. 14; see also Achy, Trade in North Africa: Assessing Regional Integration Potential in North Africa, U.N. Economic Commission for Africa Document ECA-NA/RABAT/ICE/XXI/3/I, April 2006, p. 5, available at: http://www.uneca.org/sros/na/documents/Trade.pdf.

[191] Hufbauer/Brunel, *Maghreb Regional and Global Integration: A Dream to be Fulfilled*, 2008, p. 1.

[192] Yahia, Tunis forum targets Maghreb unity as solution to economic crisis, Magharebia, 14 May 2009, available at: www.magharebia.com/cocoon/awi/xhtml1/en_GB/features/awi/features/2009/05/14/feature-03.

years, and trade exchanges between Tunisia and the AMU Member countries have more than doubled between 2005 and 2008.[193] Individual association agreements have also been signed between the EU and Algeria, Morocco and Tunisia and a free trade agreement has been entered into between Morocco and the United States. A direct trade agreement between the AMU and the EU will allow the northern African region to double its exports to the EU and increase per capita income in the region.[194] It will take an estimated 20 years for Algeria, Morocco, and Tunisia to "reach the levels of per capita income of those countries, which are at the tail-end in the development list of the Organization for Economic Co-operation and Development."[195] The World Bank claims that if the AMU pursues commercial and economic integration with the EU through bilateral treaties signed individually the AMU can achieve a 15 % increase of per capita income.[196] However, most observers using gravity models to estimate trade potentials between member countries based on geographical distance, economic size, and other characteristics have consistently found that the level of integration in the northern African region is below that what was expected.[197] These bilateral agreements have been adopted as the initial approach of the Union aiming at a broad-based liberalisation of most products proved unrealistic because of the differences in the Member States' economic, trade and social policies.[198] Attempts to extend these bilateral agreements on a multilateral basis have been unsuccessful, as the countries have found it difficult to agree on a common list of products to be freely circulated within the region.[199] There must be macroeconomic and structural reforms to harmonise the economic policies of the AMU Members as well as the harmonisation of standards such as licensing requirements.[200]

[193] Yahia, Tunis forum targets Maghreb unity as solution to economic crisis, Magharebia, 14 May 2009, available at: www.magharebia.com/cocoon/awi/xhtml1/en_GB/features/awi/features/2009/05/14/feature-03; Trade exchanges between Tunisia and the other Maghreb countries went from 1.9 billion dinars in 2005 to 4.2 billion dinars in 2008. Tunisian exports to Maghreb countries have increased from 1 billion dinars in 2005 to 1.9 billion dinars in 2008 and imports have increased from 900 million dinars in 2005 to 2.3 billion dinars in 2008.

[194] Felice, According to the World Bank, Maghreb is Key to EU Development, Medibtikar, 13 April 2007, available at: http://www.medibtikar.eu/+According-to-World-Bank-Maghreb-is+.html.

[195] Felice, According to the World Bank, Maghreb is Key to EU Development, Medibtikar, 13 April 2007, available at: http://www.medibtikar.eu/+According-to-World-Bank-Maghreb-is+.html.

[196] Felice, According to the World Bank, Maghreb is Key to EU Development, Medibtikar, 13 April 2007, available at: http://www.medibtikar.eu/+According-to-World-Bank-Maghreb-is+.html.

[197] World Bank, Regional Integration for Global Competitiveness, p. 36, available at: http://siteresources.worldbank.org/INTMENA/Resources/EDP2008_Chap_2.pdf.

[198] Finaish/Bell, The Arab Maghreb Union, IMF Working Paper No. 94/55, p. 23.

[199] Finaish/Bell, The Arab Maghreb Union, IMF Working Paper No. 94/55, p. 24.

[200] Finaish/Bell, The Arab Maghreb Union, IMF Working Paper No. 94/55, p. 24.

The Maghreb Bank for Investment and External Trade was established in 2002 to engage the private sector and promote trade and investment in the region.[201] The Bank provides finance to facilitate trade and undertake agricultural and industrial projects at a national and regional level.[202] The formation of the Maghreb Bank is argued to have the potential to lead to deeper financial integration and to allow for the freer movement of capital within the region through stabilising exchange rates and making currency fully convertible among the Member countries. Progress in lowering tariffs through bilateral preferential trade agreements with the EU and other countries has been made, although the average tariff protection is still higher than the world average.[203] Regional integration will create a large regional market, which in turn will bring efficiency gains and attract foreign investment.[204] However, regulatory and other non-tariff barriers to trade must be removed before the AMU can achieve its first goal of attaining the status of a free trade area.

Recent integration initiatives focusing on trade facilitation between Algeria, Morocco and Tunisia began in 2005 at a conference in Algiers, and Libya and Mauritania have been invited to participate in the follow-up work and subsequent conferences.[205] A work programme was formulated at the conference that focuses on seven areas:

- Harmonising trade regulations linked to the implementation of free trade areas, particularly with respect to non-tariff barriers and preferential treatment of goods from the Maghreb region, as well as rules and associated procedures of origin;
- Eliminating trade distortions in order to reduce informal trade flows;
- Continuing tariff reforms aimed at simplifying and reducing customs tariffs;
- Moving forward with customs reforms;
- Streamlining document processing;
- Improving payment systems; and
- Improving the logistical chain, including transport infrastructure and services related to trade.[206]

---

[201] UN Economic Commission for Africa/African Union, Assessing Regional Integration in Africa, Part III, 2008, p. 16, available at: http://www.iss.co.za/uploads/ARIA3NOV08.PDF.

[202] UN Economic Commission for Africa/African Union, Assessing Regional Integration in Africa, Part III, 2008, p. 16, available at: http://www.iss.co.za/uploads/ARIA3NOV08.PDF.

[203] Allain/Loko, Fresh Impetus Toward Maghreb Integration, IMF Survey Magazine, 12 September 2007, available at: http://www.imf.org/external/pubs/ft/survey/so/2007/car0912b.htm.

[204] Martinez, Algeria, the Arab Maghreb Union and Regional Integration, EuroMeSCo Paper 59, 2006, p. 6.

[205] International Monetary Fund, Regional Economic Outlook: Middle East and Central Asia, September 2006, p. 24, available at: http://www.imf.org/external/pubs/ft/reo/2006/ENG/02/mreo0906.pdf.

[206] International Monetary Fund, Regional Economic Outlook: Middle East and Central Asia, September 2006, p. 24, available at: http://www.imf.org/external/pubs/ft/reo/2006/ENG/02/mreo0906.pdf.

An action plan was drawn up by technical working groups that includes activating the intra-Maghreb Customs Committee to reduce trade distortions and informal trade caused by tariffs and non-tariff barriers; developing a one-stop document processing system; and creating a private-sector led unit to monitor the region's foreign trade.[207] Subsequent regional conferences were scheduled to deal with financial sector reforms and financial integration in the region and to address private sector development.[208]

Towards the goal of greater integration in northern Africa, the Social and Economic Council of the Arab League concluded the Agreement on the Greater Arab Free Trade Area (GAFTA) in 1997 to establish GAFTA within 10 years, beginning 1 January 2008.[209] GAFTA has seventeen Members, including Bahrain, Egypt, Iraq, Jordan, Kuwait, Lebanon, Libya, Morocco, Oman, Palestine, Qatar, Saudi Arabia, Syria, Tunisia, United Arab Emirates, Sudan and Yemen.[210] The Agreement called for the gradual reduction of tariffs and non-tariff barriers on intra-regional trade within a period of 10 years by an average rate of 10 % each year to reach full elimination by 2007.[211] However, the Social and Economic Council decided to accelerate the transition period so that it would end in 2005 instead of 2007, thus increasing the rate of tariff and non-tariff barrier reductions to 20 % for the years 2004 and 2005.[212] The Agreement is the most far-reaching trade liberalisation agreement in the region, partly because it includes the removal of not only tariffs but also administrative, monetary and quantitative non-tariff barriers to trade such as quotas and provides for trade liberalisation in agriculture.[213] It also provides for individual countries to agree to accelerate the

[207] International Monetary Fund, Regional Economic Outlook: Middle East and Central Asia, September 2006, p. 24, available at: http://www.imf.org/external/pubs/ft/reo/2006/ENG/02/mreo0906.pdf.

[208] International Monetary Fund, Regional Economic Outlook: Middle East and Central Asia, September 2006, p. 24, available at: http://www.imf.org/external/pubs/ft/reo/2006/ENG/02/mreo0906.pdf.

[209] Italian Ministry of Agricultural and Agrarian Reform, Implementation of the Great Arab Free Trade Agreement: The Case of Syria, Working Paper No. 8, p. 4, available at: http://www.napcsyr.org/dwnld-files/working_papers/en/08_gafta_en.pdf.

[210] Italian Ministry of Agricultural and Agrarian Reform, Implementation of the Great Arab Free Trade Agreement: The Case of Syria, Working Paper No. 8, p. 4, available at: http://www.napcsyr.org/dwnld-files/working_papers/en/08_gafta_en.pdf.

[211] Italian Ministry of Agricultural and Agrarian Reform, Implementation of the Great Arab Free Trade Agreement: The Case of Syria, Working Paper No. 8, p. 4, available at: http://www.napcsyr.org/dwnld-files/working_papers/en/08_gafta_en.pdf.

[212] Italian Ministry of Agricultural and Agrarian Reform, Implementation of the Great Arab Free Trade Agreement: The Case of Syria, Working Paper No. 8, p. 4, available at: http://www.napcsyr.org/dwnld-files/working_papers/en/08_gafta_en.pdf.

[213] Abedini/Péridy, The Greater Arab Free Trade Area (GAFTA): An Estimation of the Trade Effects, 2007, p. 3, available at: http://economics.ca/2007/papers/0300.pdf.

liberalisation process through bilateral or sub-regional agreements.[214] By liberalising trade among the Arab countries, the Agreement aims to increase the trade volume within the region, to distribute production among Member countries according to their comparative advantages and enhance production efficiency, create competitive domestic markets by providing greater product variety for consumers, attract more foreign direct investments by creating a larger market and to increase economic interdependence between the Arab countries to enhance the stability and security in the region.[215]

In 2005, the tariff removal schedule was completed, although the schedule for the removal of non-tariff barriers was only partially completed.[216] The benefits of GAFTA are disputed. Although intra-regional trade has increased, it is highly concentrated in a few more developed countries, as are imports and exports.[217] Concerns regarding the implementation of GAFTA include many issues beyond those affecting the general implementation of African regional integration agreements such as inadequate transport infrastructure and incompatible currencies. One of the major concerns is with the number of exemptions provided for in the Agreement, generally regarding agricultural commodities[218] and the potential for the numerous exemptions to hinder the trade liberalisation process and the growth of inter-regional trade. Furthermore, non-tariff barriers remain a constant hindrance to intra-regional trade, although a few forms are addressed by the Agreement.[219] Despite progress with respect to tariff elimination, the integration process in the Arab countries remains behind AMU's schedule.

---

[214] Abedini/Péridy, The Greater Arab Free Trade Area (GAFTA): An Estimation of the Trade Effects, 2007, p. 3, available at: http://economics.ca/2007/papers/0300.pdf.

[215] Abedini/Péridy, The Greater Arab Free Trade Area (GAFTA): An Estimation of the Trade Effects, 2007, p. 3, available at: http://economics.ca/2007/papers/0300.pdf.; see also Italian Ministry of Agricultural and Agrarian Reform, Implementation of the Great Arab Free Trade Agreement: The Case of Syria, Working Paper No. 8, p. 5.

[216] Abedini/Peridy, The Greater Arab Free Trade Area (GAFTA): An Estimation of the Trade Effects, 2007, p. 1.

[217] Abedini/Peridy, The Greater Arab Free Trade Area (GAFTA): An Estimation of the Trade Effects, 2007, p. 4.

[218] Gendrano, League of Arab States: The Greater Arab Free Trade Agreement, 2007, p. 13, available at: http://www.idia.net/Files/ConferenceCommitteeTopicFiles/149/PDFFile/U07-LAS-GreaterArabFreeTradeAgreement.pdf. With the "agricultural calendar" provision, each GAFTA state was allowed to use protectionist measures for at most ten agricultural products for seven months out of twelve months a year, with a maximum of 45 months in total for a specific commodity. The reasoning behind the exemptions was to protect certain commodities from facing competition from other states in the region, particularly states participating in GAFTA. States are abusing the exemption list by adding products potentially subject to non-Arab competition on their exception list, fearing strong competition from outside the region.

[219] Gendrano, League of Arab States: The Greater Arab Free Trade Agreement, 2007, p. 15, available at: http://www.idia.net/Files/ConferenceCommitteeTopicFiles/149/PDFFile/U07-LAS-GreaterArabFreeTradeAgreement.pdf.

Southern African Development Community

The Southern African Development Community (SADC) was formed in 1992 and it has fifteen members. They are; Angola, Botswana, the Democratic Republic of Congo, Lesotho, Madagascar, Malawi, Mauritius, Mozambique, Namibia, Seychelles, South Africa, Swaziland, Tanzania, Zambia and Zimbabwe.[220] The Treaty Establishing the SADC aims to promote integration and cooperation. In this direction, Article 22 calls for the conclusion of Protocols that spell out the objectives and scope of cooperation and integration as are necessary.[221] These protocols enter into force 30 days after ratification, and Member States can become a party to a protocol by accession. A protocol is only binding on the Member States that are party to the protocol in question.

The Protocol on Trade was created in 1996 with the objectives of furthering the liberalisation of intra-regional trade in goods, furthering economic development, diversification and industrialisation, and forming a free trade area in the SADC region. Twelve members of SADC have ratified the Protocol on Trade, and Angola and the Democratic Republic of Congo will join the SADC free trade area at a later stage. Implementation of the SADC Protocol on Trade began in September 2000.

The Protocol on Trade sets out the guidelines for the attainment of the goal of trade liberalisation. The process for the phased elimination of tariffs and non-tariff barriers is to be determined by the Committee of Ministers responsible for trade matters, who should have regard for preferential trade agreements between Member States and that the elimination of barriers to trade should be eliminated "within 8 years from the entry into force of this Protocol."[222] In determining the process for the elimination of tariffs and non-tariff barriers, the Committee is required to bear in mind that countries that may be or have been adversely affected by the removal of such barriers can apply for more time to eliminate the trade barriers, and that different tariff lines may be applied to different products during the process of eliminating tariffs and non-tariff barriers.

Under the SADC Protocol on Trade, 85 % of all intra-regional trade was to be duty-free by 2008, and the remaining 15 % of intra-regional trade, consisting of sensitive products, to be liberalised by 2012.[223] Countries were able to choose the products on which to reduce duties so long as the overall goal was achieved. Mauritius agreed to allow 65 % of imports to enter its markets duty-free in 2000,

[220] SADC currently has fifteen members: Angola, Botswana, the Democratic Republic of Congo, Lesotho, Madagascar, Malawi, Mauritius, Mozambique, Namibia, Seychelles, South Africa, Swaziland, Tanzania, Zambia and Zimbabwe. See Gendrano, League of Arab States: The Greater Arab Free Trade Agreement, 2007, p. 13, available at: http://www.idia.net/Files/ConferenceCommitteeTopicFiles/149/PDFFile/U07-LAS-GreaterArabFreeTradeAgreement.pdf.

[221] Art. 22(1) SADC Treaty.

[222] Art. 3(1) of the SADC Protocol on Trade, available at: http://www.sadc.int/english/key-documents/protocols/protocol-on-trade/.

[223] Abdoulahi, Progress Report on Regional Integration Efforts in Africa towards the Promotion of Intra-African Trade, 2005, p. 7.

although Tanzania could only offer 9 % that year with the removal of its tariffs to be staggered, 88 % lifted by 2008 and 100 % lifted by 2012.[224] SADC members that are also members of SACU are required to reduce tariffs on intra-SADC trade faster than other members. SACU provides duty-free entry for 77 % of non-SACU imports from SADC members by 2000, and 97 % by 2008. South Africa is to eliminate all tariffs by 2012.[225]

The Protocol on Trade calls for the elimination through a phased reduction of import duties on goods originating in Member States.[226] Article 4 further provides that fees and other charges that are commensurate with the costs of any services rendered are to be excluded from the provisions of that Article.[227] Article 7 of the Protocol provides that Member States shall not apply any new quantitative restrictions, and phase out existing quantitative restrictions on the import of goods originating in Member States, but Member States may apply a quota system if the tariff rate under such a system is more favourable than the rate applied under the Protocol.[228]

Article 5(1) provides that Member States cannot impose any export duties on goods for export into other Member States. However, Article 5(2) allows any Member State to apply export duties that are necessary to prevent erosion of any prohibitions or restrictions that may apply to exports outside of the SADC if no less favourable treatment is granted to Member States than to third countries.[229] The Protocol on Trade Article 8(1) additionally provides that no Member State shall apply any quantitative restrictions on exports to any other Member State. Like Article 5(2), Article 8(2) allows any Member State to take necessary measures "to prevent erosion of any prohibitions or restrictions which apply to exports outside the Community provided that no less favourable treatment is granted to Member States than to third countries."[230]

The Trade Protocol requires the Member States to phase out existing quantitative restrictions on imports and exports, and refrain from imposing any new quantitative restrictions, except where otherwise provided in the Protocol. Article 9 lists general exceptions to the phase-out requirement, provided that the measures do not

---

[224] Abdoulahi, Progress Report on Regional Integration Efforts in Africa towards the Promotion of Intra-African Trade, 2005, p. 7.

[225] Abdoulahi, Progress Report on Regional Integration Efforts in Africa towards the Promotion of Intra-African Trade, 2005, p. 7.

[226] Art. 4(1) of the SADC Protocol on Trade.

[227] Grimett, Protectionism and Compliance with the GATT Article XXIV in Selected Regional Trade Arrangements, p. 223, available at: http://eprints.ru.ac.za/208/01/grimett-thesis.pdf (arguing Article 4 is inconsistent with the provisions of Article XXIV(8)(b) of GATT since it authorises the maintenance of quantitative restrictions. However, that argument ignores the fact that the enabling clause creates independent justification for intra LDC regional cooperation outside of Article XXIV of GATT as we saw in chapter 5.).

[228] See Art. 7 of the SADC Protocol on Trade.

[229] Art. 5(2) of the SADC Protocol on Trade.

[230] Art. 8(2) of the SADC Protocol on Trade.

arbitrarily or unjustifiably discriminate between Member States or are not disguised restrictions on intra-SADC trade. Leticia Anthea Grimett argues, starting from a contestable premise, that "although the general exceptions clause contains a proviso which aims to prevent protectionism between contracting Member States, the fact that it provides for the application of these quantitative restrictions between Member States at all, could be interpreted as an infringement of Article XXIV (8)(b)."[231] GATT aims to eliminate quantitative restrictions in Article XI: General Elimination of Quantitative Restrictions. Article XI(1) reads, "No prohibitions or restrictions other than duties, taxes or other charges, whether made effective through quotas, import or export licences or other measures, shall be instituted or maintained by any contracting party on the importation of any product of the territory of any other contracting party or on the exportation or sale for export of any product destined for the territory of any other contracting party."[232] Article XI(2) lists specific exceptions when quantitative restrictions may be allowed, and Article XX lists general exceptions in similar language as that found in Article 9 of the SADC Trade Protocol. Quantitative restrictions are discouraged because they "reduce imports, so that domestic demand pushes up domestic prices until the gap between domestic demand and supply is equal to the quota."[233] Tariffs are preferred because a tariff "adds to the import price, reducing domestic demand and increasing domestic supply, so that imports are less."[234] Tariffs also yield government revenue, can be used to reduce monopolies on domestic industries, and allows for increased imports in certain circumstances that would be to the benefit of the domestic economy.

However, the claim that the SADC Protocol on trade somehow violates the provisions of Article XXIV of GATT is not well founded. Such a claim is based on textual comparisons, no conduct pursuant to the Protocol that is violative of any GATT provision is available. Second, the enabling clause provides independent justification for LDC regional trade agreements well outside of Article XXIV and that argument has not been persuasively dismissed except by reference to GATT as a Constitution. Even if GATT was to be regarded as a trade Constitution, and I have no problems with that, the interpretations of Article XXIV are so contested that they provide no benchmark at all for assessing whether particular provisions of a regional trade treaty are consistent with Article XXIV or not. Moreover, such provisions are indicative of the built-in flexibility in African regional trade agreements allowing for variable geometry. As I noted at the beginning of the

[231] Grimett, Protectionism and Compliance with the GATT Article XXIV in Selected Regional Trade Arrangements, pp. 221–222, available at: http://eprints.ru.ac.za/208/01/grimett-thesis.pdf.

[232] See Article XI(1) GATT, available at: http://www.wto.org/english/docs_e/legal_e/gatt47_01_e.htm#articleXI.

[233] See Quantitative Restrictions on Trade, a revised paper presented at the Seventh Trade Policy Coordinating Meeting of CAREC on 6 September 2007, p. 2, available at: http://www.carecprogram.org/uploads/docs/Quantitative-Restrictions-Trade.pdf.

[234] See Quantitative Restrictions on Trade, a revised paper presented at the Seventh Trade Policy Coordinating Meeting of CAREC on 6 September 2007, p. 2, available at: http://www.carecprogram.org/uploads/docs/Quantitative-Restrictions-Trade.pdf.

essay, variable geometry allows Member States to have flexibility in implementing time-tabled commitments as a way of accounting for variations in priorities between Member States within a particular RTA.

As a further example of this flexibility, the Protocol on Trade calls for the gradual reduction of tariffs through a phase-down period. All goods are broken down into four categories of tariffs: A, B, C and E. In Category A, all tariff lines are immediately eliminated from the date of implementation. For Category B goods, the principle of asymmetry applies. In this category, the SACU countries (South Africa, Botswana, Lesotho, Namibia, and Swaziland) reduce their tariff lines by equal installments from year 1 to year 8, Mauritius and Zimbabwe reduce their tariff lines by equal installments from year 4 to year 8, and the MMTZ countries (Malawi, Mozambique, Tanzania and Zambia) reduce their tariff lines by equal installments from year 6 to year 8. Category C applies to sensitive goods, which are goods of economic importance to the Member States. Tariff reduction on these goods starts after the 8-year period. Sensitive goods represent 15 % or less of tariff lines. Category E consists of very few goods that are excluded from the tariff reduction scheme, such as fire arms.[235] The Protocol on Trade provides that Member States should implement policies and measures to eliminate all forms of existing non-tariff barriers, and refrain from imposing new non-tariff barriers, in relation to intra-SADC trade.[236]

With regard to GATT Article XXIV (5)(b), Grimett argues that the SADC Trade Protocol is compliant.[237] Article XXIV(5)(b) requires an agreement leading to the formation of a free trade area not to raise or increase the restrictiveness of duties or regulations on trade with third countries that existed in the territories before the agreement or formation of the free trade area. Member States have agreed not to raise import duties beyond those that were in existence before the Trade Protocol and have also agreed not to grant less favourable treatment to third countries than they give to Member States where export duties and quantitative export restrictions are applied. These undertakings ensure that protectionism in trade with third countries will be minimal.

The Trade Protocol allows for Member States to apply for an extension to eliminate tariffs and non-tariff barriers to trade if they may be or have been adversely affected by the removal of tariffs and non-tariff barriers to trade.[238] As most of the countries, excluding South Africa, that are members of SADC are classified as developing or least-developed economies, it is not unpredictable that most will need an extension to eliminate substantially all trade barriers. However, the time period for the removal of tariffs and non-tariff barriers, according to the

[235] See the SADC FTA Brochure, p. 7, available at: http://www.sadc.int/english/regional-integration/tifi/sadc-free-trade-area/documents-and-resources/fta-brochure/.

[236] See Art. 6 of the SADC Protocol on Trade.

[237] Grimett, Protectionism and Compliance with the GATT Article XXIV in Selected Regional Trade Arrangements, p. 222, available at: http://eprints.ru.ac.za/208/01/grimett-thesis.pdf.

[238] See Art. 3(1)(c) of the SADC Protocol on Trade.

Trade Protocol, is 8 years. Thus an extension of 2 years can be granted and still conform to the provisions of GATT Article XXIV(5)(c). The Understanding on the Interpretation of Article XXIV of GATT 1994 provides that a reasonable period of time is 10 years, except in exceptional cases. In such circumstances, the country may apply for an extension to the Council for Trade in Goods. Because this provision is similar to that found in Article 3(1)(c) of the SADC Trade Protocol, and because an extension longer than 2 years is likely to be necessary only in exceptional cases, the "extension of the period for eliminating tariffs and non-tariff barriers is not an infringement of Article XXIV."[239]

The Protocol on trade was signed in 1996 and the implementation of the SADC free trade area began in 2000. The liberalisation of tariffs has taken place at different rates, generally the developed countries reducing tariffs at a faster rate. Three countries, namely South Africa, Botswana and Namibia, removed most tariffs in 2000. Middle income countries, such as Mauritius, have gradually reduced their tariffs each year between 2000 and 2008. For least developed countries, such as Mozambique and Zambia, tariff reductions have generally been introduced during 2007–2008.[240]

SADC attained the status of a free trade area in January of 2008. Since then, producers and consumers have paid no import tariffs on an estimated 85 % of all trade in Community goods in the initial 12 countries.[241] The remaining tariff lines will be eliminated by 2012.[242] The Member States have agreed to remove all non-tariff barriers and not impose any new restrictions, but removal of import and export restrictions has proved difficult and little progress has been made.[243] The reason for this is that non-tariff barriers often arise from policies that are not intended to restrict imports. For example, an outbreak of Foot and Mouth Disease may result in restrictions on the exportation of animals, meat and meat products originating in the affected area. However, such a restriction may fall within the general exceptions listed in Article 9 of the Protocol on Trade. Article 9 allows measures to be taken, as long as they are "not applied in a manner which would constitute a means of arbitrary or unjustifiable discrimination between Member States, or a disguised restriction on intra-SADC trade," if they are

a) Necessary to protect public morals or to maintain public order;
b) Necessary to protect human, animal or plant life or health;
c) Necessary to secure compliance with laws and regulations which are consistent with the provisions of the WTO;
d) Necessary to protect intellectual property rights, or to prevent deceptive trade practices;

---

[239] Grimett, Protectionism and Compliance with the GATT Article XXIV in Selected Regional Trade Arrangements, p. 222, available at: http://eprints.ru.ac.za/208/01/grimett-thesis.pdf.

[240] See the SADC FTA Web Site, available at: http://www.sadc.int/fta.

[241] See the SADC FTA Web Site, available at: http://www.sadc.int/fta.

[242] See the SADC FTA Brochure, p. 7.

[243] See the SADC FTA Leaflet, available at: http://www.sadc.int/english/regional-integration/tifi/sadc-free-trade-area/documents-and-resources/fta-leaflet/.

e) Relating to transfer of gold, silver, precious and semi-precious stones, including precious and strategic metals;
f) Imposed for the protection of national treasures of artistic, historic or archaeological value;
g) Necessary to prevent or relieve critical shortages of foodstuffs in any exporting Member State;
h) Relating to the conservation of exhaustible natural resources and the environment; or
i) Necessary to ensure compliance with existing obligations under international agreements.[244]

To solve the problem of eliminating non-tariff barriers, SADC is establishing a Trade Monitoring and Compliance Mechanism (TMCM) for monitoring the implementation of the free trade area with a specific mechanism for identifying and eliminating non-tariff barriers. "This mechanism has the potential to facilitate the movement of goods and will lead to increased trade."[245] Another concern is that the rules of origin have become increasingly restrictive and product-specific, resulting in increased administrative costs and making it more difficult for exporters to take advantage of SADC preferences.[246]

The next goal to be achieved is the establishment of a customs union that was expected to be established by 2010, which includes a common external tariff and the harmonisation of behind-the-border policies. The main challenges facing the transition from a free trade area are effective implementation, full participation by members and full engagement of the region's business community, and the public in general.[247] The Secretariat has concentrated on conducting studies leading to preparations for negotiations on the formation of the customs union, the first two focusing on the model of the customs union and the compatibility of trade policies. The SADC Council of Ministers has approved the establishment of technical working groups that will initiate work in key areas leading to the formation of the customs union including a common external tariff, revenue collection, and the harmonisation of agricultural, industrial, infrastructure, competition, and other sectoral policies.[248]

The membership of some SADC countries in the South African Customs Union, (SACU), which as a customs union is at a more advanced stage of integration than SADC, makes it necessary for all SADC Member States to reach the level of that

[244] Art. 9 of the SADC Protocol on Trade.

[245] See the SADC FTA Leaflet.

[246] Khandelwal, COMESA and SADC: Prospects and Challenges for Regional Trade Integration, IMF Working Paper WP/04/227, December 2004, p. 12, available at: http://www.imf.org/external/pubs/ft/wp/2004/wp04227.pdf.

[247] African Union, Status of Integration in Africa, p. 58, para. 198, available at: http://www.africa-union.org/root/ua/conferences/2009/mai/ea/07-08mai/status%20of%20integration%20in%20africa%2027-04-09.pdf.

[248] U.N. Economic Commission for Africa, Assessing Regional Integration in Africa, Part IV, pp. 14–15, available at: http://www.uneca.org/eca_resources/Publications/books/aria4/ARIA4Full.pdf.

customs union before the SADC Customs Union can be launched.[249] The membership of several SADC Member countries in COMESA, which established a customs union in June 2009, poses additional challenges because several SADC countries now concurrently belong to two customs unions with two different common external tariffs and different tariff schedules. Furthermore, overlapping membership has other negative consequences such as duplication of efforts, conflicting duties and obligations and spreading scarce human and financial resources too thinly, resulting in less than full participation and compliance.[250] Thus, there is a need for all of the RECs in the region to collaborate and possibly merge in order to move the integration process forward. To this end, SADC formed a Joint Task Force with COMESA in 2001 in order to harmonise their trade liberalisation policies. The Joint Task Force was expanded in 2007 with the inclusion of EAC, which had adopted a common external tariff and became a customs union in 2005. The first Tripartite Summit was held in Kampala, Uganda in 2008 and efforts to form an EAC, SADC and COMESA FTA are well underway as we saw earlier in the chapter. Such an FTA would be a step towards resolving the issue of overlapping membership and advancing integration in the region. Along with the issue of overlapping membership, challenges to the process of deepening regional integration that face the region include differentiated levels of economic integration within the region, the varied pace of implementation, inadequate infrastructure, and capacity constraints at both the Member States and the regional/Secretariat levels.[251]

The Regional Indicative Strategic Development Plan (RISDP), launched in August 2004, was designed to provide strategic direction for the SADC programmes and projects by aligning the objectives and priorities with the policies and strategies that are to be pursued in order to achieve these objectives over a 15 year period.[252] Most of the SADC policies and programmes were designed by independent sectoral committees and thus lacked coordination and had weak inter-sectoral linkages.[253] The RISDP identifies and strengthens linkages between the programmes and policies of the various sectors in order to improve efficiency and the effective implementation of the SADC Program of Action.[254] Indicative in nature, the RISDP outlines the necessary conditions to be attained towards the goal

[249] African Union, Status of Integration in Africa, p. 64, para. 216, available at: http://www.africa-union.org/root/ua/conferences/2009/mai/ea/07-08mai/status%20of%20integration%20in%20africa%2027-04-09.pdf.

[250] Khandelwal, COMESA and SADC: Prospects and Challenges for Regional Trade Integration, IMF Working Paper WP/04/227, December 2004, p. 14.

[251] African Union, Status of Integration in Africa, p. 65, para. 221.

[252] SADC Regional Indicative Strategic Development Plan, Chapter 1, § 6, available at: http://www.sadc.int/index/browse/page/104.

[253] SADC Regional Indicative Strategic Development Plan, Chapter 1, § 6, available at: http://www.sadc.int/index/browse/page/104.

[254] SADC Regional Indicative Strategic Development Plan, Chapter 1, § 6, available at: http://www.sadc.int/index/browse/page/104.

of regional integration and development, setting four targets to be reached within a reasonable and feasible time frame that takes into account constraints particular to the region.[255] The RISDP recognises the need for a flexible approach to the implementation of policy reforms and deepening regional integration due to the differences existing between Member countries.[256] Such flexibility is a central element of African RTAs.

The objectives of the Strategic Plan include enhancing economic competitiveness and the diversification of production structures and exports through the promotion of intra-regional trade, productive investment and technology cooperation.[257] The ultimate goal to be achieved through the stages of economic integration is the formation of an economic union. Towards this end, SADC drafted a Competition Policy Model and finalised the harmonisation framework expected to have been put in place by 2009 for implementation by 2010.[258] The Model, by removing barriers to competition, is to create conditions that will enable markets to function competitively to the benefit of consumers and businesses alike.[259]

SADC is working towards the establishment of a customs union. The formation of a customs union poses difficulties because the varying levels and complexity of tariff structures of individual Member countries will make it difficult to formulate a common external tariff.[260] Another difficulty facing the establishment of a common external tariff regime is harmonising the different rationales behind individual countries use of tariffs, as some are heavily dependent on customs duties for government revenue while others primarily use tariffs as protectionist measures with respect to sensitive sectors or as a part of their industrial policy goals.[261] A customs revenue collection, disbursal and sharing mechanism needs to be created in

[255] SADC Regional Indicative Strategic Development Plan, Chapter 1, § 6, available at: http://www.sadc.int/index/browse/page/104.

[256] SADC Regional Indicative Strategic Development Plan, Chapter 1, § 6, available at: http://www.sadc.int/index/browse/page/104.

[257] SADC Regional Indicative Strategic Development Plan, Annex Table 4.10, Trade and Economic Liberalization and Development, available at: http://www.sadc.int/index/browse/page/104.

[258] African Union, Status of Integration in Africa, p. 66, para. 227, available at: http://www.africa-union.org/root/ua/conferences/2009/mai/ea/07-08mai/status%20of%20integration%20in%20africa%2027-04-09.pdf.

[259] African Union, Status of Integration in Africa, p. 66, para. 227, available at: http://www.africa-union.org/root/ua/conferences/2009/mai/ea/07-08mai/status%20of%20integration%20in%20africa%2027-04-09.pdf.

[260] Elago/Kalenga, Whither the SADC Customs Union?, Monitoring Regional Integration Yearbook 2007, 2008, p. 8, available at: http://www.garnet.sciencespobordeaux.fr/Garnet%20papers%20PDF/ELAGO%20Paulina%20&%20KALENGA%20Paul.pdf.

[261] Elago/Kalenga, Whither the SADC Customs Union?, Monitoring Regional Integration Yearbook 2007, 2008, pp. 8–9, available at: http://www.garnet.sciencespobordeaux.fr/Garnet%20papers%20PDF/ELAGO%20Paulina%20&%20KALENGA%20Paul.pdf.

order to mitigate the effects of the adoption of a common external tariff policy.[262] Progress towards establishing a customs union is also hampered by overlapping membership in multiple RECs. To resolve these issues, the three RECs in the region, COMESA, SADC and EAC, met in October 2008 and agreed to form a larger free trade area, encompassing the three organisations, leading eventually to the formation of a single customs union.[263] At the 2008 meeting, the Heads of State and Government of the three RECs also agreed to develop a roadmap towards the goal of establishing the enlarged free trade area and directed the three groups to accelerate the development of joint programmes to enhance cooperation and coordination in industrial and competition policies.[264] With overlapping membership and its consequences in mind, SADC made a decision in 2009 to delay the establishment of a customs union.[265] However, SADC has failed to reach the revised deadline for adopting a customs union and it is reported that the ministerial task force on regional integration will discuss the protocol in December of 2011.[266] It has been agreed that there is a need to first continue with the consolidation of the SADC free trade area, with particular emphasis on coordinating and furthering the development of the SADC-EAC-COMESA Tripartite free trade area.[267] Another issue that has delayed the implementation of the SADC customs union is the membership of five SADC Members in SACU and the ensuing complications over the adoption of a common external tariff. Since SACU is already at the level of a customs union, the two trade blocs must work closely with one another to create complementary policies and to advance all SADC Members to the level of the SACU Members.

The SADC has made little progress as well towards the implementation of its Protocol on the Facilitation of Movement of Persons—out of the fifteen SADC Members, only nine have signed it and a mere four have ratified it.[268] Since the

[262] Elago/Kalenga, Whither the SADC Customs Union?, Monitoring Regional Integration Yearbook 2007, 2008, p. 12, available at: http://www.garnet.sciencespobordeaux.fr/Garnet%20papers%20PDF/ELAGO%20Paulina%20&%20KALENGA%20Paul.pdf.

[263] U.N. Economic Commission for Africa, Assessing Regional Integration in Africa, Part IV, p. 16.

[264] U.N. Economic Commission for Africa, Assessing Regional Integration in Africa, Part IV, p. 16.

[265] Bursvik, et al., Supporting Regional Integration in East and Southern Africa—Review of Select Issues, 2010, available at: http://www.tralac.org/2010/05/18/supporting-regional-integration-in-east-and-southern-africa-review-of-select-issues/.

[266] Botswana Press Agency, "SADC Fails to Meet Deadline", Trade Law Centre for Southern Africa, 19 August 2010, available at: http://www.tralac.org/2010/08/19/sadc-fails-to-meet-deadline/.

[267] Botswana Press Agency, "SADC Fails to Meet Deadline", Trade Law Centre for Southern Africa, 19 August 2010, available at: http://www.tralac.org/2010/08/19/sadc-fails-to-meet-deadline/.

[268] Bursvik et al., Supporting Regional Integration in East and Southern Africa—Review of Select Issues, 2010, p. 21, available at: http://www.tralac.org/2010/05/18/supporting-regional-integration-in-east-and-southern-africa-review-of-select-issues/.

2009 Meeting of the SADC Ministers of Foreign Affairs Council, the organisation has taken significant steps towards facilitating the free movement of goods and services as well, such as harmonising customs procedures and instruments such as the electronic exchange of customs data, adopting a single customs administrative document, the SADC CD, to streamline customs declarations within the region, creating a nomenclature of common tariffs, reviewing the rules of origin, and coordinating trade liberalisation through the tripartite task force between COMESA, EAC and SADC.[269] Trade policies must be harmonised and infrastructure must be improved to enhance market access and promote intra-regional trade in order to achieve deeper regional integration and sustainable development.

SADC now aims for the establishment of a customs union in 2012 when all its Member States' tariff regimes are expected to be liberalised.[270] SADC reportedly has liberalised 85 % of trade and is now in the process of phasing down tariffs for trade in sensitive goods.[271] Slowing down the process of becoming a full free trade area is the fact that not all SADC Member States are members of the free trade area, and three unnamed SADC Members that are members of the free trade area have requested extensions or deferrals of the phase-down schedule for sensitive products.[272] The organisation's pattern of delaying and extending deadlines could develop into a serious problem because Members may begin to think that they are not being held fully accountable and can renege on commitments without serious consequences. In order to prevent this mindset within the region, SADC must establish an effective implementation and monitoring mechanism whereby Members are held accountable for commitments and progress is monitored to ensure accomplishment of set goals.

Southern African Customs Union

The Southern African Customs Union (SACU), the world's oldest custom union, was initially formed as a result of the 1889 Customs Union Convention between the British Colony of Cape of Good Hope and the Orange Free State Boer Republic.[273] A new agreement, signed on 29 June 1910, was in effect until 1969. The primary goal of the customs territory was to promote economic

[269] Bursvik et al., Supporting Regional Integration in East and Southern Africa—Review of Select Issues, 2010, p. 21, available at: http://www.tralac.org/2010/05/18/supporting-regional-integration-in-east-and-southern-africa-review-of-select-issues/.

[270] Njini, SADC Limps Towards a Common Market, Trade Law Centre for Southern Africa, 13 August 2010, available at: http://www.tralac.org/2010/08/13/sadc-limps-towards-a-common-market/.

[271] Njini, SADC Limps Towards a Common Market, Trade Law Centre for Southern Africa, 13 August 2010, available at: http://www.tralac.org/2010/08/13/sadc-limps-towards-a-common-market/.

[272] Njini, SADC Limps Towards a Common Market, Trade Law Centre for Southern Africa, 13 August 2010, available at: http://www.tralac.org/2010/08/13/sadc-limps-towards-a-common-market/.

[273] SACU, History of SACU, available at: http://www.sacu.int/about.php?id=394.

development through the regional coordination of trade.[274] The 1910 agreement created a common external tariff on goods imported into the region from third countries, the free movement within the region of SACU manufactured products without any duties or quantitative restrictions, and a revenue-sharing formula for the distribution of customs and excise revenues collected by the SACU.[275] During the period where the 1910 agreement was in force, South Africa administrated the common SACU revenue pool, set SACU import duties and set excise policy.[276] After issues arose from the inequitable revenue sharing and structural issues of management and decision-making processes came into play, the British High Commission Territories called for a revision of the 1910 agreement, and negotiations began after the British High Commission Territories gained their independence in the 1960's.[277] The new agreement was signed on 11 December 1969 by Botswana, Lesotho, Swaziland and South Africa. Two major changes provided in the 1969 agreement were the inclusion of excise duties in the revenue pool and a multiplier in the revenue-sharing formula that enhanced Botswana, Lesotho and Swaziland revenues each year by 42 %.[278] However, problems similar to those under the 1910 agreement arose, particularly regarding South Africa's sole decision-making power over customs and excise policies.[279] Concerns over the fairness of the revenue-sharing formula still existed, and negotiations to reform the 1969 agreement began after the democratic transition in South Africa in November of 1994, culminating in the creation of a new agreement that was signed on 21 October 2002.[280]

The 2002 agreement, which entered into force on 16 July 2004, addressed several issues that had plagued the customs territory since its inception. First, the 2002 agreement established an independent Administrative Secretariat, with headquarters in Windhoek, Namibia, which was designed to oversee SACU.[281] Several other independent institutions were also created under the 2002 agreement in order to establish a system of joint decision-making processes where each member country participated equally.[282] Additionally, policy coordination in several areas, including agriculture, industry, competition, unfair trade practices, and protection of infant industries, was provided for in the 2002 agreement.[283] Second, the revenue-sharing formula was revised to include a customs excise and development

[274] SACU, History of SACU, available at: http://www.sacu.int/about.php?id=394.

[275] SACU, History of SACU, available at: http://www.sacu.int/about.php?id=394.

[276] SACU, History of SACU, available at: http://www.sacu.int/about.php?id=394.

[277] SACU, History of SACU, available at: http://www.sacu.int/about.php?id=394.

[278] SACU, History of SACU, available at: http://www.sacu.int/about.php?id=394.

[279] SACU, History of SACU, available at: http://www.sacu.int/about.php?id=394.

[280] SACU, History of SACU, available at: http://www.sacu.int/about.php?id=394.

[281] See Art. 3, 10 of the 2002 Southern African Customs Union Agreement, available at: http://www.sacu.int/main.php?include=docs/legislation/2002-agreement/part3.html.

[282] SACU, History of SACU, available at: http://www.sacu.int/about.php?id=394.

[283] SACU, History of SACU, available at: http://www.sacu.int/about.php?id=394.

component.[284] Under the 2002 agreement, South Africa was to manage the Common Revenue Pool for a transitional period of 2 years, after which a Member State or a SACU institution is to be appointed by the Council to manage the Pool.[285] Finally, the question of external trade was addressed, such as the need to develop strategies that enhance the region's political, social, economic and cultural integration while simultaneously taking into consideration the protection of the economies of the smaller Member States.[286]

In addition to addressing several outstanding issues, the 2002 agreement also states the objectives of SACU. Among the objectives listed in Article 2 of the 2002 agreement are the facilitation of cross-border movement of goods between Member States; the promotion of conditions of fair competition in the customs territory; to increase substantially the economic development, diversification, industrialisation and competitiveness of its members; the promotion of Member States' integration into the global economy through enhanced trade and investment; and the facilitation of the development of common policies and strategies.[287] The SACU Vision is to establish an "economic community with equitable and sustainable development" that is "dedicated to the welfare of its people for a common future."[288]

Part 5 of the 2002 SACU agreement sets forth the trade liberalisation scheme to be followed by SACU Member States. Goods imported into one Member State from another Member State that are grown, produced or manufactured in the region are to be free of customs duties and quantitative restrictions, although Member countries retain the right to impose restrictions on imports or exports for the protection of certain enumerated areas in accordance with national legislation and regulations.[289] Additionally, Members are not allowed to impose any duties on goods originally imported to a Member from outside the region upon the importation of such goods into a Member State.[290] On the recommendation of the Tariff Board, the Council is to approve customs duties that are to be applied to goods imported into the region from outside the area.[291] Further, Members are to apply identical rebates, refunds or drawbacks of customs duties on imported goods.[292]

In SACU, the trade facilitation programme is a comprehensive and integrated approach aimed towards developing a predictable, transparent, and consistent system where international trade transactions are completed. It covers all of the steps necessary to facilitate the free movement of goods across borders. Trade

[284] SACU, History of SACU, available at: http://www.sacu.int/about.php?id=394.

[285] Art. 33(1),(3) of the 2002 SACU Agreement.

[286] SACU, History of SACU.

[287] Art. 2 of the 2002 SACU Agreement.

[288] SACU, About SACU: Vision and Mission, available at: http://www.sacu.int/about.php?id=395.

[289] Art. 18 of the 2002 SACU Agreement.

[290] Art. 19 of the 2002 SACU Agreement.

[291] Art. 20(1) of the 2002 SACU Agreement.

[292] Art. 20(2) of the 2002 SACU Agreement.

facilitation in SACU is based on "internationally accepted norms and practices resulting from the simplification of formalities and procedures; the standardisation and improvement of physical infrastructure and facilities and the harmonisation of applicable laws and regulations."[293] Ultimately, trade facilitation aims to reduce transaction costs and the complexity of international trade as well as to improve the region's trading environment while optimising efficient, effective levels of governmental control and revenue collection.[294] One of SACU's primary objectives is to facilitate the cross-border movement of goods between Member States, and accordingly, the 2002 agreement provides for freedom of transit across Members' territories and the non-discrimination of transport operators from within the region.[295] The 2002 SACU agreement requires the application of similar legislation regarding customs and excise duties, customs cooperation, use of common customs documentation and common procedures and practices.[296]

Under the 2002 agreement, SACU Member States are obliged to take appropriate measures to ensure that the provisions of the agreement are effectively and harmoniously applied, including arrangements regarding customs cooperation, and Members must also take such measures as are necessary to facilitate the simplification and harmonisation of trade procedures and documentation.[297] SACU countries must apply similar legislation with regard to customs and excise duties.[298]

The 2002 SACU agreement provides for the freedom of transit of goods consigned to and from the territories of other Member States, without discrimination. However, a Member may impose conditions upon such transit as are deemed necessary to protect its legitimate interests respecting goods whose importation into the Member country is prohibited on certain grounds, such as public morals, health or security, or in pursuance of a multilateral international agreement where the Member is a party.[299] Further, under the 2002 agreement, SACU Member States "recognize the right of each Member State to prohibit or restrict the importation into or exportation from its area of any goods for economic, social, cultural or other reasons as may be agreed upon by the Council."[300] This provision does not permit the prohibition or restriction on imports of goods grown, produced or manufactured in other Member countries for the purpose of protecting the Member's own industries producing such goods.[301] The SACU Members commit to refrain from subjecting the transit of goods through their territory to transport rate discrimination by public authorities, and undertake to ensure that tariffs applicable within each

[293] SACU, Trade Facilitation: Overview, available at: http://www.sacu.int/tradef.php?id=405.
[294] SACU, Trade Facilitation: Overview, available at: http://www.sacu.int/tradef.php?id=405.
[295] Art. 2, 24, 27 of the 2002 SACU Agreement.
[296] SACU, Trade Facilitation: Overview, available at: http://www.sacu.int/tradef.php?id=405.
[297] Art. 23 of the 2002 SACU Agreement.
[298] Art. 22 of the 2002 SACU Agreement.
[299] Art. 24 of the 2002 SACU Agreement.
[300] Art. 25(1) of the 2002 SACU Agreement.
[301] Art. 25(3) of the 2002 SACU Agreement.

Member's territory to the conveyance of goods by publicly-owned transport to and from other Members' countries are equally favourable as the tariffs applicable to the carriage of similar goods within such Member's area.[302]

Under the 2002 agreement, Member States are permitted to maintain preferential trade and other similar arrangements that are in existence at the time the agreement enters into force, although Members are not allowed to negotiate or enter into new preferential trade arrangements with third parties or to amend existing arrangements without the other Members' consent.[303] For the purpose of undertaking negotiations with third parties, a common negotiating mechanism is to be established by the Member States.[304]

The 2002 SACU agreement permits the Government of Botswana, Lesotho, Namibia or Swaziland to temporarily levy additional duties on imported goods in order to enable infant industries within its territory to meet competition from other producers and manufactures in the SACU region if such duties are levied equally on goods grown, produced or manufactured in the region and similar products originating externally.[305] This provision applies irrespective of whether externally-produced goods are imported directly or from another Member State. The term 'infant industry' as used in the agreement refers to an industry that has been established in a Member State's territory for no longer than 8 years, and the protection of such infant industries is to last for a period of 8 years.[306]

In an effort to promote trade facilitation and modernise customs administrations, a consultation process was initiated in 2007 between SACU Member States and the World Customs Organization (WCO).[307] The focus of the consultation was on the identification of priority areas of intervention to be regionally implemented, which culminated in the formation of a comprehensive Customs Development programme for SACU. This programme was adopted by the SACU Council of Ministers in December of 2008. The Customs Development programme builds on the progress achieved under the five Customs Initiatives pursued by SACU since 2004. The programme's ultimate objective is to contribute to the development of a sustainable and improved economy with respect to trade, security and social protection. This is to be accomplished through the development of Customs Authorities, which are to be fair and effective trade management partners; the development of revenue collection services and modern social protection; assisting SACU Members in complying with international customs instruments; and modernising the Member

[302] Art. 27 of the 2002 SACU Agreement.

[303] Art. 31(1),(3) of the 2002 SACU Agreement.

[304] Art. 31(2) of the 2002 SACU Agreement.

[305] Art. 26(1) of the 2002 SACU Agreement.

[306] Art. 26(2),(3) of the 2002 SACU Agreement. The protection accorded to infant industries under the 2002 SACU agreement is to last for an eight year period unless "otherwise determined by the Council."

[307] SACU, Trade Facilitation: SACU-WCO Customs Development Programme, available at: http://www.sacu.int/tradef.php?id=472.

States' respective customs administrations.[308] Specifically, the programme aims to assist the Customs Authorities in designing and implementing a comprehensive regional reform programme, focusing on various areas, including regional customs policy, customs legislation, risk management, trade partnerships, standard operating procedures in the region, and information technology connectivity.[309] It is envisaged that once the programme is successfully completed and incorporated, SACU as a whole and individual Member countries will realise benefits such as reduced costs to governments and traders; predictability and transparency in procedures and legislative requirements; increased competitiveness of regional firms; improved cooperation and collaboration with various stakeholders; and sustainable customs reform and modernisation efforts in the region.[310]

One of the problems consistently plaguing SACU is the high degree of inequality in the levels of economic development between the Member States. South Africa has traditionally dominated the region and such dominance has been reflected in SACU's history, particularly South Africa's sole decision-making power over trade and industrial policies and its control and management of the revenue-sharing formula and the Common Revenue Pool. South Africa's dominance in the region is reflected in SACU's statistics, for example during the period studied in the 2009 WTO Trade Policy Review, South Africa accounted for over 90 % of the area's GDP.[311] As of November 2009, the only trade policy instruments that have been harmonised are the applied customs tariff; excuse duties; duty rebates, refunds and drawbacks; customs valuation; non-preferential rules of origin; and contingency trade remedies.[312] While the common external tariff has been somewhat simplified since 2003, internal taxes such as the value-added tax as well as customs procedures must also be harmonised in order to foster economic integration.[313] The 2009 WTO Trade Policy Review suggests that the complete implementation of the 2002 agreement would result in the further harmonisation of policies, deeper economic

[308] SACU, Trade Facilitation: SACU-WCO Customs Development Programme, available at: http://www.sacu.int/tradef.php?id=472.

[309] SACU, Trade Facilitation: SACU-WCO Customs Development Programme, available at: http://www.sacu.int/tradef.php?id=472.

[310] SACU, Trade Facilitation: SACU-WCO Customs Development Programme, available at: http://www.sacu.int/tradef.php?id=472.

[311] WTO, Trade Policy Review, Report by the Secretariat: Southern African Customs Union, WT/TPR/S/222, 30 September 2009, para. 1, available at: http://www.wto.org/english/tratop_e/tpr_e/tp322_e.htm.

[312] WTO, Trade Policy Review, Report by the Secretariat: Southern African Customs Union, WT/TPR/S/222, 30 September 2009, para. 4, available at: http://www.wto.org/english/tratop_e/tpr_e/tp322_e.htm.

[313] WTO, Trade Policy Review, Report by the Secretariat: Southern African Customs Union, WT/TPR/S/222, 30 September 2009, para. 73, available at: http://www.wto.org/english/tratop_e/tpr_e/tp322_e.htm.

integration, and more balanced development.[314] In an effort to further harmonise trade policy, SACU Members have agreed to negotiate new preferential trade arrangements with third parties as a group.[315]

SACU has made little progress on regional integration since the signing of the 2002 agreement. The 2002 agreement called for the establishment of several institutions to form a more democratic organisation, yet institutions such as the SACU Tariff Board, the Common Negotiating Mechanism and the Ad Hoc Tribunal have yet to become operational.[316] Furthermore, the 2002 agreement calls for the adoption of joint policies, but no common SACU policies are currently in place.[317] At the July 2010 Summit of the SACU Heads of State, it was agreed that SACU will work on strengthening internal matters, such as ensuring that all agreements on industrial, agricultural and competition policies, unfair trade practices and other priority commitments in the 2002 agreement are being implemented.[318] The Heads of State decided that policies and procedures must be developed that will lead to the establishment of competent institutions. It was further agreed that a SACU trade and tariff policy should be developed, along with a trade strategy that supports industrialisation within the region and initiatives to promote intra-regional trade.[319]

A step has been taken by one SACU Member towards the goal of establishing the SACU Tariff Board, which under the 2002 agreement is to make recommendations to be approved or denied by the Council as to the level and changes of customs, anti-dumping, countervailing and safeguard duties on goods imported from outside the region.[320] Each Member State is to establish a national body, whose function is to conduct preliminary investigations and to make recommendations to the Tariff Board regarding any tariff changes.[321] These national bodies are to be established by April of 2011. Botswana is expected to become the first SACU Member to

---

[314] WTO, Trade Policy Review, Report by the Secretariat: Southern African Customs Union, WT/TPR/S/222, 30 September 2009, para. 4, available at: http://www.wto.org/english/tratop_e/tpr_e/tp322_e.htm.

[315] WTO, Trade Policy Review, Report by the Secretariat: Southern African Customs Union, WT/TPR/S/222, 30 September 2009, para. 8, available at: http://www.wto.org/english/tratop_e/tpr_e/tp322_e.htm.; see also Art. 31(3) of the 2002 SACU Agreement.

[316] Erasmus, Will SACU Have a Permanent Summit?, Trade Law Centre for Southern Africa, 11 May 2010, available at: http://www.tralac.org/2010/05/11/will-sacu-have-a-permanent-summit/.

[317] Erasmus, Will SACU Have a Permanent Summit?, Trade Law Centre for Southern Africa, 11 May 2010, available at: http://www.tralac.org/2010/05/11/will-sacu-have-a-permanent-summit/.

[318] Heita, SACU Advocates Win-Win Solution on EPA Negotiations, Trade Law Centre for Southern Africa, 20 July 2010, available at: http://www.tralac.org/2010/07/20/sacu-advocates-win-win-solution-on-epa-negotiations/.

[319] Heita, SACU Advocates Win-Win Solution on EPA Negotiations, Trade Law Centre for Southern Africa, 20 July 2010, available at: http://www.tralac.org/2010/07/20/sacu-advocates-win-win-solution-on-epa-negotiations/.

[320] Art. 8(2) of the 2002 SACU Agreement.

[321] Art. 14(1) of the 2002 SACU Agreement.

establish such a national body.[322] Botswana's national body will be responsible for various trade issues, such as investigating and evaluating applications for alleged dumping or subsidised exports into the country, instituting safeguard measures, amending customs duties, determining eligibility for infant industry protection, regulating the import and export of restricted goods, and making recommendations to the SACU Tariff Board.[323] The Tariff Board was to have been established by March of 2009, but is not yet currently operational. Other issues, such as EPA negotiations with the EU and dealing with the global recession, have taken the stage and pushed the implementation of the 2002 agreement to the back burner.[324] The organisation's centenary celebration this year has brought renewed vigor to the issue of regional integration and efforts will hopefully be made towards implementing the 2002 agreement, especially regarding the establishment of effectively functioning institutions.

Differences between the SACU Member States' policies have been exacerbated by the recent EPA negotiations with the EU and the signing of an interim EPA by three of the SACU Members—Botswana, Lesotho, and Swaziland. The signing of the interim EPA by only a few of the Member States calls into question their commitment to the customs union, as under the 2002 agreement Members are bound to negotiate collectively with third parties.[325] However, Botswana and Namibia were faced with a difficult decision regarding their beef exports to the EU, since outside of the EPA the two countries would have to rely on a general system of preferences that does not include beef.[326] Without the EPAs, Botswana, Swaziland, and Lesotho would lose their preferential access to key European markets and aid.[327] After the Summit held on 15 and 16 July 2010, the Department of Trade and Industry chief director for multilateral relations, Xololwa Mlumbi-Peter, said that the Heads of State agreed that the organisation should take a unified approach and should continue to engage collectively in negotiations regarding the

[322] Mguni, Botswana Pioneers SACU Tariff Body, Trade Law Centre for Southern Africa, 28 July 2010, available at: http://www.tralac.org/2010/07/28/botswana-pioneers-sacu-tariff-body/.

[323] Mguni, Botswana Pioneers SACU Tariff Body, Trade Law Centre for Southern Africa, 28 July 2010, available at: http://www.tralac.org/2010/07/28/botswana-pioneers-sacu-tariff-body/.

[324] Mguni, Botswana Pioneers SACU Tariff Body, Trade Law Centre for Southern Africa, 28 July 2010, available at: http://www.tralac.org/2010/07/28/botswana-pioneers-sacu-tariff-body/.

[325] Pressly, Disappointing SACU Talks Fail to Resolve Disunity over EU Deals, Trade Law Centre for Southern Africa, 20 July 2010, available at: http://www.tralac.org/2010/07/20/disappointing-sacu-talks-fail-to-resolve-disunity-over-eu-deals/.

[326] Pressly, Disappointing SACU Talks Fail to Resolve Disunity over EU Deals, Trade Law Centre for Southern Africa, 20 July 2010, available at: http://www.tralac.org/2010/07/20/disappointing-sacu-talks-fail-to-resolve-disunity-over-eu-deals/, Beef is a key export item for both countries.

[327] Pressly, Disappointing SACU Talks Fail to Resolve Disunity over EU Deals, Trade Law Centre for Southern Africa, 20 July 2010, available at: http://www.tralac.org/2010/07/20/disappointing-sacu-talks-fail-to-resolve-disunity-over-eu-deals/.

EPAs.[328] SACU Executive Secretary Tswelopele Moremi stated that although following the principle of unified engagement in trade negotiations with third parties, the different levels of development between Member States and individual States' capacities must be taken into account. Moremi stated that "current calendars and strategic opportunities require that we do things in a different way to the benefit of all members of SACU."[329] A compromise must be reached between the SACU countries that have signed the EPA and South Africa and Namibia, who maintain that the EPAs undermine regional integration efforts and that the EU's increased access to the SACU markets will have a negative effect on the African countries' economies.[330]

The global recession has also created tensions within the group, as pressure on the budget mounts. The financial crisis has spurred South Africa to voice complaints regarding the revenue-sharing formula that is currently in place and the perception in South Africa that its customs receipts are bankrolling the smaller SACU nations.[331] Officially devised as a method of compensating the smaller SACU economies for their long-standing cessation of trade and industrial policy autonomy to South Africa, revenue sharing has been an outstanding issue within SACU for years.[332] At the July 2010 Summit, the SACU Heads of State agreed to reconsider the revenue-sharing formula.[333] South Africa wants to revise the formula so that it would retain some of the income generated by the tariffs on goods imported into its territory, although a move that would decrease the amount of revenue received by the other SACU Members under the formula would have drastic consequences for the smaller economies.[334] The four smaller SACU nations, in particular Swaziland and Lesotho who derive over half of their budget revenue

---

[328] Pressly, Disappointing SACU Talks Fail to Resolve Disunity over EU Deals, Trade Law Centre for Southern Africa, 20 July 2010, available at: http://www.tralac.org/2010/07/20/disappointing-sacu-talks-fail-to-resolve-disunity-over-eu-deals/.

[329] Heita, SACU Advocates Win-Win Solution on EPA Negotiations, Trade Law Centre for Southern Africa, 20 July 2010, available at: http://www.tralac.org/2010/07/20/sacu-advocates-win-win-solution-on-epa-negotiations/.

[330] Cohen, Southern African Leaders Hold Summit to Rescue 100-Year-Old Customs Union, Trade Law Centre for Southern Africa, 15 July 2010, available at: http://www.tralac.org/2010/07/15/southern-africa-leaders-hold-summit-to-rescue-100-year-old-customs-union/.

[331] Cropley, Southern Africa Grasps Trade Subsidy Nettle, Trade Law Centre for Southern Africa, 19 July 2010, available at: http://www.tralac.org/2010/07/19/southern-africa-grasps-trade-subsidy-nettle/.

[332] Cropley, Southern Africa Grasps Trade Subsidy Nettle, Trade Law Centre for Southern Africa, 19 July 2010, available at: http://www.tralac.org/2010/07/19/southern-africa-grasps-trade-subsidy-nettle/.

[333] Cropley, Southern Africa Grasps Trade Subsidy Nettle, Trade Law Centre for Southern Africa, 19 July 2010, available at: http://www.tralac.org/2010/07/19/southern-africa-grasps-trade-subsidy-nettle/.

[334] Erasmus, Will SACU Have a Permanent Summit?, Trade Law Centre for Southern Africa, 11 May 2010, available at: http://www.tralac.org/2010/05/11/will-sacu-have-a-permanent-summit/.

from SACU's income, are dependent upon the revenue received from the Common Revenue Pool and have already suffered from the decreased revenues due to the downturned economy.[335]

In order to rebound from its current unstable position, SACU must implement many changes. Most importantly, strong institutions where all Member States participate equally must be established and become operational to speak on behalf of SACU. These institutions must work to formulate joint policies and to harmonise existing policies in order to present a united front when dealing with third parties. The harmonisation of SACU policies with those of the other African RTAs is also important as plans for deeper integration are set in motion by the other organisations. An agreement must be reached with regard to the EPAs being negotiated with the EU that takes into account the divergent levels of economic development within the region while complying with the 2002 agreement's requirement of unified engagement with third parties in trade negotiations.

It has been mentioned that the 2002 SACU agreement may be renewed in a direction that would include areas that have previously been ignored, such as market and monetary integrations, trade in services, finance and investment, government procurement, and the environment.[336] Expanding the areas of cooperation and policy harmonisation will only serve to facilitate regional economic integration in the future. However, the organisation must first establish operational institutions that are capable of administering the trade arrangement and developing unified policies across the various areas of cooperation.

Community of Sahel-Saharan States

The Community of Sahel-Saharan States was established on 4 February 1998 in Tripoli.[337] Its six founding members are Burkina Faso, Chad, Libya, Mali, Niger and Sudan, but since its creation 22 other countries have joined its ranks.

Article I of the Treaty establishing CEN-SAD lists the overriding objective of the organisation to establish a comprehensive economic union based on

[335] Erasmus, Will SACU Have a Permanent Summit?, Trade Law Centre for Southern Africa, 11 May 2010, available at: http://www.tralac.org/2010/05/11/will-sacu-have-a-permanent-summit/; see also Cropley, Southern Africa Grasps Trade Subsidy Nettle, Trade Law Centre for Southern Africa, 19 July 2010, available at: http://www.tralac.org/2010/07/19/southern-africa-grasps-trade-subsidy-nettle/.

[336] Masinga, 2002 SACU Deal to be Renewed, Trade Law Centre for Southern Africa, 14 July 2010, available at: http://www.tralac.org/2010/07/14/2002-sacu-deal-to-be-renewed/.

[337] CEN-SAD, About CEN-SAD, available at: http://www.uneca.org/cen-sad/aboutcensad.htm#whatiscensad.

implementing a strategy based on a development plan to be integrated into the national development policies of its Member States.[338] The development plan is to include investment in the agricultural, industrial, energy, social and cultural fields.[339] All restrictions hampering the integration of the Member countries are to be removed by facilitating free movement of persons and capital and promoting the interests of the citizens of Member States, ensuring freedom of residence, employment, ownership and economic activity, and ensuring the free movement of services, goods and commodities of regional origin.[340] External trade is to be promoted through the formulation and implementation of an investment policy for Member States and increased provision is to be made for improvement to infrastructural links between Member States such as land, air and maritime transport and communications through the implementation of joint projects.[341] An agreement is to be reached giving citizens of the signatory countries equal rights, privileges and duties as provided in the Member countries' individual Constitutions, and all levels of educational and pedagogical systems—in the technical, scientific and cultural fields—are to be harmonised and coordinated.[342]

The trade liberalisation programme was launched in 1991 in accordance with the Abuja Treaty and with the technical assistance and guidance of the U.N. Economic Commission for Africa and the African Development Bank.[343] It also launched the process of facilitating the free movement of persons, goods and services, which is an important issue to CEN-SAD's major objectives and identified in the Treaty establishing the Community.[344] A protocol on free movement is planned and transitional measures that exempt holders of diplomatic and service passports and special envoys from visas are in place.[345]

---

[338] Letter from the Permanent Representative of Sudan to the United Nation, Observer Status for the Community of Sahel-Saharan States in the General Assembly, A/56/191, Annex 1, p. 2, available at: http://www.un.org/documents/ga/docs/56/a56191.pdf.

[339] Letter from the Permanent Representative of Sudan to the United Nation, Observer Status for the Community of Sahel-Saharan States in the General Assembly, A/56/191, Annex 1, p. 2, available at: http://www.un.org/documents/ga/docs/56/a56191.pdf.

[340] Letter from the Permanent Representative of Sudan to the United Nation, Observer Status for the Community of Sahel-Saharan States in the General Assembly, A/56/191, Annex 1, p. 2, available at: http://www.un.org/documents/ga/docs/56/a56191.pdf.

[341] Letter from the Permanent Representative of Sudan to the United Nation, Observer Status for the Community of Sahel-Saharan States in the General Assembly, A/56/191, Annex 1, p. 3, available at: http://www.un.org/documents/ga/docs/56/a56191.pdf.

[342] Letter from the Permanent Representative of Sudan to the United Nation, Observer Status for the Community of Sahel-Saharan States in the General Assembly, A/56/191, Annex 1, p. 3, available at: http://www.un.org/documents/ga/docs/56/a56191.pdf.

[343] U.N. Economic Commission for Africa, Assessing Regional Integration in Africa, Part IV, p. 17, available at: http://www.uneca.org/eca_resources/Publications/books/aria4/ARIA4Full.pdf.

[344] U.N. Economic Commission for Africa, Assessing Regional Integration in Africa, Part IV, p. 17, available at: http://www.uneca.org/eca_resources/Publications/books/aria4/ARIA4Full.pdf.

[345] U.N. Economic Commission for Africa, Assessing Regional Integration in Africa, Part IV, p. 18, available at: http://www.uneca.org/eca_resources/Publications/books/aria4/ARIA4Full.pdf.

CEN-SAD has concluded several partnership and cooperation agreements with the UN Economic Commission for Africa and the Permanent Inter-State Committee on Drought Control in the Sahel.[346] Since its establishment, CEN-SAD has been working towards the goal of creating a common market. To this end, the organisation has implemented a variety of sectoral programmes and policies with emphasis on some priority sectors such as infrastructure, food security, desertification control, and the promotion and facilitation of intra-regional trade.[347] At the sixth Ordinary Session of the Executive Council in 2001, the Council exchanged views on the economic integration process and considered that the steps taken by CEN-SAD should be based on a long-term global strategic plan.[348] This integration plan, it was determined, should take into consideration the needs of Member countries and the possibilities of integration of projects of goods and services production, as well as the financial resources.[349]

The second meeting of Ministers in charge of trade, held in Tunis in March 2003, recommended the creation of a free trade zone after analysing the intra-community trade.[350] Subsequently at the fifth Session of the Conference of Leaders and Heads of State of CEN-SAD held in Niamey in March 2003 a recommendation was made to the General Secretariat to continue the discussions both between Member States and with the international organisations with a view to meet the requirements for the creation of a free trade zone.[351] A study was conducted in 2006 by the General Secretariat in collaboration with the African Development Bank to evaluate the trade situation of Member States by identifying tariff and non-tariff obstacles and to propose a trade liberalisation programme with an implementation plan to intensify intra-regional trade.[352] The findings of the study were structured around three proposed scenarios for tariff elimination. The first scenario takes into account the differences in development levels between the Members and proposes a specific tariff elimination schedule—for least developed countries there is an annual tariff reduction of 12.5 % over a period of 8 years, and for the rest of the countries a 4-year period in which to eliminate tariffs, with the annual rate of 20 % for the first

[346] U.N. Economic Commission for Africa, Assessing Regional Integration in Africa, Part IV, pp. 3–4, available at: http://www.uneca.org/eca_resources/Publications/books/aria4/ARIA4Full.pdf.

[347] Report of the Sixth Ordinary Meeting of the Executive Council, 22–23 August 2001, available at: http://www.uneca.org/CEN-SAD/reportofthe6thordinarysessionoftheEC.htm.

[348] Report of the Sixth Ordinary Meeting of the Executive Council, 22–23 August 2001, available at: http://www.uneca.org/CEN-SAD/reportofthe6thordinarysessionoftheEC.htm.

[349] Report of the Sixth Ordinary Meeting of the Executive Council, 22–23 August 2001, available at: http://www.uneca.org/CEN-SAD/reportofthe6thordinarysessionoftheEC.htm.

[350] CEN-SAD, Trade Sector, available at: http://www.cen-sad.org/new/index.php?option=com_content&task=view&lang=en&id=150.

[351] CEN-SAD, Trade Sector, available at: http://www.cen-sad.org/new/index.php?option=com_content&task=view&lang=en&id=150.

[352] CEN-SAD, Trade Sector, available at: http://www.cen-sad.org/new/index.php?option=com_content&task=view&lang=en&id=150.

2 years and 30 % for the last 2 years.[353] The second scenario provides for an identical tariff elimination scheme for all countries alike over a 6-year period, with an annual reduction rate of 20 % for the first 2 years and 20 % for the remaining 4 years.[354] Under the third scenario, each Member State presents a tariff elimination scheme over an 8-year period, beginning 1 January 2007 and ending December 31, 2014.[355] The findings of the study were examined at a meeting of experts held in Tunis in April 2006, who concluded that the first and second scenarios were the most feasible.[356] A hybrid alternative, combining the first and second scenarios is expected.[357] The eleventh Session of the Ordinary Session of the Conference of Leaders and Heads of State of CEN-SAD held in May 2009 reasserted the pressing need to turn the African Union into a political and institutional reality and reasserted the leaders' commitment to accelerate the African integration process through the gradual harmonisation of the Members' development policies in conformity with the Abuja Treaty.[358]

Little actual progress has been made in the way of concrete steps towards integration, despite broad statements of the organisation's resolution to take action towards forming a free trade area. This is most likely a result of overlapping membership in multiple regional trade agreements—many CEN-SAD members are also members of ECOWAS, ECCAS, COMESA and other regional trade blocs that are in a more advanced stage in their integration process. This makes it difficult to coordinate trade and economic policies between members of the groups, which in turn leads to a decreased level of intra-regional trade because of trade barriers and a lack of harmonised market integration programmes.[359] Overlapping membership also results in a duplication of efforts that unnecessarily consumes

---

[353] African Union, Status of Integration in Africa, p. 94, para. 339, available at: http://www.africa-union.org/root/ua/conferences/2009/mai/ea/07-08mai/status%20of%20integration%20in%20africa%2027-04-09.pdf.

[354] African Union, Status of Integration in Africa, p. 95, para. 354, available at: http://www.africa-union.org/root/ua/conferences/2009/mai/ea/07-08mai/status%20of%20integration%20in%20africa%2027-04-09.pdf.

[355] African Union, Status of Integration in Africa, p. 95, para. 354, available at: http://www.africa-union.org/root/ua/conferences/2009/mai/ea/07-08mai/status%20of%20integration%20in%20africa%2027-04-09.pdf.

[356] African Union, Status of Integration in Africa, p. 95, para. 354, available at: http://www.africa-union.org/root/ua/conferences/2009/mai/ea/07-08mai/status%20of%20integration%20in%20africa%2027-04-09.pdf.

[357] African Union, Status of Integration in Africa, p. 95, para. 354, available at: http://www.africa-union.org/root/ua/conferences/2009/mai/ea/07-08mai/status%20of%20integration%20in%20africa%2027-04-09.pdf.

[358] CEN-SAD, 11th Ordinary Session of the Conference of Leaders and Heads of State, available at: http://www.cen-sad.org/new/index.php?option=com_content&task=view&id=282&Itemid=236.

[359] UN Economic Commission for Africa/African Union, Assessing Regional Integration in Africa, Part II, 2008, p. 55, available at: http://www.foresightfordevelopment.org/sobi2/Resources/Assessing-Regional-Integration-in-Africa-II-Rationalizing-Regional-Economic-Communities.

scarce human and financial resources.[360] As a result, more than half of CEN-SAD Member countries do not pay their required contributions.[361] Overlapping membership, therefore, serves as an obstacle to the achievement of regional integration and trade liberalisation. Consequently, the CEN-SAD free trade zone has not been implemented and likely will never be practically implemented because of its Members' overlapping membership in other African regional economic communities. To achieve the objective of establishing a free trade area, CEN-SAD should establish trade policies that are compatible with the other African RECs in order to further the goal of creating an enlarged free trade area and eventually a customs union encompassing all of the regional trading blocs. To accomplish this and increase intra-regional trade, there must be a coordinated regional and continent-wide approach to infrastructure financing, institutional harmonisation and policy coordination as well as improved transportation infrastructure.[362]

Food security remains an obstacle to integration as the food crisis cripples the economies and populations of the CEN-SAD Member States.[363] The first phase Regional Food Security programme began in January of 2004 in five CEN-SAD Member States and was satisfactorily completed in June of 2007.[364] The final programme evaluation mission conducted in January 2009 concluded that the Regional Food Security programme had achieved its objectives at an appreciable rate.[365] The second phase of the programme is to be implemented over a 5-year period and is designed to reinforce the gains of the first phase in twelve Member States at the national level and to build technical partnership at the community level.[366] In order to deal with the current food crisis, CEN-SAD Members must commit themselves to the successful implementation of the Regional Food Security

[360] UN Economic Commission for Africa/African Union, Assessing Regional Integration in Africa, Part II, 2008, p. 55, available at: http://www.foresightfordevelopment.org/sobi2/Resources/Assessing-Regional-Integration-in-Africa-II-Rationalizing-Regional-Economic-Communities.

[361] UN Economic Commission for Africa/African Union, Assessing Regional Integration in Africa, Part II, 2008, p. 59, available at: http://www.foresightfordevelopment.org/sobi2/Resources/Assessing-Regional-Integration-in-Africa-II-Rationalizing-Regional-Economic-Communities.

[362] UN Economic Commission for Africa/African Union, Assessing Regional Integration in Africa, Part II, 2008, p. 59, available at: http://www.foresightfordevelopment.org/sobi2/Resources/Assessing-Regional-Integration-in-Africa-II-Rationalizing-Regional-Economic-Communities.

[363] African Union, Status of Integration in Africa, pp. 87 et seq., available at: http://www.africa-union.org/root/ua/conferences/2009/mai/ea/07-08mai/status%20of%20integration%20in%20africa%2027-04-09.pdf.

[364] African Union, Status of Integration in Africa, p. 87, para. 307, available at: http://www.africa-union.org/root/ua/conferences/2009/mai/ea/07-08mai/status%20of%20integration%20in%20africa%2027-04-09.pdf. The five countries involved in the first phase were Burkina Faso, Mali, Niger, Chad and Sudan.

[365] African Union, Status of Integration in Africa, p. 87, para. 307, available at: http://www.africa-union.org/root/ua/conferences/2009/mai/ea/07-08mai/status%20of%20integration%20in%20africa%2027-04-09.pdf.

[366] African Union, Status of Integration in Africa, p. 88, para. 308, available at: http://www.africa-union.org/root/ua/conferences/2009/mai/ea/07-08mai/status%20of%20integration%20in%20africa%2027-04-09.pdf.

programme. Furthermore, transportation infrastructure must be improved in order to ameliorate the existing weak infrastructure that makes it difficult to link agricultural production areas to urban consumption and export markets.[367] Recognising that infrastructure and services development plays a crucial role in promoting sustainable development in the region, the CEN-SAD Community Plan aims to increase the incomes of its population to reduce or eliminate poverty.[368] Because the CEN-SAD region includes countries that belong to several other RECs, the Plan is oriented to promote their global integration through programmes of action in the transport, energy, mining and telecommunications fields that will constitute linkages between the various RECs to address the constraints that limit integration within the region.[369] The Plan will primarily involve improving the planning and coordination of actions and investments at the regional level; creating new transit routes and corridors; maintaining and improving the quality of infrastructure services; integrating and coordinating policies; harmonising laws, standards, regulations and procedures; and involving the private sector in financing joint projects.[370] In the transport sector, the main objective is to implement sufficient, efficient and integrated infrastructure in order to facilitate regional integration with the goal of eradicating poverty.[371] To this end, the specific objectives include ensuring the extension and maintenance of the transit routes and corridors network; improving the operational efficiency of the services; deregulating the regional transport market; promoting the safe and secure use of integrated systems; and improving accessibility to rural areas.[372] However, only three countries have repaved more than 50 % of their road network and only eight have railway lines.[373]

[367] African Union, Status of Integration in Africa, p. 93, para. 334, available at: http://www.africa-union.org/root/ua/conferences/2009/mai/ea/07-08mai/status%20of%20integration%20in%20africa%2027-04-09.pdf.

[368] African Union, Status of Integration in Africa, p. 89, para. 316, available at: http://www.africa-union.org/root/ua/conferences/2009/mai/ea/07-08mai/status%20of%20integration%20in%20africa%2027-04-09.pdf.

[369] African Union, Status of Integration in Africa, p. 89, para. 316, available at: http://www.africa-union.org/root/ua/conferences/2009/mai/ea/07-08mai/status%20of%20integration%20in%20africa%2027-04-09.pdf.

[370] African Union, Status of Integration in Africa, p. 90, para. 320, available at: http://www.africa-union.org/root/ua/conferences/2009/mai/ea/07-08mai/status%20of%20integration%20in%20africa%2027-04-09.pdf.

[371] African Union, Status of Integration in Africa, p. 90, para. 320, available at: http://www.africa-union.org/root/ua/conferences/2009/mai/ea/07-08mai/status%20of%20integration%20in%20africa%2027-04-09.pdf.

[372] African Union, Status of Integration in Africa, p. 90, para. 320, available at: http://www.africa-union.org/root/ua/conferences/2009/mai/ea/07-08mai/status%20of%20integration%20in%20africa%2027-04-09.pdf.

[373] African Union, Status of Integration in Africa, p. 94, para. 334, available at: http://www.africa-union.org/root/ua/conferences/2009/mai/ea/07-08mai/status%20of%20integration%20in%20africa%2027-04-09.pdf.

Economic Community of Central African States

In December 1991, the leaders of the Central African Customs and Economic Union (UDEAC) agreed in principle to form a wider community of Central African states.[374] The UDEAC members and the members of the Economic Community of the Great Lakes States established ECCAS on 18 October 1983.[375] Its members include Angola, Burundi, Cameroon, Central African Republic, Chad, Congo, Democratic Republic of Congo, Equatorial Guinea, Gabon, Rwanda, and Sao Tome and Principe.[376] The objectives of ECCAS include the promotion and strengthening of harmonious cooperation and self-sustained development in all fields of social and economic activity in order to "achieve collective self-reliance, raise the standard of living of its peoples, increase and maintain economic stability, foster close and peaceful relations between Member States and contribute to the progress and development of the African continent."[377]

The ECCAS Treaty calls for the gradual establishment of the Community over a period of 12 years, broken down into three subdivisions of 4-year stages.[378] The stages are set out in the following table.

Stage 1	Stage 2	Stage 3
• Stability of the fiscal and customs regime existing at the date of entry into force of the Treaty • Carrying out of studies to determine the timetable for the progressive removal of tariff and non-tariff barriers to intra-Community trade • Setting a timetable for increases or decreases in the customs tariffs of Member States with a view to the adoption of a common external tariff	• Creation of a free trade area (application of the timetable for the progressive elimination of tariff and non-tariff barriers to intra-Community trade)	• Establishment of the customs union (adoption of the common external tariff)

[374] African Union, Economic Community of Central African States: Profile, p. 2, available at: http://www.africa-union.org/Recs/ECCASoverview.pdf.

[375] African Union, Economic Community of Central African States: Profile, p. 2, available at: http://www.africa-union.org/Recs/ECCASoverview.pdf.

[376] African Union, Economic Community of Central African States: Profile, p. 1, available at: http://www.africa-union.org/Recs/ECCASoverview.pdf. Rwanda withdrew its membership in June 2007; Alusala, Is There Hope for ECCAS?, Institute for Security Studies, 19 October 2007, available at: http://www.iss.co.za/pgcontent.php?UID=27157.

[377] Art. 4(1) of the Treaty Establishing ECCAS.

[378] Art. 6(1) ECCAS Treaty.

The total duration of the stages may be increased or reduced only by a decision adopted by consensus and the transition period may not be reduced to 10 years or under or increasing it to more than 20 years from its initiation.[379]

During the first stage, the Member States may not establish new or increase existing customs duties between them.[380] At the end of the first stage and during the second stage, Members are to progressively reduce and ultimately eliminate customs duties between them.[381] Additionally during this time period, Members shall "eliminate differences between customs duties in their respective customs tariffs,"[382] with a view to the progressive establishment of a common external tariff that is applicable to goods imported into Member States from third countries.[383] At the end of the second stage, "no Member State shall levy customs duties on goods originating in one Member State and transferred to another Member State" or on "goods coming from third countries which are in free circulation in Member States and are transferred from one Member State to another."[384] Quota restrictions and other non-tariff barriers to intra-Community trade are to be gradually relaxed and ultimately removed by the end of the second stage, at the latest, and Member States are to refrain from imposing any further restrictions or prohibitions.[385] At the end of the second stage and during the third stage, the Council of Ministers shall propose to the Conference of Heads of State and Government the adoption of a common customs and statistical nomenclature for all Member States.[386]

The ECCAS Preferential Tariff was created as a plan to eliminate gradually tariffs on intra-regional trade. For traditional handicraft and local products, there was to be a 100 % reduction from 1 July 2004.[387] For mineral and manufactured products there was to be a 50 % reduction from 1 July 2004; a 70 % reduction from January of 2005; a 90 % reduction from January of 2006; and a 100 % reduction by January of 2007.[388] ECCAS undertook to harmonise commercial policies such as rules of origin and means of identifying the origin of a product with CEMAC. However, a WTO Trade Policy Review on the Central African Republic reported that as of March 2007, the tariff reduction process had not yet begun.[389]

---

[379] Art. 6(2) ECCAS Treaty.

[380] Art. 28(1) ECCAS Treaty.

[381] Art. 28(1) ECCAS Treaty.

[382] Art. 29(2) ECCAS Treaty.

[383] Art. 29(1) ECCAS Treaty.

[384] Art. 31(1) ECCAS Treaty.

[385] Art. 33(1) ECCAS Treaty.

[386] Art. 29(3) ECCAS Treaty.

[387] U.N. Economic Commission for Africa, Assessing Regional Integration in Africa, Part IV, p. 14, available at: http://www.uneca.org/eca_resources/Publications/books/aria4/ARIA4Full.pdf.

[388] U.N. Economic Commission for Africa, Assessing Regional Integration in Africa, Part IV, p. 14, available at: http://www.uneca.org/eca_resources/Publications/books/aria4/ARIA4Full.pdf.

[389] U.N. Economic Commission for Africa, Assessing Regional Integration in Africa, Part IV, p. 14, available at: http://www.uneca.org/eca_resources/Publications/books/aria4/ARIA4Full.pdf.

At the 1999 Conference of the Heads of State and Government, four priority fields were identified: to develop capacities to maintain peace, security and stability, all of which are essential prerequisites for economic and social development; to develop physical, economic and monetary integration; to develop a culture of human integration; and to establish an autonomous financing mechanism for ECCAS.[390]

Due to conflicts within the region, little progress has been made with respect to these economic goals. It was during the period of inactivity that it became apparent that if the organisation was to be functional again it would need to go beyond economic issues and incorporate into its wider operations efforts towards peace and security in the region.[391] ECCAS Member States created the Council for Peace and Security in Central Africa (COPAX) in February 1999 in order to promote, maintain and consolidate peace and security in Central Africa.[392] COPAX established two mechanisms, the Multinational Peace Keeping Force in Central Africa (FOMAC), and the Early Warning Observation and Monitoring System for Central Africa (MARAC), both of which have proved largely ineffective.[393] Conflicts among Member States continue, and non-payment of Member fees is still an issue, leaving ECCAS disempowered as Members continue to withdraw or join other regional economic communities. In the face of continuing challenges, ECCAS remains committed to pursuing new projects, such as the recent joint project with the EU aimed at supporting and aiding the ECCAS Department of Human Integration, Peace, Stability and Security in fulfilling its role to detect, prevent and manage conflict within the Central African region.[394] The joint project plans to equip MARAC with an early warning mechanism that will enable it to examine, analyse and react to crises in the region in a timely manner.[395] Other objectives of the joint project are to enable ECCAS to mediate conflicts between Members and to equip ECCAS to work closely with its Members in the fight against various factors promoting conflict in the region, like the illicit proliferation of small arms, cross-border crime and the illegal exploitation of the region's natural

---

[390] African Union, Economic Community of Central African States: Profile, p. 3, available at: http://www.africa-union.org/Recs/ECCASoverview.pdf.

[391] Alusala, Is There Hope for ECCAS?, Institute for Security Studies, 19 October 2007, available at: http://www.iss.co.za/pgcontent.php?UID=27157.

[392] Alusala, Is There Hope for ECCAS?, Institute for Security Studies, 19 October 2007, available at: http://www.iss.co.za/pgcontent.php?UID=27157. However, COPAX did not enter into force until 2004.

[393] Alusala, Is There Hope for ECCAS?, Institute for Security Studies, 19 October 2007, available at: http://www.iss.co.za/pgcontent.php?UID=27157.

[394] African Union, Status of Integration in Africa, p. 47, para. 145, available at: http://www.africa-union.org/root/ua/conferences/2009/mai/ea/07-08mai/status%20of%20integration%20in%20africa%2027-04-09.pdf.

[395] African Union, Status of Integration in Africa, p. 47, para. 145, available at: http://www.africa-union.org/root/ua/conferences/2009/mai/ea/07-08mai/status%20of%20integration%20in%20africa%2027-04-09.pdf.

resources.[396] Financed by the European Development Fund, the EU-ECCAS project began in February 2007 and will be implemented over a period of three and a half years.[397]

The ECCAS re-launching process was initiated in 1998 with technical assistance from the UN Economic Commission on Africa to help establish an autonomous financing mechanism and a free trade area.[398] The strategy was aimed to improve the interests of the other institutions in the region, such as CEMAC and COMESA, while avoiding conflict with the existing institutions, in order to establish a single regional market for Central Africa.[399] To this end the strategy enabled the formation of a free trade area over a period of 4 years, from 2004 to 2007, as opposed to the 12 years initially planned.[400] After the 4 year period, during which the strategy will only apply to non-CEMAC members, ECCAS is expected to be at the same level as CEMAC, which has reached the customs union stage, and will then apply uniformly and residual standards and norms will be harmonised.[401] On 24 January 2003, the EU signed a financial agreement with ECCAS and CEMAC conditional on the two African groups merging into one organisation for the purpose of ultimately concluding an Economic Partnership Agreement with Central Africa.[402]

ECCAS achieved the status of a free trade area in July 2004 and was expected to launch the ECCAS Customs Union in 2010. The customs union was initially to be launched in 2008, 4 years after the formation of the free trade area.[403] Its launch was delayed by a lack of political will and financial support within the region.[404] In order to form a customs union, ECCAS must speed up the harmonisation of the common external tariff and continue to work on the removal of non-tariff barriers as

[396] African Union, Status of Integration in Africa, p. 47, para. 145, available at: http://www.africa-union.org/root/ua/conferences/2009/mai/ea/07-08mai/status%20of%20integration%20in%20africa%2027-04-09.pdf.

[397] African Union, Status of Integration in Africa, p. 47, para. 145, available at: http://www.africa-union.org/root/ua/conferences/2009/mai/ea/07-08mai/status%20of%20integration%20in%20africa%2027-04-09.pdf.

[398] UN Economic Commission for Africa/African Union, Assessing Regional Integration in Africa, Part II, 2008, p. 50, available at: http://www.foresightfordevelopment.org/sobi2/Resources/Assessing-Regional-Integration-in-Africa-II-Rationalizing-Regional-Economic-Communities.

[399] UN Economic Commission for Africa/African Union, Assessing Regional Integration in Africa, Part II, 2008, p. 50, available at: http://www.foresightfordevelopment.org/sobi2/Resources/Assessing-Regional-Integration-in-Africa-II-Rationalizing-Regional-Economic-Communities.

[400] UN Economic Commission for Africa/African Union, Assessing Regional Integration in Africa, Part II, 2008, p. 50, available at: http://www.foresightfordevelopment.org/sobi2/Resources/Assessing-Regional-Integration-in-Africa-II-Rationalizing-Regional-Economic-Communities.

[401] UN Economic Commission for Africa/African Union, Assessing Regional Integration in Africa, Part II, 2008, p. 50, available at: http://www.foresightfordevelopment.org/sobi2/Resources/Assessing-Regional-Integration-in-Africa-II-Rationalizing-Regional-Economic-Communities.

[402] WTO Trade Policy Review, Central African Republic, WT/TPR/S/183, 7 May 2007, p. 15.

[403] WTO Trade Policy Review, Central African Republic, WT/TPR/S/183, 7 May 2007, p. 15.

[404] WTO Trade Policy Review, Central African Republic, WT/TPR/S/183, 7 May 2007, p. 15.

well as harmonising national policies so as to facilitate the free movement of persons and goods across borders.

The implementation of protocols aimed at facilitating the movement of goods and services has been hindered by lack of stability in the region and inadequate infrastructure linking the Member countries. For ECCAS, transport infrastructure is particularly important for increased intra-regional trade because 80 % of its trade is provided by ground transportation.[405] In January of 2004, a plan to develop the transportation infrastructure in the region, referred to as the Blueprint Consensus on Transport in Central Africa (PDCT-AC), was launched with the objective of providing Central Africa with secure, reliable and efficient transport infrastructure and to offer services at affordable costs.[406] The PDCT-AC, as a short-term goal, aims to make it possible to travel on paved roads from one capital in the region to another by 2010.[407] As a medium-term goal, the PDCT-AC aims to have a consensus framework for negotiations in order to mobilise investments in the transportation infrastructure field and, in the long-term, to ensure that the region has a transport system that encompasses all modes of transportation and whose infrastructure and services encourage the free movement of persons and goods.[408] However, the short-term goal to have paved roads connecting the region's capitals by 2010 has not been reached, as only two capitals are currently connected by road—Yaounde and Libreville.[409] In addition to the weak transport infrastructure and political instability, development programmes focusing on food security, the free movement of persons, health issues such as HIV/AIDS, gender issues and the environment should be created and implemented as these issues are key aspects of economic integration.

Conclusion

This article has extensively examined the trade agenda of the leading African RTAs. Each of the major RTAs has elaborate time-tabled trade liberalisation mandates. Yet, trade is only one of the many goals of African RTAs. Objectives

[405] Pibasso, ECCAS: 8000 Billion FCFA for Roads, BusinessinCamaroon.com, 25 November 2009, available at: http://www.businessincameroon.com/categories/41-real-estate-and-constructions-news/81-ceeac-8000-milliards-de-fcfa-pour-les-routes-.

[406] Mvogo, 6.41 Billion USD to Mobilize for the Tarring of Roads International Capitals, Emploi Service, 20 March 2010.

[407] African Union, Status of Integration in Africa, p. 54, para. 185, available at: http://www.africa-union.org/root/ua/conferences/2009/mai/ea/07-08mai/status%20of%20integration%20in%20africa%2027-04-09.pdf.

[408] African Union, Status of Integration in Africa, p. 54, para. 185, available at: http://www.africa-union.org/root/ua/conferences/2009/mai/ea/07-08mai/status%20of%20integration%20in%20africa%2027-04-09.pdf.

[409] Pibasso, ECCAS: 8000 Billion FCFA for Roads, BusinessinCamaroon.com, 25 November 2009, available at: http://www.businessincameroon.com/categories/41-real-estate-and-constructions-news/81-ceeac-8000-milliards-de-fcfa-pour-les-routes-.

such as those relating to resolving challenges such as telecommunications and transport as well as insecurity are regarded as necessary prerequisites for cooperation. Recent efforts to resolve the challenges of multiple memberships and the spaghetti bowl are underway within individual RTAs or as we saw in efforts such as the proposed tripartite between COMESA, EAC, and SADC. There is currently much energy in regional trade initiatives and notwithstanding the many barriers to cross-border trade in Africa, enthusiasm for regional integration is at an extremely high point.

Regional Economic Integration in Southeast Asia

Ashique Rahman and Chester Brown

Introduction

The nations of Southeast Asia are characterised by their diversity. The diversity is not only reflected in the populations, languages, cultures and politics of the region, but also in the economics. For example, the Gross Domestic Product ("GDP") per capita of one of the richest nations in the region, Singapore, is approximately 100 times that of one of the poorest nations, Myanmar.[1] There is also a significant development gap between the Member States of the Association of Southeast Asian Nations ("ASEAN"). This is clearly reflected in the fact that two members of the 10-member group—namely, Singapore and Malaysia—account for more than half of all intra-ASEAN trade.[2] These are examples of regional characteristics that have

The views expressed in this article are personal and are not necessarily those of any institutions or organisations with which the authors are presently or have in the past been affiliated.

[1] UN Data, Country Profile: Singapore, available at: http://data.un.org/CountryProfile.aspx?crName=Singapore; cf. UN Data, Country Profile: Myanmar, available at: http://data.un.org/CountryProfile.aspx?crName=Myanmar.

[2] In 2009, Singapore was responsible for USD 140,694,100,000 and Malaysia was responsible for USD 72,065,300,000 of intra-ASEAN trade (together USD 212,759,000,000), when the total of intra-ASEAN trade amounted to USD 376,207,300,000, see http://www.aseansec.org/stat/Table18.pdf.

A. Rahman (✉)
Associate, Volterra Fietta, 1 Fitzroy Square, London W1T 5HE, UK
e-mail: ashique.rahman@volterrafietta.com

C. Brown (✉)
Faculty of Law (Building F10), University of Sydney, Sydney 2006, NSW, Australia

Essex Court Chambers, London, UK

Maxwell Chambers, Singapore, Singapore
e-mail: chester.brown@sydney.edu.au

C. Herrmann et al. (eds.), *European Yearbook of International Economic Law (EYIEL), Vol. 4 (2013)*, European Yearbook of International Economic Law 4,
DOI 10.1007/978-3-642-33917-2_13,

influenced the policies adopted to promote economic liberalisation and integration in Southeast Asia. Certain external factors have also had an influence. Economic liberalisation has been precipitated in the ASEAN region by the general trend towards regional trade liberalisation, particularly through the establishment of free trade areas; the 1997 Asian financial crisis; the economic rise of China and India in the past decade; and the 2008 global economic crisis.[3]

Since the signing of the Bangkok Declaration on 8 August 1967 that created ASEAN,[4] the nations of Southeast Asia have progressively liberalised their economic policies and investment climates through use of the ASEAN framework. After the conclusion of the Treaty of Amity and Cooperation in Southeast Asia in 1976 between the Governments of Singapore, Indonesia, Malaysia, Thailand and the Philippines, where the founding States of ASEAN set out some guiding principles for the conduct of their relations with each other,[5] the first substantive steps towards regional economic integration came with the signing of the Agreement on ASEAN Preferential Trading Arrangements ("APTA") on 24 February 1977.[6] The APTA was an early attempt at regional integration through both a system of preferential tariffs and the liberalisation of non-tariff measures.[7] These policies were further developed, culminating on 28 January 1992 with the conclusion of the Framework Agreements on Enhancing Economic Cooperation ("Framework Agreements"), where the ASEAN Member States agreed to establish an ASEAN Free Trade Area ("AFTA") within 15 years.[8] The Framework Agreements introduced a comprehensive regime for the economic liberalisation of the region,

---

[3] Report of the United States International Trade Commission, ASEAN: Regional Trends in Economic Integration, Export Competitiveness, and Inbound Investment for Selected Industries, USITC Publication 4176, 2010, p. 2–1.

[4] Bangkok Declaration, signed on 8 August 1967. The original Member States were Malaysia, Indonesia, the Philippines, Singapore, and Thailand. The Declaration is available at http://www.aseansec.org/1212.htm. The original Member States were later joined by Brunei Darussalam (1984), Vietnam (1995), Laos (1997), Myanmar (1997), and Cambodia (1999), see http://www.aseansec.org/about_ASEAN.html. The Agreement on the Establishment of the ASEAN Secretariat was signed on 24 February 1976, 1331 UNTS 243. In addition, there is now a Charter of the Association of Southeast Asian States, signed 20 November 2007 and entered into force on 15 December 2008, available at http://www.aseansec.org/publications/ASEAN-Charter.pdf. See further Chesterman, Does ASEAN Exist? The Association of Southeast Asian Nations as an International Legal Person, Singapore Year Book of International Law 12 (2008), p. 199.

[5] Treaty of Amity and Cooperation in Southeast Asia, signed 24 February 1976, available at: http://www.aseansec.org/1217.htm. The guiding principles, as set out in Art. 2 of the Treaty, are: "a. Mutual respect for the independence, sovereignty, equality, territorial integrity and national identity of all nations; b. The right of every State to lead its national existence free from external interference, subversion or coercion; c. Non-interference in the internal affairs of one another; d. Settlement of differences or disputes by peaceful means; e. Renunciation of the threat or use of force; f. Effective cooperation among themselves."

[6] Agreement on ASEAN Preferential Trading Arrangements, signed 24 February 1977 and entered into force on 25 August 1977, available at: http://www.aseansec.org/1376.htm.

[7] See, for example, Art. 3 of the APTA.

[8] Framework Agreements on Enhancing Economic Cooperation, signed 28 January 1992 and entered into force on 28 January 1992, Art. 2(1), available at: http://www.aseansec.org/12374.htm.

primarily through the elimination of both tariff and non-tariff barriers to trade, and the mechanism for achieving this was the Common Effective Preferential Tariff ("CEPT") Scheme.[9] The modalities for the CEPT were set out in the Agreement on the Common Effective Preferential Tariff Scheme for the ASEAN Free Trade Area, which was signed and entered into force on the same date as the Framework Agreements.[10] Other international agreements seeking to liberalise trade in ASEAN even further have been concluded, the most recent one being the ASEAN Trade in Goods Agreement, which was signed on 26 February 2009.[11]

In addition to the removal of trade barriers, the ASEAN region has made significant progress towards liberalisation of its investment climate. Investment liberalisation was initially promoted through the 1987 ASEAN Agreement for the Promotion and Protection of Investment ("IGA") and the 1998 Framework Agreement on the ASEAN Investment Area ("AIA").[12] The two legacy agreements on investment were consolidated into the ASEAN Comprehensive Investment Agreement ("ACIA"), which was signed on 26 February 2009, and entered into force on 1 March 2012.[13]

The purpose of this article is to review the progress achieved to date in the economic integration of Southeast Asia, to examine current developments in regional economic integration, and to identify specific regional challenges to further deepening integration and economic liberalisation in the Southeast Asian region. To this end, Part I considers the existing economic integration agreements in the South East Asia, namely progress made in achieving the ASEAN FTA, the conclusion and entry into force of the ASEAN Comprehensive Investment Agreement, the conclusion of ASEAN + 1 Agreements, and the unilateral negotiation of FTAs and BITs by ASEAN Member States. Part II examines a number of recent and ongoing developments in regional economic integration, including the negotiation of the Trans-Pacific Partnership Agreement, the ASEAN Economic Community initiative, and the Government of Australia's recent announcement in relation to its trade policy. The article concludes that although there are challenges to be met, the dynamic economies of Southeast Asia are likely to continue to integrate apace.

---

[9] Framework Agreements on Enhancing Economic Cooperation, signed 28 January 1992 and entered into force on 28 January 1992, Art. 2(2), available at: http://www.aseansec.org/12374.htm.

[10] Agreement on the Common Effective Preferential Tariff Scheme for the ASEAN Free Trade Area, signed 28 January 1992 and entered into force on 28 January 1992, available at: http://www.aseansec.org/12375.htm.

[11] ASEAN Trade in Goods Agreement, signed 26 February 2009, available at: http://www.aseansec.org/12039.htm. At this website, a complete list (and copies) of the agreements and instruments relating to the ASEAN Free Trade Area can be found.

[12] Agreement among the Government of Brunei Darussalam, the Republic of Indonesia, Malaysia, the Republic of the Philippines, the Republic of Singapore and the Kingdom of Thailand for the Promotion and Protection of Investments, signed 15 December 1987 and entered into force on 2 August 1988, available at: http://www.aseansec.org/12812.htm; Framework Agreement on the ASEAN Investment Area, signed 7 October 1998 and entered into force on 25 May 1999, available at: http://www.aseansec.org/7994.pdf.

[13] ASEAN Comprehensive Investment Agreement, signed 26 February 2009 and entered into force on 1 March 2012, available at: http://www.aseansec.org/22244.htm.

Existing Economic Integration Agreements in Southeast Asia

Since the Bangkok Declaration that created ASEAN in 1967, the liberalisation of trade and investment has progressed at a steady pace in the ASEAN region. This has been achieved both through multilateral efforts using the ASEAN platform and through unilateral efforts by the Member States reflected in the negotiation of a number of bilateral free trade agreements ("FTAs") and bilateral treaties for the promotion and protection of investments ("BITs").

The ASEAN Free Trade Area

The negotiation of the AFTA marked a concerted joint effort to achieve, for the first time, free trade among Member States of the ASEAN. The purpose of the AFTA was to realise a free trading bloc primarily through the elimination of tariff and non-tariff barriers to trade. As noted above, the AFTA sought to reduce and finally eliminate intra-regional tariffs through the CEPT scheme.[14] The CEPT introduced for the first time obligations on Member States to reduce the CEPT rates to between 0 % and 5 % within a clearly defined timetable for implementation.[15] The AFTA establishes comprehensive coverage through a "negative list" approach whereby the CEPT applies to all goods originating in the ASEAN region unless expressly excluded by a member State.[16] Therefore, it has been rightly observed that the AFTA can be "considered a 'deep' FTA relative to others among developing countries because of its comprehensive coverage, ambitious liberalization to zero or near-zero rates, and timely implementation."[17]

Through the implementation of Member States' obligations under the CEPT, it is reported that the "ASEAN-6" (comprising Brunei Darussalam, Indonesia, Malaysia, Philippines, Singapore, and Thailand) have reduced their tariff rates on more than 99 % of products listed in the CEPT Inclusion List to within the 0–5 % tariff range.[18] The more recent members, Cambodia, Laos, Myanmar and Vietnam have made substantially less progress, with approximately 66 % of products in the

---

[14] Hill/Menon, ASEAN Economic Integration: Features, Fulfilment, Failures and the Future, ADB Working Paper Series on Regional Economic Integration No. 69, 2010, p. 5.

[15] Hill/Menon, ASEAN Economic Integration: Features, Fulfilment, Failures and the Future, ADB Working Paper Series on Regional Economic Integration No. 69, 2010, p. 5.

[16] Hill/Menon, ASEAN Economic Integration: Features, Fulfilment, Failures and the Future, ADB Working Paper Series on Regional Economic Integration No. 69, 2010, p. 5.

[17] Report of the United States International Trade Commission, ASEAN: Regional Trends in Economic Integration, Export Competitiveness, and Inbound Investment for Selected Industries, USITC Publication 4176, 2010, pp. 2–9.

[18] The ASEAN Free Trade Area, available at: http://www.aseansec.org/12021.htm; see also ASEAN-6 Achieves Zero Tariffs (31 December 2012), available at: http://www.aseansec.org/24146.htm.

Table 1 Average CEPT rates, by country, 1993–2003 (percent)[a]

Country	1993	1994	1995	1996	1997	1998	1999	2000	2001	2002	2003
Brunei D.	3.78	2.64	2.54	2.02	1.61	1.37	1.55	1.26	1.17	0.96	1.04
Indonesia	17.27	17.27	15.22	10.39	8.53	7.06	5.36	4.76	4.27	3.69	2.17
Malaysia	10.79	10.00	9.21	4.56	4.12	3.46	3.20	3.32	2.71	2.62	1.95
Philippines	12.45	11.37	10.65	9.55	9.22	7.72	7.34	5.18	4.48	4.13	3.82
Singapore	0.01	0.01	0.01	0.01	0.00	0.00	0.00	0.00	0.00	0.00	0.00
Thailand	19.85	19.84	18.16	14.21	12.91	10.24	9.58	6.12	5.67	4.97	4.63
ASEAN-6	**11.44**	**10.97**	**10.00**	**7.15**	**6.38**	**5.22**	**4.79**	**3.64**	**3.22**	**2.89**	**2.39**
Cambodia								10.39	10.39	8.89	7.94
Lao PDR						5.00	7.54	7.07	7.08	6.72	5.86
Myanmar						2.39	4.45	4.43	4.57	4.72	4.61
Vietnam				0.92	4.59	3.95	7.11	7.25	6.75	6.92	6.43
CLMV				**0.92**	**4.59**	**2.98**	**6.31**	**7.51**	**7.17**	**6.77**	**6.22**
ASEAN-10				**7.03**	**6.32**	**4.91**	**5.01**	**4.43**	**4.11**	**3.84**	**3.33**

[a]Austria, The Pattern of Intra-ASEAN Trade in the Priority Goods Sectors, 2004, available at: http://www.ausaid.gov.au/Publications/Documents/priority_goods_sector.pdf, p. 10

CEPT Inclusion List having achieved tariff rates within the 0–5 % range.[19] As demonstrated by the figures in Table 1, the CEPT's impact on tariff reduction has been largely successful. An average tariff rate of 11.44 % amongst the original ASEAN-6 at the time the AFTA was negotiated was reduced in the subsequent decade to an average tariff rate of 3.33 % for the ASEAN-10.[20]

Trade liberalisation under the AFTA has been complemented through the negotiation of the ASEAN Framework Agreement on Services ("AFAS") on 15 December 1995.[21] This was a natural progression in economic liberalisation as the services sector accounts for approximately 40–50 % of GDP in ASEAN countries.[22] The AFAS is designed to eliminate barriers to trade in services including market access limitations.[23] Indeed, the framework established under the AFAS goes so far as to direct Member States to adopt specific commitments that go beyond each Member States' schedule of specific commitments assumed under the General Agreement on Trade in Services ("GATS").[24]

Despite the establishment of a comprehensive framework for trade liberalisation in the ASEAN region, the effectiveness of the regime has been diminished by certain implementation constraints. For example, despite the relative success in

[19] The ASEAN Free Trade Area, available at: http://www.aseansec.org/12021.htm.

[20] Austria, The Pattern of Intra-ASEAN Trade in the Priority Goods Sectors, 2004, available at: http://www.ausaid.gov.au/Publications/Documents/priority_goods_sector.pdf, p. 10.

[21] ASEAN Framework Agreement on Services, signed 15 December 1995 and entered into force on 30 December 1998, available at: http://www.aseansec.org/6628.htm.

[22] See Services, available at: http://www.aseansec.org/6626.htm.

[23] Art. 3 AFAS.

[24] Art. 1(c), 4 AFAS.

overall tariff reduction, the effectiveness of trade liberalisation under the AFTA has been curtailed by the protection of certain product lines through their listing in the Temporary Exclusion List, the Sensitive List or the General Exception List.[25] For example, rice, deemed to be a "highly sensitive" product, remains outside the AFTA and CEPT schemes.[26] In addition, the effectiveness of tariff reduction has been diminished by a lack of implementation. It is estimated that only 5 % of intra-ASEAN trade makes use of the advantageous CEPT rates.[27] Commentators have observed that "local enterprises do not bother to go through all the necessary formalities, or just do not know that their business transactions qualify for these preferential tariff rates."[28] Therefore, while much progress has been made because of multilateral efforts through the ASEAN framework, the full benefits of trade liberalisation may be enhanced through better implementation at the national level.

The ASEAN Comprehensive Investment Agreement

ASEAN has also provided a platform for the negotiation of comprehensive commitments by Member States to promote and protect investments within the region. Investment liberalisation was initially achieved through negotiation of the IGA and AIA. These two intra-ASEAN investment agreements were consolidated by the negotiation of the ACIA on 26 February 2009. Both the IGA and AIA were terminated upon entry into force of the ACIA on 1 March 2012.[29]

The ACIA provides a comprehensive set of obligations designed to progressively liberalise the investment regimes of Member States and to provide substantive protections to ASEAN investors. Indeed, the protections afforded under the ACIA may extend to ASEAN investors who are ultimately owned or controlled by a non-ASEAN investor.[30] Investment liberalisation under the ACIA follows a formula typically adopted in the ASEAN; being the liberalisation of specific sectors, the policies for which, if successfully implemented, are progressively extended to

---

[25] Hill/Menon, ASEAN Economic Integration: Features, Fulfilment, Failures and the Future, ADB Working Paper Series on Regional Economic Integration No. 69, 2010, p. 7.

[26] See Trade, available at: http:// www.aseansec.org/12021.htm.

[27] Reyes, The ASEAN Model of Economic Integration, available at: http://www.aseansec.org/16276.htm.

[28] Cuyvers/Lombaerde/Verherstraeten, Current Status of East Asian Economic Integration, available at: http://www.cris.unu.edu/uploads/media/Antwerp.pdf, p. 7.

[29] Art. 47(1) ACIA. See "ASEAN Pact Due Tomorrow," Bangkok Post, 29 February 2012, available at: http://www.bangkokpost.com/business/economics/282103/asean-pact-due-tomorrow.

[30] Art. 4 ACIA; see also the commentary in the ASEAN Investment Report, 2008, p. 16, available at: http://www.aseansec.org/22111.pdf; Report of the United States International Trade Commission, ASEAN: Regional Trends in Economic Integration, Export Competitiveness, and Inbound Investment for Selected Industries, USITC Publication 4176, 2010, pp. 2–19.

the entire market. Specifically, the ACIA identifies the manufacturing, agricultural, fisheries, forestry, and the mining and quarrying sectors for liberalisation of investment policies.[31]

Importantly, the ACIA provides intra-ASEAN investors with protections typically found in international investment agreements. These protections include, among others, the extension of national treatment to covered investments,[32] most-favoured-nation ("MFN") treatment,[33] fair and equitable treatment,[34] full protection and security,[35] and compensation for the expropriation of investments.[36] The ACIA also contains provisions to protect senior management and the board of directors from discriminatory treatment and to provide compensation to investors who suffer losses due to armed conflict, civil strife or a state of emergency.[37]

In addition, the above substantive protection, Article 25 of the ACIA contains certain obligations for the "facilitation of investments." Pursuant to their obligations under Article 25, Member States "shall endeavour to cooperate in the facilitation of investments into and within ASEAN through," *inter alia*, "creating the necessary environment for all forms of investments."[38] Although the scope of this provision is yet to be tested, it would seem that Article 25 is at least in part designed to remove barriers to the establishment of investments within the ASEAN region.

The dispute settlement provisions of the ACIA allow investors from Member States to initiate arbitration (after a compulsory consultation and negotiation period) against an ASEAN State that has breached its obligations under the provisions of the ACIA.[39] The arbitration may be conducted under the auspices of the International Centre for Settlement of Investment Disputes ("ICSID"), pursuant to the Arbitration Rules of the United Nations Commission on International Trade Law ("UNCITRAL"), or under the rules of a regional institution such as the Kuala Lumpur Regional Centre for Arbitration.[40] In addition to the application of any institutional or *ad hoc* Rules selected by the Parties, in Articles 28 to 41, the ACIA provides detailed rules for the arbitration covering a number of procedural issues such as the selection of arbitrators, the conduct of the arbitration, confidentiality, and consolidation of proceedings.

[31] Art. 3(3) ACIA.

[32] Art. 5 ACIA.

[33] Art. 6 ACIA.

[34] Art. 11 ACIA.

[35] Art. 11 ACIA.

[36] Art. 14 ACIA.

[37] Art. 8, 12 ACIA.

[38] Art. 25 ACIA.

[39] Art. 28 to 41 ACIA.

[40] Art. 33 ACIA.

Table 2 ASEAN trade by selected partner country/region, 2009 (as of 15 July 2010)[a]

	Value			Share to total ASEAN trade		
Partner country/region	Exports	Imports	Total trade	Exports	Imports	Total trade
ASEAN	199,587.3	176,620.1	376,207.3	24.6	24.3	24.5
China	81,591.0	96,594.3	178,185.4	10.1	13.3	11.6
EU-25[b]	92,990.9	78.795.0	171,785.9	11.5	10.8	11.2
Japan	78,068.6	82,795.1	160,863.7	9.6	11.4	10.5
USA	82,201.8	67,370.3	149,572.1	10.1	9.3	9.7
Republic of Korea	34,292.9	40,447.4	74,740.3	4.2	5.6	4.9
Australia	29,039.3	14,810.8	43,850.1	3.6	2.0	2.9
India	26,520.3	12,595.5	39,115.8	3.3	1.7	2.5
Canada	5,500.4	3,539.2	9,039.6	0.7	0.5	0.6
Russia	1,660.6	5,104.9	6,765.5	0.2	0.7	0.4
New Zealand	3,137.6	2,238.6	5,376.2	0.4	0.3	0.3
Pakistan	3,833.8	469.6	4,303.4	0.5	0.1	0.3
Total selected partner countries/regions	638,424.5	581,380.8	1,219,805.2	78.8	80.0	79.4
Others[c]	172,064.7	144,973.3	317,038.0	21.2	20.0	20.6
Total ASEAN	**810,489.2**	**726,354.1**	**1,536,843.3**	**100.0**	**100.0**	**100.0**

Value in US$ million; share in percent

Source: ASEAN Merchandise Trade Statistics Database (compiled/computed from data submission, publications and/or websites of ASEAN Member State's national ASEAN Free Trade Area (AFTA) units, national statistics offices, customs departments/agencies, or central banks)

Notes: Some figures may not add up to totals due to rounding off errors. All figures are preliminary: dates exclude Cambodia and Lao PDR as they are not available

[a]ASEAN Trade by Selected Partner Country / Region, 2009 (as of 15 July 2010), available at: http://www.aseansec.org/stat/Table19.pdf

[b]Includes Austria, Belgium, Cyprus, Czech Republic, Denmark, Estonia, Finland, France, Germany, Greece, Hungary, Ireland, Italy, Latvia, Lithuania, Luxembourg, Malta, the Netherlands, Poland, Portugal, Slovakia, Slovenia, Spain, Sweden, and United Kingdom

[c]Includes of all other countries and those that could not be attributed to specific countries

ASEAN+1 Agreements

As demonstrated in Table 2, intra-ASEAN trade accounts for only a quarter of the total trade in the ASEAN region. Therefore, it is unsurprising that, in recent times, the ASEAN platform has been used to negotiate a number of multilateral FTAs with external trade partners.

On 4 November 2002, a Framework Agreement on Comprehensive Economic Cooperation was signed by the Member States of ASEAN with its biggest trading partner, China. The framework agreement paved the way for the creation of the ASEAN-China Free Trade Area ("ASEAN-China FTA") that came into effect on 1 January 2010 creating the biggest FTA in the world in terms of consumer market size.[41] The ASEAN-China FTA contains a number of enabling agreements to

[41] FTA Agreements, p. 2, available at: http://www.aseansec.org/Fact%20Sheet/AEC/AEC-12.pdf.

liberalise trade in goods and services and to promote and facilitate investments between China and the ASEAN region. An ASEAN-China FTA has important benefits for all parties. The existence of an FTA with China allows ASEAN Member States to gain access to the extensive supply chains established by China throughout Asia, while also allowing Chinese businesses to diversify operations throughout the ASEAN region and thereby reduce business and political risks.[42]

A number of additional FTAs have been negotiated with key regional trading partners including Japan, India, South Korea, Australia and New Zealand.[43] These "ASEAN+1" FTAs all purport to liberalise trade in goods and services primarily through the reduction and elimination of tariffs and also promote investments between ASEAN nations and its main regional trading partners.

Unilateral Negotiation of FTAs and BITs

In addition to the multilateral agreements in place within the ASEAN region and between the ASEAN+1 countries, a number of ASEAN States have separately negotiated FTAs and BITs with both regional trading partners and nations worldwide. Singapore has been particularly active in this practice, having separately negotiated FTAs with a number of nations and trading blocs including the European Free Trade Association ("EFTA"),[44] the United States,[45] and Australia.[46] This trend perhaps reflects the "enormous gap that exists within ASEAN, between members wanting to negotiate collectively (using the ASEAN or the ASEAN+3 framework) and other members aiming at quicker progress and thus switching to bilateral trade agreements."[47]

Added to the layers of agreements already in place is the proliferation of both intra-ASEAN BITs and BITs negotiated with nations that have historically been capital-exporting countries.[48] For example, Indonesia has separately negotiated

---

[42] Report of the United States International Trade Commission, ASEAN: Regional Trends in Economic Integration, Export Competitiveness, and Inbound Investment for Selected Industries, USITC Publication 4176, 2010, pp. 2–17.

[43] On the ASEAN–Australia–New Zealand FTA see especially Bath/Nottage, The ASEAN Comprehensive Investment Agreement and 'ASEAN-Plus': The ASEAN–Australia–New Zealand Free Trade Area and the PRC–ASEAN Investment Agreement, in: Bungenberg/Griebel/Reinisch/Hobe (eds.), *International Investment Law*, forthcoming 2012.

[44] Singapore–EFTA FTA, signed 26 June 2002 and entered into force on 1 January 2003, available at: http://www.efta.int/free-trade/free-trade-agreements/singapore.aspx.

[45] Singapore–United States FTA, signed 6 May 2003 and entered into force on 1 January 2004, available at: http://www.ustr.gov/trade-agreements/free-trade-agreements/singapore-fta.

[46] Singapore–Australia FTA, signed 17 February 2003 and entered into force on 28 July 2003, available at: http://www.dfat.gov.au/fta/safta/index.html.

[47] Cuyvers/Lombaerde/Verherstraeten, Current Status of East Asian Economic Integration, available at: http://www.cris.unu.edu/uploads/media/Antwerp.pdf, p. 19.

[48] For commentary on the proliferation of BITs in Asia see generally Nottage/Weeramantry, Investment Arbitration in Asia: Five Perspectives on Law and Practice, Arbitration International 28 (2012) 1, p. 19.

BITs with a number of ASEAN partners, including Vietnam, Malaysia, Thailand and Laos. Indonesia also has BITs with other Asian nations including India and China and with traditional capital-exporting countries including the United Kingdom and Germany.[49] Another ASEAN member State, Malaysia, has entered into 68 BITs.[50] Singapore, for its part, has 41 BITs and 14 FTAs.[51] These overlapping agreements create a "noodle bowl" of rights and obligations that, it has been observed, bring with it the potential risks of trade diversions and other market-distorting effects.[52] However, conversely, the cross-proliferation of obligations could also be advantageous for ASEAN nations as it may allow the promulgation of more liberal trade policies through the application of the MFN principle.

Recent Developments in Economic Integration in Southeast Asia

Notwithstanding the negotiation of a number of comprehensive trade and investment liberalisation agreements in recent years, the ASEAN region is pressing ahead with bolder plans for deeper regional integration and more extensive trade ties with non-Asian partners. These include in particular the negotiations for a Trans-Pacific Partnership ("TPP") Agreement and the furtherance of the ASEAN Economic Community Initiative.

Negotiation of the Trans-Pacific Partnership Agreement

On 12 November 2011, the governments of Australia, Brunei Darussalam, Chile, Malaysia, New Zealand, Peru, Singapore, the United States and Vietnam announced a broad outline of a TPP Agreement between the nine countries. The TPP Agreement has been described by its negotiating partners as a "next-generation" regional agreement that purports to not only further liberalise trade and investment between the State parties, but also to "promote innovation, economic growth and development, and support the creation and retention of jobs."[53]

---

[49] See, e.g., Butt, Foreign Investment in Indonesia: The Problem of Legal Uncertainty, in: Bath/Nottage (eds.), *Foreign Investment and Dispute Resolution Law and Practice in Asia*, 2011, pp. 112, 117–118, 129–130.

[50] See, e.g., Farrar, Foreign Investment Laws and the Role of FDI in Malaysia's 'New' Economic Model, in: Bath/Nottage (eds.), *Foreign Investment and Dispute Resolution Law and Practice in Asia*, pp. 153, 164–166.

[51] See, e.g., Ho, Singapore, in: Brown (ed.), Commentaries on Selected Model Investment Treaties (2013), pp. 623–650.

[52] Paczyński/Gasiorek (eds.), Economic Integration in South East Asia and the Impact on the EU, Centre for the Analysis of Regional Integration at Sussex, Final Report of 23 March 2011, p. 37, available at: http://trade.ec.europa.eu/doclib/docs/2011/may/tradoc_147874.pdf.

[53] Office of the US Trade Representative (USTR), The United States in the Trans-Pacific Partnership, available at: http://www.ustr.gov/about-us/press-office/fact-sheets/2011/november/united-states-trans-pacific-partnership; see also USTR, Trans-Pacific Partnership Leaders Statement, available at: http://www.ustr.gov/about-us/press-office/press-releases/2011/november/trans-pacific-partnership-leaders-statement.

At its core, the TPP Agreement is typical in that it will enhance market access through the elimination of tariffs and other barriers to goods and services trade and investment.[54] The Agreement aims to cover over 11,000 tariff lines and will seek to adopt a "negative list" procedure to maximise coverage.[55] However, beyond the elimination of tariffs, the TPP Agreement will seek to contain a number of innovative features that reflect the adoption of a holistic approach to regional economic liberalisation. For example, it is envisaged that the TPP Agreement will address the concerns of small and medium-sized enterprises regarding their understanding of the trade agreement so that small- to medium-sized businesses are better equipped to trade internationally through utilisation of the TPP Agreement. As mentioned above in the context of the AFTA, a deeper understanding of the benefits to be gained from utilisation of free trade agreements will in turn maximise the benefits of trade liberalisation through measures such as tariff cuts.

It is also envisaged that the TPP Agreement will introduce commitments on the part of State parties to establish and maintain competition laws that curtail anti-competitive behaviour.[56] Recognising the importance of implementation, the agreement will facilitate capacity building in the developing countries that are parties to the agreement so that they may effectively implement the objectives of the agreement.[57] In addition, the TPP Agreement is also likely to include comprehensive chapters on e-commerce, the environment (including, potentially, rules on climate change, biodiversity and the conservation of marine life), financial services regulation (including commitments designed to allow regulators to better react to ensure the stability and integrity of financial markets in the event of a financial crisis), investment protection, commitments on labour rights protection, and a number of commitments that build upon the framework of the World Trade Organisation ("WTO"), including rules on Technical Barriers to Trade ("TBT"), Sanitary and Phytosanitary Standards ("SPS") and Trade-Related Aspects of Intellectual Property ("TRIPS").[58]

This TPP Agreement's all-encompassing agenda has compelled the Australian Government to classify the negotiation of this agreement as its "highest regional trade negotiation priority."[59] It is envisioned that the TPP Agreement will be a "living agreement that remains relevant to emerging issues and allows for

[54] USTR, Outlines of the Trans-Pacific Partnership Agreement, available at: http://www.ustr.gov/about-us/press-office/fact-sheets/2011/november/outlines-trans-pacific-partnership-agreement.

[55] USTR, Outlines of the Trans-Pacific Partnership Agreement, available at: http://www.ustr.gov/about-us/press-office/fact-sheets/2011/november/outlines-trans-pacific-partnership-agreement.

[56] USTR, Outlines of the Trans-Pacific Partnership Agreement, available at: http://www.ustr.gov/about-us/press-office/fact-sheets/2011/november/outlines-trans-pacific-partnership-agreement.

[57] USTR, Outlines of the Trans-Pacific Partnership Agreement, available at: http://www.ustr.gov/about-us/press-office/fact-sheets/2011/november/outlines-trans-pacific-partnership-agreement.

[58] USTR, Outlines of the Trans-Pacific Partnership Agreement, available at: http://www.ustr.gov/about-us/press-office/fact-sheets/2011/november/outlines-trans-pacific-partnership-agreement.

[59] Department of Foreign Affairs and Trade, Trans-pacific Partnership Negotiations, available at: http://www.dfat.gov.au/fta/tpp.

membership expansion."[60] Towards the end of 2011, the governments of Canada, Japan, and Mexico expressed an interest in joining the talks for the negotiation of the TPP Agreement.[61] If Japan was to join the TPP Agreement, it would potentially create a regional trading bloc that is 40 % larger than the size of the European Union.[62]

The ASEAN Economic Community Initiative

At the Bali Summit in 2003, the ASEAN Member States declared that the formation of the ASEAN Economic Community ("AEC") "shall be the goal of regional economic integration."[63] In January 2007, the ASEAN Member States decided to accelerate the agenda for the formation of the AEC so that it could be established by 2015.[64] The AEC Blueprint, adopted by all members, recognises the key characteristics of the AEC. They include (a) a single market and production base; (b) a highly competitive economic region; (c) a region of equitable economic development; and (d) a region fully integrated into the global economy.[65] These four key characteristics form the basis of the AEC.

The AEC Blueprint identifies a number of elements that will need to be implemented to achieve the economic liberalisation goals of the AEC. It is expected that a single market and production base will be achieved by allowing the "free" flow of goods, services, investments, and skilled labour and the "freer" flow of capital.[66] The free flow of goods is to be achieved through measures typically found in FTAs, including, *inter alia*, the elimination of tariffs and non-tariff barriers, implementation of effective rules of origin, further trade facilitation between Member States, customs integration (although not necessarily the creation of a common tariff), and the elimination of technical barriers to trade.[67] The objective of

[60] Department of Foreign Affairs and Trade, Trans-pacific Partnership Negotiations, available at: http://www.dfat.gov.au/fta/tpp.

[61] Department of Foreign Affairs and Trade, Trans-pacific Partnership Negotiations, available at: http://www.dfat.gov.au/fta/tpp.

[62] Craig Emerson MP, "Australia Welcome's Japan's Decision on TPP," 11 November 2011, available at: http://trademinister.gov.au/releases/2011/ce_mr_111111a.html.

[63] ASEAN Economic Community Blueprint, adopted 20 November 2007, para. 2, available at: http://www.aseansec.org/21083.pdf.

[64] Cebu Declaration on the Acceleration of the Establishment of an ASEAN Community by 2015, 13 January 2007, available at: http://www.aseansec.org/19260.htm.

[65] ASEAN Economic Community Blueprint, adopted 20 November 2007, para. 8, available at: http://www.aseansec.org/21083.pdf.

[66] ASEAN Economic Community Blueprint, adopted 20 November 2007, para. 9, available at: http://www.aseansec.org/21083.pdf.

[67] ASEAN Economic Community Blueprint, adopted 20 November 2007, paras. 14–17, 19, available at: http://www.aseansec.org/21083.pdf.

creating a highly competitive economic region will focus on infrastructure development and the strengthening policies in relation to competition, consumer protection, intellectual property, taxation, and e-commerce.[68] Therefore, the AEC Blueprint highlights the adoption of a comprehensive approach towards economic liberalisation.

In addition to the above policies, the AEC builds into the agenda a number of strategies to reduce the development gap between ASEAN members. The AEC Blueprint purports to reduce the development gap by providing assistance to small and medium enterprises in the region and through the implementation of the Initiative on ASEAN Integration (a programme launched in November 2000 to reduce the development gap in the region and to improve its competitiveness).[69] Finally, the AEC Blueprint promotes the region's integration with the global economy through the development of a coherent regional approach towards external economic relations and through greater participation in global supply networks.[70] This comprehensive vision for the AEC has been described as a "hybrid FTA-plus arrangement" as it includes characteristics of a common market but does not go so far as to create a common external tariff.[71]

Australian Trade Policy Statement of April 2011

In April 2011, the Australian Government published the "Gillard Government Trade Policy Statement: Trading our Way to More Jobs and Prosperity."[72] This Trade Policy Statement dealt with a broad range of trade and investment issues. These included setting out the "five principles guiding Australia's trade policy," which were listed as being the pursuit of pro-competitive economic reform, non-discrimination, ensuring that any trade deal must be in Australia's national interest, transparency, and "the indivisibility of trade policy and economic reform."[73] It also

---

[68] ASEAN Economic Community Blueprint, adopted 20 November 2007, paras. 41–59, available at: http://www.aseansec.org/21083.pdf.

[69] ASEAN Economic Community Blueprint, adopted 20 November 2007, paras. 60–62, available at: http://www.aseansec.org/21083.pdf.

[70] ASEAN Economic Community Blueprint, adopted 20 November 2007, paras. 65–66, available at: http://www.aseansec.org/21083.pdf.

[71] Report of the United States International Trade Commission, ASEAN: Regional Trends in Economic Integration, Export Competitiveness, and Inbound Investment for Selected Industries, USITC Publication 4176, 2010, pp. 2–4.

[72] "Gillard Government Trade Policy Statement: Trading our Way to More Jobs and Prosperity," available at: http://www.dfat.gov.au/publications/trade/trading-our-way-to-more-jobs-and-prosperity.html.

[73] "Gillard Government Trade Policy Statement: Trading our Way to More Jobs and Prosperity," available at: http://www.dfat.gov.au/publications/trade/trading-our-way-to-more-jobs-and-prosperity.html.

set out Australia's commitment to the Doha Round, as well as completing various regional and bilateral trade negotiations, including the TPP Agreement, and FTAs with Japan, Korea, and China, among others.[74] However, the element of the Trade Policy Statement that appears to have attracted the most attention is the following statement:

> In the past, Australian Governments have sought the inclusion of investor-state dispute resolution procedures in trade agreements with developing countries at the behest of Australian businesses. The Gillard Government will discontinue this practice. If Australian businesses are concerned about sovereign risk in Australian trading partner countries, they will need to make their own assessments about whether they want to commit to investing in those countries.[75]

This new policy of no longer seeking to include investor-State dispute settlement provisions had its origin in the recommendation by the Productivity Commission (that is the Australian Government's "independent research and advisory body on a range of economic, social and environmental issues affecting the welfare of Australians").[76] In late 2009, the Productivity Commission had been requested to undertake a study on "the impact of bilateral and regional trade agreements on trade and investment barriers and on Australia's trade and economic performance."[77] In its study, it considered the possible benefits of including investor-State dispute settlement provisions in investment and trade agreements, and made a finding that: "There does not appear to be an underlying economic problem that necessitates the inclusion of ISDS provisions within agreements. Available evidence does not suggest that ISDS provisions have a significant impact on investment flows."[78] It then considered the possible risks of including investor-State dispute settlement provisions in investment treaties, and found that: "Experience in other countries demonstrates that there are considerable policy and financial risks arising from ISDS provisions."[79] It concluded that:

[74] "Gillard Government Trade Policy Statement: Trading our Way to More Jobs and Prosperity," available at: http://www.dfat.gov.au/publications/trade/trading-our-way-to-more-jobs-and-prosperity.html.

[75] "Gillard Government Trade Policy Statement: Trading our Way to More Jobs and Prosperity," available at: http://www.dfat.gov.au/publications/trade/trading-our-way-to-more-jobs-and-prosperity.html.

[76] See website of the Australian Government's Productivity Commission, available at: http://www.pc.gov.au.

[77] Productivity Commission, Bilateral and Regional Trade Agreements, November 2010, p. iv, available at: http://www.pc.gov.au/__data/assets/pdf_file/0010/104203/trade-agreements-report.pdf.

[78] Productivity Commission, Bilateral and Regional Trade Agreements, November 2010, p. 271, available at: http://www.pc.gov.au/__data/assets/pdf_file/0010/104203/trade-agreements-report.pdf.

[79] Productivity Commission, Bilateral and Regional Trade Agreements, November 2010, p. 274, available at: http://www.pc.gov.au/__data/assets/pdf_file/0010/104203/trade-agreements-report.pdf.

> Australia should seek to avoid accepting ISDS provisions in trade agreements that confer additional substantive or procedural rights on foreign investors over and above those already provided by the Australian legal system. Nor, in the Commission's assessment, is it advisable in trade negotiations for Australia to expend bargaining coin to seek such rights over foreign governments, as a means of managing investment risks inherent in investing in foreign countries. Other options are available to investors.[80]

The Productivity Commission added that:

> The Commission notes that, if perceptions of problems with a foreign country's legal system are sufficient to discourage investment in that country, a bilateral arrangement with Australia to provide a 'preferential legal system' for Australian investors is unlikely to generate the same benefits for that country than if its legal system was developed on a domestic non-preferential basis. To the extent that secure legal systems facilitate investment in a similar way that customs and port procedures facilitate goods trade, there may be a role for developed nations to assist through legal capacity building to develop stable and transparent legal and judicial frameworks. While not an immediate solution, over time such capacity building goes towards addressing the underlying problem, and provides benefits not only for foreign investors (including Australian investors), but all participants in the domestic economy.[81]

Accordingly, the Productivity Commission recommended that the Australian Government should "seek to avoid the inclusion of investor-state dispute settlement provisions in BRTAs that grant foreign investors in Australia substantive or procedural rights greater than those enjoyed by Australian investors."[82] As has been seen above, this recommendation found its way into the Gillard Government Trade Policy Statement of April 2011.

The Productivity Commission's Report, and the Gillard Government Trade Policy Statement, have met with criticism in some quarters,[83] but have been welcomed in others.[84] It is worth noting that, according to the Office of the US Trade Representative, the negotiations for the TPP Agreement, where Australia is participating, will seek to include "provisions for expeditious, fair, and transparent investor-State dispute settlement subject to appropriate safeguards, with discussions continuing on scope and coverage."[85] It remains to be seen how the TPP negotiations will unfold on this particular issue.

---

[80] Productivity Commission, Bilateral and Regional Trade Agreements, November 2010, p. 279, available at: http://www.pc.gov.au/__data/assets/pdf_file/0010/104203/trade-agreements-report.pdf.

[81] Productivity Commission, Bilateral and Regional Trade Agreements, November 2010, p. 279, available at: http://www.pc.gov.au/__data/assets/pdf_file/0010/104203/trade-agreements-report.pdf.

[82] Productivity Commission, Bilateral and Regional Trade Agreements, November 2010, p. 279, available at: http://www.pc.gov.au/__data/assets/pdf_file/0010/104203/trade-agreements-report.pdf. (Recommendation 4(c)).

[83] See especially Nottage, The Rise and Possible Fall of Investor-State Arbitration in Asia: A Skeptic's View of Australia's Gillard Government Trade Policy Statement, Legal Studies Research Paper No 11/32, Sydney Law School, 2011, available at: http://papers.ssrn.com.

[84] See, e.g., Tienhaara/Ranald, Australia's Rejection of Investor-State Dispute Settlement: Four Potential Contributing Factors, Investment Treaty News 4 (2011) 1, p. 6 (6–7).

[85] USTR, Outlines of the Trans-Pacific Partnership Agreement, available at: http://www.ustr.gov/about-us/press-office/fact-sheets/2011/november/outlines-trans-pacific-partnership-agreement.

Conclusion

Although the ASEAN was initially established as a quasi-political response to regional developments, it has over the years become a successful platform for the economic liberalisation of the region. In the early stages of its history, ASEAN members promoted trade liberalisation through the reduction of tariffs and other non-tariff barriers to trade. However, with the creation of the AFTA, a more holistic approach was adopted to trade and investment liberalisation in the region.

The ASEAN area is highly dependent on trade and investment originating from outside the region. Therefore, it comes as no surprise that in recent years, a number of ASEAN+1 FTAs have been negotiated with regional powers. Through the negotiation of trade and investment agreements with global reach, Southeast Asia is now entering a new phase in economic liberalisation. The successful negotiation of the TPP Agreement promises to be a landmark moment for the region. The TPP Agreement will cover a number of items that are not typically found in FTAs, including, for example, current issues such as climate change and regulatory responses to an economic crisis.

Finally, the formation of the AEC is expected to be the culmination of trade and economic liberalisation in the ASEAN region. The AEC embodies the region's on-going efforts to create free trade and investment. However, beyond this, the AEC seeks to address structural concerns through policies designed to ameliorate the development gap between ASEAN nations. This is perhaps recognition that going forward such key structural issues will form the focus of efforts to deepen regional integration within the ASEAN region.

Part III
International Economic Institutions

Recent Quota and Governance Reforms at the International Monetary Fund

Wolfgang Bergthaler and Andrew Giddings

Introduction

This article discusses the significant quota and governance reforms recently undertaken at the International Monetary Fund which is the international financial institution at the center of the global financial system, over the past few years. The IMF approved two ad hoc quota increases (2006 and 2008), completed one periodic quota review with a doubling of quotas (2010), and approved two amendments to its charter related to quota and governance (2008 and 2010) setting out major changes to the IMF's governance structure. Considering the widespread consensus that is necessary to achieve reform in this crucial area, the reforms are remarkable in their extent and dimension. This is particularly pronounced when comparing the degree and extent of IMF quota and governance reforms at other international organizations and the fact that, at the same time, the IMF has been at the center of resolving the global financial crisis.

The global financial system has undergone dramatic change since the International Monetary Fund was established in 1946. The Bretton Woods gold-based exchange system broke down in the 1970s, capital flows were liberalized over the following decades, the IMF transformed into a truly global institution in the 1990s with near-universal membership (of currently 188 members), the sophistication of financial markets increased, and the financial sector became a major part of countries' economies. These developments were interrupted by periodic regional

The views expressed herein are those of the authors and should not be attributed to the IMF, its Executive Board, or IMF management. The authors would like to thank Ross Leckow, Deputy General Counsel, and Damien Eastman, Senior Counsel, for their guidance on this article. This article reflects the status as of May 2012.

W. Bergthaler (✉) • A. Giddings
Legal Department, International Monetary Fund, 700 19th Street, N.W., Washington, DC 20431, USA
e-mail: wbergthaler@imf.org; agiddings@imf.org

C. Herrmann et al. (eds.), *European Yearbook of International Economic Law (EYIEL), Vol. 4 (2013)*, European Yearbook of International Economic Law 4,
DOI 10.1007/978-3-642-33917-2_14,

financial crises, such as those of Latin American and Asia in the 1980s and 1990s, and most recently by the ongoing global financial crises, requiring strong international cooperation in addressing and resolving these crises.

The IMF is the international financial institution at the center of the global financial system and even though these developments and events have affected the institution, the IMF's main objective and purpose—the stability of the international monetary system—remains unchanged. The IMF's purposes include:

(i) "to promote exchange stability, to maintain orderly exchange arrangements among members, and to avoid competitive exchange depreciation" and
(ii) "to give confidence to members by making the general resources of the Fund temporarily available to them under adequate safeguards, thus providing them with opportunity to correct maladjustments in their balance of payments without resorting to measures destructive of national or international prosperity."[1]

IMF quota and governance reform has been at the center of reform discussions in recent years.[2] As in other international financial organizations, in the IMF a member's voice (its voting power) is determined by its quota contribution to the IMF rather than based on the principle of one member, one vote, which is used in a number of other international organizations.

In the last 70 years, not only has the global financial system evolved but the economic weight among IMF members has also shifted significantly; first, to Western Europe and Japan, and more recently to emerging nations in Asia, Latin America, and Africa. In the context of this shift, it was recognized that the IMF's decision-making needs to reflect the relative economic weight of its membership in order to retain its legitimacy and accountability. The quota structure, on which the IMF's funding and representation is based, may change relatively flexibly through periodic quota reviews every 5 years,[3] thus enabling the institution to adapt to the changes in members' relative positions in the world economy. However, the governance structure of the IMF is enshrined in the IMF's Articles of Agreement (the "IMF's Articles"), the institution's charter,[4] and thus can only be modified by way of amendments to such Articles, which are difficult to achieve given that a double majority of the membership in terms of total voting power and number of IMF members needs to accept an amendment to the IMF's Articles.[5]

---

[1] See Art. I(iii) and (v) of the IMF's Articles.

[2] See for instance, United Nations, Report of the Commission of Experts of the President of the United Nations General Assembly on Reforms of the International Monetary and Financial System, 2009, available at: http://www.un.org/ga/econcrisissummit/docs/FinalReport_CoE.pdf; IEO, Governance of the IMF. An evaluation, 2008, available at: http://www.ieo-imf.org/ieo/pages/IEOPreview.aspx?img=i6nZpr3iSlU%3D&mappingid=K1g%2BWj0GTnY%3D.

[3] Art. III, Section 2 of the IMF's Articles.

[4] See the IMF Articles of Agreement, available at: http://www.imf.org/external/pubs/ft/aa/index.htm.

[5] Art. XXVIII of the IMF's Articles. Certain amendments to the IMF's Articles require acceptance by all IMF members (see Art. XXVIII(b)(i) through (iii) of the IMF's Articles).

The IMF's reform efforts have yielded significant results over the past few years: the IMF approved two ad hoc quota increases (2006 and 2008), completed one periodic quota review with a doubling of quotas (2010), and approved two amendments to its Articles related to quota and governance (2008 and 2010) setting out major changes to the governance structure. This is also significant since the IMF has been, at the same time, at the center of resolving the ongoing global financial crisis.

In light of these developments, this article discusses the following: (i) an overview of the IMF governance structure; (ii) the major governance reforms that focused on quota and voice, the reform of the IMF Executive Board, ministerial involvement in IMF decision-making, and the selection of the Managing Director; and (iii) an outlook for the future.

Overview of IMF Governance

An overview of the basic governance structure of the IMF seems appropriate at the outset of this article. The basic governance structure as set out in the IMF's Articles has remained largely unchanged since 1946. In this respect, the IMF's governance structure comprises three organs: the Board of Governors; the Executive Board; and the Managing Director.[6]

The Board of Governors is the highest decision-making body of the IMF. It is comprised of one governor and one alternate governor appointed by each member country, who is usually the minister of finance or the governor of the central bank. All powers of the IMF not directly conferred by the IMF's Articles on the Board of Governors, the Executive Board, or the Managing Director are vested in the Board of Governors.[7] The Board of Governors may delegate to the Executive Board all powers, except for certain powers specifically reserved to it,[8] and the Board of Governors has exercised such authority by delegating all those powers to the Executive Board.[9] The Board of Governors normally meets annually.[10] The Board of Governors takes major decisions for the institution, such as changes in IMF member's quota or admission of new members.[11]

[6] Art. XII, Section 1 of the IMF's Articles.

[7] Art. XII, Section 2(a) of the IMF's Articles.

[8] Art. XII, Section 2(b) of the IMF's Articles.

[9] Section 15 of the By-Laws. Therefore, the Executive Board may exercise all competences under the IMF's Articles not specially conferred on the Board of Governors and the Managing Director.

[10] Joint IMF and World Bank Annual Meetings, usually in the fall, for example the October 2012 meeting in Tokyo, Japan.

[11] See for instance, Art. II and III of the IMF's Articles.

Consistent with the authority of the Board of Governors to establish committees (that are advisory in nature),[12] the Interim Committee was established in 1974, and was transformed into the International Monetary and Financial Committee (the "IMFC") in 1999.[13] The IMFC meets bi-annually and advises the Board of Governors on a range of matters including the supervision, management and adaptation of the international monetary and financial system, reviewing developments in global liquidity and the transfer of resources to developing countries, considering proposals by the Executive Board to amend the IMF's Articles, and dealing with disturbances that might threaten the system. The IMFC has 24 members who are IMF governors, ministers, or others of comparable rank, and the membership reflects the composition of the IMF Executive Board.

The Executive Board is responsible for "conducting the business of the Fund."[14] It is currently composed of 24 Executive Directors[15]—who are either appointed or elected by members or groups of members—and the Managing Director, who serves as its chairman. Members with the five largest quotas in the IMF (currently, the United States, Japan, Germany, France, and the United Kingdom) are required to appoint an Executive Director while the remainder of IMF members participate in the election of 19 Executive Directors every 2 years.[16] The Executive Board sits in "continuous session" and in practice meets several times per week. The Executive Board exercises various important functions for the institution:

(i) A regulatory function (such as surveillance under Article IV of the IMF's Articles and IMF jurisdiction under Article VIII, Sections 2(a), 3, and 4 of the IMF's Articles);
(ii) A legislative function (such as establishment of legal frameworks of general applicability in the area of the use of IMF resources under Article V of the IMF's Articles or surveillance under Article IV of the IMF's Articles); and

---

[12] Art. XII, Section 2(f) of the IMF's Articles. Another committee is the Development Committee, which is a joint committee with the World Bank.

[13] IMF, Board of Governors Resolution No. 29-8, adopted on 2 October 1974, as repealed by Board of Governors Resolution No. 54-9, adopted on 30 September 1999, Selected Decisions and Selected Documents of the International Monetary Fund, 35th issue, 2011, pp. 853-858, available at: http://www.imf.org/external/pubs/ft/sd/2011/123110.pdf.

[14] Art. XII, Section 3(a) of the IMF's Articles.

[15] The Board of Governors may by an 85% majority increase or decrease the number of Executive Directors at the IMF Executive Board in the context of each regular biannual election. See Art. XII, Section 3(b) of the IMF's Articles.

[16] Art. XII, Section 3(b) of the IMF's Articles. In the Executive Board, Executive Directors elected by a multi-member constituency must cast their votes in a unit and therefore, may not split their votes; see Art. XII, Section 3(i)(iv), second sentence, of the IMF's Articles. See Gianviti, Decision Making in the International Monetary Fund, in: IMF (ed.), *Current Developments in Monetary and Financial Law*, Vol. 1, 1999, p. 46.

(iii) A financing function (such as approving individual IMF arrangements or completing reviews under IMF arrangement under Article V of the IMF's Articles).[17]

The Managing Director is selected by the Executive Board and conducts, under the direction of the Executive Board, the "ordinary business" of the IMF.[18] In practice, the Managing Director exercises the initiative with respect to the Executive Board's agenda and thus exercises a role that is akin to an executive function within the institution. Subject to the general control of the Executive Board, the Managing Director is responsible for the organization, appointment, and dismissal of staff. The Managing Director acts as Chairman of the Executive Board, though has no vote except a deciding vote in case of an equal division.[19] In addition, the Managing Director may participate in meetings of the Board of Governors and the IMFC, but cannot vote at Board of Governors' meetings.[20] The Managing Director serves for a 5-year term and may be re-elected subject to certain age limits.[21]

Recent Quota and Governance Reforms

This section discusses the elements of quota and governance reforms in the IMF over the past few years,[22] which can be divided into the following four broad categories, specifically: (i) quota and voice reform; (ii) reform of the Executive Board; (iii) ministerial involvement in IMF decision making; and (iv) the selection of the Managing Director.

The 2008 and 2010 Quota and Voice Reform

The recent quota and governance reforms must be considered in light of the relevance and role of a member's quota within the IMF. A member's quota is the

[17] See Committee on IMF Governance, Final Report, 2009, p. 16, available at: http://www.imf.org/external/np/omd/2009/govref/032409.pdf.

[18] Art. XII, Section 4(a) and (b) of the IMF's Articles.

[19] Art. XII, Section 4(a) of the IMF's Articles.

[20] See paragraph 1(d) of Board of Governors Resolution No. 54-9 of 30 September 1999.

[21] Section 14(c) of the By-Laws.

[22] See Hagan, Reforming the IMF, in: Giovanoli/Devos (eds.), *International Monetary and Financial Law. The Global Crisis*, 2010, pp. 40–68; Bergthaler/Bossu, Recent legal developments in the International Monetary Fund, in: Herrmann/Terhechte (eds.), *European Yearbook of International Economic Law 2010*, 2010, pp. 391–404.

key metric for a member's participation in the IMF. More specifically, each IMF member's voting power (and, *inter alia*, a member's access to financing and its contribution as well as its participation in the Special Drawings Rights Department) is determined by its quota in the General Resources Account ("GRA").[23] Each IMF member is assigned a quota expressed in Special Drawing Rights ("SDRs"), the IMF's unit of account, reflecting its relative weight in the world economy. The IMF uses a quota formula to help guide the decision regarding the size and distribution of members' actual quotas.[24]

Given the special majority of 85 % of the IMF's total voting power required to approve an increase in IMF quotas, reforms are typically approved in the context of a package consisting of different elements. For instance, past quota increases included minimum consent requirements (such as 70 % or 85 % of quotas before quota increases become effective) or were tied, with respect to their effectiveness, to an amendment to the IMF's Articles that in itself requires a double majority (in terms of voting power and number of Fund members) to enter into force.[25]

The IMF's Articles call for a review of quotas every 5 years to ensure that quota resources remain adequate and reflect the members' relative share in the world economy.[26] Prior to 2006, the last effective quota increase was adopted in January 1998 in the context of the Eleventh General Review of Quotas. While the world economy had grown significantly since 1998, the IMF membership decided to complete the Twelfth and Thirteenth General Reviews of Quotas without any quota increases.[27] Accordingly, the general sense emerged among the IMF membership that IMF quotas were no longer adequate and particularly did not reflect the relative share of members in world economy (i.e. some members were overrepresented while others were underrepresented relative to their economic weight in terms of IMF quota).

[23] Total approved quotas currently amount to SDR 238.116 billion. The quotas of individual members range from SDR 42.122 billion in the case of the United States, the IMF member with the largest quota, to SDR 1.8 million in the case of Tuvalu, the IMF's member with the smallest quota. For individual IMF member country quota information, see: http://www.imf.org/external/np/sec/memdir/members.htm; see also, Steinki/Bergthaler, Recent Reforms of the Finances of the International Monetary Fund: An Overview, in: Herrmann/Terhechte (eds.), *European Yearbook of International Economic Law 2012*, 2012, pp. 635–666 (651).

[24] Given the importance of quotas in the IMF, the quota formula itself is subject to debate.

[25] See Art. XXVIII(a) and (b) of the IMF's Articles. For instance, the Sixth General Review of Quotas only became effective once the Second Amendment to the IMF's Articles had entered into force.

[26] Art. III, Section 1 of the IMF's Articles. Quotas are subject to periodic reviews, at least every five years, but can also be changed on an ad-hoc basis (Art. III, Section 2 of the IMF's Articles). Any change in quotas must be adopted by the Board of Governors with an 85% majority of the total voting power.

[27] IMF Press Release No. 03/14, IMF Board of Governors Approves Conclusion of Quota Review, 4 February 2003, available at: http://www.imf.org/external/np/sec/pr/2003/pr0314.htm; IMF Press Release No. 08/13, IMF Board of Governors Approves Conclusion of Quota Review, 4 February 2008, available at: http://www.imf.org/external/np/sec/pr/2008/pr0813.htm.

In September 2006, after an intensive work program and many consultations,[28] the Board of Governors adopted a resolution providing for a 2-year plan of action aimed at: (i) better aligning members' quota shares with their economic weight in the world economy; and (ii) enhancing the participation of low-income countries in the governance of the IMF.[29]

As an immediate step, in 2006, the IMF approved initial ad hoc increases in quotas for a small group of the countries with a "robust standard of underrepresentedness," comprising China, Korea, Mexico, and Turkey.[30] There was a concern that, given the shortcomings of the existing quota formulas, any ad hoc increases without agreement on a revised quota formula could create new distortions in the distribution of quota shares. Given these concerns, while the existing quota formulas were decided to be a starting point for determining eligibility for an ad hoc increase, these needed to be supplemented by other metrics or filters.

In 2007, the IMF changed the quota formula, which now constitutes the new calculated basis that helps determine actual members' quotas.[31]

As the next step, in April 2008, as part of the IMF's broader quota and voice reform discussion[32], the IMF Board of Governors approved increases in the quotas of 54 members that were underrepresented according to the newly-adopted quota formula, and requested that the IMF Executive Board recommend further realignments of members' quota shares in the context of the next regular review of quotas, the 14th General Quota Review.[33] The effectiveness of the ad hoc quota

[28] See the Communiqué of the International Monetary and Financial Committee of the Board of Governors of the International Monetary Fund of 22 April 2006, available at: http://www.imf.org/external/np/cm/2006/042206.htm.

[29] Board of Governors Resolution No. 61-5 of 18 September 2006.

[30] See IMF, Quotas and Voice: Further Thoughts on Approaches to Reform, 2006, available at: http://www.imf.org/external/np/pp/eng/2006/062306.pdf; IMF, Press Release No. 06/189, IMF Executive Board Recommends Quota and Related Governance Reforms, 1 September 2006, available at: http://www.imf.org/external/np/sec/pr/2006/pr06189.htm.

[31] The current quota formula is a weighted average of GDP (weight of 50 percent), openness (30 percent), economic variability (15 percent), and international reserves (5 percent). For this purpose, GDP is measured as a blend of GDP based on market exchange rates (weight of 60 percent) and on PPP exchange rates (40 percent). IMF, A New Quota Formula—Additional Considerations, Statistical Appendix, and Statement by the Managing Director, 2007, available at: http://www.imf.org/external/np/pp/2007/eng/031407.pdf; IMF, Reform of Quota and Voice in the International Monetary Fund-Draft Report of the Executive Board to the Board of Governors, 2008, available at: http://www.imf.org/external/np/pp/eng/2008/032108.pdf.

[32] Committee on IMF Governance, Final Report, 2009, pp. 5, 13–15, 21, 23, available at: http://www.imf.org/external/np/omd/2009/govref/032409.pdf, noted "the inadequate voice and representation and hence ownership of emerging markets and developing countries in the IMF."

[33] IMF, Board of Governors Resolution No. 63-2, adopted on 28 April 2008, Selected Decisions and Selected Documents of the International Monetary Fund, 35th issue, 2011, p. 9, available at: http://www.imf.org/external/pubs/ft/sd/2011/123110.pdf. Following the entry into force of the Sixth Amendment on 3 March 2011, ad hoc quota increases for 54 eligible members under the 2008 quota and voice reform have become effective for those members that have consented

increase was conditioned upon the entry into force of the 2008 proposed amendment, the Sixth Amendment.

The second aspect of the 2008 reforms was aimed at enhancing the voice of low income countries' participation, by reforming the number (and future calculation) of "basic votes" provided for in the IMF's Articles.[34] Under the IMF's Articles (as amended by the Sixth Amendment), a member's voting power comprises two elements:

(i) A fixed number of "basic votes," which are the same number for every member. These basic votes of each member are the number of votes that results from the equal distribution among all the members of 5.502 percent of the aggregate sum of the total voting power of all the members;[35] and
(ii) "Quota-based votes," which are the votes allocated to members according to their quota share, give each IMF member one additional vote for each SDR 100,000 of quota.

This essentially led to a tripling of basic votes for all IMF members (to about 750 each) and included a formula to maintain the share of basic votes as a percentage of to the total voting power going forward (to approximately 5.5 %). The net effect of this reform was to boost low-income members' voting power at the IMF as well as prevent erosion of basic votes going forward by linking them to total quotas.

Before the 2008 amendment to the IMF's Articles (the Sixth Amendment), the share of basic votes—the set number of votes that are the same for each member—was fixed by the IMF's Articles at 250 votes per member. Over time, as the membership of the IMF expanded and quota-related voting shares were increased, the proportion of basic votes as a share of total voting power was significantly eroded. To illustrate this point, basic votes comprised approximately 11.3 % of the total voting power in 1946, and by 2008, comprised only 2.1 % of the total voting power.[36]

---

to, and paid for, their increases. See IMF, Quota and Voice Reform—Key Elements of a Potential Package of Reforms, 2008, available at: http://www.imf.org/external/np/pp/eng/2008/022608.pdf.

[34] IMF, Proposed Amendment of the Articles of Agreement Regarding Basic Votes— Preliminary Considerations and Chairman's Summing Up, 2006, available at: http://www.imf.org/external/np/pp/eng/2006/122206a.pdf; IMF, Reform of Quota and Voice in the International Monetary Fund—Report of the Executive Board to the Board of Governors, 2008, available at: http://www.imf.org/external/np/pp/eng/2008/032108.pdf. The Sixth Amendment was adopted by the Board of Governors Resolution No. 63-2 effective 28 April 2008 and entered into force on 3 March 2011. Acceptance of the Proposed Amendments of the Articles of Agreement at: http://www.imf.org/external/np/sec/misc/consents.htm#a2.

[35] Art. XII, Section 5 of the IMF's Articles.

[36] IMF, Proposed Amendment of the Articles of Agreement Regarding Basic Votes—Preliminary Considerations and Chairman's Summing Up, 2006, available at: http://www.imf.org/external/np/pp/eng/2006/122206a.pdf.

Finally, in 2010, with the onset of the global financial crisis[37] and picking up from its commitment to complete the next periodic quota review earlier, the Board of Governors completed the 14th General Review of Quotas[38] and decided to double IMF members' quotas. Given that quota resources also constitute the main financing power for the IMF, the IMF also discussed the size of the IMF's resources in this context.[39] This quota review supported "a shift in quota share to dynamic emerging market and developing countries of at least five percent from over-represented countries to under-represented countries using the current quota formula as the basis to work from" and committed to "protecting the voting share of the poorest members." If the criteria for the effectiveness are met,[40] IMF quotas would reflect members relative share in the economy; in particular, fast growing emerging markets like Brazil, China, India, and Russia (commonly referred to as "BRIC") will see their quotas increase substantially and all BRIC members will be among the IMF's ten largest quota holders.

---

[37] Statement Issued by the G20 Leaders, 2 April 2009, available at: http://www.g20.utoronto.ca/2009/2009communique0402.html; G20 Leaders Statement: The Pittsburgh Summit, 24–25 September 2009, available at: http://www.g20.utoronto.ca/2009/2009communique0925.html; The G20 Seoul Summit Leaders' Declaration 12 November 2010, available at: http://www.g20.utoronto.ca/2010/g20seoul.html; Communiqué of the International Monetary and Financial Committee of the Board of Governors of the International Monetary Fund, 25 April 2009, available at: http://www.imf.org/external/np/cm/2009/042509.htm; Communiqué of the International Monetary and Financial Committee of the Board of Governors of the International Monetary Fund, 4 October 2009, available at: http://www.imf.org/external/np/cm/2009/100409.htm; Communiqué of the Twenty-First Meeting of the International Monetary and Financial Committee of the Board of Governors of the International Monetary Fund, 24 April 2010, available at: http://www.imf.org/external/np/cm/2010/042410.htm; Communiqué of the Twenty-Second Meeting of the International Monetary and Financial Committee of the Board of Governors of the International Monetary Fund, 9 October 2010, available at: http://www.imf.org/external/np/cm/2010/100910.htm.

[38] IMF, Board of Governors Resolution No. 66-2 of 15 December 2010, Selected Decisions and Selected Documents of the International Monetary Fund, 35th issue, 2011, p. 9, available at: http://www.imf.org/external/pubs/ft/sd/2011/123110.pdf.

[39] The IMF makes its resources available to members under Art. V of the IMF's Articles; see Steinki/Bergthaler, Recent Reforms of the Finances of the International Monetary Fund: An Overview, in: Herrmann/Terhechte (eds.), *European Yearbook of International Economic Law 2012*, 2012, pp. 651, 652; IMF, Fourteenth General Review of Quotas—The Size of the Fund: Initial Considerations and The Chairman's Concluding Remarks, 2010, available at: http://www.imf.org/external/np/pp/eng/2010/031210.pdf.

[40] This requires two remaining conditions (see Board of Governors Resolution No. 66-2 of 15 December 2010) to be met: (i) consents to the quota increases under the 14th General Review of Quotas by members having not less than seventy percent of the total of quotas on 5 November 2010 consenting to the increases in their quotas; and (ii) entry into force of the proposed board reform amendment that happens once the Fund certifies that three-fifths of the members (currently 113 members), representing eighty-five percent of the total voting power have accepted the proposed amendment. At the time of writing, these requirements have not yet been met. For an updated list of acceptances and consents, see http://www.imf.org/external/np/sec/misc/consents.htm.

In the context of the 2010 Board of Governors resolution, the Board of Governors also committed to accelerate the next periodic review of quotas, the 15th General Review of Quotas, to January 2014 and again to review the quota formula, for which the initial step occurred in 2012.[41]

Executive Board Reform

The Executive Board is at the heart of the governance structure of the IMF and, as described above, plays an important role in the strategic and day-to-day operations of the IMF.

The 2008 Reforms

In addition to the quota and voice reforms and the reforms to members' basic votes, the 2008 quota and voice reforms also addressed another aspect of "voice," which was to provide for the appointment of a Second Alternate Executive Director for Directors elected by a certain number of members.

Prior to this amendment, each Executive Director was required to appoint one Alternate Executive Director who had the power to act for the Executive Director when the Executive Director was not present in meetings of the Executive Board.[42] With the growth of the IMF's membership and the average size of constituencies increasing over time, concerns arose over the burdens placed on Executive Directors representing large constituencies.

To address these concerns, Article XII, Section 3(e) of the IMF's Articles (as amended by the Sixth Amendment[43]) entitles, but does not require, Executive Directors elected by a specified number of members to appoint a second Alternate Executive Director. This provision strengthens the offices of those Executive Directors and facilitates the execution of their responsibilities under the IMF's Articles. For instance, the two chairs at the Executive Board representing African constituencies are elected by a large number of IMF members, thereby making it challenging for the Executive Director and his/her office to adequately represent their interests without sufficient resources and personnel.

---

[41] IMF, Quota Formula Review—Initial Considerations, 2012, available at: http://www.imf.org/external/np/pp/eng/2012/021012.pdf.

[42] Art. XII, Section 3(e) of the IMF's Articles in the version before the Sixth Amendment.

[43] The IMF's Articles were amended effective 3 March 2011 by the modifications approved by the Board of Governors in Resolution No. 63-2, adopted 28 April 2008 ("Sixth Amendment"); Board of Governors Resolution No. 63-2 of 28 April 2008; IMF, Reform of Quota and Voice in the International Monetary Fund—Report of the Executive Board to the Board of Governors, 2008, available at: www.imf.org/external/np/pp/eng/2008/032108.pdf.

To provide for future flexibility, Article XII, Section 3(e) of the IMF's Articles permits the Board of Governors to revise the specified number in the context of each regular election of Executive Directors. In this regard, as part of the 2010 reforms discussed below, the Board of Governors decided that following the 2012 regular election of Executive Directors, an Executive Director elected by seven or more members will be entitled (but not required) to appoint an additional Alternate Executive Director (this was set as nineteen or more in 2008).[44]

The 2010 Reforms

Governance reform discussions were accelerated following different studies on IMF governance reform inside and outside the IMF.[45]

The Managing Director appointed a Committee on IMF Governance Reform, a group of eminent persons chaired by Trevor Manuel, the then-Minister of Finance for the Republic of South Africa. The group issued its final report on IMF governance in March 2009 (the "Manuel Report")[46], which cited drawbacks in the governance structure of the IMF that were resulting in the IMF's advice losing traction and effectiveness.[47] It proposed a package of reforms, some but not all of

[44] See IMF, Board of Governors Resolution No. 63-2 of 28 April 2008 and Board of Governors Resolution No. 66-2 of 15 December 2010, Selected Decisions and Selected Documents of the International Monetary Fund, 35th issue, 2011, p. 3, available at: http://www.imf.org/external/pubs/ft/sd/2011/123110.pdf.

[45] See for a summary: IMF, IMF Governance—Summary of Issues and Reform Options, 2009, available at: http://www.imf.org/external/np/pp/eng/2009/070109.pdf; Moser, et al., Report of the Executive Board Working Group on IMF Corporate Governance, 31 July 2008, available at: http://www.imf.org/external/np/pp/eng/2008/073108.pdf; IEO, Governance of the IMF. An evaluation, 2008, available at: http://www.ieoimf.org/ieo/pages/IEOPreview.aspx?img=i6nZpr3iSlU%3D&mappingid=K1g%2BWj0GTnY%3D; G-20, Final Report of G-20 Working Group 3: Reform of the IMF, 4 March 2009, available at: http://www.g20.org/Documents/g20_wg3_010409.pdf; Boorman, Reform of the Global Financial System and the Role of the International Monetary Fund, 2009 Latin America Emerging Markets Forum (2008); Boorman, An Agenda for Reform of the International Monetary Fund, Dialogue on Globalization, Occasional Paper No. 38, (2008); Truman (ed.), *Reforming the IMF for the 21st Century*, 2006; Truman, Governance of the Bretton Woods Sisters: Making Progress on the Agenda, Essay for the Petersen Institute for International Economics, 2009, available at: http://www.iie.com/publications/papers/paper.cfm?ResearchID=1150.

[46] See Committee on IMF Governance, Final Report, 24 March 2009, available at: http://www.imf.org/external/np/omd/2009/govref/032409.pdf.

[47] The Manuel Report noted the governance drawbacks including the excessive involvement of the Executive Board in day-to-day operational activities that undermines its effectiveness and in general a lack of clarity in the roles and responsibilities of the Board, IMFC, and IMF management. See Committee on IMF Governance, Final Report, 2009, pp. 11, 15, available at: http://www.imf.org/external/np/omd/2009/govref/032409.pdf.

which were ultimately incorporated into the 2010 quota and governance reform.[48] The Executive Board intensely debated these proposals, as well as proposals from staff on possible governance reforms.[49]

In November 2010, the Board of Governors adopted a package of major reforms on quota and governance, which—if the criteria for effectiveness are met[50]—will represent a significant change in the structure and representation at the IMF.[51] The reforms agreed by the Board of Governors consisted of one amendment to the IMF's Articles and two political commitments:

(i) A move to an all-elected Executive Board (the "Seventh Amendment");
(ii) A commitment of the membership to maintain Executive Board size at 24 and, after the conditions for effectiveness of the quota increases under the 14th General Quota Review are met, to review Board composition every 8 years; and
(iii) A commitment to two fewer advanced European chairs, based on an agreed metric (occupancy of the Executive Director position pro-rated to the time spent in it)—to be implemented no later than the first regular election after the conditions for effectiveness of the quota increases under the 14th Review are met.

First, with respect to the move to an all-elected Board, the IMF's current Articles establish two categories of Executive Directors: those who are appointed, and those who are elected. This longstanding principle of appointments is similar to provisions in charters of other international organizations, such as the United Nations Security Council or the World Bank's Board of Directors.[52] The 2010 proposed amendment eliminates the category of appointed Executive

[48] The Manuel Report's proposals included a re-composition of the Executive Board to allow for greater representation of emerging market economies, including removing the requirement of five appointed Executive Directors and undertaking constituency reforms to achieve consolidation, to reduce the size of the Executive Board to 20, and a clear delineation of roles and responsibilities including elevating the Executive Board from day-to-day operational decisions to advising an activated Council on strategic issues and overseeing management (see section on Ministerial Involvement in IMF Decision-Making, *infra*). See Committee on IMF Governance, Final Report, 2009, pp. 3, 15, 16, 23, available at: http://www.imf.org/external/np/omd/2009/govref/032409.pdf.

[49] IMF, IMF Governance—Summary of Issues and Reform Options, 2009, available at: http://www.imf.org/external/np/pp/eng/2009/070109.pdf; IMF, IMF Governance Reform, 2010, available at: http://www.imf.org/external/np/pp/eng/2010/070710.pdf.

[50] This requires two remaining conditions (see Board of Governors resolution No 66-2 of 15 December 2010) to be met: (i) consents to the quota increases under the 14th General Review of Quotas by members having not less than seventy percent of the total of quotas on 5 November 2010 consenting to the increases in their quotas and (ii) entry into force of the proposed board reform amendment that happens once the Fund certifies that three-fifths of the members (currently 113 members), representing eighty-five percent of the total voting power have accepted the proposed amendment. At the time of writing, these requirements have not yet been met. For an updated list of acceptances, see http://www.imf.org/external/np/sec/misc/consents.htm.

[51] See IMF News Release, G-20 Ministers Agree 'Historic' Reforms in IMF Governance, available at: http://www.imf.org/external/pubs/ft/survey/so/2010/NEW102310A.htm.

[52] See e.g., Art. V Section V of the IBRD Articles of Agreement, under which five Executive Directors shall be appointed, one by each of the five members having the largest number of shares.

Directors and requires that all Executive Directors be elected.[53] This change also requires a corresponding amendment to the biannual election rules for Executive Directors.[54] There are also a number of other provisions in the IMF's Articles that refer to appointed Executive Directors that would be deleted or amended.[55]

Second, the IMF's Articles currently provide for an Executive Board composed of 20 Executive Directors (5 appointed and 15 elected), but authorize the Board of Governors to increase or decrease the number of elected Executive Directors for each regular election. The proposed amendment would maintain both the general rule regarding the total size of the Executive Board and the mechanism by which this size may be adjusted. Under the proposed amendment, while the Executive Board would consist of 20 Executive Directors (all elected), the IMF's Articles would continue to authorize the Board of Governors, by an 85 % majority of the total voting power, to increase or decrease the number of Executive Directors for each regular election of Executive Directors. As a legal matter, the commitment to an Executive Board of 24 members would not obviate the need for the Board of Governors to take a decision to increase the number of Executive Directors to 24 at the time of each regular election—nor would it require the Board of Governors to approve such an increase.

Third, there have been long-standing calls for European members "to make room" for more emerging market country representation at the IMF Executive Board.[56] This call was addressed in the 2010 reforms, though it was well accepted that representation at the Executive Board must continue to be based on the principle of voluntary constituency formation. Therefore, facilitating a re-composition of the Executive Board requires the pro-active participation of members to consolidate constituencies and otherwise develop mechanisms for sharing an Executive Director's chair. The Board of Governors Resolution notes a commitment to reduce the number of Executive Directors representing advanced European countries by two in favor of dynamic emerging market and developing countries.[57] The reduction would be implemented no later than the first election

[53] Upon the entry into force of the amendment, there would no longer be a category of appointed Executive Directors under the Articles. However, there would be Executive Directors in office who had been appointed pursuant to the relevant provisions of the current Articles of Agreement. To address the transition to an Executive Board comprised solely of elected Executive Directors, the proposed amendment includes provisions to govern the period between the entry into force of the amendment and the first election following such entry into force. See Schedule E of the IMF's Articles under the proposed amendment.

[54] In this regard, the rules contained in Schedule E of the IMF's Articles will be replaced with rules to be adopted by the Board of Governors biannually.

[55] These provisions are as follows: Art. XII, Sections 3(f), 3(i)(i)-(v), 3(j) and 8; Art. XXI(a)(ii); Art. XXIX(a); Schedule D, paragraphs 1(a), 5(e) and 5(f); Schedule E; and Schedule L, paragraphs 1(b) and 3(c).

[56] This was addressed, inter alia, at the G-20 Ministerial Meeting in Korea in 2010. See IMF News Release, G-20 Ministers Agree 'Historic' Reforms in IMF Governance, available at: http://www.imf.org/external/pubs/ft/survey/so/2010/NEW102310A.htm.

[57] This is to be measured by the time pro-rated in the Executive Director's chair (e.g., rotation of an EMDC into an advanced European Executive Director chair for one period out of two counts as ½).

after the general conditions for the effectiveness of quota increases under the 14th General Review (that requires the consent to the quota increase, and the entry into force of the Seventh Amendment).

In terms of process, the Board of Governors endorsed a timeline that calls for the quota and governance reforms to become effective by the IMF-World Bank Annual Meetings in October 2012 in Tokyo, Japan.[58]

However, it has been understood that the changes may have to be reviewed and further changes may be required.[59] In the context of the 2010 reforms, it was agreed that the composition of the Board will be reviewed every 8 years, starting when the quota reform related to the 14th General Review of Quotas takes effect.

Ministerial Involvement in IMF Decision-Making

Another aspect of IMF governance is the role of ministerial or high-level political involvement in the IMF's decision-making process. The Executive Board is comprised mostly of civil servants rather than political representatives, and the Manuel Report noted that Executive Directors are often removed from actual policy making.[60] With the increase in IMF membership, the Board of Governors became a larger body (comprising today of 188 Governors), making discussions more challenging.

The debate on ministerial involvement in IMF decision making is not new.[61] The First Amendment to the IMF's Articles[62] was discussed and agreed upon in bodies outside the IMF. In 1972, the IMF membership set up a temporary body, the Group of Twenty (or the "ad hoc Committee of the Board of Governors on Reform of the International Monetary System and Related Issues") to discuss IMF governance reform in order to enable ministerial and political influence *within* the IMF rather

[58] This requires two remaining conditions (see Board of Governors resolution No 66-2 of 15 December 2010) to be met: (i) consents to the quota increases under the 14th General Review of Quotas by members having not less than seventy percent of the total of quotas on 5 November 2010 consenting to the increases in their quotas and (ii) entry into force of the proposed board reform amendment that happens once the Fund certifies that three-fifths of the members (currently 113 members), representing eighty-five percent of the total voting power have accepted the proposed amendment. At the time of writing, these requirements have not yet been met. For an updated list of acceptances, see http://www.imf.org/external/np/sec/misc/consents.htm.

[59] See IMF Press Release No. 11/246, Statement by Agustín Carstens to IMF Executive Board, 21 June 2011, available at: http://www.imf.org/external/np/sec/pr/2011/pr11246.htm.

[60] See Committee on IMF Governance, Final Report, 2009, p. 9, available at: http://www.imf.org/external/np/omd/2009/govref/032409.pdf.

[61] See IMF, IMF Governance—Summary of Issues and Reform Options, 2009, p. 6, available at: http://www.imf.org/external/np/pp/eng/2009/070109.pdf.

[62] The IMF's Articles were amended effective 28 July 1969, by the modifications approved by the Board of Governors in Resolution No. 23-5, adopted on 31 May 1968 ("First Amendment").

than outside.[63] In 1974, the IMF membership agreed to establish the Interim Committee, until the discussions on what was to be known as the Second Amendment were to be concluded.[64]

In the context of the Second Amendment, the IMF membership introduced a new organ, the Council, into the IMF's Articles. The Council would be established as part of the IMF's Articles but not immediately "activated." A decision of the Board of Governors with an 85 % majority under Article XII, Section 1 of the IMF's Articles is required to activate the organ.

The Council would be an intermediate organ between the Board of Governors and the Executive Board.[65] It would be similar in competence and composition to the IMFC but with formal decision-making powers.[66] While calls have been made intermittently to activate the Council, to date the Council has not yet been activated, given that the necessary 85 % majority required for a Board of Governors resolution has not yet been attained.[67]

In 2008, an Independent Evaluation Office ("IEO") report called for the activation of the Council and the Council to exercise oversight over the IMF on behalf of the Board of Governors. The IEO also recommended a few procedural improvements such as the selection of chairman in the form of a troika model and preparation of the agenda.[68] In 2009, the Manuel Report also called for enhancing political voice in the IMF's decision making and thus for the activation of the Council.[69]

The Executive Board discussed the activation of the Council in 2009 but "many Directors considered that such a move would weaken member voice, consensus-based decision making, and the system of checks and balances vis-à-vis staff and management, and emphasized that the activation of the Council, as set out in the Articles of Agreement, had very limited support among Executive Directors."[70]

---

[63] De Vries, *The International Monetary Fund 1972–1978, Volume I: Narrative and Analysis*, 1985, pp. 141, 148.

[64] The IMF's Articles were amended effective 1 April 1978, by the modifications approved by the Board of Governors in Resolution No. 31–4, adopted on 30 April 1976 ("Second Amendment").

[65] See also: Schedule D of the IMF's Articles and Gianviti, Decision Making in the International Monetary Fund in: IMF (ed.), *Current Developments in Monetary and Financial Law*, Vol. 1, 1999, pp. 64 et seq.

[66] However, one difference, for instance would be that a Councillor appointed by a multi-country constituency would be able to split his/her votes; see paragraph 3(b) of Schedule D of the IMF's Articles.

[67] IMF, IMF Governance—Summary of Issues and Reform Options, 2009, p. 6, available at: http://www.imf.org/external/np/pp/eng/2009/070109.pdf.

[68] IEO, Governance of the IMF. An evaluation, 2008, p. 20, available at: http://www.ieo-imf.org/ieo/pages/IEOPreview.aspx?img=i6nZpr3iSlU%3D&mappingid=K1g%2BWj0GTnY%3D.

[69] Committee on IMF Governance Reform, Final Report, 2009, p. 21, available at: http://www.imf.org/external/np/omd/2009/govref/032409.pdf. Specifically, the Manuel report noted the "absence of high-level political representation that provides strategic and policy direction and oversight" and thus called for the activation of a ministerial-level Council envisioned in the IMF's Articles (Schedule D).

[70] IMF Public Information Notice No. 09/98, IMF Executive Board Discusses Governance Reform, 4 August 2009, available at: http://www.imf.org/external/np/sec/pn/2009/pn0998.htm.

In 2010, given the limited support to activate the Council in its current form, the Executive Board discussed an alternative—the creation of an International Monetary and Financial Board (the "IMFB") to be established under the IMF's Articles—that would resemble the IMFC today, except that it would also have certain decision-making powers.[71] In this regard, the Executive Board considered a proposal to establish the IMFB and to amend the IMF's Articles to permit the Board of Governors to delegate to the IMFB certain decisions that are exclusively reserved for the Board of Governors under the existing IMF's Articles. In addition, a few powers currently residing with the Executive Board—such as the selection of the Managing Director and strategic aspects of global surveillance—would be transferred to the IMFB. The Executive Board would continue its central role in conducting the business of the Fund. As under the existing IMF's Articles, the legal framework would be sufficiently flexible to allow for the Board of Governors to shift the allocation of responsibilities among the various organs of the Fund over time. Importantly, the Board of Governors would retain its power to delegate decision-making authority, and to take it back.

The Executive Board decided not to pursue this proposal in the context of the 2010 reforms since "many Directors remained unconvinced of the need for a ministerial-level decision making body. They saw little difference between the IMFB and the Council, and felt that the decisions proposed to be taken up by such bodies require an understanding of institutional detail and process beyond the time and inclination of ministers and governors."[72]

As noted above, to date the Council has not been activated.

Selection of the Managing Director

The position of Managing Director of the IMF has long been seen as a vital position in international financial affairs and at the IMF as an institution. In light of the key role played by the Managing Director, there have been calls to make the selection process transparent, fair, merit-based, and independent of nationality, particularly as the Managing Director, since the inception of the IMF, has been a European national (just as the President of the World Bank has been an American).[73]

---

[71] IMF, Governance Reform, 2010, available at: http://www.imf.org/external/np/exr/govern/index.htm.

[72] Public Information Notice No. 10/108, IMF Executive Board Discusses IMF Governance Reform, 2 August 2010, available at: http://www.imf.org/external/np/sec/pn/2010/pn10108.htm.

[73] For instance, the Manuel Report called for the selection process for the Managing Director to be open, transparent, and merit-based with the Managing Director appointed by the Council. See Committee on IMF Governance, Final Report, 2009, pp. 4, 12, 17–18, 22, available at: http://www.imf.org/external/np/omd/2009/govref/032409.pdf.

The legal framework for the selection of the IMF's Managing Director is set out in the IMF's Articles and By-Laws: Article XII, Section 4(a) provides that "[t]he Executive Board shall select the Managing Director who shall not be a Governor or an Executive Director." Section 14(c) of the Fund's By-Laws provides that "[t]he contract of the Managing Director shall be for a term of 5 years and may be renewed for the same term or a shorter term at the discretion of the Executive Board, provided that no person shall be appointed to the post of Managing Director after he has reached his sixty-fifth birthday and that no Managing Director shall hold such post beyond his seventieth birthday."[74]

As early as 2001, Executive Directors at the IMF and the World Bank agreed that a concurrent review of the selection process was timely and necessary, and working groups were established in each institution to undertake this task.[75] In 2006, it was noted the IMF Executive Board would consider whether further steps would be needed, as part of the overall 2-year program of governance reforms.[76] In this light, the IMF has endeavored to improve the selection process of the Managing Director, with significant changes in the last two selections; i.e. in 2007, and, following the reform discussions in 2010, also in 2011.[77]

2011 Selection Process

It has been recognized that the selection of the Managing Director needs to be made through an open, transparent, and merit-based process.[78] As such, the 2011 process for selection of the Managing Director built off improvements from 2007.[79]

---

[74] IMF, IMF Governance—Summary of Issues and Reform Options, 2009, p. 19, available at: http://www.imf.org/external/np/pp/eng/2009/070109.pdf.

[75] In April, 2001, the Bank Working Group and the IMF Working Group issued a Draft Joint Report, setting out suggestions for how to improve the process of selecting the Managing Director. See World Bank/IMF, Draft Joint Report, 25 April 2001, available at: http://www.imf.org/external/spring/2001/imfc/select.htm.

[76] IMF, Report of the Managing Director to the International Monetary and Financial Committee on IMF Quota and Voice Reform, 14 September 2006, available at: http://www.imf.org/external/np/pp/eng/2006/091406q.pdf; see also IMF, The Managing Director's Report on Implementing the Fund's Medium-Term Strategy, 5 April 2006, available at: http://www.imf.org/external/np/pp/eng/2006/040506.pdf.

[77] IMF, IMF Governance—Summary of Issues and Reform Options, 2009, p. 19, available at: http://www.imf.org/external/np/pp/eng/2009/070109.pdf.

[78] See e.g., IMF News Release, G-20 Backs Sustained Crisis Response, Shift in IMF Representation, 25th September 2009, available at: http://www.imf.org/external/pubs/ft/survey/so/2009/NEW092509A.htm.

[79] The Executive Board adopted a process including, consistent with past practice, that any Executive Director could submit a nomination, regardless of nationality, for the position. The Executive Board also set out specific criteria, including on the qualifications for Managing Director and that consideration of a candidate by the Executive Board would be without geographical preference; see IMF Press Release No. 07/156, Statement by IMF Executive Board on Managing Director Selection Process, 9 July 2007, available at: http://www.imf.org/external/np/sec/pr/2007/pr07156.htm.

In 2011 and as before, any national of the IMF's members could be nominated. The framework adopted by the Executive Board permitted both Governors and Executive Directors to nominate candidates (previously, only Executive Directors could nominate candidates). The rationale was to allow Governors, who are closely aligned politically with the respective member (i.e. they are generally a Minister of Finance, Central bank governor, or equivalent position) to put forward nominations. As in 2007, the Executive Board considered the candidates without geographical preferences. In addition, the 2011 framework included a process of "short-listing" where, at the end of the nomination period, the IMF's Secretary announces to the Executive Board the names of those nominees who have confirmed their desire to be candidates. The rationale was for a confidential nomination process, in effect to enable a wide and diverse pool of candidates.[80] From these nominees, the Executive Board would draw up a shortlist of three candidates that would be published. The Executive Board would meet with the shortlisted candidates (or all candidates if there are fewer than four) at the IMF's headquarters in Washington, D.C.

In 2011, there were two nominated candidates: Agustín Carstens and Christine Lagarde. A third candidate, Stanley Fisher, was considered for a nomination, but he was above the age limit of 65 as set out in the IMF By-Laws and there was insufficient support in the Executive Board to recommend that the Board of Governors amend the By-Laws.[81] Both nominated candidates submitted statements to the IMF Executive Board[82] and the Executive Board met with the candidates.

On June 28, 2011, after considering all relevant information, the Executive Board selected Christine Lagarde as Managing Director by consensus.[83] Christine Lagarde became the IMF's eleventh Managing Director on July 5, 2011 and was appointed for a 5-year term.

---

[80] IMF, Q&A Managing Director selection, available at: http://www.imf.org/external/np/exr/faq/mdselection.htm.

[81] See IMF, Letter Submitted by Mr. Shakour Shaalan of the IMF's Executive Board to the New York Times, 15 June 2011, available at: http://www.imf.org/external/np/vc/2011/061511.htm. The By-Laws of the IMF, Section 14(c), states, inter alia, "[t]he contract of the Managing Director shall be for a term of five years and may be renewed for the same term or for a shorter term at the discretion of the Executive Board, provided that no person shall be initially appointed to the post of Managing Director after he has reached his sixty-fifth birthday and that no Managing Director shall hold such post beyond his seventieth birthday."

[82] IMF Press Release No. 11/246, Statement by Agustín Carstens to IMF Executive Board, 21 June 2011, available at: http://www.imf.org/external/np/sec/pr/2011/pr11246.htm; IMF Press Release No. 11/253, Statement by Christine Lagarde to the IMF Executive Board, 23 June 2011, available at: http://www.imf.org/external/np/sec/pr/2011/pr11253.htm.

[83] IMF Press Release No. 11/259, IMF Executive Board Selects Christine Lagarde as Managing Director, 28 June 2011, available at: http://www.imf.org/external/np/sec/pr/2011/pr11259.htm; the terms of appointment were made publicly available as well: IMF Press Release No. 11/270, Terms of Appointment of Christine Lagarde as Managing Director of the International Monetary Fund, 5 July 2011, available at: http://www.imf.org/external/np/sec/pr/2011/pr11270.htm.

Outlook

As this article has shown, in the last few years, the IMF achieved major quota and governance reform. Considering the widespread consensus that is necessary to achieve significant reform in this crucial area, the reforms are remarkable in their extent and dimension. This is particularly pronounced when comparing the degree and extent of IMF quota and governance reform to developments in other international organizations.

Recognizing the need to continue to consider developments in quota and governance, the IMF membership has put on track further quota and governance reforms. These steps include a review in the composition of the Executive Board every 8 years, and in the context of the regular quota reviews, an advancing of the 15th General Review of Quotas including a review of the quota formula.

The IMF and its membership also acknowledge that the IMF needs to continue to regularly reflect and discuss on ways to improve its legitimacy and accountability. In this regard, the IMF will continue the discourse with multiple parties and take into account their statements and views. This may include re-visiting certain proposed reforms that were not adopted during the major reform process discussed herein, as well as considering new proposals as experiences with the reforms are evaluated.

The Valuation of Goods for Customs Purposes

Hans-Michael Wolffgang and Christopher Dallimore

Introduction

The purpose of this contribution is to provide the reader with a general introduction to customs valuation[1] with particular emphasis on the activities of the World Customs Organisation ("WCO") and World Trade Organisation ("WTO").

The "valuation of goods for customs purposes" concerns the methods by which customs authorities determine "the value of the goods for the purposes of levying

[1] The WTO, WCO, and academic literature provide detailed overviews of the determination of customs value, whereas the World Bank and Organization for Economic Co-operation and Development have provided surveys on the implementation of the current WTO customs valuation agreement in developing countries. See generally World Customs Organization, Customs Valuation Compendium, 2009, http://wcoomdpublications.org/valuation/compendium-customs-valuation.html; specifically within the context of the European Union, see Compendium of Customs Valuation Texts of the Customs Code Committee, Customs Valuation Section, TAXUD/800/2002 (Update), January 2007, p. 62, available at: http://ec.europa.eu/taxation_customs/resources/documents/customs/customs_duties/declared_goods/european/compendium_2007_en.pdf; Rosenow/O'Shea, *A Handbook on the WTO Customs Valuation Agreement*, 2010; Wolfrum/Stoll/Hestermeyer (eds.), *WTO – Trade in Goods*, 2011; De Wulf/Sokol (eds.), *Customs Modernization Handbook*, 2005. Considering the importance of commercial practices to customs valuation, see also the OECD Trade Policy Working Papers Series, available at: http://www.oecd.org/document/40/0,3746,en_2649_37431_44756840_1_1_1_37431,00.html and the WTO's Trade Policy Review Gateway, available at: http://www.wto.org/english/tratop_e/tpr_e/tpr_e.htm.

H.-M. Wolffgang
Universität Münster, Rechtswiss. Fakultät, Universitätsstr. 14-16, Münster 48143, Germany
e-mail: Wolffgang@uni-muenster.de

C. Dallimore (✉)
Department of Customs and Excise, Department for Taxation, University of Münster, Universitätsstr. 14-16, Münster 48143, Germany
e-mail: Dallimore@wwu.de

C. Herrmann et al. (eds.), *European Yearbook of International Economic Law (EYIEL), Vol. 4 (2013)*, European Yearbook of International Economic Law 4,
DOI 10.1007/978-3-642-33917-2_15,

ad valorem duties of customs on imported goods."[2] This process takes place at the border and is a condition for the release of goods into free circulation.[3] Customs valuation is regulated by Art. VII of the GATT and the Agreement on Implementation of Article VII of the General Agreement of Tariffs and Trade 1994, also known as the Customs Valuation Agreement ("CVA").

The contribution is divided into five sections: the development of an international standard for customs valuation; an overview of the CVA; practical issues relating to the transaction value; challenges facing developing countries in implementing the CVA and a summary of the findings.

The Harmonisation of Customs Valuation

Customs authorities traditionally valued goods in accordance with national law. However, as early as the Havana Conference[4] it was recognised that the lack of harmonisation in this area constituted a barrier to trade insofar as it enabled states to easily circumvent tariff bindings agreed at trade rounds,[5] create uncertainty in trading relations and provide protection for domestic industries that was particularly detrimental to developing countries.[6] For these reasons, an international standard for customs valuation was considered essential in realising the aims of the GATT.

---

[2] See Art. 15.1(a) of the Agreement on Implementation of Article VII of the General Agreement on Tariffs and Trade 1994 ("CVA"). The vast majority of WTO members calculate duties on an *ad valorem* basis. In the case of specific duties, no valuation is necessary because the duties are levied by weight (e.g. 20 cents per kilo). Switzerland is one example of a state that still uses specific duties. The CVA is available at: http://www.wto.org/english/docs_e/legal_e/20-val.pdf.

[3] For example, according to Art. 201(1)(a) and (2) of the Customs Code, Council Regulation (EEC) No. 2913/92, OJ [1992] L 302/1, the acceptance of the customs declaration for the release of goods into free circulation also gives rise to the customs debt on importation. The customs declarant is also the customs debtor and must therefore either pay the due amount immediately or provide a security (Art. 201(3), Art. 74 CC). The Code is available at: http://eur-lex.europa.eu/LexUriServ/LexUriServ.do?uri=CONSLEG:1992R2913:20070101:EN:PDF.

[4] See Jackson, *World Trade and the Law of GATT. A Legal Analysis of the General Agreement on Tariffs and Trade*, 1969, p. 447.

[5] E.g. the notorious American Selling Price (ASP), see Jackson, *World Trade and the Law of GATT. A Legal Analysis of the General Agreement on Tariffs and Trade*, 1969, pp. 446–447 (at fn. 2). It is still possible for states to circumvent the CVA, e.g. by using a secret system of reference prices. See e.g. Executive Office of the President of the United States, United States Trade Representative, 2011 Report to Congress on China's WTO Compliance, December 2011, pp. 28–30, available at: http://www.ustr.gov/webfm_send/3189.

[6] See e.g. De Wulf/Sokol (eds.), *Customs Modernization Handbook*, 2005, p. 157.

Article VII of the General Agreement on Tariffs and Trade (GATT)

Article VII of the GATT 1994 establishes general principles regarding customs valuation and procedures. However, it provides an inadequate basis for harmonisation because it leaves the actual method of valuation to the Member States. As a result, it simply represents "the constitutional position – the background against which laws are to be framed"[7] and cannot be read in isolation from the CVA.

The central provision is Article VII:2, which provides the basis for customs valuation. It requires customs authorities to calculate customs duties using the "actual value" of the imported goods and not "arbitrary or fictitious values." According to Article VII:2 (a) "actual value" is to be understood as follows:

> [T]he price at which, at a time and place determined by the legislation of the country of importation such or like merchandise is sold or offered for sale in the ordinary course of trade under fully competitive conditions.

The provision bases the value of goods on a *bona fide* commercial transaction. However, it does not contain any detailed provisions on how the price is to be determined. Accordingly, the "actual value" of goods could be interpreted by referring either to their sale price as agreed by the contractual parties (i.e. a 'positive' value) or to a theoretical value set by the customs administration (i.e. a 'notional' value).[8]

It is a measure of the vague wording of this provision that, prior to the CVA 1994, many Contracting Parties were using widely different methods of valuation, confident that theirs complied with Article VII of the GATT (and that others constituted a barrier to trade).[9]

The Convention on the Valuation of Goods for Customs Purposes 1950

The European Study Group on European Customs Union was established in 1947 to examine the pre-conditions for a European customs union.[10] This led to the Convention on the Valuation of Goods for Customs Purposes, which was enacted

---

[7] Statement by Mr. F. Edmond-Smith, Representative of the European Customs Union Study Group, Working Party I on the International Chamber of Commerce Resolutions, General Agreement on Tariffs and Trade, W.7/8, 7 October 1952, p. 2.

[8] In this respect, Ad Art. VII(2)(1) of GATT 1947 Annex I states that the invoice price (after adjustments) can be seen as representative of the actual price. The American Selling Price (ASP) was particularly notorious, see Jackson, *World Trade and the Law of GATT. A Legal Analysis of the General Agreement on Tariffs and Trade*, 1969, pp. 446–447 (at note 2).

[9] GATT, Committee on Trade in Industrial Products, Working Group 2 on Non-Tariff Barriers, COM.IND/W/47, 18 December 1970, p. 3: "Because of the vagueness of Article VII and the use of procedures of exception, no country considered that its system was inconsistent with the terms of that Article."

[10] See Wolffgang/Dallimore, The World Customs Organization and its Role in the System of World Trade, in: Herrmann/Terhechte (eds.), *European Yearbook of International Economic Law 2012*, pp. 617–618.

on 15 December 1950 (the same day as the Convention Establishing a Customs Co-operation Council). It was designed as an international standard[11] and administered by the CCC, which had the task of ensuring its uniform interpretation and application.[12]

The Convention determined the "actual value" of goods using a notional value prescribed by customs administrations in accordance with national legislation.[13] Article I (1) of Annex I required valuation to be based on the "normal price" of goods that was defined as "the price which they would fetch at the time when the duty becomes payable on a sale in the open market between buyer and seller independent of each other." This method became known as the Brussels Declaration of Value ("BDV").

Although the CCC also stated that the invoice price would generally be acceptable as the "normal price," situations often arose where the two values diverged.[14] Based on the BDV, customs authorities would therefore adjust the declared value ("uplifts") to reflect the notional value prescribed by national legislation.

The BDV was criticised by the International Chamber of Commerce (ICC) for being a theoretical standard that gave too much discretion to customs authorities.[15] The 1950 Convention also valued imports on a c.i.f. basis (apparently in reflection of European trading conditions)[16] that was unacceptable to countries that valued the goods at f.o.b. level.[17]

---

[11] This is made clear in the preamble to the Convention on the Valuation of Goods for Customs Purposes 1950, which refers to the desire to facilitate international trade and explicitly declares the convention to be international in nature. That said, the Convention reflected European conditions in one important respect, namely the adoption of the c.i.f. value.

[12] See Art. V(a) of the 1950 Valuation Convention. Along with the nomenclature of goods, customs valuation has represented a basic function of the Customs Co-operation Council since its inception. Art. III(b) of the CCC states that the function of the CCC shall be to "[. . .] ensure the highest degree of harmony and uniformity."

[13] Many provisions of the 1950 Valuation Convention reflected the principles of Art. VII GATT. For example, note 5 of Annex II underlined that the object of the "normal price" was to make it possible to calculate the duties payable based on the ordinary course of trade under competitive conditions and Art. II(1)(b) provided that the price could not be based on fictitious values. Art. VI (a) provided for transparency in national legislation. Art. X(b) accommodated existing obligations under international agreement incurred by the Contracting Parties.

[14] This would be the case, for example, if the shipment were delayed with a resultant drop in the value of the goods. Alternatively, the goods could be damaged during shipment with the result that their actual value would also be far less than their sale price. See statement by Mr. F. Edmond-Smith, Representative of the European Customs Union Study Group, Working Party I on the International Chamber of Commerce Resolutions, General Agreement on Tariffs and Trade (W.7/8), 7 October 1952, p. 2.

[15] The International Chamber of Commerce (ICC) also criticised the BDV for its "length, looseness and susceptibility to differences of interpretation." See GATT, Working Party I on the International Chamber of Commerce Resolutions, Statement by Mr. M. Dreyfus, Chairman of the International Chamber of Commerce Delegation, General Agreement on Tariffs and Trade (W.7/54), 31 October 1952, p. 2.

[16] See Kreider, Valuation for Customs, The Quarterly Journal of Economics 56 (1941) 1, p. 157.

[17] This provision was later amended but before it was ratified by members, the GATT Valuation Agreement entered into force.

The Agreement on Implementation of Article VII of the General Agreement on Tariffs and Trade 1981

When the Tokyo Round (1973–1979) started, the BDV was well-established and applied in over 100 countries.[18] However, despite the efforts of the CCC, it was not adopted by the GATT as an international standard[19] because the United States and other major trading states opposed the notional value for not taking sufficient account of commercial practices.

In November 1977, the European Union and United States agreed on a system based on a positive value.[20] This led to the adoption of the Agreement on Implementation of Article VII of the General Agreement on Tariffs and Trade (also known as the "GATT Valuation Code").[21] The Code officially entered into force on 1 January 1981. As a result of the Uruguay Round, the GATT Valuation Code was incorporated into the WTO framework largely unchanged.

Owing to the single undertaking approach, membership of the WTO was conditional on accepting all results of the Uruguay Round. Finally, almost 50 years after the GATT, a legally-binding agreement on the determination of customs value had been achieved.

Overview of the Agreement on Implementation of Article VII of the General Agreement on Tariffs and Trade 1994

The Agreement on Implementation of Article VII of the General Agreement on Tariffs and Trade 1994—also known as the Customs Valuation Agreement ("CVA")—regulates the customs valuation of imports and is divided into three parts. The general introduction and preamble list the main objectives of the agreement.[22] The operative provisions stipulate the methods of valuation outlined

[18] See also Trujillo, in: Wolfrum/Scholl/Hestermeyer (eds.), *WTO – Trade in Goods*, 2011, p. 223.

[19] GATT Multilateral Trade Negotiations, Group "Non-Tariff Measures," Sub-Group "Customs Matters:" Communication from the Customs Co-operation Council, MTN/NTM/W/17, 26 August 1975, p. 1.

[20] See Rege, Developing Country Participation in Negotiations Leading to the Adoption of WTO Agreements on Customs Valuation and Preshipment Inspection. A Public Choice Analysis, World Competition 22 (1999) 1, p. 37 (42–43). The reason for this was the belief that import duties were likely to decline in importance in the near future and the need to ensure that European exports were not exposed to high rates of duties.

[21] See Multilateral Trade Negotiations, Group "Non-Tariff Measures," Sub-Group "Customs Matters," Statement made by the Commission of the European Communities at the Meeting of the Sub-Group of 15 November 1977, MTN/NTM/W/126, 21 November 1977.

[22] These include: to secure additional benefits for the international trade of developing countries; to provide greater uniformity and certainty in the implementation of Article VII; to establish a fair, uniform and neutral system for the valuation of goods for customs purposes that precludes the use of arbitrary of fictitious customs values.

in Articles 1 to 7, rights of appeal and the administration of the agreement. Finally, guidance on the application of the agreement is provided in the interpretative notes. All three parts must be referred to when interpreting the agreement.[23] According to the general rule of interpretation in WTO law, conflicts between the GATT and the CVA are to be decided in favour of the latter.[24]

Although the CVA has often given rise to disputes between WTO members, few Panel reports deal with its interpretation.[25] In practice, its administration, interpretation and promotion are largely the responsibility of the WCO.

The heart of the CVA comprises the primary method of valuation and five secondary methods that the customs administration is to apply in a fixed order (with one exception).

Primary Valuation Method

According to Article 1 CVA, the primary method of determining the value of goods for customs purposes is the transaction value. This consists of two components: the sale for export and price paid or payable as adjusted.[26]

Sold for Export

The transaction value is based on a *bona fide* commercial transaction. The CVA does not define "sold for export" and contractual formation is determined by the contract law of Member States. However, the Technical Committee on Customs Valuation ("TCCV") has recommended that the term "sale" be interpreted in "the widest sense." It also provides examples where a sale would not exist.[27]

---

[23] See also Liu, in: Wolfrum/Scholl/Hestermeyer (eds.), *WTO – Trade in Goods*, 2011, pp. 867, 880.

[24] The Interpretative Note to Annex 1a of the Agreement Establishing the World Trade Organization states: "In the event of conflict between a provision of the General Agreement on Tariffs and Trade 1994 and a provision of another agreement in Annex 1A to the Agreement Establishing the World Trade Organization (referred to in the agreements in Annex 1A as the "WTO Agreement"), the provision of the other agreement shall prevail to the extent of the conflict."

[25] Report of the Panel, *Argentina—Measures Affecting Imports of Footwear, Textiles, Apparel and Other Items*, WT/DS56/R; Report of the Panel, *Colombia—Indicative Prices and Restrictions on Ports of Entry*, WT/DS366/R; Report of the Panel, *Thailand—Customs and Fiscal Measures on Cigarettes from the Philippines*, WT/DS371/R; Report of the Panel, *Argentina—Definitive Anti-Dumping Duties on Poultry from Brazil*, WT/DS241/R. The WTO website provides a list of disputes that refer to the CVA: http://www.wto.org/english/tratop_e/dispu_e/cases_e/ds241_e.htm.

[26] According to Art. 1, the transaction value itself is not simply the price stated on the invoice price but is to be adjusted according to Art. 8 "on the basis of objective and quantifiable data," Art. 8(3).

[27] See Technical Committee on Customs Valuation, Advisory Opinion 1.1: The Concept of "Sale" in the Agreement.

Overview of customs valuation methods under the CVA[28]

The transaction value method (Art.1)	The customs authority is bound to accept the value stated on the invoice unless it has good reason not to do so
The value of identical goods (Art. 2)	The customs value is the transaction value of identical goods sold for export to the same country of importation and export at or about the same time as the goods being valued
The value of similar goods (Art. 3)	The customs value is the transaction value of similar goods sold for export to the same country of importation and export at or about the same time as the goods being valued
Article 4	Enables reversal of the deductive and computed method
The deductive value (Art. 5)	The customs value is based on the unit price at that the imported goods or identical or similar imported goods are so sold in the greatest aggregate quantity, at or about the time of the importation of the goods being valued, to persons who are not related to the persons from whom the buy the goods subject to the deductions in Art. 5 (i)–(iv)
The computed value (Art. 6)	Computed value consists of (a) the cost or value of materials and fabrication or other processing in producing the goods; (b) an amount for profit and general expenses usually reflected in sales of the same class or kind; (c) cost or value of all other expenses necessary to reflect the valuation option (Art. 8:2)
The fall-back method (Art. 7)	Customs value is determined using a reasonable means consistent with the principles and general provisions of the CVA and Article VII of the GATT and on the basis of data available in the country of exportation

The formation of contract requires the necessary legal capacity. For example, a transaction between a parent and subsidiary would qualify as a sale between two independent legal entities whereas a transaction involving a branch office could only constitute a transfer of goods owing to its lack of legal personality.[29]

If there is a *bona fide* sale, the customs authority is obliged to accept the declared value even if it is far lower than the usual sale price of such goods.[30] Generally, however, customs accepts the invoice price as representing the transaction value in

[28] Summarised from the provisions of the CVA. For a detailed analysis of all valuation methods see Liu/Wolffgang, in: Wolfrum/Stoll/Hestermeyer (eds.), *WTO – Trade in Goods*, 2011, pp. 875–929

[29] See Conclusion No. 5: Imports by branches, Compendium of Customs Valuation Texts of the Customs Code Committee, Customs Valuation Section, TAXUD/800/2002 (Update), January 2007, p. 62, available at: http://ec.europa.eu/taxation_customs/resources/documents/customs/customs_duties/declared_goods/european/compendium_2007_en.pdf.

[30] This is reflected in the preamble to the CVA that states that the "valuation procedure should not be used to combat dumping." In addition, contract law also permits goods to be sold at far less than their actual value. In common law systems, it has been held that good consideration can be "adequate but not sufficient." As a result, a valid contract of sale only requires a nominal sale price. See *Thomas vs. Thomas* [1842] 2 Q.B. 851, 114 E.R. 330: "A court will not look into the adequacy of consideration or the reasons for the bargain, if there is a real bargain between the parties."

the vast majority of cases. This can be evidenced by commercial invoices, contracts, purchase order etc.[31]

By obliging customs authorities to use the transaction value as far as possible, the CVA reflects the fact that each transaction value is a result of the unique circumstances of the transaction.[32] Thereby, the CVA finally ensures that sufficient regard is paid to commercial practices as requested by the International Chamber of Commerce 40 years previously.[33]

The Price Actually Paid or Payable

Article 1 states that the customs value of the imported goods is to be the transaction value or "the price actually paid or payable." This is defined as the "total payment" made to the buyer for the imported goods and "all payments actually made or to be made as a condition of the sale."[34] Article 1 (a)–(d) also provides a list of situations where the transaction price will not be deemed acceptable.

If necessary, the price paid or payable must be adjusted to include certain elements incurred by the buyer that form part of the customs value.[35] The permissible adjustments are listed in Art. 8[36] and are divided into four types: costs, assists, licences and royalties as well as subsequent proceeds.

Article 8.1(a) provides for the addition of commissions paid to the importer's agent, as well as the cost of containers and packing. The Member States are free to decide whether the transaction value should include costs of transportation, transhipment and insurance (Art. 8.2). Accordingly, value is determined either "cost, insurance, freight" (c.i.f.) or "free on board" (f.o.b.).[37]

---

[31] See World Customs Organisation, *Customs Valuation Control Handbook*, Part I, p. 1, para. 1; the Handbook also defines an invoice as "[a] document which lists the goods shipped, sent or consigned, together with the relevant prices of the goods an charges for their dispatch. [...] It is usually the document against which payment for the goods is required to be made." See Part II, Chapter 4, p. 3, para. 5.

[32] For example, the sale price reflects the parties' respective bargaining power during contractual negotiations, prevalent external economic conditions as well as marketing considerations including branding and consumer behaviour. See e.g. Kristensen/Gabrielsen/Zaichkowsky, How Valuable is a Well-Crafted Design and Name Brand? Recognition and Willingness to Pay, Journal of Consumer Behaviour 11(2012) 1, p. 44 (46):
"It is very important for firms to charge the maximum amount the consumer is willing to pay for their goods. However, answering the question what the consumer is willing to pay is not that easy [...]," available at: http://onlinelibrary.wiley.com/doi/10.1002/cb.368/pdf.

[33] See GATT, Working Party I on the International Chamber of Commerce Resolutions, Statement by Mr. M. Dreyfus, Chairman of the International Chamber of Commerce Delegation, General Agreement on Tariffs and Trade, W.7/54, 31 October 1952, pp. 2–3.

[34] See interpretative note 1 to Article 1 CVA Annex I as well as Paragraph 7 CVA Annex III.

[35] See Paragraph 1 of the General Introductory Commentary to the CVA. See also Rosenow/O'Shea, *A Handbook on the WTO Customs Valuation Agreement*, 2010, p. 30.

[36] According to Art. 8(4) CVA, this list is final.

[37] See e.g. Art. 32(1)(e)(i) of the Community Customs Code, which provides for the inclusion of transportation costs "to the place of introduction into the customs territory of the Community."

Sub-paragraph (b) deals with assists, i.e. "goods or services supplied by the importer to the foreign manufacturer, free of charge or at a reduced cost, for use in connection with the production of the imported goods for export."[38] Such non-monetary supplies must first be categorised under Article 8:1(b) then valued and finally apportioned.[39]

Fees for royalties and licence fees can also be added (Art.8.1(c)). These must be related to the goods being valued and paid by the buyer. The classification as a royalty or licence fee depends on the legislation of the Member State.[40]

The final adjustment in Art. 8.1(d) requires the addition of proceeds from a subsequent resale, disposal or use of the imported goods. The proceeds must relate to the imported goods and so do not include e.g. dividends.[41]

Secondary Valuation Methods

The secondary valuation methods are listed in Articles 2–7 of the CVA and can only be used if the declared value is unacceptable in accordance with Art. 1.1(a)–(d). They are to be applied in sequential order.[42]

First, the value is to be determined using the transaction value of identical or similar goods "sold for export to the same country of importation" in consultation with the customs authority. According to Art. 4, if this is not possible then the deductive (Art. 5) and computed value methods (Art. 6) are to be used. Finally, if none of these methods is successful in determining the customs value, then the "fall-back method" in Art. 7 is available as a method of last resort. This vaguely worded provision requires members to determine the customs value by "reasonable means."[43]

The secondary valuation methods are to be based as far as possible on commercial criteria. At no point are customs administrations permitted to apply a theoretical or notional value. Therefore, this approach reduces the possibility of using "fictional" or "arbitrary" values to an absolute minimum. At the same time, it only permits the customs authority to challenge the declared value within carefully defined limits.

---

[38] Collins, The Concept of Assist as Applied to Customs Valuation of Imported Merchandise, Detroit College of Law Review 239 (1991) 1, pp. 243–244; see also Technical Committee on Customs Valuation, Advisory Opinion 24.1 (Determination of the Value of an Assist under Article 8.1(b) of the Agreement).

[39] See interpretative note to Art. 8(1)(b)(ii) CVA.

[40] See also Liu, in: Wolfrum/Stoll/Hestermeyer (eds.), *WTO – Trade in Goods*, 2011, p. 947.

[41] See World Customs Organisation, WTO Agreement & Texts of the Technical Committee on Customs Valuation, Case Study 2.1 (Application of Art. 8.1(d) of the Agreement) and Case Study 2.2 (Treatment of Proceeds under Art. 8.1(d)).

[42] See Report of the Panel, *Thailand—Customs and Fiscal Measures on Cigarettes from the Philippines*, WT/DS371/R, para. 7.154.

[43] The interpretative notes provide limited guidance in this respect. They simply refer to the use of previously determined values and a flexible application of Art. 1-6.

In practice, the secondary valuation methods are difficult to apply due to their onerous information requirements (that is why Art. 4 gives the importer the right to reverse the order of the deductive and computed value methods). Particularly in developing countries, importers may not be in a position to provide sufficient evidence to support the declared value or customs administrations may not have the resources to perform post-clearance audits.[44] For this reason, the latter often compare value declarations against reference values.

Procedural and Administrative Provisions

According to Art. 22.1, all 153 members of the WTO must "ensure [...] the conformity of its laws, regulations and administrative procedures with the provisions of [the CVA]." Although the transaction valuation method appears a "simple rule of thumb,"[45] its implementation requires complex procedural and administrative arrangements.

Therefore, the procedural provisions of the CVA serve to implement the overarching objectives of Art. VII:5 GATT. Article 12 requires members to publish their valuation laws in accordance with Art. X of the GATT 1994 promptly,[46] thereby enabling governments and traders to become acquainted with them.[47] In accordance with Art. 11, members are to notify the appellant in writing of the decision and provide an appeals procedure against customs valuation rulings. Article 19 directs members to settle disputes between themselves in accordance with the WTO Dispute Settlement Understanding.[48] As a concession for developing countries, Art. 20 grants a 5 year transition period that can be extended on request.[49]

The administration of the CVA is the joint responsibility of the WTO and WCO. Article 18.1 establishes a Committee on Customs Valuation (CCV) under the auspices of the World Trade Organisation. It meets annually and is attended by

[44] Art. 13 allows the importer to withdraw the goods from customs supervision provided that he provides a sufficient guarantee. See e.g. Art. 74 of the Community Customs Code.

[45] General Agreement on Tariffs and Trade, Resolutions Submitted by the International Chamber of Commerce on Valuation, Nationality of Manufactured Goods and Formalities Connected with Quantitative Restrictions, G/22, 29 August 1952, p. 2.

[46] It may be possible to obtain advance rulings on customs valuation. See Moïsé/Orliac/Minor, Trade Facilitation Indicators: The Impact on Trade Costs, OECD Trade Policy Working Papers, (2011) 118, p. 16, available at: http://dx.doi.org/10.1787/5kg6nk654hmr-en.

[47] Art. X(3)(a) also requires each Contracting Party to administer customs valuation laws in a uniform, impartial and reasonable manner and Art. X(3)(b) requires review tribunals to be independent of administrative enforcement agencies.

[48] See the Understanding on Rules and Procedures Governing the Settlement of Disputes 1994. The GATT Customs Valuation Agreement provided for a self-contained procedure. Compare Art. XI of the Customs Valuation Convention 1950 with Art. 19 of the CVA 1994.

[49] See CVA Annex III, Paragraphs 1, 3 and 4. Nowadays, no member maintains an extension to the delay period. See World Trade Organization, Report of the Committee on Customs Valuation, G/VAL/W/203, 2011, p. 1.

representatives of each member and observers.[50] The CCV gives members the opportunity to consult on the administration of the Customs valuation system[51] and it also submits an annual report on the implementation and operation of the Agreement to the Council for Trade in Goods (Art. 17).

Article 18.2 establishes a Technical Committee on Customs Valuation (hereinafter "TCCV") to ensure uniformity in interpretation and application of the CVA at a technical level.[52] According to its terms of reference, the TCCV deals with everyday technical problems, undertakes studies into aspects of valuation, reports annually on the CVA's operation and provides technical assistance to members.[53] In performing its function, the TCCV uses the following instruments[54]:

- *Advisory opinion*: answers a question raised on the application of the agreement to a particular set of facts, actual or theoretical.
- *Commentary*: clarifies the literal meaning of a text by providing illustrative examples. They are of general application.
- *Explanatory note*: elucidates the TCCV's views on general questions arising from one or more provisions of the Agreement. Thereby, it examines trade practices.
- *Case study*: an exposition of a complex set of facts based on an actual commercial transaction.
- *Study*: the result of an in-depth examination on any question related to the agreement under para. 2 (b) of Annex II and not covered by any other instruments. Not for general publication.[55]

These instruments are not legally-binding on members. However, they can generate considerable persuasive force and members may incorporate them in their national legislation.[56] One notable example is Commentary 22.1 (see below).

---

[50] In April 1997, the Committee granted observer status to UNCTAD, WCO, ACP, IADB. The World Bank and IMF also have observer status. See WTO, Draft Report of the Committee on Customs Valuation to the Council for Trade in Goods, G/VAL/W/197, 4 November 2010, para. 3.

[51] The rules of procedure are those of the General Council with the necessary modifications. See rules of Procedure for Meetings of the Committee on Customs Valuation, approved by the Council for Trade in Goods on 1 December 1995, G/L/146, 24 February 1997.

[52] See CVA Annex II.

[53] The Terms of Reference of the Technical Committee on Customs Valuation are available online at: http://www.wcoomd.org/files/1.%20Public%20files/PDFandDocuments/About%20Us/Terms%20Reference%20WB%20E_Rev20090513.pdf.

[54] An issue can be dealt with by more than one instrument. For example, related party transactions are dealt with by AO 7.1, AO 21.1; Com. 10.1, Com. 14.1; EN. 4.1; CS. 9.1, CS 10.1, CS. 11.1.

[55] World Customs Organisation, Customs Valuation Compendium, Technical Committee Texts, General Part (G3-G4).

[56] World Customs Organization, Customs Valuation Compendium, Technical Committee Texts, General Part (G5, paras. 25–26).

The WCO forms an integral part of the WTO's regulation of customs valuation.[57] Considering that there have been few decisions and Ministerial Decisions on customs valuation, it could be argued that it is the TCCV that plays the leading role in implementing, promoting and further developing the CVA.[58]

Customs Valuation Control

Under the CVA, the valuation of goods is wholly based on the information provided by the importer.[59] Therefore, valuation control assumes crucial importance not only in relation to revenue collection but also law enforcement.[60] Accordingly, customs authorities must be able to verify the accuracy of the declared value in cases of doubt. In this respect, the importer is liable for the accuracy of the declaration of value (notwithstanding his use of a customs broker).[61] The incorrect declaration of customs value can give rise to administrative penalties and criminal prosecution.[62]

Article 17 and Annex III para. 6 CVA protect the right of customs to carry out valuation controls. However, during the Uruguay Round, developing countries expressed their concerns that these provisions had undermined customs controls by placing the burden of proof on customs administrations regarding challenges to the truth, accuracy or completeness of the declared value.[63]

In order to clarify the right of administrations to perform valuation controls, the CVC issued a Ministerial Decision in 1995.[64] It provides that where the customs

---

[57] Another example would be the express reference to the United Nations in Art. XXI of the GATT.

[58] For the legal implications on decisions interpreting the WTO Agreements (within the context of the discussions concerning the valuation of computer software), see GATT Committee on Customs Valuation, Minutes of the Meeting Held on 10 May 1983, VAL/M/7, 7 July 1983, pp. 8–9.

[59] Examples of incorrect information provided by the importer include undervaluation or overvaluation, an incorrect description of the goods or failing to make the necessary adjustments required by Art. 8.

[60] For example, customs duties still represent an important source of revenue for the state in many countries; undervaluation can give an importer an unfair advantage over his competitors and last but not least, valuation fraud is connected to organised crime such as money laundering and smuggling. See Report of the Panel, *Columbia—Indicative Prices and Restrictions on Ports of Entry*, WT/DS366/R, p. 3 (para. 2.5).

[61] World Customs Organization, *Customs Valuation Control Handbook*, Part II, Chapter 1, p. 1, paras. 4–5; Report of the Panel, *Thailand – Customs and Fiscal Measures on Cigarettes from the Philippines*, WT/DS371/R, para. 7.160.

[62] See Report of the Panel, *Argentina – Measures Affecting Imports of Footwear, Textiles*, Apparel and Other Items, WT/DS56/R, para. 6.44.

[63] See Committee on Customs Valuation, Justification for India's Proposal on the Burden of Proof, VAL/W/51, 10 October 1989, p. 1.

[64] Available at: http://www.wto.org/english/docs_e/legal_e/42-dval1.pdf.

authority has reasonable doubts as to the truth or accuracy of the declared value, the importer will bear the burden of proving the declared value is correct.[65]

Although the term "reasonable doubt" is not defined in the decision, the TCCV has recommended that customs authorities review value declarations using risk assessment techniques.[66] For example, a relationship between the parties and a particularly low invoice may constitute reasonable grounds for confirming that the relationship has not influenced the price paid or payable.[67] This approach recognises customs' limited resources[68] and minimises delays to the clearance of goods.

The TCCV has also issued Advisory Opinion 19.1 that provides that, subject to the CVA, the rights and obligations of importers and customs can be determined by national laws and regulations.[69] In addition, the WTO Panel has also affirmed the power of members to control declarations of value.[70]

[65] See De Wulf/Sokol (eds.), *Customs Modernization Handbook*, 2005, p. 158. See also Liu, in: Wolfrum/Scholl/Hestermeyer (eds.), *WTO – Trade in Goods*, 2011, p. 981, deeming the legal effects of the Decision "controversial" and emphasising that it "does not and should not shake the fundamental basis of the agreement, which is that the primary base for customs value is the transaction value." However, from the importer's point of view, it is difficult to reconcile the obligation to prove compliance with the rule of law according to which the burden of proof is to be borne by the accuser of wrongdoing. See Abad, Forging a Translation: The "Circumstances of Sale" Criterion, Transfer Pricing, and Economics, Global Trade and Customs Journal 5 (2010) 9, p. 335 (338).

[66] E.g. rating the transaction according to a checklist of risk factors such as undervaluation, no-sale situations, subsequent sale etc. See World Customs Organization, *Customs Valuation Control Handbook*, Part III, Chapter 1, Appendix to Chapter 1 (III), "Risk Rating," p. 4. See also World Customs Organization, Guidelines on the Development and Use of a National Valuation Database as a Risk Assessment Tool, available at: http://www.wcoomd.org/files/1.%20Public%20files/PDFandDocuments/Valuation/guidelines_national_db.pdf. See also World Customs Organization, *Customs Valuation Control Handbook*, Part V on the computerisation of valuation.

[67] See Shin, Implementation of the WTO Customs Valuation Agreement in Developing Countries, Issues and Recommendation, Journal of World Trade 33 (1999) 1, p. 124 (132–133).

[68] Diaz Gavier/Pierola, Related Parties and Customs Valuation: Guidance Derived from the Panel Report Thailand—Cigarettes, Global Trade and Customs Journal 7 (2012) 1, p. 7 (9).

[69] In this respect, the 19 U.S.C. s. 1401a(b)(2)(B) imposes the unique obligation on importers to exercise "reasonable care." See US Customs and Border Protection Bureau, Reasonable Care (A Checklist for Compliance), April 2004, p. 3, available at:http://www.cbp.gov/linkhandler/cgov/trade/legal/informed_compliance_pubs/icp021.ctt/icp021.pdf. See also Abad, Forging a Translation: The "Circumstances of Sale" Criterion, Transfer Pricing, and Economics, Global Trade and Customs Journal 5 (2010) 9, p. 335 (337–339), who argued that the concept implicitly imposes an "obligation to prospectively evaluate and document RPTs" and further, that its breach "may result in civil customs penalties, even when the imported goods are free of duty."

[70] See Report of the Panel, *Columbia – Indicative Prices and Restrictions on Ports of Entry*, WT/DS366/R, p. 109, (para. 7.155), "[. . .] the Panel recognizes that WTO members have a legitimate right to apply measures aimed at combating under-invoicing, smuggling and money laundering. However, these measures should be WTO-consistent [. . .]." See also Report of the Panel, *Thailand – Customs and Fiscal Measures on Cigarettes from the Philippines*, WT/DS371/R, para. 7.159, where the Panel stated that "any situation giving rise to a reason(s) for questioning the transaction value would naturally demand the customs authorities' critical consideration of, inquiry into, and investigation of, the relevant situation."

General Issues in the Application of the CVA

The growth in international trade has seen companies expand across national frontiers.[71] These so-called 'multi-national enterprises' (or MNEs) maintain a global business presence through sites in several countries.[72] This business organisation gives rise to a number of issues relating to customs valuation, namely the sales between related entities, series of sales and transfer pricing. In addition, the application of the CVA can be problematic in developing countries.

Acceptability of Transactions between Related Parties

Article 15.4 (a)–(h) of the CVA, provides a list of related persons. The major question arising from a sales transaction between related parties is whether the relationship has influenced the price paid for the goods. If this is the case, the transaction value method cannot apply and the parties must demonstrate the absence of a relationship using certain test values under Art. 1.2 (b).[73]

According to Article 2(a) and its interpretative notes, the fact that the parties are related does not necessarily mean the transaction value is unacceptable. An examination should only be carried out if there are doubts about the acceptability of the price.[74] In this case, the customs authorities must refer to the circumstances surrounding the sale in order to confirm that it was not influenced by the relationship.

According to the Panel in Thailand—Cigarettes (2010)[75] if the customs authority has doubts about the price, it should give the importer the chance to supply further information to enable it to examine the circumstances of the sale. In this respect, the authority "must actively seek out pertinent information."[76] In addition,

---

[71] See Diaz Gavier/Pierola, Related Parties and Customs Valuation: Guidance Derived from the Panel Report Thailand-Cigarettes, Global Trade and Customs Journal 7 (2012) 1, p. 7, pointing out that in 2009, such trade accounted for approx. 48% of imports into the United States.

[72] See OECD Guidelines for Multinational Enterprises, p. 12, para. 3, available at: http://www.oecd.org/dataoecd/56/36/1922428.pdf, which state that MNEs "usually comprise companies or other entities established in more than one country and so linked that they may co-ordinate their operations in various ways."

[73] According to the TCCV, importers "are more likely to be able to show that the price was not influenced than they will be able to demonstrate that the transaction value meets one of the tests in Art. 1.2 (b)." See World Customs Organization, *Customs Valuation Control Handbook*, Part III, Chapter 7, p. 1, para. 2.

[74] The interpretative notes to Art. 1, Paragraph 2 CVA Annex I state that "Where the customs administration have no doubts about the acceptability of the price, it should be accepted without requesting further information from the importer."

[75] Report of the Panel, *Thailand – Customs and Fiscal Measures on Cigarettes from the Philippines*, WT/DS371/R. For a brief analysis see Krallmann, WTO Dispute Settlement: Current Cases, in: Herrmann/Terhechte, *European Yearbook of International Economic Law 2012*, p. 590.

[76] See Report of the Panel, *Thailand – Customs and Fiscal Measures on Cigarettes from the Philippines*, WT/DS371/R, para. 7164, drawing a parallel with the Agreement on Safeguards.

Advisory Opinion 14.1 states that "the importer has an obligation to ensure to the greatest extent possible that the price is not influenced."[77] However, it may be difficult for the importer to prove this, especially where two related entities have agreed a low sale price.[78]

Series of Sales

Very often in international trade, goods are subject to several transactions before they are imported to the destination country. The transaction value of each sale will be different because each reseller includes a mark-up to reflect costs and profit margins. Often, the transaction value of the first sale will be significantly less than that of the last sale.[79] Companies (MNEs) will often prefer to use the first sale because it results in less dutiable value.

The CVA is silent on this issue. Article 1 simply refers to "the price actually paid or payable for the goods when sold for export to the country of importation." It does not state when or where the contract is to be concluded. Provided that the first sale and the last sale are based on *bona fide* contracts, the CVA would appear to accommodate both alternatives. In addition, Advisory Opinion 14.1 does not deal with the meaning of sold for export within the context of a series of sales.[80] Therefore, until recently, this question was regulated at national level.[81]

---

[77] See World Customs Organization, *Customs Valuation Control Handbook*, Part III, Chapter 7, p. 1.

[78] See Diaz Gavier/Pierola, Related Parties and Customs Valuation: Guidance Derived from the Panel Report Thailand-Cigarettes, Global Trade and Customs Journal 7 (2012) 1, p. 7 (8).

[79] See Desiderio/Desiderio, Thoughts on the "First Sale" Rule, World Customs Journal 4 (2010) 1, p. 39, stating that using the first sale can reduce the amount of *ad valorem* duties payable by up to 50%. The article is available at: http://www.worldcustomsjournal.org/media/wcj/-2010/1/Desiderio.pdf.

[80] Technical Committee on Customs Valuation, Advisory Opinion 14.1: Meaning of the Expression "Sold for Export to the Country of Importation" (in response to the question "How should this be interpreted?"). In Example 2, the TCCV states: "It is not necessary that the sale takes place in a specific country of exportation."

[81] For example, Art. 147 of the Customs Code Implementing Provisions, Commission Regulation (EEC) No. 2454/93, OJ [1993] L 253/1 (the Code is available online at: http://eur-lex.europa.eu/LexUriServ/LexUriServ.do?uri=CONSLEG:1992R2913:20070101:EN:PDF), allows Member States to accept the first sale rule. This provision states that, in the case of successive sales before valuation, "each price resulting from these sales may, subject to the provisions of Articles 178 to 181, be taken as a basis for valuation." This is supported by Commentary No. 7 of the Customs Code Committee (Customs Valuation Section) on the application of Article 147 of Commission Regulation (EEC) No. 2454/93, available in Compendium of Customs Valuation Texts of the Customs Code Committee, Customs Valuation Section, TAXUD/800/2002 (Update), January 2007, pp. 40 et seq., available at: http://ec.europa.eu/taxation_customs/resources/documents/customs/customs_duties/declared_goods/european/compendium_2007_en.pdf.

In order to clarify the meaning of AO 14.1 with regard to a series of sales, the TCCV issued Commentary 22.1 dealing with the meaning of the expression "sold for export to the country of importation." Here, the TCCV stated that "guidance must be sought from the purpose and overall text of the agreement, including an analysis of its provisions."[82] In view of various indications in the General Introductory Commentary and operative provisions, it concluded that the last sale rule would be consistent with the purpose and overall text of the CVA.

These arguments have been described as "fragile" by commentators[83] and criticised by commerce for failing to take into account commercial realities. As current EU legislation shows, it is also a subject that can be effectively regulated by the Member States themselves. It could also be argued that the TCCV's interpretation does not give sufficient weight to the practice of Member States in interpreting this provision.[84]

Although the Advisory Opinion is non-binding, the fact that the last sale rule operates to the benefit of customs administrations makes it more likely to be adopted in national legislation.[85] The European Commission had planned to incorporate the ruling in the Modernized Customs Code that was due to enter into force in June 2013.[86] According to the Commission, this would have corrected the unfair advantage that related companies with access to earlier sale invoices enjoy under the first sale rule.[87]

---

[82] Cf. the approach stipulated by Art. 31 and 32 of the Vienna Convention on the Law of Treaties 1969.

[83] Ruessmann/Willems, Revisiting The First Sale For Export Rule: An Attempt to Remove Fairness in the Interests of Raising Revenues Without Improving Legal Certainty, World Customs Journal 3 (2009) 1, p. 45 (48), available at: http://worldcustomsjournal.org/media/wcj/-2009/1/Willems-Ruessmann.pdf.

[84] As required by Art. 31(3) of the Vienna Convention on the Law of Treaties 1969. This treaty represents customary international law and is expressly followed by the Panel and Appellate Body. The provision requires "any subsequent practice between the parties regarding the interpretation of the treaty or application of its provisions" to be taken into account together with the context.

[85] In the United States, CBP's attempt to incorporate A.O. 22.1 in national law failed due to the protest of commerce and legislative requirements. For an overview see Desiderio/Desiderio, Thoughts on the "First Sale" Rule, World Customs Journal 4 (2010) 1, p. 39 (40–42), available at: http://www.worldcustomsjournal.org/media/wcj/-2010/1/Desiderio.pdf.

[86] Regulation (EC) No. 450/2008 of the European Parliament and of the Council, OJ [2008] L 145/1 ("Modernised Customs Code," available at: http://eur-lex.europa.eu/LexUriServ/LexUriServ.do?uri=OJ:L:2008:145:0001:0064:EN:PDF), entered into force on 24 June 2008 but could not be applied without its implementing provisions. These were due to be issued by June 2012. However, in February 2012, the Commission replaced the code with a Proposal of the European Parliament and of the Council laying down the Union Customs Code, COM(2012) 64 final, available at: http://ec.europa.eu/taxation_customs/resources/documents/common/legislation/proposals/customs/com%282012%2964_en.pdf. It will take a number of years before the code enters into force.

[87] Parliamentary Questions, Answer given by Mr. Šemeta on behalf of the Commission, 2 May 2011 (E-002959/2011), available at: http://www.europarl.europa.eu/sides/getAllAnswers.do?reference=E-2011-002959&language=EN.

Transfer Pricing

Transfer pricing refers to the transfer of goods, services and assets within MNEs in different tax jurisdictions.[88] Thereby, MNEs must comply with the regulations of both customs and tax authorities.[89] The extent to which satisfaction of customs valuation requirements also satisfy transfer pricing requirements depends on national regulations.[90]

This situation begs the question whether it would be possible to harmonise the rules of taxation and customs relating to transfer pricing. One set of documentation satisfying the requirements of both regimes would increase compliance and transparency.

There are two international instruments regulating transfer pricing: customs authorities use the CVA whereas tax authorities generally follow the OECD's Transfer Pricing Guidelines for Multinational Enterprises and Tax Administrations.[91] Although both share the same broad objective (i.e. to establish whether the price has been influenced by the parties' relationship),[92] the subjects of investigation differ: the CVA seeks to determine the value of a product whereas the OECD's Guidelines determine the taxable proceeds of a transaction.[93] In this respect, it has been pointed out that although tax rules tend to be clearer than the CVA, failure to comply with the latter could lead to fines and penalties.[94]

---

[88] Liu, Transfer Pricing and Customs Valuation: Exploring Convergence, Global Trade and Customs Journal 2 (2007) 3, p. 117.

[89] Concerning the European Union, Council Directive 2006/112/EC of 28 November 2006, OJ [2006] L 347/1, Art. 85 states: "In respect of the importation of goods, the taxable amount shall be the value for customs purposes, determined in accordance with the Community provisions in force." It is available at: http://eur-lex.europa.eu/LexUriServ/LexUriServ.do?uri=CELEX:32006L0112:EN:HTML.

[90] In this respect, it is significant that the United States has stated that an importer who relies solely on an APA or transfer pricing study will fail not only to satisfy the transaction value method of customs valuation but also to discharge the burden of reasonable care imposed by US law. See US Customs and Border Protection Bureau, Determining the Acceptability of Transaction Value for Related Party Transactions, April 2007, p. 17, available at: http://www.cbp.gov/linkhandler/cgov/trade/legal/informed_compliance_pubs/icp089.ctt/icp089.pdf.

[91] See OECD Guidelines for Multinational Enterprises, available at: http://www.oecd.org/dataoecd/56/36/1922428.pdf.

[92] In this respect, the CVA prohibits the use of a transaction price that has been influenced through a relationship between the buyer and seller. The OECD's Guidelines uses the concept of an "arm's length transaction." See OECD Guidelines for Multinational Enterprises, Principle X (Taxation), available at: http://www.oecd.org/dataoecd/56/36/1922428.pdf.

[93] This makes it difficult for MNEs to satisfy the requirements of both regimes in a way that operates to their advantage. An advantage under the CVA requires a low transaction value whereas an advantage under the OECD Guidelines requires the highest possible deductible value.

[94] See Abad, Forging a Translation: The "Circumstances of Sale" Criterion, Transfer Pricing, and Economics, Global Trade and Customs Journal 5 (2010) 9, p. 335 (336–337). Annex I offers only vague guidance on the methodology to use and this is often reflected in national legislation.

Owing to the differing methodologies and requirements of both regimes, it is questionable whether harmonisation is possible or even desirable.[95] As matters stand, neither authority is bound to accept the values determined by the other. The way forward appears to lie in greater cooperation between customs and taxation authorities on the one hand, and the customs and taxation departments within MNEs on the other.[96]

Challenges Facing Developing Countries

The conditions affecting customs valuation is very different in developing and industrialised countries. The former are heavily dependent on customs receipts and are therefore particularly concerned to prevent the loss of revenue.[97] However, inadequate customs procedures and the informal nature of trade in developing countries[98] exacerbate the problem of valuation fraud.[99]

During the Tokyo Round (1973–1979), developing countries opposed the use of the transaction value method, believing it would provide importers with greater opportunity for fraud by reducing the power of customs authorities to perform valuation control.[100] For that reason, they supported the BDV, which allowed

[95] For example, under s.482 of the US Internal Revenue Code, taxpayers can prove an arm's length transaction in relation to an aggregate value of transactions. By contrast, customs authorities are required to examine in each and every transaction whether a relationship between the parties has influenced the transaction price pursuant to 19 U.S.C. §1401a(b)(2)(A)(iv). See Murphy/Files, The Intersection of Transfer Pricing and Customs Valuation: Challenges (and Opportunities) for Multinational Enterprises, International Trade Law and Regulation15 (2009) 5, p. 149 (152).

[96] See Liu, in: Wolfrum/Scholl/Hestermeyer (eds.), *WTO – Trade in Goods*, 2011, pp. 900–902.

[97] See Weerth, Tariffs of the World: Are Customs Duties Really Growing Unimportant?, Global Trade and Customs Journal 4 (2009) 2, p. 53 (55): According to data from the WCO, the revenue from tariffs accounts for between 30-50% of revenue in 27 countries.

[98] The informal sector is estimated to represent 43% of the GDP in Africa, almost equivalent to the formal sector. See Organisation for Economic Co-operation and Development, Trade and Agriculture Directorate Trade Committee, Working Party of the Trade Committee, Informal Cross-Border Trade and Trade Facilitation Reform in Sub-Saharan Africa, OECD Trade Policy Working Paper No. 86, TAD/TC/WP(2008)13/FINAL, 18 February 2009, p. 8, available at: http://www.oecd.org/dataoecd/24/6/42222094.pdf.

[99] See Satapathy, Implementation of WTO Agreement on Customs Valuation, Economic and Political Weekly, 17 June 2000, p. 2098, who refers to "fraudulent re-invoicing in third countries, double invoicing with the connivance of the foreign suppliers, misdeclaration of description, quantity and quality of imported goods to suppress value, overvaluation of exempted and low-rated imports to transfer hard currency abroad and overvaluation of exports to get additional export incentives."

[100] See comments by Belize in Report by the Technical Committee on Customs Valuation Concerning the Effects of False Invoicing on Customs Valuation, GATT Committee on Customs Valuation, VAL/W/32, 7 November 1985. See also GATT, Committee on Customs Valuation, Justification for India's Proposal on the Burden of Proof, VAL/W/51, 10 October 1989, paras. 4–5.

customs authorities to challenge suspiciously low value declarations ("undervaluation").[101] However, under the CVA, a low value would only justify a request for further information.[102] For this reason, developing countries often use reference pricing, valuation databases and pre-shipment inspections to verify transaction values.

Owing to their weak bargaining position, developing countries could not influence negotiations at the Tokyo or Uruguay rounds to ensure the CVA reflected their needs adequately.[103] The resultant difficulties experienced by developing countries in the implementation of Article VII GATT were recognised in a decision by the WTO Ministerial Conference on Implementation-related issues and concerns of November 2001.[104]

In developing countries, both customs and business need capacity building in order to implement the agreement.[105] On the one hand, customs officers must know how to apply the relevant legal provisions and be able to examine the relevant facts.[106] On the other, the private sector must maintain adequate commercial records.

Concerning the first aspect, the CVA can only be implemented as part of a customs modernisation programme based on the Revised Kyoto Convention.[107] In this respect, the WCO provides comprehensive capacity building measures for administrations in accordance with the guiding principles of its Capacity Building Strategy.[108] More specifically, it has acknowledged the need for capacity building in revenue collection

---

[101] E.g. by using official indicative values based on the average prices of imports as well as minimum values. See GATT, Non-Tariff Measures Affecting Trade of Developing Countries: Note by the Secretariat, MTN/3B/23, 31 December 1974, p. 24, para. 58.

[102] See Rosenow/O'Shea, *A Handbook on the WTO Customs Valuation Agreement*, 2010, pp. 29–30.

[103] For an explanation of the weak negotiating position of developing countries in trade negotiations see Rege, Developing Country Participation in Negotiations Leading to the Adoption of the WTO Agreements on Customs Valuation and Preshipment Inspection, A Public Choice Analysis, World Competition 22 (1999) 1, p. 37 (38). See also Finger/Schuler, Implementation of Uruguay Round Commitments: The Development Challenge, World Bank Policy Working Paper No. 2215, October 1999, p. 11, available at: http://elibrary.worldbank.org/content/workingpaper/10.1596/1813-9450-2215.

[104] Ministerial conference, 4th Session (Doha, November 2001)—Decision on Implementation-related issues and concerns, WT/MIN(01)/17, 20 November 2001, available at: http://www.wto.org/english/thewto_e/minist_e/min01_e/mindecl_implementation_e.pdf.

[105] See Duran/Sokol, Policy and Operational Lessons Learned From Eight Country Case Studies, in: De Wulf/Sokol (eds.), *Customs Modernization Handbook*, 2005, pp. 116–119.

[106] See World Customs Organization, *Customs Valuation Control Handbook*, Part II, Chapter 1, p. 1, para. 1.

[107] Finger/Schuler, Implementation of Uruguay Round Commitments: The Development Challenge, World Bank Policy Working Paper No. 2215, October 1999, p. 12, available at: http://elibrary.worldbank.org/content/workingpaper/10.1596/1813-9450-2215.

[108] See World Customs Organization, Capacity Building Strategy, 2003, pp. 4–5, available at: http://www.wcoomd.org/files/1.%20Public%20files/PDFandDocuments/Capacity%20Building/Cap%20buil%20strat.pdf.

in view of the economic crisis.[109] The Technical Valuation Committee also provides support and training measures to members on request. On the other hand, capacity building in the private sector presents a great challenge owing to the informal nature of trade in developing countries. One solution is to use trade facilitation measures as a means of encouraging traders to adopt more formal practices.[110]

It is also important that customs valuation controls often found in developing countries do not constitute trade barriers.[111] For example, reference prices and valuation databases must not be used as systems of valuation in their own right but only as indicators of risk.[112] Pre-shipment inspections must also comply with the provisions of the WTO's Agreement on Pre-shipment Inspection ("PSI").[113]

Conclusion

The drafters of Art. VII GATT used the broadest wording to secure agreement on a delicate subject,[114] which had hitherto been the preserve of Member States. However, as was recognised at the Bretton Woods Conference, a liberal, stable and peaceful international trade regime could not be realised by abstract principles alone.[115] Therefore, an additional agreement on the method of customs valuation was necessary to implement Article VII.

[109] See Resolution of the Customs Cooperation Council passed in June 2009 to enhance delivery of capacity building as a response to declining revenue collection caused by the economic downturn, available at: http://www.wcoomd.org/files/1.%20Public%20files/PDFandDocuments/About%20Us/Annex%20%20-%20Resolution%20Global%20Economic%20Downturn.pdf. See also, World Customs Organization, Revenue Collection Package, 2011, pp. 4–5, available at: http://www.wcoomd.org/files/1.%20Public%20files/english/revenue_package/revenue_package.pdf.

[110] See Lesser/Moisé-Leeman, Organisation for Economic Co-operation and Development, Trade and Agriculture Directorate Trade Committee, Working Party of the Trade Committee, Informal Cross-Border Trade and Trade Facilitation Reform in Sub-Saharan Africa, OECD Trade Policy Working Paper No. 86, TAD/TC/WP(2008)13/FINAL, 18 February 2009, pp. 43–45, available at: http://www.oecd.org/dataoecd/24/6/42222094.pdf.

[111] Accordingly, reference values can be used to check the customs values but not to calculate the duties themselves. See Report of the Panel, *Columbia – Indicative Prices and Restrictions on Ports of Entry*, WT/DS366/R, p. 103 (para. 7.129): The Panel rejected Columbia's argument that the payment made by the importer was a guarantee because the importer could only have the goods released if he paid the customs duties and sales tax based on indicative prices. In the event, the Panel held the system of indicative pricing contravened Art. 1-3, 5-6, and 7.2(b) and (f) of the CVA.

[112] See also World Customs Organization, Guidelines on the Development and Use of a National Valuation Database as a Risk Assessment Tool, Preamble, para. 1, available at: http://www.wcoomd.org/files/1.%20Public%20files/PDFandDocuments/Valuation/guidelines_national_db.pdf.

[113] The preamble to this agreement recognises that developing countries need to verify price of imported goods but also that PSI programmes must not give rise to unnecessary delays or unequal treatment. The PSI agreement is available at: http://www.wto.org/english/docs_e/legal_e/21-psi.pdf.

[114] Asakura, *World History of the Customs and Tariffs*, 2003, p. 173: "[C]ustoms valuation is always a delicate business."

[115] Pehle, The Bretton Woods Institutions, The Yale Law Journal 55 (1946) 5, p. 1127.

Considering that the CVA 1994 has now been in force for almost 20 years, sufficient time has elapsed to ask whether the agreement has achieved its objectives. Generally speaking, the answer depends on whether the member is an industrialised or developing country. In the former, customs and commerce have the necessary procedures in place to enable effective implementation of the CVA. However, this is not the case in developing countries where customs administrations lack the resources to perform audits and trade is largely informal.

In developing countries, a lack of information may force customs authorities to negotiate a mutually acceptable value with the importer using the vaguely worded fall-back method. This not only creates legal uncertainty for trade and but also endangers customs receipts—that still remain a significant source of revenue in many developing countries.[116] However, implemented in conjunction with customs modernisation and best commercial practices, there is evidence that CVA can enhance revenue collection, combat corruption and facilitate trade in developing countries.[117] In this respect, the WCO, acting through the TCCV, plays a fundamental role in promoting and implementing the CVA 'on the ground', through its wide range of instruments and capacity building measures.

[116] See Weerth, Tariffs of the World: Are Customs Duties Really Growing Unimportant?, Global Trade and Customs Journal 4 (2009) 2, p. 53 (55).

[117] See e.g. Clarete, Managing the Challenges of WTO Participation, Case Study 37, Philippines: Adopting the Transaction Basis for Customs Valuation, in: Gallagher/Low/Stoler (eds.), *Managing the Challenges of WTO Participation – 45 Case Studies*, 2005, also available at: http://www.wto.org/english/res_e/booksp_e/casestudies_e/case37_e.htm.

WIPO and the Public–Private Web of Global Intellectual Property Governance

Andrea Wechsler

Introduction

The *World Intellectual Property Organization* (WIPO) has always been recognized as important international economic institution for the global governance of intellectual property (IP) law. Moreover, its role in promoting, facilitating and supporting national, regional and local governance of IP law worldwide has long been uncontested. However, ever since the late 1980s, fundamental transformations in the IP landscape have challenged the established position of WIPO in global IP governance.

First, increasing perceptions of the interconnectedness of IP issues with larger global development issues have required substantial adaptations in WIPO's policy formulations. Second, fragmentation and horizontal forum-shifting of IP issues from WIPO to both complementary and competing international institutions, such as the *World Trade Organization* (WTO), have challenged the uncontested role of WIPO in global IP governance. Likewise, vertical forum-shifting from multilateral to bilateral law-making has necessitated strategic adaptations on the part of WIPO. And third, the rise of private regulation in IP law as well as new soft law regulatory approaches have pressurized WIPO into redefining its own position towards public actors, private actors and civil society.

The author wishes to thank the Max Weber Programme of the European University Institute (EUI) and the Max Planck Institute for Intellectual Property and Competition Law for their funding of this research and expresses her gratitude to Prof. Hans-W. Micklitz and Prof. Reto M. Hilty for their inspiration and encouragement. Of course, the author takes full responsibility for any mistakes or omissions.

A. Wechsler (✉)
Max Weber Fellow, European University Institute, Villa La Fonte, Via delle Fontanelle, 10, 50014 San Domenico di Fiesole (Firenze), Italy
e-mail: andrea.wechsler@eui.eu

C. Herrmann et al. (eds.), *European Yearbook of International Economic Law (EYIEL), Vol. 4 (2013)*, European Yearbook of International Economic Law 4,
DOI 10.1007/978-3-642-33917-2_16, © Springer-Verlag Berlin Heidelberg 2013

In the light of these transformations, the following chapter introduces, discusses and evaluates the mission, role and activities of WIPO as international economic institution for the global governance of intellectual property. It discusses, first, the larger public–private web of global IP governance where WIPO operates. It then introduces in detail WIPO as international economic institution for IP governance. This introduction is followed by a discussion of WIPO's mission and strategic goals as well as an overview over its core activities. The conclusions evaluate WIPO's current positioning and provide recommendations for WIPO's further establishment in the public–private web of global IP governance.

The Public–Private Web of Global Intellectual Property Governance

With WIPO having been one of the first international institutions for the global governance of IP law in the twentieth century, its position has dramatically changed at the beginning of the twenty-first century. At the time of writing, WIPO constitutes merely one of a multiplicity of actors, organizations and institutions that claim their role and share in the public–private web of global IP governance. Its having been embedded into a system of global governance corresponds to the tremendous rise in academic governance literature and increasingly so in literature revolving around the global governance of IP law.[1] This rising focus on governance reflects the fading trust in traditional modes of regulation and the Westphalian system in capturing and controlling current dimensions of global IP protection.[2] These developments warrant a closer look at and discussion of the transformations of global IP governance and the factors that have driven such transformation. Thus, the following section introduces and discusses the growing interconnectedness of IP law with related policy issues that is herein termed "IP and . . ."-approach, horizontal and vertical forum-shifting and novel regulatory modes.

The "IP and . . ."-Approach

One of the driving factors for changes in the global IP governance structure were both the growing realities of and increasing perceptions about the interrelationship of IP issues with larger global policy issues related to, *inter alia*, civil society,

---

[1] Sand, Polycontextuality as an Alternative to Constitutionalism, in: Joerges/Sand/Teubner (eds.), *Transnational Governance and Constitutionalism*, 2004, pp. 41, 44.

[2] Burris/Kempa/Shearing, Changes in Governance: A Cross-Disciplinary Review of Current Scholarship, Akron Law Review 41 (2008) 1, p. 1 (2).

development, human rights, biodiversity and the environment.[3] While IP law and its realities had long been regarded a highly technical legal field, it is in particular the adoption of the *Agreement on Trade-Related Aspects of Intellectual Property Rights* (*TRIPS Agreement*)[4] that has brought the interconnectedness of IP to the forefront of attention.

Prior to the realities of the *TRIPS Agreement*[5] itself, it has primarily been the *US Trade Act*[6] that has exposed the linkage between IP and trade. However, subsequent to the *TRIPS Agreement,*[7] the trade-relatedness of IPRs has become widely acknowledged.[8] As a result of the effects of the *TRIPS Agreement* on national policy space,[9] the perceptions about the trade-relatedness of IPRs have closely been followed by perceptions about the impact of IP protection on development.[10] In particular, the impact of IP protection on public health was the subject of intense debate and eventually pressures for policy adaptations through, for instance, the *Doha Declaration.*[11] In recent years, further public interests have come to feature prominently in the IP debate—amongst them IP and human rights and IP and the environment.[12] In consequence, the changing face of the global IP debate in recent years is herewith characterized as having led to an "IP and . . ."-approach to IP policy debates and formations.

Moreover, recent years have seen a growing infiltration of economic analysis into IP policy discussions.[13] Having arisen out of re-conceptualizing IP law as

---

[3] For a discussion of further challenges see Yu, TRIPS and Its Achilles' Heel, Journal of Intellectual Property Law 18 (2011) 2, p. 479.

[4] Marrakesh, Agreement Establishing the World Trade Organization, Annex 1C, 1869 U.N.T.S. 299, 33 I.L.M. 1125, 1197.

[5] Marrakesh, Agreement Establishing the World Trade Organization, Annex 1C, 1869 U.N.T.S. 299, 33 I.L.M. 1125, 1197.

[6] Cf. US Trade Act (Section 301), see Gervais, *The TRIPS Agreement: Drafting History and Analysis*, (3rd ed.) 2008, p. 154.

[7] Marrakesh, Agreement Establishing the World Trade Organization, Annex 1C, 1869 U.N.T.S. 299, 33 I.L.M. 1125, 1197.

[8] Gervais, Intellectual Property and Human Rights: Learning to Live Together, in: Torremans (ed.), *Intellectual Property and Human Rights*, 2008, p. 15.

[9] Taubman, TRIPS Jurisprudence in the Balance. Between the Realist Defense of Policy Space and a Shared Utilitarian Ethic, in: Lenk, et al. (eds), *Ethics and Law of Intellectual Property, Current Problems in Politics, Science and Technology*, 2007, pp. 90–93.

[10] Gervais, TRIPS and Development, in: Gervais (ed.), *Intellectual Property, Trade and Development. Strategies to Optimize Economic Development in a TRIPS-Plus Era*, 2007, p. 21.

[11] Declaration on the TRIPS Agreement and Public Health, adopted on 14 November 2001, WT/MIN(01)/DEC/W/2. See also Sell, The Quest for Global Governance in Intellectual Property and Public Health: Structural, Discursive, and Institutional Dimensions, Temple Law Review 77 (2004) 2, p. 363.

[12] E.g. Stoeva, *New Norms and Knowledge in World Politics: Protecting people, intellectual property and the environment*, 2009, p. 12.

[13] Drexl, Is there a 'more economic approach' to intellectual property and competition law?, in: Drexl (ed.), *Research Handbook on Intellectual Property and Competition Law*, 2008, p. 3.

complementary to competition law and thereby approximating IP analyses with the more economic approach in competition law, a more economic approach to IP law in itself is on the rise.[14] The economic analysis of IP law is focusing on almost all aspects of IPRs.[15] However, particular emphasis is placed on the interrelationship of patents and innovation and patents and technology.[16] This growing emphasis on economic perspectives on IP protection testifies to an increasing instrumental and functional use of IP law for the promotion of domestic innovation capacities and economic development goals.[17] Yet, critical voices have also pointed to the methodological and substantive limitations of economic analysis for guiding the policy formation process in IP law.[18]

From these transformations of IP policy discussions, it not only follows that new perspectives on IP policy elements and powerful novel methodologies have emerged. It follows also that new experts, new actors, new agents and new governing institutions have entered the stage claiming their share in shaping the IP environment of the twenty-first century.

Proliferation of Governing Bodies

The entry of new actors and new governing institutions into international IP law has led to both a proliferation of governing bodies in the sense of horizontal forum-shifting and to vertical forum-shifting for IP policy issues. The fragmentation of IP law-making and its enforcement in the international realm is thereby one of the most striking features of global IP law in the twenty-first century.

First, fragmentation and horizontal forum-shifting of IP issues from WIPO to both complementary and competing international institutions, such as the WTO, have challenged the uncontested role of WIPO in global IP governance.[19] The very beginnings of transnational IP governance were marked by a very limited number of fora with the foundation of WIPO in 1967 signalling the concentration of IP governance and standard-setting in one specialized agency of the *United*

[14] For early beginnings see Posner, Intellectual Property: The Law and Economics Approach, Journal of Economic Perspectives 19 (2005) 2, p. 57.

[15] E.g. Elkin-Koren/Salzberger, *The Law and Economics of Intellectual Property in the Digital Age*, 2011.

[16] E.g. Blair/Cottier, *Intellectual Property. Economic and Legal Dimensions of Rights and Remedies*, 2005, pp. 13–20.

[17] Wechsler, Intellectual Property Law in the P.R. China: A Powerful Economic Tool for Innovation and Development, China-EU Law Journal 1 (2011) 1/2, p. 3.

[18] Wechsler, Criminal Enforcement of Intellectual Property Law—An Economic Approach, in: Geiger (ed.), *Criminal Enforcement of Intellectual Property: A Handbook of Contemporary Research*, forthcoming in 2012, copy on file with author.

[19] Oguamanam, Beyond Theories: Intellectual Property Dynamics in the Global Knowledge Economy, Wake Forest Intellectual Property Law Journal 9 (2009) 2, p. 104 (110).

Nations (UN). However, in 1994, the *TRIPS Agreement*[20] formally brought IP rules into the WTO framework and opened the floodgates for numerous novel IP policymaking initiatives and thereby institutional competition.[21] Organizations—such as the *Organization for Economic Co-operation and Development* (OECD),[22] the *World Health Organization* (WHO),[23] the *United Nations Conference on Trade and Development* (UNCTAD),[24] and the *Convention on Biological Diversity* (CBD)[25]—started to integrate questions of IP protection into their agendas. Helfer conceptualizes these new forms of IP law-making as having focused on four different international regimes: "biodiversity, plant genetic resources for food and agriculture (PGRs), public health, and human rights."[26] Yet, the multiplication of IP sources, fora, and processes has stretched far beyond those four substantive regimes and has led to the integration of countless policy dimension and institutions into IP policy-making.[27] This proliferation of international fora for the governance of IP law has been termed horizontal forum-shifting—a process that is, however, rightly so still seen to be "under construction."[28]

Second, and quite distinct from horizontal forum-shifting, vertical forum-shifting from multilateral to bilateral and individual law-making has necessitated strategic adaptations on the part of WIPO. Vertical forum-shifting is taken to denote a top-down shifting in IP norm-setting, rule-making, implementation and enforcement.[29] More precisely, Sell has conceptualized vertical forum-shifting along four dimensions. The first dimension denotes a trend towards bilateral and regional negotiations and treaties and is reflected in an increasing number of bilateral trade agreements, such as for instance *Free Trade Agreements* (FTAs).[30] By 2010, the US had concluded FTAs with no less than 17 countries while the number

[20] Marrakesh, Agreement Establishing the World Trade Organization, Annex 1C, 1869 U.N.T.S. 299, 33 I.L.M. 1125, 1197.

[21] Helfer, Regime Shifting: The TRIPS Agreement and New Dynamics of International Intellectual Property Lawmaking, Yale Journal International Law 29 (2004) 1, p. 1 (2).

[22] See http://www.oecd.org.

[23] See http://www.who.int.

[24] See http://www.unctad.org.

[25] See http://www.cbd.int.

[26] Helfer, Regime Shifting: The TRIPS Agreement and New Dynamics of International Intellectual Property Lawmaking, Yale Journal of International Law 29 (2004) 1, p. 1 (27).

[27] Cf. Dutfield, *Literature Survey on Intellectual Property Rights and Sustainable Human Development*, 2003.

[28] Chon, Global Intellectual Property Governance (Under Construction), Theoretical Inquiries in Law 12 (2011) 1, p. 349 (349–350).

[29] Sell, TRIPS Was Never Enough: Vertical Forum Shifting, FTAs, ACTA, and TPP, Journal of Intellectual Property Law 18 (2011) 2, p. 447 (452–454).

[30] For an overview on the *European Partnership Agreements* (EPA) by the European Union see http://ec.europa.eu/trade/creating-opportunities/bilateral-relations.

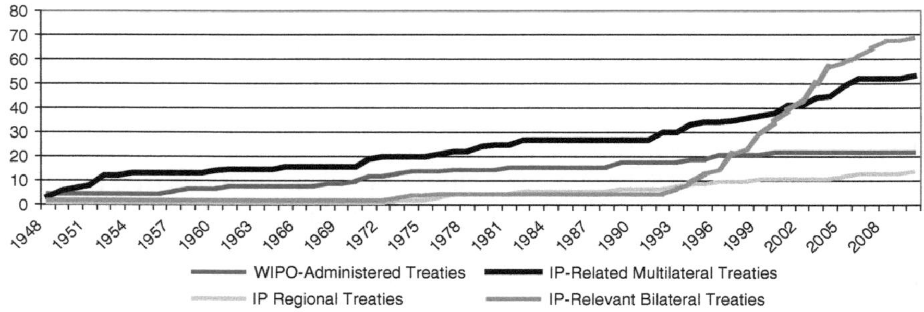

Fig. 1 Number of IP-related treaties, 1948–2010

of *Bilateral Investment Treaties* (BITs) came up to 40.[31] While such FTAs and BITs govern issues of IP protection amongst other policy areas, there are even 30 more specific treaties called *Intellectual Property Rights Agreements* that focus exclusively on IP issues.[32] On a global scale, Fig. 1 graphically depicts this trend towards bilateral treaty-making as opposed to more traditional modes of multilateral and regional treaty-making. The second dimension of vertical forum-shifting denotes a trend towards law-making amongst a small group of like-minded countries. A most recent example of this second dimension is provided by the negotiations towards the *Anti-Counterfeiting Trade Agreement* (ACTA).[33] A third dimension of vertical forum-shifting is the intensifying of trans-pacific partnership (TPP) negotiations as reflected in a number of TRIPS-plus initiatives.[34] And a fourth dimension of vertical forum-shifting arises out of the increasing tendency to enforce IP interests at the lowest regional level through direct contact with stakeholders, governments and sub-state actors.[35] This latter dimension of vertical forum-shifting constitutes a first expression of the rising power of private parties in determining the shape of global IP law and policy.

---

[31] See Office of the United States Trade Representative, http://www.ustr.gov/trade-agreements and Trade Compliance Center, available at: http://tcc.export.gov/Trade_Agreements/Bilateral_Investment_Treaties/index.asp.

[32] E.g. the 1992 People's Republic of China Intellectual Property Rights Memorandum of Understanding, the 1995 People's Republic of China Intellectual Property Rights Memorandum of Understanding, the 1996 People's Republic of China Implementation of the 1995 Intellectual Property Rights Agreement, available at: http://tcc.export.gov/Trade_Agreements/Intellectual_Property_Rights/index.asp.

[33] See Opinion of European Academics on ACTA: http://www.iri.uni-hannover.de/acta-1668.html.

[34] For more information see http://www.ustr.gov/tpp.

[35] Sell, TRIPS Was Never Enough: Vertical Forum Shifting, FTAs, ACTA, and TPP, Journal of Intellectual Property Law 18 (2011) 2, p. 447 (452–454).

Cumulative number of IP-related treaties, 1948–2010 (including prior treaties), distinguishing between WIPO-Administered Treaties, IP-Related Multilateral Treaties, IP Regional Treaties, and IP-Relevant Bilateral Treaties.[36]

It follows from this proliferation of fora and the attendant forum-shifting that new levels of IP politics have assumed greater importance in recent years. These new levels are not only threatening the role of established governing bodies but also the global *acquis* on the normative underpinnings of the IP law regime that had found expression in the IP policies of more traditional bodies of global IP governance.

Novel Regulatory Modes

Not only the actors and institutions in global IP governance have changed. It is also the regulatory modes that have undergone substantial transformation. On the one hand, particular emphasis shall herein be placed on the changing nature of IP law through the rise of soft law initiatives. On the other hand, particular emphasis shall be placed on the changing sources of regulation—especially the rise of private regulatory approaches in the form of self- and co-regulation.

First, soft law is defined as referring to "non-legally binding instruments, such as guidelines, standards, criteria, code of practice, resolutions, decisions, and principles or declarations."[37] In global IP governance, reliance on soft law has grown tremendously in comparison to treaty-making whose lengthy procedures appear to be less adapted to the rapidly changing and technologically driven area of IP law. Examples of such soft law reliance are both the *Joint Recommendation Concerning Provisions on the Protection of Well-Known Marks*[38] and the *Recommended Standards for Industrial Property*.[39] The rationale of such swiftly enacted soft laws lies in their immediate reaction to new economic and technological developments.[40] Their theoretical justification as suggested by constructivists lies in the capacity of soft laws to define shared norms and a sense of commonality without being endangered by the threat of potential litigation.[41] However, the

[36] Data sources: http://www.wipo.int/wipolex/en/other_treaties and http://docs.law.gwu.edu/burns/research/tools/IPTreatyFinder.pdf.

[37] Chopra, et al., *Ecosystems and Human Well-Being, Volume 3: Policy Responses*, 2005, p. 42.

[38] WIPO Doc. No. A/34/13 at 3 (August 1999), available at: http://www.wipo.int/about-ip/en/development_iplaw/pub833.htm.

[39] Available at: http://www.osim.ro/brevete/manuale.osim/manualompi/handbook/eng/03/e030001.pdf.

[40] Dinwoodie, The International Intellectual Property System: Treaties, Norms, National Courts and Private Ordering, in: Gervais (ed.), *Intellectual Property, Trade and Development. Strategies to Optimize Economic Development in a TRIPS-Plus Era*, 2007, p. 80.

[41] Shaffer/Pollack, Hard vs. Soft Law: Alternatives, Complements, and Antagonists in International Governance, Minnesota Law Review 94 (2010) 3, p. 706.

disadvantage of this transformation of the nature of IP protection lies not only in the danger of solidification of such soft laws and the rising inconsistencies between hard and soft laws but in the fact that developing countries, whose traditional focus has been on treaty-making, have not fully grasped the implications of a greater reliance on soft-law thereby tipping the IP-balance in favor of industrialized nations.[42]

Second, the rise of private regulation in IP law has pressurized WIPO into redefining its own position towards public actors, private actors and civil society. In a comparative institutional analysis, the institutional frameworks involved in governing IPRs, essential complementarities between public and private institutions have long been recognized.[43] Thus, it was shown that reliance on interindividual governance structures (IGS) could lead to efficient cost-shifting towards private agents for regime governance.[44] However, recent years have seen an entirely new dimension of private regulation in global IP law that not only refers to regime governance but to the law-making entities themselves. Essentially, various dimensions of privatization—that is the rise of private commercial actors, the rise of private rule-making, and reduction of state involvement in the enforcement of private law—are identifiable in IP law and policy. A first example of private ordering is the creation of norms by information intermediaries, such as Internet services providers (ISP) in response to allegations of copyright infringement by their subscribers.[45] A second example is the evolution of digital rights management (DRM) norms through copyright owners for the prevention of user activities that are, however, authorized by copyright law. Yet another well-known example of extensively permissive, and consequently widely hailed, model of private governance of online content constitutes the governance of the *Apple Computer's iTunes Music Store*.[46] A third example is set by the regulation of collective rights management organizations in Norway. Both TONO as Norway's Performing Rights Society for authors and composers of musical works[47] and

[42] Dinwoodie, The International Intellectual Property System: Treaties, Norms, National Courts and Private Ordering, in: Gervais (ed.), *Intellectual Property, Trade and Development. Strategies to Optimize Economic Development in a TRIPS-Plus Era*, 2007, p. 83.

[43] Brousseau/Bessy, Public and private institutions in the governance of intellectual property rights, in: Andersen (ed.), *Intellectual Property Rights: Innovation, Governance and the Institutional Environment*, 2006, p. 243.

[44] Brousseau/Bessy, Public and private institutions in the governance of intellectual property rights, in: Andersen (ed.), *Intellectual Property Rights: Innovation, Governance and the Institutional Environment*, 2006, p. 247.

[45] Dinwoodie, The International Intellectual Property System: Treaties, Norms, National Courts and Private Ordering, in: Gervais (ed.), *Intellectual Property, Trade and Development. Strategies to Optimize Economic Development in a TRIPS-Plus Era*, 2007, p. 65.

[46] Armstrong, Digital Rights Management and the Process of Fair Use, Harvard Journal of Law & Technology, 20 (2006) 1, p. 49 (64); Digital Media Project, The Berkman Center for Internet & Society at Harvard Law School, iTunes: How Copyright, Contract, and Technology Shape the Business of Digital Media—A Case Study, 2004, p. 40–48.

[47] See http://www.tono.no.

Kopinor as collecting society for books, newspaper, and comparable publications[48] are owned and governed by its members as opposed to being under governmental supervision.[49] The rise of private actors in law-making and regulation is by no means confined to the realms of IP law. It is traceable in a variety of legal areas, such as food safety regulation.[50] However, what all of these areas of law have in common is as of yet a certain insecurity of how to theoretically and practically deal with the rise of private power.

In consequence, this discussion of novel regulatory modes has shown both a trend towards soft law initiatives and a trend towards private regulation. Both of these trends have major implications for an institution—such as WIPO—that has traditionally relied on classical modes and sources of international law-making.

WIPO as International Economic Institution

Against the above-discussed background of transformations and the emerging public–private web of global IP governance, the following section introduces WIPO as international economic institution. It focuses, in particular, on the history, establishment and evolution of WIPO, relevant facts and figures, and WIPO's institutional structure.

History, Establishment and Evolution

The history, establishment, and evolution of WIPO show its changing rationale, nature, and role in global IP governance. Created originally and primarily for norm administration, it has gradually expanded its global ambit as specialized agency of the UN towards a service-oriented global player in IP governance that transgresses the traditional borders of international organizations in the Westphalian model.[51]

Historically, WIPO's predecessor was designed for norm administration of global international IP treaties. WIPO was preceded by the *United International*

[48] See http://www.kopinor.no.

[49] Compare the German governmental supervisory system under the "Gesetz über die Wahrnehmung von Urheberrechten und verwandten Schutzrechten (Urheberrechtswahrnehmungsgesetz)" of 9 November 1965, BGBl. I, p. 1294, last revision on 26 October 2007, BGBl. I, pp. 2513, 2517.

[50] See Cafaggi, Private Regulation, Supply Chain and Contractual Networks: The Case of Food Safety, EUI Working Paper RSCAS 10 (2010).

[51] See also Yu, The Global Intellectual Property Order and Its Undetermined Future, The WIPO Journal 1 (2009) 1, p. 1 (2).

Bureaux for the Protection of Intellectual Property (BIRPI)[52] that was set up in 1839 up for the administration of the 1883 *Paris Convention for the Protection of Industrial Property*[53] and the 1886 *Berne Convention for the Protection of Literary and Artistic Works* (*Berne Convention*).[54] Having originally been based in Berne, its offices were moved to Geneva in 1960 for closer proximity with the UN and further international organizations. This moving to Geneva indicated the beginning of the changing role of the institution from pure norm administration to a more sophisticated governing body in international IP norm creation and administration.

In 1967, the international consensus about the need for a more pronounced and advanced institution of global IP governance translated into the *Convention Establishing the World Intellectual Property Organization* (*WIPO Convention*).[55] On April 26, 1970, WIPO was established in Geneva and has ever since governed global IP law. The extended mission of WIPO to contribute to a better understanding and cooperation among States, to encourage creative activity and to promote IP protection reflects the changing rationale of the institution.[56] The convention clearly reflects a state-oriented approach to international policy-making in the Westphalian tradition that disregards at that time further and today firmly established economic agents in global IP governance.

In 1974, the *Agreement between the United Nations and the World Intellectual Property Organization*[57] made it one of the now 17 specialized agencies of the UN. Article 1 of the above mentioned agreement entrusted WIPO with the responsibility to take "appropriate action in accordance with its basic instruments, treaties and agreements administered by it." Such appropriate action should be designed "inter alia, for promoting creative intellectual activity and for facilitating the transfer of technology related to industrial property to the developing countries in order to accelerate economic, social, and cultural development."[58] In thus being entrusted as specialized agency, WIPO has assumed responsibilities in all areas of IP law ranging from industrial property, copyright and related rights to issues of traditional knowledge and traditional cultural expressions.[59] The closer attachment of the institution to the UN again shows the then prominent role ascribed to the UN and its agencies in governing policy issues of global relevance with and amongst states.

In consequence, the history of WIPO demonstrates its evolution from an institution of norm administration towards a member-state-oriented international economic institution for global IP governance in the Westphalian tradition. However,

[52] BIRPI is the acronym for the French term Bureaux Internationaux Réunis pour la Protection de la Propriété Intellectuelle.

[53] 21 U.S.T. 1581, 828 U.N.T.S. 305.

[54] S. Treaty Doc. No. 99-27 (1986), 1161 U.N.T.S. 3.

[55] 14 July 1967, as amended 18 September 1979, 21 U.S.T. 1749, 828 U.N.T.S. 3.

[56] Preamble, WIPO Convention, 21 U.S.T. 1749, 828 U.N.T.S. 3.

[57] Available at: http://www.wipo.int/treaties/en/agreement/index.html.

[58] Art. 1 of the Agreement, available at: http://www.wipo.int/treaties/en/agreement/index.html.

[59] See coverage of their activities, available at: http://www.wipo.int/about-ip/en.

as further analysis of the development of WIPO's mission and strategic goals will show,[60] the changing IP infrastructure has forced WIPO into further strategic realignment in the sense of redefining its core mission and strategies for global IP governance.

Facts and Figures

Almost five decades after its establishment, WIPO is still based in Geneva with recently having moved to new headquarters[61]; however, it also entertains external offices in New York, Rio de Janeiro, Singapore and Tokyo. At the time of writing, Francis Gurry is the Director General of WIPO. He was appointed on October 1, 2008 with his 6-year term running until September 2014.[62] Since his coming into office, he has launched an extensive programme of strategic realignment of the work and direction of WIPO.[63] The implementation of this programme is assisted by *WIPO's Senior Management Team*[64] that consists of four Deputy Directors General, three Assistant Director Generals and the Chief of Staff as well as over 1,200 WIPO employees from more than 100 countries.

Since its establishment, WIPO has grown to a membership of 185 countries that constitutes over 90% of the world's countries.[65] In addition and testifying a growing trend towards embracing non-state actors, some 284 non-governmental organizations (NGOs)—such as the *International Trademark Association* (INTA)—and 69 intergovernmental organizations (IGOs)—such as the *European Patent Organization* (EPO)—are accredited as observers at WIPO meetings.[66] WIPO itself provides funds through the *WIPO Voluntary Fund*[67] in order to allow indigenous and local communities to take an active part in the discussions of the *Intergovernmental Committee on Intellectual Property and Genetic Resources, Traditional Knowledge and Folklore* (IGC). Thereby, WIPO fulfils its mission of close cooperation with its Member States and stakeholders to improve understanding and respect for IP worldwide.

---

[60] See the sections on "Strategic Realignment" and "WIPO's IP Policy Direction."

[61] See WIPO, Inauguration of the New WIPO Building, 26 September, 2011, available at: http://www.wipo.int/pressroom/en/articles/2011/article_0023.html.

[62] Available at: http://www.wipo.int/about-wipo/en/dgo.

[63] See the section on "Strategic Realignment."

[64] Available at: http://www.wipo.int/about-wipo/en/management.html.

[65] WIPO, A Users' Guide, An Introduction to the Organization, 2011, see http://www.wipo.int/export/sites/www/freepublications/en/general/1040/wipo_pub_1040.pdf.

[66] For an overview on WIPO observers see List of Observers, available at: http://www.wipo.int/members/en/organizations.jsp.

[67] Available at: http://www.wipo.int/tk/en/ngoparticipation/voluntary_fund.

One of the striking features of WIPO—in comparison to other UN organizations—is that it is largely self-financing. Over 90% of the budgeted expenditure of 618.8 million Swiss francs for the 2010–2011 biennium was covered by WIPO revenues.[68] For the 2012–2013 biennium, the organization projects a coverage of 93% of its budget by revenues from the fee-paid services it provides to its customers.[69] Such revenues stem primarily from WIPO global IP services, i.e. the *Patent Cooperation Treaty* (PCT),[70] the Madrid, Hague and Lisbon systems. Further contributions stem from WIPO's arbitration and mediation services as well as contributions from its Member States. In its financial activities, WIPO adheres to the principles of accountability, transparency and oversight that are guaranteed and enforced by various oversight measures.[71] As a result of their self-financing mechanisms and, thus, the relevance of quality service-provision for WIPO, the organization has increasingly displayed a service-oriented stance towards its customers—primarily private companies—and has, therefore, made a substantial contribution to the emerging public–private web of global IP governance.

Institutional Structure

The institutional structure of WIPO is composed of its main governing bodies, its standing committees, its permanent committees and its working groups. Furthermore, WIPO entertains a close web of outside relations with the multilateral system that is introduced in the following section.

The primary policy and decision-making bodies of WIPO are the *WIPO General Assembly*, the *WIPO Conferences* and the *WIPO Coordination Committee*. Article 6 of the *WIPO Convention*[72] sets out in more detail the set-up, obligations and working mode of the General Assembly. It meets once in every calendar year in ordinary session. Article 7 of the *WIPO Convention*[73] determines the framework for WIPO Conferences. In particular, it shall "discuss matters of general interest in the field of intellectual property and may adopt recommendations relating to such matters."[74] Further details on the WIPO Coordination Committee are set out in

[68] WIPO, 2010–2011 Budget, available at: http://www.wipo.int/export/sites/www/about-wipo/en/budget/pdf/budget_2010_2011.pdf.

[69] WIPO, Results, Budget and Performance, available at: http://www.wipo.int/about-wipo/en/budget.

[70] 28 U.S.T. 7645, 1160 U.N.T.S. 231.

[71] E.g. the Internal Audit and Oversight Division (IAOD) and the Financial Regulations and Rules, available at: http://www.wipo.int/about-wipo/en/pdf/wipo_financial_regulation.pdf.

[72] 14 July 1967, as amended 18 September 1979, 21 U.S.T. 1749, 828 U.N.T.S. 3.

[73] 14 July 1967, as amended 18 September 1979, 21 U.S.T. 1749, 828 U.N.T.S. 3.

[74] Art. 6(2)(i), 14 July 1967, as amended 18 September 1979, 21 U.S.T. 1749, 828 U.N.T.S. 3.

Article 8 of the *WIPO Convention*.[75] The Committee gives advice to "the organs of the Union, the General Assembly, the Conference, and the Director General, on all administrative, financial and other matters of common interest."[76]

In addition to WIPO's main governing bodies, WIPO entertains standing committees that the *General Assembly* establishes for a particular purpose. Currently, there is, first, the *Standing Committee on the Law of Patents* (SCP) that is—after the adoption of the *Patent Law Treaty* (PTL)[77]—primarily concerned with negotiations on a draft Substantive Patent Law Treaty (SPLT).[78] There is, second, the *Standing Committee on the Law of Trademarks, Industrial Designs and Geographical Indications* (SCT) that was established in 1998 and focuses on recommendations in the area of trademarks, industrial designs and geographical indications.[79] Third, there is the *Standing Committee on Copyright and Related Rights* (SCCR) that presently discusses, inter alia, the issue of limitations and exceptions in copyright law as well as the protection of broadcasting organizations.[80] All of the standing committees may ask the *General Assembly* to decide on the convention of a *Diplomatic Conference* to finalize negotiations on a new treaty and for the adoption of such a new treaty.

Standing committees as well as any of the assemblies can establish working groups for the in-depth examination of a particular issue. Thus, there has been a variety of working groups on a variety of areas, such as the *Working Group on the Legal Development of the Madrid System for the International Registration of Marks*. Further working groups are the *PCT Working Group*[81] and the *Standards and Documentation Working Group*.

In addition to the WIPO standing committees, there are permanent committees that deal with a specific sub-theme of WIPO, such as IP and development. Examples of such permanent committees are the CDIP, the IGC, the *Program and Budget Committee*, the *Advisory Committee on Enforcement* (ACE) and permanent committees on the international classification treaties.[82] The task of the latter permanent committees is the periodical revision and update of the respective classification systems.

This internal web of governing bodies, committees and working groups is also entrusted with entertaining a close network of interrelationships with other international institutions and the multilateral system. Close relations are, for instance, entertained with the WTO. In 1996, WTO and WIPO signed the *Agreement*

[75] 14 July 1967, as amended 18 September 1979, 21 U.S.T. 1749, 828 U.N.T.S. 3.

[76] Art. 7(3)(i), 14 July 1967, as amended 18 September 1979, 21 U.S.T. 1749, 828 U.N.T.S. 3.

[77] 39 I.L.M. 1047.

[78] For more information see http://www.wipo.int/patent-law/en/harmonization.htm.

[79] For more information see http://www.wipo.int/trademarks/en/sct.html.

[80] For more information see http://www.wipo.int/copyright/en.

[81] For more information see http://www.wipo.int/pct-wg/en/index.html.

[82] E.g. Locarno (industrial designs), Nice (marks), Strasbourg (patents), Vienna (figurative elements of marks).

Between the World Intellectual Property Organization and the World Trade Organization[83] that aims at establishing "a mutually supportive relationship" between the two organizations "with a view to establishing appropriate arrangements for cooperation between them."[84] More specifically, the Agreement provides for cooperation in three main fields: first, notification of, access to and translation of national IP laws, second, implementation of procedures for the protection of national emblems,[85] and third, technical cooperation.[86] Following the 1996 Agreement, the WTO and WIPO have concluded two further technical cooperation agreements in 1998 and 2001 for the promotion of TRIPS-compliance.[87] Furthermore, the two institutions have established a Common Portal[88] for IP offices and national trade offices and entertain various other substantive co-operations, such as the *WHO, WIPO, WTO Trilateral Cooperation on* Public *Health, Intellectual Property and Trade*.[89] It follows that the horizontal forum-shifting of IP issues from WIPO to the WTO has not only led to increased governance competition for WIPO but also to a strong coalition between WIPO and the WTO in international IP governance.[90] The same holds true for WIPO's relations with related international organizations.

WIPO's Mission and Strategic Goals

Altogether, WIPO's institutional framework aims at the attainment of WIPO's mission and strategic goals that had already been formulated at the time of WIPO's establishment. However, the above-discussed transformations in the global IP landscape and its governance structure have led to increasing pressures upon WIPO for strategic realignment and policy adaptations. The following section introduces and reflects upon WIPO's mission and strategic goals in the light of the emerging public–private web of global IP governance and its expectations towards WIPO.

[83] Of 22 December 1995, 35 I.L.M. 754.

[84] Preamble, 35 I.L.M. 754.

[85] Art. 2 and 4, 35 I.L.M. 754.

[86] Art. 4, 35 I.L.M. 754.

[87] See e.g. Legal and Technical Assistance to Developing Countries for Implementation of the TRIPS Agreement from January 1, 1996 to March 31, 1999, WO/GA/24/5, see http://www.wipo.int/meetings/en/doc_details.jsp?doc_id=1009.

[88] See WIPO-WTO Common Portal, available at: http://www.wipo.int/wipolex/en/common_portal.html.

[89] See http://www.wipo.int/globalchallenges/en/health/trilateral_cooperation.html for more information.

[90] See also Salomon, Cooperation Between the World Intellectual Property Organization (WIPO) and the World Trade Organization (WTO), St. John's Journal of Legal Commentary 17 (2003) 3, p. 429 (430).

Core Mission

However, the core mission of WIPO is set out in the *WIPO Convention*[91] with the Member States determining the strategic direction and activities of WIPO in assemblies, committees and working groups on an on-going basis.

Article 3 of the *WIPO Convention* sets out the objectives of the organization and stresses thereby the objective of WIPO "to promote the protection of intellectual property throughout the world through cooperation among States." The tone of Article 3 of the *WIPO Convention* reflects the content of the Preamble of the Convention that stresses, on the one hand, the overarching objective of contributing "to better understanding and cooperation among States" and, on the other hand, the objective of encouraging creative activity and of promoting the protection of intellectual property throughout the world.

Building upon the Preamble and Article 3 of the *WIPO Convention*, Article 4 of the Convention entitled "Functions" sets out in even more detail the strategies to be pursued by WIPO to attain the objectives as set out in Article 3. Thus, Article 4 entrusts WIPO with the task of promoting, creating and harmonizing measures for the protection of intellectual property throughout the world through, for instance, the conclusion of international agreements.[92] It further allows WIPO to provide legal-technical assistance to its Member States in the field of intellectual property[93] and to take appropriate action in the educational, informational and service-related field to facilitate the protection of IP.[94]

This core mission has remained largely unchanged. It has indeed recently been reinforced in the inscription of the cupola in the new WIPO headquarters that reads: "Human genius is the source of all works of art and invention; these works are the guarantee of a life worthy of men; it is the duty of the State to ensure with diligence the protection of the arts and inventions."[95] Nevertheless, the rise of new global challenges related to IP together with the emergence of new modes, institutions and fora of IP governance have necessitated the formulation of new directions and a strategic realignment of WIPO in recent years.

[91] 14 July 1967, as amended 18 September 1979, 21 U.S.T. 1749, 828 U.N.T.S. 3.

[92] See Art. 4(i), 4(ii), 4(iii), 4(iv) of the WIPO Convention, 14 July 1967, as amended 18 September 1979, 21 U.S.T. 1749, 828 U.N.T.S. 3.

[93] See Art. 4(v) of the WIPO Convention, 14 July 1967, as amended 18 September 1979, 21 U.S.T. 1749, 828 U.N.T.S. 3.

[94] See Art. 4(vi), 4(vii), 4(viii) of the WIPO Convention, 14 July 1967, as amended 18 September 1979, 21 U.S.T. 1749, 828 U.N.T.S. 3.

[95] WIPO, A Users' Guide, An Introduction to the Organization, 2011, p. 19.

WIPO Development Agenda

The growing concern of WIPO's developing Member States about sufficient regard to development issues in the wake of the *TRIPS Agreement*, led WIPO into the incorporation of development concerns into its policies. Thus, in 2007, the WIPO General Assembly adopted the *WIPO Development Agenda*[96] with the initiative for the drafting of a development agenda having gone back to the governments of Brazil and Argentina in 2004.[97] The purpose of its adoption was to ensure that development considerations feature prominently in the work of WIPO.[98] The Agenda thereby recognizes the importance of policy space and flexibilities for nation states to implement IP systems that are most suited to national and regional circumstances and capacities.[99]

The *WIPO Development Agenda* represents a set of 45 recommendations that are divided into 6 clusters. Cluster A deals with technical assistance and capacity building, Cluster B with norm-setting flexibilities, public policy and public domain, Cluster C with technology transfer, information and communication technologies (ICT) and access to knowledge, Cluster D with assessment evaluation and impact studies, Cluster E with institutional matters including mandate and governance and Cluster F with other issues.

Following the adoption of the *WIPO Development Agenda,* all of WIPO's activities are to be conducted by mainstreaming the Agenda's principles and activities into the respective activities. Such implementation is to be directed by the newly established *Committee on Development and Intellectual Property* (CDIP) that has been mandated to develop, monitor, assess and discuss a work-programme for the implementation of the recommendations. It is composed of all WIPO Member States and is open to the participation of observers.

To the present day, 21 dedicated projects responding to specific recommendations are under way with four having been completed. A great number of the projects have either been or are still focusing on recommendation Nr. 10 that establishes the CDIP's mandate to "develop and improve national intellectual property institutional capacity

---

[96] WIPO Development Agenda 2007, available at: http://www.wipo.int/ip-development/en/agenda.

[97] WIPO, Proposal to Establish a Development Agenda for the World Intellectual Property Organization (WIPO). An Elaboration of Issues Raised in Document WO/GA/31/11. Submission by the Group of Friends of Development, 2005 (Document IIM/1/4).

[98] Sell, Everything old is new again: the development agenda now and then, The WIPO Journal 3 (2011) 1, p. 17 (19).

[99] For a related discussion on the use of flexibilities in the People's Republic of China see Wechsler, Intellectual Property Law in the P.R. China: A Powerful Economic Tool for Innovation and Development, China-EU Law Journal 1 (2011), p. 3.

through further development of infrastructure and other facilities with a view of making national intellectual property institutions more efficient and promote fair balance between intellectual property protection and the public interest."[100] One project has, for instance, been a pilot project for the establishment of "start-up" national IP academies.[101]

The *WIPO Development Agenda* has received rather positive assessments. While WIPO itself hails the Agenda a "milestone"[102] in its policy development, the Agenda has equally been highly recognized by academics and commentators. Yu has, for instance, seen the Agenda as representing a "New Agenda" as opposed to the "Old Agenda" of the 1960s and 1970s that had found expression in the formation of WIPO, the Stockholm Protocol, the establishment of the International Code of Conduct and the revision of the *Paris Convention*.[103] The new development agenda by contrast, reflected the extent to which IP issues had been transformed from narrow, technical domestic issues to ones that are multi-faceted and central to the international policy agenda.[104] Critical voices, however, pointed to the lack of resources for the provision of technical assistance in the respective IP community.[105] Nevertheless, the potential of the *WIPO Development Agenda* to revolutionize the international governance of intellectual property law and policy is widely recognized and extensive efforts are being undertaken to assess the success of its implementation.[106]

Strategic Realignment

Rather than responding to the request of developing countries for consideration of a development dimension and rather than focusing on policy development in its Member States, the WIPO *Strategic Realignment Programme* (SRP) has responded

[100] WIPO Development Agenda 2007, available at: http://www.wipo.int/ip-development/en/agenda.

[101] WIPO, Document CDIP/3INF/2.

[102] See WIPO, Overview of the Development Agenda, http://www.wipo.int/ip-development/en/agenda/overview.html.

[103] Yu, A Tale of Two Development Agendas, Ohio Northern University Law Review 35 (2009) 2, p. 465 (471).

[104] Yu, A Tale of Two Development Agendas, Ohio Northern University Law Review 35 (2009) 2, p. 465 (511).

[105] Trainer, Intellectual Property Enforcement: A Reality Gap (Insufficient Assistance, Ineffective Implementation)?, Johhn Marshall Review of Intellectual Property Law 8 (2008) 1, p. 47 (69).

[106] Beer, *Implementing the World Intellectual Property Organization's Development Agenda*, 2009, p. 3.

to a rapidly changing IP environment at a larger scale. Thereby it responded, in particular, to the greater interaction between public, private and civil society sectors in global IP governance.[107] It can thus be evaluated as an attempt to establish novel participatory and dynamic legal mechanisms for the global governance of IPRs.[108]

In essence, the SRP redefined WIPO's strategic-level goals. The definition of new goals was seen as rendering WIPO a "responsive, efficient organization, equipped to achieve its strategic goals and to provide global leadership on IP issues."[109] Nine strategic goals were defined ranging from a "balanced evolution of the international normative framework for IP" to the "provision of premier global IP services."[110] The new strategic goals are supported by the definition of "core values" that encompass, first, service orientation, second, working as one, third, accountability for results, and fourth, environmental, social and governance responsibility.[111] Following the redefinition of its strategic goals, WIPO embarked on progressively bringing the Organization's structures, processes, resources and cultural values into alignment with its new goals.

After the initial restructuring of programme and resources, the SRP is focusing on 19 initiatives that implement the above-defined four core values.[112] First, in implementing service orientation, WIPO is aiming at increasing its responsiveness to global stakeholders. Second, in acting as integrated entity, WIPO is aiming at increasing its level of efficiency and responsiveness. Third, in stressing its accountability for results, WIPO is aiming at increasing its ownership of performance. Fourth, in taking environmental, social and governance responsibility, WIPO is aiming at ethical performance and behaviour towards staff, community and environment.

The success of the implementation was measured using the *SRP Results Framework*[113] in December 2011 and will undergo final evaluation in December 2012.[114]

---

[107] Chon, Global Intellectual Property Governance (Under Construction), Theoretical Inquiries in Law 12 (2011) 1, p. 349 (349–350).

[108] See Oguamanam, *Intellectual Property in Global Governance: A Development Question*, 2011, p. 2.

[109] WIPO Strategic Realignment Programme, Introduction, available at: http://www.wipo.int/about-wipo/en/strategic_realignment.

[110] Further goals are "facilitating the use of IP for development, coordination and development of global IP infrastructure, world reference source for IP information and analysis, international cooperation on building respect for IP, addressing IP in relation to global policy issues, a responsive communications interface between WIPO, its Member States and other stakeholders, an efficient administrative and financial support structure to enable WIPO to deliver its programs," cf. WIPO, A Users' Guide, An Introduction to the Organization, 2011, p. 13.

[111] WIPO Strategic Realignment Programme, Introduction, available at: http://www.wipo.int/about-wipo/en/strategic_realignment.

[112] WIPO, A Users' Guide, An Introduction to the Organization, 2011, p. 16.

[113] WIPO, SRP Results Framework, available at: http://www.wipo.int/about-wipo/en/strategic_realignment/results_framework.html.

[114] See already WIPO, Strategic Realignment Program Results Framework, Baseline Report, March 2011.

Every individual initiative is measured with a set of 16 detailed outcome indicators to which 47 detailed indicators contribute. For instance, in relation to the PCT system, the customer satisfaction is evaluated by measuring the timeliness of formality examination, the timeliness for publication and the translation quality.[115] While progress has already been made in achieving the SRP strategic goals, it will remain to be seen to what extent the SRP will have been successful at the end of its implementation period in December 2012.[116]

WIPO's IP Policy Directions

Closely related to WIPO's strategic realignment and an integral part of the SRP are recent adaptations in WIPO's methodological and strategic choices. On the one hand, WIPO has incorporated a more economic approach into its policy-making. On the other hand, WIPO has committed itself to a new strategic framework for "the promotion of innovation and creativity for the economic, social and cultural development of all countries, through a balanced and effective international intellectual property system."[117]

First and in following the trend towards a more economic approach, WIPO has committed itself to promote a better understanding of the economic effects of different IPRs and has offered itself as entry point for anyone seeking information on the economics of IP.[118] More specifically it has installed a Chief Economist in the institution in 2009—currently Carsten Fink—who oversees the various activities of WIPO in the area of the economics of IP.[119] One of the activities that are now entertained by the newly created division is the *WIPO Seminar Series on the Economics of IP* that invites state-of-the-art economists for the presentation of their latest research findings on IP economics.[120] However, reaching far beyond such informational and networking activities, WIPO has incorporated economic thinking in all of their core activities and provides a large variety of publications in the form of *WIPO Economic Research Working Papers* and the *World Intellectual Property Report 2011*.[121] Furthermore, WIPO has engaged in a close dialogue with other international governance institutions, such as the OECD and the Worldbank

---

[115] WIPO, Strategic Realignment Program Results Framework, Baseline Report, March 2011, p. 8.

[116] For the progress made so far see WIPO, Measuring Success, available at: http://www.wipo.int/about-wipo/en/strategic_realignment/progress.html.

[117] WIPO, Assemblies of the Member States of WIPO, Medium Term Strategic Work Plan for WIPO, 2010–2015, p. 3, available at: http://www.wipo.int/about-wipo/en/pdf/mtsp.pdf.

[118] WIPO, The Economics of IP, available at: http://www.wipo.int/econ_stat/en/economics.

[119] See Intellectual Property Watch, "WIPO Names First-Ever Chief Economist," 2 June 2009.

[120] See http://www.wipo.int/econ_stat/en/economics/seminars.html.

[121] WIPO, World Intellectual Property Report 2011, available at: http://www.wipo.int/econ_stat/en/economics/publications.html.

and participates in the creation of a *Global Network of IP Office Economists*.[122] In consequence, WIPO is actively participating in the establishment of a close network of global IP governance that incorporates the latest methodological approaches to IP policy.

Second, and stretching far beyond a more economic approach, WIPO has defined a *Medium Term Strategic Plan* for WIPO that sets strategic directions from 2010 to 2015.[123] The Plan constitutes a deliberate response to the changing landscape of the knowledge and digital economy, of the geography of science and technology and of the internationalization of science and technology production. In the light of this changing landscape, the *Medium Term Strategic Plan* defines seven substantive goals and two enabling goals. The seven substantive goals are, first, balanced evolution of the international normative framework for IP, second, provision of premier global IP services, third, facilitating the use of IP for development, fourth, coordination and development of global IP infrastructure, fifth, world reference source for IP information and analysis, sixth, international cooperation on building respect for IP, and seventh, addressing IP in relation to global policy issues. The two enabling goals are, first, a responsive communications interface between WIPO, its Member States and all stakeholders, and second, an efficient administrative and financial support structure to enable WIPO to deliver its programmes.[124] The attainment of these strategic goals will be measured by outcome indicators in what is termed *WIPO's Results Based Management (RBM) Framework*.[125] Thus, these overarching goals are intended to build a stable overall strategic framework for WIPO's development that relies substantially on a fruitful dialogue with WIPO's Member States, stakeholders and other international organizations. Most remarkable in this regard is the ever stronger orientation of WIPO towards non-state stakeholders.

In the light of these novel policy directions, the rigor of this strategic-reorientation is most striking. It resembles closely strategy formulations by private enterprises and, as such, corresponds very much so to the self-financing and service-oriented nature of WIPO. It follows that WIPO's novel policy directions testify to the changing nature of WIPO from a traditional international organization and specialized agency of the UN in the Westphalian tradition to a global governing body that efficiently and effectively merges characteristics of private and public governance.

---

[122] Cf. http://www.wipo.int/econ_stat/en/news/2010/news_0001.html, available at: http://www.wipo.int/econ_stat/en/economics/publications.html.

[123] WIPO, Assemblies of the Member States of WIPO, Medium Term Strategic Work Plan for WIPO, 2010–2015, available at: http://www.wipo.int/about-wipo/en/pdf/mtsp.pdf.

[124] WIPO, Assemblies of the Member States of WIPO, Medium Term Strategic Work Plan for WIPO, 2010–2015, p. 4–54, available at: http://www.wipo.int/about-wipo/en/pdf/mtsp.pdf.

[125] WIPO, Assemblies of the Member States of WIPO, Medium Term Strategic Work Plan for WIPO, 2010–2015, p. 59, available at: http://www.wipo.int/about-wipo/en/pdf/mtsp.pdf.

WIPO's Core Activities

Ever since its establishment, WIPO has conducted a variety of activities ranging from norm creation and administration, the provision of global IP services to technical assistance, infrastructure support and awareness building. Thereby, the range of WIPO activities reflects a most diversified approach to global IP governance that entails most specific elements for a variety of stakeholders ranging from nation states to private stakeholders. The following section discusses a selection of WIPO core activities in the light of the emerging public–private web of global IP governance and its expectations towards WIPO.

Norm Creation and Administration

Norm creation and administration are two of the core activities of WIPO.[126] They are conducted in cooperation with its Member States and in collaboration with other stakeholders and global governance institutions.[127] While WIPO's predecessor BIRPI administered only four international treaties at its time, WIPO administers 24 multilateral treaties today that are exhaustively listed in Table 1.[128] Through these activities, WIPO plays an important governing role in identifying and regulating policy responses to global IP challenges that reach across national borders. WIPO has, thus, assumed a role as facilitator between nation states and global stakeholders in establishing the global IP law regime.

Until the 1990s, WIPO's engagement in norm creation and administration was largely confined to establishing the legal and administrative framework for the transnational protection of patents, trademarks, designs, appellations of origin and protection of state emblems.[129] It facilitated cooperation between nation states in setting up an efficient system for the international registration of IP. Thereafter, however, the nature of WIPO's norm creation and administration has changed by drawing more substantially on the involvement of non-state actors and by driving substantive global IP law standards and their enforcement in colation with both public and private actors.

Testifying to this development, one of the most recent milestones in WIPO's norm creation and administration is WIPO's rising role in regulating ICT and Internet policies. Until the 1990s and because of the minimal role IP law played in regulating the digital era, WIPO did not feature in norm creation and

[126] For a critical stance on norm creation at WIPO see Visser, The Policy-Making Dynamics in Intergovernmental Organizations: A comment on the Remarks of Geoffrey Yu, Chicago-Kent Law Review 82 (2007) 3, p. 1457.

[127] WIPO, A Users' Guide, An Introduction to the Organization, 2012, p. 5.

[128] WIPO, WIPO Treaties—General Information, available at: http://www.wipo.int/treaties/en/general.

[129] See Table 1.

Table 1 WIPO treaties and number of contracting parties

Classification	Treaty	Parties
IP protection	1883 Paris Convention for the Protection of Industrial Property	173
	1886 Berne Convention for the Protection of Literary and Artistic Works	164
	1891 The Madrid Agreement for the Repression of False or Deceptive Indications of Source on Goods	35
	1961 International Convention for the Protection of Performers, Producers of Phonograms and Broadcasting Organizations	91
	1971 The Convention for the Protection of Producers of Phonograms Against Unauthorized Duplication of Their Phonograms	77
	1974 Brussels Convention Relating to the Distribution of Programme-Carrying Signals Transmitted by Satellite	45
	1981 The Nairobi Treaty on the Protection of the Olympic Symbol	50
	1989 Treaty on Intellectual Property in Respect of Integrated Circuits	Pending
	1994 The Trademark Law Treaty	50
	1996 WIPO Copyright Treaty (WCT)	89
	1996 WIPO Performances and Phonogram Treaty (WPPT)	89
	2000 The Patent Law Treaty	32
	2006 Singapore Treaty on the Law of Trademarks	24
Protection system	1891 Madrid Agreement Concerning the International Registration of Marks	85
	1934/1960 Hague Agreement Concerning the International Registration of Industrial Designs	58
	1958 Lisbon Agreement for the Protection of Appellations of Origin and Their International Registration	27
	1970 Patent Cooperation Treaty (PCT)	144
	1980 Budapest Treaty on the International Recognition of the Deposit of Microorganisms for the Purposes of Patent Procedure	75
	1989 Protocol Relating to the Madrid Agreement Concerning the International Registration of Marks	84
Classification	1968 Locarno Agreement Establishing an International Classification for Industrial Designs	52
	1957 Nice Agreement Concerning the International Classification of Goods and Services for the Purposes of the Registration of Marks	83
	1971 Strasbourg Agreement Concerning the International Patent Classification	62
	1973 Vienna Agreement Establishing an International Classification of the Figurative Elements of Marks	31

administration in the area of ICT. However, fostered by an increasingly transnational business environment and the need for global regulation, WIPO initiated—at the request of IP right-holders—the so-called "Internet Treaties" in the early 1990s. Both the *WIPO Copyright Treaty* (WCT)[130] and the *WIPO Performances and Phonograms Treaty* (WPPT)[131] were adopted in 1996. They allowed for the first

[130] See Treaty Doc. No. 105-17, at 1 (1997), 36 I.L.M. 65.

[131] See Treaty Doc. No. 105-17, at 18 (1997), 36 I.L.M. 67.

time in the history of IP law the use of technological measures for the protection of copyrighted works in digital media. Through their implementation in the form of the *Digital Millennium Copyright Act* (DMCA)[132] in the United States (US) and the *Directive 2001/29/EC of the European Parliament and of the Council of 22 May 2001 on the harmonisation of certain aspects of copyright and related rights in the information society*[133] both treaties have substantially determined and shaped national policy directions worldwide.

Following up on these two treaties, WIPO has continuously engaged in attempts to further structure and regulate transnational ICT relations. Thus, the *Standing Committee on Copyright and Related Rights* has persistently been working on a *Treaty on the Protection of Broadcasting Organizations*.[134] With negotiations having stalled in 2007 because of differences on the treatment of webcasting, treaty negotiations were revived in 2011 with the aim of scheduling a Diplomatic Conference in 2012 for the final adoption of the treaty.[135] While the success of these initiatives is yet to be seen, WIPO's engagement clearly testifies to its continued interest in establishing itself as a major player in global ICT regulation.

The same holds true for WIPO's interest in establishing itself as important player in Internet governance. This interest is reflected in a multiplicity of initiatives. First, WIPO is closely cooperating with the *International Corporation for Assigned Names and Number* (ICANN)[136] in setting up its *Uniform Domain-Name Dispute-Resolution Policy* (UDRP).[137] Second, WIPO participated in larger UN initiatives for Internet governance, such as the *UN World Summit on the Information Society* 2003–2005 (WSIS), and has been given a seat on the *UN Working Group on Internet Governance* (WGIG).[138] Nevertheless, it has been pointed out that WIPO has not taken full responsibility for appropriately regulating IP issues in the construction of global Internet governance as it has only played a minor role in the *UN Internet Governance Forum* (IGF).[139] Therefore, it remains to be seen whether WIPO's strategic realignment will also lead to a more intense engagement in the realm of Internet governance.

---

[132] 17 U.S.C. §§ 1201-1205.

[133] OJ [2001] L167/10.

[134] See Revised Consolidated Text for a Treaty on the Protection of Broadcasting Organizations, SCCR/12/2, 4 October 2004, available at: http://www.wipo.int/edocs/mdocs/copyright/en/sccr_12/sccr_12_2.pdf.

[135] Intellectual Property Watch, "WIPO Sees Progress on Broadcaster Rights, Library Exceptions; Treaty for Blind Readers Slips," 5 December 2011, available at: http://www.ip-watch.org.

[136] For the organization's website see http://www.icann.org.

[137] See below "Relations with other IP Governance Institutions" for a more detailed account of WIPO's Internet cooperation.

[138] For the website of the forum see http://www.wgig.org.

[139] For criticism see Global Information Society Watch, World Intellectual Property Organization (WIPO), 2007, available at: http://www.giswatch.org/institutional-overview/civil-society-participation/world-intellectual-property-organisation-wipo. For the website of the forum see http://www.intgovforum.org/cms.

Provision of Global IP Services

In response to the assumption of global responsibility in global IP law-making, WIPO is now providing a variety of global IP services for private entities. The type of such services is twofold: on the one hand, WIPO supports the international protection of patents (PCT), trademarks (Madrid system), designs (Hague system), appellations of origin (Lisbon system), protection of state emblems (Article 6ter), domain name dispute resolution (cf. ICANN) and international classification by entertaining the respective administrative services. On the other hand, WIPO provides arbitration, mediation and other alternative dispute resolution (ADR) services. As the latter IP services are growing substantially in importance and testify to a growing trend towards private dispute resolution, the following section introduces those latter services in more detail.[140]

In 1994, the *WIPO Arbitration and Mediation Centre* (the Centre) was established and has ever since been based in both Geneva and in Singapore. In the beginning, the driving force behind the creation of the *Arbitration and Mediation Centre* was an informal working group composed of representatives of largely private associations: the *International Federation of Industrial Property Attorneys* (FICPI), the *International Association for the Protection of Industrial Property* (AIPPI) and the *Licensing Executives Society International* (LESI).[141] In response to the private impetus provided by these associations, WIPO convened a *Working Group of Non-Governmental Organizations on Arbitration and other Extra-Judicial Mechanisms for the Resolution of Intellectual Property Disputes Between Private Parties,*[142] composed of a multiplicity of stakeholders from 1992–1993. Building upon the work done by the *Working Group*, the *WIPO General Assembly* established WIPO dispute resolution services and the Centre in September 1993.[143]

One of the first tasks of the newly established Centre was the drafting and adoption of the *WIPO Mediation, Arbitration and Expedited Arbitration Rules*, which entered into force on October 1, 1993.[144] Ever since, WIPO has adopted a variety of rules for a variety of purposes: first, the *WIPO Arbitration Rules*,[145] second, the *WIPO Expedited Arbitration Rules*,[146] third, the *WIPO Mediation*

---

[140] For further information on the IP services relating to patents (PCT), trademarks (Madrid system), designs (Hague system), appellations of origin (Lisbon system), protection of state emblems (Article 6ter of the Paris Convention), domain name dispute resolution and international classification see: http://www.wipo.int/services/en and WIPO, Guide to WIPO Services, available at: http://www.wipo.int/export/sites/www/freepublications/en/general/1020/wipo_pub_1020.pdf.

[141] For an overview over the developments see http://www.wipo.int/amc/en/history.

[142] See http://www.wipo.int/amc/en/history.

[143] Document WO/GA/XIV/1 and 4.

[144] WIPO Publication No. 446.

[145] WIPO Publication No. 446.

[146] See http://www.wipo.int/amc/en/arbitration/expedited-rules/index.html.

Rules,[147] and fourth, since 2007 the *Expert Determination Rules*.[148] Furthermore, WIPO has provided for the *Recommended WIPO Contract Clauses and Submission Agreements*[149] that could govern submission of disputes to the Centre. Yet two further areas that the Centre focuses on are the resolution of domain name disputes and the provision of alternative dispute resolution (ADR) for specific sectors, for instance, art and cultural heritage and sports.[150]

In acting on these Rules and procedures, the Centre has advised numerous clients and parties and administered more than 270 mediation and arbitration cases with an ever faster growth rate in case adoption.[151] Forty-two percent of the WIPO Mediation and Arbitration Cases were thereby in the realm of patent law, 23% in IT law, 12% in trademarks, 6% in copyright, and 17% in other areas. Remedies varied substantially between 20,000 USD and several hundred million USD with a settlement rate of 68%.[152] In the area of domain names, a total number of 22,840 cases has been filed since 1999, again with an impressive growth rate in recent years.[153]

By entering the market of mediation, ADR and arbitration, WIPO has strategically positioned itself in an ever-growing commercial market of non-judicial dispute resolution.[154] This positioning of WIPO has clearly required an adaptation of WIPO to its now primarily private clients that partially explains the move towards service-orientation in WIPO's strategic realignment. Furthermore, the positioning in a market of non-coercive enforcement mechanisms flows logically from the lack of coercive enforcement mechanisms on the part of WIPO—as opposed to the possibilities of the WTO Dispute Settlement Body.[155] Finally, the positioning in the market of voluntary compliance dispute resolution flows rather logically from the nature of WIPO as governing body based on voluntary and reputation-based compliance models.[156]

---

[147] See http://www.wipo.int/amc/en/mediation/rules/index.html.

[148] See http://www.wipo.int/amc/en/clauses.

[149] See http://www.wipo.int/amc/en/clauses.

[150] See http://www.wipo.int/amc/en/center/specific-sectors/sports.

[151] For a WIPO caseload summary see http://www.wipo.int/amc/en/center/caseload.html.

[152] For a WIPO caseload summary see http://www.wipo.int/amc/en/center/caseload.html.

[153] For domain name dispute resolution statistics see http://www.wipo.int/amc/en/domains/statistics/cases.jsp. There was only one case in 1999 but the figure shot skyhigh soon after, reaching 1100 cases in 2003 and 2764 cases in 2011.

[154] Petersmann, Justice as Conflict Resolution: Proliferation, Fragmentation, and Decentralization of Dispute Settlement in International Trade, University of Pennsylvania Journal of International Economic Law 27 (2006) 2, p. 273 (273–276).

[155] Davey, The WTO Dispute Settlement System: The First Ten Years, Journal of International Economic Law 8 (2005) 1, p. 17.

[156] Cf. Hathaway/Shapiro, Outcasting: Enforcement in Domestic and International Law, Yale Law Journal 121 (2011) 2, p. 252.

Technical Assistance, Infrastructure Support and Awareness Building

In addition to the above-discussed core activities of norm creation and administration, on the one hand, and of provision of global IP services, on the other hand, WIPO has defined two further core areas for its activities: first, technical assistance and infrastructure support, and second, awareness building.[157]

Rather distinct from most of the global IP services provided to private parties is the technical assistance and infrastructure support offered by WIPO.[158] As opposed to the provision of global IP services, the pledge to the construction of a global IP infrastructure is mainly directed at IP institutions and authorities and capacity building and support centers and, thus, Member States and other stakeholders. WIPO has committed itself to the establishment of a sustainable infrastructure for the global protection of IPRs. More specifically, for instance, WIPO provides technical assistance to support the efficient establishment of online services in national and regional IP offices and supports the integration of regional and international networks of IP offices. These initiatives correspond to WIPO's overarching strategic goal IV, to the mandate in Article 4(v) of the *WIPO Convention*,[159] to the *WIPO Development Agenda*[160] and to the provisions of further WIPO-administered treaties, such as the PCT.[161] In so taking responsibility for the development of the global IP infrastructure, WIPO has committed itself to becoming a most relevant transnational actor in global IP governance that aims not only at services provision to private parties but also to narrowing the knowledge gap and the empowerment of developing countries.[162]

Another prominent role is played by WIPO in the area of awareness building that is largely directed towards civil society. Awareness building entails elements such as building respect for IP as laid out in the Strategic Goal VI.[163] Awareness building is thereby seen as a concept related to enforcement—as a result of which it is also dealt with in the *Advisory Committee on Enforcement*—albeit one that is more encompassing than a narrow enforcement conception.[164] In December 2011, the *Advisory Committee on Enforcement* was presented with a list of recent activities in

---

[157] WIPO, A Users' Guide, An Introduction to the Organization, 2011, p. 7.

[158] See http://www.wipo.int/global_ip/en.

[159] 14 July 1967, as amended 18 September 1979, 21 U.S.T. 1749, 828 U.N.T.S. 3.

[160] WIPO Development Agenda 2007, available at: http://www.wipo.int/ip-development/en/agenda.

[161] 28 U.S.T. 7645, 1160 U.N.T.S. 231.

[162] For WIPO's efforts to close the knowledge gap see also http://www.wipo.int/global_ip/en/knowledge_gap.html.

[163] WIPO, Assemblies of the Member States of WIPO, Medium Term Strategic Work Plan for WIPO, 2010–2015, available at: http://www.wipo.int/about-wipo/en/pdf/mtsp.pdf.

[164] For the activities of the Committee see http://www.wipo.int/meetings/en/details.jsp?meeting_id=22170.

the area of building respect for IP by the secretariat.[165] However, closer inspection of the list demonstrates the strong focus of the initiatives on combatting counterfeiting and piracy and upholding IPRs rather than a more comprehensive and balanced approach to awareness building.[166] Yet, another and more balanced approach to awareness building is reflected in the activities of the *WIPO Academy* that was founded in 1998.[167] The *WIPO Academy* offers a wide range of learning and development opportunities in the form of distance learning, summer schools, professional trainings, executive programmes and startup academies.[168] Through its enhancement of human capital worldwide, the *WIPO Academy* has contributed substantially to awareness and knowledge building as well as global networking in the relevant global community.

In consequence, this brief introduction to the core activities of WIPO in the areas of technical assistance and infrastructure support, on the one hand, and awareness building, on the other hand, has shown that WIPO aims at global IP infrastructure building through interaction not only with private stakeholders but with a large variety of global actors in the IP landscape and civil society. As such, the core activities of WIPO today show a tremendous evolution from the initial rationale for the foundation of BIRPI.

Conclusion: WIPO in a New Pluralist IP Order

In conclusion, the above introduction of WIPO as international economic institution in the public–private web of global IP governance has shown the changing mission and strategic goals of the organization. It has further shown how its mission and strategic goals have changed in an ever more rapidly evolving IP landscape and have eventually translated into a large variety of activities that are directed at various IP stakeholders. The discussion has further shown how the changing mission, goals and activities are slowly transforming WIPO from a traditional international economic institution corresponding to Westphalian notions international governance into a service-oriented governing body that combines elements of public institutions and private entities. In fact, it is in particular the evolving type of activities that WIPO conducts and its increasing role in the provision of diverse IP services for IP rightholders that has led it to draw in perspectives not only from all

165 WIPO, Advisory Committee on Enforcement, Seventh Session, 30 November–2 December 2011, Recent Activities of WIPO in the Field of Building Respect for Intellectual Property (IP), WIPO/ACE/7/2.

166 For a critical stance see also Drahos, Securing the Future of Intellectual Property: Intellectual Property Owners and Their Nodally Coordinated Enforcement Pyramid, Case Western Reserve Journal of International Law 36 (2004) 1, p. 53 (55).

167 See http://www.wipo.int/academy/en.

168 For the full 2012 portfolio see WIPO, WIPO Academy Education and Training Program Portfolio, 2011.

of its Member States but private actors, international organizations, interest groups and civil society.

This transformation is exactly where some of the criticism can be directed to. The overriding importance that WIPO has given to private interests as opposed to the public interest in recent years should be closely monitored and corrected if needed. Closely related to this criticism is the unique and somewhat detached role that WIPO places within the larger UN governing framework. While profitability should certainly be retained, closer alignment with the overarching goals of the UN would be of great benefit to the global public interest. Moreover, WIPO should broaden its perspectives towards a more critical stance to IP protection. For instance, awareness building should no longer be associated or even be governed by enforcement circles. Rather it should be focused upon the larger interest in spurring and promoting creativity and innovation. Moreover, further reciprocity and mutuality with developing countries should be on WIPO's Agenda for the twenty-first century. Instead of focusing primarily on the one-way provision of assistance and support for developing countries, WIPO should actively solicit views, suggestions and policies from developing countries and new global players such as China, India and Brazil.

If WIPO is to face the global IP challenges of the twenty-first century, it must—as any other institution of global governance[169]—look out for novel avenues, novel partnerships and novel modes of governance for the establishment of a balanced and sustainable global IP environment. It should take up the challenge of constantly realigning itself as international actor that contributes meaningfully to the rational, just and sustainable management of our world. Furthermore, it should take an active role in constructing a new pluralist IP order that represents the diversity of all global IP interests in an ever more fragmented international IP order.

[169] Cf. Charnovitz, Triangulating the World Trade Organization, American Journal of International Law 96 (2002) 1, p. 28 (28–30).

Developments in International Investment Law

Marc Bungenberg and Catharine Titi

General Remarks

A vibrant and constantly evolving legal field, international investment law continues to grow in significance and, as a corollary, it remains at the forefront of an increasing amount of attention—and scrutiny—from both public policymakers and relevant sections of the public. Developments at the regional as well as at the global level continue to contribute to this increased interest in international investment law. This report will highlight recent developments in international investment law and will provide an outlook onto the further evolution of this at the moment most dynamic field of international economic law.

Continually expanding, already at the end of 2010 the international investment regime comprised 2,807 bilateral investment treaties (BITs), 2,976 double taxation treaties (DTTs) and 309 other international investment agreements (IIAs) ('other IIAs' in UNCTAD parlance)[1] broadly corresponding to the estimated US $1.66 trillion of global foreign direct investment (FDI) outflows in 2011, that marked a 16% increase on 2010 levels and above pre-economic-and-financial-crisis numbers.[2] The continued presence and proliferation of these agreements is seen as a cardinal factor in the stabilisation and increase of investment flows. The significance of these agreements, in particular that of BITs and 'other IIAs,' consists in the setting in place of an investment promotion and protection system, that guarantees investors what may be called a charter of basic investor rights, including, *inter alia*, fair and equitable treatment,

[1] UNCTAD, World Investment Report 2011: Non-Equity Modes of International Production and Development, 2011, p. 100.

[2] UNCTAD. Global Investment Trends Monitor, No. 9, 12 April 2012, advanced unedited copy, p. 1, available at: http://www.unctad.org/en/PublicationsLibrary/webdiaeia2012d19_en.pdf.

M. Bungenberg (✉) • C. Titi
Universität Siegen, Fak. III, Campus Hölderlinstraße, Hölderlinstraße 3, 57076 Siegen-Weidenau, Germany
e-mail: Marc.Bungenberg@gmx.de; cathy_titi@hotmail.com

C. Herrmann et al. (eds.), *European Yearbook of International Economic Law (EYIEL), Vol. 4 (2013)*, European Yearbook of International Economic Law 4,
DOI 10.1007/978-3-642-33917-2_17,

most-favoured-nation (MFN) treatment, compensation in the event of expropriation, but also access to a highly-developed legal system of international investor-state arbitration, that to a greater or lesser extent guarantees impartial and politically independent adjudication beyond the context of domestic judiciaries.

Overall, G20 members have reaffirmed and 'continued to honour' their commitment not to regress into investment protectionism and, despite the introduction of a few restrictions, the majority of new policy measures adopted has been in the general direction of liberalising capital flows and enhancing clarity to the benefit of investors.[3] As demonstrated in reports prepared by the OECD and UNCTAD, a handful of countries have revised their investment policies relating to national security[4] while a resurgence of turmoil in financial markets has led some countries to assist ailing companies and impose some restrictions on inter-bank lending activity.[5]

At the same time that financial turbulence has sent new shivers up the spine of developed economies, the Arab Spring movement has contributed to intensely increase foreign investors' risk perceptions and raise questions around investor confidence and recovery of investment flows.[6] More recently, Argentina has found itself in the headlines for the nationalisation of Spanish-controlled oil company YPF.[7]

Although FDI outflows from the developing world 'appeared to lose some momentum in 2011'[8], recent years have witnessed an increase in the importance of the developing world as a source of investment; a development not without repercussions for investment policymakers. Concepts such as the protection of nationally strategic industries have been informed with the first experiences of

---

[3] OECD/UNCTAD. Fifth Report on G20 Investment Measures, 24 May 2011, available at: http://unctad.org/en/docs/unctad_oecd2011d5_en.pdf, p. 6; OECD/UNCTAD, Sixth Report on G20 Investment Measures, 25 October 2011, p. 54, available at: http://www.oecd.org/dataoecd/24/31/48941943.pdf,; OECD, Inventory of investment measures taken between 1 November 2011 and 29 February 2012, April 2012, p. 6, available at: http://www.oecd.org/dataoecd/36/61/50053970.pdf.

[4] China and Russia are examples in this respect. See OECD, Inventory of investment measures taken between 16 February 2011 and 31 October 2011, January 2012, p. 5, available at: http://www.oecd.org/dataoecd/27/12/49449570.pdf; OECD/UNCTAD, Sixth Report on G20 Investment Measures, 25 October 2011, p. 53 and OECD, Inventory of investment measures taken between 1 November 2011 and 29 February 2012, April 2012, p. 6.

[5] OECD, Inventory of investment measures taken between 16 February 2011 and 31 October 2011, January 2012, p. 5 and OECD, Inventory of investment measures taken between 1 November 2011 and 29 February 2012, April 2012, p. 6.

[6] Barbour, et al., The Arab Spring: How soon will foreign investors return? Columbia FDI Perspectives No. 67, 2012.

[7] On this see e.g. Hernandez, "YPF nationalisation: Is Argentina playing with fire?," BBC News, 17 April 2012, available at: http://www.bbc.co.uk/news/world-europe-17740393. See also OECD/UNCTAD, Seventh Report on G20 Investment Measures, May 2012, pp. 3, 9, available at: http://unctad.org/en/PublicationsLibrary/unctad_oecd2012d7_en.pdf.

[8] UNCTAD, Global Investment Trends Monitor, No. 9, 12 April 2012, advanced unedited copy, p. 4, available at: http://www.unctad.org/en/PublicationsLibrary/webdiaeia2012d19_en.pdf.

developing economies accessing national industries in developed economies in a sphere previously reserved for national companies.[9]

This contribution will in the following section summarise some of the most important institutional developments in the international investment law landscape. Furthermore, it will deal with the practice of arbitral tribunals in investment matters. In 2011, at least 26 decisions were rendered, most of these under the International Centre for Settlement of Investment Disputes (ICSID) Convention; therefore the report cannot be exhaustive, but it will highlight some specific awards; in a first step, it will concentrate on procedural and jurisdictional issues, it will continue by addressing a particular jurisdictional question, namely the notion of investment and investor, before turning to substantive standards of protection. The final section will also provide a brief conclusion and outlook.

Institutional Developments and the Politics of International Investment Law

Developments Within the EU Context

The entry into force of the Treaty of Lisbon has led to far-reaching discussions on the extent of EU competence in the area of investment law as well as the overall strategy of the EU as a new actor in this policy field. Foreign direct investment is fully comprised in the EU competence laid down in Article 207 of the Treaty on the Functioning of the European Union (TFEU). Not only legal scholars argue on the concept, extent, and scope of the European international investment policy,[10]

---

[9] See UNCTAD, The Protection of National Security in IIAs, UNCTAD/DIAE/IA/2008/5, UNCTAD Series on International Investment Policies for Development, pp. 16–17, available at: http://www.unctad.org/en/docs/diaeia20085_en.pdf.

[10] Bungenberg/Griebel/Hindelang (eds.), *European Yearbook of International Economic Law, Special Issue: International Investment Law and EU Law*, 2011; Bungenberg, The Politics of the European Union's Investment Treaty-Making, in: Broude/Busch/Porges (eds.), *The Politics of International Economic Law*, 2011; Bungenberg. Going Global? The EU Common Commercial Policy After Lisbon, in: Herrmann/Terhechte (eds.), *European Yearbook of International Economic Law 2010*, 2010, pp. 123 et seq.; Burgstaller, European Law and Investment Treaties, Journal of International Arbitration 26 (2009) 2, p. 181; Dimopoulos, *EU Foreign Investment Law*, 2011; Eilmansberger, Bilateral Investment Treaties and EU Law, Common Market Law Review 46 (2009) 2, p. 383; Griebel, Überlegungen zur Wahrnehmung der neuen EU-Kompetenz für ausländische Direktinvestitionen nach Inkrafttreten des Vertrags von Lissabon, Recht der Internationalen Wirtschaft 55 (2009) 7, p. 473; Griebel, Der Weg seit Lissabon—Die neue Kommissionsstrategie im Bereich der Direktinvestitionen, in: Bungenberg/Herrmann (eds.), *Die Gemeinsame Handelspolitik der Europäischen Union nach Lissabon*, 2011, pp. 193 et seq.; Herrmann, Die Zukunft der mitgliedstaatlichen Investitionspolitik nach dem Vertrag von Lissabon, Europäische Zeitschrift für Wirtschaftsrecht 21 (2010) 6, p. 207; Johannsen, Die Kompetenz der Europäischen Union für ausländische Direktinvestitionen nach dem Vertrag von Lissabon, Beiträge

but the EU institutions do so as well. Following the EU Commission's Communication 'Towards a Comprehensive European International Investment Policy' of July 2010[11] with an emphasis, *inter alia*, on achieving a 'state-of-the-art investor state dispute settlement' mechanism and on starting negotiations with a handful of preferred partners (Canada, Singapore, India, Mercosur, and then Russia and China), the Council reacted with its 'Conclusions on a comprehensive European international investment policy'[12], reiterating the need to keep in mind the effectiveness of the new EU system of investment protection. The Council's Conclusions were followed by the European Parliament's 'Resolution on the future European international investment policy' in April 2011.[13] In the latter, the European Parliament stressed the need to protect the right to regulate in EU investment agreements as well as the necessity to take into account sustainable development, corporate social responsibility and other investor obligations.

Following this procedure the Commission reacted again to the European Parliament.[14] Generally, whereas the Commission had highlighted its exclusive competence, the Council later stressed the 'mixed competence' shared between the EU and its Member States for the negotiation of new international investment agreements in 'negotiating mandates.' On 12 September 2011, the Council adopted negotiating mandates[15] concerning investment chapters in the currently ongoing negotiations

zum Transnationalen Wirtschaftsrecht (2009) 90, available at: http://telc.jura.uni-halle.de/sites/default/files/altbestand/Heft_90.pdf; Leal-Arcas, The European Union's Trade and Investment Policy after the Treaty of Lisbon, Journal of World Investment and Trade 11 (2010) 4, p. 463; Mestral, The Lisbon Treaty and the Expansion of EU Competence over Foreign Direct Investment and the Implications for Investor-State Arbitration, in: Sauvant (ed.) *Yearbook on International Investment Law & Policy 2009-2010*, 2010; Tietje, Die Außenwirtschaftsverfassung der EU nach dem Vertrag von Lissabon, Beiträge zum Transnationalen Wirtschaftsrecht 2009 (83); Tietje, EU-Investitionsschutz und –förderung zwischen Übergangsregelungen und umfassender europäischer Auslandsinvestitionspolitik, Europäische Zeitschrift für Wirtschaftsrecht 21 (2010) 17, p. 647; Wehland, Intra-EU Investment Agreements and Arbitration: Is European Community Law an Obstacle? International and Comparative Law Quarterly 58 (2009) 2, p. 297.

[11] Commission Communication, Towards a comprehensive European international investment policy, COM(2010)343 final, 7 July 2010, available at: http://trade.ec.europa.eu/doclib/docs/2010/july/tradoc_146307.pdf.

[12] Council of the European Union, Conclusions on a comprehensive European international investment policy, 25 October 2010, available at: http://www.consilium.europa.eu/uedocs/cms_data/docs/pressdata/EN/foraff/117328.pdf.

[13] European Parliament, Resolution on the future European international investment policy, 2010/2203(INI), 6 April 2011, available at: http://www.europarl.europa.eu/oeil/FindByProcnum.do?lang=2&procnum=INI/2010/2203.

[14] European Commission, Follow up to the European Parliament Resolution on the future European international investment policy, adopted by the Commission on 5 July 2011, SP(2011)5857, available at: http://www.europarl.europa.eu/oeil/popups/ficheprocedure.do?id=587223#documentGateway.

[15] For the press release concerning the negotiating mandate see http://www.consilium.europa.eu/ueDocs/cms_Data/docs/pressData/EN/genaff/124579.pdf; the guidelines of the mandate themselves have been published on an NGO website: http://www.s2bnetwork.org/themes/eu-investment-policy/eu-documents/text-of-the-mandates.html.

for FTAs with Canada, India, and Singapore.[16] The text of the negotiating mandates provides for typical BIT standards and provisions (fair and equitable treatment, national and most-favoured-nation treatment, protection against direct and indirect expropriation, full protection and security of investors and investments, an umbrella clause, free transfers of capital, rules on subrogation) as well as for an 'effective' investor-state dispute settlement mechanism. The mandates further provide for an inclusion of the 'right to regulate.' With respect to the latter, it specifies that (each) agreement shall provide 'for a level playing field for investors in Canada/India/ Singapore and in the EU and shall be without prejudice to the right of the EU and the Member States to adopt and enforce, in accordance with their respective competences, measures necessary to pursue legitimate public policy objectives such as social, environmental, security, public health and safety in a non-discriminatory manner. The agreement shall respect the policies of the EU and its Member States for the promotion and protection of cultural diversity.'

The EU is likely to start negotiations of investment chapters in broader economic agreements with more countries and probably international organisations in the near future. In December 2011, the opening of negotiations on 'deep and comprehensive free trade agreements' comprising provisions on investment protection with Egypt, Jordan, Morocco and Tunisia was authorised[17], although these negotiations appear to be temporarily suspended. At the same time, the launch of EU-Australia negotiations in October 2011 for a Framework Agreement may offer the necessary impetus for a future inclusion of an investment chapter.[18] Investment chapters could also be negotiated within the context of EU FTAs sought with ASEAN countries. In the wake of yet another stalemate reached in the WTO-Doha negotiations in December 2011, German Chancellor Angela Merkel and UK Prime Minister David Cameron brought up the idea of an EU-US FTA, following on from an earlier idea advanced by Angela Merkel and French President Nicolas Sarkozy and reflected in statements by other European leaders.[19] At the EU level, a European Council statement of 30 January 2012 noted the desire to

[16] See also the Commission Communication, Towards a comprehensive European international investment policy, COM(2010)343 final, 7 July 2010, available at: http://trade.ec.europa.eu/doclib/docs/2010/july/tradoc_146307.pdf.

[17] See EU agrees to start trade negotiations with Egypt, Jordan, Morocco and Tunisia, Brussels, 14 December 2011, http://trade.ec.europa.eu/doclib/press/index.cfm?id=766.

[18] On the Framework Agreement, see Australia-European Union Ministerial Consultations, 31 October 2011, available at: http://eeas.europa.eu/delegations/australia/press_corner/all_news/news/2011/20111111_02_en.htm; see also the Joint Statement of President Barroso and Prime Minister Gillard, 5 September 2011, available at: http://www.pm.gov.au/press-office/joint-statement-president-european-commission.

[19] Murphy, "Toward a Transatlantic Trade Agreement: Gaining Momentum," Free Enterprise, 10 February 2012, available at: http://www.freeenterprise.com/international/toward-transatlantic-trade-agreement-gaining-momentum-0.

'consider all options for boosting EU/US trade and investment'[20], however other than in this noncommital language, the proposal has not yet been followed upon in other official *fora*. Discussions of an EU-China Agreement have started after an Executive-to-Executive meeting in April 2010 between Commission President Barroso and Chinese Premier Wen Jiabao. A 'Joint EU-China Investment Task Force' was launched over the course of the summer of 2010 in order to 'explore the scope for deeper cooperation on investment, including considerations of a possible standalone investment agreement'[21]; the Commission consequently launched a public consultation on this matter.[22]

A further step in influencing the development of international investment law has been taken by the EU together with the US. In the framework of the Transatlantic Economic Council, the EU and the US 'have developed a blueprint for creating and maintaining stable, predictable and transparent investment regimes'[23]. Parallel to an endorsement of the standards of non-discrimination and transparency, a high level of investment protection and a fair and binding dispute settlement mechanism, including investor-state arbitration, host states are expected to 'maintain the right to regulate in order to pursue legitimate public policy objectives'[24].

Especially the implementation of an investor-state arbitration mechanism in future agreements—mentioned in the negotiating mandates and the EU-US blueprint—will remain difficult from an EU law perspective, after the Court of Justice of the European Union (CJEU) imposed strict limitations for the creation of a body outside the EU system, especially in its Opinion 1/09.[25]

In parallel to its July 2010 policy proposal, the Commission had published a 'Proposal for a Regulation [. . .] establishing transitional arrangements for bilateral investment agreements between Member States and third countries'[26]; the

[20] European Council, Towards Growth-Friendly Consolidation and Job-Friendly Growth, 20 January 2012, available at: http://www.consilium.europa.eu/uedocs/cms_data/docs/pressdata/en/ec/127599.pdf.

[21] Public Consultation on the future investment relationship between the EU and China, available at: http://trade.ec.europa.eu/consultations/?consul_id=153.

[22] Public Consultation on the future investment relationship between the EU and China, available at: http://trade.ec.europa.eu/consultations/?consul_id=153.

[23] See the Commission Press release, EU and US adopt blueprint for open and stable investment climates, 10 April 2012, available at: http://trade.ec.europa.eu/doclib/press/index.cfm?id=796, and the Statement of the European Union and the United States on Shared Principles for International Investment, available at: http://trade.ec.europa.eu/doclib/docs/2012/april/tradoc_149331.pdf.

[24] See the Commission Press release, EU and US adopt blueprint for open and stable investment climates, 10 April 2012, available at: http://trade.ec.europa.eu/doclib/press/index.cfm?id=796.

[25] ECJ, Opinion 1/09, ECR [2011] not yet available; on this see for example Lavranos, Designing an international investor-to-state arbitration system after Opinion 1/09, in: Bungenberg/Herrmann (eds.), *CCP after Lisbon, Special Issue to the EYIEL 2013*, forthcoming.

[26] European Commission, Proposal for a Regulation of the European Parliament and of the Council establishing transitional arrangements for bilateral investment agreements between Member States and third countries, COM(2010)344 final, 2010/0197 (COD), 7 July 2010, available at: http://trade.ec.europa.eu/doclib/docs/2010/july/tradoc_146308.pdf.

European Parliament reacted to this with a Resolution of 10 May 2011 'on the proposal for a regulation establishing transitional arrangements for bilateral investment agreements between Member States and third countries.' Regarding the 1,300 concluded Member State BITs, the Commission pointed out that they remain in force but are required to be notified to it. If necessary in cases of an incompatibility with EU law, the Commission would ask the specific Member States for a modification of the specific agreements. Case law involving intra-EU BITs will be dealt with in the section on developments in arbitral jurisprudence.

Developments in Asia and Beyond

Three recent agreements in the ASEAN context are seeing their first years of operation. Namely, the ASEAN Comprehensive Investment Agreement (ACIA), the ASEAN-Australia-New Zealand Free Trade Agreement (AANZFTA) and the ASEAN-China Free Trade Agreement (ACFTA) demonstrate a strong commitment to investment liberalisation,[27] while parallel developments, notably Australia's rejection of investor-state arbitration, may affect the region's future stance on investor-state (ISDS). Although in the short time that these treaties have been operative it is not possible to appreciate their long-term impact on investment promotion and protection in the ASEAN region, it is nonetheless remarkable that these agreements make a pledge to adhere to the principles that have informed investment treaties in the last few decades.

2011 saw the announcement of the sketched outlines of a comprehensive Trans-Pacific Partnership Agreement (TPPA) with an investment chapter, including provision for the state's right to regulate. The ambitious Agreement is currently being negotiated between eleven countries: Australia, Brunei Darussalam, Canada, Chile, Malaysia, Mexico, New Zealand, Peru, Singapore, Vietnam, and the United States,[28] while at least Japan has declared an interest in joining the negotiations.[29]

It is noteworthy that the TPPA is negotiated among parties that have already in the past concluded international investment agreements between them. The US for instance has previously concluded FTAs with Australia, Chile, Peru and Singapore, and, of course, with Canada and Mexico. With respect to the latter, the question arises how the TPPA's relationship to the NAFTA will be shaped.[30] The case of the US-Australia FTA is also worth looking into for a different reason.

[27] On these three agreements see generally Bath/Nottage, The ASEAN Comprehensive Investment Agreement and 'ASEAN Plus,' in: Bungenberg/Griebel/Hobe/Reinisch (eds.), *International Investment Law – A Handbook*, forthcoming 2013, and for the comment in particular 4. Conclusions and Outlook.

[28] On the TPPA negotiations and other developments, see for instance http://www.ustr.gov/tpp.

[29] See also Bungenberg, M. (2013). Preferential Trade and Investment Agreements and Regionalism. In Hofmann, R., Tams, C. and Schill, S., eds. Preferential Trade and Investment Agreements: A New Ordering Paradigm for International Investment Relations? (forthcoming, Nomos 2013).

[30] See also ibid.

Already in 2004, the then concluded Australia-US FTA famously excluded investor-state dispute settlement from its provisions. In removing an essential investor protection mechanism, this rather astonishing move has been both canvassed and criticised at length,[31] but until recently it appeared to probably reflect an exceptional decision, rather than the beginning of a trend for Australia. New developments in 2011 cast some considerable doubt on this observation.

In a public statement dating from April 2011, Australia's Gillard Government expressed its rejection of investor-state dispute resolution provisions. The Australian Government justified its position on the basis of, *inter alia*, a reluctance to confer preferential treatment on foreign as opposed to domestic businesses or to encourage provisions that may limit the state's ability to proceed to social, environmental or economic regulation or 'to put health warnings or plain packaging requirements on tobacco products'[32]. It went on to unequivocally declare that it will not seek to include investor-state dispute settlement provisions in its future trade (and investment) agreements,[33] a policy choice apparently also evinced in the Pacific country's unwillingness to embrace such provisions in the TPPA.[34]

Australia's rejection of investor-state dispute settlement, sporadically mirrored in some recent Asian IIAs,[35] ties in with a new preoccupation that appears most recently to have made its way into the investment arena: that of creating a level playing field for all investors. A concern perhaps inspired in part by trade and competition policy,[36] the pursuit of a level playing field may be to some extent the result of closer co-existence of investment and trade matters in new comprehensive treaties that cover both disciplines.[37] The Australian Government's insistence on

[31] See on this e.g. Dodge, Investor-State Dispute Settlement between Developed Countries: Reflections on the Australia-United States Free Trade Agreement, Vanderbilt Journal of Transnational Law 39 (2006) 1, p. 1.

[32] Australian Government Department of Foreign Affairs and Trade, Trading our way to more jobs and prosperity, April 2011, available at: http://www.dfat.gov.au/publications/trade/trading-ourway-to-more-jobs-and-prosperity.pdf. It is notable that this statement *precedes* initiation of the *Philip Morris* proceedings, relying on Australia's tobacco packaging regulation.

[33] Australian Government Department of Foreign Affairs and Trade, Trading our way to more jobs and prosperity, April 2011, available at: http://www.dfat.gov.au/publications/trade/trading-ourway-to-more-jobs-and-prosperity.pdf.

[34] Australian Government, Department of Foreign Affairs and Trade (2011). Gillard Government Trade Policy Statement: *Trading our way to more jobs and prosperity*. April 2011. http://www.dfat.gov.au/publications/trade/trading-our-way-to-more-jobs-and-prosperity.pdf.

[35] E.g. see Art. 107 of the Japan-Philippines Economic Partnership Agreement.

[36] Comment by David Gaukrodger, speaking in his personal capacity, during the Frankfurt Investment Law Workshop 2012 on Preferential Trade and Investment Agreements: A New Ordering Paradigm for International Investment Relations? 16–17 March 2012. On the level playing field as a recent concern in investment law, see also Gaukrodger/Gordon, Investor-State Dispute Settlement—Public Consultation: 16 May–9 July 2012, Draft scoping paper issued for public consultation at the request of the OECD-hosted Freedom of Investment Roundtable, 2012, pp. 53, 57 (see also p. 25 ft. 55), available at: http://www.oecd.org/dataoecd/61/29/50291642.pdf.

[37] The issue on the interaction between investment and trade issues brought under the umbrella of the same treaty is one that attracts increasing attention. For instance, it constituted the core of the

not conferring greater rights on foreign than domestic investors, including through granting the former access to international arbitration, reflects this level-playing-field reasoning.[38] As already noted, the level playing field is also explicitly cited in the EU's negotiating mandate of September 2011.

Developments in the Americas

Some further institutional developments have revealed some uneasiness with the system. Venezuela's denunciation of the ICSID Convention in January 2012[39] came probably as little surprise, following in the steps of earlier denunciations by Bolivia and Ecuador (in 2007 and 2009 respectively).[40] Withdrawal from the ICSID Convention, the multilateral treaty establishing the International Centre for Settlement of Investment Disputes (ICSID)—admittedly the principal investment arbitration institution—and governing conciliation and arbitration proceedings, may be interpreted as tantamount to a rejection of an important aspect of the international investment law system and involves serious questions around post-ICSID-withdrawal investment protections.[41] The move comes to be added to a growing concern about the system's legitimacy, a so-called *backlash* against the international investment law regime[42] that has raised voices in certain quarters calling for systemic reforms. It appears uncertain at this stage whether this new withdrawal from the ICSID Convention is likely to produce a domino effect.

---

aforementioned Frankfurt Investment Law Workshop 2012. The co-existence of investment and trade issues is also apparent in other recent developments, such as Argentina's nationalisation of YPF and claims around cigarette packaging, giving rise to potential disputes both based on investment treaties and the WTO framework. See e.g., McGrady, Implications of Ongoing Trade and Investment Disputes Concerning Tobacco: Philip Morris v. Uruguay, in: Voon, et al. (eds.), *Public Health and Plain Packaging of Cigarettes: Legal Issues*, 2012.

[38] David Gaukrodger, in his personal capacity, during the Frankfurt Investment Law Workshop 2012 on Preferential Trade and Investment Agreements: A New Ordering Paradigm for International Investment Relations? 16–17 March 2012.

[39] See ICSID News Release, Venezuela Submits a Notice under Article 71 of the ICSID Convention, available at: http://icsid.worldbank.org/ICSID/FrontServlet?requestType=CasesRH&actionVal=OpenPage&PageType=AnnouncementsFrame&FromPage=Announcements&pageName=Announcement100.

[40] See UNCTAD, Denunciation of the ICSID Convention and BITs: Impact on Investor-State Claims, IIA Issues Note, No. 2, December 2010, available at: http://www.unctad.org/diae.

[41] On this hotly-debated topic see Schreuer, Denunciation of the ICSID Convention and Consent to Arbitration, in: Waibel/Kaushal/Chung/Balchin (eds.), *The Backlash against Investment Arbitration*, 2010; Tietje/Nowrot/Wackernagel, Once and Forever? The Legal Effects of a Denunciation of ICSID, Beiträge zum Transnationalen Wirtschaftsrecht, 2008 (74), available at: http://telc.jura.uni-halle.de/sites/default/files/altbestand/Heft74.pdf; UNCTAD (2010), Denunciation of the ICSID Convention and BITs: Impact on Investor-State Claims, IIA Issues Note, No. 2, December 2010, available at: http://www.unctad.org/diae.

[42] E.g. see Waibel, M., Kaushal, A., Chung, K.-H. and Balchin, C. eds. (2010). *The Backlash against Investment Arbitration*. Alphen aan den Rijn: Kluwer Law International.

However, not all arbitration-related systemic developments in the field have been of a nature to raise concerns about the legitimacy or popularity of the system.

At the same time that Bolivia, Ecuador and Venezuela reject the ICSID Convention and investor-state dispute settlement, a new regional economic integration organisation (REIO) treaty that incorporates all three 'ICSID recalcitrant' Latin American countries among its members—i.e. Bolivia, Ecuador and Venezuela—sees the day with the entry into force in 2011 of the Union of South American Nations (UNASUR) Constitutive Treaty.[43] Although its significance from an investment viewpoint remains only speculative at this stage, UNASUR introduces proposals regarding investor-state arbitration, including awards endowed with *stare decisis* effect and the creation of an appellate tribunal that, if adopted, may impact on the face of investment arbitration as we know it.[44]

Reforms of Guidelines and Procedural Rules

OECD Guidelines

Another considerable and much-discussed development is the 2011 Update of the OECD Guidelines for Multinational Enterprises, the fifth update since their adoption in 1976 and the first one since 2000. The 2011 Update of the Guidelines, notably coinciding with the OECD's 50th anniversary, marked a restatement of government determination to promote this canon of responsible business conduct. The Guidelines are government recommendations addressed to multinational enterprises encompassing corporate conduct in a large range of business areas, including ethics, compliance, human rights, labour, the environment, anti-corruption, consumer interests and other recognised standards.[45] The update of the OECD Guidelines was followed in the UN context by the formal endorsement by the UN Human Rights Council of new 'Guiding Principles on Business and Human Rights' in June 2011.[46] The Guiding Principles summarise the work of the Secretary-General's Special Representative for Business and Human Rights, John Ruggie, from 2005 to 2011, which has been canvassed in the context of the update of the OECD Guidelines.

---

[43] The Constitutive Treaty is available through the official UNASUR website at: http://www.unasursg.org/index.php?option=com_content&view=article&id=290&Itemid=339.

[44] On the UNASUR Treaty see Leathley, What will the recent entry into force of the UNASUR Treaty mean for investment arbitration in South America?, Kluwer Arbitration Blog, 13 April 2011, available at: http://kluwerarbitrationblog.com/blog/2011/04/13/unasur-treaty-and-investment-arbitration-in-south-america/.

[45] For the OECD Guidelines and the 2011 update, see https://www.oecd.org/document/28/0,3746,en_2649_34893_2397532_1_1_1_1,00.html.

[46] For the Guiding Principles, see http://www.ohchr.org/documents/issues/business/A.HRC.17.31.pdf.

ICC Arbitration Rules

Following the revision of the UNCITRAL Arbitration Rules in 2010, and the emphasis on the theme of transparency in investor-state arbitration, the Paris-based International Chamber of Commerce (ICC) revised its arbitration rules in September 2011. The revised version of ICC Rules has been in the general direction of maintaining the flexibility of the Rules and, *inter alia*, improving time- and cost-management of the arbitration process. The revised Rules constitute part-'codification' of practices developed by ICC arbitrators.[47]

Revision of the French Legislation on Arbitration

Another update with potentially significant ramifications for international arbitration is the revision of the French legislation on arbitration with the *décret n° 2011–48 portant ré forme de l'arbitrage* of 13 January 2011.[48] The new law, that presents a major overhaul of international as of domestic French arbitration rules, the first one since the early 1980s, keeps up with the tradition of arbitration-friendly legislation that has established Paris as one of the most attractive arbitration centres worldwide.[49] Conserving and reinforcing arbitral authority and independence, at the same time as establishing the parties' autonomy in selecting arbitration as a mode of dispute settlement,[50] the decree aims to consolidate part of the *acquis* of arbitral case law, improve efficacy of the legal text and introduce innovations inspired by foreign legislation with proved utility.[51] The new legislation has already received a hearty welcome from the business world[52] and has been hailed as modernising and liberalising arbitration rules and contributing to further enhancing the popularity of Paris as an arbitration centre.[53]

---

[47] For a concise overview of the revision of the ICC Rules see "The New ICC Rules Uncovered," Hogan Lovells, 12 September 2011, http://emailcc.com/rv/ff0002066ed8f9886072c40645469f43102ac622, and Hogan Lovells, The 2011 ICC Rules of Arbitration and the 1998 ICC Rules of Arbitration: A Comparison, available at: http://www.hoganlovells.com/newsmedia/pubDetail.aspx?publication=7273.

[48] Décret n° 2011-48 du 13 janvier 2011 portant réforme de l'arbitrage, JORF du 14 janvier 2011, texte : 9.

[49] Scherer/Born, "Long-Awaited New French Arbitration Law Revealed," Kluwer Arbitration Blog, 15 January 2011, available at: http://kluwerarbitrationblog.com/blog/2011/01/15/long-awaited-new-french-arbitration-law-revealed/.

[50] Fortier, La nouvelle loi française sur l'arbitrage : vues d'Outre-Atlantique, Presentation at the Conférence annuelle de l'Association française d'arbitrage, 28 September 2011, p. 17, available at: http://www.arbitration-icca.org/media/1/13282757006560/la_nouvelle_loi_francaise_sur_larbitrage.pdf.

[51] See Rapport au Premier ministre relatif au décret n° 2011-48 du 13 janvier 2011 portant réforme de l'arbitrage. JORF du 14 janvier 2011, texte : 8. http://www.legifrance.gouv.fr/jopdf/common/jo_pdf.jsp?numJO=0&dateJO=20110114&numTexte=8&pageDebut=00773&pageFin=00777.

[52] See Bellan, "Arbitrage : Paris veut conserver son leadership," Les Echos, 14 January 2011, available at: http://archives.lesechos.fr/archives/2011/LesEchos/20848-18-ECH.htm.

[53] Gaillard/de Lapasse, Le nouveau droit français de l'arbitrage interne et international, Recueil Dalloz 3, 20 January 2011, para. 45.

Jurisprudence of Arbitral Tribunals

General Observations

After a relative slump at the turn of the decade, 2011 saw the highest number of investment arbitration cases known to have been initiated in any one year. Despite an apparent resurgence of state-to-state dispute settlement,[54] the present contribution will concentrate on *investor*-state dispute settlement, as by far the most popular form of investment arbitration and the one that continues to shape the international investment law system as we know it today. While only 25 new cases were known to have been filed in 2010,[55] 2011 marked an all-time annual high of at least 46 initiated cases, bringing the total of known cases to 450.[56] Twenty-six awards are known to have been rendered in 2011.[57]

Out of 450 cases, 351 cases had been registered under the ICSID Convention and the ICSID Additional Facility Rules,[58] rendering the World Bank institution the most popular investment arbitration *forum*. The actual number of initiated cases is higher, since, unlike ICSID, not all arbitration *fora* are required to publicise their awards. In the vast majority of cases, developing economies or economies in transition have been the typical respondents, with developed countries attracting only a fraction of this number of cases.[59]

However, some of the most prominent among the recently initiated arbitrations also involve developed economies. These cases bring to the table seminal public policy themes[60] and raise significant questions regarding the scope of government regulatory capacity for policymaking relating, *inter alia*, to measures affecting public health and the environment, or, in other words, the right of the government

---

[54] E.g. initiation of state-to-state arbitration by Ecuador against the US in the context of the *Chevron vs. Ecuador* case. See also on this: Peterson, "Ecuador initiates unusual state-to-state arbitration against United States in bid to clarify scope of investment treaty obligation," IA Reporter, 4 July 2011. On another state-to-state arbitration, see Hepburn/Peterson, "Cuba prevails in rare state-to-state investment treaty arbitration initiated by Italy on behalf of Italian nationals," IA Reporter, 4 July 2011.

[55] UNCTAD, Latest Developments in Investor-State Dispute Settlement, IIA Issues Note No. 1, March 2011, UNCTAD/WEB/DIAE/IA/2011/3, advance unedited version, p. 1, available at: http://www.unctad.org/diae.

[56] UNCTAD, Latest Developments in Investor-State Dispute Settlement, IIA Issues Note, No. 1, April 2012, p. 1, available at: http://www.unctad.org/diae.

[57] UNCTAD, Latest Developments in Investor-State Dispute Settlement, IIA Issues Note, No. 1, April 2012, pp. 1–2, available at: http://www.unctad.org/diae.

[58] ICSID, ICSID 2011 Annual Report, p. 22, available at: http://icsid.worldbank.org/ICSID/FrontServlet?requestType=ICSIDPublicationsRH&actionVal=ViewAnnualReports&year=2011_Eng.

[59] UNCTAD, Latest Developments in Investor-State Dispute Settlement, IIA Issues Note, No. 1, April 2012, p. 2, available at: http://www.unctad.org/diae.

[60] UNCTAD, Latest Developments in Investor-State Dispute Settlement, IIA Issues Note, No. 1, April 2012, pp. 1, 14, available at: http://www.unctad.org/diae.

to regulate in the public interest. Three cases deserve a particular mention in this context.

The *Philip Morris v. Uruguay*[61] and the more recent *Philip Morris v. Australia*[62] cases involve tobacco regulation regarding cigarette packaging in order to protect public health. *Philip Morris v. Australia* is the first known case initiated against Australia. It is noteworthy that Australia's decision to discontinue ISDS predates institution of the *Philip Morris* arbitral proceeding against it,[63] although the public statement's mention of government concerns over its freedom to adopt tobacco packaging legislation may indicate anticipation of potential investor claims, possibly triggered by the institution of the *Philip Morris v. Uruguay* case. A legal opinion in the context of the latter predicts that the investor's claims should fail.[64] Another recent case involving significant public policy aspects (*Vattenfall I*) was eventually settled out of arbitration.[65] A *Vattenfall II* case could well bring to the table further important policy issues regarding Germany's nuclear phase-out.

Of the 26 arbitral awards that are known to have been rendered in 2011, 11 dealt with substantive matters, eight with jurisdictional matters, one concerned an annulment proceeding, while the rest are not in the public domain.[66] Some of these awards, but also 2012 awards, will be looked at closer in subsequent sections of this contribution. After reporting on the relationship between EU law and international investment law as reflected in arbitral jurisprudence, the focus will shift to the treatment of procedural and jurisdictional issues, followed by a particular emphasis on the notion of investor and investment, before ultimately turning to substantive issues in recent case law.

Intra-EU BITs and the Relationship Between EU Law and International Investment Law

A controversial and intensely-debated topic is the treatment of intra-EU BITs and the interaction between EU law and international investment law where a case instituted

[61] ICSID, ARB/10/7, *Philip Morris Brand Sàrl, Philip Morris Products S.A. and Abal Hermanos S.A. vs. Oriental Republic of Uruguay.*

[62] UNCITRAL, *Philip Morris Asia Limited vs. Australia, available at:* http://italaw.com/cases/851.

[63] These date to April and June 2011 respectively. On Australia's decision to discontinue investor-state dispute settlement, see *supra.*

[64] Weiler, Preliminary legal opinion on Philip Morris vs. Uruguay: An Analysis of Tobacco Control Measures in the Context of International Investment Law, Report #1 for Physicians for a Smoke Free Canada, 28 July 2010, available at: http://italaw.com/documents/WeilerOpinion-PMI-Uruguay.pdf.

[65] See ICSID, ARB/09/6, *Vattenfall AB, Vattenfall Europe AG, Vattenfall Europe Generation AG* vs. *The Federal Republic of Germany*, Award.

[66] UNCTAD, Latest Developments in Investor-State Dispute Settlement, IIA Issues Note, No. 1, April 2012, pp. 1–2, available at: http://www.unctad.org/diae.

before an arbitral jurisdiction involves an intra-EU BIT.[67] Arbitral tribunals have considered the validity of intra-EU BITs and the applicability of EU law in investment disputes, while the European Commission has regularly challenged the validity of intra-EU BITs. In the cases of *Eastern Sugar*,[68] *Binder*,[69] *Eureko*[70] and *AES*,[71] tribunals each time confirmed the BITs' applicability. The latter two awards will be dealt with in the following section; even though they date back to 2010, it is worth focusing on these decisions. Other awards based on intra-EU BITs, such as the *Nordzucker v. Poland* Award, have not been released.

In the *AES* case, the Tribunal pointed out that the dispute did not concern a conflict between the EU law and the Energy Charter Treaty (ECT), but rather the conformity or non-conformity of Hungary's acts and measures with the ECT and therefore, it was the behaviour of the state that had to be analysed in light of the ECT, in order to determine whether the measures, or the manner in which they were introduced, violated the ECT. The Tribunal stated that '[t]he question of whether Hungary was, may have been, or may have felt obliged under [EU] law to act as it did, is only an element to be considered by this Tribunal when determining the "rationality," "reasonableness," "arbitrariness" and "transparency" of the reintroduction of administrative pricing and the Price Decrees'[72]. Article 351 TFEU is applicable to agreements between Member States and non-Member States only and, the Tribunal concluded, this Article was 'not applicable, as such, in this arbitration'[73].

If a state measure is motivated by a legal obligation arising from European Union law, it would constitute a rational public policy measure; such would have been the case, should Hungary have been motivated to introduce measures with a view to addressing EU state aid concerns[74]; but 'as long as the Commission's state aid decision was not issued, Hungary had no legal obligation to act in accordance with what it believed could be the result of the decision and to start a limitation of

---

[67] See on this topic for example Lavranos, Bilateral Investment Treaties (BITs) and EU Law, 2010, available at: http://ssrn.com/abstract=1683348; Reinisch, Articles 30 and 59 of the Vienna Convention and the Law of Treaties in Action: The Decisions on Jurisdiction in the Eastern Sugar and Eureko Investment Arbitrations, Legal Issues of Economic Integration 39 (2012) 2, p. 157.

[68] SCC Case 88/2004, *Eastern Sugar vs. Czech Republic*, Partial Award; on this case see e.g. Chalker, Case Note: Eastern Sugar B.V. v. The Czech Republic, Transnational Dispute Management 1 (2009).

[69] *Rupert Joseph Binder vs. Czech Republic*, Award on Jurisdiction.

[70] UNCITRAL, PCA Case No. 2008-13, *Eureko B.V. vs. Slovakia*, Award on Jurisdiction, Arbitrability and Suspension.

[71] ICSID, ARB/07/22, *AES Summit Generation Limited and AES-Tisza Erömü Kft. vs. Hungary*, Award.

[72] ICSID, ARB/07/22, *AES Summit Generation Limited and AES-Tisza Erömü Kft. vs. Hungary*, Award, para. 7.6.9.

[73] ICSID, ARB/07/22, *AES Summit Generation Limited and AES-Tisza Erömü Kft. vs. Hungary*, Award, paras. 7.6.11 and 7.6.10, see also paras. 7.6.7. et seq.

[74] ICSID, ARB/07/22, *AES Summit Generation Limited and AES-Tisza Erömü Kft. vs. Hungary*, Award, para. 10.3.16.

potential state aid'[75]. The law of the European Union would have to be considered as a fact by a tribunal. In particular, the *AES* Tribunal noted that the EU competition law regime 'has a dual nature: on the one hand, it is an international law regime, on the other hand, once introduced in the national legal orders, it is part of these legal orders. It is common ground that in an international arbitration, national laws are to be considered as facts. Both parties having pleading [*sic*] that the [EU] competition law regime should be considered as a fact, it will be considered by this Tribunal as a fact, always taking into account that a state may not invoke its domestic law as an excuse for alleged breaches of its international obligations'[76].

In the *Eureko* case, the Tribunal stated that, where jurisdiction is challenged, analysis of the relevant arguments needs to take place first within 'the framework applicable to the legal instrument from which the Tribunal derives its *prima facie* jurisdiction,' i.e. 'the BIT and international law, including applicable EU law'[77]. 'Whatever legal consequences may result from the application of EU law, those consequences must be applied by this Tribunal within the framework of the rules of international law and not in disregard of those rules. Those consequences may operate in a number of distinct ways. For example, EU law may affect the capacity of a State to consent to an international treaty, or may affect the performance of obligations under the treaty, or may be part of the law applicable to determine the scope of obligations under the treaty, or may affect the manner in which disputes arising under the treaty must be settled and the jurisdiction of tribunals established outside the EU legal order'[78].

Furthermore, the Tribunal stated that EU law does not prohibit investor-state arbitration; on the contrary, 'transnational arbitration is a commonplace throughout the EU, including arbitrations between legal persons and States; and the [Court of Justice of the European Union] has given several indications of how questions of EU law should be handled in the course of arbitrations, including important questions of public policy. It cannot be asserted that all arbitrations that involve any question of EU law are conducted in violation of EU law. The argument that the availability of arbitration for some but not all EU investors would amount to discrimination in violation of EU law was addressed above, where it was decided that the answer is to extend rights and not to cancel them'[79]. There would be 'no reason, legal or practical, why an EU Member State should not accord to investors of all other EU Member States rights equivalent to those which the State has bound

[75] ICSID, ARB/07/22, *AES Summit Generation Limited and AES-Tisza Erömü Kft. vs. Hungary*, Award, para. 10.3.16.

[76] ICSID, ARB/07/22, *AES Summit Generation Limited and AES-Tisza Erömü Kft. vs. Hungary*, Award, para. 7.6.6.

[77] UNCITRAL, PCA Case No. 2008-13, *Eureko B.V. vs. Slovakia*, Award on Jurisdiction, Arbitrability and Suspension, para. 228.

[78] UNCITRAL, PCA Case No. 2008-13, *Eureko B.V. vs. Slovakia*, Award on Jurisdiction, Arbitrability and Suspension, para. 229.

[79] UNCITRAL, PCA Case No. 2008-13, *Eureko B.V. vs. Slovakia*, Award on Jurisdiction, Arbitrability and Suspension, para. 274, footnotes omitted.

itself to accord to investors of its EU bilateral investment treaty partners—or, indeed, to investors from States that are not members of the EU'[80].

Furthermore, the Tribunal stated that the Judgment of the Court of Justice in the *MOX Plant* case does not apply to investor-state disputes. It noted in particular that '[t]here is no suggestion here that every dispute that arises between a Member State and an individual must be put before the [CJEU]; nor would the [Court] have the jurisdiction (let alone the capacity) to decide all such cases'[81] and that '[t]he argument that the [CJEU] has an "interpretative monopoly" and that the Tribunal therefore cannot consider and apply EU law, is incorrect. The [Court] has no such monopoly. Courts and arbitration tribunals throughout the EU interpret and apply EU law daily. What the [Court of Justice] has is a monopoly on the final and authoritative interpretation of EU law: but that is quite different'[82]. 'The fact that, at the merits stage, the Tribunal might have to consider and apply provisions of EU law does not deprive the Tribunal of jurisdiction. The Tribunal can consider and apply EU law, if required, both as a matter of international law and as a matter of German law. This jurisdictional objection therefore is rejected'[83].

In comparing the fair and equitable treatment (FET) standard with the prohibition of discrimination in EU Law, the Tribunal did not accept that the FET standard 'is entirely covered by a prohibition on discrimination' noting further that the respondent in the case did not 'allege that there is any principle of EU law that specifically forbids treatment that is not fair and equitable. The Tribunal does not consider that any such principle, independent of concepts of non-discrimination, proportionality, legitimate expectation and of procedural fairness, is yet established in EU law'[84]. 'Treatment might be unfair and inequitable even if it is imposed on everyone regardless of nationality or, indeed, of any other distinguishing characteristic'[85]. Indeed, the Tribunal held that the rights offered investors under the BIT, including the FET standard, full protection and security and protection against expropriation, exceed protections afforded under EU law,[86] while access to

[80] UNCITRAL, PCA Case No. 2008-13, *Eureko B.V. vs. Slovakia*, Award on Jurisdiction, Arbitrability and Suspension, para. 267.

[81] UNCITRAL, PCA Case No. 2008-13, *Eureko B.V. vs. Slovakia*, Award on Jurisdiction, Arbitrability and Suspension, para. 276.

[82] UNCITRAL, PCA Case No. 2008-13, *Eureko B.V. vs. Slovakia*, Award on Jurisdiction, Arbitrability and Suspension, para. 282.

[83] UNCITRAL, PCA Case No. 2008-13, *Eureko B.V. vs. Slovakia*, Award on Jurisdiction, Arbitrability and Suspension, para. 283.

[84] UNCITRAL, PCA Case No. 2008-13, *Eureko B.V. vs. Slovakia*, Award on Jurisdiction, Arbitrability and Suspension para. 250, footnote omitted.

[85] UNCITRAL, PCA Case No. 2008-13, *Eureko B.V. vs. Slovakia*, Award on Jurisdiction, Arbitrability and Suspension, para. 251, footnote omitted.

[86] UNCITRAL, PCA Case No. 2008-13, *Eureko B.V. vs. Slovakia*, Award on Jurisdiction, Arbitrability and Suspension, para. 263, see also paras. 259 et seq.

international arbitration under an investment treaty 'cannot be equated' with access to the host state's domestic judiciary.[87]

Meanwhile the OLG Frankfurt[88] has confirmed in the *Eureko* case that EU law does not affect the validity of the arbitration clause, as Article 344 TFEU[89] only applies to disputes between Member States but not to disputes between an investor and an EU Member State. The OLG Frankfurt declined to refer the matter to the Court of Justice for a preliminary ruling on questions of EU law. A statement that Article 344 TFEU would also be applicable to investor-state proceedings could not, in the Court's view, be premised on the basis of remarks the Commission has made.

A discussion is just starting regarding the potential arbitration claims against Greece in relation to bond swaps that may have led to property expropriation of German bondholders as well as a violation of the FET standard. However, it has to be noted that the intra-EU BIT between Germany and Greece does not contain a clause on investor-state dispute settlement.

Procedural and Jurisdictional Aspects in Arbitral Jurisprudence

On Consent to Arbitration

Determining state consent to arbitration presents a multifaceted dilemma, whose resolution involves issues as different as investor-state dispute resolution language in an IIA or the question of most-favoured-nation treatment extension to investor-state dispute settlement provisions. State consent has been examined or touched upon in a number of awards rendered in recent arbitrations.

In determining the existence of consent on the basis of national legislation, the *Brandes* Tribunal held that interpretation of the pertinent domestic provision, as a unilateral declaration of the host state, must 'be conducted within the parameters set by the [host state's] legal system,' but, as such interpretation has the effect of deciding whether consent under Article 25 ICSID Convention exists, 'it is necessary to take account of the principles of International Law'[90]. The *Brandes* Tribunal

[87] UNCITRAL, PCA Case No. 2008-13, *Eureko B.V. vs. Slovakia*, Award on Jurisdiction, Arbitrability and Suspension, para. 264.

[88] 26 SchH 11-10, Decision of the Oberlandesgericht Frankfurt am Main, *Eureko BV vs. The Slovak Republic.*

[89] Article 344 TFEU provides: "Member States undertake not to submit a dispute concerning the interpretation or application of the Treaties to any method of settlement other than those provided for therein."

[90] ICSID, ARB/08/3, *Brandes Investment Partners, LP vs. Venezuela*, para. 81, see also paras. 82, 36.

further noted that national courts' interpretation of the national provision determining whether it offers consent are not binding on the Tribunal[91] that remains the judge of its own competence.[92]

On Waiting Clauses

In *Alps Finance v. Slovakia*, the Tribunal pointed out the rationale of a waiting clause, requiring consultations between the parties before initiation of arbitration: the purpose of the waiting clause is to give a state the opportunity to discuss the matter with the other party.[93] If the state has been given this opportunity, the waiting clause is satisfied, even if the investor 'did not employ the most perfect forms' when it first notified the respondent state of the dispute.[94] Similar conclusions regarding the purpose of waiting clauses had been reached by earlier tribunals, such as in the 2010 *Burlington Resources* Award, which noted that the waiting clause 'is designed precisely to provide the State with an opportunity to redress the dispute' prior to the investor's decision to resort to arbitration'[95].

MFN Extension to ISDS

After a relative calm in the post-*Maffezini*[96] era and the controversy it invited over the potential extension of an IIA's most-favoured-nation clause to investor-state dispute settlement provisions, probably one of the most important jurisdictional developments of the last few months is a particularly animated resurfacing of this heated debate. The topic was rekindled with Brigitte Stern's 32-page-long Dissenting Opinion in the 2011 *Impregilo v. Argentina* Award,[97] in a way that it appears unlikely that interpretative consensus may be reached any time soon.

While the majority of the *Impregilo* Tribunal found that the MFN clause allowed the claimant to bypass a requirement to pursue domestic remedies for 18 months (limited local remedies clause) before instituting international arbitral proceedings,[98] Stern's Dissenting Opinion concurs with earlier arbitral decisions,

---

[91] ICSID, ARB/08/3, *Brandes Investment Partners, LP vs. Venezuela*, para. 98.

[92] ICSID, ARB/08/3, *Brandes Investment Partners, LP vs. Venezuela*, para. 99, citing the *Cemex* Tribunal.

[93] *Alps Finance vs. Slovakia*, Award, para. 209, available at: http://arbitrationlaw.com/node/45893.

[94] *Alps Finance vs. Slovakia*, Award, paras. 200 et seq., available at: http://arbitrationlaw.com/node/45893.

[95] ICSID, ARB/08/5, *Burlington Resources Inc. vs. Ecuador*, Decision on Jurisdiction, para. 312.

[96] ICSID, ARB/97/7, *Emilio Agustín Maffezini vs. Kingdom of Spain*, Decision on Jurisdiction.

[97] ICSID, ARB/07/17, *Impregilo S.p.A. vs. Argentina*, Award.

[98] ICSID, ARB/07/17, *Impregilo S.p.A. vs. Argentina*, Award, para. 108.

such as the *Plama* Award,[99] that rejected MFN extension to ISDS.[100] Stern founds her proposed analysis on a 'distinction between qualifying conditions for access to rights and rights'[101], observing that 'an MFN clause can only concern the rights that an investor can enjoy, it cannot modify the fundamental conditions for the enjoyment of such rights, in other words, the insuperable conditions of access to the rights granted in the BIT'[102].

Stern's Dissenting Opinion notes that the most-favoured-nation clause cannot alter the state's consent to arbitration and that '[u]nless specifically stated to the contrary, the qualifying conditions put by the State in order to accept to be sued directly on the international level by foreign investors cannot be displaced by an MFN clause, and a conditional right to ICSID cannot magically be transformed into an unconditional right by the grace of the MFN clause'[103].

Stern's arguments are likely to lead to new discussions on MFN coverage of ISDS. After the *Impregilo* Award, the *Hochtief* Tribunal, accepting in its majority MFN extension to ISDS in order to bypass a limited local remedies clause and including in its reasoning an apparent response to a comment in Stern's Dissenting Opinion,[104] has no less been accompanied by a Dissenting Opinion. Echoing in certain respects Stern's Dissenting Opinion, J. Christopher Thomas remarks that, in his opinion, the Tribunal may not 'apply the Treaty's substantive terms (including the MFN clause) so as to *create* its jurisdiction'[105], as well as that the MFN treatment does not extend to dispute resolution.[106]

But the argument in favour of non-extension of the MFN provision to ISDS has not been limited to dissenting opinions. In February 2012, the *ICS Inspection and Control Services v Argentina* Tribunal, faced with claimant non-compliance with an 18-month local remedies clause, determined that state consent could not be surmised 'in the face of ambiguity' and that the term 'treatment,' absent any

[99] ICSID, ARB/03/24, *Plama Consortium Limited vs. Bulgaria*, Decision on Jurisdiction.

[100] ICSID, ARB/07/17, *Impregilo S.p.A. vs. Argentina*, Dissenting Opinion of Brigitte Stern, paras. 14–15.

[101] ICSID, ARB/07/17, *Impregilo S.p.A. vs. Argentina*, Dissenting Opinion of Brigitte Stern, paras. 44 et seq.

[102] ICSID, ARB/07/17, *Impregilo S.p.A. vs. Argentina*, Dissenting Opinion of Brigitte Stern, para. 47, emphasis in the original.

[103] ICSID, ARB/07/17, *Impregilo S.p.A. vs. Argentina*, Dissenting Opinion of Brigitte Stern, para. 80, see also para. 97, for the citation para. 99.

[104] ICSID, ARB/07/31, *Hochtief AG vs. Argentina*, Decision on Jurisdiction, para. 98. See ICSID, ARB/07/17, *Impregilo S.p.A. vs. Argentina*, Dissenting Opinion of Brigitte Stern, paras. 106–107, also para. 12.

[105] ICSID, ARB/07/31, *Hochtief AG vs. Argentina*, Separate and Dissenting Opinion of Christopher Thomas, para. 39.

[106] See for instance ICSID, ARB/07/31, *Hochtief AG vs. Argentina*, Separate and Dissenting Opinion of Christopher Thomas, para. 63, where he notes that "when taking the opportunity to give interpretative guidance as to what actually constitutes "less favourable treatment" within the meaning of Article 3(2), the examples used by the States Parties were far removed from the conditions of access to international jurisdiction stipulated in Article 10 of the Treaty."

provision to the contrary within the treaty, does not encompass dispute settlement provisions.[107] Finally, in the context of another recent case, that of the *BG v. Argentina* Award, Argentina's *Petition to vacate* the award was granted by the US Court of Appeals for the District of Columbia Circuit (17 January 2012) on grounds of non-extension of the most-favoured-nation provision to investor-state dispute settlement provisions.

The controversial question of MFN extension to ISDS seems unlikely to be settled for some time to come, while new awards will have to deal with the issue. For instance, in the currently ongoing *Philip Morris v. Uruguay* case, Uruguay has raised, *inter alia*, a jurisdictional objection on the basis of the investor's non-respect of a 6-month waiting clause and an 18-month local remedies clause.[108]

Domestic Remedies

Another case concerning domestic proceedings was decided by the *Commerce Group v. El Salvador* Tribunal.[109] In interpreting the 'waiver provision' of Article 10.18.2(b) CAFTA, the Tribunal determined that the obligation to file a formal written waiver has to be satisfied at the same date as all other requirements of jurisdiction.[110] Waivers 'must comply with both a formal and a material element' and 'to understand the concept of waiver in any other way would render it devoid of meaning'[111]. In particular, the waiver clause requires the claimant to actively discontinue any domestic court proceedings.[112]

Counterclaims

The *Spyridon Roussalis* Tribunal rejected the respondent state's counterclaim because hearing counterclaims would overstep the parties' consent to arbitration.[113] This is the first such rejection of a counterclaim on the basis of lack of consent.[114]

[107] PCA Case No. 2010-9, *ICS Inspection and Control Services Limited (United Kingdom) vs. Argentina*, Award on Jurisdiction, paras. 280 and 285–296 respectively; see further paras. 314–317.

[108] ICSID, ARB/10/7, *Philip Morris Brand Sàrl, Philip Morris Products S.A. and Abal Hermanos S.A. vs. Oriental Republic of Uruguay*, Uruguay's Memorial on Jurisdiction, paras. 37 et seq.

[109] ICSID, ARB/09/17, *Commerce Group Corp. and San Sebastian Gold Mines, Inc. vs. El Salvador*, Award.

[110] ICSID, ARB/09/17, *Commerce Group Corp. and San Sebastian Gold Mines, Inc. vs. El Salvador*, Award, paras. 96–97.

[111], ICSID, ARB/09/17, *Commerce Group Corp. and San Sebastian Gold Mines, Inc. vs. El Salvador*, Award paras. 79–80.

[112] ICSID, ARB/09/17, *Commerce Group Corp. and San Sebastian Gold Mines, Inc. vs. El Salvador*, Award, paras. 81 et seq.

[113] ICSID, ARB/06/1, *Spyridon Roussalis vs. Romania*, Award, paras. 864–872.

[114] See W. M. Reisman's partial dissent (Declaration) attached to the Award.

More particularly, the Tribunal determined that '[t]he investor's consent to the BIT's arbitration clause can only exist in relation to counterclaims if such counterclaims come within the consent of the host State as expressed in the BIT'[115]. The dispute settlement provision of the BIT in question provided for '[d]isputes between an investor of a Contracting Party and the other Contracting Party concerning *an obligation of the latter* under this Agreement, in relation to an investment of the former'[116]. The Tribunal considered that the text of this provision 'undoubtedly limit[s] jurisdiction to claims brought by investors about obligations of the host State. Accordingly, the BIT does not provide for counterclaims to be introduced by the host state in relation to obligations of the investor'[117]. The Tribunal held that 'the BIT imposes no obligations on investors, only on contracting States. Therefore, where the BIT does specify that the applicable law is the BIT itself, counterclaims fall outside the tribunal's jurisdiction'[118].

The Tribunal further reasoned that the identified lack of consent to adjudicate the counterclaim could not be bypassed by application of the umbrella clause in the treaty under interpretation.[119]

Jurisdiction over the respondent state's counterclaims, the *Spyridon Roussalis* Tribunal broke ground for rejecting jurisdiction over counterclaims on account of lack of consent.[120] The Award's doctrinal importance nonetheless consists also in Reisman's partial dissent (*Declaration*) observing, *inter alia*, that the tribunal's finding of a lack of jurisdiction over counterclaims 'perforce directs the respondent State to pursue its claims in its own courts where the very investor who had sought a forum outside the state apparatus is now constrained to become the defendant.' Reisman noted the potential duplication of proceedings and the resulting inefficiency that leads to 'an ironic, if not absurd, outcome, at odds [. . .] with the objectives of international investment law'[121].

Attempts at Arbitrator Disqualifications

A further noteworthy procedural issue, having acquired some significance due to their recurrent presence in recent disputes, is that of how tribunals have dealt with attempts at arbitrator disqualifications. Arbitrator disqualifications under the ICSID Convention are regulated by Chapter V of the same Convention (Articles 56-58). In interpreting Article 57 of the ISCID Convention that provides, *inter alia*, for a

[115] ICSID, ARB/06/1, *Spyridon Roussalis vs. Romania*, Award, para. 866. This follows from Art. 46 ICSID Convention.

[116] Art. 9(1) Greece-Romania BIT (1997), emphasis added.

[117] ICSID, ARB/06/1, *Spyridon Roussalis vs. Romania*, Award, para. 869.

[118] ICSID, ARB/06/1, *Spyridon Roussalis vs. Romania*, Award, para. 871.

[119] ICSID, ARB/06/1, *Spyridon Roussalis vs. Romania*, Award, paras. 873.

[120] W. M. Reisman's partial dissent (Declaration) attached to the *Spyridon Roussalis* Award.

[121] W. M. Reisman's partial dissent (Declaration) attached to the *Spyridon Roussalis* Award.

'manifest lack of the qualities required' of an arbitrator for a disqualification,[122] the *Universal Compression* Tribunal cited earlier jurisprudence to support its argument that ' "manifest" means "obvious" or "evident," and that it imposes a "relatively heavy burden of proof on the party making the proposal" '[123]. The Tribunal further noted that the International Bar Association (IBA) Guidelines on Conflicts of Interest in International Arbitration, while broadly recognised for the assessment of arbitrator conflicts, are 'indicative only' in the context of an ICSID adjudication.[124] On the question of whether multiple appointments manifestly compromise the independence or impartiality of the arbitrator, the Tribunal responded in the negative, provided 'no objective fact' is adduced to 'suggest' that such independence or impartiality has been impacted upon,[125] while it equally rejected the claimant's contention that similar issues arising in other cases where the same arbitrator is appointed would be an obstacle to an impartial and independent judgment.[126] The Tribunal rejected both proposals for disqualification under examination.[127]

---

[122] Art. 57 ICSID Convention provides: "A party may propose to a Commission or Tribunal the disqualification of any of its members on account of any fact indicating a manifest lack of the qualities required by paragraph (1) of Article 14. A party to arbitration proceedings may, in addition, propose the disqualification of an arbitrator on the ground that he was ineligible for appointment to the Tribunal under Section 2 of Chapter IV."

[123] ICSID, ARB/10/9, *Universal Compression International Holdings, S.L.U. vs. Venezuela*, Decision on the proposal to disqualify Prof. Brigitte Stern and Prof. Guido Santiago Tawil, Arbitrators, para. 71, citing ICSID Cases ARB/03/17 and ARB/03/19, *Suez, Sociedad General de Aguas de Barcelona S.A. and InterAguas Servicios Integrales del Agua S.A. vs. The Argentine Republic*, Decision on the Proposal for the Disqualification of a Member of the Arbitral Tribunal.

[124] ICSID, ARB/10/9, *Universal Compression International Holdings, S.L.U. vs. Venezuela*, Decision on the proposal to disqualify Prof. Brigitte Stern and Prof. Guido Santiago Tawil, Arbitrators, para. 74, further citing ICSID, ARB/08/17, *Participaciones Inversiones Portuarias SARL vs. Gabonese Republic*.

[125] ICSID, ARB/10/9, *Universal Compression International Holdings, S.L.U. vs. Venezuela*, Decision on the proposal to disqualify Prof. Brigitte Stern and Prof. Guido Santiago Tawil, Arbitrators, paras. 75, 77.

[126] ICSID, ARB/10/9, *Universal Compression International Holdings, S.L.U. vs. Venezuela*, Decision on the proposal to disqualify Prof. Brigitte Stern and Prof. Guido Santiago Tawil, Arbitrators, para. 85, also paras. 80 et seq.

[127] ICSID, ARB/10/9, *Universal Compression International Holdings, S.L.U. vs. Venezuela*, Decision on the proposal to disqualify Prof. Brigitte Stern and Prof. Guido Santiago Tawil, Arbitrators, paras. 96, 107.

Particular Jurisdictional Issues in Investment Arbitration Including the Notions of Investor and Investment

Notion of Investor and Investment

The determination of which persons and actions are protected by the international investment law regime delineates the scope of application of the specific standards of treatment laid down in international investment agreements; only investors that have made an investment within the meaning of an IIA enjoy the latter's protection. The semantic content of the notions of investor and investment differs from agreement to agreement and a case-by-case/agreement-by-agreement examination is necessary; nevertheless, common approaches and terminology offer a basis for an analysis of case law in this matter.

In *Alps Finance v. Slovakia*,[128] the Tribunal was confronted with problems regarding the 'nationality' of the investor. Article 1(1)(b) and (c) of the Slovakia-Switzerland BIT, the agreement under interpretation in the case, requires that an entity be constituted under the laws of Switzerland, that its seat be in Switzerland and that it perform real economic activities in Switzerland. Therefore, the Tribunal determined that the BIT requires '*more than*' 'mere incorporation in one of the contracting parties'[129]; rather, the wording of the treaty Article is intended to 'exclude from treaty-protection 'mailbox' or 'paper' companies'[130]. Article 1(1)(b)'s requirement for a Swiss 'seat' as an additional element separate from the 'constitution and organization under Swiss law' would make evident that mere incorporation in Switzerland is in itself insufficient to establish a 'seat' within the meaning of the BIT.[131] In examining the issue of whether an investor had 'real economic activities,' the Tribunal further reasoned that 'the good faith ordinary meaning of the word 'real' cannot but be 'actual,' or 'effective,' or 'genuine,' or 'verifiable,' or 'visible,' or 'tangible,' or 'objective' ' and that the BIT's preamble would indicate that the intention of the contracting parties was to intensify 'the economic cooperation to the mutual benefit of both States and [to foster] their economic prosperity [...] No

---

[128] *Alps Finance vs. Slovakia*, Award, available at: http://italaw.com/documents/AFTvSlovakRepublic_5Mar2011_Part1.pdf and http://italaw.com/documents/AFTvSlovakRepublic_5Mar2011_Part2.pdf.

[129] *Alps Finance vs. Slovakia*, Award, para. 224, emphasis in original, available at: http://italaw.com/documents/AFTvSlovakRepublic_5Mar2011_Part1.pdf and http://italaw.com/documents/AFTvSlovakRepublic_5Mar2011_Part2.pdf.

[130] *Alps Finance vs. Slovakia*, Award, para. 224, available at: http://italaw.com/documents/AFTvSlovakRepublic_5Mar2011_Part1.pdf and http://italaw.com/documents/AFTvSlovakRepublic_5Mar2011_Part2.pdf.

[131] *Alps Finance vs. Slovakia*, Award, para. 216, available at: http://italaw.com/documents/AFTvSlovakRepublic_5Mar2011_Part1.pdf and http://italaw.com/documents/AFTvSlovakRepublic_5Mar2011_Part2.pdf.

State is anxious to promise special guarantees, privileges and protections to investors which bring no benefit to its economy'[132].

Still on the issue of real activities, the Tribunal determined that the claimant was not an investor[133] making particular note of the fact that the investor's tax return pointed to 'a quite modest turnover' as well as the fact that the claimant was unable to establish a number of elements such as the number and type of its clients or the contracts it entered into, further admitting that there was no employed personnel.[134] Although finding that the claimant was not an investor based on the above reasoning was sufficient to establish its lack of jurisdiction, the *Alps Finance* Tribunal preferred—'for the sake of completeness'—to address some further questions.[135] In examining whether the claimant's operations in the host country constituted an investment on the basis of the BIT's 'every kind of asset,' the Tribunal held that for claims arising out of a contract, 'the contract itself should qualify as an investment' and therefore it would need to meet some requirements, 'such as duration, contribution and risk'[136]; as a result, despite the 'very broad definition of the term "investment" ' in the BIT, the Tribunal could not concede the existence of an investment under the circumstances.[137] The Tribunal backed up its reasoning by referring to an 'objective' definition of investment to be found in 'international law'[138]. Therefore, the Tribunal concluded that the claimant's operations did not qualify as an investment neither under the BIT nor under international law rules.

The *Abaclat v. Argentina* Tribunal followed the typical two-pronged test adopted by tribunals when determining whether the dispute at hand relates to an investment; namely, an examination of the existence of an investment under the

[132] *Alps Finance vs. Slovakia*, Award, para. 226, available at: http://italaw.com/documents/AFTvSlovakRepublic_5Mar2011_Part1.pdf and http://italaw.com/documents/AFTvSlovakRepublic_5Mar2011_Part2.pdf.

[133] *Alps Finance vs. Slovakia*, Award, para. 227, available at: http://italaw.com/documents/AFTvSlovakRepublic_5Mar2011_Part1.pdf and http://italaw.com/documents/AFTvSlovakRepublic_5Mar2011_Part2.pdf.

[134] *Alps Finance vs. Slovakia*, Award, para. 219, available at: http://italaw.com/documents/AFTvSlovakRepublic_5Mar2011_Part1.pdf and http://italaw.com/documents/AFTvSlovakRepublic_5Mar2011_Part2.pdf.

[135] *Alps Finance vs. Slovakia*, Award, para. 229, available at: http://italaw.com/documents/AFTvSlovakRepublic_5Mar2011_Part1.pdf and http://italaw.com/documents/AFTvSlovakRepublic_5Mar2011_Part2.pdf.

[136] *Alps Finance vs. Slovakia*, Award, para. 231, available at: http://italaw.com/documents/AFTvSlovakRepublic_5Mar2011_Part1.pdf and http://italaw.com/documents/AFTvSlovakRepublic_5Mar2011_Part2.pdf.

[137] *Alps Finance vs. Slovakia*, Award, para. 238, available at: http://italaw.com/documents/AFTvSlovakRepublic_5Mar2011_Part1.pdf and http://italaw.com/documents/AFTvSlovakRepublic_5Mar2011_Part2.pdf.

[138] *Alps Finance vs. Slovakia*, Award, paras. 239 et seq., available at: http://italaw.com/documents/AFTvSlovakRepublic_5Mar2011_Part1.pdf and http://italaw.com/documents/AFTvSlovakRepublic_5Mar2011_Part2.pdf.

pertinent BIT and under the ICSID Convention.[139] In analysing the meaning of investment, the Tribunal noted that two aspects may be identified: '(i) the contribution that constitutes the investment, and (ii) the rights and the value that derive from that contribution'[140] and observed further that '[t]hese two aspects are addressed somewhat differently by the BIT and the ICSID Convention'[141]. The definition in Article 1(1) of the BIT *in casu*, including the list of examples provided, describes the 'rights and values' that may be at risk through host state measures, e.-g. an expropriation, and that 'deserve protection under the BIT'[142]. 'Thus the focus here is on the rights and the value that potential contributions from investors may generate. Nevertheless, this definition is of course based on the premise of the existence of such contribution'[143]. On the other hand, the Tribunal remarked, the notion of investment in the ICSID Convention 'relates more to the contribution itself' and 'a number arbitral tribunals have attempted to further define the concept of investment under Article 25 ICSID Convention. This has been regularly done by reference to some or all of the so-called *Salini* factors [...] This definition focuses on the nature of the contribution constituting the investment, and not on the rights and value deriving therefrom'[144]. The Tribunal further stated that the two aspects may be perceived as complementary and 'merely reflect a two-folded approach of the BIT and the ICSID Convention towards investment'[145]. 'Thus, within this interpretation, as it arises further from the wording of Article 1(1) and the aim of the BIT, the definition of investment provided in the BIT focuses on what is to be protected, i.e. the fruits and value generated by the investment, whilst the general definitions developed with regard to Article 25 ICSID Convention focus on the contributions, which constitute the investment and create the fruits and value. In summary, a certain value may only be protected if generated by a specific contribution, and—vice versa—contributions may only be protected to the extent they generate a certain value, which the investor may be deprived of'[146].

---

[139] ICSID, ARB/07/5, *Abaclat and Others vs. Argentina*, Decision on Jurisdiction and Admissibility, para. 344.

[140] ICSID, ARB/07/5, *Abaclat and Others vs. Argentina*, Decision on Jurisdiction and Admissibility, para. 346.

[141] ICSID, ARB/07/5, *Abaclat and Others vs. Argentina*, Decision on Jurisdiction and Admissibility, para. 347.

[142] ICSID, ARB/07/5, *Abaclat and Others vs. Argentina*, Decision on Jurisdiction and Admissibility, para. 347.

[143] ICSID, ARB/07/5, *Abaclat and Others vs. Argentina*, Decision on Jurisdiction and Admissibility, para. 347.

[144] ICSID, ARB/07/5, *Abaclat and Others vs. Argentina*, Decision on Jurisdiction and Admissibility, para. 347.

[145] ICSID, ARB/07/5, *Abaclat and Others vs. Argentina*, Decision on Jurisdiction and Admissibility, para. 349.

[146] ICSID, ARB/07/5, *Abaclat and Others vs. Argentina*, Decision on Jurisdiction and Admissibility, para. 350.

On the question of shares, the *Abaclat* Tribunal decided that the bonds and securities in question constituted investments within the meaning of Article 1(1) of the BIT and, furthermore, regarding the definition of investment in Article 25 ICSID Convention, a majority of the Tribunal after rejecting the application of the *Salini* test found that the purchase of securities bonds constitutes a contribution leading to an investment within the meaning of that Article.

The conclusion that minority shareholdings can constitute investments was one of the outcomes of the *El Paso* Award.[147] Since in that case the Tribunal determined that El Paso had a *substantial* shareholding interest in the companies in question, it did not proceed to examine whether the minority shareholding interest needs to be 'a substantial one or whether even a single share could give rise to a claim'[148].

The *Paushok, et al.* Tribunal concluded that a company 100% of whose shares are owned by the claimant constitutes an investment. In this regard, the Tribunal stated clearly that '[i]f "shares" in companies can constitute "investment," it would be absurd to argue that a company the shares of which are owned 100% by an investor would not constitute an "investment" as defined in the Treaty'[149]. On the question of whether nominal shareholdings may constitute an investment, the Tribunal indirectly conceded the case. In response to the respondent's argument that the claimants did not qualify as investors since they were nominal shareholders, it observed that the claimants owned 'shares having a significant value by any standard and those shares come under the definition of "investment" under the Treaty'[150].

Also in *Hicee v. Slovakia*, the Tribunal held that the admissibility of shareholder claims is contingent upon IIA clauses that very often 'make provision to allow for shareholder claims, either explicitly or by necessary implication'[151]. The Tribunal further noted that 'the phrase "invested either directly or through an investor of a third State", as it appears in the Agreement in question, is capable, as a matter of ordinary meaning, of bearing two meanings: a directional meaning, where it refers to the investment's origin, the place from which it comes; or a relational meaning, in which it refers to the connection between the investor and the investment'[152]. In *Malicorp v. Egypt*, the Tribunal held that the definitions of 'investment' in a BIT

---

[147] ICSID, ARB/03/15, *El Paso Energy International Company vs. Argentina*, Award.

[148] ICSID, ARB/03/15, *El Paso Energy International Company vs. Argentina*, Award, paras. 211–212.

[149] UNCITRAL, *Sergei Paushok, CJSC Golden East Company and CJSC Vostokneftegaz Company vs. Mongolia*, Award on Jurisdiction and Liability, para. 201, see also paras. 202 et seq., also referring to the *Azurix vs. Argentina* case, available at: http://italaw.com/documents/PaushokAward.pdf.

[150] UNCITRAL, *Sergei Paushok, CJSC Golden East Company and CJSC Vostokneftegaz Company vs. Mongolia*, Award on Jurisdiction and Liability, paras. 205–206, available at: http://italaw.com/documents/PaushokAward.pdf.

[151] UNCITRAL, PCA Case No. 2009-11, *Hicee B.V. vs. Slovakia*, Partial Award, para. 147, footnote omitted.

[152] UNCITRAL, PCA Case No. 2009-11, *Hicee B.V. vs. Slovakia*, Partial Award, para. 116.

and in Article 25 ICSID Convention are complementary.[153] The typical definition in IIAs does not, in the opinion of the Tribunal, 'so much stress the contributions made by the party acting, as the rights and assets that such contributions have generated for it' but the wording of other IIA provisions clearly presupposes the existence of contributions.[154] The requirements of the *Salini* test for the existence of investment pursuant to Article 25 ICSID Convention 'are not at all absolute and must be regarded as attempts to pin down the notion'[155]. As echoed later in the *Abaclat* Award,[156] the IIA definition of investment 'emphasises the fruits and assets resulting from the investment, which must be protected, whereas the definitions generally used in relation to Article 25 of the ICSID Convention lay stress on the contributions that have created such fruits and assets. It can be inferred from this that assets cannot be protected unless they result from contributions, and contributions will not be protected unless they have actually produced the assets of which the investor claims to have been deprived'[157]. Furthermore, the Tribunal held that 'costs incurred during negotiations with a view to concluding a contract do not constitute an investment if in the end the State finally refuses to sign it'[158]. Once the contract is concluded, the commitment is tantamount to an investment, since 'it entails the promise to make contributions in the future for the performance of which that party is henceforth contractually bound'[159].

In examining the concept of investment, the *GEA v. Ukraine* Tribunal held that an arbitral award deciding on contractual rights and obligations does not in itself constitute an investment.[160] 'Properly analysed, [the Award] is a legal instrument, which provides for the disposition of rights and obligations [...] [T]he fact that the Award rules upon rights and obligations arising out of an investment does not equate the Award with the investment itself'[161]. By contrast, the Tribunal determined that an investment may arise out of a contract that 'confers "rights to the exercise of an economic activity" '[162]. In the case at hand, the Tribunal determined that the contract satisfied the criteria both of the BIT definition of investment as, establishing the existence of the 'commonly applied elements' of investment definition under the Convention, of the ICSID Convention.[163]

---

[153] ICSID, ARB/08/18, *Malicorp Limited vs. Egypt*, Award, para. 110.

[154] ICSID, ARB/08/18, *Malicorp Limited vs. Egypt*, Award, para. 108.

[155] ICSID, ARB/08/18, *Malicorp Limited vs. Egypt*, Award, para. 109.

[156] ICSID, ARB/07/5, *Abaclat and Others vs. Argentina*, Decision on Jurisdiction and Admissibility, para. 347

[157] ICSID, ARB/08/18, *Malicorp Limited vs. Egypt*, Award, para. 110.

[158] ICSID, ARB/08/18, *Malicorp Limited vs. Egypt*, Award, para. 113, with further citations.

[159] ICSID, ARB/08/18, *Malicorp Limited vs. Egypt*, Award, para. 113.

[160] ICSID, ARB/08/16, *GEA Group Aktiengesellschaft vs. Ukraine*, Award, paras. 158–164.

[161] ICSID, ARB/08/16, *GEA Group Aktiengesellschaft vs. Ukraine*, Award, paras. 161–162.

[162] ICSID, ARB/08/16, *GEA Group Aktiengesellschaft vs. Ukraine*, Award, para. 150.

[163] ICSID, ARB/08/16, *GEA Group Aktiengesellschaft vs. Ukraine*, Award, paras. 146–153.

The *White Industries v. India* Tribunal, in the matter of an UNCITRAL arbitration, held, that, since the *Salini* test was developed to determine the existence of investment under the ICSID Convention, it was not relevant *in casu* and noted that that test requires 'a higher standard than simply resolving whether there is an "investment" for the purposes of a particular BIT'[164]. Considering a counterfactual, the Tribunal determined that even if the *Salini* test was found to be applicable, the claimant had showed that its elements were satisfied.[165] As long as the IIA does not contain a contrary stipulation, the investment does not need to be a right *in rem* or to display certain economic elements.[166] The Tribunal further held that rights established under bank guarantees do not constitute an investment, since they do not grant or create substantive rights and may accordingly not be considered an asset.[167] In contrast with the aforementioned *GEA* Tribunal's finding that an arbitral award does not constitute an investment, the *White Industries* Tribunal expressly rejecting that approach,[168] concurred with the claimant that the Award in question constituted an investment 'because it constitutes a "right to money or to any performance having a financial value, contractual or otherwise" ' and that 'rights under the Award constitute part of [the claimant's] original investment' and that, as such, they were entitled to protection under the BIT.[169]

The *Grand River Enterprises Six Nations* Tribunal[170] reached the conclusion that amounts paid into escrow accounts did not constitute an investment within the meaning of Article 1139 NAFTA, since, in the case, the obligation to respect 'escrow and other regulatory requirements existed solely because of sales of cigarettes' thus being a case of 'commercial contracts for the sale of goods or services', which typically do not constitute investment within the meaning of NAFTA Article 1139.[171]

Finally, the *Perenco v. Ecuador* Tribunal had to deal with the issue of the nationality of juridical persons as investors. It pointed out that Article 25(2)(b) ICSID Convention second sentence 'addresses the nationality of juridical persons

---

[164] UNCITRAL, *White Industries Australia Limited vs. India*, Final Award, paras. 7.4.8-7.4.9, available at: http://italaw.com/sites/default/files/case-documents/ita0906.pdf.

[165] UNCITRAL, *White Industries Australia Limited vs. India*, Final Award, para. 7.4.10, available at: http://italaw.com/sites/default/files/case-documents/ita0906.pdf.

[166] UNCITRAL, *White Industries Australia Limited vs. India*, Final Award, paras. 7.3.2-7.3.8, available at: http://italaw.com/sites/default/files/case-documents/ita0906.pdf.

[167] UNCITRAL, *White Industries Australia Limited vs. India*, Final Award, para. 7.5.7, available at: http://italaw.com/sites/default/files/case-documents/ita0906.pdf.

[168] UNCITRAL, *White Industries Australia Limited vs. India*, Final Award, paras. 7.6.7-7.6.8, available at: http://italaw.com/sites/default/files/case-documents/ita0906.pdf.

[169] UNCITRAL, *White Industries Australia Limited vs. India*, Final Award, paras. 7.6.1-7.6.10, available at: http://italaw.com/sites/default/files/case-documents/ita0906.pdf.

[170] *Grand River Enterprises Six Nations, Ltd., et al. vs. United States of America*, Award, available at: http://italaw.com/sites/default/files/case-documents/ita0384.pdf.

[171] *Grand River Enterprises Six Nations, Ltd., et al. vs. United States of America*, Award, paras. 114–116, available at: http://italaw.com/sites/default/files/case-documents/ita0384.pdf.

created under the law of the Contracting State party to the dispute. Although the Convention recognizes that any such person has the nationality of the Contracting State party to the dispute, it can be treated as a national of another Contracting State where "because of foreign control, the parties have agreed [it] should be treated as a national of another Contracting State..." In this way the ICSID Convention provides a means for parties to agree that a national of a State that ordinarily could not bring an international claim against its own State would be granted standing under the Convention'[172].

Conduct Attributable to a State

The *White Industries v. India* Tribunal held that, in determining whether a conduct is attributable to a state within the meaning of Article 8 of the International Law Commission's Draft Articles on Responsibility of States for Internationally Wrongful Acts (hereinafter ILC Draft Articles on State Responsibility),[173] the entity's organisational structure, the manner where directors are appointed and the frequency of consultations, e.g. on pricing are irrelevant.[174] Making direct reference to the wording of Article 8 ILC Draft Articles on State Responsibility,[175] the Tribunal noted that public international law imposes a high threshold in order to determine whether the conduct of a person or a group of persons is 'controlled' or 'directed' by a state, and pointed to the *Military and Paramilitary Activities in and against Nicaragua* Judgment of the International Court of Justice (ICJ) and its test of 'effective control'[176]. The ICJ reaffirmed the latter (test of 'effective control') in the Genocide case in 2007, where it held that: '[I]t has to be proved that [the persons or groups] acted in accordance with that State's instructions or under its 'effective control.' However, it must be shown that this 'effective control' was exercised, or that the State's instructions were given, in respect of each operation in which the alleged violations occurred, not generally in respect of the overall actions taken by the persons or groups of persons having committed the violations'[177].

[172] ICSID, ARB/08/6, *Perenco Ecuador Ltd. vs. Ecuador and Empresa Estatal Petróleos del Ecuador (PETROECUADOR)*, Decision on Jurisdiction, para. 70.

[173] Art. 8 (*Conduct directed or controlled by a State*) ILC Draft Articles on State Responsibility provides: "The conduct of a person or group of persons shall be considered an act of a State under international law if the person or group of persons is in fact acting on the instructions of, or under the direction or control of, that State in carrying out the conduct."

[174] UNCITRAL, *White Industries Australia Limited vs. India*, Final Award, para. 8.1.6, available at: http://italaw.com/sites/default/files/case-documents/ita0906.pdf.

[175] UNCITRAL, *White Industries Australia Limited vs. India*, Final Award, para. 8.1.3, 8.1.7, available at: http://italaw.com/sites/default/files/case-documents/ita0906.pdf.

[176] UNCITRAL, *White Industries Australia Limited vs. India*, Final Award, paras. 8.1.10 et seq., available at: http://italaw.com/sites/default/files/case-documents/ita0906.pdf; See ICJ, *The Republic of Nicaragua vs. The United States of America*, ICJ Reports (1986), pp. 116 et seq.

[177] UNCITRAL, *White Industries Australia Limited vs. India*, Final Award, para. 8.1.14, available at: http://italaw.com/sites/default/files/case-documents/ita0906.pdf; See ICJ, *Bosnia and*

The *White Industries* Tribunal proceeded to consider the ICJ's test of 'effective control' as transposed to the *Jan de Nul N.V. and Dredging Intemational N.V. v. Egypt* arbitration, where the Tribunal stated that '[i]nternational jurisprudence is very demanding in order to attribute the act of a person or entity to a State, as it requires both a general control of the State over the person or entity and a specific control of the State over the act the attribution of which is at stake; this is known as the 'effective control' test'[178].

Following on from this analysis, the *White Industries* Tribunal concluded that for the wrongful conduct of an entity to give rise to the responsibility of a state, the latter should be shown to have both general control over the entity and specific control over the acts in question.[179]

In the *GEA Group v. Ukraine* case, the Tribunal decided that acts (a misrepresentation) committed by separate legal entities acting in a commercial capacity and independent of the state are not attributable to the latter.[180] Finally, in determining a claim not directly concerning whether the act was attributable to the state, rather whether there was a legal act (measure) in the first place, the *Commerce Group v. El Salvador* Tribunal considered that a mining ban policy and the revocation of the relevant permits did not constitute a measure *per se*; rather the ban was 'a policy of the Government as opposed to a "measure" taken by it'[181]. By contrast, the Tribunal decided, the revocation of environmental permits pursuant to that government policy 'squarely constitutes a measure'[182].

The attribution of acts to states was also elaborated in the *Paushok, et al.* adjudication, with the Tribunal deciding, *inter alia*, that a state may be held liable under an investment treaty 'in connection with legislation passed by its legislative body', unless otherwise provided in that treaty.[183] Acts by state entities and not organs of the state may also be attributable to a state, if the acts are *de iure imperii*.[184] As in the *White*

Herzegowina vs. Serbia and Montenegro (Application of the Convention and Punishment of Genocide), International Legal Materials 46 (2007) 2, pp. 185 et seq.

178 UNCITRAL, *White Industries Australia Limited vs. India*, Final Award, para. 8.1.16, available at: http://italaw.com/sites/default/files/case-documents/ita0906.pdf; ICSID, ARB/04/13, *Jan de Nul N.V. and Dredging Intemational N.V. vs. Egypt*, Award.

179 UNCITRAL, *White Industries Australia Limited vs. India*, Final Award, paras. 8.1.18, available at: http://italaw.com/sites/default/files/case-documents/ita0906.pdf.

180 ICSID, ARB/08/16, *GEA Group Aktiengesellschaft vs. Ukraine*, Award, paras. 262 et seq.

181 ICSID, ARB/09/17, *Commerce Group Corp. and San Sebastian Gold Mines*, Inc. vs. El Salvador, Award, para. 112.

182 ICSID, ARB/09/17, *Commerce Group Corp. and San Sebastian Gold Mines*, Inc. vs. El Salvador, Award, para. 112.

183 UNCITRAL, *Sergei Paushok, CJSC Golden East Company and CJSC Vostokneftegaz Company vs. Mongolia*, Award on Jurisdiction and Liability, para. 298, see also para. 299, available at: http://italaw.com/documents/PaushokAward.pdf.

184 UNCITRAL, *Sergei Paushok, CJSC Golden East Company and CJSC Vostokneftegaz Company vs. Mongolia*, Award on Jurisdiction and Liability, paras. 574 et seq., available at: http://italaw.com/documents/PaushokAward.pdf.

Industries Award (see above), the Tribunal pointed out the need to examine whether the actions of the entity in question may be attributed to the state 'under the international law rules of attribution' and for this purpose it made direct reference to Articles 4, 5 and 9 ILC Draft Articles on State Responsibility, generally deemed to reflect customary international law.[185] Finally, the Tribunal determined that even if the act by the entity in question is not in conformity with domestic law, this fact is not sufficient to release the respondent from liability under international law.[186]

Substantive Matters of International Investment Law in Arbitral Jurisprudence

Various awards of 2011 had to deal with the 'rather vague and generally worded standards of treatment'[187] provided for in IIAs. Typically, multiple standards can be found in one single article, as it is for example the case in German BIT practice.[188] A separate provision deals with the problem of expropriation and compensation in this latter instance.[189] These standards regularly include—besides expropriation—national treatment, fair and equitable treatment, full protection and security, most-favoured-nation treatment, non-impairment of the investment through arbitrary or discriminatory measures and the free transfer of capital. It is not relevant whether a measure or other conduct attributable to a state is directed against the investor or the investment, as long as there is a violation of an IIA obligation—such as the aforementioned standards—harming the investment.[190]

Law of Aliens and the Minimum Standard of Treatment

In exploring the content of Article 1105 NAFTA (fair and equitable treatment equated with the minimum international standard) the *Grand River Enterprises Six Nations* Tribunal determined that, even if a rule of customary international law enjoins host states to consult indigenous populations as collective communities, such a requirement would not hold for individual investors[191] and even if it did 'it

---

[185] UNCITRAL, *Sergei Paushok, CJSC Golden East Company and CJSC Vostokneftegaz Company vs. Mongolia*, Award on Jurisdiction and Liability, para. 576, available at: http://italaw.com/documents/PaushokAward.pdf.

[186] UNCITRAL, *Sergei Paushok, CJSC Golden East Company and CJSC Vostokneftegaz Company vs. Mongolia*, Award on Jurisdiction and Liability, para. 606, available at: http://italaw.com/documents/PaushokAward.pdf.

[187] Reinisch, Preface, in: Reinisch (ed.), *Standards of Investment Protection*, 2008.

[188] E.g. see Articles 2 and 3 German Model BIT (2009).

[189] See Article 4 German Model BIT (2009).

[190] ICSID, ARB/06/1, *Spyridon Roussalis vs. Romania*, Award, para. 594.

[191] *Grand River Enterprises Six Nations, Ltd., et al. vs. United States of America*, Award, paras. 210 et seq., 213, available at: http://italaw.com/sites/default/files/case-documents/ita0384.pdf.

would be difficult to construe such a rule as part of the customary minimum standard of protection that must be accorded to every foreign investment pursuant to Article 1105 NAFTA. The notion of specialized procedural rights protecting some investors, but not others, cannot readily be reconciled with the idea of a minimum customary standard of treatment due to all investments'[192].

The same Tribunal further determined that neither Article 1105 NAFTA nor customary international law offer a general prohibition of discrimination against foreign investments.[193]

Non-Impairment of Investment by Arbitrary or Discriminatory Measures

With reference to the requirement that a host state does not impair the investment with arbitrary or discriminatory measures, the *Spyridon Roussalis* Tribunal reasoned, quoting the *Saluka* and *Rumeli* Tribunals, that the non-impairment standard is not violated where 'the conduct *"bears a reasonable relationship to some rational policy, whereas the standard of "non-discrimination" requires a rational justification of any differential treatment of a foreign investor"* '[194]. On the topic of non-discrimination in another case, the *Paushok, et al.* Tribunal stated that 'the "non-impairment" standard does not provide a blanket protection for investors against any measure that might be adopted by the State'[195].

With respect to taxation measures differentiating between industry sectors or between products within the same sector, the *Paushok, et al.* Tribunal observed that tax legislation in many countries 'treats various industries differently from one another' and 'there is nothing in the Treaty or in international law which generally prohibits' a host state from imposing different tax regimes on different industry sectors.[196] Under these circumstances, the Tribunal concluded that the differential treatment of different industries did not constitute 'illegal discrimination'[197]. By the same token, the Tribunal held that the differential tax regime regulating two different products (gold and copper) within the same sector did not give rise to a violation of the

---

[192] *Grand River Enterprises Six Nations, Ltd., et al. vs. United States of America*, Award, para. 213, see also paras. 214–215, available at: http://italaw.com/sites/default/files/case-documents/ita0384.pdf.

[193] *Grand River Enterprises Six Nations, Ltd., et al. vs. United States of America*, Award, paras. 15, 208–209, available at: http://italaw.com/sites/default/files/case-documents/ita0384.pdf.

[194] ICSID, ARB/06/1, *Spyridon Roussalis vs. Romania*, Award, para. 594.

[195] UNCITRAL, *Sergei Paushok, CJSC Golden East Company and CJSC Vostokneftegaz Company vs. Mongolia*, Award on Jurisdiction and Liability, para. 307, available at: http://italaw.com/documents/PaushokAward.pdf.

[196] UNCITRAL, *Sergei Paushok, CJSC Golden East Company and CJSC Vostokneftegaz Company vs. Mongolia*, Award on Jurisdiction and Liability, para. 310, available at: http://italaw.com/documents/PaushokAward.pdf.

[197] UNCITRAL, *Sergei Paushok, CJSC Golden East Company and CJSC Vostokneftegaz Company vs. Mongolia*, Award on Jurisdiction and Liability, para. 310, available at: http://italaw.com/documents/PaushokAward.pdf.

Treaty.[198] On a final question of discrimination, the *Paushok, et al.* Award stated that restrictions imposed on hiring foreign workers, including an outright ban on hiring foreign workers, do not automatically signal a treaty breach.[199]

Indirect Expropriation

In examining whether there had been an indirect expropriation, the *Spyridon Roussalis* Tribunal, adopted the *sole effect* doctrine.[200] According to this jurisprudential construct, the sole determinant of the existence of an indirect expropriation is the effect of the state measure, while state intentions in adopting it are immaterial. As did other tribunals before it, the *Spyridon Roussalis* Tribunal reasoned that 'in order to determine whether an indirect expropriation has taken place, the determination of the *effect* of the measure is the key question'[201]. In a minor digression from the sole effect doctrine, the Tribunal proceeded further to note that '[t]he intention or purpose of the State is *relevant* but is not *decisive* of the question whether there has been an expropriation'[202].

The sole effect doctrine is not the only jurisprudential doctrine employed in order to determine the existence of an indirect expropriation. On the other side of the doctrinal debate, the state police powers doctrine, in partial consistency with some provisions de-characterising a confiscatory state measure as such (e.g. Annexes to US and Canadian BITs), recognises that whatever falls within the generally-accepted police powers of a state may not constitute indirect expropriation.

Adjudicating another claim of indirect expropriation, the *El Paso* Tribunal expressed doubts regarding tax measures and the investor's legitimate expectations in the context of expropriation. More particularly, the Tribunal disagreed with the claimant that investors may hold 'a reasonable and legitimate expectation to be able to adjust their fixed assets for tax purposes in periods of high inflation' and concluded that a state is not under an obligation to 'adapt its tax regime to the best interests of foreign investors. An unfavourable calculation of taxes cannot be equated with an expropriation'[203]. It is noteworthy that in that case the claimant had not quantified its alleged losses.[204]

---

[198] UNCITRAL, *Sergei Paushok, CJSC Golden East Company and CJSC Vostokneftegaz Company vs. Mongolia*, Award on Jurisdiction and Liability, para. 311, available at: http://italaw.com/documents/PaushokAward.pdf.

[199] UNCITRAL, *Sergei Paushok, CJSC Golden East Company and CJSC Vostokneftegaz Company vs. Mongolia*, Award on Jurisdiction and Liability, para. 364, available at: http://italaw.com/documents/PaushokAward.pdf.

[200] ICSID, ARB/06/1, *Spyridon Roussalis vs. Romania*, Award, paras. 328–330.

[201] ICSID, ARB/06/1, *Spyridon Roussalis vs. Romania*, Award, para. 328, emphasis added.

[202] ICSID, ARB/06/1, *Spyridon Roussalis vs. Romania*, Award, para. 330, emphasis added.

[203] ICSID, ARB/03/15, *El Paso Energy International Company vs. Argentina*, Award, para. 295.

[204] ICSID, ARB/03/15, *El Paso Energy International Company vs. Argentina*, Award, para. 295.

Fair and Equitable Treatment

The fair and equitable treatment standard (FET) has evolved to become probably the most-frequently applied as well as discussed[205] standard in international investment practice. FET is an absolute and general standard and it has continued to be interpreted in a flexible and potentially unpredictable manner, with a variable—and expanding—geometry of potential coverage.[206]

The investor's legitimate expectations were discussed at length in several recent awards. The *White Industries* Award disagreed with the *Tecmed* dictum that the fair and equitable treatment standard enjoins a state to treat investment in a way that it 'does not affect the *basic expectations that were taken into account* by the foreign investor to make the investment'[207] and cited Newcombe and Paradell to the effect that, *inter alia*, '[investment treaty] jurisprudence highlights that, to create legitimate expectations, State conduct needs to be specific and unambiguous. Encouraging remarks from government officials do not by themselves give rise to legitimate expectations. There must be an 'unambiguous affirmation' or a 'definitive, unambiguous and repeated assurances''[208].

On the basis of the above analysis, the *White Industries* Tribunal found that the alleged representations to the claimant were general and vague and as such they did not give rise to 'reasonable legitimate expectations' that would fall within the protection of the fair and equitable treatment,[209] while it further accepted that undue delay to rule on a dispute may amount to a denial of justice, although it did not find that the facts of the case pointed to denial of justice.[210]

Another novel contribution to the interpretation of the fair and equitable treatment standard is offered by the *El Paso* Tribunal.[211] Adjudicating in the context of a dispute involving Argentina's crisis, the Tribunal introduced the concept of 'creeping' violation of the fair and equitable treatment. It defined the creeping violation of the FET standard as 'a process extending over time and comprising a succession or

---

[205] For some recent publications, see for example Kläger, *'Fair and Equitable Treatment' in International Investment Law*, 2011; Tudor, *The Fair and Equitable Treatment Standard in the International Law of Foreign Investment*, 2008; UNCTAD, Fair and Equitable Treatment: A Sequel, UNCTAD Series on Issues in International Investment Agreements II, 2012.

[206] UNCTAD, Latest Developments in Investor-State Dispute Settlement, IIA Issues Note, No. 1, April 2012, p. 7, available at: http://www.unctad.org/diae.

[207] UNCITRAL, *White Industries Australia Limited vs. India*, Final Award, para. 10.3.5, citing the *Tecmed* Award, footnote omitted, emphasis in original; see also paras. 10.3.6 et seq., available at: http://italaw.com/sites/default/files/case-documents/ita0906.pdf.

[208] UNCITRAL, *White Industries Australia Limited vs. India*, Final Award, para. 10.3.7, footnote omitted, available at: http://italaw.com/sites/default/files/case-documents/ita0906.pdf.

[209] UNCITRAL, *White Industries Australia Limited vs. India*, Final Award, paras. 10.3.17, 10.3.9 et seq., available at: http://italaw.com/sites/default/files/case-documents/ita0906.pdf.

[210] UNCITRAL, *White Industries Australia Limited vs. India*, Final Award, paras. 10.4.5 et seq., available at: http://italaw.com/sites/default/files/case-documents/ita0906.pdf.

[211] ICSID, ARB/03/15, *El Paso Energy International Company vs. Argentina*, Award.

an accumulation of measures which, taken separately, would not breach that standard but, when taken together, do lead to such a result'[212]. In keeping with this reasoning, although the measures adopted by Argentina when seen in isolation were not found to violate the fair and equitable treatment standard, the Tribunal considered, as in the case of creeping expropriation, that the cumulative effect of these measures—the latter being seen as a 'composite act'[213]—was tantamount to a violation of the FET standard.[214] In support of this finding, the Tribunal had noted earlier in the Award that although this series of measures 'may be seen in isolation as reasonable measures to cope with a difficult economic situation, the measures examined can be viewed as cumulative steps which individually do not qualify as violations of FET [. . .] but which amount to a violation if their cumulative effect is considered. It is quite possible to hold [. . .] that a combination of all these measures completely altered the overall framework'[215].

Notably, on the question of the relationship between the fair and equitable treatment and the minimum standard of treatment, the *El Paso* Tribunal had deemed the 'discussion to be somewhat futile, as the scope and content of the minimum standard of international law is as little defined as the BITs' FET standard, and as the true question is to decide what substantive protection is granted to foreign investors through the FET. The issue is not one of comparing two undefined or weakly defined standards; it is to ascertain the content and define the BIT standard of fair and equitable treatment'[216]. However, 'the position according to which FET is equivalent to the international minimum standard is more in line with the evolution of investment law and international law and with the identical role assigned to FET and to the international minimum standard'[217].

The *El Paso* Tribunal further linked the FET standard to 'the objective reasonable legitimate expectations of the investors' and noted that these '*can only be examined by having due regard to the general proposition that the State should not unreasonably modify the legal framework or modify it in contradiction with a specific commitment not to do so*'[218]. The Tribunal reasoned that the fair and equitable treatment standard requires that there shall be no *unreasonable* or *unjustified* alteration of the host state's legal landscape, provided that no contrary 'specific commitments' have been made to the investor.[219] The Tribunal was at

[212] ICSID, ARB/03/15, *El Paso Energy International Company vs. Argentina*, Award, para. 518.

[213] ICSID, ARB/03/15, *El Paso Energy International Company vs. Argentina*, Award, see para. 516.

[214] ICSID, ARB/03/15, *El Paso Energy International Company vs. Argentina*, Award, para. 519.

[215] ICSID, ARB/03/15, *El Paso Energy International Company vs. Argentina*, Award, para. 515.

[216] ICSID, ARB/03/15, *El Paso Energy International Company vs. Argentina*, Award, para. 335.

[217] ICSID, ARB/03/15, *El Paso Energy International Company vs. Argentina*, Award, para. 336, footnote omitted.

[218] ICSID, ARB/03/15, *El Paso Energy International Company vs. Argentina*, Award, para. 364, *framework or modify*.

[219] ICSID, ARB/03/15, *El Paso Energy International Company vs. Argentina*, Award, paras. 365 et seq.

pains to stress that the FET standard does not guarantee the stability of the legal and business framework within which investors operate.[220] Indeed, it is not 'the BITs' purpose that States guarantee that the economic and legal conditions in which investments take place will remain unaltered *ad infinitum*'[221] nor does the fair and equitable treatment standard 'play the role assumed by stabilisation clauses'[222]. The Tribunal went on further to describe the FET standard as one that entails 'reasonableness and proportionality'[223] and reiterated that '[t]here can be no legitimate expectation for anyone that the legal framework will remain unchanged in the face of an extremely severe economic crisis. No reasonable investor can have such an expectation unless very specific commitments have been made towards it or unless the alteration of the legal framework is total'[224].

In some respects, the *El Paso* Award echoes the decision of another recent Tribunal adjudicating an Argentine dispute. The *Total* Tribunal noted that 'changes to general legislation, in the absence of specific stabilization promises to the foreign investor, reflect a legitimate exercise of the host State's governmental powers that are not prevented by a BIT's fair and equitable treatment standard and are not in breach of the same'[225]. In the same context, the *Total* Tribunal further stressed '[t]he host State's right to regulate domestic matters in the public interest'[226]. Furthermore, in this case, Herrera Marcano questioned whether the fair and equitable treatment contains the investor's legitimate expectations.[227]

The investors' legitimate expectations were further discussed in detail in other recent awards. Following in the steps of the above as well as earlier arbitral jurisprudence, such as the 2007 *Parkerings-Compagniet* Award,[228] in examining the investor's legitimate expectations in the context of the fair and equitable treatment, the *Impregilo* Tribunal determined that, although foreign investors need to be protected from 'unreasonable modifications' of the host state's regulatory framework, the investor's legitimate expectations 'cannot be that the State

[220] See ICSID, ARB/03/15, *El Paso Energy International Company vs. Argentina*, Award, paras. 350, 365 et seq.

[221] ICSID, ARB/03/15, *El Paso Energy International Company vs. Argentina*, Award, para. 350, see also para. 352.

[222] ICSID, ARB/03/15, *El Paso Energy International Company vs. Argentina*, Award, para. 368.

[223] ICSID, ARB/03/15, *El Paso Energy International Company vs. Argentina*, Award, para. 373.

[224] ICSID, ARB/03/15, *El Paso Energy International Company vs. Argentina*, Award, para. 374.

[225] ICSID, ARB/04/1, *Total S.A. vs. Argentine Republic*, Decision on Liability, para. 164, footnote omitted, see also para. 117.

[226] ICSID, ARB/04/1, *Total S.A. vs. Argentine Republic*, Decision on Liability, para. 123.

[227] See Peterson, "Co-arbitrators in Total v. Argentina case take widely-divergent views of Argentina's Fair and Equitable Treatment obligation under investment treaty," IA Reporter, 11 April 2011.

[228] ICSID, ARB/05/8, *Parkerings-Compagniet AS vs. The Republic of Lithuania*, Award, para. 332.

will never modify the legal framework, especially in times of crisis'[229]. However, the Tribunal ended by finding a violation of the fair and equitable treatment standard. In another case that examined the investor's legitimate expectations, the *Paushok, et al.* Tribunal ended by finding no violation of the fair and equitable treatment standard. Similarly with the *Parkerings-Compagniet* and the *Impregilo* Awards, the *Paushok, et al.* Tribunal observed that the investor may not hold a legitimate expectation to the effect that 'investors cannot legitimately expect that the taxation environment which they face at the time of their first investment will not be substantially altered with the passage of time and the evolution of events'[230]. Further echoing the *Parkerings-Compagniet* Tribunal,[231] the *Paushok, et al.* Award indicated that, should an investor wish to be shielded against changes in host state legislation, it must seek a 'stability agreement'[232].

Finally, another decision worth quoting in the context of the FET standard analysis is that of the *Malicorp* Tribunal,[233] which determined that an allegation of expropriation already implies an unfair and inequitable treatment; thus, an additional allegation of breach of the fair and equitable treatment has to be based on another state measure. In particular, the Tribunal noted that 'when an investor bases its action principally on the fact that it has been the victim of an expropriation, that measure necessarily implies treatment that was, precisely, neither fair nor equitable. In order to rely on both provisions, the investor must be able to establish that it has also been the victim of other measures, different from expropriation'[234].

Full Protection and Security

On the issue of full protection and security, the *Spyridon Roussalis* Tribunal endorsed earlier jurisprudence by confirming that the standard that 'does not create absolute liability'[235], further observing that full protection and security extends

[229] ICSID, ARB/07/17, *Impregilo S.p.A. vs. Argentina*, Award, para. 291.

[230] UNCITRAL, *Sergei Paushok, CJSC Golden East Company and CJSC Vostokneftegaz Company vs. Mongolia*, Award on Jurisdiction and Liability, para. 370, available at: http://italaw.com/documents/PaushokAward.pdf.

[231] ICSID, ARB/05/8, *Parkerings-Compagniet AS vs. The Republic of Lithuania*, Award, para. 332.

[232] UNCITRAL, *Sergei Paushok, CJSC Golden East Company and CJSC Vostokneftegaz Company vs. Mongolia*, Award on Jurisdiction and Liability, para. 370, available at: http://italaw.com/documents/PaushokAward.pdf. See also ICSID, ARB/05/8, *Parkerings-Compagniet AS vs. The Republic of Lithuania*, Award, para. 332 and ICSID, ARB/04/1, *Total S.A. vs. Argentina*, Decision on Liability, para. 117.

[233] ICSID, ARB/08/18, *Malicorp Limited vs. Egypt*, Award.

[234] ICSID, ARB/08/18, *Malicorp Limited vs. Egypt*, Award, para. 124.

[235] ICSID, ARB/06/1, *Spyridon Roussalis vs. Romania*, Award, para. 322; for the earlier jurisprudence cited by the Tribunal: *Elettronica Sicula Spa (ELSI), AAPL vs. Sri Lanka, Tecmed vs. Mexico, Noble Ventures vs. Romania, Rumeli vs. Kazakhstan* and *American Manufacturing & Trading vs. Republic of Zaire*.

'beyond safeguard from physical violence and requires *legal* protection for the investor'[236]. Another 2011 Tribunal, in the *Paushok, et al.* case, adjudicating on the basis of treaty language providing specifically for 'full *legal* protection and security', came to very similar conclusions regarding the requirement for legal as well as physical protection of investments.[237] The *El Paso* Tribunal in its turn, determined that 'the full protection and security standard is no more than the traditional obligation to protect aliens under international customary law and that it is a residual obligation provided for those cases in which the acts challenged may not themselves be attributed to the Government, but to a third party'[238]. *Inter alia*, on the authority of earlier awards,[239] both the *Paushok, et al.* Tribunal and the later *El Paso* Tribunal noted in verbatim language that the full protection and security standard 'imposes an obligation of vigilance and due diligence upon the government'[240]. As regards the 'minimum standard of vigilance and care set by international law,' again both Tribunals noted that the latter 'comprises a duty of prevention and a duty of repression' and that states must exercise ' "due diligence" to prevent wrongful injuries to the person or property of aliens' caused by third parties within their territory, and, 'if they did not succeed, to exercise at least "due diligence" to punish such injuries'[241]. The *Paushok, et al.* and *El Paso* Tribunals further emphasised that the obligation to show "due diligence" does not enjoin the state to prevent every possible injury; '[r]ather, the obligation is generally understood as requiring that the State take reasonable actions within its power to avoid injury when it is, or should be, aware that there is a risk of injury'[242].

[236] ICSID, ARB/06/1, *Spyridon Roussalis vs. Romania*, Award, para. 321, further citing the *Biwater Gauff Tribunal*, emphasis added.

[237] UNCITRAL, *Sergei Paushok, CJSC Golden East Company and CJSC Vostokneftegaz Company vs. Mongolia*, Award on Jurisdiction and Liability, para. 326, available at: http://italaw.com/documents/PaushokAward.pdf.

[238] ICSID, ARB/03/15, *El Paso Energy International Company vs. Argentina*, Award, para. 522.

[239] ICSID, ARB/87/3, *AAPL vs. Sri Lanka and ICSID*, ARB/93/1, *American Manufacturing & Trading vs. Republic of Zaire*, also cited by the Tribunal in ICSID, ARB/06/1, *Spyridon Roussalis vs. Romania*.

[240] UNCITRAL, *Sergei Paushok, CJSC Golden East Company and CJSC Vostokneftegaz Company vs. Mongolia*, Award on Jurisdiction and Liability, para. 323, available at: http://italaw.com/documents/PaushokAward.pdf; ICSID, ARB/03/15, *El Paso Energy International Company vs. Argentina*, Award, para. 522. The two Tribunals shared Brigitte Stern as arbitrator.

[241] UNCITRAL, *Sergei Paushok, CJSC Golden East Company and CJSC Vostokneftegaz Company vs. Mongolia*, Award on Jurisdiction and Liability, para. 324, available at: http://italaw.com/documents/PaushokAward.pdf; ICSID, ARB/03/15, *El Paso Energy International Company vs. Argentina*, Award, 31 October 2011, para. 523.

[242] UNCITRAL, *Sergei Paushok, CJSC Golden East Company and CJSC Vostokneftegaz Company vs. Mongolia*, Award on Jurisdiction and Liability, para. 325, available at: http://italaw.com/documents/PaushokAward.pdf; ICSID, ARB/03/15, *El Paso Energy International Company vs. Argentina*, Award, para. 523.

Interpretation of the Essential Security Interests Exception

In determining the meaning of the essential security interests exception in the US-Argentina BIT, the *El Paso* Award[243] comes to be added to the set of Argentine decisions that essentially side-step the treaty-based exception in order to employ requirements found in the, however different, necessity defence under customary international law. The *El Paso* Tribunal employed the principle of systemic integration to import *one* of the requirements of necessity under customary law, that of state non-contribution to the state of necessity, into the essential security interests exception in the US-Argentina BIT.[244] As a result, the Tribunal rejected Argentina's relevant defence.[245] Annulment proceedings have already been instituted in the context of the *El Paso* Award.

Conclusion and Outlook

Bearing in mind the initiated arbitrations, the near future will probably reveal new issues in international investment law. While it is uncertain how resurgence of financial turbulence in Europe may affect international investment, and the cases that may result from it—the issue may prove of particular significance in that, should cases arise, they will open Pandora's Box of questions on the interaction between EU law and international investment law –, another movement, the Arab Spring has already produced its first cases. What these recent and initiated cases have in common is that they raise questions around essential security interests and, in the case of the *Philip Morris* and *Vattenfall* cases, regulation in the public interest involving health and environmental issues. A new potential emphasis placed on the balance of interests between investors and host states and on the right to regulate will probably dominate the debate on future investment treaties as in international investment arbitration. Finally, it will remain interesting to watch out for developments regarding the future conclusion of more plurilateral investment agreements as well as the evolution and developments in the still new field of EU investment policy.

[243] ICSID, ARB/03/15, *El Paso Energy International Company vs. Argentina*, Award.

[244] ICSID, ARB/03/15, *El Paso Energy International Company vs. Argentina*, Award, paras. 552 et seq.

[245] ICSID, ARB/03/15, *El Paso Energy International Company vs. Argentina*, Award, para. 665.

The Future of the Doha Development Agenda

Edwini Kessie

Introduction

For many observers, the Doha Round cannot be concluded in the form it was originally envisaged by WTO Members in November 2001. Some even go as far as to say that the Doha Round has been dead for some time[1] and that the stench will become too powerful to conceal with the passing of time and that individual WTO Members, particularly the key players, just do not want to admit for fear of being blamed for its demise. The failure of the April 2011 texts[2] to gain any traction among the Members and encourage them to work hard to bridge their differences signaled that the Eighth WTO Ministerial Conference in December 2011 was not going to produce any breakthrough in the negotiations and that, if anything at all, it was going to confirm what had been obvious all along that the Round was beyond redemption and that it was high time to think seriously about the next steps. Pretending that the Round was alive and that it could be concluded on the basis

The views expressed in this paper are those of the author and should not in any way be attributed to the OCTA or the WTO.

[1] Lehmann, End the Charade in Talks on Global Trade, Financial Times, 24 August 2011.

[2] The April 2011 texts were comprehensive and presented a complete picture of where the negotiations stood in different areas. As noted by WTO Director-General Pascal Lamy: "This document is the product of work since the launch of the negotiations in 2001. For the first time in 10 years, Members have had the opportunity to consider the entire Doha package in all market access and regulatory areas. The package includes texts in areas where these had not been possible before. It reflects extensive work in vital technical issues and presents options that show the commitment and creativity of negotiators. In sum, the documents leave no-one in doubt about the value of what is on the table, but also reveals the issues that still divide Members": Report of WTO Director General to the Ministerial Conference, WT/MIN(11)/5; 18 November 2011, p. 4.

E. Kessie (✉)
Chief Trade Adviser, Office of the Chief Trade Adviser (OCTA), Independence Park, PO Box 561, Port Vila, Vanuatu
e-mail: ekessie@octapic.org

C. Herrmann et al. (eds.), *European Yearbook of International Economic Law (EYIEL), Vol. 4 (2013)*, European Yearbook of International Economic Law 4,
DOI 10.1007/978-3-642-33917-2_18, © Springer-Verlag Berlin Heidelberg 2013

of the single undertaking was wishful thinking and did not reflect the reality on the ground.

The Eighth Ministerial conference was unremarkable in that no key decisions on the Doha Round were made. The Declaration acknowledged the different perspectives on the possibility of achieving results in all areas of the single undertaking and stated that it was "unlikely that all elements of the Doha Development Round could be concluded simultaneously in the future."[3] It further also encouraged WTO Members to explore other negotiating strategies, while respecting the principles of transparency and inclusiveness.[4] In effect, the Declaration signaled the death of the single undertaking approach and gave the nod for countries to explore the possibility of concluding individual agreements, where possible, pursuant to paragraph 47 of the Doha Ministerial Declaration (paragraph 47),[5] or arguably plurilateral agreements that not all WTO Members would be signatories. Since then, some WTO Members have been exploring the possibility of concluding a plurilateral agreement on trade in services.[6] With such a development, it is clear that it would be extremely difficult to revive the Doha Round when the fundamental differences over the negotiating issues continue to persist.

In his report to the General Council on 25 July 2012, the WTO Director-General, Mr. Pascal Lamy, recalled the views of some WTO Members that whatever outcomes were agreed pursuant to paragraph 47 did not imply the end of the Doha Round.[7] While it is technically possible for agreements to be reached on all the negotiating subjects at separate times, it is highly unlikely that would happen. One of the main advantages of the single undertaking approach is that it encourages countries to agree to tradeoffs in order to reach agreements. Thus, in evaluating the overall balance of a package, countries would look not only at the internal balance in each agreement, but across all the negotiated agreements to decide whether a careful balance has been struck between competing interests. Should linkages not be made between negotiating issues, it would be more difficult for agreements to be reached, as most countries would like to see internal balance in each and every agreement which, in practice, is difficult to achieve unless the negotiating parties have common interests.

The current stalemate in the negotiations is mainly because some countries believe that a number of the draft texts on the table lack internal balance and inadvertently promote the interests of one group over the other. With this prevailing view, it is difficult to see how abandoning the single undertaking will make it any easier for agreements to be reached. In the case of agriculture, some developed

[3] WTO, Elements for Political Guidance, WT/MIN(11)/W/2; 1 December 2011, p. 3.

[4] WTO, Elements for Political Guidance, WT/MIN(11)/W/2; 1 December 2011, p. 3.

[5] WTO, Elements for Political Guidance, WT/MIN(11)/W/2; 1 December 2011, p. 3.

[6] See, for example, http://www.exportnz.org.nz/news-and-info/features/trade-update-services-trade-negotiations-to-go-plurilateral. See further, WTO official Argues Against Services Plurilateral Favoured by the US in Inside US Trade, 16 December 2011.

[7] http://www.wto.org/english/news_e/news12_e/gc_rpt_25jul12_e.htm.

countries are of the view that there are too many exceptions for developing country Members, particularly the emerging economies and would like to see stringent rules governing, for example, when developing countries can have recourse to the proposed special safeguard mechanism. By contrast, some developing countries believe that given the substantial subsidies provided by developed country Members to support their agriculture sector, they will need to protect their farmers through a mix of high tariffs, designating as many products as special and sensitive in order to make no or minimal tariff cuts and the use of the special safeguard mechanism in times of import surges or significant price declines. With respect to the non-agricultural market access negotiations, there is a fundamental difference in view as to the level of commitments to be assumed by the emerging economies in the sectoral negotiations. These intractable issues will remain regardless of whether they are negotiated separately or together with other issues in different negotiating areas.

By contrast, progress can be made on certain negotiating issues, if participation is limited to like-minded countries. An example is the plurilateral initiative on trade in services being led by the United States. Currently, there are 17 WTO Members counting the EU-27 as one participating in the discussions, 21 namely Australia, Canada, Chile, Chinese Taipei, Costa Rica, Colombia, European Union, Hong Kong (China), Israel, Japan, Mexico, New Zealand, Norway, Pakistan, Panama, Peru, Singapore, South Korea, Switzerland, Turkey and United States. The value of this initiative has been questioned when key emerging economies such as Brazil, China, India, Russia and South Africa, whose share in services trade is rising very fast, will not be participating in it.[8] Proponents argue that since the participating countries account for around 70 % of global services trade, an agreement will not be a symbolic one but one that would have teeth, especially if they assume far-reaching obligations comparable to those assumed by Korea and the United States under their free trade agreement.

There is the belief among the participating countries that the emerging countries would see the logic in joining once the agreement enters into force. The emerging countries have thus far not shown any inclination of joining the plurilateral negotiations, mainly because they still have hope that the Doha Round can be revived with the single undertaking at its core, provided there was sufficient political will.[9] Being the leaders of developing countries, their joining the plurilateral negotiations would be seen as an act of betrayal by most developing countries, particularly the LDCs who increasingly are relying on them to further their interests in the multilateral trading system. Further, there is the perception that

[8] See, for example, http://www.exportnz.org.nz/news-and-info/features/trade-update-services-trade-negotiations-to-go-plurilateral. See further, WTO official Argues Against Services Plurilateral Favoured by the US in Inside US Trade, 16 December 2011.

[9] See reported comments of the Ambassador of Brazil to the WTO, Mr. Roberto Azevedo, that Brazil does not support the plurilateral negotiations on services, as it leaves the DDA aside and leaves no room for trade-offs: http://itrade.gov.il/switzerland/plurilateral-trade-agreements-session-by-the-graduate-institute.

as the developed countries are the demandeurs of liberalisation of services trade, they should give concessions in other areas, particularly agriculture. In effect, they believe that their chances of getting a better deal are much greater when the agreement is negotiated multilaterally rather than plurilaterally. A high-ranking official from the European Union has cast doubts on the long-term sustainability and benefits of an agreement without the participation of the emerging economies.[10]

A strict interpretation of paragraph 47 will seem to exclude plurilateral agreements and also agreements on issues that are not covered under the Doha Declaration. What is envisaged under this paragraph is the possibility of WTO Members implementing an agreement on any of the negotiating issues ahead of the rest. It is implicit that all WTO Members would be signatories to that agreement. Conscious of this limitation, the 21 WTO Members participating in the plurilateral services initiative have signaled their intention to invoke Article V as the basis of any eventual agreement. Thus, in the absence of a fully-fledged regional trade agreement, plurilateral negotiations cannot be launched, unless there is explicit authorisation from the Ministerial Conference or the General Council.

While the plurilateral route can eventually strengthen the multilateral trading system when more countries subsequently accede to the agreement or when the benefits are multilateralised as was the case under the Information Technology Agreement, it would eventually result in the dismembering of the Doha Round. Should a plurilateral agreement on services be concluded and the results not multilateralised, the parties would be unlikely to admit new countries unless they are prepared to match the concessions that they gave or go beyond them. Where the results are multilateralised, it would be in their interests to get concessions, whatever the level, from the aspiring entrants who even without any concessions would be entitled to the benefits under the agreement anyway.

It is clear from the foregoing that both alternatives cannot be perfect substitutes for the single undertaking approach. The pursuit of any of them would ultimately make it difficult for WTO Members to revive and conclude the Doha Round.

Why Has It Been Difficult to Conclude the Doha Round?

The question that is now being asked is why have WTO Members given up on the Doha Round, which at its inception, was presented as a key element in strengthening the multilateral trading system and making it relevant to the needs of the twenty-first century and reviving the slumping global economy, which had

---

[10] See comments of Mr. Marc Vanheukelen, Head of Cabinet of the European Union's Trade Directorate, reported in the Washington Trade Daily. See further http://www.ecipe.org/media/publication_pdfs/ISA-revised30mar.pdf and http://www.mutrap.org.vn/en/Newsletter/Doha%20Round%20Bulletin%20Vol.%201-2%202012.pdf.

faced a severe assault following the September 2001 attacks. The argument has been advanced that we are living in a different world to the one that was in existence when the Round was launched.[11] The Round could have helped revive the global economy had it been concluded by 1 January 2005, as had been envisaged in the Ministerial Declaration. By not meeting that deadline, and with so many events having taken place since then to fundamentally alter the character of the global economy, the Round has little contribution to make, hence the indifference by countries that were once its champions.

According to this theory, events such as the global financial crisis in 2008 have made countries to look inward for solutions to their economic problems. The debt crisis engulfing many Western European countries has focused the attention of the European Union on saving the "Euro" rather than on the Doha Round that, for many European citizens, is inconsequential. The United States is coping with high unemployment rates and trade with countries such as China and India is being blamed for the loss of jobs. With elections around the corner, it would be difficult for the United States Administration to push for the conclusion of the Round, assuming it was even satisfied with what was on the table. Major developing countries such as Brazil, China, India, and South Africa have grown their economies in the intervening period and have avoided to some extent the economic problems of their developed counterparts. These countries believe that they are being asked to do too much in the Doha Round and that some of the proposals would threaten their future growth and economic development, hence their opposition, for example, to proposals on sectoral negotiations in NAMA tabled by the developed countries. They believe that the relevant industries that would be affected by the sectoral agreements are still growing and that it would be necessary to shield them from competition until such time that they mature. Likewise, they are opposed to proposals that would curtail their rights to impose export duties and other related measures to ensure the availability of cheaper raw materials to their local industries.

Some developing countries are also concerned about rising food prices and would like broad flexibility to adopt policies that would ensure their long-term food security. There is also the concern about the competitive devaluation of currencies by the leading trading nations. Whereas the United States and the European Union have been pressuring China to allow its currency to appreciate, other emerging economies, including Brazil have also accused the United States of not doing much to boost the value of the dollar. Rounds of quantitative easing have weakened the dollar boosting American exports and hampering imports. For these emerging economies, it would be suicidal to give substantive commitments in agriculture and NAMA when their currencies are overvalued making their exports expensive and uncompetitive in international markets. There is also the concern that as a result of climate change, they would need to provide

[11] Gallagher, Challenging Opportunities for the Multilateral Trade Regime, in: Heléndez-Orliz et al. (eds.), *The Future and the WTO: Confronting the Challenges*, 2012.

subsidies to their domestic industries to develop clean technologies. As such, they are opposed to a tightening of WTO rules that would make it difficult for them to support the growth of environment-friendly industries.

It has been suggested that it was probably a mistake to make an explicit reference to development in the Doha Ministerial Declaration.[12] This has created an expectation among developing countries that the Round would automatically lead to development, which was not necessarily the case. Very much depended on supporting domestic policies adopted by countries as well as donor countries and international institutions providing adequate aid for trade to enable countries address supply-side constraints and other challenges inhibiting an increase and diversification of exports. Proponents of this view note that trade negotiations have traditionally not had development as an objective, even though trade liberalisation could boost exports and improve competitiveness with a positive impact on growth and the alleviation of poverty. There was an indirect link between trade negotiations and development, but this should not have been explicitly recognised as it has encouraged developing countries to approach the negotiations through only the prism of development.

The way the negotiations have been conducted has also been blamed for the current stalemate. The former Ambassador of Switzerland and Chairman of the NAMA Negotiating Group, Mr. Luis Wasescha, has stated that in retrospect ministerial involvement in the negotiations was a mistake.[13] Given that several of them were not technical people, it was relatively easy for them to be manipulated in taking decisions that led to gridlock in the negotiations. The bulk of the work should have been done in Geneva by the technical people who could have worked through differences and achieve a result. Once Ministers adhered to certain positions, it was difficult for the technical people to get them to reverse these positions.

The most probable cause of the stalemate in the negotiations could be the perceived gains and losses from the Round.[14] While there have been a number of studies estimating the benefits of the Doha Round to the global economy, they are inconclusive. According to the Peterson Institute for International Economics, a successfully concluded Doha Round could deliver about US$ 300 billion in additional world output, boosting markets and growth opportunities. These benefits are expected to increase over time and strengthen the global economy. The OECD also postulates that an agreement on trade facilitation could potentially reduce trade transaction costs by 9 %, through more transparent and predictable border procedures. A 1 % reduction in worldwide trade transaction costs could generate US$ 43 billion in worldwide welfare gains, of which 65 % would accrue to

[12] Ancharaz, Can the Doha Round be Saved?, in: Heléndez-Orliz et al. (eds.), *The Future and the WTO: Confronting the Challenges*, 2012.

[13] Interview with the Washington Trade Daily, 10 July 2012.

[14] See generally Kessie, The Doha Development Agenda at a Crossroads: What are the Remaining Obstacles to the Conclusion of the Round—Part III?, in: Herrmann/Terhechte (eds.), *European Yearbook of International Economic Law Vol. 3*, 2012.

developing countries. According to former Director-General Peter Sutherland, failure to conclude the Round could cost the global economy US$ 700 billion in additional income.[15]

A study conducted by the World Bank in 2005 was more cautious about the gains to be derived from the Doha Round.[16] It estimates that gains from global trade liberalisation in 2015 will only yield US$ 96 billion, with developed countries gaining US$ 80 billion and developing countries only US$ 16 billion. Given that it is estimated that developing countries could lose up to US$ 64 billion as a result of the reduction of tariffs on industrial goods alone, there is the perception and belief among some developing countries that the Doha Round is not worth the investment. It was supposed to be a development Round in the sense of putting the interests of developing countries at the core of the negotiations and ensuring that they derive significant benefits from the Round, but it appears the opposite is true, as most of the gains will accrue to developed countries. For some developed countries, the estimated gains are not substantial considering that the Trans-Pacific Partnership Agreement is expected to yield annual global income gains of US$ 295 billion, with US$ 78 billion accruing to the United States alone.[17] The Petersen Institute further postulates that a free trade agreement with countries in the Asia-Pacific region could yield potential gains of US$1.9 trillion.[18]

Whatever be the reasons for the stalemate in the Doha negotiations, there is recognition by WTO Members that a different approach is needed to save the Doha Round or salvage what is left. As alluded to earlier, they have been considering two alternative negotiating approaches, namely the conclusion and implementation of individual agreements on the basis of paragraph 47 and the conclusion of plurilateral agreements among like-minded countries that could be extended to other WTO Members at a later stage. These are addressed in turn.

New Negotiating Approaches

Early Harvest Agreements

As a general matter, concluding and implementing agreements pursuant to paragraph 47 would seem to be preferable from a multilateral perspective to plurilateral agreements in that all WTO Members will be parties to those agreements, and there

[15] http://www.project-syndicate.org/commentary/sutherland2/English.

[16] Gallagher, Challenging Opportunities for the Multilateral Trade Regime, in: Heléndez-Orliz et al. (eds.), *The Future and the WTO: Confronting the Challenges*, 2012.

[17] Petri/Plummer, The Trans-Pacific Partnership and Asia-Pacific Integration: Policy Implications. Available at: http://www.piie.com/publications/pb/pb12-16.pdf.

[18] Petri/Plummer, The Trans-Pacific Partnership and Asia-Pacific Integration: Policy Implications. Available at: http://www.piie.com/publications/pb/pb12-16.pdf.

is the implicit understanding that they will continue to work on the other negotiating issues after the implementation of the concluded agreements. However, the reality may be different as there is the possibility that some Members may not show enthusiasm for the remaining negotiations if they have more defensive interests, which could lead to the collapse of the negotiations on the outstanding issues. Even if that should happen, it would still be preferable to have agreements on some issues than to have nothing at all as is the case now with the stalemate in the Doha Round.

The experience with the Eighth Ministerial Conference has shown that it is not easy to reach agreements pursuant to paragraph 47. In the run up to the Ministerial Conference, WTO Members had initially grouped informally the negotiating issues into four categories. Category I featured issues of importance to least-developed countries, including duty-free quota-free market access with simplified rules of origin and implementation of LDC modalities to enhance their participation in services trade. Category II issues were those on which Members had identified key points of convergence and which could possibly be harvested before or at the Ministerial meeting in December. These included agricultural export subsidies, trade facilitation, and the SDT monitoring mechanism. Category III issues were those on which progress had been made but agreement hinged on the level of detail of obligations to be assumed by Members. Among the issues in this category were non-tariff barriers in the NAMA negotiations, dispute settlement and fisheries subsidies. Category IV issues were those that were difficult and in respect of which Members positions were far apart. Among the issues in this category were trade remedies and market access issues in agriculture, NAMA, and services.

After several rounds of discussions, it was suggested that work should focus on an "LDC Package," as Members were more likely to support the adoption of a raft of measures that would promote their trade. However, some Members demanded the inclusion of issues of importance to them. There were several rounds of negotiations on an "LDC Plus" package, but it became clear in no time that was not going to work. As noted by the Director-General Lamy in his Report to the Eighth Ministerial Conference:

> Following the realisation that the full DDA would not be possible by the end of the year, we embarked on a process aimed at delivering a smaller package by the Eighth Ministerial Conference. It was understood that this was not going to be the final package, but rather a step forward to demonstrate with facts that we could deliver on the entire DDA at a later stage. From the start, it was clear that Least-developed Countries (LDCs) issues were a priority. But some Members felt that this component alone would not address their constituencies' requirements and that there had to be a "plus" element. We therefore explored the possibility of building an "LDC Plus" package which could include trade facilitation, a special and differential treatment monitoring mechanism, export competition in agriculture, a step forward on environmental goods and services, and a step forward on fisheries subsidies. In July [2011], it became clear that the "LDC Plus" package as Members had framed it was not taking shape.[19]

[19] WTO, Elements for Political Guidance, WT/MIN(11)/W/2; 1 December 2011, p. 3.

In the end, Members were only able to adopt a handful of decisions, including the Services waiver. Overall, the decisions were not significant and fell far below the expectations of LDCs. They served to demonstrate that in picking up issues for early harvest careful consideration should be given to the balance of rights and obligations of Members. Some Members were opposed to certain issues presented as LDC issues, primarily because the proposed decisions on those issues were not going to benefit only LDCs. A case in point is the proposed decision on cotton subsidies. Whereas it is true that a decision to cut more steeply cotton subsidies would have certainly benefitted least-developed countries, they were not the only ones going to benefit from such a decision. In fact, other Members were going to benefit more from such a decision given their large market share in world trade in cotton. Had the decision been adopted, these countries would have been free riders, as they would have gotten benefits without giving reciprocal commitments.

It follows that if WTO Members were decide to follow this path, they will need to select issues with broad appeal for the entire membership such as dispute settlement, trade facilitation and strengthened disciplines on regional trade agreements. With respect to the dispute settlement, it is in the interest of each and every WTO Member to have an improved and robust mechanism for settling trade disputes. It is because of this reason that Members decided to exclude the negotiations on dispute settlement from the single undertaking. However, it should be noted that the DSU negotiations were supposed to have been concluded in 2003 but they are still ongoing possibly indicating that Members are waiting for the outcomes of the negotiations in other areas. Regarding trade facilitation, there is broad consensus among the WTO membership that an agreement would reduce red tape, transactions costs and expedite the movement of goods across borders. As previously stated, the OECD postulates that an agreement on trade facilitation could potentially reduce trade transaction costs by 9 % amounting to over US$ 350 billion in worldwide welfare gains.

With respect to tighter disciplines on regional trade agreements, there is a shared concern among WTO membership about the proliferation of these agreements is challenging the dominance of the multilateral trading system. Some studies indicate that over half of world trade is already taking place under bilateral and regional trade agreements and this figure will rise sharply if some of the agreements under negotiations such as the Trans-Pacific Partnership Agreement were to be concluded. The decision to implement the transparency mechanism in 2006 underscores the determination of WTO Members to discipline these agreements and ensure that they operate in a manner supportive of the multilateral trading system. An agreement on tighter disciplines would benefit each and every WTO Member considering the potential impact of some agreements to divert trade and in the process raise barriers to the trade of third countries.

Another possible candidate for early harvest would be special and differential treatment for developing countries, specifically the adoption of the decisions on the 28 agreement-specific proposals and the monitoring mechanism. With regard to the former, the decisions were agreed in the run-up to the Cancun Ministerial Conference in 2003. The formal adoption of these decisions would signal the commitment of the membership to the development dimension of the Doha Round. Significant work has been undertaken on the monitoring mechanism and it would be in the interests of all Members to have such a mechanism in place. It will afford all Members an opportunity to review the operation of special and differential treatment within the framework of the WTO Agreement.

As regards the other negotiating issues, particularly the market access negotiations in agriculture, NAMA, and services, it would be difficult for agreements to be reached on them and implemented on the basis of paragraph 47. This is primarily because an agreement would entail certain Members having to modify their existing policies or assuming new obligations that they would be reluctant to do unless they get reciprocal commitments from other Members either within the framework of the same agreement being negotiated or other agreements. In the context of agriculture, the draft modalities text would require all Members with the exception of LDCs and recently acceded members to reduce their tariffs according to the agreed tiered formula. For some countries, it would be difficult to make the proposed tariff cuts unless they are satisfied with the cuts others would make to their domestic support, as they would not like locally produced goods to be displaced by the subsidised exports. From the perspective of agricultural exporting countries, the proposals on special products, sensitive products and the special safeguard mechanism are also not cost neutral, as they could affect their potential export earnings. Therefore, they are likely to insist on tighter disciplines to ensure that their restrained use.

It will also be difficult for an agreement to be reached on NAMA and implemented on the basis of paragraph 47 considering the stakes involved. For some developing countries, the costs will be substantial, as they would lose tariff revenue, especially if the new bound rates were to be below their current applied rates. For others, substantial tariff cuts would erode their policy space and compromise their ability to protect infant industries. It is for these reasons that the emerging economies are reluctant to participate in the sectoral negotiations, which would eliminate or substantially reduce tariffs on the relevant products. For developed countries, the draft NAMA text contains too many exceptions that would hamper market access for their exporters. For a start, not many developing countries will be applying the formula. Least-developed countries, small and vulnerable economies, recently acceded members and countries that have bound less than 35 % of their tariff lines will not be applying the formula. A fair number of developing countries that will be applying the formula using higher co-efficients are seeking special treatment meaning that there will not be significant improvement in market access for their exporters in many developing countries. With these difficult issues at stake and varying commercial interests, it would not be easy for an agreement to be reached and implemented on the basis of paragraph 47. Countries would like to see an internal balance, which may prove elusive considering the hardening of positions of the key players in the negotiations.

Given that the services negotiations are not also cost-neutral, it would be difficult to reach agreement on the basis of paragraph 47. Whereas the developed countries are expecting substantive commitments from emerging countries, they are hesitant about the commitments that would be made under mode 4 by developed countries and also under other agreements, particularly agriculture and NAMA. From the viewpoint of developed countries, a substantive result is needed in the trade in services negotiations to balance the commitments that they would be assuming in agriculture and NAMA. They have expressed their disappointment with the offers on the table and were hoping that the plurilateral negotiations agreed to during the Hong Kong Ministerial Conference in 2005 would result in improved offers from developing countries. They want the level of ambition in trade in services to be comparable to those of agriculture and NAMA. Several developing countries do not share that view. They maintain that the essential character of the GATS as a framework agreement should be preserved and that it should be entirely up to a country to decide which services sectors it wants to liberalise taking into account its development priorities. Considering the high stakes involved and the potential costs to countries, it would not be easy to conclude and implement an agreement on the basis of paragraph 47. It is perhaps in recognition of this difficulty that a group of countries is seeking to conclude a plurilateral agreement on the basis of Article V of the GATS. Contentious issues such as antidumping and fisheries subsidies would also be difficult to negotiate, primarily because of the costs they could entail.

It is clear from the foregoing that very few agreements can be concluded and implemented on the basis of paragraph 47. Due care has to be exercised in selecting candidates for early harvest. As the negotiations in the lead up to the December 2011 Ministerial Conference showed, it is only subjects where all WTO Members have a broad systemic interest such as the dispute settlement system have the possibility of attracting consensus. The decision by WTO Members to implement the transparency mechanism for bilateral and regional trade agreements in 2006 buttresses this point.

Plurilateral Agreements

Plurilateral agreements have a long history in the GATT/WTO. During the Tokyo Round, the agreements reached on non-tariff issues such as the Standards Code and the Antidumping Code were not expected to be adhered to by all GATT contracting parties. The *à la carte* approach was seen as flexible and permitting countries that were not ready to opt out of agreements, which they could join at a later stage. The results of these plurilateral negotiations were not multilateralised creating a two-tier membership of the GATT. Developing countries, particularly the least-developed countries felt marginalised not only in the multilateral trading system, but also in the GATT. They detested this system that relegated them to the lower rungs and sought to make fundamental changes during the Uruguay Round. The adoption of the single undertaking approach represented a victory for developing countries, but also for the multilateral trading system as it broadened its appeal and shook off the view that it existed primarily to serve the interests of the developed and a handful of developing countries. From an economic point of view, the single undertaking also made sense, as it simplified the GATT/WTO legal framework and promoted uniformity that, in turn, reduced transaction costs and facilitated trade. While four plurilateral agreements were concluded during the Uruguay Round, their impact on world trade have been very minimal and, in any case, only two are still in force.[20]

Following the implementation of the WTO Agreement in 1995, a number of plurilateral agreements have been concluded by WTO Members accounting for the bulk of world trade in those relevant sectors. These include the agreements on financial services, telecommunications, and information technology. One of the distinguishing features of these agreements is that while they were negotiated mostly by developed countries and a few developing countries, the results were multilateralised broadening their appeal and enabling them to have a greater impact as if there were multilateral trade agreements. The reaction of most WTO Members to these plurilateral agreements has been generally positive. They are seen as having enhanced global welfare and strengthened the multilateral trading system.[21]

With the stalemate in the Doha negotiations and the search for alternative negotiating approaches, a number of WTO Members, particularly the developed countries, have been urging the jettisoning of the single undertaking approach and the embrace of plurilateral negotiations as one of the most flexible and practicable ways to break the deadlock and make progress in the negotiations. While developing countries had hitherto not expressed strong proposals on the conclusion of plurilateral trade agreements, they have expressed alarm at the proposals of developed country Members. They believe that going the plurilateral route would spell the end of the Doha Round where they had invested valuable time and resources. They are reluctant to return to the Tokyo Round days, where there was effectively a two-tier system that gave short shrift to issues of concern to them.

The context where plurilateral agreements are now being discussed is different. During the Uruguay Round and after the entry into force of the WTO Agreement, it was understood that the plurilateral agreements would supplement the multilateral trade agreements and not replace them. It was implicitly accepted that as compared to the multilateral trade agreements, they were secondary in importance within the WTO legal framework. However, with the current proposals, they would rival existing multilateral trade agreements and, to some extent, undermine their effectiveness. A plurilateral agreement on trade in services among the leading trading nations would rival the GATS, especially where they undertake obligations far exceeding their WTO commitments.

As pointed out previously, there is no basis for plurilateral trade agreements under the Doha Declaration. Paragraph 47 envisages the early implementation of multilateral trade agreements concluded within the framework of the Doha Round.

[20] The Agreements were the Agreement on Trade in Civil Aircraft, Agreement on Government Procurement, International Dairy Agreement, and the International Bovine Meat Agreement. The latter two are no longer in force since December 1997.

[21] See statement of Pascal Lamy on the 15th anniversary of the entry into force of the Information Technology Agreement. Available at: http://www.wto.org/english/news_e/sppl_e/sppl228_e.htm.

Put differently, plurilateral agreements concluded among a subset of WTO Members cannot be implemented on the basis of this paragraph. Indeed, the seventeen WTO Members that are negotiating the plurilateral agreement on trade in services have not asserted otherwise. They have stated that Article V of the GATS permits WTO Members to conclude economic integration agreements, provided the agreement would have substantial sectoral coverage and meet the other requirements specified in the Article. It follows that apart from the recognised derogations, plurilateral agreements can only be concluded with the express consent of all WTO Members.

To allay the fears of developing countries, particularly least-developed countries and ensure that plurilateral agreements strengthen the multilateral trading system, it would be useful for Members to agree on the broad parameters for authorising the conclusion of such agreements. First, countries wishing to form such agreements should account for the bulk of world trade in that particular sector or sub-sector. Second, plurilateral agreements should be encouraged in areas where the WTO does not currently have disciplines. Third, they should not impose onerous commitments on WTO Members that want to accede to the agreement. In that context, special and differential treatment must be accorded to least-developed and developing countries depending on their unique circumstances. Fourth, the benefits of the agreement should be extended to all WTO Members within a time period to be agreed between the parties to the agreement and other WTO Members. Last but not least, the parties should make every effort to convert the agreement into a multilateral agreement within a reasonable period of time following its entry into force.

Concluding Remarks

It is clear from the foregoing that there are several factors responsible for the gridlock in the Doha negotiations. While it is useful to analyse them for future lessons, what needs to be addressed urgently is what should be the next steps in the Doha Round? Should the Doha Round be declared dead as has been suggested by some analysts and a new Round commenced, or should WTO Members recommit themselves to it and begin the serious process of deciding which negotiating strategy or strategies should be adopted to ensure substantive progress and the modalities for participation in the negotiations. In deciding which course of action to take, it is important to bear in mind that substantive progress has been made in all areas of the negotiations and that there are very few issues, particularly in agriculture and NAMA where it has not been possible to achieve convergence.

With that in mind, it is clear that it is premature to call for the jettisoning of the Doha Round and the commencement of a new Round. It would be difficult for developing countries to accept this considering the resources they have expended on the Doha Round and the fact that agreement has been reached on the bulk of the negotiating issues. There is no guarantee that the launching of a new Round will miraculously solve the outstanding issues. Abandoning the Round will be an easy option but not necessarily the correct one. It would be better to address head-on the issues on which agreement has eluded the membership. Despite public protestations, there has not been any serious engagement by WTO Members, particularly the key players, in recent months. They have been distracted by domestic and regional issues and have not made serious efforts to reach compromises.

The call for other negotiating strategies has been made more out of frustration rather than their pure merits. The proponents of the 'early harvest' or plurilateral approaches admit that that conclusion of the Doha Round on the basis of the single undertaking would generate more economic benefits and strengthen the multilateral trading system and enable it to provide holistic responses to the challenges of the twenty-first century, including fully integrating least-developed countries into the multilateral trading system and the nexus trade and climate change. Given the broad acceptance of this by WTO Members, resort to other negotiating approaches should only be made after good faith negotiations have failed to resolve the outstanding issues.

While some of the outstanding issues in the negotiations are admittedly very difficult, they are not insurmountable if countries are prepared to negotiate and exercise flexibility where appropriate. It has almost become ideological for some countries to insist on their positions without making any effort to listen to or accommodate the views of other Members. Trade is not a zero sum game and countries should always bear that in mind. A collective effort is needed to breathe new life into the negotiations. Attempts to put the blame at the door of one country or group of countries are not helpful and will not break the impasse in the negotiations. The key players bear a huge responsibility in that regard. They should exercise leadership and bring along the rest of the membership to the finishing line. The contribution that has been made by the rules-based multilateral trading system to global prosperity came about because countries looked beyond their narrow interests and agreed on measures that strengthened the system to the benefit of all countries.

The Doha Round may have been on life support for a long time, but it is capable of being resuscitated to enable it deliver on development and strengthen the multilateral trading system for the benefit of all countries. WTO Members should not be in a hurry to write the obituary of the Round. They should step back from the brink and approach the negotiations in a spirit of true partnership and make the necessary compromises that would pave the way for the Round's conclusion. Should Doha be allowed to die, it would have severe ramifications for the rules-based multilateral trading system and threaten its very foundations. The loss of trust and confidence in the system by developing countries would take some time to rebuild if ever at all.

WTO Dispute Settlement: Current Cases

Andreas Krallmann

Introduction

2011 has been an important year for the WTO dispute settlement system: the Appellate Body issued six reports and ten panels published their reports.[1] This chapter—like its two predecessors in the previous two editions of this Yearbook—will provide an overview of all these 16 decisions.[2] The main factual aspects of the cases and its findings, as well as selected systemic implications will be sketched out. The aim of this series is to give the reader a condensed overview. At the same time, the extensive use of references by way of footnotes referring to the relevant passages in the single reports should allow and encourage the reader to dive into areas of his or her particular interest in more depth.[3]

Arguably, the systemically most important case of the year 2011 is the *China-Raw Materials* case. For the very first time, a panel did not look at import restrictions of a member but at export restraints that a member enacted in order to limit the exports of its natural resources. Though the decision was appealed, it will play a decisive role in the WTO's jurisprudence and on the concept of how a

The views expressed in this article are those of the author and should not in any way be attributed to the German government.

[1] All reports are publicly available at the WTO website: http://www.wto.org/english/tratop_e/dispu_e/dispu_status_e.htm.

[2] For a brief overview of the different types of rulings and stages of WTO dispute settlement cf. Krallmann, WTO Dispute Settlement—The Establishment of 'Binding Guidance' by the Appellate Body in *US Stainless Steel* and Recent Dispute Settlement Rulings, in: Herrmann/Terhechte (eds.), *European Yearbook of International Economic Law 2011*, p. 417 (419–420).

[3] Throughout the chapter, language is taken from the respective decisions. However, quotes with inverted commas are reserved for special terms and longer quotes.

A. Krallmann (✉)
Federal Ministry of Economics and Technology, Berlin, Germany
e-mail: andreas.krallmann@web.de

C. Herrmann et al. (eds.), *European Yearbook of International Economic Law (EYIEL), Vol. 4 (2013)*, European Yearbook of International Economic Law 4,
DOI 10.1007/978-3-642-33917-2_19, © Springer-Verlag Berlin Heidelberg 2013

member is seen to have limited its state sovereignty over its natural resources by having joined the WTO. Furthermore, the decision clarified in how far China could justify its restrictions to preserve its natural reserves and protect the environment according to Article XX of the GATT 1994.

The most voluminous decisions were the aircraft disputes. In 2011, the Appellate Body delivered the result of the appeal in the *Airbus* case. The Airbus appeal was not only important from a political point of view but also had important implications on WTO jurisprudence in general: the Appellate Body defined when a subsidy qualifies as 'export contingent.' To this end, it established a test that all future panels will have to apply if it comes to the question of whether a subsidy is export contingent. It furthermore elaborated on the effect of subsidies, explaining that subsidies diminish over time, which may have important implications on the implementation of subsidy cases in the future. For the first time the Appellate Body also interpreted key concepts of Article 6.1 of the SCM Agreement.

Five years after its establishment, a panel issued the report in the *Boeing* case. In the second aircraft case, the panel held that Boeing has been massively subsidised through tax advantages and R&D programmes. A concept that the panel had to look at was if and under what circumstances the purchase of services by a government had to be qualified as subsidies.

An area of WTO law that hugely benefited from dispute settlement procedures was the Agreement on Technical Barriers to Trade (TBT Agreement). Three cases emerged that touched on basic concepts and definitions of the TBT Agreement. The fact that three cases on technical barriers arose shows the growing importance of technical regulations and standards in today's global trade. All three decisions were appealed so that the Appellate Body will give further guidance on the interpretation of the TBT Agreement.

In *US Clove Cigarettes,* the panel for the first time had to define how the key term 'likeness' should be determined in the TBT Agreement. However, the reader should be cautious about the outcome because the Appellate Body reversed the panel's systemic analysis. The case is also interesting from a public health point of view because it touches on the fight against nicotine addiction.

Similarly, in *US Tuna II,* the technical barrier touched on environmental questions. More important than what the tuna panel decided may arguably be what it did not decide: the panel did not attempt to clarify the fiercely debated question whether two products are not alike if, despite the physical identity of the two products in question, one of the two has been produced or harvested in a different way. This refers to the problem of the so-called process and production methods.

The third TBT case, *US COOL,* concerned a labelling regime on meat. Labelling requirements will, arguably, play a much more important role in international trade in the future.

A common feature that *US tuna II* and *US COOL* share is that both are disputes that arose amongst NAFTA partners. For some reason, Mexico and Canada preferred to bring their disputes to the WTO rather than seeking a solution under NAFTA. This highlights the role of WTO dispute settlement, since the parties could also have tried to solve the issues under the dispute settlement mechanism established under NAFTA.

Some panels and the Appellate Body also had to decide on some classical GATT 1994 questions: *Philippines Distilled Spirits* is a textbook case on Article III:2 of the GATT 1994 and gave the panel and the Appellate Body another opportunity to elaborate on the well-known question of like products. Similarly, *Thailand Cigarettes* elaborated on article III:2 and 4 of the GATT 1994.

Furthermore, some of the decisions were classical trade remedy cases. In *EC Fasteners,* the Appellate Body defined the term 'domestic industry.' In that decision, the Appellate Body adopted a narrow interpretation of the Chinese Protocol of Accession, which forced the EU to change its anti-dumping legislation.

In *US Anti-Dumping and Countervailing Duties,* the Appellate Body ruled on the prohibition of double remedies in the case of non-market economies and came up with an unexpected definition of 'public body.' Furthermore, it showed how benchmarks for identifying benefits to the Chinese industry have to be chosen.

The *EU Footwear* case was another classical anti-dumping case.

Unfortunately, in 2011 there were still more cases on the so-called zeroing methodology. Zeroing is a methodology applied by the USA for calculating dumping margins. Although the WTO dispute settlement had clearly stated that zeroing is inconsistent with the Anti-Dumping Agreement, three more panels had to rule on zeroing and clarify its inconsistency with the Agreement.

The last case presented in this chapter deals with a safeguard measure. However, the basis for the application of that US safeguard measure was not the multilateral Safeguards Agreement but the Chinese Protocol of Accession.

Many of the decisions issued in 2011 will be regarded as landmark cases in WTO jurisprudence. Even though some of the decisions and clarifications may have come as a surprise to some of the members, the WTO dispute settlement is of paramount importance for the WTO and world trade.[4] G.C. Hufbauer put it like this: 'The Appellate Body has earned worldwide respect for thoughtful decisions on complex matters rendered by impartial judges. The Doha Round may be dead in the water, but the dispute settlement system remains a well-functioning part of the World Trade Organization.'[5]

Panel *China – Measures Related to the Exportation of Various Raw Materials* (DS 394, 395 and 398)

Facts of the Case

The USA, Mexico and the EU called upon the dispute settlement of the WTO because China restricted exports of nine raw materials through export duties, export

[4] Cf. a previous contribution on the role of WTO jurisprudence in Krallmann, WTO Dispute Settlement—The Establishment of 'Binding Guidance' by the Appellate Body in *US Stainless Steel* and Recent Dispute Settlement Rulings, in: Herrmann/Terhechte (eds.), *European Yearbook of International Economic Law 2011*, p. 417 (417–418).

[5] Hufbauer, WTO Judicial Appointments: Bad Omen for the Trading System, http://www.piie.com/blogs/?p=2209.

quotas, export licensing and minimum price requirements. The nine essential raw materials in dispute were bauxite, coke, fluorspar, magnesium, manganese, silicon carbide, silicon metal, yellow phosphorus and zinc.[6]

Important Aspects of the Findings

One procedural aspect that deserves attention was that many of the measures that the complainants tried to tackle in their panel request expired or were modified and replaced by new Chinese measures after the establishment of the panel and before the parties submitted their written submissions.[7] In line with the jurisprudence on zeroing, the panel held that annually reviewed measures must not evade a review simply because they expire at the end of a year, and therefore also assessed these new measures.[8]

Paragraph 11.3 of China's Accession Protocol stipulates that China has to 'eliminate all taxes and charges applied to exports unless specifically provided for in Annex 6 of' the Protocol. The existing export duties were found to violate Paragraph 11.3 of the Accession Protocol since bauxite, coke, fluorspar, magnesium, manganese, silicon metal and zinc were not included in the 84 products that the aforementioned Annex lists.[9]

China argued that a justification according to Article XX of the GATT 1994 should also be applicable to its obligation arising out of Paragraph 11.3 of the Chinese Accession Protocol. The panel, however, elaborated that the 'deliberate choice of some language providing for exceptions in Paragraph 11.3, together with the omission of general references to the WTO Agreement or to the GATT 1994' suggests 'that the WTO Members and China did not intend to incorporate' that defence.[10] For this particular obligation, China was thus barred from invoking the defence of Article XX of the GATT 1994.[11] Another, more general question was whether China could justify the export restrictions with the 'inherent and sovereign right of every WTO member to regulate trade.' The panel acknowledged China's state sovereignty but rightly concluded that China exercised this right in negotiating

[6] Report of the Panel, *China – Measures Related to the Exportation of Various Raw Materials*, WT/DS394/R, para. 2.1.

[7] Report of the Panel, *China – Measures Related to the Exportation of Various Raw Materials*, WT/DS394/R, para. 7.5.

[8] Report of the Panel, *China – Measures Related to the Exportation of Various Raw Materials*, WT/DS394/R, paras. 7.33 and 7.218.

[9] Report of the Panel, *China – Measures Related to the Exportation of Various Raw Materials*, WT/DS394/R, paras. 7.105 and 7.122.

[10] Report of the Panel, *China – Measures Related to the Exportation of Various Raw Materials*, WT/DS394/R, paras. 7.129 and 7.138.

[11] Report of the Panel, *China – Measures Related to the Exportation of Various Raw Materials*, WT/DS394/R, paras. 7.139 and 7.158 et seq.

and ratifying its terms of conditions upon accession to the WTO. The Accession Protocol and its obligations were held to be 'the ultimate expression of China's sovereignty.'[12]

The panel furthermore found that a series of Chinese measures, 'when operating in concert,'[13] worked as export quotas applied to bauxite, coke, fluorspar, silicon carbide and zinc. Their effect was to cause export restrictions and or prohibitions, and were thus inconsistent with the obligation contained in Article XI:1 of the GATT 1994.[14] In summary, Article XI:1 of the GATT 1994 'forbids import and export restrictions or prohibitions, including those made effective through. . .quotas . . .on the exportation . . .of any product.'[15]

China, however, argued that its export quota on refractory-grade bauxite was justified pursuant to Article XI:2 lit. a of the GATT 1994 that allows restrictions if they are 'temporarily applied to prevent or relieve critical shortages of [. . .] products essential to the exporting' member. The panel interpreted these terms and required that such a measure could be in existence 'for a limited time' only and had to concern an important, necessary or indispensable product for the member.[16] In order to qualify as a justification for the restriction, the export prohibitions also had to 'prevent a critical shortage.' The panel clarified that Article XI:2 lit. a of the GATT 1994 addresses a different situation than Article XX lit. g of the GATT 1994 and interpreted the term 'critical shortage' to refer to a situation 'that may be relieved or prevented through the application of measures on a temporary and not indefinite or permanent, basis.'[17] China could neither justify its restrictions on refractory-grade bauxite according to Article XI:2 lit. a of the GATT 1994 since China's measures were not temporarily applied,[18] nor could China justify its restrictions according to Article XX lit. g of the GATT 1994. The panel explained that Article XX lit. g of the GATT 1994 would allow a justification if the inconsistent measure was accompanied by a parallel domestic restriction for the conservation of natural resources. China could not prove that its restrictions on bauxite and

[12] Report of the Panel, *China – Measures Related to the Exportation of Various Raw Materials*, WT/DS394/R, paras. 7.156 et seq.

[13] Report of the Panel, *China – Measures Related to the Exportation of Various Raw Materials*, WT/DS394/R, para. 7.218; cf. the explanation in para. 7.224 that some of the individual Chinese measures could be WTO consistent but that these measures 'operating in concert' are inconsistent with Article XI(1) of the GATT 1994.

[14] Report of the Panel, *China – Measures Related to the Exportation of Various Raw Materials*, WT/DS394/R, para. 7.218.

[15] Report of the Panel, *China – Measures Related to the Exportation of Various Raw Materials*, WT/DS394/R, para. 7.205.

[16] Report of the Panel, *China – Measures Related to the Exportation of Various Raw Materials*, WT/DS394/R, paras. 7.260 and 7.282.

[17] Report of the Panel, *China – Measures Related to the Exportation of Various Raw Materials*, WT/DS394/R, paras. 7.299 and 7.306.

[18] Report of the Panel, *China – Measures Related to the Exportation of Various Raw Materials*, WT/DS394/R, para. 7.355.

fluorspar related to conservation and did not demonstrate that there was an even-handed burden on domestic consumers.[19] China also failed to justify its restrictions on scrap products from magnesium, manganese and zinc and energy-intensive, highly polluting, resource based products (coke, magnesium metal and manganese metal) pursuant to Article XX lit. b of the GATT 1994. The panel was of the view that there would have been less trade restrictive and WTO-consistent alternatives available to China. Accordingly, the restrictions were not found to be necessary. Inter alia, China could not explain why it did not simply apply stricter environmental standards to address the problem of pollution. China had also not proven that these restrictions made a material contribution to the objective of reducing pollution; the panel rather found some indications that, on the contrary, the measures served the economic goal of moving up the value chain.[20]

The complainants furthermore challenged aspects of the allocation and administration of export quotas that required the demonstration of prior export performance and minimum capital requirements in order to be granted quota allocation for bauxite, coke, fluorspar and silicon carbide.[21] The panel found that the requirement of prior export performance and the capital requirements were inconsistent with the trading rights China agreed to in its Protocol of Accession.[22] The ability to reject foreign bidders if they cannot prove a necessary 'business management capacity' in the absence of guidelines of how this criterion should be applied was found to be in breach of Article X:3 lit. a of the GATT 1994.[23] China, however, successfully defended itself against the claim that the quota allocation rules themselves were inconsistent with that provision.[24] In the same vein, the USA and Mexico could not demonstrate that payment of a bid-winning price for the right to export under the quota were inconsistent with Article VIII:1 lit. a of the GATT 1994 or Paragraph 11.3 of China's Accession Protocol.[25]

With regard to the export licensing framework through which China administered its export quotas, the panel held that it is not per se inconsistent with Article XI:1 of the GATT 1994.[26]

---

[19] Report of the Panel, *China – Measures Related to the Exportation of Various Raw Materials*, WT/DS394/R, paras. 7.408, 7.435 and 7.466.

[20] Report of the Panel, *China – Measures Related to the Exportation of Various Raw Materials*, WT/DS394/R, paras. 7.512 et seq., 7.577, 7.590 and 7.604.

[21] Report of the Panel, *China – Measures Related to the Exportation of Various Raw Materials*, WT/DS394/R, paras. 7.627-7.628.

[22] Report of the Panel, *China – Measures Related to the Exportation of Various Raw Materials*, WT/DS394/R, paras. 7.669-7.670.

[23] Report of the Panel, *China – Measures Related to the Exportation of Various Raw Materials*, WT/DS394/R, paras. 7.679 and 7.756.

[24] Report of the Panel, *China – Measures Related to the Exportation of Various Raw Materials*, WT/DS394/R, paras. 7.757 and 7.797.

[25] Report of the Panel, *China – Measures Related to the Exportation of Various Raw Materials*, WT/DS394/R, paras. 7.808 and 7.861.

[26] Report of the Panel, *China – Measures Related to the Exportation of Various Raw Materials*, WT/DS394/R, para. 7.958.

The complainants also attacked the minimum export prices for certain raw materials. The panel decided that the minimum export price had a limiting or restricting effect on trade and thus violated Article XI:1 of the GATT 1994.[27]

Panel *United States – Measures Affecting the Production and Sale of Clove Cigarettes* (DS 406)

Facts of the Case

The USA prohibited the importation and sale of flavoured cigarettes other than tobacco or menthol. The alleged reason for the prohibition of all other flavours was to reduce the number of young smokers. Studies had shown that young smokers consume flavoured cigarettes more often than adult smokers. Most US smokers smoke regular tobacco cigarettes, roughly one quarter of smokers uses menthol cigarettes. Imported clove cigarettes accounted for 0.1 % of the US market.[28]

Both clove and menthol cigarettes are predominantly composed of tobacco. According to a WHO study, the additives menthol and clove both cause a reduction in the harshness of smoking, enabling the smoker to take in more dependence-causing and toxic substances. At the same time, the added flavour contributes to the perception that flavoured cigarettes are less harmful.[29]

Indonesia successfully argued that its clove cigarettes exports were unfairly discriminated by the US ban, thereby violating the Agreement on Technical Barriers to Trade (TBT Agreement).

Important Aspects of the Findings

The panel started by recognising the WTO members' right to adopt measures to protect human health. WTO rules, however, would require that this autonomy is exercised in a non-discriminatory way that is compatible with the rules of the WTO.[30] The panel found that the relevant provision of the Federal Food, Drug and Cosmetic Act was a mandatory technical regulation within the meaning of the

---

[27] Report of the Panel, *China – Measures Related to the Exportation of Various Raw Materials*, WT/DS394/R, para. 7.1082.

[28] Report of the Panel, *United States – Measures Affecting the Production and Sale of Clove Cigarettes*, WT/DS406/R, paras. 2.1-2.8 and 2.24-2.25.

[29] Report of the Panel, *United States – Measures Affecting the Production and Sale of Clove Cigarettes*, WT/DS406/R, paras. 7.178 and 7.182.

[30] Report of the Panel, *United States – Measures Affecting the Production and Sale of Clove Cigarettes*, WT/DS406/R, paras. 7.2-7.3.

TBT Agreement.[31] The panel then assessed whether the ban of the flavour clove constituted a breach of the national treatment obligation that is contained in Article 2.1 of the TBT Agreement. Since the decision was published prior to the *US Tuna II* and *US COOL* case, it became the first panel to interpret the concept of *likeness* in Article 2.1 of the TBT Agreement. The panel applied a systemic analysis on some of the key concepts of the TBT Agreement and emphasised that the likeness in Article 2.1 of the TBT Agreement has to be assessed in light of its context, i.e. primarily as a technical regulation.

Although there is some similarity between Article III:4 of the GATT 1994 and the national treatment provision in Article 2.1 of the TBT Agreement, the panel refused to automatically transpose 'the competition-oriented approach to likeness under Article III:4 of the GATT 1994 to Article 2.1 of the TBT Agreement.'[32] Instead, the panel looked at the measure from the point of view of a technical regulation. It emphasised 'the fact that' the technical regulation had the 'immediate purpose to regulate product characteristics' that should have 'potentially great weight, in the determination of whether the products at issue are like.'[33] Furthermore, 'in the context of the TBT Agreement and in the light of its object and purpose expressed by the preambular recitals' the panel bore in mind the 'significance of the public health objective of a technical regulation.' Therefore, the reduction of youth smoking had to 'permeate and inform' the likeness analysis.[34] The panel then examined the four traditional criteria of likeness that are known from the likeness test in Article III of the GATT 1994. However, when applying these criteria *it assessed the likeness from the angle of Article 2.1 of the TBT Agreement*. Taking into account that the purpose of the technical regulation was the regulation of flavoured cigarettes, the panel held that both cigarettes contain tobacco and an additive with a characteristic flavour. Both appeal to young smokers because the additive masks the harshness of tobacco. Bearing in mind the purpose of the technical regulation, i.e. reduction in the number of young smokers, the panel held that clove and menthol cigarettes are alike. The physical differences of the masking agents clove and menthol were held to be irrelevant in this case, but the panel elaborated that the two flavoured cigarettes may be regarded as different products if their likeness is assessed in a different context.[35] Thus, the USA was in

---

[31] Report of the Panel, *United States – Measures Affecting the Production and Sale of Clove Cigarettes*, WT/DS406/R, para. 7.41.

[32] Report of the Panel, *United States – Measures Affecting the Production and Sale of Clove Cigarettes*, WT/DS406/R, para. 7.99. Though 'Article 2.1 of the TBT Agreement seems to be modelled on Article III:4 of the GATT 1994,' 'the absence in the TBT Agreement of language such as that in Article III:1 of the GATT 1994' was taken into account, cf. paras. 7.95 and 7.103.

[33] Report of the Panel, *United States – Measures Affecting the Production and Sale of Clove Cigarettes*, WT/DS406/R, para. 7.109.

[34] Report of the Panel, *United States – Measures Affecting the Production and Sale of Clove Cigarettes*, WT/DS406/R, para. 7.116.

[35] Report of the Panel, *United States – Measures Affecting the Production and Sale of Clove Cigarettes*, WT/DS406/R, paras. 7.188, 7.231, 7.244 and 7.246-7.247.

breach of Article 2.1 of the TBT Agreement because imported clove cigarettes were banned and domestic menthol cigarettes remained in the US market.[36] Upon appeal, however, the Appellate Body made clear that it did not agree with the panel's interpretation and legal standard of the term 'like.'

Indonesia, on the other hand, failed to show that the US ban was more trade-restrictive than necessary to fulfil a legitimate objective within the meaning of Article 2.2 of the TBT Agreement. According to the panel, Article 2.2 of the TBT Agreement requires a two-step analysis: the US ban was found to serve the reduction of smoking by persons under the age of 18, thus serving the legitimate aim of protecting human health.[37] In a second step, Indonesia would have had to convince the panel that the US ban was more trade-restrictive than necessary.

The systemically important question that the panel solved was whether the jurisprudence developed under Article XX lit. b of the GATT 1994 ('measures ... necessary to protect human ... health') is of relevance to the interpretation of the term 'more trade-restrictive than necessary' in Article 2.2 of the TBT Agreement. The panel found that not only the wording of paragraph 2 of Article 2 of the TBT Agreement showed a high degree of similarity but recalled that the sixth recital of the TBT Agreement reproduces the wording of Article XX of the GATT 1994. Thus, Article 2.2 of the TBT Agreement should not 'be given a radically different interpretation from Article XX(b) of the GATT 1994.'[38] The panel, however, cautioned that there may be certain aspects of the jurisprudence on Article XX lit. b of the GATT 1994 that could not be transposed to Article 2.2 of the TBT Agreement.[39] In other words, it may not be exactly the same standard and thus there is no automatic transposition in its entirety.

The panel in this concrete case was not convinced that the measure was more trade-restrictive than necessary since it agreed with the USA that a ban on flavoured cigarettes could indeed lead to a reduction of youth smoking and that Indonesia failed to demonstrate that there were less-trade restrictive alternatives available.[40]

The panel was, however, of the view that the USA failed to notify the ban according to the requirements set out in Article 2.9.2 of the TBT Agreement.[41] Furthermore, the panel interpreted the wording 'reasonable interval' between

---

[36] Report of the Panel, *United States – Measures Affecting the Production and Sale of Clove Cigarettes*, WT/DS406/R, para. 7.281.

[37] Report of the Panel, *United States – Measures Affecting the Production and Sale of Clove Cigarettes*, WT/DS406/R, paras. 7.343 and 7.347.

[38] Report of the Panel, *United States – Measures Affecting the Production and Sale of Clove Cigarettes*, WT/DS406/R, paras. 7.358-7.361. However, note should be taken that the burden of proof is on the complainant, para. 7.364.

[39] Report of the Panel, *United States – Measures Affecting the Production and Sale of Clove Cigarettes*, WT/DS406/R, para. 7.369.

[40] Report of the Panel, *United States – Measures Affecting the Production and Sale of Clove Cigarettes*, WT/DS406/R, paras. 7.415 and 7.421.

[41] Report of the Panel, *United States – Measures Affecting the Production and Sale of Clove Cigarettes*, WT/DS406/R, para. 7.550.

publication and entry into force of the TBT measure in Article 2.12 of the TBT Agreement to normally mean a 6 month period: the panel referred to Paragraph 5.2 of the Doha Ministerial Decision that states that 'the phrase reasonable interval shall be understood to mean normally a period of not less than 6 months.' The panel found that it must be guided by this interpretation of the term reasonable interval since all members agreed on this clarification at the ministerial level.[42]

Panel *United States – Measures Concerning the Importation, Marketing and Sale of Tuna and Tuna Products* (DS 381)

Facts of the Case

Mexico brought its second tuna related case against the USA because Mexico alleged that the US regulation for labelling tuna products as 'dolphin-free' was in breach of the TBT Agreement. The complex US stipulations laid down in detail the preconditions for using such a label on tuna products. The extensive provisions differentiated between different fishing methods in different fishing grounds. The dolphin-safe label must, for example, not be used if the tuna was caught on the high seas by a vessel using the technique of driftnet fishing. In other waters, it could be sufficient to obtain a declaration by the captain of the vessel and an observer that no dolphins were killed or seriously injured when the tuna was caught.[43]

Mexico and the USA are parties to the Agreement on International Dolphin Conservation Program (AIDCP). A resolution adopted under the regime of the AIDCP defines dolphin safe as tuna that is 'captured in sets in which there is no mortality or serious injury of dolphins.' The application of that resolution is, however, voluntary for the parties, especially if it is inconsistent with domestic law of one of the parties.[44]

The underlying problem is that there are dolphin schools where certain tuna swim with the dolphins. Some of the commercial fishing vessels exploit this association by 'setting on dolphins': They encircle the pod with nets to catch the tuna beneath the dolphins. That creates the danger of entangling, injuring or killing some of the dolphins.[45]

---

[42] Report of the Panel, *United States – Measures Affecting the Production and Sale of Clove Cigarettes*, WT/DS406/R, paras. 7.572 et seq.

[43] Report of the Panel, *United States – Measures Concerning the Importation, Marketing and Sale of Tuna and Tuna Products*, WT/DS381/R, paras. 2.3 et seq.

[44] Report of the Panel, *United States – Measures Concerning the Importation, Marketing and Sale of Tuna and Tuna Products*, WT/DS381/R, paras. 2.34 et seq.

[45] http://en.wikipedia.org/wiki/Tuna.

Important Aspects of the Findings

In 1991, a GATT panel ruled on the US requirement for tuna entering the USA. The USA, however, blocked the adoption of that GATT panel report. The current case is a kind of remake of that old case and will be referred to as the *US Tuna II*-case.

First of all, it is important to clarify what the decision did not do: The panel report does not decide whether or not processes and production methods, so called *ppm*s, change the identity of an otherwise like product. There is a long and extensive debate whether a product that has the same physical characteristics but was produced or harvested in another way has to be regarded as a 'like' product under WTO law. The *tuna II* decision, arguably, mentions the problem of *ppm*s but does not answer the general question.

Another interesting aspect of the decision is that one of the panellists delivered a well-reasoned dissenting opinion on the fundamental question whether or not the US labelling requirements constituted a voluntary or mandatory regime.

The panel first looked at the alleged violation of Article 2.1 of the TBT-Agreement. The first precondition for the application of Article 2.1 of the TBT Agreement would be that the labelling requirement is qualified as a technical regulation according to the definition in Annex 1.1 of the TBT Agreement which includes that the labelling is mandatory.

The majority of panellists qualified the labelling scheme as mandatory because it was the only standard available to address the issue of the safety of dolphins. It prohibited the use of other terms relating to dolphins if the conditions of that labelling scheme were not met. It thus left no discretion to inform consumers on its dolphin-safety unless those specific requirements were met.[46] The third panellist, however, disagreed with a well-reasoned and well-founded dissenting opinion. He was of the view that labelling requirements of any given label must always be fulfilled. That would be the very nature of a label. If parties, on the contrary, were free not to stick to these preconditions, the label would become meaningless. He consequently concluded that '[i]n a voluntary labelling scheme, labelling requirements are thus not mandatory for marketing products.'[47] Instead, 'the measures at issue set out the requirements for dolphin-safe labelling but they impose no obligation to label (or not to label) tuna as "dolphin-safe".'[48] 'The requirements to be allowed to use a label would have to be clearly distinguished from the obligation to use a label.'[49] It would be the voluntary decision of commercial agents to use the label, even though the label may *de facto* be mandatory if a commercial agent wants to market tuna in the USA.[50]

---

[46] Report of the Panel, *United States – Measures Concerning the Importation, Marketing and Sale of Tuna and Tuna Products*, WT/DS381/R, paras. 7.143-7.144.

[47] Report of the Panel, *United States – Measures Concerning the Importation, Marketing and Sale of Tuna and Tuna Products*, WT/DS381/R, para. 7.150

[48] Report of the Panel, *United States – Measures Concerning the Importation, Marketing and Sale of Tuna and Tuna Products*, WT/DS381/R, para. 7.153.

[49] Report of the Panel, *United States – Measures Concerning the Importation, Marketing and Sale of Tuna and Tuna Products*, WT/DS381/R, para. 7.155.

[50] Report of the Panel, *United States – Measures Concerning the Importation, Marketing and Sale of Tuna and Tuna Products*, WT/DS381/R, paras. 7.156 and 7.175.

Since the majority was of the opinion that the labelling scheme is mandatory, the panel assessed whether (*i*) a like product had been (*ii*) discriminated by the labelling scheme.

(i) Mexican and American tuna share the same physical characteristics, end uses and tariff classifications; they are identical products, processed in different countries.[51] The panel clearly stated that it did not compare dolphin-safe and non dolphin-safe tuna. The panel was not persuaded that the consumer preferences of US consumers would change its assessment of the likeness. The basis for the panel's analysis was a comparison between US and Mexican tuna. A comparison of the dolphin-safe status on the contrary would effectively have implied that Mexican tuna is not dolphin-safe.[52] Arguably, the panel thereby did not illuminate the question of *ppm*s.

(ii) 'Less favourable treatment' in the provision's sense would afford that the foreign tuna products were at a disadvantage compared to the domestic tuna.[53] The panel agreed with Mexico that the label provided a commercial advantage but it disagreed with the complainant that Mexican tuna was discriminated. It appeared to the panel 'that the measures at issue, in applying the same origin-neutral requirement to all tuna products, do not inherently discriminate on the basis of the origin of the products, and that they also do not make it impossible for Mexican tuna products to comply with this requirement.' Instead, the adverse impact on Mexican tuna was primarily the result of circumstances that were not related to the foreign origin of that product, including the choices of Mexican fishing fleets.[54] Mexico had argued that the USA would 'unilaterally exert pressure on the Mexican fleet to change fishing areas and/or fishing methods,' 'including unincorporated processes and production methods.'[55] The panel, however, held that the 'incentive for fleets setting on dolphins to discontinue that practice [. . .] applies also to the US fleet.'[56]

The US labelling requirements were, however, found to be unnecessary obstacles to international trade because, according to Article 2.2, second sentence of the TBT Agreement, the technical regulation was more trade-restrictive than necessary to fulfil a legitimate objective. The panel accepted that the US measure served the purposes of consumer information and the protection of dolphins and that both objectives were legitimate within the meaning of Article 2.2. of the TBT

---

[51] Report of the Panel, *United States – Measures Concerning the Importation, Marketing and Sale of Tuna and Tuna Products*, WT/DS381/R, para. 7.246.

[52] Report of the Panel, *United States – Measures Concerning the Importation, Marketing and Sale of Tuna and Tuna Products*, WT/DS381/R, paras. 7.246-7.250

[53] Report of the Panel, *United States – Measures Concerning the Importation, Marketing and Sale of Tuna and Tuna Products*, WT/DS381/R, para. 7.278.

[54] Report of the Panel, *United States – Measures Concerning the Importation, Marketing and Sale of Tuna and Tuna Products*, WT/DS381/R, paras. 7.291 and 7.377-7.378.

[55] Report of the Panel, *United States – Measures Concerning the Importation, Marketing and Sale of Tuna and Tuna Products*, WT/DS381/R, para. 7.369

[56] Report of the Panel, *United States – Measures Concerning the Importation, Marketing and Sale of Tuna and Tuna Products*, WT/DS381/R, para. 7.373.

Agreement.[57] The panel held that a measure would be 'more trade restrictive than necessary' if 'it would be possible to achieve the same objective through a less trade restrictive measure, than the measure at issue.'[58] However, like the panel in *US-COOL*, the panel gave the member the freedom to choose the level of protection for itself.[59] Therefore, a panel would have to assess whether there is an alternative measure reasonably available that is less trade-restrictive and 'achieve[s] the challenged measure's objective at the same level.'[60] Mexico successfully identified the label under the AIDCP regime as a less trade restrictive measure: the US label was found to have a misleading effect on consumers because it allowed tuna to be labelled 'dolphin-safe' if the US preconditions were met, even if dolphin killings or serious injuries occurred during the catch. The panel found that the consumers would not be mislead to a greater extent 'if the AIDCP label were allowed to co-exist with the US dolphin-safe provisions.'[61]

Panel *United States – Certain Country of Origin Labelling (COOL) Requirements* (DS 384 and 386)

Facts of the Case

Mexico and Canada claimed that certain US country of origin labelling ('COOL') requirements for meat products were inconsistent with Article 2 of the TBT Agreement. The market for livestock in the NAFTA countries is highly integrated; different stages of the production are often performed in more than one country.[62]

---

[57] Report of the Panel, *United States – Measures Concerning the Importation, Marketing and Sale of Tuna and Tuna Products*, WT/DS381/R, paras. 7.425 and 7.444.

[58] Report of the Panel, *United States – Measures Concerning the Importation, Marketing and Sale of Tuna and Tuna Products*, WT/DS381/R, paras. 7.453 et seq.

[59] Report of the Panel, *United States – Measures Concerning the Importation, Marketing and Sale of Tuna and Tuna Products*, WT/DS381/R, para. 7.460.

[60] Report of the Panel, *United States – Measures Concerning the Importation, Marketing and Sale of Tuna and Tuna Products*, WT/DS381/R, para. 7.465.

[61] Report of the Panel, *United States – Measures Concerning the Importation, Marketing and Sale of Tuna and Tuna Products*, WT/DS 381/R, paras. 7.573 and 7.578; the panel found the US labelling requirements to be consistent with Article 2.4 of the TBT Agreement. The provision was regarded to be a relevant international standard and that the US failed to base its own labelling requirements thereon. However, Mexico failed to demonstrate that the AIDCP standard *taken on its own* would be sufficient to fulfil the set US objectives, cf. paras. 7.707, 7.716 and 7.740.

To avoid confusion of these seemingly contradictory findings: In contrast to this isolated application of the measure under Article 2.4 of the TBT Agreement, the panel held under its assessment of Article 2.2 of the TBT Agreement that the dolphin-safe requirements of the AIDCP *in conjunction* with the existing standard of the US regime would be possible, cf. para. 7.577.

The panel exercised judicial economy with regard to Mexico's claim under the GATT 1994 since materially all aspects had been addressed under the panel's assessment under the TBT Agreement, cf. para. 7.748.

[62] Report of the Panel, *United States – Certain Country of Origin Labelling (COOL) Requirements*, WT/DS384/R, para. 7.140.

The US COOL law established that US retailers had to inform the consumer on the country of origin of certain meat.[63] In practice, the labelling requirement meant that beef and pork could not be labelled 'product of USA' if the cattle and hogs were raised at least to some extent outside the USA, even if they were finally slaughtered in the USA. Instead, they had to be labelled as 'product of the US, product of country x' (or vice versa) or as 'product of country x.'[64] The US labelling requirements were laid down in different pieces of legislation and a letter from the US Secretary of Agriculture, the so-called Vilsack letter. The letter recommended a certain implementation of the COOL law by suggesting that the industry 'voluntarily' adapt certain practices for the information of consumers.[65]

Important Aspects of the Findings

The panel stated that the key concepts of Article 2 of the TBT Agreement had not been interpreted previously.[66] However, this is not correct since prior to the publication of the COOL case the two other TBT decisions, i.e. *US Clove Cigarettes* and *US Tuna II,* were published. Arguably, the panel in *US Clove Cigarettes* adopted a more systemic interpretation of some of the key terms of the TBT Agreement.

According to Article 2.1 of the TBT Agreement, members shall ensure that technical regulations do not accord treatment less favourable to like imported products.

The threshold question for Article 2.1 of the TBT Agreement was whether the COOL measures were a technical regulation according to Annex 1.1 of the TBT Agreement. For that question, the panel followed the test the Appellate Body had established in *EC Sardines* and according to which three criteria need to be fulfilled: the measure must apply to an identifiable product; the document has to lay down the characteristics of the product; and compliance needs to be mandatory.[67] Applying these criteria to the present case, the panel found that the COOL measure was a technical regulation but that the Vilsack letter did not qualify since it was voluntary in nature.[68]

---

[63] Report of the Panel, *United States – Certain Country of Origin Labelling (COOL) Requirements*, WT/DS384/R, paras. 2.1 and 7.87.

[64] Report of the Panel, *United States – Certain Country of Origin Labelling (COOL) Requirements*, WT/DS384/R, paras. 7.65 and 7.100; examples of concrete labels used can be found in paras. 7.113 et seq.

[65] Report of the Panel, *United States – Certain Country of Origin Labelling (COOL) Requirements*, WT/DS384/R, paras. 2.2 and 7.123.

[66] Report of the Panel, *United States – Certain Country of Origin Labelling (COOL) Requirements*, WT/DS384/R, paras. 7.228 and 7.550.

[67] Report of the Panel, *United States – Certain Country of Origin Labelling (COOL) Requirements*, WT/DS384/R, para. 7.147.

[68] Report of the Panel, *United States – Certain Country of Origin Labelling (COOL) Requirements*, WT/DS384/R, paras. 7.162, 7.196 and 7.216.

The USA did not contest that imported Canadian and Mexican meat was 'like' domestic American meat.[69]

Furthermore, for a violation of Article 2.1 of the TBT Agreement the US measure had to be discriminative in nature. The complainants argued that the measure was a *de facto* discrimination that raised the question whether Article 2.1 of the TBT Agreement covers only *de iure* or also *de facto* discriminatory treatment. The panel clarified that Article 2.1 of the TBT Agreement—like Article III:4 of the GATT 1994—would cover both *de iure* and *de facto* discrimination. 'To effectively ensure equality of competitive conditions [the provision] cannot exclude measures that discriminate in effect.' The panel continued to explain that 'the TBT Agreement serves to further the objectives of [the] GATT 1994' and that it would therefore be 'incongruous to interpret Article 2.1 of the TBT Agreement as excluding *de facto* discriminatory treatment.'[70] The panel found that some of the COOL measures indeed discriminated against imported livestock from Canada and Mexico because they created 'an incentive in favour of processing exclusively domestic [American] livestock and a disincentive against handling imported livestock.'[71]

Noteworthy is the panel's analysis of a violation of Article 2.2 of the TBT Agreement, especially its assessment of the member's purpose of enacting the regulation. The provision stipulates that a technical regulation must not have the effect of creating unnecessary obstacles to international trade, i.e. they shall not be more trade-restrictive than necessary to fulfil a *legitimate objective*. The panel had already established that the COOL measures were discriminatory in nature. Canada and Mexico argued that the COOL measures served a protectionist intent, the US was of the view that it served the purpose of informing consumers.[72] The panel held that there is a rebuttable presumption of good faith in favour of the defendant: According to 'the principle of good faith... as embodied in Article 26 of the Vienna Convention on the Law of Treaties' the USA was assumed to have truthfully notified the WTO of the objectives of the COOL measures, i.e. consumer information.[73] A panel would not need to 'consider the *alleged intent* behind' the technical regulation in identifying the objective of the technical regulation. Instead, the panel assumed that there is a prerogative of members to pursue their own policy goals. Therefore, members are free to adopt technical regulations and the assessment would have to be based on the information provided by that member. The task of a panel, in contrast, would be to assess whether the pursued objective was

---

[69] Report of the Panel, *United States – Certain Country of Origin Labelling (COOL) Requirements*, WT/DS384/R, para. 7.256.

[70] Report of the Panel, *United States – Certain Country of Origin Labelling (COOL) Requirements*, WT/DS384/R, paras. 7.299 et seq.

[71] Report of the Panel, *United States – Certain Country of Origin Labelling (COOL) Requirements*, WT/DS384/R, paras. 7.420 and 7.546.

[72] Report of the Panel, *United States – Certain Country of Origin Labelling (COOL) Requirements*, WT/DS384/R, para. 7.596.

[73] Report of the Panel, *United States – Certain Country of Origin Labelling (COOL) Requirements*, WT/DS384/R, para. 7.605.

legitimate.[74] Therefore, the panel accepted that the US objective was to inform consumers about the precise origin of the meat.[75] The panel furthermore accepted that the provision of consumer information is a legitimate objective[76] but it found that the US COOL law was more trade-restrictive than necessary to fulfil this legitimate objective. For the assessment of the necessity, the panel referred to the legal tests established under the jurisprudence of Article XX of the GATT 1994 because of the textual similarities between Article XX of the GATT 1994 and Article 2.2 of the TBT Agreement and since the TBT Agreement serves the same objectives as the GATT 1994.[77] The panel thus assessed whether there was 'a genuine relationship of ends and means between the objective pursued and the measure at issue.' The COOL labelling, however, was found to fall short of accurately and clearly providing the consumer with information on the country of origin. For example, the meaning of the label 'product of the US, Mexico' would not be clear and rather confuse the average consumer.[78] Since the labelling requirements did not inform the consumer accurately on the origin of the product, the COOL measures were held not to fulfil the objective of consumer information. Thus, they were found to be in violation of Article 2.2 of the TBT Agreement.[79]

Appellate Body *European Communities and Certain Member States – Measures Affecting Trade in Large Civil Aircraft* (DS 316)

Facts of the Case

On appeal, the Appellate Body had to decide on whether different European support measures to the European aircraft manufacturer Airbus were subsidies within the meaning of the SCM Agreement. The facts of the Airbus case and the panel's decision were presented in more detail in last year's contribution.[80] It should, however, be kept in mind that the Airbus case is just the first of the two aircraft

---

[74] Report of the Panel, *United States – Certain Country of Origin Labelling (COOL) Requirements*, WT/DS384/R, paras. 7.609-7.613.

[75] Report of the Panel, *United States – Certain Country of Origin Labelling (COOL) Requirements*, WT/DS384/R, para. 7.620.

[76] Report of the Panel, *United States – Certain Country of Origin Labelling (COOL) Requirements*, WT/DS384/R, para. 7.651.

[77] Report of the Panel, *United States – Certain Country of Origin Labelling (COOL) Requirements*, WT/DS384/R, paras. 7.670 and 7.693.

[78] Report of the Panel, *United States – Certain Country of Origin Labelling (COOL) Requirements*, WT/DS384/R, paras. 7.700-7.701 and 7.716 et seq.

[79] Report of the Panel, *United States – Certain Country of Origin Labelling (COOL) Requirements*, WT/DS384/R, paras. 7.719-7.719.

[80] Krallmann, WTO Dispute Settlement: Current Cases, in: Herrmann/Terhechte (eds.), *European Yearbook of International Economic Law 2012*, p. 577 (602–608).

cases. To see the whole picture, the reader should also refer to the results of the Boeing case where the subsidies of the USA to Boeing were assessed. The two cases are thus two faces of the same coin, i.e. support measures to the two large aircraft manufacturing companies.

Important Aspects of the Findings

An interesting preliminary question of public international law that the Appellate Body had to solve was whether Article 5 of the SCM Agreement applies to subsidies that had been granted prior to the existence of the WTO, i.e. 1 January 1995. The EU argued that measures prior to 1995 fell outside the temporal scope of the Agreement because Article 28 of the Vienna Convention sets out that treaty provisions cannot be applied retrospectively.[81]

The Appellate Body interpreted Article 5 of the SCM Agreement to mean that members were obliged as of 1 January 1995 not to cause adverse effects through the use of subsidies.[82] It then looked at Paragraph 7 of Annex IV of the SCM Agreement that deals with the factoring in of subsidies granted prior to the coming into existence of the WTO when calculating the overall amount of subsidies. This provision would demonstrate that subsidies granted before 1995 are capable of causing adverse effects. The question of retroactivity would thus hinge on whether or not the causing of the adverse effects continued or had been completed, rather than the point in time of granting the subsidy.[83]

Furthermore, the EU argued that the SCM Agreement required the USA to demonstrate a *continuing benefit*. According to the EU, a subsidy would diminish over time and thus a panel would have to determine if the subsidy still confers a benefit.[84] In an important ruling, the Appellate Body held that Article 4.7 and 7.8 of the SCM Agreement would prove that a subsidy would not simply cease to exist after it was granted. However, a panel would have to 'take into account that a subsidy provided accrues and diminishes over time, and [would] have a finite life.' Separately, a panel would also have to 'assess whether there are 'intervening events' that occurred after the grant of the subsidy.' Therefore, a panel would have to take into account how a subsidy had materialised over time.[85] The fact that the effects of a subsidy diminish over time would not mean that the subsidies and

[81] Report of the Appellate Body, *European Communities and Certain Member States – Measures Affecting Trade in Large Civil Aircraft*, WT/DS316/AB/R, para. 650.

[82] Report of the Appellate Body, *European Communities and Certain Member States – Measures Affecting Trade in Large Civil Aircraft*, WT/DS316/AB/R, para. 659.

[83] Report of the Appellate Body, *European Communities and Certain Member States – Measures Affecting Trade in Large Civil Aircraft*, WT/DS316/AB/R, paras. 667 and 684.

[84] Report of the Appellate Body, *European Communities and Certain Member States – Measures Affecting Trade in Large Civil Aircraft*, WT/DS316/AB/R, para. 698.

[85] Report of the Appellate Body, *European Communities and Certain Member States – Measures Affecting Trade in Large Civil Aircraft*, WT/DS316/AB/R, paras. 708–710.

the benefits have to be present; the Appellate Body did not exclude that there may be occasions when a subsidy that no longer exists may still cause adverse effects. However, a complainant would not have to demonstrate that a benefit continues for the purposes of the adverse effect analysis.[86] Thus, in future cases the complaining party does not have to substantiate that there is a continuing benefit BUT the ruling will, arguably, have an impact on the implementation of future cases: According to Article 7.9 of the SCM Agreement, actionable subsidies that were found to be incompatible with the SCM Agreement either have to be withdrawn or the defendant has to 'remove the adverse effects of the subsidy.' Since the Appellate Body held that subsidies diminish over time—which would most probably also be true for the adverse effect caused by that subsidy—the harming effect of a subsidy may decrease automatically and thereby reduce the burden of implementation for the member.

The Appellate Body then assessed whether intervening events in this case occurred after the grant of the subsidies to Airbus. The EU argued that one intervening event that extinguished the subsidies granted to Airbus was the sale of shares between private Airbus entities and sales that were conducted in the process of a partial privatisation. After recalling the principles that apply to privatisation and the effects on the existence of a subsidy[87] the Appellate Body found that the existing case law did not apply to the Airbus case. More interestingly, the members of the Appellate Body could not agree on a common standard for the assessment of the 'extinction of subsidies in the context of partial privatisations and private-to-private sales.'[88] Although divided on the right standard for the assessment, the Appellate Body members held that the panel had failed to make sufficient factual findings on these sales transactions and found that the analysis could not be completed due to insufficient factual findings.[89]

On the launch aid/member state finance (in the following '*msf*') to Airbus that was at the centre of the dispute, the Appellate Body first of all denied finding that there was an unwritten European programme in the form of an on-going conduct that provides subsidies to every new Airbus model. The Appellate Body held that such a request was not sufficiently identified in the US request for the establishment of the panel.[90]

The panel then examined whether French, German, British and Spanish msf for different Airbus models in the past (not, however, the A350) were actionable

[86] Report of the Appellate Body, *European Communities and Certain Member States – Measures Affecting Trade in Large Civil Aircraft*, WT/DS316/AB/R, paras. 712 and 715.

[87] Report of the Appellate Body, *European Communities and Certain Member States – Measures Affecting Trade in Large Civil Aircraft*, WT/DS316/AB/R, paras. 722–723.

[88] Report of the Appellate Body, *European Communities and Certain Member States – Measures Affecting Trade in Large Civil Aircraft*, WT/DS316/AB/R, paras. 726 et seq.

[89] Report of the Appellate Body, *European Communities and Certain Member States – Measures Affecting Trade in Large Civil Aircraft*, WT/DS316/AB/R, paras. 735–736.

[90] Report of the Appellate Body, *European Communities and Certain Member States – Measures Affecting Trade in Large Civil Aircraft*, WT/DS316/AB/R, paras. 795–796.

subsidies within the meaning of the SCM Agreement. To assess whether the respective governments had conferred a benefit on Airbus, the Appellate Body compared the conditions of the individual loans at the time when they were made 'to the terms and conditions that would have been offered by the market at that time.'[91] Looking at the concrete conditions of the loans, the Appellate Body held that the challenged msf indeed conferred a benefit to Airbus since the loans 'were provided at a rate of return that was below the market benchmark.'[92] In its comparison of the actual conditions and the market situation, the Appellate Body rejected both the benchmark suggested by the USA and the EU.[93]

The Appellate Body furthermore confirmed that certain R&D grants that were provided to Airbus through several EC Framework Programmes were specific within the meaning of Article 2.1 lit. a of the SCM Agreement.[94]

The Appellate Body also modified the panel's findings on infrastructure measures that were provided by Germany and France. The leasing agreement between Airbus and Hamburg for Airbus' facilities at the Mühlenberger Loch was found to confer a benefit to Airbus. The Appellate Body, however, clarified that the benefit did not consist in the *creation* of the infrastructure in question but the *lease* of the land and special facilities at the Mühlenberger Loch. Similarly, the right to use an extended runway at the airport in Bremen and the sale and lease of facilities in Toulouse also conferred a benefit to Airbus.[95] When trying to quantify the benefit, the Appellate Body clarified that the panel could not simply rely on the *investments* borne by the government *to create* the facilities in order to define the market rate, thus equating the investment costs with the market value. Instead, a *price* that reflects supply and demand of sellers and buyers in the relevant market would have to be established as the proper benchmark.[96]

---

[91] Report of the Appellate Body, *European Communities and Certain Member States – Measures Affecting Trade in Large Civil Aircraft*, WT/DS316/AB/R, para. 838.

[92] Report of the Appellate Body, *European Communities and Certain Member States – Measures Affecting Trade in Large Civil Aircraft*, WT/DS316/AB/R, paras. 927 and 929.

[93] Report of the Appellate Body, *European Communities and Certain Member States – Measures Affecting Trade in Large Civil Aircraft*, WT/DS316/AB/R, para. 894 on the US benchmark and paras. 921–922 on the EU benchmark. The Appellate Body furthermore rejected the EU argument that the maximum ceilings of support for Airbus and Boeing as agreed upon in the bilateral Agreement between the EU and the USA on trade in large civil aircraft, which was concluded in 1992, defined the ceilings of when a benefit would be conferred, cf. for more detail para. 851.

[94] Report of the Appellate Body, *European Communities and Certain Member States – Measures Affecting Trade in Large Civil Aircraft*, WT/DS316/AB/R, para. 952.

[95] Report of the Appellate Body, *European Communities and Certain Member States – Measures Affecting Trade in Large Civil Aircraft*, WT/DS316/AB/R, para. 967.

[96] Report of the Appellate Body, *European Communities and Certain Member States – Measures Affecting Trade in Large Civil Aircraft*, WT/DS316/AB/R, paras. 980–981. For some of the facilities in question the Appellate Body could not fully complete the analysis based on this correct benchmark: the lease of land in Hamburg and the use of the extended runway in Bremen were found to be a benefit, whereas the Appellate Body could not complete its analysis on special purpose facilities in Hamburg and infrastructure in Toulouse, cf. paras. 984 et seq.

Furthermore, the Appellate Body upheld the panel's finding that equity infusions in Aérospatiale by France conferred a benefit since the capital investments were inconsistent with the usual practice of private investors.[97]

The Appellate Body reversed the panel's findings that the German, Spanish and British msf for the A380 were prohibited subsidies because they were tied to anticipated exportation and thus in breach of Article 3.1 lit. a of the SCM Agreement. The starting point of the Appellate Body's analysis was what would have to be 'demonstrated in order to establish that a subsidy is in fact *tied to*… anticipated exportation within the meaning of footnote 4 of the SCM Agreement.'[98] In an important ruling, the Appellate Body laid down a 'test' that will be the benchmark for future cases: 'is the granting of the subsidy *geared to induce the promotion of future export performance* by the recipient?'[99] This standard would not simply be met 'because the granting of the subsidy is designed to increase a recipient's production, even if the increased production is exported in whole.' Rather, 'the standard for *de facto* export contingency under Article 3.1(a) and footnote 4 of the SCM Agreement would be met when the subsidy is granted *so as to provide an incentive to the recipient to export in a way that is not simply reflective of the conditions of supply and demand in the domestic and export markets undistorted by the granting of the subsidy*.'[100] For example, a subsidy would not be judged to be export contingent if 'the anticipated ratio of [the additional] export sales to domestic sales is not greater than the existing ratio.' If however, on the contrary, the recipient's additional exports were expected to increase that ratio, the subsidies would be regarded to be export contingent.[101] The example the Appellate Body uses is a recipient that used to export 40 % of his products. If the subsidy enables the recipient to produce five more products of which a maximum of two would be expected to be exported, then there would be no export contingency. If the subsidising government would however expect that at least three of the additional produced goods would be exported, the subsidy would be found to be export contingent.

However, that 'conditional relationship between the granting of the subsidy and export performance must be *objectively observable* on the basis of evidence in order for the subsidy to be geared to induce the promotion of future export performance

[97] Report of the Appellate Body, *European Communities and Certain Member States – Measures Affecting Trade in Large Civil Aircraft*, WT/DS316/AB/R, para. 1012. However, the Appellate Body could not decide whether a transfer of shares in Dassault Aviation to Aérospatiale by the French government was a benefit, cf. para. 1027.

[98] Report of the Appellate Body, *European Communities and Certain Member States – Measures Affecting Trade in Large Civil Aircraft*, WT/DS316/AB/R, para. 1042.

[99] Report of the Appellate Body, *European Communities and Certain Member States – Measures Affecting Trade in Large Civil Aircraft*, WT/DS316/AB/R, para. 1044.

[100] Report of the Appellate Body, *European Communities and Certain Member States – Measures Affecting Trade in Large Civil Aircraft*, WT/DS316/AB/R, para. 1045.

[101] Report of the Appellate Body, *European Communities and Certain Member States – Measures Affecting Trade in Large Civil Aircraft*, WT/DS316/AB/R, para. 1048.

by the recipient.' In contrast, the Appellate Body was 'not satisfied by the subjective motivation of the granting government to promote the future export performance of the recipient.' The Appellate Body clarified that it 'must be determined by assessing the subsidy itself, in the light of the relevant factual circumstances, rather than by reference to the granting authority's reason for the measure.'[102] According to the Appellate Body the panel that had found the German, Spanish and British msf to be export contingent erroneously 'equated the standard of export contingency with the reason(s) for granting a subsidy.' 'The authority's reasons [...] may provide some evidence [...] but it is not to be equated with that standard.'[103] The Appellate Body acknowledged that the large aircraft market is a global market. It judged that the projected exports showed that Airbus was an export-oriented company. However, there would not be evidence to 'clearly indicate the proportion of export and domestic sales Airbus would be expected to make under the LA/MSF contracts in question.'[104] The panel's findings with regard to export contingency were reversed because it was not sufficient for the USA to show that anticipated exportation was the reason for granting the subsidy. The Appellate Body held that there was not enough evidence to show 'the extent to which Airbus would be expected to export in the absence of the granting of these LA/MSF subsidies.'[105] Since there were not enough undisputed facts before the Appellate Body that would show that the above mentioned ratio would change in the required way, the Appellate Body could not find a prohibited subsidy.

In the last part of its decision the Appellate Body assessed whether the European subsidies caused serious prejudice to Boeing. For the first time, the Appellate Body had to interpret a case of 'displacement' and 'lost sales' under Article 6.3 lit. a, b and c of the SCM Agreement.[106] As described in last year's contribution, the USA and EU did not agree on how the market had to be assessed for the purposes of Article 6 of the SCM Agreement. The Appellate Body clarified that the scope of the relevant market would probably vary from case to case but that it would 'depend on the nature and degree of competition between the products' of the complainant and respondent. The panel would thus have been required to make an independent assessment of the US serious prejudice claim including the question whether it was appropriate to compare all Airbus aircraft as a single subsidised product with

[102] Report of the Appellate Body, *European Communities and Certain Member States – Measures Affecting Trade in Large Civil Aircraft*, WT/DS316/AB/R, paras. 1050–1051.

[103] Report of the Appellate Body, *European Communities and Certain Member States – Measures Affecting Trade in Large Civil Aircraft*, WT/DS316/AB/R, para. 1063.

[104] Report of the Appellate Body, *European Communities and Certain Member States – Measures Affecting Trade in Large Civil Aircraft*, WT/DS316/AB/R, paras. 1092–1093.

[105] Report of the Appellate Body, *European Communities and Certain Member States – Measures Affecting Trade in Large Civil Aircraft*, WT/DS316/AB/R, paras. 1097–1098.

[106] Report of the Appellate Body, *European Communities and Certain Member States – Measures Affecting Trade in Large Civil Aircraft*, WT/DS316/AB/R, paras. 1115 et seq. and 1213.

all Boeing aircraft models as a single like product for the adverse effects assessment. Since the panel failed to make such an objective assessment of that question, the panel's finding that there was a single subsidised Airbus product and one single corresponding like product from Boeing could not stand. However, the Appellate Body itself could not complete the legal analysis of whether there was one or several aircraft product markets.[107]

Displacement was interpreted to mean a situation where the products of the competitor are substituted by the subsidised product.[108] For its analysis, the Appellate Body *de facto* divided the market into three segments: the single-aisle, the twin-aisle and the very large aircraft market, and assessed the market developments in some countries. In some markets it found displacement, in others the USA could not show displacement.[109]

A 'lost sale' was defined as a sale that a supplier 'failed to obtain.' However, Article 6.3 lit. c of the SCM Agreement requires that the lost sales are 'significant.' According to the Appellate Body, this would best be assessed through a counterfactual analysis, i.e. a comparison of the sales of the competitor's product with a hypothetical scenario where the respondent's products were not subsidised. Lost sales would be established if in the counterfactual scenario, the sales would have been made by the complaining party's company instead.[110] The Appellate Body then applied this test to the sale of Airbus A380 aircraft to Emirates Airlines and confirmed that Boeing lost these sales.[111] The Appellate Body also confirmed the chain of causation for the displacement and the lost sales.[112] Although the panel's analysis showed some deficiencies, the Appellate Body also agreed with the panel that the msf 'was a necessary precondition for Airbus' launch in 2000 of the A380.'[113] The Appellate Body, however, denied that the USA had established a causal link for the European R&D subsidies.[114]

[107] Report of the Appellate Body, *European Communities and Certain Member States – Measures Affecting Trade in Large Civil Aircraft*, WT/DS316/AB/R, paras. 1123, 1130, 1137 and 1147.

[108] Report of the Appellate Body, *European Communities and Certain Member States – Measures Affecting Trade in Large Civil Aircraft*, WT/DS316/AB/R, para. 1170.

[109] Report of the Appellate Body, *European Communities and Certain Member States – Measures Affecting Trade in Large Civil Aircraft*, WT/DS316/AB/R, paras. 1178–1204.

[110] Report of the Appellate Body, *European Communities and Certain Member States – Measures Affecting Trade in Large Civil Aircraft*, WT/DS316/AB/R, paras. 1214 et seq.

[111] Report of the Appellate Body, *European Communities and Certain Member States – Measures Affecting Trade in Large Civil Aircraft*, WT/DS316/AB/R, para. 1228.

[112] Report of the Appellate Body, *European Communities and Certain Member States – Measures Affecting Trade in Large Civil Aircraft*, WT/DS316/AB/R, para. 1300.

[113] Report of the Appellate Body, *European Communities and Certain Member States – Measures Affecting Trade in Large Civil Aircraft*, WT/DS316/AB/R, para. 1356.

[114] Report of the Appellate Body, *European Communities and Certain Member States – Measures Affecting Trade in Large Civil Aircraft*, WT/DS316/AB/R, para. 1411.

Panel *United States – Measures Affecting Trade in Large Civil Aircraft (Second Complaint)* (DS 353)

Facts of the Case

The Boeing case is the second case in the aircraft disputes between the USA and the EU. In this case, a panel had to decide on an EU claim that Boeing was illegally subsidised by different programmes and tax regimes of the US federal government, single US States and their municipalities. The panel assessed whether certain transfers of NASA, the US Department of Defence, the US Department of Commerce and the US Department of Labour were subsidies within the meaning of the SCM Agreement. At the sub-federal level, the panel looked into measures in the States of Washington, Kansas and Illinois where several transfers had been made to Boeing's research, development production and headquarters.[115] The Boeing case is, as mentioned before, the second chapter in the aircraft dispute. The decision of the Appellate Body in the Boeing case was published in 2012 and by and large confirmed the panel's finding.

Important Aspects of the Findings

When assessing whether or not the US tax regime for Boeing in Washington qualified as a financial contribution within the meaning of Article 1 of the SCM Agreement, the panel recalled that the basis for the determination of what 'would otherwise have been due' according to Article 1.1(a)(1)(ii) of the SCM Agreement 'must be the tax rules applied by the Member in question.'[116] Applying this standard, the panel held that there was a tax exemption for Boeing's manufacturing activities that deviated from the standard rate for manufacturing. However, for that reduction, Boeing would have had to pay higher taxes.[117] Similarly, Boeing profited from tax exemptions in Kansas. Furthermore, e.g. the City of Everett offered Boeing tax reductions on non-market terms and thereby conferred a subsidy on Boeing.[118] The subsidies also took the form of a workforce programme.[119]

---

[115] Report of the Panel, *United States – Measures Affecting Trade in Large Civil Aircraft (Second Complaint)*, WT/DS 353/R, para. 2.1.

[116] Report of the Panel, *United States – Measures Affecting Trade in Large Civil Aircraft (Second Complaint)*, WT/DS 353/R, para. 7.116.

[117] Report of the Panel, *United States – Measures Affecting Trade in Large Civil Aircraft (Second Complaint)*, WT/DS 353/R, paras. 7.121, 7.126 and 7.133.

[118] Report of the Panel, *United States – Measures Affecting Trade in Large Civil Aircraft (Second Complaint)*, WT/DS 353/R, paras. 7.332-7.333.

[119] Report of the Panel, *United States – Measures Affecting Trade in Large Civil Aircraft (Second Complaint)*, WT/DS 353/R, para. 7.589.

On the other hand, e.g. certain infrastructure measures in Everett and the waiver of landing fees in Snohomish County, were not found to be a subsidy to Boeing.[120]

Subsidies in Kansas amounting to $ 476 million were also held to be specific since disproportionately large amounts of the programme in question had been paid to Boeing and another company and were thus *de facto* specific according to Article 2.1 lit. c of the SCM Agreement.[121] The EU, however, could not demonstrate that other bonds that had been issued in Kansas had passed through to Boeing.[122] The panel found additional *de facto* specific subsidies in the form of property tax abatements and refunds in Illinois that were granted in consideration of Boeing's decision to relocate its headquarters.[123]

The panel furthermore assessed R&D programmes that NASA provided for Boeing. An interesting question of systemic nature here was whether certain support by NASA could be qualified as 'purchases of services' within the meaning of Article 1.1(a)(1) of the SCM Agreement. For the first time a panel had to decide 'whether transactions properly characterized as purchases of services are excluded from the scope of Article 1.1.(a)(1)(i) of the SCM Agreement.'[124] The panel held 'that the negotiators of the GATS were unable to reach agreement on disciplines regarding governmental purchases of services' and that the omission or exclusion of '"purchases" of "services" from Article 1 [of the SCM Agreement] can only be seen as a deliberate choice' of the drafters. The panel thus held that 'purchases of services are excluded from the scope of Article 1.1(a)(1)(i) of the SCM Agreement.'[125] Precondition for that, however, is that the measure in question is properly characterised as a purchase of a service. This would depend on 'whether or not the work performed was principally for the benefit or use of the government [...] or rather principally for the benefit or use of the "service" "seller" itself.' The panel was of the view that in this case 'the work that Boeing performed under its aeronautics R&D contracts with NASA was principally for its own benefit or use, rather than for the benefit or use of the US Government.'[126] Since these benefits also conferred a

[120] Report of the Panel, *United States – Measures Affecting Trade in Large Civil Aircraft (Second Complaint)*, WT/DS 353/R, paras. 7.480 and 7.515.

[121] Report of the Panel, *United States – Measures Affecting Trade in Large Civil Aircraft (Second Complaint)*, WT/DS 353/R, paras. 7.779 and 7.819.

[122] Report of the Panel, *United States – Measures Affecting Trade in Large Civil Aircraft (Second Complaint)*, WT/DS 353/R, para. 7.889.

[123] Report of the Panel, *United States – Measures Affecting Trade in Large Civil Aircraft (Second Complaint)*, WT/DS 353/R, paras. 7.927 and 7.939.

[124] Report of the Panel, *United States – Measures Affecting Trade in Large Civil Aircraft (Second Complaint)*, WT/DS 353/R, para. 7.953.

[125] Report of the Panel, *United States – Measures Affecting Trade in Large Civil Aircraft (Second Complaint)*, WT/DS 353/R, paras. 7.968-7.970.

[126] Report of the Panel, *United States – Measures Affecting Trade in Large Civil Aircraft (Second Complaint)*, WT/DS 353/R, para. 7.1027. Furthermore, the provision of access to NASA's facilities, its equipment and its employees was seen as the provision of goods and services to Boeing.

benefit upon Boeing, the R&D programmes were found to be subsidies within the meaning of the SCM.[127] The amount of these specific subsidies in the form of R&D programmes granted from 1989 to 2006 was valued to be $ 2.6 billion.[128]

Regarding a R&D contract of Boeing with the US Department of Defence, the panel held that some parts of the work Boeing had performed was primarily for the benefit of the Department of Defence and thus qualified as the purchase of services and no subsidy. Other parts, so-called assistance instruments of that programme were principally for the benefit of Boeing itself.[129]

Payments that the US Department of Commerce made to joint ventures where Boeing participated were subsidies but these subsidies were not specific within the meaning of Article 2 of the SCM Agreement.[130]

The EU also alleged that Boeing was subsidised through certain patent rights and data rights. The panel was, however, unable to see how certain intellectual property rights that Boeing obtained under the R&D contracts could be seen as a separate financial contribution to Boeing.[131]

In a second step the panel assessed whether the USA had also granted prohibited subsidies within the meaning of Article 3 of the SCM Agreement. It held that the US Foreign Sales Corporation (FSC) and Extraterritorial Income programmes were prohibited subsidies according to Articles 3.1 lit. a and 3.2 of the SCM Agreement because they were export-contingent. That came as no surprise since the Appellate Body had already qualified the FSC to be prohibited subsidies in the *US FSC* case.[132] The EU furthermore argued that the aforementioned tax reductions granted by the State of Washington were export contingent and thus prohibited subsidies. The panel's interpretation of the term export contingency may be of little relevance since the Appellate Body determined the meaning of that term in the Airbus case as described above. The panel was not satisfied that the grant of the subsidy was actually *tied* to the anticipated exportation. In light of Boeing's additional production capacity that was created in Washington, it held that there may be such a link but was not convinced by the evidence that was brought forward by the EU.[133] Thus, the panel did not find that the Washington tax programme was a prohibited subsidy.[134]

[127] Report of the Panel, *United States – Measures Affecting Trade in Large Civil Aircraft (Second Complaint)*, WT/DS 353/R, paras. 7.1040-7.1041.

[128] Report of the Panel, *United States – Measures Affecting Trade in Large Civil Aircraft (Second Complaint)*, WT/DS 353/R, para. 7.1110.

[129] Report of the Panel, *United States – Measures Affecting Trade in Large Civil Aircraft (Second Complaint)*, WT/DS 353/R, para. 7.1171.

[130] Report of the Panel, *United States – Measures Affecting Trade in Large Civil Aircraft (Second Complaint)*, WT/DS 353/R, para. 7.1257.

[131] Report of the Panel, *United States – Measures Affecting Trade in Large Civil Aircraft (Second Complaint)*, WT/DS 353/R, para. 7.1311.

[132] Report of the Panel, *United States – Measures Affecting Trade in Large Civil Aircraft (Second Complaint)*, WT/DS 353/R, paras. 7.1452 et seq. and 7.1463.

[133] Report of the Panel, *United States – Measures Affecting Trade in Large Civil Aircraft (Second Complaint)*, WT/DS 353/R, para. 7.1577.

[134] Report of the Panel, *United States – Measures Affecting Trade in Large Civil Aircraft (Second Complaint)*, WT/DS 353/R, para. 7.1590.

In the last part of its decision, the panel assessed whether the subsidies for Boeing caused adverse effects to the European rival, i.e. Airbus. It held that the EU was free to structure its serious prejudice claim. The EU divided the global market for large aircraft into five separate market segments: single-aisle aircraft with 100–200 seats, wide-body aircraft with 200–300, 300–400 and 400–500 seats, and super wide-body aircraft for more than 500 passengers. The EU then formed three groups of like products.[135] The panel found adverse effects to Airbus' different aircraft.[136]

Panel *Philippines – Taxes on Distilled Spirits* (DS 396 and 403)

Facts of the Case

The Philippines' excise tax regime for spirits distinguished between the raw materials from which the spirits were distilled and where that process took place: spirits produced from, e.g., syrup or sugar of the cane that were produced in the country where they were processed into distilled spirits were subject to a flat tax. All other spirits were subject to a much higher taxation. In effect, taxes on the vast majority of imported spirits were 10 to 40 times the rate imposed on domestic spirits that fulfilled the aforementioned criteria.[137] Not surprisingly, imported spirits accounted for only 2.3 % of the Philippine market.[138]

Important Aspects of the Findings

The case that was initiated jointly by the USA and the EU is a classic text book case on Article III of the GATT 1994. It conjugates the well-known criteria of likeness. The panel found a violation of Article III:2, first sentence of the GATT 1994 because the imported and domestic spirits were found to be like products and imported spirits were taxed in excess of the domestic ones.

The panel recalled the relevant test according to which the likeness of two products within the meaning of Article III of the GATT 1994 needs to 'be determined on a case-by-case basis, by examining all relevant factors.'

[135] Report of the Panel, *United States – Measures Affecting Trade in Large Civil Aircraft (Second Complaint)*, WT/DS 353/R, paras. 7.1667 and 7.1669-7.1670.

[136] Report of the Panel, *United States – Measures Affecting Trade in Large Civil Aircraft (Second Complaint)*, WT/DS 353/R, para. 7.1854.

[137] Report of the Panel, *Philippines – Taxes on Distilled Spirits*, WT/DS396/R, paras. 2.3-2.4, 7.88 and 7.183.

[138] Report of the Panel, *Philippines – Taxes on Distilled Spirits*, WT/DS396/R, para. 2.34.

This test—which is well-established under WTO jurisprudence—includes four criteria: (1) 'the product's properties, nature and quality'; (2) 'the product's end uses in a given market'; (3) 'consumers' tastes and habits that change from country to country'; and (4) 'the tariff classification.'[139] The panel held that since all products at issue were potable alcohols processed through distillation, the likeness analysis had to focus on the physical characteristics of the final product and not on the raw materials used.[140] There was, however, no difference in colour, flavour or aroma between the imported and domestic spirits, not even in their chemical composition.[141] The different spirits also shared the same end use and tariff classification. Furthermore, consumers in the Philippines were willing to consume spirits irrespective of their raw materials.[142]

The panel also found that there is a direct competitive relationship between the alcoholic beverages at issue and thus a violation of Article III:2, second sentence of the GATT 1994.[143]

Appellate Body *Philippines – Taxes on Distilled Spirits* (DS 396 and 403)

The Appellate Body largely[144] confirmed the panel's finding. The Appellate Body clarified that 'in spite of the differences in the raw materials used to make the products, if these differences do not affect the final products, these products can still be found to be "like"' since Article III:2, first sentence of the GATT 1994 would refer to like products, 'not to their raw material base.'[145] The ethyl alcohol distilled from sugar cane molasses would be stripped off its congeners and would therefore be a neutral spirit; domestic and imported distilled spirits would be presented to consumers as indistinguishable.[146]

---

[139] Report of the Panel, *Philippines – Taxes on Distilled Spirits*, WT/DS396/R, para. 7.31.

[140] Report of the Panel, *Philippines – Taxes on Distilled Spirits*, WT/DS396/R, paras. 7.35 and 7.37.

[141] Report of the Panel, *Philippines – Taxes on Distilled Spirits*, WT/DS396/R, paras. 7.39-7.40.

[142] Report of the Panel, *Philippines – Taxes on Distilled Spirits*, WT/DS396/R, paras. 7.48 and 7.62-7.63.

[143] Report of the Panel, *Philippines – Taxes on Distilled Spirits*, WT/DS396/R, para. 7.137; the discrimination was also more than *de minimis*, cf. para. 7.154.

[144] However, the panel narrowed the scope of imported products that would have to be regarded as like products, cf. Report of the Appellate Body, *Philippines—Taxes on Distilled Spirits,WT/DS396/AB/R*, para. 183 in conjunction with para. 174. Furthermore, the Appellate Body also reversed the panel on a procedural issue since it misinterpreted a claim of the EU, cf. paras. 191 and 260.

[145] Report of the Appellate Body, *Philippines – Taxes on Distilled Spirits*,WT/DS396/AB/R, para. 125.

[146] Report of the Appellate Body, *Philippines – Taxes on Distilled Spirits*,WT/DS396/AB/R, paras. 126 and 128.

Appellate Body *Thailand – Customs and Fiscal Measures on Cigarettes from the Philippines (DS 371)*

As described in last year's contribution[147] a panel had to rule on a dispute that arose about Philip Morris Thailand's importation of cigarettes manufactured in the Philippines by another Philip Morris subsidiary, Philip Morris Thailand. The Philippines successfully claimed that Thai Customs breached the multilateral WTO Customs Valuation Agreement by incorrectly determining the tax value of the goods and by disclosing certain confidential information to the public. Furthermore, imported cigarettes had been taxed in excess of domestic cigarettes which was held to be a violation of Article III:2, first sentence of the GATT 1994. The Philippines appealed certain aspects of the finding that relate to alleged violations of the GATT 1994. In contrast, the panel's findings with regard to the violations of the Customs Violations Agreement were not contested.[148]

Important Aspects of the Findings

The Appellate Body confirmed the violation of Article III:2, first sentence of the GATT 1994 since Thailand indeed discriminated like imported cigarettes. The Thai argument that Article III:2 of the GATT 1994 would not be applicable because the measure at issue was no tax but an administrative requirement was rejected by the Appellate Body.[149] It also held that Thailand had violated Article III:4 and X:3 lit. b of the GATT 1994.[150]

More interesting than the little surprising clarifications on Article III of the GATT 1994 was a procedural issue. Thailand argued that the panel had violated Thailand's due process rights by not allowing Thailand to comment on a piece of evidence that was submitted by the Philippines.[151] The Appellate Body confirmed that '[d]ue process is a fundamental principle of WTO dispute settlement' and that generally each party must be 'afforded a meaningful opportunity to comment on the arguments and evidence adduced by the other party.' However, it would be the

---

[147] Krallmann, WTO Dispute Settlement: Current Cases, in: Herrmann/Terhechte (eds.), *European Yearbook of International Economic Law 2012*, p. 577 (589–591).

[148] Report of the Appellate Body, *Thailand – Customs and Fiscal Measures on Cigarettes from the Philippines*, WT/DS371/AB/R, para. 82.

[149] Report of the Appellate Body, *Thailand – Customs and Fiscal Measures on Cigarettes from the Philippines*, WT/DS371/AB/R, paras. 108, 114 and 119.

[150] Report of the Appellate Body, *Thailand – Customs and Fiscal Measures on Cigarettes from the Philippines*, WT/DS371/AB/R, paras. 181 and 222. The Appellate Body corrected an error by the panel on Thailand's justification according to Article XX of the GATT 1994 but Thailand failed to establish the necessary elements for a justification, cf. paras. 169–170 and 180.

[151] Report of the Appellate Body, *Thailand – Customs and Fiscal Measures on Cigarettes from the Philippines*, WT/DS371/AB/R, para. 145.

party's responsibility to 'bring alleged procedural deficiencies to the attention of a panel at the earliest possible opportunity.'[152] Thailand, however, only objected to the Philippine submission 7 months after the submission (in its comments on the interim report), of the panel, although it could have requested to respond earlier. Thus, Thailand did not establish a failure of due process.[153] This procedural ruling could cause parties of future disputes to engage more widely in objecting submissions by the other party in order to be on the safe side. That, in turn, could lead to more cumbersome panel proceedings.

Appellate Body *European Communities – Definitive Anti-Dumping Measures on Certain Iron or Steel Fasteners from China* (DS 397)

Facts of the Case

The Appellate Body confirmed the panel's finding that Article 9(5) of the European Basic Anti-Dumping Regulation was in breach of the Anti-Dumping Agreement. The provision allowed the European anti-dumping authorities to apply a country-wide anti-dumping duty to all exporters if the country concerned was a non-market economy and if the exporter could not qualify for a certain exception. For a description of the case and more details on the provision the reader is kindly referred to last year's contribution that sets out the facts of the case and the panel's decision.[154]

Important Aspects of the Findings

The EU had argued that China's Accession Protocol would allow members to treat China as a non-market economy for the purpose of applying anti-dumping duties. The Appellate Body interpreted Section 15 of China's Accession Protocol narrowly: Section 15 of the Accession Protocol would place the burden on China's producers to prove that market economy conditions prevail in the industry that allegedly dumps and that does not want to be treated as a non-market economy producer. However, the Appellate Body read Section 15 lit. a of the Chinese Accession Protocol to regulate only how the normal value can be determined in

[152] Report of the Appellate Body, *Thailand – Customs and Fiscal Measures on Cigarettes from the Philippines*, WT/DS371/AB/R, paras. 147 and 150.

[153] Report of the Appellate Body, *Thailand – Customs and Fiscal Measures on Cigarettes from the Philippines*, WT/DS371/AB/R, paras. 156 and 160–161.

[154] Krallmann, WTO Dispute Settlement: Current Cases, in: Herrmann/Terhechte (eds.), *European Yearbook of International Economic Law 2012*, p. 577 (609–612).

anti-dumping proceedings with Chinese exporters. In the narrow interpretation of the Appellate Body this would not include an authorisation of 'WTO Members to treat China differently from other Members *except for the determination of price-comparability* in respect of domestic prices and costs in China, which relates to the determination of normal value.' In other words, Section 15 of the Chinese Accession Protocol would not be an open-ended exception to treat China differently in other aspects of the anti-dumping investigations.[155] It would not 'pronounce generally on China's status as a market economy or' non-market economy.[156] The Appellate Body furthermore sided with the panel that Article 9(5) of the European Basic Anti-Dumping Regulation would not only concern the imposition of anti-dumping duties but also the calculation of the dumping margins.[157] Since Section 15 of the Accession Protocol does not address the export price aspect of the price comparability it cannot be viewed as an exception to the requirement in Article 6.10 of the Anti-Dumping Agreement to determine individual dumping margins.[158] Furthermore, Article 9.2, third sentence of the Anti-Dumping Agreement would only allow members to name the supplying country concerned when it is *impracticable* to name individual suppliers but it does not permit naming the supplying country when the imposition of individual duties is *ineffective*. Therefore, investigating authorities would have to specify an individual duty for each supplier unless it is *impracticable*. The Appellate Body held that this would not allow the EU to impose country-wide duties on exporters from non-market economies that do not meet the additional requirements that are set out in Article 9(5) of the European Basic Anti-Dumping Regulation because the imposition of individual duties might otherwise be ineffective.[159]

Furthermore, the EU could not establish that the economic structure in China would allow a general presumption that the Chinese government and all Chinese exporters constitute a single entity.[160] The Appellate Body explicitly stated that a member could materially influence the prices and output of its exporters so that the state and the exporters could be regarded as a single exporter for the purposes of the Anti-Dumping Agreement. However, in the Appellate Body's view the test set out in Article 9(5) of the European Basic Anti-Dumping Regulation did not have that function.[161]

[155] Report of the Appellate Body, *European Communities – Definitive Anti-Dumping Measures on Certain Iron or Steel Fasteners from China*, WT/DS 397/AB/R, paras. 287 and 289–290.

[156] Report of the Appellate Body, *European Communities – Definitive Anti-Dumping Measures on Certain Iron or Steel Fasteners from China*, WT/DS 397/AB/R, para. 366.

[157] Report of the Appellate Body, *European Communities – Definitive Anti-Dumping Measures on Certain Iron or Steel Fasteners from China*, WT/DS 397/AB/R, para. 308.

[158] Report of the Appellate Body, *European Communities – Definitive Anti-Dumping Measures on Certain Iron or Steel Fasteners from China*, WT/DS 397/AB/R, para. 328.

[159] Report of the Appellate Body, *European Communities – Definitive Anti-Dumping Measures on Certain Iron or Steel Fasteners from China*, WT/DS 397/AB/R, paras. 348, 351 and 354.

[160] Report of the Appellate Body, *European Communities – Definitive Anti-Dumping Measures on Certain Iron or Steel Fasteners from China*, WT/DS 397/AB/R, para. 369.

[161] Report of the Appellate Body, *European Communities – Definitive Anti-Dumping Measures on Certain Iron or Steel Fasteners from China*, WT/DS 397/AB/R, para. 376.

Thus, the provision of Article 9(5) of the European Basic Anti-Dumping Regulation *as such* was found to be in breach of Articles 6.10 and 9.2 of the Anti-Dumping Agreement.[162] Since the law was found to be inconsistent as such, the report forced the EU to change its legislation.

The Appellate Body also judged on some aspects of the definitive anti-dumping duties that the EU applied on certain iron and steel fasteners from China.

First of all, it logically concluded that the application of Article 9(5) of the European Basic Anti-Dumping Regulation in this case ('*as applied*') had been inconsistent with the WTO obligations as well.[163] The Appellate Body also determined how 'domestic industry' has to be defined in the context of Articles 4.1 and 3.1 of the Anti-Dumping Agreement. Article 4.1 of the Anti-Dumping Agreement stipulates that the domestic industry is being referred to as 'domestic producers as a whole of the like product' or 'those of them whose collective output of the product constitutes a major proportion of the total domestic production,' leaving room for two exceptions that were of no relevance in this case. When determining the domestic industry, the investigating authorities 'must not act so as to give rise to a material risk of distortion in defining the domestic industry' but on the other hand the Appellate Body acknowledged that the investigating authorities have 'some flexibility to define the domestic industry in the light of what is reasonable and practically possible.'[164] Article 5.4 of the Anti-Dumping Agreement would concern a different question, i.e. whether an application is made by or on behalf of the domestic industry. There, a benchmark of 25 % of the total production is required. However, this benchmark would not define domestic industry *itself*.[165] The EU's application of a 25 % benchmark for the purpose of domestic industry thus did not address the right question. However, the Appellate Body declined further appeals made by China in regard to other aspects of Articles 3.1 and 4.1 of the Anti-Dumping Agreement.[166]

Thereafter, the Appellate Body assessed other aspects of the definitive anti-dumping duties on steel fasteners, e.g. the treatment of confidential information and the protection of anonymous supporters of the anti-dumping investigation against steel fasteners from China.

[162] Report of the Appellate Body, *European Communities – Definitive Anti-Dumping Measures on Certain Iron or Steel Fasteners from China*, WT/DS 397/AB/R, para. 385.

[163] Report of the Appellate Body, *European Communities – Definitive Anti-Dumping Measures on Certain Iron or Steel Fasteners from China*, WT/DS 397/AB/R, para. 409.

[164] Report of the Appellate Body, *European Communities – Definitive Anti-Dumping Measures on Certain Iron or Steel Fasteners from China*, WT/DS 397/AB/R, paras. 411 et seq.

[165] Report of the Appellate Body, *European Communities – Definitive Anti-Dumping Measures on Certain Iron or Steel Fasteners from China*, WT/DS 397/AB/R, para. 418.

[166] Report of the Appellate Body, *European Communities – Definitive Anti-Dumping Measures on Certain Iron or Steel Fasteners from China*, WT/DS 397/AB/R, paras. 430 and 468.

Appellate Body *United States – Definitive Anti-Dumping and Countervailing Duties on Certain Products from China* (DS 379)

Facts of the Case

The USA had imposed cumulatively definitive anti-dumping and countervailing duties on four different categories of goods from China. Furthermore, the US measures targeted the provision of preferential loans for Chinese producers by state-owned commercial banks. The case touched upon systemically important aspects: whether a member needs to restrict itself to either anti-dumping sanctions or countervailing duties when faced with products that are both dumped and subsidised; the definition of the term 'public body' in Article 1 of the SCM Agreement since the panel had to decide whether the Chinese state-owned banks and enterprises had to be qualified as governmental bodies within the meaning of the SCM Agreement; and how the relevant benchmarks for the comparison of interest rates for commercial loans should be established in a case involving China and its state-owned commercial banks. The main facts of the case and the panel's decision are set out in last year's edition.[167]

Important Aspects of the Findings

The Appellate Body first looked at the concept of public body in Article 1.1 lit. a (1) of the SCM Agreement and provided a significant but unexpected clarification of this key term. According to the Appellate Body's definition, a 'public body within the meaning of Article 1.1.(a)(1) of the SCM Agreement must be an entity that possesses, exercises or is vested with governmental authority. Yet, just as no two governments are exactly alike, the precise contours and characteristics of a public body are bound to differ from entity to entity, State to State, and case to case.'[168] Future panels will thus have to carefully assess and evaluate the core features of the entity that grants the subsidy. It may also be possible that an entity may have characteristics that may suggest that it is a public body and features suggesting that it is a private body. 'What matters is whether an entity is vested with authority to exercise governmental functions, rather than how that is achieved.'[169] In that context, the Appellate Body stressed that the existence of

---

[167] Krallmann, WTO Dispute Settlement: Current Cases, in: Herrmann/Terhechte (eds.), *European Yearbook of International Economic Law 2012*, p. 577 (584–588).

[168] Report of the Appellate Body, *United States – Definitive Anti-Dumping and Countervailing Duties on Certain Products from China*, WT/DS 379/AB/R, para. 317.

[169] Report of the Appellate Body, *United States – Definitive Anti-Dumping and Countervailing Duties on Certain Products from China*, WT/DS 379/AB/R, para. 318.

'mere formal links between an entity and government in the narrow sense is unlikely to suffice to establish the necessary possession of governmental authority.' The Appellate Body thereby disagreed with the panel's interpretation of the term public body. The Appellate Body demands a complex and difficult evaluation of the entity whereas the control of the entity in question by the government in itself will not be sufficient to establish that it is indeed a public body.[170] Since the US determination that the producers of steel, rubber and petrochemical inputs were public entities relied principally on the information of the ownership of these companies instead of evidence that they were meaningfully controlled by China, the US determination was found to be inconsistent with the SCM Agreement. However, the USA was right in characterising the Chinese state owned commercial banks as public bodies.[171] As a consequence of this ruling, the determination of whether an entity is a public body will be much more complicated and cumbersome for investigating authorities in the future.

The Appellate Body also interpreted, for the first time, certain aspects of specificity according to Article 2 of the SCM Agreement. The question before the Appellate Body was whether a subsidy is only then specific within the meaning of Article 2.1 of the SCM Agreement if the granting authority 'explicitly limits access both to the financial contribution and to its corresponding benefits' or 'whether, as the panel found, an explicit limitation on access either to the financial contribution or to the benefit may prove sufficient.' The Appellate Body agreed with the panel, it could be made effective through a limitation on either.[172]

The Appellate Body also had to rule on the question of the right benchmark according to Article 14 lit. d of the SCM Agreement. China alleged that the panel was wrong in allowing the USA to reject in-country private prices in China as the proper benchmark. The Appellate Body gave an instructive overview of how the benchmark according to Article 14 lit. d of the SCM Agreement had to be chosen.[173] It concluded that the USA in this case where China itself supplied more than 96 % of the products[174] was allowed to reject the Chinese private prices as a basis for the comparison. '[A]n investigating authority may reject in-country private prices if it reaches the conclusion that these are *too distorted due to the predominant participation of the government* as a supplier in the market, thus rendering the comparison required under Article 14(d) of the SCM Agreement circular.'[175]

[170] Report of the Appellate Body, *United States – Definitive Anti-Dumping and Countervailing Duties on Certain Products from China*, WT/DS 379/AB/R, paras. 319–320.

[171] Report of the Appellate Body, *United States – Definitive Anti-Dumping and Countervailing Duties on Certain Products from China*, WT/DS 379/AB/R, paras. 346–347 and 356.

[172] Report of the Appellate Body, *United States – Definitive Anti-Dumping and Countervailing Duties on Certain Products from China*, WT/DS 379/AB/R, paras. 377–378.

[173] Report of the Appellate Body, *United States – Definitive Anti-Dumping and Countervailing Duties on Certain Products from China*, WT/DS 379/AB/R, paras. 431 et seq.

[174] Report of the Appellate Body, *United States – Definitive Anti-Dumping and Countervailing Duties on Certain Products from China*, WT/DS 379/AB/R, para. 456.

[175] Report of the Appellate Body, *United States – Definitive Anti-Dumping and Countervailing Duties on Certain Products from China*, WT/DS 379/AB/R, para. 446.

Similarly, the Appellate Body also had to decide on the proper benchmark for the comparison of the interest rates of Chinese state-owned commercial banks. Unlike Article 14 lit. d of the SCM Agreement, Article 14 lit. b lays down a benchmark for loans without mentioning territoriality. The Appellate Body for the very first time in history applied Article 14 lit. b and clarified that the provision does not specify any geographical scope for the relevant market. The selection of a benchmark within the meaning of this provision would thus entail a 'progressive search for a comparable commercial loan, starting with the commercial loan that is closest to the investigated loan [. . .] and moving to less similar commercial loans while adjusting them.' Article 14 lit. b of the SCM Agreement would not bar investigating authorities from using (adjusted) benchmarks interest loans denominated in other currencies or a proxy.[176]

Lastly but very importantly, the Appellate Body had to decide on the concept of double remedies or double counting. These terms refer to 'circumstances in which the simultaneous application of anti-dumping and countervailing duties on the same imported products results, at least to some extent, in the offsetting of the same subsidization twice.' This is a problem that may occur in the context of investigations in non-market economies since here the comparison of the export price with the normal value can be based on surrogate costs or prices from an analogue third country. Under these circumstances the subsidisation of the product may be included in the overall dumping margin and may cause a double counting.[177] The Appellate Body held that such an imposition of double remedies is inconsistent with Article 19.3 of the SCM Agreement that requires the investigating authorities to impose appropriate amounts. The objective of the SCM Agreement would be to offset the damaging subsidisation and to remove the injury to the domestic industry. The appropriateness of the amount of the countervailing duty would not be unrelated to the injury that is being caused. The Appellate Body explained that the panel's interpretation of Article VI:5 of the GATT 1994 was flawed: the panel concluded that the prohibition of double remedies would only apply to export subsidies. *E contrario*, the panel concluded that members did not want a prohibition of double remedies in the case of domestic subsidies.[178] However, the Appellate Body stressed that the term 'same situation' would be central for the interpretation of the prohibition of the cumulative appliance of anti-dumping and countervailing duties in Article VI:5 of the GATT 1994: '[w]e recall that, in principle, an export subsidy will result in a *pro rata* reduction in the export price of a product, but will not affect the price of domestic sales of that product. That is, the subsidy will lead to increased price discrimination and a higher

[176] Report of the Appellate Body, *United States – Definitive Anti-Dumping and Countervailing Duties on Certain Products from China*, WT/DS 379/AB/R, paras. 486 et seq.

[177] Report of the Appellate Body, *United States – Definitive Anti-Dumping and Countervailing Duties on Certain Products from China*, WT/DS 379/AB/R, paras. 541 et seq.

[178] Report of the Appellate Body, *United States – Definitive Anti-Dumping and Countervailing Duties on Certain Products from China*, WT/DS 379/AB/R, paras. 547 et seq.

margin of dumping. In such circumstances, the situation of subsidization and the situation of dumping are the "same situation," and the application of concurrent duties would amount to the application of "double remedies" to compensate for, or offset, that situation. By comparison, domestic subsidies will, in principle, affect the prices at which a producer sells its goods in the domestic market and in export markets in the same way and to the same extent. Since any lowering of prices attributable to the subsidy will be reflected on both sides of the dumping margin calculation, the overall dumping margin will not be affected by the subsidization. In such circumstances, the concurrent application of duties would not compensate for the same situation, because no part of the dumping margin would be attributable to the subsidization. Only the countervailing duty would offset such subsidization.'[179] The Anti-Dumping Agreement and the SCM Agreement taken together would suggest that a double remedy 'would circumvent the standard of appropriateness that the two agreements separately establish for their respective remedies.'[180] Thus, the Appellate Body concluded that the imposition of double remedies was inconsistent with Article 19.3 of the SCM Agreement.[181]

Panel *European Union – Anti-Dumping Measures on Certain Footwear from China* (DS 405)

Facts of the Case

This case was another anti-dumping case that China brought against the EU. The core issue in this case, like in the steel fasteners case, was an *as such* claim against Article 9(5) of the European Basic Anti-Dumping Regulation according to which the EU could apply nation-wide anti-dumping duties for all Chinese producers. This time the EU charged duties on Chinese imports of certain footwear with uppers of leather.[182] China argued that both the European Definitive Regulation that set out the background of the investigation against the leather shoes and formed the basis for the imposition of the duties and the Review Regulation that extended the anti-dumping duties that were originally set out in the aforementioned Definitive Regulation were inconsistent with the requirements of the Anti-Dumping Agreement.[183]

[179] Report of the Appellate Body, *United States – Definitive Anti-Dumping and Countervailing Duties on Certain Products from China*, WT/DS 379/AB/R, para. 568.

[180] Report of the Appellate Body, *United States – Definitive Anti-Dumping and Countervailing Duties on Certain Products from China*, WT/DS 379/AB/R, para. 572.

[181] Report of the Appellate Body, *United States – Definitive Anti-Dumping and Countervailing Duties on Certain Products from China*, WT/DS 379/AB/R, para. 583.

[182] Report of the Panel, *European Union – Anti-Dumping Measures on Certain Footwear from China*, WT/DS405/R, para. 2.

[183] Report of the Panel, *European Union – Anti-Dumping Measures on Certain Footwear from China*, WT/DS405/R, paras. 7.115 and 7.121.

Important Aspects of the Findings

In its decision, the panel followed the reasoning of the steel fasteners decision: the panel agreed with the panel in *EC Fasteners* that Article 9(5) of the European Basic Anti-Dumping Regulation as such and as applied could not be reconciled with the provisions of Articles 6.10 and 9.2 of the Anti-Dumping Agreement.[184] The panel also held that the European Anti-Dumping Regulation constituted a violation of the most-favoured-nation principle contained in Article I:1 of the GATT 1994.[185]

The panel assessed whether the EU had kept the procedural requirements in its anti-dumping proceedings. The panel found that the EU was in breach of Article 6.5.1 of the Anti-Dumping Agreement by failing to ensure that producers who had submitted confidential production data did supply an adequate non-confidential summary of this data or provide an explanation why this summary could not be made.[186]

The vast majority of alleged procedural breaches in the European anti-dumping procedures on leather shoes were, however, not founded: China was of the view that the other members had committed themselves in Paragraph 151 of China's Working Party Report to provide Chinese producers with certain information. The panel made clear that this stipulation of China's Working Party Report could not be understood to have imposed legally binding obligations on the other members.[187] Nor did Paragraph 15(a)(ii) of China's Accession Protocol suggest that the other members 'must consider whether individual producers can show that market economy conditions prevail with respect to each of the individual producers or any of them.'[188] The EU, furthermore, committed no error in selecting the relevant samples for the dumping determination.[189] Also, the panel found no mistake in the EU selecting Brazil as the analogue country for determining normal value.[190] Furthermore, the samples used by the EU were found to be sufficiently representative of the European industry.[191] China also failed to demonstrate that the EU was

---

[184] Report of the Panel, *European Union – Anti-Dumping Measures on Certain Footwear from China*, WT/DS405/R, paras. 7.83 et seq. for the *as such* claim and paras. 7.140 and 7.147 for the *as applied* claim.

[185] Report of the Panel, *European Union – Anti-Dumping Measures on Certain Footwear from China*, WT/DS405/R, para. 7.105.

[186] Report of the Panel, *European Union – Anti-Dumping Measures on Certain Footwear from China*, WT/DS405/R, para. 7.709.

[187] Report of the Panel, *European Union – Anti-Dumping Measures on Certain Footwear from China*, WT/DS405/R, paras. 7.180f.

[188] Report of the Panel, *European Union – Anti-Dumping Measures on Certain Footwear from China*, WT/DS405/R, para. 7.194.

[189] Report of the Panel, *European Union – Anti-Dumping Measures on Certain Footwear from China*, WT/DS405/R, paras. 7.215 and 7.226.

[190] Report of the Panel, *European Union – Anti-Dumping Measures on Certain Footwear from China*, WT/DS405/R, para. 7.266.

[191] Report of the Panel, *European Union – Anti-Dumping Measures on Certain Footwear from China*, WT/DS405/R, paras. 7.388 and 7.391.

in breach of Article 3.5 of the Anti-Dumping Agreement 'by failing to examine known factors other than the dumped imports' that were causing injury to the EU industry.[192]

Panel *United States – Use of Zeroing in Anti-Dumping Measures Involving Products from Korea* (DS 402)

This case was yet another zeroing case brought against the USA, this time by Korea.

Zeroing is a methodology applied by the US authorities when calculating the margins of dumping for anti-dumping duties. During anti-dumping investigations some of the individual products may show a positive margin of dumping that means that they have been dumped. Other products may show negative margins of dumping, i.e. they are not dumped. When making an assessment for the whole group of products under consideration, some of the positive and negative margins would cancel each other out. However, zeroing means that any negative margin is valued as zero, thus the margins of anti-dumping duties are artificially increased.[193]

In light of numerous decisions of panels and the Appellate Body that condemn the zeroing methodology,[194] it came as no surprise that the panel found once again that the zeroing method does not comply with the Anti-Dumping Agreement. As one Appellate Body member put it in *US Continued Zeroing*: The Appellate Body 'has spoken definitely' on that question, 'there must be an end to every great debate.'[195] Despite this clarification by the Appellate Body, the USA still applied the zeroing methodology and was consequently facing several cases by other members that defended themselves against this illegal practice.

This time the panel assessed zeroing on dumping margins for Korean exporters of certain steel products and diamond sawblades.[196] Although the USA did not

[192] Report of the Panel, *European Union – Anti-Dumping Measures on Certain Footwear from China*, WT/DS405/R, paras. 7.541.

[193] Goode, *Dictionary of Trade Policy Terms*, (5th ed.) 2007, p. 491.

[194] For more information on the technique of zeroing and other cases that condemned the use of zeroing, cf. Krallmann, WTO Dispute Settlement—The Establishment of 'Binding Guidance' by the Appellate Body in *US Stainless Steel* and Recent Dispute Settlement Rulings, in: Herrmann/Terhechte (eds.), *European Yearbook of International Economic Law 2011*, p. 417 (438–446) and Krallmann, WTO Dispute Settlement: Current Cases, in: Herrmann/Terhechte (eds.), *European Yearbook of International Economic Law 2012*, p. 577 (591–592).

[195] Report of the Appellate Body, *United States – Continued Existence and Application of Zeroing Methodology*, WT/DS350/AB/R, para. 312.

[196] Report of the Panel, *United States – Use of Zeroing in Anti-Dumping Measures Involving Products from Korea*, WT/DS402/R, para. 2.1.

contest the inconsistency of the measure with the AD Agreement, the panel examined in its very short decision whether Korea had made a *prima facie* case for the illegality of the zeroing measure.[197] The Korean submissions were found to be satisfactory and thus the USA was found to have violated Article 2.4.2 of the Anti-Dumping Agreement.[198] The USA did not appeal the ruling.

Panel *United States – Anti-Dumping Administrative Reviews and Other Measures Related to Imports of Certain Orange Juice from Brazil* (DS 382)

The second zeroing case that had been decided in 2011 dealt with the so-called variant of 'simple zeroing' in administrative reviews of anti-dumping duties against orange juice imports from Brazil.[199] Again, the measure was found not to be in compliance with Article 2.4 of the Anti-Dumping Agreement.[200]

More interesting than the result is that one of the panellists had concerns about this well discussed question. Article 2.4 of the Anti-Dumping Agreement would not be as clear as previous panels and the Appellate Body had suggested. However, 'on balance and in the light of the systemic considerations [...], the view of the Appellate Body should be followed on this issue.'[201] Although the above mentioned panel in *US Zeroing Korea* rightly held that 'panels are not bound by Appellate Body reasoning,'[202] there arguably exists the principle of *binding guidance*.[203] This decision proves that the first instance panels of the WTO dispute settlement feel obliged to follow the Appellate Body's guidance.

Again, as in the previous case with Korea, the USA did not appeal the ruling.

---

[197] Report of the Panel, *United States – Use of Zeroing in Anti-Dumping Measures Involving Products from Korea*, WT/DS402/R, paras. 7.12 and 7.20.

[198] Report of the Panel, *United States – Use of Zeroing in Anti-Dumping Measures Involving Products from Korea*, WT/DS402/R, para. 7.35.

[199] Report of the Panel, *United States – Anti-Dumping Administrative Reviews and Other Measures Related to Imports of Certain Orange Juice from Brazil*, WT/DS382/R, paras. 2.1-2.2 and 7.130.

[200] Report of the Panel, *United States – Anti-Dumping Administrative Reviews and Other Measures Related to Imports of Certain Orange Juice from Brazil*, WT/DS382/R, paras. 7.154, 7.161 and 7.193.

[201] Report of the Panel, *United States – Anti-Dumping Administrative Reviews and Other Measures Related to Imports of Certain Orange Juice from Brazil*, WT/DS382/R, para. 7.143.

[202] Report of the Panel, *United States – Use of Zeroing in Anti-Dumping Measures Involving Products from Korea*, WT/DS402/R, para. 7.31.

[203] Krallmann, WTO Dispute Settlement—The Establishment of 'Binding Guidance' by the Appellate Body in *US Stainless Steel* and Recent Dispute Settlement Rulings, in: Herrmann/Terhechte (eds.), *European Yearbook of International Economic Law 2011*, p. 417 (420–429).

Panel *United States – Anti-Dumping Measures on Certain Shrimp from Viet Nam* (DS 404)

Facts of the Case

In Vietnam's first case ever as a party in a WTO dispute settlement case, Vietnam attacked the imposition of anti-dumping duties on shrimp exported to the USA. The first claim once again related to the application of the zeroing methodology in the calculation of the anti-dumping margins. Furthermore, Vietnam claimed that the USA wrongly applied a country-wide anti-dumping rate on all Vietnamese exporters, regardless of some exporters' declaration to be independent of the Vietnamese state. Additionally, the USA allegedly limited the number of Vietnamese producers or exporters of shrimp selected for individual investigation or review and did not correctly apply the so called all 'others rate.'[204]

Important Aspects of the Findings

Again, it came as no surprise that yet another panel condemned the US practice of zeroing to be incompatible with Articles 2.4 and 9.3 of the Anti-Dumping Agreement and Article VI:2 of the GATT 1994.[205] Due to the use of the zeroing methodology, the determination of the second and third administrative review in question was, furthermore, found to be in breach of Article 9.4 of the AD-Agreement.[206]

Vietnam, on the contrary, was not successful in arguing that the USA was in breach of several Articles of the Anti-Dumping Agreement because it did not issue individual margins for all exporters of shrimp. The panel clarified that Article 6.10 of the Anti-Dumping Agreement leaves no doubt that *in general* there would be a preference for the determination of individual margins but that there are also clear exceptions that allow the investigating authorities not to determine individual margins for all exporters.[207]

---

[204] Report of the Panel, *United States – Anti-Dumping Measures on Certain Shrimp from Viet Nam*, WT/DS404/R, paras. 2.1 et seq.

[205] Report of the Panel, *United States – Anti-Dumping Measures on Certain Shrimp from Viet Nam*, WT/DS404/R, paras. 7.95 and 7.142.

[206] Report of the Panel, *United States – Anti-Dumping Measures on Certain Shrimp from Viet Nam*, WT/DS404/R, para. 7.227.

[207] Report of the Panel, *United States – Anti-Dumping Measures on Certain Shrimp from Viet Nam*, WT/DS404/R, para. 7.167; cf. para. 7.191 on the question whether one of the exporters was discouraged to voluntarily respond to the US investigating authority.

The USA treated Vietnam as a non-market economy and applied a rebuttable assumption that all shrimp exporters were controlled by the government and treated all government controlled units collectively as a single exporter. Exporters that could establish their independence from government control were either treated individually or assigned the 'all others rate.' All exporters that did not prove that they were independent from the Vietnamese state were subject to a rate that was determined to the Vietnam wide state entity. This rate was set above 25 %, more than five times the all others rate.[208] The panel found that neither the wording of Article 9.4 of the Anti-Dumping Agreement nor the Vietnamese Working Party Report allowed for an application of this all others rate subject to additional requirements that are not mentioned in Article 9.4 of the Anti-Dumping Agreement. The panel thus found the US determination to be inconsistent with Article 9.4 of the Anti-Dumping Agreement.[209]

Neither party appealed the panel's decision.

Appellate Body United States - Measures Affecting Imports of Certain Passenger Vehicle and Light Truck Tyres from China (DS 399)

Facts of the Case

As described in more detail in last year's contribution, a panel found that the USA correctly applied safeguard duties on imported tyres from China for a period of 3 years. The peculiarity of this US safeguard measure was that the safeguard duties were not based on the multilateral WTO Safeguards Agreement but on the transitional product-specific safeguard mechanism under the Chinese Accession Protocol. This special mechanism allows other members to limit Chinese imports if they enter the other members' territories 'in such increased quantities or under such conditions as to cause or threaten to cause market disruption.'[210] In contrast to a 'normal' safeguard measure according to the multilateral Safeguards Agreement, a safeguard measure taken under the Chinese Accession Protocol does not affect imports from other WTO members.

---

[208] Report of the Panel, *United States – Anti-Dumping Measures on Certain Shrimp from Viet Nam*, WT/DS404/R, paras. 7.237-7.238.

[209] Report of the Panel, *United States – Anti-Dumping Measures on Certain Shrimp from Viet Nam*, WT/DS404/R, paras. 7.237 et seq.

[210] Krallmann, WTO Dispute Settlement: Current Cases, in: Herrmann/Terhechte (eds.), *European Yearbook of International Economic Law 2012*, p. 577 (593–595).

Important Aspects of the Findings

The Appellate Body confirmed that the conditions for the application of the safeguard measures were fulfilled. The Appellate Body defined 'increasing rapidly' imports that are required by Paragraph 16.4 of the Chinese Protocol of Accession to impose safeguards as imports that are 'increasing at great speed or swiftly, either in relative or absolute terms.' The increases have to 'be occurring over a short and recent period of time, and must be of a sufficient absolute or relative magnitude so as to be a significant cause of material injury to the domestic industry.'[211] When looking at the increase of Chinese tyres in the US market, the Appellate Body furthermore clarified that 'a decline in the yearly rate of increase does not necessarily preclude a finding that imports are increasing rapidly.'[212] The Appellate Body applied these benchmarks to the case and agreed with the panel that the imports of Chinese tyres were increasing rapidly.[213]

The Appellate Body also clarified that Paragraph 16.4 of the Chinese Accession Protocol defines a different standard of causation than the multilateral Safeguards Agreement. It requires 'an important contribution in bringing about material injury to the domestic industry.'[214] The Appellate Body confirmed the coincidence between the upward movement in Chinese tyre imports and the downward movement in the US tyre industry.[215] The panel furthermore properly evaluated injury for the US industry that was caused by others factors.[216]

In sum, the Appellate Body rejected all arguments raised by China and confirmed the panel's findings that the preconditions for imposing safeguard duties were given.

---

[211] Report of the Appellate Body, *United States – Measures Affecting Imports of Certain Passenger Vehicle and Light Truck Tyres from China*, WT/DS399/AB/R, para. 140.

[212] Report of the Appellate Body, *United States – Measures Affecting Imports of Certain Passenger Vehicle and Light Truck Tyres from China*, WT/DS399/AB/R, para. 158.

[213] Report of the Appellate Body, *United States – Measures Affecting Imports of Certain Passenger Vehicle and Light Truck Tyres from China*, WT/DS399/AB/R, paras. 169–170.

[214] Report of the Appellate Body, *United States – Measures Affecting Imports of Certain Passenger Vehicle and Light Truck Tyres from China*, WT/DS399/AB/R, para. 185, cf. also para. 195 in more detail.

[215] Report of the Appellate Body, *United States – Measures Affecting Imports of Certain Passenger Vehicle and Light Truck Tyres from China*, WT/DS399/AB/R, paras. 241 and 249.

[216] Report of the Appellate Body, *United States – Measures Affecting Imports of Certain Passenger Vehicle and Light Truck Tyres from China*, WT/DS399/AB/R, para. 319.

UNCTAD's Role in Addressing International Investment Trends and Challenges

Elisabeth Tuerk and Diana Rosert

Introductory Remarks

On the occasion of the thirteenth session of the United Nations Conference on Trade and Development (UNCTAD), held in Doha, Qatar, from 21 to 26 April 2012, this contribution is dedicated to UNCTAD, the United Nations (UN) focal point for the integrated treatment of trade, investment and development. It first offers a brief overview of UNCTAD's historical evolution and its organisational structure. It then presents UNCTAD's contribution to one area of international economic relations: international investment and, more specifically, international investment agreements (IIAs). In so doing, this contribution shows how UNCTAD has, over time, adapted to a changing context for development policy-making and implemented a comprehensive approach that integrates three pillars of activities: research and analysis, capacity-building, and intergovernmental consensus-building.

UNCTAD's Historical Evolution and Organisational Structure

Within the United Nations system, UNCTAD is the focal point for the integrated analysis of trade, investment and development-related questions. The organisation's full name refers to its founding Conference held in Geneva from 23 March to 16 June

The views expressed in this chapter are those of the authors and do not necessarily reflect the views of the UNCTAD secretariat or its Member States.

E. Tuerk (✉) • D. Rosert
UNCTAD, International Investment Agreements Section, Division on Investment and Enterprise, Palais des Nations, 8-14 Av. de la Paix, 1211 Geneva, Switzerland
e-mail: Elisabeth.Tuerk@unctad.org; Diana.Rosert@unctad.org

C. Herrmann et al. (eds.), *European Yearbook of International Economic Law (EYIEL), Vol. 4 (2013)*, European Yearbook of International Economic Law 4,
DOI 10.1007/978-3-642-33917-2_20, © Springer-Verlag Berlin Heidelberg 2013

1964. Following a proposal of the UN Economic and Social Council,[1] the UN General Assembly (GA)[2] decided to convene UNCTAD by 1964.[3] The first UNCTAD Conference in 1964 turned out to be a great success: it attracted representatives of 120 states, a number that outgrew the 115 member states the UN counted at that time.[4] The final act adopted by states at the end of the Conference promised "to ensure that all countries—regardless of size, of wealth, of economic and social system—enjoy the benefits of international trade for their economic development and social progress."[5]

Six months later, UNCTAD was formally established as a permanent organ of the UN GA.[6] Its creation responded to the need for sustained efforts through a specialised agency on trade and development[7] and UNCTAD was given the mission to use trade co-operation as a tool to "further economic progress throughout the world", to create common wealth and prosperity.[8] Along these lines, UNCTAD's original mandate was to promote international trade and economic development, negotiate international trade matters and formulate trade principles, co-ordinate other international organisations' activities and assist its member states to develop appropriate trade and development policies.[9]

Over time, UNCTAD has established itself as a UN think-tank that deals with an increasingly broad range of interrelated policy areas, going well beyond 'traditional' trade issues. Today, its work encompasses services, tourism, technology, foreign direct investment (FDI), enterprise development, social entrepreneurship and delivering on trade and investment related aspects of the Millennium Development Goals, such as poverty reduction, gender equality and environmental sustainability.[10] UNCTAD also responded to recent challenges to the well-functioning of the

---

[1] UN Economic and Social Council, Resolution 917 (XXXIV), 1962.

[2] UN General Assembly, Resolution 1785 (XVII), 1962.

[3] Despite the initial opposition of developed countries, eventually, all UN Member States were "determined to do their utmost to lay the foundations of a better world economic order," UN General Assembly, Resolution 1785 (XVII), 1962, para. 5, and collectively established UNCTAD as a development body to contribute to this objective, see UNCTAD, Proceedings of the United Nations Conference on Trade and Development, Vol. 1, Final Act and Report, 1964, pp. 4 and 6 (Final Act, paras. 9 and 19–20).

[4] The former are listed in UNCTAD, Proceedings of the United Nations Conference on Trade and Development, Vol. 1, Final Act and Report, 1964, p. 103 (Report of the Conference, para. 15). For a listing of the latter, see http://www.un.org/en/members/growth.shtml#text.

[5] UNCTAD, Proceedings of the United Nations Conference on Trade and Development, Vol. 1, Final Act and Report, 1964, p. 3 (Final Act, para. 1).

[6] UN General Assembly, Resolution 1995 (XIX), 1964, para. 3.

[7] UNCTAD, Proceedings of the United Nations Conference on Trade and Development, Vol. 1, Final Act and Report, 1964, p. 9 (Final Act, paras. 52 and 53).

[8] UNCTAD, Proceedings of the United Nations Conference on Trade and Development, Vol. 1, Final Act and Report, 1964, p. 4 (Final Act, para. 6).

[9] UN General Assembly, Resolution 1995 (XIX), 1964, para. 3.

[10] UN General Assembly, United Nations Millennium Declaration, 2000, available at: http://www.un.org/millennium/declaration/ares552e.pdf.

globalised economy in areas such as monetary, financial and economic crises, food crises, and climate change, since they as well interact with trade, investment and development policies. Throughout, UNCTAD's objective has been to analyse and draw attention to the possibilities for renewed cooperation on development and for linking economic policies with development strategies and other policy areas.[11]

Being a deliberative forum for its currently 194 member states as well as an operational agency, UNCTAD consists of the Ministerial Conference, the Trade and Development Board (TDB) and its subsidiary intergovernmental bodies, as well as the secretariat. The Conference is UNCTAD's highest decision-making body and forum for member states to address trade, investment and development issues and develop policy options. The TDB is the executive body of the Conference, while the secretariat is its operational agency. The Conference is convened every 4 years with the last one—the thirteenth UNCTAD Ministerial Conference (the Doha Conference)—having taken place in April 2012 in Doha, Qatar.

The substantive work carried out by the UNCTAD secretariat[12] is organised along five divisions: Africa, Least Developed Countries and Special Programmes; Globalization and Development Strategies; International Trade and Commodities; Investment and Enterprise; and Technology and Logistics.[13] It interacts with member states through technical cooperation activities, usually specifically tailored to the needs of the developing and least developed beneficiary countries and conducts research and analysis, published through its flagship reports, numerous publication series and databases.[14] The secretariat's operational mandate to deliver on three pillars of activities—intergovernmental consensus-building, research and analysis, and capacity-building –, metaphorically speaking, turns UNCTAD into the UN's one stop shop for trade, investment and development services. More specifically, the organisation serves as (1) a forum for intergovernmental deliberations and consensus building; (2) a think-tank for research and analysis on key and emerging development issues; and (3) a demand-driven provider of tailored technical assistance to respond to the needs of developing countries and countries with economies in transition in implementing development strategies.[15] This offers a unique potential for synergies and cross-fertilisation: The secretariat's research and analysis feeds into technical cooperation activities and into policy advice for member states that supports consensus-building on substantive issues and vice versa.

---

[11] UNCTAD, Annual Report, 2011, available at: http://unctad.org/en/PublicationsLibrary/dom2012d1_en.pdf.

[12] The secretariat is composed of about 500 staff members with an annual regular budget of approximately 68 million US dollars and 44 million US dollars of extra-budgetary technical assistance funds.

[13] See organisational chart, available at: http://archive.unctad.org/sections/about/docs/Secretariat_organi.pdf.

[14] UNCTAD's flagship publications include, amongst others, the reports on World Investment, Trade and Development, Economic Development in Africa and Least Developed Countries.

[15] In terms of delivery in 2011, UNCTAD implemented some 240 projects in more than 75 countries, with annual expenditures of 39 million dollars, see UNCTAD, Annual Report 2011, available at: http://unctad.org/en/PublicationsLibrary/dom2012d1_en.pdf.

At the Doha Conference, member states reaffirmed UNCTAD's mandate adopted at the twelfth Ministerial Conference, held in Accra, Ghana, in 2008 (the Accra Conference)[16] stating that "UNCTAD remains the focal point in the United Nations for the integrated treatment of trade and development, and interrelated issues in the areas of finance, technology, investment and sustainable development. UNCTAD should continue to work within its mandate—through its three pillars, delivering meaningful results, utilizing available resources, while enhancing synergies and promoting complementarities with the work of other international organizations."[17]

International Investment and Sustainable Development

Delivering on New Policy Needs

Throughout its existence, the organisation has closely followed trends and developments in the global economy, and responded with a constant alignment of its research and policy advice to the new needs of its member states and emerging issues in the world economy. One issue that has emerged since the creation of UNCTAD in the 1960s and developed into a key issue of international economic relations is international investment. Today, international investment is regarded as one of the main drivers of economic growth and development. Over the years, UNCTAD "established itself as the leading international agency in addressing investment issues."[18]

For example, UNCTAD has been at the forefront of organisations accompanying the emergence of transnational business activities, the rapid growth in FDI flows, and, most recently, the emergence of global value chains (GVCs) and non-equity modes (NEMs) of international production. UNCTAD's comprehensive data sets on international investment-related issues in the past 20 years and its analytical work have captured the boom and bust cycles of FDI and the evolution of national and international investment policies.

The establishment of UNCTAD's investment-related activities followed the growing importance of foreign investment, transnational corporations (TNCs) and international investment policy-making. At the beginning of the 1970s, the globalisation of business activities and the emergence of TNCs gained increasing attention in international policy circles and became a recurring item on the international agenda. Policy-makers' interest in understanding TNCs led the UN, more precisely its Economic and Social Council (ECOSOC), to create the Commission

[16] UNCTAD, UNCTAD XII: Accra Accord and the Accra Declaration, 2008, p. 12 (Accra Accord, para. 9).

[17] UNCTAD, The Doha Mandate, 2012, p. 3, para. 18.

[18] UN, Report of the Panel of Eminent Persons: Enhancing the Development Role and Impact of UNCTAD, 2006, para. 24(e).

on Transnational Corporations and, under its supervision, the Centre on Transnational Corporations (UNCTC) in 1975.[19] At that time, TNCs were regarded with some suspicion by (developing) countries and the international community seemed inclined to increase State control and regulation of TNCs. The Commission and the UNCTC were thus mandated to provide research on TNCs and to develop a Code of Conduct, which should regulate transnational business activities with a view to avoiding adverse effects on development.

By the 1980s, most developing countries, joined by transition economies in the 1990s, became more open to TNCs and FDI and less focussed on introducing new restrictions on business.[20] An increasing number of states aimed at attracting TNCs as a source of capital to stimulate growth and development. Eventually, the draft Code of Conduct on Transnational Corporations, firstly presented in 1983, failed to be ratified[21] and the Centre was abolished and integrated into UNCTAD in 1993.[22] The ninth UNCTAD Ministerial Conference, held in Midrand, South Africa, in 1996 (the Midrand Conference) spelled out UNCTAD's comprehensive mandate on international investment, namely to improve the general understanding of investment and development issues through UNCTAD's report on world investment, to enhance the capacity of developing countries and transition economies to improve their overall investment climate, to undertake investment policy reviews and to facilitate exchange of experiences between countries, with a view to promoting FDI opportunities. The mandate also referred to a wide range of substantive issues to be addressed by UNCTAD's activities, including trends in FDI flows, the interrelationships between FDI, trade, technology and development, and issues related to TNCs and their contribution to development. It also covered activities "relevant to a possible multilateral framework on investment."[23]

---

[19] ECOSOC Resolution E/RES/1913(LVII) created the Commission on Transnational Corporations, while ECOSOC Resolution E/RES/1908(LVII) established the UNCTC. See also Sagafi-Nejad, *The UN and Transnational Corporations: From Code of Conduct to Global Compact*, 2008, p. 89.

[20] Fredriksson/Zimny, Foreign Direct Investment and Transnational Corporations, in: UNCTAD (ed.), *Beyond Conventional Wisdom in Development Policy: An Intellectual History of UNCTAD 1964–2004*, 2004, p. 127 (130).

[21] For the text of the draft United Nations Code of Conduct on Transnational Corporations (1983 version), see UNCTAD, International Investment Instruments: Compendium, Vol. 1, 1996, p. 161, available at: http://www.unctad.org/templates/Download.asp?docid=1838&lang=1&intItemID=2323.

[22] Fredriksson, Forty years of UNCTAD research on FDI, Transnational Corporations 12 (2003) 3, p. 1 (5); Smith/Taylor, *United Nations Conference on Trade and Development (UNCTAD)*, 2007, p. 26.

[23] See UNCTAD, Midrand Declaration and a Partnership for Growth and Development, Adopted by the United Nations Conference on Trade and Development at its ninth session, 1996, paras. 88 et seq.; see also UN Economic and Social Council, Resolution 1994/1, 1994, available at: http://www.un.org/documents/ecosoc/res/1994/eres1994-1.htm; for a discussion of the Midrand Mandate, see Smith/Taylor, *The United Nations Conference on Trade and Development (UNCTAD)*, 2007, p. 26.

In line with its mandate, UNCTAD's work on international investment has been carried out by the Division on Investment and Enterprise (DIAE) with its branches focussing on investment trends and issues, investment policies, and investment capacity-building and enterprise. UNCTAD's annual World Investment Report (WIR), one of the organisation's most cited and acknowledged products[24] exemplifies the implementation of its investment mandate. Over the two decades of its existence, the WIR series captured all major trends and emerging issues regarding foreign investment: While in the 1990s the Triad—Japan, the European Community and the United States—shaped foreign investment patterns (WIR 1991), in the 2000s developing countries and transitions economies emerged as new sources of outward investment (WIR 2006). A substantial shift towards FDI in services (WIR 2004), opportunities and challenges arising from FDI in agriculture (WIR 2009), the need to promote low-carbon foreign investment (WIR 2010) and the emergence of non-equity modalities (NEMs) of international production (WIR 2011) all were subject to in-depth analysis in the WIR series.

Another example is the WIR 2011 that highlights important developments with respect to trends in FDI flows as well as trends in new emerging forms of investment. Regarding the former, important changes occur in the geography of international investment flows: WIR 2011 highlighted that, in 2010, developing and transition economies for the first time absorbed more than half of global FDI inflows and constituted half of the top-20 host economies for FDI.[25] Moreover, it showed that these countries were increasingly becoming capital exporters. Due to a strong increase in 2010, FDI outflows from developing and transition economies accounted for 29 % of global outflows. Second, the WIR 2011 showed that today's international investment landscape is characterised by new forms of investment: new investment patterns emerge due to the increasing importance of global value chains (GVCs) and NEMs for TNCs operate in developing economies through a broadening array of production and investment models. Different forms of NEMs such as contract-manufacturing and farming, service outsourcing, franchising and licensing also effectively started to blur the lines between trade and investment.[26]

UNCTAD's most recent work on international investment pays tribute to the fact that the world economy is entering a new phase of globalisation where inclusive and

[24] WIR has a diverse audience ranging from policy-makers to academics, civil society to business. The complete WIR series is available at: http://unctad.org/en/Pages/DIAE/World%20Investment%20Report/WIR-Series.aspx; Fredriksson, Forty years of UNCTAD research on FDI, Transnational Corporations 12 (2003) 3, p. 1 (10).

[25] UNCTAD, *World Investment Report 2011: Non-Equity Modes of International Production and Development*, 2011. For quarterly FDI data, see UNCTAD's Global Investment Trends Monitors, available at: http://www.unctad.org/Templates/Page.asp?intItemID=5801&lang=1.

[26] Whereas FDI (i.e. the establishment of local operations directly owned and controlled by a parent company) is a "purely" intra-firm phenomenon and trade is "purely" inter-firm, NEMs partake of both. NEMs represent long-term contractual arrangements between TNCs and local partners; the latter are formally independent (there is no equity involved), but are tied closely to the former both by virtue of being a part of their global value chain/network and because of their dependence on key resources. See further UNCTAD, *World Investment Report 2011: Non-Equity Modes of International Production and Development*, 2011, available at: http://www.unctad-docs.org/files/UNCTAD-WIR2011-Full-en.pdf.

sustainable development is imperative. Recognising that the attraction of foreign investment is not an end in itself, UNCTAD intensifies its work with countries to maximise the sustainable development benefits of foreign investment. For example, the Investment and Enterprise Division embraces the mission of "investing in the poor, for the poor and with the poor" that translates into efforts to encourage investment projects relating to poverty alleviation, the crowding in of domestic investment through linkages, and the production of accessible and affordable goods and services for the poor. Having observed the emergence of a new generation of investment policies, UNCTAD is also committed to assist.

In bringing about policies that pursue a broader and more intricate development agenda, within a framework that seeks to maintain a favourable investment climate.

International Investment Agreements: Increasing Sustainable Development Benefits from Foreign Investment

Introduction

Drawing lessons from changes in members' national investment policies and adjusting to new policy challenges such as increased sustainability considerations, also has concrete implications for UNCTAD's work on International Investment Agreements (IIAs).

Since the 1990s, UNCTAD has monitored the proliferation of Bilateral Investment Treaties (BITs) and other IIAs and set up a specific programme to analyse this investment policy trend. Reflecting the fact that IIAs are a key instrument in the strategies of countries, particularly developing countries, to attract FDI, the issue became an integral part of the Division's work agenda. Building on the mandate of the Accra Conference, UNCTAD's IIA work programme is the focal point of the UN for dealing with all matters related to IIAs, and provides a forum to advance the understanding of IIAs and their development implications.[27]

In the last years, the programme has focussed its attention on responding to the new challenges that have arisen from the growing, increasingly diverse and complex IIA regime. In the absence of a multilateral agreement on investment, the network of IIAs has grown to more than 3,000 core investment treaties (by end 2010), including 2807 BITs and 309 "other IIAs."[28] After more than 50 years of continuing growth and expansion—with the first BIT signed between Germany and Pakistan in 1959—and with many ongoing negotiations and multiple dispute-settlement mechanisms, the IIA regime is at a crossroads. Today, all countries are

[27] UNCTAD, UNCTAD XII: Accra Accord and the Accra Declaration, 2008, p. 60 (Accra Accord, para. 151).

[28] Today, the IIA system offers protection to two thirds of global FDI stock. Yet, despite its continuous growth, it covers only one fifth of all bilateral investment relationships. A full coverage would require a further 14,100 bilateral treaties, see UNCTAD, *World Investment Report 2011: Non-Equity Modes of International Production and Development*, 2011, p. 100.

parties to at least one IIA and on average, more than one new IIA is signed per week. However, this rapid growth of IIAs has raised concerns that the IIA regime has become "too big and complex to handle for governments and investors alike."[29]

Nonetheless, IIAs are one determinant among others that can increase a developing country's attractiveness for FDI by complementing domestic policies to ensure an open, transparent and predictable investment climate.[30] This implies that the conclusion of IIAs needs to be embedded in a country's broader FDI policies, covering all determinants of foreign investment, and in a country's overall sustainable development strategy. Likewise important is the particular design of an IIA that should take into account ways to accommodate the concern that IIAs can also constrain a country's policy space for development.[31] Today, voices in the international development as well as the investment community contend that the current IIA regime lacks a clear development dimension and needs to be rebalanced.[32] As has been stressed at the Doha Conference, developing and developed countries share sustainable growth and development objectives[33] and their investment policy-makers strive to integrate IIAs into their countries' economic growth and sustainable development policies.

Aside from noting changes in the discourse on IIAs, UNCTAD's work has documented the systemic changes that the IIA regime has experienced over time. The WIR 2010 featured such developments, notably the trend towards a more integrated, inclusive and elaborated approach to IIAs.[34] It identified new, more sophisticated and precise treaty language in recent IIAs, countries' individual efforts to review their model BITs and treaty network,[35] and discussed potential reasons for this development.[36]

---

[29] UNCTAD, *World Investment Report 2011: Non-Equity Modes of International Production and Development*, 2011, p. 93.

[30] UNCTAD, *The Role of International Investment Agreements in Attracting Foreign Direct Investment to Developing Countries*, 2009.

[31] UNCTAD has discussed this fundamental trade-off in several publications. For example see UNCTAD, *International Investment Agreements: Flexibility for Development*, 2000.

[32] See UNCTAD, Report of the Multi-year Expert Meeting on Investment for Development on its fourth session, 2011, pp. 5–7, available at: http://www.unctad.org/en/docs/ciimem3d12_en.pdf. See also UNCTAD, World Investment Forum—International Investment Agreements Annual Conference, UNCTAD XIII Summary prepared by the UNCTAD secretariat, 2012, available at: http://www.unctad.org/meetings/en/SessionalDocuments/td472_en.pdf.

[33] See UNCTAD, The Doha Manar, p. 3, para. 13: "Development is a universal concern today, and development-centred globalization is our common cause."

[34] See UNCTAD, *World Investment Report 2010: Investing in a low-carbon economy*, 2010, pp. 83 et seq.

[35] For example, South Africa started a review of their IIAs and in 2009 the United States initiated the revision of the 2004 model BIT, see http://www.info.gov.za/view/DownloadFileAction?id=103768 and http://www.ustr.gov/about-us/press-office/press-releases/2009/july/public-meeting-regarding-us-model-bilateral-investmen.

[36] For example, this trend partly reflects policy-makers' response to arbitral awards that had revealed difficulties arising from the rather broad language of older IIAs. See UNCTAD, *World Investment Report 2010: Investing in a low-carbon economy*, 2010, pp. 83 et seq.

To make IIAs work better for sustainable development, UNCTAD's activities today aim at strengthening the development dimension of IIAs, balancing the rights and obligations of states and investors, and managing the systemic complexity of the IIA regime. Led by these objectives, UNCTAD's IIA programme operates along three pillars of activities: It (1) supports the sharing of experiences on investment policy-making among member states and other IIA stakeholders; (2) conducts research and policy analysis to strengthen the understanding of IIA issues and their sustainable development dimension[37]; and (3) provides technical assistance to help member states, especially developing countries, to participate more effectively in international investment rulemaking.[38]

Trends and Challenges in Investor-State Dispute Settlement

UNCTAD's work on IIAs has gained increasing attention over the years, because of the rising number of investor-State dispute settlement (ISDS) cases and the significant public policy dimension of some recent cases.

[37] In its research and policy analysis work, the IIA programme monitors trends, identifies and analyses emerging issues in international investment rulemaking from a sustainable development perspective, and provides up-to-date and comprehensive information on the IIA system. The main publications are the series on Issues in IIAs (known as the Pink Series), which offer an in-depth analysis of clauses, the series on International Investment Policies for Development (known as the Yellow Series), and the joint UNCTAD-OECD Reports on G20 Investment Measures, together with seminal studies on broader issues. Facilitating informed investment policy making, UNCTAD also publishes its Investment Policy Monitor (IPM), a quarterly publication giving country-specific information on national and international policy developments. As regards their international dimension, IPMs feature the number of new IIAs (i.e. BITs, DTTs and "other IIAs"), the number of countries involved and, to the extent it is available, information about the agreements' content. IPMs also report on other notable developments in the field of international investment policies (e.g. the adoption of policy statements) and complement UNCTAD's Global Investment Trends Monitor. All issues of the IPM are available at: http://unctad.org/en/pages/publications/Investment-Policy-Monitor.aspx. The latter is available at: http://unctad.org/en/pages/publications/Global-Investment-Trends-Monitor-(Series).aspx. UNCTAD also maintains a series of online databases on IIA related issues, including (i) the online database of bilateral investment treaties, which contains a country-by-country listing of more than 2,820 BITs and a compilation of more than 2,310 BIT texts; (ii) the online database of double-taxation treaties, which contains a country-by-country listing of more than 2,990 DTTs; and (iii) the online compendium of international investment instruments. The latter contains texts of around 300 instruments dealing with investment at the bilateral, regional and multilateral levels, as well as country model texts of BITs.

[38] Based on its research, UNCTAD further provides ad hoc technical assistance on the request of Member States and regional organisations on all matters related to the negotiation and implementation of IIAs, including the management of ISDS cases. This support ranges from advisory work on specific IIA negotiations, the development of model BITs, the drafting of investment laws in follow-up to recommendations of UNCTAD's Investment Policy Reviews (IPRs), seminars on FDI and IIAs for government officials from different ministries and other stakeholders.

Following the early NAFTA investment disputes,[39] a number of recent ISDS cases have involved essential public policy issues such as environmental regulations in *Vattenfall v. Germany*,[40] legislation on black economic empowerment in *Foresti v. South Africa*,[41] and the right to water in *Biwater Gauff v. Tanzania*.[42] The public policy dimension of ISDS cases has also become evident through the recent *Abaclat cases*,[43] involving the restructuring of Argentina's sovereign debt.[44] Most recently, Philip Morris brought two cases against Uruguay and Australia, challenging the countries' regulations on tobacco plain packaging that were partly put in place in the context of the entry into force of WHO Framework Convention on Tobacco Control (FCTC) in 2005[45] and Germany faced a second challenge by Vattenfall, this time directed against the country's nuclear phase out.[46] These cases raise questions about coherence and consistency

---

[39] For example, ICSID, ARB(AF)/97/1, *Metalclad Corp. vs. United Mexican States*, Award; NAFTA, *Ethyl Corp. vs. Government of Canada*, Award on jurisdiction; NAFTA, *SD Myers, Inc. vs. Government of Canada*, Partial Award.

[40] ICSID ARB/09/6, *Vattenfall AB, Vattenfall Europe AG, Vattenfall Europe Generation AG vs. Federal Republic of Germany*; see further Bernasconi, IISD Background paper on Background paper on Vattenfall vs. Germany arbitration, 2009, available at: http://www.iisd.org/pdf/2009/background_vattenfall_vs_germany.pdf.

[41] ICSID, ARB(AF)/07/1, *Piero Foresti, Laura de Carli and others vs. Republic of South Africa.*

[42] ICSID, ARB/05/22, *Biwater Gauff (Tanzania) Ltd vs. United Republic Of Tanzania.*

[43] ICSID, ARB/07/5, *Giovanna a Beccara and Others vs. Argentine Republic* (also known as *Abaclat, et al. vs. Argentina*).

[44] The issue has been discussed in several recent publications: See UNCTAD, Sovereign Debt Restructuring and International Investment Agreements, IIA Issues Note No. 2, July 2011, available at: http://unctad.org/en/docs/webdiaepcb2011d3_en.pdf. See also Gallagher, The New Vulture Culture: Sovereign debt restructuring and trade and investment treaties, IDEAs Working Paper No. 02/2011, IDEAs. See also UNCTAD, Latest Developments in Investor-State Dispute Settlement, IIA Issues Note No. 1, April 2012, available at: http://www.unctad.org/en/Publications Library/webdiaeia2012d10_en.pdf.

[45] ICSID ARB/10/7, *FTR Holding S.A. (Switzerland), Philip Morris Products S.A. (Switzerland) and Abal Hermanos S.A. (Uruguay) vs. Oriental Republic of Uruguay*, and UNCITRAL, *Philip Morris vs. Australia*. Invoking provisions from the Switzerland-Uruguay and the Australia-Hong Kong BIT respectively, Philip Morris alleges indirect expropriation with regard to the effects of tobacco marketing regulations. However, the FCTC makes it mandatory for all State members—including Uruguay and Australia—to implement the obligation to control and reduce tobacco consumption that includes binding labelling and packaging requirements for tobacco products under Art. 11. For a discussion of the issue, see Voon/Mitchell, Time to quit? Assessing International Investment Claims against Plain Tobacco Packaging in Australia, Journal of International Economic Law 14 (2011) 3, p. 515 (529). See also Peterson, "Philip Morris files first-known investment treaty claim against tobacco regulations," IA reporter, 3 March 2010, available at: http://www.iareporter.com/articles/20100303. See further, Weiler, Philip Morris vs. Uruguay. An Analysis of Tobacco Control Measures in the Context of International Investment Law, Report #1 for Physicians for a Smoke Free Canada, July 2010, available at: http://italaw.com/documents/WeilerOpinion-PMI-Uruguay.pdf. For a general introduction to public health and IIAs, see Vadi, Reconciling Public Health and Investor Rights: The Case of Tobacco, in: Dupuy/Francioni/Petersmann (eds.), *Human Rights in International Investment Law and Arbitration*, 2010, p. 452.

[46] ICSID ARB/12/12, *Vattenfall AB, Vattenfall Europe AG, Vattenfall Europe Nuclear Energy GmbH, Kernkraftwerk Brunsbüttel GmbH und Co. oHG, Kernkraftwerk Krümmel GmbH und Co.*

between the international investment regime and other international and national policy regimes relevant for public health, environmental and social issues (e.g. labour and human rights standards),[47] as well as broader issues related to the transparency, due process and legitimacy of the IIA regime.

Against this background, states have started responding to IIA related challenges.[48] Ecuador, for example, withdrew from the ICSID Convention—following Bolivia's withdrawal in 2007—and announced to refrain from signing new IIAs and started a process of terminating existing ones, a move that raised a number of legal and practical questions.[49] Venezuela joined Ecuador and Bolivia in announcing its withdrawal from ICSID in January 2012.[50] Other countries, most prominently South Africa,[51] have started a review of their IIAs, sometimes combined with an effort to develop a new model BIT and usually giving careful consideration to ISDS provisions. The government of Australia announced in April 2011 that it would stop including ISDS clauses into its future IIAs.[52] In 2009, the United States initiated the revision of the

oHG vs. Federal Republic of Germany, see also UNCTAD, Latest Developments in Investor-State Dispute Settlement, IIA Issues Note No. 1, April 2012, available at: http://www.unctad.org/en/PublicationsLibrary/webdiaeia2012d10_en.pdf.

[47] For IIAs and human rights, see UNCTAD, Selected Recent Developments in IIA Arbitration and Human Rights, IIA Monitor No. 2 (2009), available at http://unctad.org/en/docs/webdiaeia20097_en.pdf.

[48] See UNCTAD, *World Investment Report 2010: Investing in a low-carbon economy*, 2010. See also UNCTAD, *World Investment Report 2011: Non-Equity Modes of International Production and Development*, 2011.

[49] The Plurinational State of Bolivia's notification of its withdrawal from the ICSID Convention was received by ICSID on 2 May 2007 and took effect on 3 November 2007. Ecuador's denunciation notification was received on 6 July 2009 and took effect on 7 January 2010. In 2008, Ecuador terminated nine BITs. Other denounced BITs include those between El Salvador and Nicaragua, and the Netherlands and the Bolivarian Republic of Venezuela. In 2010, Ecuador's Constitutional Court declared arbitration provisions of six BITs to be inconsistent with the country's Constitution. It is possible that Ecuador will take action to terminate these (and possibly other) BITs. However, the termination of BITs is complicated by so-called "survival clauses", included in many agreements, which make IIA provision to retain their force for another ten, or sometimes even twenty years, after a termination of a treaty has been notified. See UNCTAD, Denunciation of the ICSID Convention and BITs: Impact on Investor-State Claims, IIA Issues Note, No. 2, 2010.

[50] Venezuela's official announcement of 24 January 2012 is available at: http://www.mre.gov.ve/index.php?option=com_content&view=article&id=18939:mppre&catid=3:comunicados&Itemid=108.

[51] See Republic of South Africa, Department of Trade and Industry, Bilateral Investment Treaty Framework Review, Executive Summary of Government Position Paper, June 2009, available at: http://www.info.gov.za/view/DownloadFileAction?id=103768.

[52] See Australian Government, Gillard Government Trade Policy Statement: Trading our way to more jobs and prosperity, April 2011, p. 14, available at: http://www.dfat.gov.au/publications/trade/trading-our-way-to-more-jobs-and-prosperity.pdf: "In the past, Australian Governments have sought the inclusion of investor-state dispute resolution procedures in trade agreements with developing countries at the behest of Australian businesses. The Gillard Government will discontinue this practice."

2004 model BIT,[53] which was completed in April 2012. Already in its 2004 model, and also kept in its 2012 version, the US model BIT contains important innovations with respect to ISDS provisions (e.g. limitations on the consent to arbitration, the participation of non-disputing parties and amicus curiae submissions and the transparency of arbitration proceedings).[54] UNCTAD, in turn, documents and analyses these developments, provides a forum for sharing of experiences and demand-driven technical assistance, thus offering comprehensive responses through its three pillars of activities.

In terms of research and analysis, for example, UNCTAD has been one of the top providers of freely accessible, comprehensive and up-to-date information on ISDS cases through its ISDS database[55] and its annual publication on ISDS related developments.[56] UNCTAD's most recent Issues Note reports that in 2011, the number of known treaty-based ISDS cases grew by at least 46, bringing the total number of known treaty-based cases to 450 by the end of 2011.[57] This constitutes the highest number of known treaty-based disputes ever filed in 1 year, noting that the total number of actual treaty-based cases could be higher. Since most arbitration forums do not maintain a public registry of claims, UNCTAD's work on ISDS delivers on the information need of investment stakeholders in the absence of a designated focal point on ISDS-related issues.[58]

UNCTAD also directs its research and analysis to specific ISDS-related policy needs in a demand-driven way. In 2011, an UNCTAD publication was devoted to the challenges arising from the lack of sound reasoning in awards, inconsistent readings of key provisions in IIAs and poor treaty interpretation, resulting in an overall lack of the predictability of ISDS proceedings. The UNCTAD IIA Issues Note suggests that states are the drafters and masters of their IIAs, and hence in a

---

[53] See official press release, Office of the United States Trade Representative, July 2009, available at: http://www.ustr.gov/about-us/press-office/press-releases/2009/july/public-meeting-regarding-us-model-bilateral-investmen.

[54] See official press release, Office of the United States Trade Representative, April 2012, available at: http://www.ustr.gov/about-us/press-office/press-releases/2012/april/united-states-concludes-review-model-bilateral-inves. The new US model BIT is available at: http://www.ustr.gov/sites/default/files/BIT%20text%20for%20ACIEP%20Meeting.pdf.

[55] Available at: http://archive.unctad.org/iia-dbcases.

[56] UNCTAD, Latest Developments in Investor-State Dispute Settlement, IIA Issues Note No. 1, April 2012, available at: http://www.unctad.org/en/PublicationsLibrary/webdiaeia2012d10_en.pdf.

[57] This number does not include cases that are exclusively based on investment contracts (State contracts) and cases where a party has so far only signaled its intention to submit a claim to arbitration, but has not yet commenced the arbitration (notice of intent).

[58] UNCTAD's database on investor-State dispute settlement cases, available at www.unctad.org/iia, is continuously updated. The annual IIA Issues Note on ISDS complements quantitative information on new cases with a discussion of the key findings in decisions rendered by investment treaty tribunals during the reporting period.

unique position to help ameliorate the current situation. Accordingly, states could consider providing more guidance to arbitral tribunals with respect to the interpretation of IIAs.[59]

Another example for UNCTAD's work in the field of ISDS are the Sequels in the Series on Issues in International Investment Agreements (the Pink Series Sequels), each of which addresses one specific IIA clause, giving an overview of treaty practices, arbitral awards and policy options.[60] The new series of Sequels recognises that since the publication of the first generation of the Pink Series in 1999, the policy environment for IIAs has changed tremendously. For example, the last years have brought about new issue areas and technical challenges for countries in general and IIA negotiators in particular. Transparency considerations,[61] the predictability of international arbitration and concerns about policy space have come to the forefront of the debate—and so has the objective of ensuring coherence between IIAs and other areas of public policy. The Sequels move beyond a merely descriptive role and offer policy options for IIA negotiators that better take into account the sustainable development needs of host countries and enhance the stability and predictability of the legal system.[62]

Furthermore, UNCTAD's technical assistance has worked to assist developing countries respond to the challenges posed by ISDS. Among others, UNCTAD offers special training courses on ISDS, frequently undertaken in cooperation with other

---

[59] See UNCTAD, Interpretation of IIAs: What States Can Do, IIA Issues Note, No. 3, December 2011, available at: http://unctad.org/en/docs/webdiaeia2011d10_en.pdf. For an in-depth analysis of the states' role in the process, see Roberts, Power and Persuasion in Investment Treaty Interpretation: The Dual Role of States, American Journal of International Law 104 (2010) 1, p. 179 (201–202). For an academic treatment of treaty interpretation, see Schreuer, Diversity and Harmonization of Treaty Interpretation in Investment Arbitration, in: Elias/Fitzmaurice/Merkouris (eds.), *Treaty Interpretation and the Vienna Convention on the Law of Treaties: 30 Years On*, 2010, p. 129. For inconsistent decisions in ISDS proceedings and legitimacy considerations, see for example Franck, The Legitimacy Crisis in Investment Treaty Arbitration: Privatizing Public International Law through Inconsistent Decisions, Fordham Law Review 73 (2005) 4, p. 1521.

[60] The Pink Series has been designed to address key concepts and issues relevant to international investment agreements. All issues are available at: http://www.unctad.org/en/Pages/DIAE/International%20Investment%20Agreements%20(IIA)/UNCTAD-Series-on-issues-on-international-investment-agreements.aspx.

[61] This involves discussions on third parties' access to ISDS proceedings, amicus curiae submissions and the publication of awards. See Magraw/Amerasinghe, Transparency and Public Participation in Investor-State Arbitration, ILSA Journal of International & Comparative Law 15 (2009) 2, p. 337. VanDuzer, Enhancing the Procedural Legitimacy of Investor-State Arbitration Through Transparency and Amicus Curiae Participation, McGill Law Journal 52 (2007) 4, p. 681. For a general discussion of transparency and IIAs, see Bjorklund, Emerging Civilization of Investment Arbitration, Penn State Law Review 113 (2009) 4, p. 1269. See also Knahr/Reinisch, Transparency versus Confidentiality in International Investment Arbitration—The *Biwater Gauff* Compromise, Law and Practice of International Courts and Tribunals 6 (2007) 1, p. 97.

[62] The updated Sequels on Expropriation, Transparency, Scope and Definition, Most-favoured Nation Treatment and Fair and Equitable Treatment are available at: http://www.unctad.org/en/Pages/DIAE/International%20Investment%20Agreements%20(IIA)/Issues-in-International-Investment-Agreements-II.aspx.

intergovernmental agencies and organisations. In 2011, for example, UNCTAD conducted a workshop on IIAs and ISDS together with the Asia-Pacific Economic Cooperation (APEC), aimed at building human and institutional capacities of APEC economies to deal with ISDS.[63] Another example is the regional workshop on ISDS and international rule-making, conducted jointly with the Islamic Development Bank (IDB) in the same year.[64]

Since 2008/2009, UNCTAD has also drawn attention to the possibility of establishing a facility that developing countries could draw on for advice on investment law and ISDS.[65] Initial steps to set up such a facility have been taken in the Latin American context, where countries discussed the creation of an "Advisory Facility for International Investment Law and Investor-State Dispute Settlement", a process supported by the UNCTAD secretariat.

Another way of addressing the challenges of ISDS is by promoting alternative methods for settling disputes (also known as alternative dispute resolution (ADR)) and dispute prevention policies (DPPs). Through a series of meetings and related publications,[66] UNCTAD has drawn attention to the opportunities that lie in strengthening consensual and less adversarial mechanisms for solving investment disputes at an early stage and prevent such conflicts between foreign investors and states. ADR and DPPs can effectively help host states to maintain or improve a trust relationship with foreign investors, solve (potential) disputes faster and less costly

---

[63] The workshop took place on 22–24 June 2011 in Manila, the Philippines. 63 officials from 14 APEC members participated in this training including China, Indonesia, Japan, Republic of Korea, Malaysia, Mexico, Papua New Guinea, Peru, Philippines, Russian Federation, Singapore, Taiwan Province of China, Thailand and Vietnam.

[64] This workshop took place on 22–25 March 2011 in Casablanca, Morocco and was financed by the IDB's Investment Promotion Technical Assistance Program (ITAP). 29 participants from 26 countries attended it, including 16 LDCs (Afghanistan, Algeria, Azerbaijan, Bangladesh, Benin, Burkina Faso, Cameroon, Chad, Comoros, Djibouti, The Gambia, Guinea-Bissau, Indonesia, Jordan, Kazakhstan, Kirgizstan, Mauritania, Morocco, Mozambique, Niger, Senegal, Sudan, Tajikistan, Togo, Tunisia and Uganda).

[65] UNCTAD, Latest Developments in Investor-State Dispute Settlement, IIA Monitor, No. 1 (2009), available at: http://unctad.org/en/Docs/webdiaeia20096_en.pdf. This had also been discussed at an expert meeting in 2009. See UNCTAD, Report of the Multi-year Expert Meeting on Investment for Development on its first session, 2009, available at http://archive.unctad.org/en/docs/ciimem3d3_en.pdf. A meeting on a possible advisory facility on international investment law and ISDS for Latin American countries with the members of the advisory group took place on 13 January 2011 in Washington, United States. For academic discussions on the issue, see for example, Gottwald, Leveling the Playing Field: Is It Time for a Legal Assistance Center for Developing Nations in Investment Treaty Arbitration?, American University International Law Review 22 (2007) 2, p. 237.

[66] UNCTAD, *Investor-State Disputes: Prevention and Alternatives to Arbitration*, 2010, also available online at: http://archive.unctad.org/en/docs/diaeia200911_en.pdf. Documenting the proceedings of the Washington and Lee University and UNCTAD Joint Symposium on International Investment and Alternative Dispute Resolution, held on 29 March 2010 in Lexington, Virginia, United States of America, see UNCTAD, *Investor-State Disputes: Prevention and Alternatives to Arbitration II*, 2011, available at: http://archive.unctad.org/en/docs/webdiaeia20108_en.pdf.

and contribute to the transparency and predictability of regulatory practices and investors' perception of good governance. Furthermore, UNCTAD's technical assistance has increasingly focused on ADR. For example, UNCTAD has developed a Curriculum on DPPs for Angola that supported the creation of a distance learning training course on DPPs (together with the World Trade Institute (WTI) and UNCTAD's Train for Trade programme).

UNCTAD's research and analysis and technical assistance on ISDS is complemented by an additional stream of activities, notably the recently launched series of "Brainstorming Conversations on Improvements to the ISDS System." This initiative was taken with a view to provide an informal, universal and inclusive platform to hear from investment stakeholders on how to improve the ISDS mechanism. It involves practitioners, negotiators, civil society and academia, and is organised in an informal setting in a number of countries around the world, usually in conjunction with an ongoing regional meeting and/or technical assistance activity. Topics addressed in most recent "Fireplace Conversations" include how to establish an appellate mechanism for investor-State cases, how to promote consistency in ISDS, how to improve the designation and quality of arbitrators (avoiding entrenchment and fostering diversity),[67] and how to, more broadly, foster the legitimacy of the ISDS system.

Insights from the above activities also feed into UNCTAD's facilitation of intergovernmental and multi-stakeholder deliberations on investment issues. For example, during the World Investment Forum (WIF) 2012,[68] the IIA Conference discussed the evolution of the ISDS regime with a particular focus on new developments spurred by the concerns articulated by different investment stakeholders. The Conference allowed IIA stakeholders, including policy-makers, academic experts and others, to share their experiences with recent disputes

[67] For a discussion of the role of arbitrators, see Bottini, Should Arbitrator Live on Mars—Challenge of Arbitrators in Investment Arbitration, Suffolk Transnational Law Review 32 (2009) 2, p. 341; see also Malintoppi, Remarks on Arbitrators' Independence, Impartiality and Duty to Disclose in Investment Arbitration, The Law & Practice of International Courts and Tribunals 7 (2008) 3, p. 351; Franck, Role of International Arbitrators, ILSA Journal of International & Comparative Law 12 (2006) 2, p. 499.

[68] UNCTAD's biennial WIF establishes a global platform at the highest policy-making level and a forum for discussion on international investment trends among all investment stakeholders. The WIF 2012, held in Qatar, attracted more than 1400 investment stakeholders from 145 countries participated, including Heads of State and Government, ministerial-level officials, senior business executives, leading academic experts. It addressed the diverse challenges the investment community faced and paved the way for a new era of international investment policy-making. The programme and background documents on all events are available at: http://www.unctad-worldinvestmentforum.org. The WIF 2012 was convened back to back with the UNCTAD XIII Conference in Doha and aimed at defining investment policies and strategies for globalisation in the post crisis era that created the need for sustainable and inclusive development paths. The WIF thus addressed the investment challenges and opportunities arising from the changing global economic governance, with a view to boosting investment in the real economy so as to restart the engine of growth and generate employment in the wake of the crisis.

touching upon public policy issues and suggest options towards making the IIA regime work better for sustainable development.[69]

All of this shows how the Division's research and policy analysis responds to the systemic challenges in the field of IIAs and harnesses the potential for cross-fertilisation between UNCTAD's three pillars of work. UNCTAD's publications, its technical assistance and international deliberations on IIA related issues exemplify the comprehensive and dynamic approach of the organisation to investment and development issues.

Guiding the Way Ahead: UNCTAD's IPFSD

The above-mentioned IIA-related trends and challenges manifest themselves at a time when persistent crises and pressing economic, social and environmental challenges, support the recognition that harnessing economic growth for sustainable and inclusive development is more important than ever. In response, a new generation of investment policies is emerging that pursues a broader and more intricate development policy agenda within a framework that seeks to maintain a generally favourable investment climate. Despite the progress made, and despite the lessons learned, important questions remain unanswered for policy-makers. Some perceived or acknowledged shortcomings in investment policy regimes are only partially addressed, or not at all, by existing models and frameworks intended to support policy-makers.

With this in mind, UNCTAD seeks to address investment policy challenges in a more systematic manner and has thus designed an investment policy framework for sustainable development (IPFSD), which encourages a new, more integrated and comprehensive approach to investment policy-making.[70] IPFSD offers a set of core

[69] Participants also discussed their countries' general approach to IIAs and specific strategic IIA related decisions (e.g. review of model BITs), development in the Arab region and the way forward for the IIA regime. For the outcome of the IIA conference, see UNCTAD, World Investment Forum—International Investment Agreements Annual Conference, UNCTAD XIII Summary prepared by the UNCTAD secretariat, 2012, available at: http://www.unctad.org/meetings/en/SessionalDocuments/td472_en.pdf. IIAs were also referred to by ministers in the Ministerial Round Table 2 in the context of WIF/UNCTAD XIII. See UNCTAD, Round Table 2 Promoting investment, trade, entrepreneurship and related development policies to foster sustained economic growth for sustainable and inclusive development, UNCTAD XIII Summary prepared by the UNCTAD secretariat, 2012, available at: http://www.unctad.org/meetings/en/SessionalDocuments/tdL421_en.pdf. See also UNCTAD, UNCTAD XIII Round Table II—Addressing the policy challenges for sustainable investment and enterprise development, Issues note prepared by the UNCTAD secretariat, 2012, available at: http://www.unctad.org/meetings/en/SessionalDocuments/td457_en.pdf.

[70] See also UNCTAD, Round Table 2 Promoting investment, trade, entrepreneurship and related development policies to foster sustained economic growth for sustainable and inclusive development, UNCTAD XIII Summary prepared by the UNCTAD secretariat, 2012, available at: http://www.unctad.org/meetings/en/SessionalDocuments/tdL421_en.pdf; UNCTAD, UNCTAD XIII Round Table II—Addressing the policy challenges for sustainable investment and enterprise development, Issues note prepared by the UNCTAD secretariat, 2012, available at: http://www.unctad.org/meetings/en/SessionalDocuments/td457_en.pdf.

principles for national and international investment policy-making, and guidance for policy-makers on how to engage in the international investment policy regime. Through concrete suggestions for the design of national policies and IIAs, IPFSD aims to offer a practical toolbox for policy-makers. It is designed to serve as a reference for policy-makers in formulating national investment policies and in negotiating IIAs or revising existing ones. IPFSD can also serve as the basis for technical assistance and capacity-building for member states by UNCTAD or other international organisations. It may come to act as a point of convergence for international cooperation on investment issues.[71]

IPFSD options for IIAs give concrete inputs to the ongoing debate on a range of pressing issues such as the balance between the rights and obligations of states and investors, ISDS, states' right to regulate in pursuit of public policy objectives related to health, environment and labour, transparency vis-à-vis stakeholders, and developed countries' obligations vis-à-vis developing countries.

IPFSD was pre-launched at the Doha Conference and WIF 2012 in Doha[72] and subsequently constituted a main chapter of the WIR 2012. Since it is designed as a dynamic framework—a "living document"—UNCTAD will continuously update its contents, based on feedback from intergovernmental and multi-stakeholder meetings and web-based policy fora. IPFSD thereby responds to the practical needs of policy-makers as identified through UNCTAD's technical assistance, its research and analysis activities, and intergovernmental meetings.

Conclusions

Throughout its almost 50 years of existence, UNCTAD has made important contributions to international policy-making and negotiations as well as policy research and analysis. The organisation has continuously adapted to the changing international context and reflected the evolution of the global economy. Development has always been the cornerstone of its activities, while the concept of

[71] UNCTAD, Investment Policy Framework for Sustainable Development, 2102, available at: http://unctad.org/en/PublicationsLibrary/webdiaepcb2012d6_en.pdf. See also UNCTAD, *World Investment Report 2012*: Towards a New Generation of Investment Policies, 2012.

[72] For the IPFSD-related discussion of the IIA conference, see UNCTAD, World Investment Forum—International Investment Agreements Annual Conference, UNCTAD XIII Summary prepared by the UNCTAD secretariat, 2012, available at: http://www.unctad.org/meetings/en/SessionalDocuments/td472_en.pdf. See also UNCTAD, Round Table 2 Promoting investment, trade, entrepreneurship and related development policies to foster sustained economic growth for sustainable and inclusive development, UNCTAD XIII Summary prepared by the UNCTAD secretariat, 2012, available at: http://www.unctad.org/meetings/en/SessionalDocuments/tdL421_en.pdf; UNCTAD, UNCTAD XIII Round Table II—Addressing the policy challenges for sustainable investment and enterprise development, Issues note prepared by the UNCTAD secretariat, 2012, available at: http://www.unctad.org/meetings/en/SessionalDocuments/td457_en.pdf.

"sustainable development" as a common concern for developed and developing countries alike is increasingly mainstreamed into its programmes today.

Being an international agency with long-standing expertise on international investment, UNCTAD has an important role to play in terms of research, capacity-building and multilateral consensus-building in this area and, not at last, with regard to IIAs. UNCTAD's IPFSD and the WIR 2012 synthesize the past decades' work and research findings on investment for development and provide a sound basis for future investment policy-making. While UNCTAD indeed "has earned a strong reputation for contributing to mainstream thinking on the subject",[73] its tradition also suggests moving beyond conventional thinking. The new IPFSD is an innovative approach towards rebalancing investment policies in favour of sustainable development that is based on the insight that "rebalancing is not a narrow technocratic challenge", but it "will involve a change of attitudes, morals and values."[74]

Through its IPFSD, which recognises the different needs and expectations of investment stakeholders in terms of transparency, predictability and inclusiveness of investment policies, the IIA Programme also responds to the Doha Mandate, which calls upon UNCTAD to "[u]ndertake analytical work on international investment agreements, weighing the interests of all stakeholders, and continue to provide technical assistance, as well as fostering the international sharing of experiences and best practices on key issues relating to their negotiation and implementation."[75]

[73] Fredriksson/Zimny, Foreign Direct Investment and Transnational Corporations, in: UNCTAD (ed.), *Beyond Conventional Wisdom in Development Policy: An Intellectual History of UNCTAD 1964–2004*, 2004, p. 127.

[74] UNCTAD, Report of the Secretary-General of UNCTAD to UNCTAD XIII. Development-led globalization: Towards sustainable and inclusive development paths, 2011, p. 9, available at: http://www.unctad.org/en/docs/tdxiii_report_en.pdf.

[75] UNCTAD, The Doha Mandate, 2012, p. 15 (para. 65(k)).

Part IV
Book Reviews

Lars Markert, Streitschlichtungsklauseln in Investitionsschutzabkommen. Zur Notwendigkeit der Differenzierung Von jurisdiction und Admissibility in Investitionsschiedsverfahren

Nomos/Dike/facultas.wuv, 2010; ISBN 978-3-8329-6136-7

Christian J. Tams

Given the major interest in investment arbitration, it is puzzling to see how much of the academic debate remains case-specific, tracing and evaluating the reasoning of specific awards. Only gradually, questions of procedure in investment arbitration are being approached in a conceptual and systemic way. Lars Markert's book is part of the new trend: it approaches procedural conditions of investment arbitration systematically and puts forward a framework within which objections lodged against the jurisdiction of tribunals, or the admissibility of claims, can be analysed. Even those who do not agree with each and every argument made are likely to find the analytical framework useful and will appreciate the systematic approach informing it.

Markert's concern throughout is with objections raised against the jurisdiction and/or admissibility of ICSID proceedings. As he rightly notes, such objections are a common feature of investment proceedings, often leading to separate awards on jurisdiction or jurisdiction and admissibility. However, practice has so far not produced clear rules on how to address them—with tribunals typically stressing their competence to determine jurisdiction, while occasionally playing down the relevance of objections going to the admissibility of proceedings. Markert's approach is different. He suggests a clearer distinction between different categories of objections, from which he deduces different legal effects. His starting point is the distinction between consent to jurisdiction on the one hand and other procedural conditions (waiver, waiting clauses, fork in the road etc.) on the other. This in itself is not novel (even though the practical need for the distinction has been questioned); yet Markert suggests a nuanced approach that goes beyond the existing literature. In his view, 'other procedural objections' are to be treated as jurisdictional objections

C.J. Tams (✉)
University of Glasgow, International Law Chair, 5-9 Stair Building, The Square, G12 8QQ Glasgow, Scotland
e-mail: christian.tams@glasgow.ac.uk

DOI 10.1007/978-3-642-33917-2_21,

if the parties formulate them as preconditions to consent. Examples include 'linkage clauses' such as Article 1121 NAFTA, pursuant to which an investor can submit claims "*only if*" it accepts "arbitration in accordance with the procedures set out in this Agreement"; or Article 26 of the Canadian Model BIT that clarifies that failure to comply with waiting clauses and other procedural requirements nullifies consent to jurisdiction. While it may be a matter for debate whether a particular procedural requirement amounts to a precondition of consent, this approach, in principle, seems correct.

In Markert's view, the distinction between jurisdictional and other procedural objections is warranted because the two produce different legal effects. A successful jurisdictional objection—that much is undisputed—results in the claim being dismissed. Matters are more complicated with respect to other procedural objections not affecting or tainting consent to jurisdiction. These can result in the claim being inadmissible, but could also—a remedy emphasised by Markert—entail the suspension of proceedings until the objection has been met.

In the main part of his analysis, Markert applies his analytical framework to the most 'popular' objections raised in investment proceedings. His analysis illustrates the ad hoc approach often informing arbitral practice and thus affirms the need for a systematic understanding. The discussion at times could have been more concise; but readers will appreciate the author's genuine attempt to apply his approach to specific problems facing investment tribunals. Markert's main concern is with the unwillingness of some tribunals to take procedural objections seriously. In his view, to take just as few examples, non-compliance with waiting clauses (requiring a lapse of time before a claim is instituted) should result in the suspension of proceedings; failure to comply with waiver clauses would render the claim inadmissible; and an investor not pursuing local remedies (to the extent required) by an investment agreement should not have his arbitral claim entertained. None of this is revolutionary; but the fact that Markert—unlike much of the preceding literature—argues within a sound analytical framework strengthens his analysis.

Of course, that framework in itself is fairly flexible. Notably, parties—determining the procedural requirements of a claim—can always turn a mere ('other') procedural objection into a precondition to jurisdiction by providing so in the BIT or other jurisdiction-conferring instrument. Recent treaty-making practice in fact suggests that they increasingly do: Article 26 of Canada's Model BIT—emphasising that failure to comply with procedural requirements nullifies consent to jurisdiction—is but a particular clear example. As Markert notes, more attentive treaty drafting could remove some of the uncertainties affecting arbitral practice. However, to expect much of treaty drafters (who, traditionally, have seemed fairly happy to establish a system of investment law on the basis of vague and general clauses) may be overly optimistic, and in any event would not entail immediate results. In the meantime, those concerned about the continued success of investment arbitration as a dispute resolution mechanism might hope for academic debate to suggest balanced and analytically sound solutions. Markert's book is an important contribution to that debate.

Irmgard Marboe, Calculation of Compensation and Damages in International Investment Law

Oxford University Press, 2009; ISBN 978-0-19-955171-2

Moritz Keller

The calculation of the amount of damages to be paid to the Claimant in arbitration proceedings is of considerable importance to the party suffering said damages: However, as Irmgard Marboe illustrates at the outset of her book by quoting Waelde and Sabahi "the issue of compensation and damages is the poor cousin when the royal battle rages first about jurisdiction and then about the merits." While it is certainly true that both arbitral tribunals and legal scholars have to some extent in the past neglected the issues of compensation and damages in their awards, one might get a different impression as a spectator in a large number of arbitration proceedings: The parties tend to fight with the same passion about the numbers as they do about the questions of liability and jurisdiction.

Nowadays more authors tackle the issue of compensation and damages in investment arbitration in their writings. In addition to the book by Mark Kantor, the works of Sergey Ripinsky and Kevin Williams come to mind, as does the recently published book by Borzu Sabahi. However, in 2007 when the German version of Marboe's book was accepted as a post-doctoral thesis, her Habilitationsschrift at the University of Vienna, it was difficult to find scholarly writings on the subject. The thesis earned her a position as professor at the University of Vienna and has since then been updated, translated into English and was eventually published by Oxford University Press in 2009—a welcome addition to the still limited number of scholarly writing on the topic.

The book provides a comprehensive analysis of how international courts and tribunals have handled the issue of calculation of compensation and damages in investment disputes and, at the same time, endeavors to provide a systematic foundation and framework going forward.

In the chapter on the "Function of Compensation and Damages," the first substantive chapter of the book (chapter 2), Marboe draws a distinction between compensation and damages. She analyses the relevant case law and arrives at the

M. Keller (✉)
Freshfields Bruckhaus Deringer LLP, Bockenheimer Anlage 44, 60322 Frankfurt, Germany
e-mail: moritz.keller@freshfields.com

C. Herrmann et al. (eds.), *European Yearbook of International Economic Law (EYIEL), Vol. 4 (2013)*, European Yearbook of International Economic Law 4,
DOI 10.1007/978-3-642-33917-2_22, © Springer-Verlag Berlin Heidelberg 2013

conclusion that the main function of compensation (restitution of value) is the replacement of the expropriated property's value, whereas, the main function of damages (reparation) is the full reparation for the breach of legal obligations. At the same time, Marboe does admit that this distinction is not unanimously applied or accepted.

However, Marboe believes the distinction to be essential as the different functions in her view lead to different approaches in calculating the loss suffered. Hence, Marboe concludes that the proper analysis of the claim brought and the different functions of compensation and damages should be the starting point for selecting the right valuation method in investment arbitration proceedings.

In the next chapter, Valuations Standards and Criteria (chapter 3), Marboe presents and analyses the standards and criteria for the calculation of compensation and damages in four subsections.

In the first section of chapter 3, Marboe scrutinises the standards and criteria of compensation for expropriation, beginning with an analysis of the discussion under customary international law (such as the Hull formula of prompt, adequate and effective compensation), investment treaty law (providing an overview about the diversity of compensation clauses) and international case law (finding a preference for in her view objective valuation criteria such as fair market value).

In the following, Marboe gives an overview on the development of the question whether the payment of compensation is a requirement for the lawfulness of an expropriation. While she rightly concludes that the content and meaning of the specific provisions applicable to a dispute need to be analysed carefully, she finds that generally any State not paying compensation or even foreseeing a procedure for the payment of such compensation violates its investment treaty obligations. Marboe also holds that in cases of indirect expropriation, States will usually not comply with, inter alia, their obligation to pay compensation and these expropriation are therefore, in Marboe's view, often unlawful.

Marboe goes on to discuss the consequences of a violation of a stabilisation clause for the payment of compensation and eventually presents her findings on the importance of distinguishing between lawful and unlawful expropriations. Starting with a discussion of the view that, in cases of unlawful expropriation, lost profits should be recoverable (lucrum cessans), while in lawful expropriations the State would only be obliged to make up for the owner's losses (damnum emergens), Marboe quickly finds that the theory should be dismissed. Rather, Marboe argues that in cases of unlawful expropriation the State is obliged to pay damages for the violation of its obligation, while in cases of lawful expropriation compensation is due. While she finds some support in the ICSID awards in ADC v. Hungary, Siemens v. Argentina and Vivendi v. Argentina, Marboe freely admits that the differentiation is "not yet generally accepted."

In the second section of chapter 3, Marboe analyses the criteria and standards applied to reparation and damages and begins by distinguishing (investment) treaty violation and breaches of a private law contracts. She starts with an analysis of the criteria and standards applied in cases where treaty obligations have been violated. In her view, the best approach to evaluate the damages incurred in these cases is the differential approach. Under the differential approach, the difference between the hypothetical situation the injured person would be in if the unlawful act would not have been committed and the actual financial situation equals the amount of damages. While she finds that a number of courts and tribunals apply the differential approach, she also holds that, in some cases, tribunals have applied an objective valuation, such as fair market value or market value, by means of an analogy to expropriation cases. Others have chosen such an approach based on the pleadings of the parties.

As regards the breaches of private law contracts, Marboe finds the situation far more complex. In principle, the applicable law (often by means of a choice of law clause) regulates the applicable criteria and standards. At the same time, she identifies several considerations usually of salient importance in the international investment context. She elaborates in detail on the relevant considerations for the questions of whether or not lost profits or lost opportunities need to be compensated for. The section concludes with a brief discussion of parallel violations of treaty and private law contract obligations, as well as contributory negligence and mitigation of damages.

The third section of chapter 3 then deals with the valuation date highlighting that, according to her findings, for expropriation, violations of treaty obligations and breaches of private law contracts, different valuation dates might come into play based on the individual circumstances of the case and the damages or compensation due.

In the fourth and last section of chapter 3, Marboe presents her findings on the exercise of equity considerations and discretion. After analysing the case law, she highlights that international tribunals have a certain discretion as the calculation of compensation and damages naturally involves some uncertainty and imprecision. At the same time, she formulates an urgent plea that equitable principles should not be used as an "excuse for not doing the job." Marboe finally discusses the relevance of the Respondent State's economic situation, observing that economic difficulties are usually not accepted in order to lower damages. At the same time, she suggests that economic realities such as financial crises—a problem some tribunals might have to deal with in the near future—should be reflected in the tribunal's findings by, e.g. deferrals of payments and appropriate application of subjective and objective valuation methods.

In the next chapter (chapter 4), on "International Valuation Standards and Bases of Value" the author presents a comprehensive overview of the international valuation standards and bases of value that were developed over the years in different jurisdictions. As regards Europe, the author presents the "Guide for Carrying Business Valuations" (2001) that was published by the Fédération des Experts Comptables Européens (FEE). Although the guide is a non-binding instrument, it was in Marboe's view broadly accepted as the standard of business valuation in Europe. As regards the United States, Marboe presents the Uniform Standards of Professional Appraisal Practice (USPAP) and the American Institute of Certified Public Accountants' (AICPA) Valuation Standards.

Moreover, the author discusses international initiatives in setting up the international standards for valuation. Marboe presents, inter alia, that the International Valuation Standard Committee (IVSC) has published International Valuation Standards that reflect both European and American approaches, as well as subjective and objective methods. In addition, as Marboe notes, the World Bank Guidelines on the Treatment of Foreign Direct Investment also provide some guidance on the valuation of companies. A discussion of the bases of value (market value vs. other bases such as investment value or contractual value) and a brief overview on transparency and experts in arbitration proceedings concludes chapter 4.

The next chapter (chapter 5), "Methods of Valuation in International Practice" is entirely devoted to valuation methods. In this part of the book, the author goes into detail with regard to valuation standards used in international practice. Marboe begins by defining the market or sales comparison approach that establishes a value by comparing the sales of similar or substitute properties. In practice, it is hard to apply the methodology of this approach in the area of foreign direct investment because some projects are unique in nature. There are different variations of the approach that are applicable depending on the specific nature of the project and based on various different indicators such as stock prices or multiples (based on figures such as EBIT or EBITDA).

The next important approach that is considered by the author is the income based approach, the aim of which is to appraise the expected future financial benefits after discounting them to present value. The objective of the income based approach can be achieved by employing the capitalisation of earnings method and the discounted cash flow (DCF) method, the latter being one of the most frequently used by international tribunals in assessing the value within the income based approach. Marboe discusses varieties of the approach and their respective particularities in depth, including the application by international arbitral tribunals. For any counsel or arbitrator dealing with specific questions in applying such an approach, the discussion, it appears, will be tremendously helpful.

The last of the three important valuation approaches considered by the author is the asset-based or cost approach, which assumes that the value of different component parts determines the overall value of an object. Marboe analyses the various particularities of the approach, such as the methods to determine the past and present cost of assets, among which are the book value, the replacement value and the liquidation value. Again, the discussion is supplemented by an analysis of cases applying or rejecting the approach.

After discussing other approaches, that have been occasionally applied by international arbitration tribunals, such as mixed methods and tax value methods, in the last section on valuation methods, Marboe turns her attention to consequential damages in the final section of chapter 5. She presents an overview on all kinds of consequential damages such as a loss of goodwill or creditworthiness, as well as the costs and expenses for pursuing the claim, and discusses the underlying reasoning of tribunals, which have dealt with requests for such damages.

The last chapter of the book, (chapter 6) "Interest," is dedicated to the calculation of interest in international investment arbitration proceedings. As the author rightly highlights at the outset of the chapter, the importance of interest in the context of damages and compensation is often underestimated, although interest might amount to a substantial amount of the damages. In this chapter, the author analyses and explains the decisive criteria for the calculation of interest. She emphasises the three most important questions that have to be answered in dealing with calculation of interest which are: (1) the rate of interest, (2) the period of interest and, (3) whether the interest should be compounded. Further, the author differentiates between the pre-award and post-award interest, since the former relates to the compensation or damages and the latter to the default on charges for the non-payment of a debt. Despite the limited discussion on this topic in the literature, the author gives a meaningful insight on the calculation of interest by analysing various relevant decisions by arbitral tribunals on the matter.

Overall, there is no doubt that this book is a new comprehensive source for counsels, advisors, judges and arbitrators in international judicial proceedings. It can be highly recommended, first of all, because it provides a comprehensive and thorough analysis of the practice of international courts and tribunals such as arbitration tribunals under ICSID Rules, the Iran-US Claims Tribunal, the European Court of Human Rights, the UN Compensation Commission and ad hoc arbitrations under UNCITRAL and other rules, in the calculation of damages in investment claims. Moreover, the emphasis of the author on the accurate identification of the legal basis for a claim, in order to identify the appropriate valuation approach, will give future tribunals and counsel food for thought. The book will certainly become a great asset for arbitrators and other legal practitioners alike as it provides a thorough analysis of valuation approaches accompanied by reference to relevant case law and legal literature. If one were to make a wish for the next edition, it would be a wish for an extra chapter on the procedural intricacies of dealing with issues of calculation of compensation and damages. The book already contains a short chapter on experts and several references to arbitral practice upon which certainly could be built.

Tracey Epps and Andrew Green, Reconciling Trade and Climate: How the WTO Can Help Address Climate Change

Edward Elgar, 2010; ISBN 978-1-84980-006-8

Alexander Proelss

This important book deals with the relationship between world trade law and climate change policy. It takes a different perspective than the majority of publications in the field. While the rules of the World Trade Organization (WTO), to the extent that they support continuing liberalisation and generally unrestricted international trade, have come to be seen as a central part of the problem, Epps and Green argue that the objectives of mitigating climate change on the one hand and deterring protectionism on the other do not necessarily conflict with each other. On the contrary, their hypothesis is that synergies exist between these goals, and, through the manner where they reinforce each other, that they have potential to increase social welfare. The authors thus assess the potential of international trade law as a tool for addressing the challenges of climate change. In light of this, the WTO is not considered as the "bad guy" in international relations, whose regime prevents States from implementing trade-related measures in order to be able to achieve the ultimate aim of safeguarding that the increase in global temperature should be below 2 degrees Celsius, but rather as a key actor with regard to the fulfillment of that target. While "WTO Members have very different perceptions of what the trading system ought to do on climate change" (*Pascal Lamy*), the approach followed in this book may ultimately have a stronger impact on the attitude of States concerning the relationship between WTO law and the climate change regime than the somewhat fruitless repeated pleas for "greening" the WTO.

Following a carefully phrased introduction where the interrelationship between the goals of mitigating climate change, deterring protectionism and further development of developing States is expounded, Epps and Green explore the economic and theoretical background of the linkages between trade and climate change (chapter 2) and introduce the reader to the existing trade and climate change frameworks (chapter 3) as well as to the role of trade measures in addressing

A. Proelss (✉)
Department of Law, University of Trier, Universitätsring 15, 54296 Trier, Germany
e-mail: proelss@uni-trier.de

DOI 10.1007/978-3-642-33917-2_23,

climate change (chapter 4) in the second part of their treatise. The authors consider climate change and widespread poverty as two of the greatest crises facing the world. That climate change cannot be approached without reference to market considerations is emphasized by reference to the "Stern Review" of 2007, where the basis for greenhouse gas (GHG) emissions was put in the perspective of a massive market failure, i.e. that individuals who benefit from activities that lead to GHG emissions do not at the same time bear the full costs of these activities. Consequently, Epps and Green identify the public goods nature and the free-riding problem deriving therefrom as the core problems of climate change. With regard to the question why States act, they convincingly reject idealistic solutions, but base their conclusions on the simple assumption that States are self-interested and focused on maximising national welfare. This realistic approach may render the study particularly relevant for the future debate on the relevance of the WTO in the context of combating global warming. The brief introduction to the existing legal rules concerning world trade and combating climate change is sound and in a suitable manner prepares the ground for the subsequent detailed assessment of the legal dimensions of the subject matter.

The following analysis is divided into three major parts that correspond to the three ways where trade and climate change policy, according to the authors, interact: (1) implications of trade rules for domestic climate policy, (2) unilateral measures to induce other countries to take action on climate change, and (3) multilateral solutions. The first dimension of interaction, i.e. the implications of trade rules for domestic climate policy, is addressed in chapters five to ten of the study. The authors start with an examination of three different forms of regulatory measures that address climate change, namely standards for particular goods or activities (e.g., emission levels), required disclosure of information (e.g., through product labelling) and domestic emissions trading programmes. Each of these categories is then measured against the requirements of WTO law such as the national treatment principle (Art. III GATT) and the TBT Agreement. Naturally, special attention is paid to the practice of the GATT panels and the Appellate Body, in particular with regard to the highly relevant question whether two products are "like" in terms of Art. III.4 GATT. This passage is extremely informative due to the authors' effort to comprehensively evaluate as well as systematise the reports of the panels and Appellate Body. Whether or not violations of Art. III GATT can be justified under Art. XX GATT is discussed at a later stage in chapter 9 of the treatise.

Chapter 6 deals with the imposition of taxes addressing climate change. This matter is particularly important in light of the fact that a (upstream) carbon tax is widely considered by economists to be one of or even the most cost-effective way to stabilise and reduce GHG concentrations in the atmosphere. The authors do not ignore that the imposition of taxes is likely to attract strong opposition by affected groups; notwithstanding this, the decisive legal question that needs to be answered is whether carbon taxes can be imposed in conformity with Art. III.2 GATT. Epps and Green look into this subject in detail and on the basis of the pertinent panel and Appellate Body reports (Korea—Taxes on Alcoholic Beverages; Japan—Taxes on Alcoholic Beverages), but convincingly refrain from giving a clear answer due to the high degree of dependence on the factual evidence available in a given situation. In the following chapter, the authors turn to the issue of subsidies that are provided, e.g., for climate friendly energy. Again, they overcome the temptation to militate in favour of the need for such instruments in an undifferentiated manner, but rather refer to the disadvantages of the use of subsidies in light of the collective action problems involved. Concerning the lawfulness under WTO law, the use of subsidies is discussed by reference to the categories established by the SCM Agreement. Recourse to border tax adjustments (BTAs) is then addressed in chapter 8. Epps and Green start with a helpful outline concerning the issues of competitiveness and leakage that may result from pricing carbon through regulations or taxes. BTAs are then distinguished from border taxes insofar as they are generally trade neutral. The compatibility of BTAs is analysed by way of differentiation between BTAs on import (Art. II.2(a) GATT) and on exports (Art. XVI GATT and Art. I.1(ii) SCM Agreement). In result, all forms of BTAs are, according to the authors, characterised by a considerable degree of legal uncertainty. As concerns emissions trading schemes, Epps and Green discuss in detail the question whether the domestic obligation to hold an emission permit qualifies as a measure in terms of Art. II.2(a) GATT. They conclude that again no clear answer can be given but that the situation depends on the specific requirements of the relevant emissions trading scheme.

Chapter 9 is then dedicated to the role of environmental exceptions, in particular Art. XX GATT. Experts in WTO law will not gain many new insights from this chapter, but the authors' efforts concerning the systematisation of the pertinent panel and Appellate Body practice again deserve special notice. In any event, the focus on regulatory measures that address climate change renders the analysis particularly worth reading. The third part of the treatise ends with a discussion of the major disadvantages of WTO rules for the implementation of trade-related policies, namely a considerable lack of flexibility, an equally considerable lack of certainty, and a lack of enforcement that is founded on the authors' convincing diagnosis that the remedial provisions of the WTO regime potentially lead to differing abilities and willingness of Member States to make use of the WTO dispute settlement system. Again, the analysis shows that virtually every regulatory measure that a State might adopt in order to address climate change gives cause for certain legal concerns.

In the fourth part of the study, Epps and Green address the second dimension of interaction between trade and climate policy. The possibilities of unilateral action of States to force other countries to take climate change action are examined by differentiating between positive ("carrots") and negative ("sticks") incentives. While the first category includes technical assistance, capacity building, increased investment, debt forgiveness and, in particular, the extension of preferential treatment, the second category covers measures such as the imposition of punitive tariffs and bans or restrictive quotas on particular products. By relying on the panel report concerning EC – Conditions for the Granting of Preferences to Developing Countries, the authors analyse the central question whether and, in the affirmative, to what extent a preference-giving country may differentiate among beneficiaries.

They argue that the answer to this question strongly depends on whether climate change can be considered a development need, that, again, cannot be clearly decided on a general level. Also in light of the sensitive nature of the economic sectors that may be affected by preferential treatment as well as the equity and justice concerns involved in their selected granting, Epps and Green conclude that an isolated recourse to "carrots" will generally not create sufficient motivation to developing countries to take action for mitigating climate change. Concerning "sticks," reference is being made to Art. 3.5 UNFCCC that implies that trade restrictions not only face serious challenges as to their compatibility with world trade law but also give rise to legal doubts within the climate change regime. Furthermore, measures such as product bans or quantitative restrictions must comply with Art. XI GATT or at least be justified under Art. XX GATT. While the authors refer to the Appellate Body's report in US – Shrimp to conclude that complete bans on trade can, depending on the circumstances of the individual case, be justified, they express their concern that such measures are particularly open to protectionist influences. Additionally, chapter 12 shows that unilateral trade measures such as BTAs only have little potential to dismantle the roadblocks that stand in the way for States taking action to mitigate climate change, and that such measures have the potential to undermine the common but differentiated responsibilities principle as codified in the UNFCCC and the Kyoto Protocol. The authors convincingly point to the fact that unilateral measures will usually not be implemented only to increase global welfare, but primarily for purposes of protection of domestic industries. This reflects the general ("realistic") approach taken by Epps and Green in respect of why States act.

The fifth part is dedicated to the last way identified by the authors where trade and climate change policy interact, namely the issue of multilateral solutions. Epps and Green start by examining the possibilities to include trade measures within a future multilateral climate agreement such as a post-Kyoto Protocol. In this respect, they argue that the Montreal Protocol on Substances that Deplete the Ozone Layer, being the most important precedent to date, could serve as a regulatory model. However, the fact that the relationship between WTO law and multilateral environmental agreements (MEAs) has been the subject of long-running, but yet unresolved discussions in the Committee on Trade and Environment of the WTO, that the connection between MEAs and the WTO is one of the areas of negotiation of the unfinished Doha Round, and that the approach taken by the GATT panels in respect of interpreting WTO law in accordance with the obligations stemming from MEAs varies to a considerable degree prompts them to take a careful approach to the central question whether a future MEA is likely to make use of trade regulations as a means to foster combating climate change. On the other hand, Epps and Green identify the issue of trade in environmental goods and services (EGS) as one of the fields where liberalisation can support both future development and protection of the environment. While they argue that liberalisation of EGS could best be achieved through the current GATT tariff-reduction structure, they clearly show that differences of opinion on the definition of the concept of EGS could give rise to a second-best solution, i.e. negotiation of a stand-alone multilateral agreement on EGS.

The reciprocal idea of including climate protection into a future WTO Climate Change Agreement, or at least amending the existing WTO agreements to incorporate measures that could help to effectively tackle climate change, is explored in the final conclusions. The approach taken by the authors, according to which a staged process within the WTO seems to be the most promising course of action from a near-term perspective, is well-reasoned. Having said this, the chances of success for adopting the necessary amendments within the WTO do not seem to be too high.

Epps and Green have submitted an excellently written, innovative, and well-balanced study that deserves a wide readership. Their conclusions are drawn based on a comprehensive and well-documented examination of existing WTO law and practice of the GATT panels and the Appellate Body. The authors do not limit themselves to a purely legal analysis, but also include the necessary considerations of political theory and economy. Above all, they deserve the credit for having rejected the traditional antagonism between trade and protection of the environment. Epps and Green insist on the assumption that global welfare is not composed solely of either economic growth or of environmental protection, but includes both. That said, the only critical point one might feel called upon to make is that the detailed analysis of the requirements of WTO law undertaken by the authors in respect of the interactions between trade and climate change policy does not fully justify their optimism concerning the nature of WTO law as a tool for fostering climate change mitigation. Rather, the study shows that the potential of the existing trade rules in this respect is characterised by considerable uncertainties.

Meredith Kolsky Lewis/Susy Frankel (eds.), International Economic Law and National Autonomy

Cambridge University Press, 2010; ISBN 987-0-521-11460-8

Wolfgang Weiß

The volume collects thirteen essays written by experts of international economic law (with one exception: a legal theorist) from several continents and diverse nations. The chapters are grouped in four parts and reflect the contributions of the authors at the inaugural conference of the New Zealand Centre of International Economic Law on December 2007 entitled International Economic Law and National Autonomy: Convergence or Divergence? As diverse as the contributors are, as diverse are their topics and lenses. They approach the overall book theme of national autonomy in international economic law from different points of view (in Part I) and from different agreement-specific issues and contexts (in Parts II to IV) that cover the main areas of WTO law, i.e. trade in goods (GATT, SPS), trade in services (GATS), TRIPS and dispute settlement, and aspects of international investment law and preferential trade agreements.

The first part comprises three papers (written by *Howse*, *Fukunga,* and *Beckett*) that address horizontal, non-agreement-specific issues. *Robert Howse* thematizes in his chapter "The end of the globalization debate: continued" the globalization debate and explores how the struggle between pro- and anti-globalists has been replaced by the debate about how globalization can be shaped as even anti-globalists have gone global since their focus shifted on the global proliferation of values and on global problems that cannot be solved autonomously by nation states, a fact that people increasingly understand. Globalization does not meet societies like an unavoidable curse, but can and must be shaped by its actors, and the nation states can play a pivotal role therein. *Yuka Fukunga* ("Global economic institutions and the autonomy of development policy: a pluralist approach") deals with the proposals to combat the democratic deficit and the alleged economic bias of international economic institutions and critizes their theoretical bases for simplistically transferring domestic concepts into the international realm without considering the

W. Weiß (✉)
Deutsche Universität für Verwaltungswissenschaften Speyer, Postfach 14 09-67324 Speyer, Freiherr-vom-Stein-Str. 2, D-67346 Speyer, Germany
e-mail: weiss@dhv-speyer.de

C. Herrmann et al. (eds.), *European Yearbook of International Economic Law (EYIEL), Vol. 4 (2013)*, European Yearbook of International Economic Law 4,
DOI 10.1007/978-3-642-33917-2_24,

diversity and plurality of the global legal order that he terms "discontinuity between international and the domestic legal order." *Fukunga* well-foundedly exemplifies the practical implications of his approach. *Jason Beckett* in his contribution "Fragmentation, openness and hegemony: adjudication and the WTO" finally presents a critical exploration of the fragmentation topos in international law and assesses its particular relevance for WTO adjudication. He ultimately advises against the introduction of a meta-system to overcome problems of fragmentation, and tribunals should not carry the responsibility to reconcile different regimes.

The remaining three parts of the book consist of three to four contributions each that address agreement specific interpretational issues like the responsibility of WTO members for private food standards under the SPS agreement (*Tracey Epp*, "Demanding perfection: private food standards and the SPS Agreement" reasons why private standards are not covered by the SPS agreement, and explores their implications for World trade), or the interference of the TRIPS agreement's minimum standards and other international intellectual property regulation with domestic autonomy (see *Susy Frankel*'s chapter "Eroding national autonomy from the TRIPS Agreement"). *Alberta Fabbricotti* ("The WTO and RTAs: a 'bottom-up' interpretation of RTAs' autonomy over WTO law") offers a new solution for the problem of how to reconcile regional trade agreements with Article XXIV GATT standards. She advocates a new customary rule of tacit consent since state practice appears not to be concerned about technical WTO compliance.

Henning Grosse Ruse-Kahn in chapter 7 ('Gambling' with sovereignty: complying with international obligations or upholding national autonomy) addresses the power paradox problem in WTO dispute understanding: Whereas the dispute settlement process is rule based, its enforcement is still depending on the choice of the states, and the effectiveness of retaliation is directly related to the economic power of the parties, even with regard to suspension of TRIPS obligations shows that for small countries even suspending TRIPS will not be an effective tool for enforcing dispute settlement decisions given the usually restricted industrial capabilities of the retaliating state. And re-negotiation of its WTO commitments by the perpetrator, e.g. under Article XXI GATS, in response to a DSB statement of breach of WTO violation does not offer viable means for small economies to protect their interests against trade heavyweights.

Meredith Kolsky Lewis deals with the relevance of safety standards for indigenous products in her contribution entitled "Safety standards and indigenous products: what role for traditional knowledge?" She advocates a decisive role for traditional knowledge of indigenous communities insofar when balancing safety demands against other public interests under the SPS agreement, taking kava—a traditional drink from Pacific islands countries—as an example. Otherwise, SPS rules might justify very strict regulation of indigenous products. *Rafael Leal-Arcas* explores the impact of GATS rules on temporary labour force migration. The reality of service provision under mode 4 depends on national migration policies that present substantive obstacles to the use of mode 4 for providing services. Hence, *Leal-Arcas* analyzes ways for increased liberalization of supply of services under mode 4 (The GATS and temporary migration policy). In the last chapter of part III,

Pinar Artiran turns to interpretive difficulties enshrined in Article XXIV GATT on the formation of preferential trade agreements focusing on regulatory standards. He identifies problems when increasingly harmonized regulatory standards are adopted in preferential trade areas as this might induce trade barriers to third countries that might come in conflict with requirements of Article XXIV.

The last part commences with the contribution by *Ko-Yung Tung* (Foreign investors vs sovereign states: towards a global framework, BIT by BIT) who advocates a global framework for bilateral investment treaties setting clear and harmonized standards for treatment of foreign investment. He identifies several developments causing increased diversification, in particular as regards the assessment of domestic rules by investment tribunals.

Jane Kelsey in her chapter "How 'trade in services' transforms the regulation of temporary migration for remittances in poor countries" describes the transformation of service provision by the developments enshrined in the establishment of a transnational services economy. This trend was strengthened by GATS rules and a new generation of further international agreements that deepened and expanded the regulatory framework for international services trade focusing on highly skilled workforce, like in the EU EPAs. *Kelsey* explores the negative effects of these changes for migrant workers from poor countries. She criticizes the deceptive neutrality of the GATS mode 4 definition in face of GATS positive list approach and the narrow redefinition of mode 4 in more recent agreements.

"Reconceptualising international investment law: bringing the public interest into private business" is the final contribution written by *Kate Miles*. *Miles* here complains about international investment law lagging behind other areas of international law insofar as it lacks rules and procedures to incorporate non-economic interests and proposes remedies for this deficit.

The book is a welcome addition to the literature on a very hotly disputed current topic of international economic law. Its unique benefit is the collection of studies from different areas of international economic law. What one could miss is a generalized conceptual stance with the aim to offer solutions to the problems described.

Nico Krisch, Beyond Constitutionalism, The Pluralist Structure of Postnational Law

Oxford University Press, 2010; ISBN 9780199228317

Joost Pauwelyn

Introduction

Beyond Constitutionalism is a wonderfully structured and eloquently written book, of interest to both constitutional and international lawyers. The book, written by Hertie School of Governance Professor Nico Krisch (formerly connected to NYU and one of the founding fathers of Global Administrative Law) can be unpacked in four steps: (1) law in crisis, (2) postnational law, (3) postnational pluralism and (4) individual autonomy.

Law in Crisis

The starting point of the book (step one) is that both constitutional law and international law are in a deep crisis. "In the twenty years since the end of the Cold War, the modern framework of law and politics has plunged from one of its greatest successes into one of its most serious crises" (p. 3). Constitutional law "is struggling" because global governance has become "increasingly effective, thus removing key issues from the reach of ... domestic political processes." But also international law is in trouble, "because its thin, consent-oriented legitimacy base" appears no longer "adequate to the task" and is "overly formalistic and undemocratic" (p. 3).

Step one is a profound and fully convincing diagnosis of a broad, overarching problem that challenges law and the legitimacy/effectiveness of law's constraining and justifying force across the traditional boundaries of national and international

J. Pauwelyn (✉)
Graduate Institute of International and Development Studies, Rue Richard Wagner 1, 5th floor, 1201 Geneva, Switzerland
e-mail: joost.pauwelyn@graduateinstitute.ch

C. Herrmann et al. (eds.), *European Yearbook of International Economic Law (EYIEL), Vol. 4 (2013)*, European Yearbook of International Economic Law 4,
DOI 10.1007/978-3-642-33917-2_25,

law. As Krisch puts it later in the book: "In the classical picture, thick (but diverse) sources of domestic legitimacy (liberal democracy, people's democracy, theocracy, etc.) could coexist and find coordination in an international legal order based on the thin ground of consent. As the line of separation between the layers fades away, this division of labour no longer holds" (p. 297). Or elsewhere: "We have arrived at a point where political and functional needs bar a return to the old order of international law in which difference was processed through consent-based law-making and strictly domestic mechanisms of implementation."

Postnational Law

Step two of the book is more controversial. Based on this blurring of the lines between domestic and international law/legitimacy, Krisch sees a world where law has become "postnational—the national sphere retains importance, but it is no longer the paradigmatic anchor of the whole order" (p. 4). Domestic and international law, formal and informal cooperation are increasingly blurred and interwoven. The classical picture of separate spheres, monism and dualism, has disappeared. This narrowing down of the problem or phenomenon (described in step one above) to a world of "postnational law" (Krisch's step two, and also the subtitle of the book) may be less convincing, for several reasons.

Descriptively no one can contest that law is increasingly expressed at a multiplicity of levels (local, national, regional, international). At the same time, Krisch may be going too far and not far enough. Too far in that he does not convincingly demonstrate that the national level is no longer "the paradigmatic anchor of the whole order" (p. 4). At several turns he underestimates, for example, the diversity of ways where domestic legal processes can internalize and legitimize new forms of transnational normativity, beyond the traditional process of parliamentary approval of treaties (finding, at p. 301, for example, that "[d]omestic actors typically only play a marginal role in formal processes of regime design on the global level"; this is highly contestable[1]). These processes include checks and balances offered by parliamentary oversight of negotiating mandates and locally-adjusted implementation of international standards, domestic administrative law principles and agency in the operation and implementation of transnational networks, and judicial review by domestic courts of both international norms and their domestic implementation. Similarly, Krisch may be going too far in seeing just "one space" of postnational law whereas reality continues to depict different layers of law or regimes with some more central than (or hierarchical superior to) others, and most activity happening within each layer with clashes between layers remaining few and far between and more organized than Krisch would have it.

[1] See Pauwelyn/Wessel/Wouters (eds.), *Informal International Lawmaking*, 2012, in particular Part IV on Domestic Elaboration and Implementation of Informal International Lawmaking.

At the same time, Krisch's depiction of postnational law may not go far enough. The biggest challenge does not seem to be different layers or expressions of formal public authority (be it local, national, regional or international) but rather normative arrangements emanating from private sources or a combination of public and private authorities, often outside the formalities of law (e.g. professional organizations setting standards or technical experts issuing benchmarks on issues ranging from safety and climate change to conflict of interest rules for arbitrators and educational rankings). The main or newest transformation is not so much a multiplicity of layers (other than or beyond the national) but rather a multiplicity of forms, processes and actors or sources of authority (referred to elsewhere as "informal international lawmaking"[2]): forms as in the multiplication of informal standards or guidelines; processes as in the importance of transnational networks (falling outside both traditional domestic agencies and international organizations); actors as in the emergence of new sources of authority other than that stemming from public officials (private regulators, businesses, NGOs, experts, etc.).

Indeed, all three of Krisch's examples offered in the book to illustrate postnational law—first, human rights law in Europe and the tension between national constitutional courts, the ECJ and ECHR; second, UN sanctions and their implementation in Europe pitting the UN Security Council against the ECJ (*Kadi*) and domestic courts; third, the EU-US GMO dispute playing out within the EU, before the WTO and at the UN—are very much within the traditional realm of formal, inter-state treaties, how they interact with other such treaties and how they are received and contested within traditional, state-centered regional and national legal orders. The new frontier is hardly there: it is where formal treaties meet informal international lawmaking; where transnational networks are created at the edge of international and domestic regimes; where public authority meets and is contested by private or public–private authority, standard-setting or regulatory activity. None of the norms issued in these three examples are particularly new. What is new is that the different layers increasingly interact before international and domestic courts and tribunals. Moreover it is not that the solutions offered to these interactions were once based on clear hierarchies or a global constitution and have now changed in the face of postnational law. Rather, the solutions offered for those interactions (that, in and of themselves, are new with the proliferation of international tribunals) have, from the start, been incremental, case-by-case and avoiding grand theories of hierarchy (I will return to whether these solutions are genuine examples of disorder or pluralism in a moment). None of Krisch's examples deal with the more difficult problem of interaction between formal law and informal norms, public and private authority.

Finally, one might question the idea of "postnational law" as it only offers a negative definition, that is, the end of nation-based law, without positively defining what is behind the corner.

[2] See Pauwelyn/Wessel/Wouters (eds.), *Informal International Lawmaking*, 2012 and Pauwelyn/Wessel/Wouters/Berman/Duquet, *Informal International Lawmaking: Case Studies*, 2012.

Postnational Pluralism

If step two of the book (postnational law) could be described as the problem or disease identified by Krisch, step three is a discussion of the possible solution or cure. Contrasting it to "postnational constitutionalism," Krisch offers as the all-encompassing cure to postnational law the idea of "postnational pluralism." Krisch defines "postnational constitutionalism" (PC) as an "overarching legal framework that determines the relationships of the different levels" (p. 23); based on an anxiety of the new, PC is a "promise to tame" the space of postnational law, to "organize it in a rational way," an "attempt to establish continuity with central political concepts and domestic traditions" with "utopian overtones" (p. 67). Postnational pluralism (PP), in contrast, is defined as a response where an "overarching framework" is "neither practically possible nor normatively desirable," a model of order relying on the "heterarchical interaction of the various layers of law" (p. 23), a "normative rupture" to "explore alternative visions of politics—to risk a break with what we are familiar with and look beyond constitutionalism for guidance and inspiration" (p. 68); "it is typical for pluralism that relations with other orders are assessed and governed by each order itself—*how* they are governed may then vary widely" (p. 172); under PP there is "no independent standpoint that could have provided a decision—only the competing, fundamentally diverging perspectives of the different systems" (p. 175).

Krisch defends PP both descriptively, as something that is happening in the real world, and normatively, as something that is a good thing and works. However, at times it is unclear whether this normative position is genuine or whether Krisch would himself not prefer the "utopian overtones" of PC. At one point, for example, he states: "There is little doubt that in an ideal world constitutionalism would be the best option for structuring global law. It would provide us with a reasoned framework ... common values ... civilized, institutional mechanisms ... coherence ... Yet the world is not ideal, and our models of order have to cope with the actual constraints politics and social structures on the global level impose on us" (p. 187).

Reformulating the PC v. PP debate into three options in response to postnational law, Krisch refers to two options that remain within constitutionalism: (1) "containment" (where the "only hope for legitimate governance lies in the domestic constitutional framework," p. 14) and (2) "transfer" (of key domestic concepts and institutions to regional and global levels offering a "global constitutionalism as 'compensating' for deficiencies in the domestic realm," p. 16). After rejecting both "containment" and "transfer," Krisch offers a third option he refers to as "break." It comes as no surprise that "break" is then equated to pluralism (although other types of breaks could be imagined). Under the "break" scenario, "more pluralist models" of law and legitimacy are to be put in place going beyond traditional accountability mechanisms, focusing on "output over input legitimacy" and including an "exploration of non-electoral accountability mechanisms" (p. 16).

Krisch's defense of the virtues of pluralism is convincing and novel. He explains how pluralism can offer greater adaptability, transformative capacity and contestatory space through conflicting claims to authority (p. 70); how pluralism may keep power in check through novel types of checks and balances, interacting networks, and the absence of an overarching hierarchical structure.

As with step two (identification of the problem as "postnational law"), Krisch's proposed solution under step three ("postnational pluralism") is not without problems. First, it remains unclear whether the vision of pluralism can offer an all-encompassing cure to the challenges of postnational law. Surely, pluralism addresses interactions between regimes and the different layers, but can it also offer a theory to keep activity within each layer legitimate and effective? As interesting as the clashes between the courts in Karlsruhe, Luxembourg and Strasbourg may be in terms of human rights protection in Europe (Krisch's first example), these clashes or interactions touch only upon a small fraction of the debates within Europe over human rights. In many ways, Krisch collapses and confuses the problem/disease (blurring of legal borders as in "postnational law") with the solution/cure (blurring of legal borders as in "pluralism"). The genuine cure we must be looking for is: how can we keep this brave new world of novel and interacting legal regimes both effective *and* accountable to the people. This raises questions internal to each of these orders or regimes. Their interaction and how it should be organized (or not) is only a relatively small element of this bigger picture.

Secondly, as with postnational law, Krisch defines "postnational pluralism" only in the negative, that is, by contrasting it to constitutionalism, defining it as the absence of clear hierarchies. And even here it often seems that Krisch sets up constitutionalism as little more than a straw man. Constitutionalism and pluralism have more in common than Krisch cares to admit. In all three examples used in the book (human rights, UN sanctions, GMOs), it is not as if hierarchies or rules on regime interaction are absent. They are simply different, in flux and decided more incrementally. Under international law, the relation between UN law and EU law remains pretty clear (UN charter obligations prevail, as even the ECJ admits). That in *Kadi* the ECJ double-checked the domestic implementation of UN Security Council sanctions against EU fundamental rights is nothing new (or postnational) either: under traditional dualism, and for purposes of domestic law, it remains for each state to decide whether or not to incorporate its international obligations in national law. Similarly, it is not in doubt that EU regulations on imported GMOs are, as a matter of international law, inferior to the EU's obligations at the WTO and that those WTO obligations, in turn, are hierarchically of the same order as obligations under the Biosafety Protocol. One may validly point out that the conflict rules in the Vienna Convention no longer make sense, but that is an argument on which hierarchical rule or solution to use, not evidence of the absence of hierarchy. Changing or competing decisions on hierarchy is not the same as absence of hierarchy.

Krisch's best example of pluralism, as in unsettled hierarchies, may be that of human rights in Europe (and even there the battle lines or hierarchies, e.g. when Karlsruhe or the ECHR will step in against the EU or ECJ, are relatively clearly drawn; in the case of the ECHR, for example, using a "manifest deficiency" standard). Yet, when it comes to human rights in Europe we may be closer to the realm of interlocking segments within a domestic (here European) order rather than a truly postnational order. As Krisch himself points out, with reference to Carl Schmitt, "indecision on ultimate supremacy could only work in homogeneous societies" (p. 235). At the international level, where diversity dominates, pluralism risks unsettling or relativizing the strength of any regime, opening doors especially for powerful actors. In the GMO debate, Krisch takes the EU's contestation of WTO rulings against the EU both domestically and at the international level (e.g. in negotiations of the UN Biosafety Protocol as a counter-weight against the WTO) as evidence of "pluralism." For others, pluralism is a euphemism for non-compliance (or how would Krisch approach a situation where, say, China or Russia loses a human rights dispute but then turns its back to contest the outcome at home or in other international fora: pluralism or non-compliance?). As Krisch at one point admits, "in the worst case, rival supremacy claims can become excuses for non-compliance whenever a rule or decision goes against the interests of an actor. Here, pluralism risks creating a slippery slope."

In any event, it is too bad that all three of the examples discussed in *Beyond Constitutionalism* are set or focused on Europe. A less Eurocentric perspective could have enriched the analysis. Ultimately, it is far from clear that the three examples discussed in the book do, indeed, portray a picture of "a rugged, mountaineous terrain: highly uneven, difficult to get a grasp of, and certainly not formed according to neat and clear principles" (p. 225). It may look like chaos to a German constitutional scholar. To a US, common law lawyer embedded in US federalism it may well look like standard practice.

Individual Autonomy

The obvious next question (once "pluralism" identified as the cure under step three) leads us to the fourth and final step of the book: admitting that under "pluralism," a panoply of regimes interact and no clear hierarchies exist, how should we nonetheless go about balancing or weighing the relative value of, or interactions between, regimes? And here is probably Krisch's most innovative and interesting proposal: his benchmark would be individual autonomy.

Krisch admits that pluralism "does not grant ultimate authority to any collective or process" but usefully adds that it "can help bring the competing visions into an informal balance" (p. 183). Unlike many proponents of pluralism he then goes on and offers a benchmark to put this in practice. For Krisch, the foundation of pluralism is "individuals' choices of the associations they want to form part of" (p. 91). From this perspective, the "postnational order" is not a top-down structure set up by states, governments or international organizations, but reflects individual, social practices of a multiplicity of identities and loyalties, an order that "disperses ultimate authority" (p. 100). Consequently, when faced with different regimes or one regime having to weigh the importance of another, the respect or weight to be given to a regime, order or polity depends on "the degree to which they are based on practices of public autonomy"; "the weight of a collective's claim will follow from the strength of its social grounding, of the participatory practices that support it as well as the plausibility of its attempt to balance inclusiveness and particularity" (p. 101). In other words, what matters is the "public autonomy credentials" of a particular layer or order. No respect is due for polities or institutions "if they are based on exclusion, leaving out substantial parts of those affected by its decisions, without providing a compelling justification."

Krisch thereby powerfully and convincingly grounds pluralism in individual freedom and puts it to work in line with basic rules of procedural integrity. Other times he goes further and refers also to substantive, value-based criteria (at p. 103: "to deserve the attribute of 'public autonomy' social practices have to meet substantial conditions—if not in legal, then in moral terms"). Whereas procedural rules may fit the idea of pluralism, it is less clear, however, how such substantive values could go hand in hand with genuine pluralism.

In addition, even if one accepts the benchmark of individual autonomy to loosely rank or weigh regimes in a pluralist order, how exactly is one to do this? How exactly can we make sure or weigh the extent to which a norm or institution reflects the preferences, loyalty or allegiance of individuals; which individuals count and for how much? What is the weight of a group of elected government officials as compared to a group of renowned scientists or a coalition of NGOs or private businesses or professional organizations that have issued a norm? And, most importantly, who is to make this decision?

Finally, assuming we can operationalize the "individual autonomy" benchmark suggested by Krisch would we then not simply replace one hierarchy with another, rather than hierarchy with pluralism?

Stephan W. Schill (ed.). International Investment Law and Comparative Public Law

Oxford University Press, 2010; ISBN 9780199589104

Rhea Tamara Hoffmann

Introduction

One of the main debates of international investment law and arbitration, which divided the investment law community,[1] concerns the legitimacy of the system. Some perceive a legitimacy crisis, while others disagree.[2] The book under review addresses and attempts to solve this crisis by a distinct methodology.

Concerns about the legitimacy of international investment law have different origins. Host states are concerned about a shrinking of domestic policy space as they experience or observe high compensation claims on the part of foreign investors before investment arbitral tribunals, that might, in the end, lead to a "chilling effect" on governmental regulatory measures aimed at public interests. In addition, several aspects, rooted in the structure and content of international investment law and arbitration, have led to a certain amount of criticism, which is also represented in the public statement of several academics.[3] One aspect is that the vague and open-ended formulations of investment protection obligations that

---

[1] Schill, Public or Private Dispute Settlement? The Culture Clash in Investment Treaty Arbitration and its Impact on the Role of the Arbitrator, in: Weiler/Baetens (eds.), *New Directions in International Economic Law, In Memoriam Thomas Wälde*, 2011, p. 23.

[2] Instead of many, see on the one hand, Franck, The Legitimacy Crisis in Investment Treaty Arbitration: Privatizing Public International Law through Inconsistent Decisions, Fordham Law Review 73 (2005) 4, p. 1521. On the other hand, see Krishan, Thinking about BITs and BIT Arbitration: The Legitimacy Crisis that Never Was, in: Weiler/Baetens (eds.), *New Directions in International Economic Law, In Memoriam Thomas Wälde*, 2011, p. 107.

[3] See the "Public statement on the international investment regime," 31 August 2010, available at: http://osgoode.yorku.ca/public_statement.

R.T. Hoffmann (✉)
Goethe University Frankfurt am Main, Cluster of Excellence "The Formation of Normative Orders", Research Group "The Change in Transnational Labour and Economic Law", Feldmannshof, 57223 Kreuztal, Germany
e-mail: rhea.hoffmann@gmail.com

C. Herrmann et al. (eds.), *European Yearbook of International Economic Law (EYIEL), Vol. 4 (2013)*, European Yearbook of International Economic Law 4,
DOI 10.1007/978-3-642-33917-2_26,

restrict state sovereignty are left to the interpretation of arbitral tribunals without clear guidance. Furthermore, arbitral awards have led to conflicting and inconsistent decisions. Moreover, the system of investment arbitration lacks objective safeguards, such as judicial independence and impartiality, which leads to a perceived bias that arbitrators might favour investor interests over legitimate non-investment policies.

The late Thomas Wälde, to whose memory the book *International Investment Law and Comparative Public Law* is dedicated, was one of the first investment experts who admitted that, both in substance and in function, investment arbitration is not very close to commercial arbitration,[4] although it originally stemmed from this type of law. Statements like this have led to the conclusion, that much of investment treaty arbitration today must be understood as public law. This motivates two interpretations of international investment law. The first is associated with the Global Administrative Law project at New York University, for example:

> Investor-State arbitration is not only a mechanism to settle disputes between an investor and a State arising out of an investment, [but] it is also a form of global governance that involves the exercise of power by arbitral tribunals in the global administrative space.[5]

The second approach concerns international investment law from a comparative public law perspective that the book under review adopts. This approach goes well beyond the emerging paradigm of global administrative law, as it also includes comparative constitutional law and other public international law regimes, such as human rights and international trade law, in order to make use of the public law understanding of international investment law and arbitration. The success story of international investment law and arbitration might come to a premature end without addressing the concerns about the legitimacy of the system. There have been a number of proposal for changes both revolutionaly and reformist. In this context, the book under review has been characterised as "a critical step in saving investment arbitration",[6] as opposed to "killing"[7] it. The book aims at re-injecting legitimacy into investment law by offering a new medicine to the reluctant patient.

---

[4] See UNCITRAL/NAFTA, Arbitral Award, *International Thunderbird Gaming Corp vs. United Mexican States*, 26 January 2006, Separate Opinion by Thomas Wälde, paras. 12 et seq.

[5] Kingsbury/Schill, Investor-State Arbitration as Governance: Fair and Equitable Treatment, Proportionality, and the Emerging Global Administrative Law, IILJ Working Paper 2009/6, Abstract; see also, Van Harten/Loughlin, Investment Treaty Arbitration as a Species of Global Administrative Law, European Journal of International Law 17 (2006) 1, p. 121 (145–150), stressing the public law nature of investment treaty arbitration; Montt, *State Liability in Investment Treaty Arbitration – Global Constitutional and Administrative Law in the BIT Generation*, 2009.

[6] Caron, who comments on the book under review, see http://ukcatalogue.oup.com/product/9780199589104.do.

[7] Schill, The public law challenge: Killing or rethinking international investment law?, Columbia FDI Perspectives, No. 58, 30 January 2012.

The book is comprised of 25 contributions on some of the most important and most discussed issues concerning international investment law and arbitration. All issues are investigated from a comparative public law perspective. The scope of the contributions, some of which acknowledge the legitimacy crisis, some of which do not, is broad, and covers substantive investment protection standards[8] as well as the institutional and procedural structure of investor-state arbitration.[9] The concept and foundations of the new public law approach, contained in the first three contributions of the volume, are the basis for further comparative analysis in the following chapters of the book. Besides the three basic chapters, the 22 other chapters focus on "Investor Rights in Comparative Perspective", "Comparative Administrative and Comparative Constitutional Law on selected issues", and, finally, aspects relating to "Dispute Settlement, Arbitral Procedure, and Remedies."

A New Public Law Approach: The Concept and Foundations of "International Investment Law and Comparative Public Law"

The concept and foundations of *International Investment Law and Comparative Public Law* are examined in the first three chapters of the book.

The Public Law Nature of International Investment Law

In the introductory chapter, written by the editor, Stephan W. Schill, the background of the comparative public law project, its aspirations, and its motivations are explained in depth. Schill reasons that, without legally and doctrinally conceptualising international investment law and arbitration, complaints about a growing legitimacy crisis cannot be rejected. International investment law, as the fastest and the most successful growing field of public international law, is facing more and more criticism. However, before taking a closer look at the concept, the underlying understanding of international investment law has to be scrutinised.

The book argues for a new public law approach to international investment law and arbitration. The hybrid nature of international investment law, combining public and private law aspects, due to its dispute settlement procedures, has led to discussions about a "public/private distinction" in this law field (p. 10). Investment treaty arbitration has a hybrid nature that combines public international law (with

[8] Investment protection standards covered by the contributions include direct and indirect expropriation, fair and equitable treatment, full protection and security, national treatment, remedies against denial of justice, and transfer of funds.

[9] Institutional and procedural issues relate to the applied standards of review, remedies, and transparency.

regard to its substance) with elements of international commercial arbitration (mainly with regard to procedure). However, Schill argues that investment treaty arbitration differs both from traditional public international law and from international commercial arbitration in several aspects. Due to the paradigm shift in international investment law, which allows foreign investors to sue host states in international arbitration directly, "[...] states today retain much less control over dispute settlement and enforcement of investment treaty obligations" (p. 13), than in traditional public international law. Compared with international commercial arbitration, investment treaty arbitration differs from the former with regard to "[...] the subject matter of the disputes [which often involve public law rather than private law issues], the relationship of the parties, the nature of the obligations at play, and the nature and scope of the host state's consent to arbitration." (p. 14 et seq.).

Bearing these differences in mind, the conceptual framework of the book sees international investment law as a public law discipline for two reasons. First, Schill argues that the essence of investment treaty arbitration is public law, as it involves public law issues. These issues are of a highly public law nature (for example, public health and safety, environmental and social issues, emergency measures, etc.). Second, investment treaty arbitration imposes restraints on state measures and the exercise of sovereign powers concerning foreign investors. Arbitral tribunals review the legality of state measures. Thus, investment treaty law and arbitration involving states and private actors can be classified as public law because it is functionally more akin to the judicial control of governmental action provided for by national administrative and constitutional law than to either classic inter-state dispute resolution or international commercial arbitration (pp. 14–17).

Thus, regardless of the commercial aspects, Schill argues that international investment law and arbitration are, at their core, an objective review and control of state action (public authority) with regard to private investors (p. 17). Against the background of understanding international investment law as a public law framework that imposes limitations on the conduct of states, the new public law approach tries to solve concerns about the legitimacy crisis of international investment law by means of a distinct methodology that takes account of this finding.

The Concept and Methodology of the New Public Law Approach

Furthermore, the introductory chapter argues that, based upon the assumption that reforms are improbable, the comparative public law approach should become the standard methodology of international investment law in order to achieve the doctrinal clarity that is still lacking. *International Investment Law and Comparative Public Law* is a system-internal approach, which tries to solve the deficits, described above, from within the system (p. 9).

Based upon the finding that international investment law is functionally analogous to public law, the approach tries to develop general principles of law, as laid down in Article 38(1)(c) of the ICJ Statute, which have to be taken into consideration in the application and interpretation of international investment treaties.

The *International Investment Law and Comparative Public Law* concept has its origin in a Separate Opinion of Thomas Wälde in the case International Thunderbird,[10] which led to the idea of engaging in a broader comparative law undertaking. Wälde stated that, instead of recurring to commercial arbitration,

> [...] more appropriate for investor-state arbitration are analogies with judicial review relating to governmental conduct – be it international judicial review [...] or national administrative courts judging the disputes of individual citizens over alleged abuse by public bodies of their governmental powers.[11]

To the extent that a comparative survey might yield general principles of law, those could be considered as a source of international law in the sense of Article 38(1)(c) of the ICJ Statute. Given that they have acquired the status of general principles, they could inform the interpretation of treaty provisions pursuant to what is the principle of systemic integration as set out in Article 31(3)(c) of the Vienna Convention on the Law of Treaties (VCLT). In this way, this approach seeks to specify and clarify the interpretation of vague investment protection standards (de lege lata) in the decision-making process of arbitral tribunals by employing a comparative analysis of domestic legal systems as well as other public international law regimes, such as human rights and trade law. Furthermore, based upon a comparative analysis, public law concepts to review governmental measures could be found, which would help arbitral tribunals to balance investors' rights and state regulatory actions in the public interest. Besides the interpretation of investment treaties by arbitral tribunals, it is argued that general principles could be helpful in the investment treaty-making process (de lege ferenda). Schill concludes that nothing precludes using principles of domestic public law as a means of construing and interpreting international investment law, or of adopting new international rules following domestic models (pp. 23–25). However, currently, the interpretation of the existing international rules is primarily driven by considerations drawing on international rules rather than domestic law. Thus, the generation of new rules is generally much more open to relying on comparative public law than the interpretation of the existing rules.

The positive effects promised by the use of the comparative public law concept are twofold. On the one hand, more precise investment standards and new standards of review developed from comparative public law should lead to consistency among public international law regimes, thereby reducing the fragmentation of international law. On the other hand, the approach aims at legitimising "[...] existing arbitral jurisprudence by showing that the solutions adopted [...] are analogous to the ones adopted by domestic courts or other international courts or tribunals [...]." (p. 26).

---

[10] UNCITRAL/NAFTA, Arbitral Award, *International Thunderbird Gaming Corp vs. United Mexican States*, 26 January 2006.

[11] UNCITRAL/NAFTA, Arbitral Award, *International Thunderbird Gaming Corp vs. United Mexican States*, 26 January 2006, Separate Opinion by Thomas Wälde, para. 12.

Generally, due to the customary rules of treaty interpretation as re-stated in the VCLT, arbitrators may use analogies and judicial borrowing. While reference to the jurisprudence of the host and home state of the investors in order to clarify investment standards seems unproblematical, references to other courts are a more sensitive issue. Furthermore, arbitrators may detect general principles of law in the sense of Article 38(1)(c) of the ICJ Statute, which could inform the treaty interpretation. However, the use of comparative public law cannot be an uncritical undertaking. Case selections and the selection of the compared legal orders (tertium comparationis) may affect the outcome of the comparative engagement. If one looks at comparative law as a neutral process of fact-finding with regard to whether there is a general principle of law, there might be nothing against it. However, comparative law (including comparative public law) is not always a neutral process.[12] The compared legal orders mainly consist of examinations of European and North-American legal systems. The legal orders referred to most are those of the United States, the United Kingdom, Germany and France. Consequently, the comparative method needs to be both sensitive and cautious.

The book is very insightful with regard to general knowledge about different legal systems and topics that are of high importance in international investment law. However, the insights into the finding of general principles of law that can be used to improve international investment law are generally limited due to the diversity of both the legal systems and the applied approaches. The legal systems analysed in the book in order to find general principles of law according to Article 38(1)(c) of the ICJ Statute represent only a fraction of all the legal systems that exist in the world. Furthermore, it has to be borne in mind that the range of the jurisdictions chosen is restricted by limitations of space and reflects the authors' backgrounds rather than the diversity of the world's domestic legal systems. This can either mean that there might be more general principles that could be evaluated through the comparative public law approach, or that it is even impossible to find general principles.

Clearly, irrespective of whether the comparative public law analysis leads to general principles that could then be applied by investment tribunals, the examined domestic solutions found could elucidate the ordinary meaning of a term used in a treaty or clarify the intention of the parties. However, where the formulation of a treaty rule leaves no room for doubt, the impact of domestic law remains limited.

To sum up, *International Investment Law and Comparative Public Law* is more than the title suggests. It is not just "find, compare, and think about it", but is, instead, a new public law approach that aims at generating general principles of law in order to solve the legitimacy crisis of international investment law.

---

[12] Similar Vadi, Critical Comparisons: The Role of Comparative Law in Investment Treaty Arbitration, Denver Journal for International Law and Policy 39 (2010) 1, p. 67 (84); Frankenberg, Critical Comparisons: Rethinking Comparative Law, Harvard International Law Journal 26 (1985) 2, p. 411, engaged in a critique of the discourse on comparative law by arguing that comparative legal scholarship's faith in an objectivity allows culturally biased perspectives to be represented as "neutral." Contrary to this, critical comparisons have to take into account "[...] the comparatist's cultural, historical, and personal preconceptions [which] inevitably shape the way she perceives and compares" (p. 416).

The Concept of Proportionality

Despite the theoretical and methodological conception of the comparative public law approach and the assumption that the general principles of law found through the approach are minimum standards, the concept of proportionality as a standard of review for investment arbitration builds the third pillar of the *International Investment Law and Comparative Public Law* framework.

The chapter entitled "Public Law Concepts to Balance Investors' Rights with State Regulatory Action in the Public Interest – the Concept of Proportionality" (pp. 75–104) written by Benedict Kingsbury and Stephan W. Schill correctly observes that investment treaty tribunals are increasingly confronted with the task of resolving conflicts between investment protection and competing public policy concerns, such as the protection of the environment, human rights, labour and social standards, or even measures taken in response to a financial crisis (p. 77). Some reasons for this dilemma lie in the absence of investor obligations, the absence of conditions under which the host state could restrict the rights of investors, and the predominant absence of exception clauses (p. 76). Thus, this contribution addresses the challenge that lies at the heart of the book. As a solution, the chapter suggests that arbitral tribunals could resolve such conflicts by drawing on proportionality analysis as a public law concept (p. 77) as "[...] the emergence of a general principle may be involved." (p. 80).

The second part of the chapter illustrates how proportionality analysis as a judicial technique has spread from its origins as a concept of German public law to many other legal systems (Canada, South Africa, and the European Union) as well as international courts and dispute settlement systems (The Court of Justice of the European Union, the International Court of Justice, WTO law and the European Court of Human Rights) (pp. 80–85). After providing the basic elements of the principle, this contribution argues that proportionality analysis can also be applied, and, in fact, has been applied in the case *Tecnicas Medioambientales Tecmed SA v United Mexican States*, for example (p. 91 et seq.), as an interpretative technique in investment treaty interpretation. The authors find much room for its application not only in the context of indirect expropriation (p. 89 et seq.) and fair and equitable treatment (p. 96 et seq.), but also in the application of necessity-related clauses, such as non-precluded measures clauses (p. 98 et seq.).

In the conclusion, the chapter openly exposes itself to criticism and throws some of the counter-arguments against the use of the proportionality analysis overboard.

As the concept of proportionality is one of the principles where scholars see general principles emerging, as well as a core concept that is touched upon in several contributions or even promoted throughout the book, and, more importantly, in the part of the book that builds the concept and foundations, the usefulness of a general principle found in the comparative law manner will be evaluated in the following in order to give a distinct idea of what a critique has to face.

In their chapter, Kingsbury and Schill argue that proportionality analysis should play a vital role in balancing investor and state interests with regard to several investment protection standards in order to improve the reasoning, legitimacy and accountability of arbitral tribunals.

> Intense concerns about legitimacy in the system [...] should drive a rapid adoption of proportionality analysis as a standard technique.[13]

With regard to the proportionality concept, it is useful to bear in mind that this concept is already viewed as an emerging worldwide consensus in constitutional matters by some scholars.[14] The adoption of the principle of proportionality beyond the framework of adjudication of constitutional courts to international investment arbitration is a straightforward suggestion.[15] However, it does present some potential difficulties. From a constitutional- and legal-theory perspective, the adoption of the principle of proportionality to international investment arbitration is problematical. Whether or not one agrees that proportionality analysis in the context of domestic constitutional law has its difficulties or not, the application in the context of international investment law and arbitration has certainly to be regarded with scepticism. Compared to courts in the domestic realm, investment tribunals are not part of an institutional setting that comply with the separation of powers between the legislative, the judiciary and the executive. If investment tribunals have the power to review state regulatory measures, they exercise public authority and power that is normally the responsibility of domestic courts and cannot even be reversed by any higher instance. Furthermore, it is true that "proportionality" is a term with a sound judicial lineage, but it can serve different purposes. Thus, balancing may, contrary to the initial intention, result in a dangerous strengthening of investor rights. The weight given to investment protection might be greater than that given to regulatory measures in the public interest, especially if proportionality analysis is applied in the light of the specific purpose of investment treaties. This argument

---

[13] Kingsbury/Schill, Public Law Concepts to Balance Investors' Rights with State Regulatory Actions in the Public Interest—the Concept of Proportionality, in: Schill (ed.), *International Investment Law and Comparative Public Law*, 2010, pp. 75 et seq. (104).

[14] Beatty, *The Ultimate Rule of Law*, 2004; Stone Sweet/Mathews, Proportionality Balancing and Global Constitutionalism, Columbia Journal of Transnational Law 47 (2008) 1, p. 73; Kumm, The Cosmopolitan Turn in Constitutionalism: On the Relationship Between Constitutionalism in and Beyond the State, in: Dunhoff/Trachtman (eds.), *Ruling the World? Constitutionalism, International Law and Global Governance*, 2009, p. 258.

[15] Despite the argumentations found in the book under review, this suggestion has already been made in a prominent article written by Alec Stone Sweet; see Stone Sweet, Investor-State Arbitration: Proportionality's New Frontier, Law & Ethics of Human Rights 4 (2010) 1, p. 47. Moreover, Alec Stone Sweet and Jud Mathews have engaged in a broad comparative study; see Stone Sweet/Mathews, Proportionality Balancing and Global Constitutionalism, Columbia Journal of Transnational Law 47 (2008) 1, p. 73.

becomes even stronger if we look at the institutional role of the arbitrator, who lacks the institutional safeguard of independence and impartiality due to the construction of the arbitration system, rather than to perceived personal bias.

Bearing this in mind, it is obvious that arbitral tribunals have a very powerful role, as they are isolated from the domestic democratic institutional surroundings (constitutional democracies). However, this not enough, given that, from a constitutional-theory perspective, international investment law and arbitral awards do have the potential to undermine domestic constitutional compromises due to the effectiveness of public international law and the effectiveness of investment arbitration. Investment arbitral tribunals can *de facto* ignore a democratic consensus by obliging the state to pay compensation. This indirect circumvention of democracy should not be forgotten, as the power of international arbitration to review regulatory state measures, which lacks the high amount of democratic legitimacy of national courts, is conferred upon arbitral tribunals by the principle of proportionality upon a regular basis.

Besides this theoretical examination of a doubtful application of the principle of proportionality, there is also a practical difficulty. Generally, domestic courts are in a better position to review state regulatory measures as they are embedded in the political, legal and social environment of the host state.[16] Furthermore, the already witnessed use of the principle of proportionality in investment arbitration casts doubts on its usefulness.[17]

Moreover, the comparative public law approach depends on arbitrators, to whom the application of comparative standards, such as proportionality, is conferred. Here, the role of arbitrators in the process comes into play. Their role might be overburdened if they had to handle such a comparative analysis.

To sum up, within the domestic realm that provides a constitutional framework, the principle of proportionality might be an "appropriate" mechanism for judicial balancing, whereas, in the light of the features of international investment arbitration, the weakness of the principle weighs heavily.

---

[16] Similarly, Burke-White/von Staden, The Need for Public Law Standards of Review in Investor-State Arbitration, in: Schill (ed.), *International Investment Law and Comparative Public Law*, 2010, p. 689 (711 et seq.).

[17] For a closer examination on this point, see Leonhardsen, Looking for Legitimacy: Exploring Proportionality Analysis in Investment Treaty Arbitration, Journal of International Dispute Settlement 3 (2011) 1, p. 89, who argues that, firstly, the proportionality principle has been applied precisely in the type of cases that has caused most controversy, and, secondly, that there does not seem to be a strong legal basis for the application in the cases where it has been applied. See further, Pirker, Seeing the Forest without the Trees—The Doubtful Case for Proportionality Analysis in International Investment Arbitration, in: Herwig/Joerges/Pavlakos (eds.), *Proportionality and Post-National Constitutionalism*, forthcoming. Pirker rejects the conceptualisation of investment arbitration as a developing constitutional regime. He suggests that the conceptual foundations for using proportionality analysis are shaky, both based upon the nature of the rights typically enshrined in bilateral investment treaties and upon the features of investment arbitration.

Responses to the Ongoing Legitimacy Crisis in International Investment Law: Examination of Further Contributions

Investor Rights in Comparative Perspective

The Concept of Indirect Expropriation

The chapter on "The Concept of Indirect Expropriation in Comparative Public Law – Searching for Light in the Dark" written by Markus Perkams compares the concept of indirect expropriations under the European Convention on Human Rights (ECHR) and domestic legal orders (US constitutional law, German constitutional law and the law of the European Union) after examining diverse approaches to the concept in international investment law as it stands.

The jurisprudence of the European Court of Human Rights (ECtHR) as a comparative legal order is very interesting, as investment arbitration awards have already been referred to it in order to clarify the concept of indirect expropriations. Based upon the jurisprudence of Article 1 of the First Protocol of the ECHR, which deals with the protection of property rights, the ECtHR has also dealt with forms of regulatory interference into property rights (that can be described as indirect expropriations). After a useful examination of important cases, such as Sporrong and Lönnroth and Pine Valley (pp. 113–120), Perkams finds two types of circumstances in the ECHR jurisprudence where "compensation is mandatory if without it the fair balance between the public interest pursued and the burden imposed on the individual is disturbed." (p. 121). These are what Perkams calls a *de facto* expropriation (the whole economic value of the property is affected by a governmental measure) and a situation where such a *de facto* expropriation is not the case but the measure is disproportionate. The jurisprudence of the ECtHR applied the principle of proportionality. This chapter reveals, in the same way as the above-mentioned chapter by Schill and Kingsbury, that this balancing approach has been used in investment treaty arbitration in order to clarify whether an indirect expropriation has occurred (p. 110). More importantly, the proportionality analysis is regarded as a general principle of law due to the concept of the comparative public law approach. Furthermore, besides many differences, the chapter discovers the same two types of circumstances, where compensation clearly has to be paid in US and German constitutional law, as well as in the law of the European Union. After the chapter's insightful separate analyses of the legal orders, some interesting commonalities with regard to indirect expropriations are mentioned in order to sum up the analytical value of the comparative public law approach: two per se rules (always indicating an indirect expropriation) can be found in all of the four legal orders compared, which are a "permanent physical occupation" and a "deprivation of all economically viable use" of the property affected (p. 149 f.). Moreover, all the legal orders under comparison balance the public interest of the governmental measure and the effect of the measure on the property in question (p. 149).

However, the distinct legal orders do not draw absolute or clear lines to determine indirect expropriations or the like, nor does the comparison between these legal orders lead to a breakthrough that goes beyond the two per se rules and the fact that, in domestic legal orders, a proportionality analysis is somehow settled as a legal principle that informs a case-by-case analysis of the courts.

Fair and Equitable Treatment

Stephan W. Schill's chapter on "Fair and Equitable Treatment, the Rule of Law, and Comparative Public Law" (pp. 151–182) proposes that fair and equitable treatment (FET) be understood as an embodiment of the rule of law. Thus, he argues that the normative content of one of the core concepts in international investment law could be concretised by looking at "the sub-elements of fair and equitable treatment that appear in recurrent fashion" (p. 154) through a comparative public law lens.

Understanding FET as a "rule of law" feature, the investment standard for host state behaviour acquires a "quasi-constitutional function." (p. 154).

> In this perspective, arbitral jurisprudence does not appear as a fragmented and disordered aggregate of awards but as part of the emerging global regime governing foreign investments and limiting the conduct of host states relating to it. (p. 154).

The chapter examines how the jurisprudence of investment tribunals on fair and equitable treatment can be summarised under a primarily institutional and procedural concept of the rule for law that has parallels in the major domestic legal systems of liberal democracies (p. 158).

On the one hand, this formal understanding of the rule of law, he argues, translates into procedural requirements that restrict the exercise of the sovereign powers of the host state. Applying this thought, Schill finds seven clusters that derive from FET by interpreting it as the embodiment of the rule of law, which he examines in depth: (1) stability, predictability, and consistency, (2) legality, (3) protection of legitimate expectations, (4) administrative due process and denial of justice, (5) protection against arbitrariness and discrimination, (6) transparency, and (7) reasonableness and proportionality. It is interesting that the chapter finds legitimate expectations as one of the seven principles derived from FET as an embodiment of the rule of law even though some states have restricted the possibility of interpreting fair and equitable treatment through the notion of legitimate expectations as a basis for review. The binding interpretation by NAFTA's Free Trade Commission, for example, states that fair and equitable treatment in Article 1105(1) of NAFTA means no more than the international minimum standards in customary international law.

On the other hand, the interpretation of FET as an embodiment of the rule of law translates into "specific requirements that national legal systems have to live up to" (p. 170), such as the existence of a minimal separation of powers in host states and the possibility of having recourse to courts.

In order to justify his approach to interpret FET as the embodiment of the rule of law, Schill argues that such an understanding can be normatively grounded in the objective of international investment treaties that aim at protecting investor rights in order to promote economic growth. Generally, the contribution interprets FET as an investment standard read in the light of the object and purpose of investment treaties that follow the goal of protecting investments against governmental interference.

Comparative Administrative and Comparative Constitutional Law on Selected Issues

Comparative State Liability

The twelfth chapter of the book, written by Irmgard Marboe, deals with "State Responsibility and Comparative State Liability for Administrative and Legislative Harm to Economic Interests" (pp. 377–411). It compares the concepts of state responsibility under international law and state liability for economic harm suffered by private persons.

The purpose of the chapter, which focuses on liability for unlawful state conduct, is to identify "general principles of law in the field of state liability for administrative and legislative harm to economic interest", (p. 378) in order to find out whether these conclusions about general principles of law could be applicable to investor-state disputes under investment treaties (p. 379). Thus, the contribution by Marboe contains a comparison of the rules on state liability (for the damage caused to individuals by unlawful acts) in France, the United Kingdom, Germany, the United States, Spain, Italy, Switzerland, and Austria (p. 382 et seq.). As the compared legal systems are partly common law countries, but mainly civil law countries, the examination of the different state liability approaches shows "considerable variety" (p. 408) rather than general principles.

The law of state liability in the common law countries, the United Kingdom and the United States, is rather complicated and restrictive with regard to the standard of judicial review (p. 385 and p. 392). In addition, most of the legal systems take the complexity of state decisions into account and thus apply standards of review that leave more discretion, such as a "discretionary function exception" (as in the United States, p. 392) or a restrictive approach to "the duty of care" (as the English courts do in order to avoid opening the "floodgates" of litigation, p. 385), or the criterion of the necessity of *faute lourde* in France by the *Conseil d'État* (the highest French administrative court, p. 384).

The chapter concludes that the rules on state liability generally try to balance the interests of the individuals who have suffered harm with the rights and duties of the state (p. 408). The interests of the general public that are taken into consideration include the protection of public funds, the so-called "floodgate-concern" (p. 385; protection against indeterminate litigation against public authorities), as well as considerations of the distribution of power within a state and the efficient conduct of governmental duties. Thus, the logical consequence following the results of the comparative analysis would be to suggest that the most obvious commonality between the various legal systems is that the exercise of competences by regulatory and supervising authorities should not be controlled or second-guessed by courts in actions for damages. However, Marboe concludes that caution should be taken in introducing such new criteria as limiting devices to state liability into international investment law as general principles of law because "the privileged position of the state is increasingly regarded as ill-founded and lacking legitimacy" (p. 411).

Altogether, the chapter, which is very informative about the different approaches to state liability, shows that the comparative public law approach with regard to state liability would mainly lead to a greater deference for state conduct, although Marboe is convinced that this discretion is shrinking, and thereby reflects the changing role of the state in modern society (p. 408). As a result, she is doubtful as "to what extent 'principles of law' can be used to introduce new elements concerning liability and responsibility in international investment law." (p. 410 et seq.).

Economic Emergency Powers

Chapter Sixteen, written by Christina Binder and August Reinisch, about "Economic Emergency Powers: A Comparative Law Perspective" (p. 503–540) deals with economic emergency powers, an issue that has been one of the most discussed topics in international investment law since the Argentinian financial crisis (2001/2002).

Applying the comparative public law perspective here seems highly important, as this might show whether the approach is capable of offering solutions to specific questions of high political and economic value. This is even more true when one bears the present global financial and sovereign debt crisis in mind.

After examining the necessity defence under (customary) international law with a brief historical appraisal, and then taking the case-law of investment tribunals into account, the chapter examines the emergency regimes of four representative legal systems (the United Kingdom, France, Germany, and the United States) for additional insights that might assist in more closely delineating a state's emergency powers in times of (economic) crisis. The chapter's evaluation of the investment awards against Argentina offers interesting insights into the difficulties of applying the necessity defence in situations of economic emergencies and crisis. Binder and Reinisch find the abstract and general wording of the customary international law defence to be "ill-suited for situations of economic emergencies" (p. 513) mainly because the requirement that the state measure has to be the "only way/means" (p. 510) and the criterion that necessity may not be invoked when there was a "contribution" (p. 512) to the situation on the part of the state.

Generally, the examination of the four legal systems has shown that, in domestic law, problems relating to divergent interests (public interest to solve the crisis efficiently versus private interest not to suffer from those measures) are often solved by a broader concept than under the customary international law defence of necessity. Reinisch and Binder conclude that:

> [i]t is generally accepted in all of the legal systems examined that emergency situations extend a state's scope of action. (p. 540).

Moreover, none of the domestic legal systems examined in the contribution makes use of the concept of whether the state has contributed to the economic emergency crisis, a question that increases in importance the more we are aware that economic crises are mainly influenced by both internal and external factors.

The comparative assessment of a state's powers in economic emergency situations, in particular concerning the conditions governing the adoption of emergency measures and the consequences thereof, shows that the domestic legal systems are more reluctant and try to offer more deference to state authorities than the current international investment regime does.

Dispute Settlement, Arbitral Procedure, and Remedies

Procedural Fairness and the Rule of Law

Contrary to Schill's rule of law approach, Gus Van Harten's contribution "Investment Treaty Arbitration, Procedural Fairness, and the Rule of Law" (pp. 627–657) mainly uses the rule of law in order to criticise the current arrangement of investment arbitration. Moreover, Schill's rule of law analysis leads to substantive principles that clarify fair and equitable treatment, whereas Van Harten focuses on the procedural and institutional elements of investment arbitration. Before Van Harten begins to examine two features of the rule of law with regard to investment arbitration (procedural fairness and judicial independence), his contribution raises awareness of the fact that the rule of law is a very general concept of law that has a positive connotation—he describes the reaction to the rule of law by using the word "Hurrah" (p. 634)—but that it is also open to abuse for several reasons.

His main claim is that investment treaty arbitration is often promoted as a fair and rule-based system that advances the rule of law (p. 634 et seq.), without complying with rule of law principles, such as fairness and judicial independence (p. 643–656). The chapter's argument is mainly based upon five factors. Firstly, the combination of arbitration and public law results in a unique form of public law arbitration (p. 643). Secondly, the asymmetrical claims structure of investment arbitration "[...] where only one class of parties brings the claim [...]" (p. 643) leads to the suspicion that arbitrators might favour investor interests, as arbitrators might promote the system from which they make money. The third argument refers to the appointment of arbitrators, as investment treaty arbitration relies on executive officials to make case-by-case appointments. This governance structure and distribution of voting power, Van Harten argues, "appears very likely to favour the priorities of major capital-exporting states or foreign investors, or both." (p. 643). Moreover, as a fifth argument, he mentions the attenuation of judicial oversight of investment treaty arbitration as the system of investment arbitration sets final and binding decisions about state liability without establishing judicial independence through an appellate process (p. 637). All of these basic assumptions refer to the institutional and procedural aspects of the adjudicative process and do not explicitly refer to an actual bias on the part of individual arbitrators.

Bearing in mind the shortfalls of the system, Van Harten examines how investment arbitration as a global enforcer of the rule of law leads to an *ad absurdum* situation. Thus, Van Hartens contribution sheds new light on the rule of law, that, in his view, can be read in at least two ways with regard to international investment law. One way is to "advocate a limited role of the state, based on an espoused preference for fairness, individual freedom, and market efficiency." This is what he calls the "rule of law advocacy." The contrary approach bears in mind that the rule of law advocacy is advocating the rule of law in a way that aims to advance "business freedom as a higher goal" (p. 635), thereby undermining governmental choices aimed at promoting public good. Van Harten mirrors the described elements of the rule of law (procedural fairness and judicial independence) with concerns about independence in investment treaty arbitration in the last part of the chapter.

Public Law Standards of Review

The chapter by William Burke-White and Andreas von Staden on "The Need for Public Law Standards of Review in Investor-State Arbitrations" (pp. 689–720) provides, at its core, a comparative analysis of the standards of review in international public law adjudication that is the basis of the subsequent approach to reach a "consistent and theoretically grounded international approach to standards of review in public law adjudication." (p. 707 et seq.). The main argument is that investment tribunals should use a margin of appreciation that allows more leeway for the state to make decisions, instead of applying a proportionality analysis when reviewing governmental measures. While affirming that any consistently applied public law standard of review that recognises the competing public interests at stake in investment arbitration would be preferable to the *status quo* (p. 715), the chapter argues that, for reasons of institutional capacity, expertise, and embeddedness, the margin of appreciation, as developed by the European Court of Human Rights, may offer the best path forward (p. 717). A consistent application of a margin of appreciation when reviewing the public law regulatory activities of states would allow arbitral tribunals to grant the appropriate deference to national authorities while simultaneously protecting investor rights, thereby helping to close the growing legitimacy gap in investor-state arbitration. Besides the appraisal of the margin of appreciation, the contribution provides a further insightful analysis of what it means to treat "Investment Law as Public Law" (p. 691 et seq.) and of the interconnection between standards of review in investment arbitration and a "growing legitimacy crisis." (p. 695 et seq.). Approaches used by arbitral tribunals constituted under the Convention of the International Centre for the Settlement of Investment Disputes (ICSID), are examined in the context of the Argentinian financial crisis. Burke-White and von Staden conclude that some tribunals "operated as if the only fundamental rights at stake were those of investors and as if they were enforcing a narrowly drawn private law contract divorced from its public law context." (p. 696).

Burke White and von Staden offer a comparative overview of a legal test that could be applied instead of the principle of proportionality. In their eyes, the principle of proportionality is a too far-reaching standard of review because of the ill-suited position of investment tribunals that are not embedded in the policy considerations that underlie the state measure (p. 717). Reviewing public international law, in particular WTO law, as well as the ECHR jurisprudence, they find three other possible standards of review. First, the "least restrictive means test" as in WTO law. Second, the margin of appreciation used in the jurisprudence of the ECtHR, and finally, the good faith review in international law.

The chapter argues that, although international investment arbitration has rapidly shifted to include disputes of a public law nature (p. 691 et seq.), arbitral tribunals nonetheless continue to apply standards of review derived from the private law origins of international arbitration (p. 691, 695). Investment arbitration tribunals have not recognised the new public law context of these disputes, and have failed to develop a coherent jurisprudence with regard to the applicable standard for reviewing the public regulatory activities of the state (p. 695).

Generally, it is convincing—as the chapter argues—that a margin of appreciation would be more suitable than the concept of proportionality. However, it is not totally clear whether the margin of appreciation is the solution to the legitimacy crisis of international investment law as the very same problems regarding the principle of proportionality can be identified. Although the margin of appreciation involves only a residual balancing compared to a direct balancing under the principle of proportionality, the lack of embeddedness of arbitral tribunals into the polities over which they exercise control, for example, remains. Thus, the application of a margin of appreciation does not change much when compared to the principle of proportionality, as it also involves balancing by arbitral tribunals.

Transparency and Public Interest

The last chapter of the book deals with "Transparency and the Public Interest in Investment Treaty Arbitration", a theme that has often been used to describe the legitimacy crisis of international investment law. Seeing this as one of the core debates, the authors, Alessandra Asteriti and Christian Tams, note that the "[...] criticism seemed to take the investment community by surprise. Yet in retrospect, one cannot wonder why it took so long to be articulated [as] international investment arbitration has distinct public policy implications." (p. 791).

The debate about transparency and public interest representation in international investment arbitration can be summed up in the contradiction between "the traditional need for confidentiality and privacy", on the one hand, and "the new demand for transparency and inclusiveness", on the other hand (p. 795). The chapter analyses the "orthodox approach" to transparency and public interest representation within the International Chamber of Commerce, the London Court of International Arbitration, the Stockholm Chamber of Commerce, and the normative framework of the UNCITRAL Rules (still allowing for absolute confidentiality), and the rather "moderate orthodoxy" of the ICSID Convention (that is, generally speaking, open with regard to transparency, but only if both parties agree) before examining transparency and public interest representation in selected domestic legal systems (the United States, the United Kingdom, Germany, France and Greece). After assessing the domestic legal systems, the authors conclude that these systems are able to address the important topic of transparency and public interests, but each system does so pursuant to its own specific different legal avenues (for example, inquisitorial versus adversarial models) (p. 813). This means that all the public law systems examined respect the most important criteria of transparency, provide for some form of public interest representation (with regard to the model of proceedings), and also provide for some form of public interest representation by non-disputing parties.

Making use of the comparative public law approach in this context could mean "[...] argu[ing] in favour of a regular registration of cases, of public access to proceedings, and of general access to awards (though not necessarily written documents)." (p. 815). Moreover, with regard to public interest representation, "[d]omestic legal systems [...] have sought to strike a balance between privacy and inclusiveness, leading them to embrace different forms and degrees of public interest representation, ranging from non-party to party representation and distinguishing between centralized and decentralized representatives of public interests." (p. 815). Moreover, after analysing public interest representations in domestic legal systems, the chapter concludes that international investment arbitration is far from including public interest litigation, which has been subject to crucial debates at national level: "[...] investment tribunals would simply have no jurisdiction to entertain suits brought by NGOs or associations seeking to vindicate societal concerns in proceedings against states or investors [...]." (p. 815). The chapter concludes with a request to the international investment community to whom the *International Investment Law and Comparative Public Law* approach is addressed:

> Having gradually begun to free itself from its 'commercial arbitration' legacy, the international investment community would be well advised not to ignore these [domestic public law as a guide to international investment law] signals. (p. 816).

International Investment Law's Legitimacy Crisis: Lost in Comparison?

Rethinking international investment law and arbitration is the right task. However, enhancing the legitimacy of the international investment regime requires us not only to acknowledge legitimacy problems, but also to provide effective solutions. This is especially true with regard to the application of comparative public law to the arbitration system itself. In contrast to substantive investment law, which can be interpreted using a comparative method, the arbitration system has to be institutionally and procedurally reformed. *International Investment Law and Comparative Public Law* is an inspiring and rich volume worth reading by those following its approach and by its critiques.

Even though *International Investment Law and Comparative Public Law* does not aim at institutional reforms, it is based upon the assumption and the acknowledgement of a need for change in international investment law and arbitration. Regardless of whether there is a crisis or not, all the contributions endeavour to improve the unbalanced starting-point as they observe international investments law's discontents.

Clearly, comparative public law and domestic analogies can encourage a reconsideration of the status quo. This might lead to a broader change in the framework of international investment protection, which was once intentionally isolated from legal principles, such as greater deference for governmental measures in the public interest and procedural rules, and transparency, in order to achieve the goal of a strong system of investment protection. However, whether the investment law community is heading in this direction remains to be seen.

Comparative public law may play a positive role in investment treaty arbitration, as it could abandon the clinical isolation of international investment law and arbitration to a certain degree. However, even if the comparative public law approach may further the judicial dialogue among international courts and tribunals, and legal transplants may constitute the possibility of inserting human rights aspects into investment arbitration, for example, the potential of the approach might be limited by an interpretation of arbitral tribunals that reflects the object and purpose of investment treaties.

All the contributions offer great insights into comparative public law, including comparisons of many different issues regarding comparative administrative and constitutional law, as well as comparative analyses of investor rights, such as full protection and security, remedies against denial of justice, national treatment, non-discrimination clauses, umbrella clauses, and the right to free transfer of funds. Furthermore, the contributions offer a wealth of good sources both with regard to the case law on investment disputes and the literature on the issues with which international investment law is struggling most. Notwithstanding this, the success of the comparative public law approach promises remains questionable.

Two Distinct Readings of the Public Law Nature of International Investment Law and Arbitration

International investment law is a field that belongs to public international law. However, the settlement of investment disputes is based upon commercial arbitration having a private law nature. This hybrid nature makes it more difficult to analyse international investment law and arbitration in the public law manner. Notwithstanding this, international investment law and arbitration cannot be read in a public law fashion alone. Instead, it is caught somewhere between quasi-administrative and quasi-constitutional adjudication, on the one hand, and commercial arbitration, on the other.

There are two distinct readings of international investment law and arbitration, which have already been relied upon in the introductory part. Whereas many agree, correctly, that international investment law and arbitration concern public law issues, and that investment arbitration is "functionally" analogous to administrative and constitutional adjudication, there is a remaining difference behind this consensus: an affirmative reading would suggest that investment arbitration has gained a quasi-constitutional character that is to be welcomed, as it subjects host state measures to the review of international investment arbitration. This reading sees the quasi-constitutional character (the public law nature) accompanied by universal standards of investment protection, a strong rule of law in investment law, which contributes to compliance with it in the domestic realm. This reading results in international investment law as global governance. The concept of the book under review falls into this category. The contradictory reading, which generally agrees with the public law nature, is still critical of investment arbitration because it adjudicates public law issues upon the basis of private commercial arbitration.

In addition, the respective reading reveals the importance of how we look at the functional similarities between constitutional adjudication and investment arbitration. While the book concentrates on the functional similarities, the potential negative implications of international investment law and arbitration are somewhat neglected.

International Investment Law's Negative Implications on Domestic Public Law

Besides the conceptual approach to reading international investment law as a public law discipline, it is worth mentioning that international investment law and arbitration must provide legitimacy and accountability for the exercise of public power. However, the democratic legitimacy of "judicial" review by private arbitrators beyond domestic legal systems is not evaluated as an issue of general relevance in the volume. Even though the contribution of Van Harten, which has been discussed above, criticises these circumstances, too, it is, however, no substitute for an in-depth evaluation of the democratic legitimacy of arbitral tribunals that review state measures and even engage in "judicial" law-making that results in a decoupling of law and politics somewhere beyond the domestic constitutional framework.[18]

Moreover, these inadequacies further exacerbate the negative implications of international investment law on domestic law. While international investment awards do not change the domestic legal system directly, and "only" involve monetary damages, investment arbitration not only has effects on both investors and states, but also on the public at large. While monetary compensation is the usual remedy, it is often under-estimated that monetary compensation may have wider impact on the structure of domestic legal systems. The larger the amount of potential compensation, the more likely it is that the state may change or amend its laws or policies. This phenomenon has become known as the "chilling effect" of international investment law and arbitration. Furthermore, the negative implications of international investment law on the domestic realm are mirrored in the theoretical potential of international investment law and arbitration to undermine domestic constitutional compromises. We have already experienced that this theoretical threat can become reality.[19] Schill definitely raises awareness of the fact that international arbitrators "[...] exercise interpretive powers over the content of investment treaty obligations and [...] are *de facto* able to restrict even policy choices made by democratically elected legislators." (p. 7). However, this circumstance is not evaluated in depth due to the conception of the book.

[18] See von Bogdandy/Venzke, Beyond Dispute: International Institutions as Lawmakers, German Law Journal 12 (2011) 5, p. 979 (993 et seq.).

[19] One striking example is the ICSID Case No. ARB (AF)/07/01, *Piero Foresti, Laura de Carli, et al. vs. Republic of South Africa*. International investment law and arbitration have influenced the implementation of South African Black Economic Empowerment Politics, which originate from the constitutional protection against discrimination as a reaction to the Apartheid regime.

MIX
Papier aus verantwortungsvollen Quellen
Paper from responsible sources
FSC® C105338

If you have any concerns about our products,
you can contact us on
ProductSafety@springernature.com

In case Publisher is established outside the EU,
the EU authorized representative is:
Springer Nature Customer Service Center GmbH
Europaplatz 3, 69115 Heidelberg, Germany

Printed by Libri Plureos GmbH
in Hamburg, Germany